Open Boundaries: A Canadian Women's Studies Reader

Third Edition

Barbara A. Crow
York University

Lise Gotell
University of Alberta

Toronto

Library and Archives Canada Cataloguing in Publication

Crow, Barbara A., 1960–
Open boundaries: a Canadian women's studies reader / Barbara A. Crow, Lise Gotell.—3rd ed.

Includes bibliographical references and index.
ISBN 978-0-13-241353-4

1. Feminism—Canada. 2. Women—Canada. I. Gotell, Lise II. Title.

HQ1181.C3C76 2009 305.420971 C2007-905516-8

ISBN-13: 978-0-13-241353-4
ISBN-10: 0-13-241353-1

Vice President, Editorial Director: Gary Bennett
Senior Acquisitions Editor: Laura Paterson Forbes
Marketing Manager: Sally Aspinall
Supervising Developmental Editor: Suzanne Schaan
Production Editor: Pearl Saban
Copy Editor: Melissa Hajek
Proofreader: Kelly Brenton
Senior Production Coordinator: Patricia Ciardullo
Compositon: Laserwords
Art Director: Miguel Angel Acevedo
Cover Design: Sharon Lucas
Cover Image: Masterfile

4 5 6 HI 12 11 10

Printed and bound in Canada.

Dedicated to the memory of strong women who have marked our lives:

Helen Daly, Anna Pellatt and Anita Odelle Watterson

Contents

Preface ix

Acknowledgments xiii

Credits xv

INTRODUCTION: What Is Women's Studies? *Lise Gotell and Barbara A. Crow* 1

CHAPTER 1: Who Is the Woman of Canadian Women's Studies? Theoretical Interventions 11

To Write Society: Adrift on the Edge of Reality and Fiction, *Nicole Brossard* 17

Philosophical Investigations (in a Feminist Voice), *Cressida Heyes* 20

Introducing Racism: Notes Towards an Anti-Racist Feminism, *Himani Bannerji* 29

Canadian Anti-Racist Feminist Thought: Scratching the Surface, *Enakshi Dua* 35

Invocation, *Jeanette Armstrong* 49

Origin Stories and Magical Signs in Women's Studies, *Ann Braithwaite* 51

Feminism in Waves: Re-Imagining a Watery Metaphor, *Kim Sawchuk* 58

Riding the Feminist Waves: In with the Thirds, *Natasha Pinterics* 65

CHAPTER 2: The Changing Context of Activisms 71

Assessing Gender Equality: Trends in the Situation of Women and Men in Canada, *Status of Women Canada* 78

Thinking It Through: Women, Work and Caring in the New Millennium, *Pat Armstrong and Hugh Armstrong* 86

The Great Undoing: State Formation, Gender Politics and Social Policy in Canada, *Janine Brodie* 95

Intersecting Identities and Inclusive Institutions: Women and the Future of Transformative Politics, *Alexandra Dobrowolsky* 104

Managing Trade Engagements?: Mapping the Contours of State Feminism and Women's Political Activism, *Christina Gabriel and Laura Macdonald* 115

Why Women Still Ain't Satisfied: Politics and Activism in Canadian Childcare, *Martha Friendly* 127

Confronting Power: Aboriginal Women and Justice Reform, *Patricia A. Monture* 132

War and the Politics of Truth-Making in Canada, *Sunera Thobani* 140

Rooting Out Injustice: Discussions with Radical Young Women in Toronto, Canada, *Jennifer Plyler* 149

Riding the Third Wave: Women-Produced Zines and Feminisms, *Brandi Bell* 156

CHAPTER 3: Engendering Violence 165

Husband Abuse: Equality with a Vengeance?, *Joanne C. Minaker and Laureen Snider* 170

Erasing Race: The Story of Reena Virk, *Yasmin Jiwani* 180

Gendered Racial Violence and Spatialized Justice: The Murder of Pamela George, *Sherene Razack* 190

Does No "No" Mean Reasonable Doubt? Assessing the Impact of *Ewanchuk* on Determinations of Consent, *Rakhi Ruparelia* 202

Is Canada Peaceful and Safe for Aboriginal Women?, *Anita Olsen Harper* 207

The Ultimate Rape Victim, *Jane Doe* 216

CHAPTER 4: The Body: Reproduction and Femininity 223

A Special Report to Celebrate the 15th Anniversary of the Decriminalization of Abortion: Protecting Abortion Rights in Canada, *CARAL* 226

Abortion, *Susan Wendell* 228

Between Body and Culture: Beauty, Ability and Growing Up Female, *Carla Rice* 233

The Flight from the Rejected Body, *Susan Wendell* 245

From Airbrushing to Liposuction: The Technological Reconstruction of the Female Body, *Dr. Fabienne Darling-Wolf* 251

Feminizing the Mobile: Gender Scripting of Mobiles in North America, *Leslie Regan Shade* 257

CHAPTER 5: Sexuality 263

Heterosexuality and Feminist Theory, *Christine Overall* 267

Moving Beyond "No Means No": Understanding Heterosexual Casual Sex and Consent, *Melanie Beres* 275

Desire as Interruption: Young Women and Sexuality Education in Ontario, Canada, *Erin Connell* 283

Isn't Love a Given?, *Lee Maracle* 289

The Respectable Same-Sex Couple: A New Entity in the History of Sexuality, *Mariana Valverde* 295

Losing the Feminist Voice: Debates on the Legal Recognition of Same-Sex Partnerships in Canada, *Claire Young and Susan B. Boyd* 299

The Silencing of Sexuality, *Cassandra Lord* 311

Does a Lesbian Need a Vagina Like a Fish Needs a Bicycle? Or, Would the "Real" Lesbian Please Stand Up!, *Amber Dean* 314

Sons of the Movement: Feminism, Female Masculinity and Female to Male (FTM) Transexual Men, *Jean Bobby Noble* 325

Bibliography 335

Suggested Readings 339

Index 353

Preface

Rather than a field contained within fixed borders, Canadian Women's Studies is marked by a sense of mobility and "open boundaries." Our challenge as Women's Studies scholars is to continue the feminist work of "asking questions" and to sustain a place where such questions can be posed. While the controversies that mark feminist scholarship are not settled, we believe that Women's Studies is a vital intellectual place where questions can be asked, appreciated, and debated. As Jean Robinson written, "Women's Studies is still a place where resistant ideas are voiced, where opposition to cultural and social norms is accepted, and where the very subjects of study still have to be justified to a doubting, highly critical academic community" (Robinson, 2002, p. 209).

When we were asked to do a third edition of *Open Boundaries*, we realized that the sense of mobility and questioning that had animated the first and second editions could only be sustained by rethinking the content of a new reader. In the first edition of *Open Boundaries*, our focus was on the formative texts in Canadian Women's Studies—interventions that had inaugurated and shaped this field of intellectual inquiry. In the second edition and now third edition of *Open Boundaries*, our emphasis has shifted towards the contemporary. In this reader, we continue to introduce students to the crucial questions, debates, and issues that together comprise the still open and unsettled terrain of Canadian Women's Studies.

This collection is shaped by our own intellectual trajectories. We trained together as graduate students (in Political Science and Sociology) at York University from the mid-1980s to the early 1990s. As students committed to feminist inquiry, we were forced to seek out relevant courses, often outside our own disciplines, at a time when feminist challenges had yet to fundamentally reshape the nature of disciplinary projects. We studied feminist theory from a generation of scholars who had been the driving force behind the establishment of the first Women's Studies programs. We were introduced to rich debates around the origins and dynamics of women's oppression and we were fundamentally influenced by the socialist feminist approaches that grounded the works of many of our professors.

We are, in many ways, part of a bridge between what has been referred to as "second wave" feminism and the "third wave." As graduate students, we were engaged in the second wave feminist project of constructing a grand theory of women's subordination. As our own work as Women's Studies scholars began in the early 1990s, we were profoundly affected by the challenges that rocked the second wave feminist project of "grand theorizing." In the face of postmodern insights about the irreducible complexities and uncertainties of the social world, the insistence on the social constructedness of analytic frameworks, and anti-racist and anti-essentialist feminist critiques of the exclusiveness of the feminist project, our own intellectual work was reconfigured. It was reconfigured in ways that might be seen as quite consistent with the defiant critical project of third wave feminism.

Third wave feminism has been primarily concerned with race and sexuality, with a deep skepticism about the unity of the category "women" and an interrogation of the orthodoxies that are perceived to reside within second wave feminism. For many of our own students, no matter how much our own concerns overlap with the thrust of third wave feminism, we are aligned with second wave feminism. Perhaps this is a function of our graying hair; perhaps it is also because we encourage our students to appreciate the complex contributions of second wave feminism alongside their own concerns with differences and contradiction. The position of "imbetweenness" that we occupy—this bridge, this ambiguous inter-generational space between the second and third waves of Canadian feminism—places feminists of our generation in a position to construct and mediate a conversation between second and third wave feminisms. This third edition of *Open Boundaries* provides a place for this conversation.

The sense of open boundaries that we believe is integral to Women's Studies made it difficult to determine the content of this reader. We are not trying to define the contemporary contours of the "discipline" in this reader; Women's Studies is by necessity interdisciplinary and feminist "definitions" are temporary and changing. Our approach has been to bracket some central topics, questions, and contributions. There were many pieces we wanted to include, but space requirements limited our selections. We debated how to include as many pieces as possible. Most of the pieces have been abridged to allow us to capture the main points of a wide variety of feminist authors. We selected five topics that have been central areas of analytic inquiry and debate within contemporary Canadian feminism: "Who is the Woman of Canadian Women's Studies?: Theoretical Interventions;" "The Changing Context of Activisms"; "Engendering Violence"; "The Body: Reproduction and Femininity"; and "Sexuality." These five areas are ones that frame the organization of many introductory courses.

The first chapter, "Who Is the Woman of Canadian Women's Studies? Theoretical Interventions," sketches out the terrain of Canadian Women's Studies by grappling with the deep tensions that have marked efforts to define its object of inquiry. Whereas many Women's Studies texts have begun by laying out competing feminist theories (liberal feminism, radical feminism, socialist feminism, postmodern feminism, and so on), we believe a rethinking of this typical point of departure is now necessary. It is necessary for Women's Studies students to appreciate the continued importance of analyzing women's oppression, especially within a context of backlash that denies the continued existence of gender-based disadvantage. At the same time, however, we must acknowledge that contemporary feminist theory is no longer preoccupied with the search for grand explanatory frameworks. Postmodern feminism, with its rejection of grand theory and its attention to "women" as a constructed category, has shifted the terrain of feminist inquiry. Anti-essentialist feminism has called attention to the exclusions that accompany any effort to define a homogenous women's experience that would serve as the ground of feminist theory. Canadian anti-racist and indigenous feminisms are rich and diverse traditions. Analyses of differences and power relations among women, especially racial differences, have produced a re-articulation of feminist understandings of gender, contesting overarching concepts such as women's oppression and patriarchy as inadequate descriptions of social worlds that are marked by multiple axes of power and differential positions within a context of colonialism. Third wave feminism, with its embrace of differences and contradiction, embodies the shift away from grand explanatory frameworks. It is these tensions and theoretical shifts that we seek to capture in the first chapter of the reader. We do not mean to suggest, however, that the questions of essentialism, differences has supplanted the insights and contributions of established feminist frameworks. In fact, as we see in the contributions in later chapters, liberal feminist concerns have shaped inquiries into women's political under-representation, radical feminist theory underpins and shapes much contemporary work on gendered violence, and Canadian socialist feminists have continued to develop internationally recognized analyses of the contemporary contours of the gendered division of labour.

Other chapters of this text reveal how Canadian feminist analysis has developed and sustained a dialogue around key issues in a contemporary context marked by backlash and complexity. In Chapter 2, "The Changing Context of Activisms," we explore feminist efforts to create and reshape political activism in an era characterized by severe obstacles to national feminist organizing and by the disappearance of systemic disadvantage as a legitimate object of public policy. Even as empirical studies confirm the persistence of the sexual division of labour and gendered, racialized and class-based inequalities, Canadian governments have cut back and cut off the public funding that helped to sustain critical feminist engagement in public policy. Historically, the Canadian women's movement has had an engaged relationship with the state, and has lobbied the government to encourage equality through the extension of the welfare state. The embrace of neo-liberal and neo-conservative agendas, decreased funding for social programs, and the construction of social movements as "special interest groups" have had an extremely damaging impact on feminist activism. While Canadian feminists continue to struggle to increase women's representation in traditional political institutions and to sustain national feminist organizing, it is also clear that political strategies are taking on new forms. The literature on the Canadian feminist activism reveals significant theoretical and activist engagement with race, gender, class, and sexuality. Aboriginal women are organizing in diverse ways to contest the damaging impacts of colonialism. Moreover, in the post-9/11 context of the "War against Terrorism," Canadian feminists have intervened to contest American militarism and to forge global links among women of the north and south. Young feminists now engage in diverse forms of social justice work and inspired by third wave ideas, they increasingly define culture as an important site of struggle. These various interventions reveal the way in which feminist activism is being rethought and enacted.

Just as the shape of activism is being reconfigured, so too are the social, material, and political conditions which Canadian feminists confront. In Chapter 3, "Engendering Violence," we reveal the importance of rethinking antiviolence activism in a context where systemic feminist analyses of violence are being silenced. We interrogate the contradictory impacts of the criminal regulation of sexual violence and we highlight the national crisis of violence against Canadian aboriginal women. In Chapter 4, "The Body: Reproduction and Femininity," we confront feminist efforts to contest the continued regulation of reproduction and the disciplinary norms of femininity, through exploring the questions of access to abortion and challenges to "beauty norms" built upon racialized and ablelist foundations. Finally, in Chapter 5, "Sexuality," we highlight the ways in which Canadian feminism has confronted the institution of heterosexuality, from the insights of lesbian feminists to queer theory. The readings in this chapter together undermine heterosexual privilege and compulsory heterosexuality by giving voice to lesbian and transgender identities and interrogating the racialization of sexuality.

As we emphasize in the reader as a whole, the creation and sustenance of feminist knowledge is vitally important. Without the rich spaces offered by Women's Studies programs, this project would not continue. Women's Studies plays a particular role in the university. Its interdisciplinary approach allows students to look at topics from a broad range of academic disciplines. It takes a problem-based approach to thinking, and encourages this thinking as a development in contemporary higher education. The kind of rigourous critical thinking that Women's Studies promotes is essential if universities are to fulfill their role in helping people find their place in an increasing plural, interdependent, and changing world. Certainly, Women's Studies confronts multiple challenges at the beginning of the 21st century, but this is also a time of exciting possibilities.

Acknowledgments

I would like to once again thank my good friend and colleague Lise Gotell for continuing to work on this project.

– Barbara Crow

Without the enthusiasm and commitment of my friend and colleague Barbara Crow, this collection would not have materialized. Barbara once again dragged me into this project kicking and screaming, but I am very pleased with the book that has emerged. I would also like to thank my partner, Adien Dubbelboer, for her support and double-duty childcare while I was in the middle of a tight schedule. To my son, Liam Gotell, I owe much quality time. Finally, I am grateful for many conversations with my colleagues—especially Claudine Potvin, Mebbie Bell, Heather Tapley, Dallas Cullen and Jo-Ann Wallace. These conversations shaped my thinking on this collection.

– Lise Gotell

We would like to thank the research assistants who worked on the third edition—Janice Leung and Linnet Fawcett.

We are enormously appreciative of the editorial staff we have worked with at Pearson. We have particularly appreciated the support and work of Joel Gladstone, Shelley Murchison, and Pearl Saban.

We are grateful to the following reviewers for their thoughtful comments and suggestions: Seema Ahluwalia, Kwantlen University College; Ann Braithwaite, University of PEI; Rhiannon Bury, University of Waterloo; Lara Campbell, Simon Fraser University; Elizabeth Dennis, University College of the Fraser Valley; Linda Derksen, Malaspina University College; Annalee Lepp, University of Victoria; Ann McKinnon, Okanagan College; Shelley Moore, Douglas College; Anne Quema, Acadia University; Justyna Sempruch, Queen's University; Norman Smith, University of Guelph; Heather Tapley, University of Alberta.

Finally, we are indebted to the many voices that mark the diverse, rich and contested terrain of Canadian feminist thought. This is the ground from which this collection has grown.

Credits

Jeannette Armstrong. (1996). Invocation: The real power of aboriginal women. In Christine Miller and Patricia Chuchryk (Eds.), *Women of the First Nations: Power, wisdom and strength* (pp. ix–xii). Winnipeg, MN: University of Manitoba Press. Reprinted with permission of the publisher.

Pat Armstrong and Hugh Armstrong. (2002). Thinking it through: Women, work and caring in the new millennium. *Canadian Woman Studies/les cahiers de la femme*, 21/22: 4/1, 44–50. Reprinted with permission of the authors and by *Canadian Woman Studies/Les Cahiers de la femme.*

Himani Bannerji. (1987). Introducing racism: Notes towards an anti-racist feminism. *Resources for Feminist Research/Documentation sur la recherche feministe*, 16:1, 10-12. Reprinted with permission of the author and *Resources for Feminist Research.*

Brandi Leigh-Ann Bell. (2002). Riding the third wave: Woman-produced zines and feminisms. *Resources for Feminist Research*, 29:3, pp. 187–198. Reprinted with permission of the author and *Resources for Feminist Research.*

Melanie Beres. (2006). Sexual consent to casual heterosexual sex. Sexual consent to heterosexual casual sex among young adults living in Jasper. Doctoral dissertation. Department of Sociology, University of Alberta, Edmonton, AB.

Ann Braithwaite. (2007). Origin stories and magical signs in Women's Studies. Solicited for this collection.

Janine Brodie. (2002). The great undoing: State formation, gender politics, and social policy in Canada. In Catherine Kingfisher (Ed.), *Western welfare in decline: Globalization and women's poverty* (pp. 90–110). Philadelphia, PA: University of Pennsylvania Press. Reprinted with permission of the author and the University of Pennsylvania Press.

Nicole Brossard. (2005). To write society: Adrift on the edge of reality and fiction. In *Fluid arguments* (pp. 222–241). Toronto, ON: Mercury. Reprinted with permission of the author and the publisher.

CARAL. (2003). A special report to celebrate the 15th anniversary of the decriminalization of abortion: Protecting abortion rights in Canada. Canadian Abortion Rights Action League.

Erin Connell. (2005). Desire as interruption: Young women and sexuality education in Ontario Canada. *Sex Education.* 5:3, 253–268. Reprinted by permission of the publisher (Taylor & Francis Ltd, http://www.informaworld.com).

Amber Dean. (2005). Does a lesbian need a vagina like a fish needs a bicycle? Or would the real lesbian please stand up?, *Canadian Woman Studies/les cahiers de la femme*, 24:2-3, 92–101. Reprinted with permission of the author and *Canadian Woman Studies/Les Cahiers de la femme.*

Alexandra Dobrowolsky. (2000). Intersecting identities and inclusive institutions: Women and a future transformative politics. *Journal of Canadian Studies*, 35:1, 240–261. Reprinted with permission of University of Toronto Press Incorporated (*www.utpjournals.com*).

Jane Doe. (2006). The ultimate rape victim. *Canadian Woman Studies/les cahiers de la femme*, 25:1–2, 77. Excerpted from *The Story of Jane Doe: A Book About Rape*. Copyright © 2003 Jane Doe. Reprinted with permission of Random House Canada.

Enakshi Dua. (1999). Canadian anti-racist feminist thought: Scratching the surface. In *Scratching the surface: Canadian anti-racist feminist thought* (pp. 7–31). Toronto, ON: Women's Press. Reprinted with permission of the author and Women's Press.

Martha Friendly. (2007). Why women still ain't satisified: Politics and activism in Canadian child care, *Canadian Woman Studies/les cahiers de la femme*, 25:3–4, 41–46. Reprinted with permission of the author and *Canadian Woman Studies/Les Cahiers de la femme*.

Chris Gabriel and Laura Macdonald. (2005). Managing trade agreements?: Mapping the contours of state feminism and women's political activism. *Canadian Foreign Policy,* 12:1, 71–88. Reprinted with permission of Canadian Scholar 's Press Inc. and/or Women 's Press.

Fabienne Darling-Wolf. (2000). From airbrushing to liposuction: The technological reconstruction of the female body. In Baukje Miedema et al. (Eds.), *Women's bodies, women's lives* (pp. 277–293). Toronto, ON: Sumach Press. Reprinted with permission of the publisher.

Anita Olsen Harper. (2006). Is Canada peaceful and safe for Aboriginal women? *Canadian Woman Studies/les cahiers de la femme*, 25:1–2, 33–39. Reprinted with permission of the author and *Canadian Woman Studies/Les Cahiers de la femme.*

Cressida J. Heyes. (2000). Philosophical investigations (in a feminist voice). In *Line drawings: Defining women through feminist practice* (pp. 77–102). Ithaca, NY: Cornell University Press. Reprinted from Cressida J. Heyes, *Line Drawings: Defining Women through Feminist Practice*. Copyright © 2000 by Cornell University. Used by permission of the publisher, Cornell University Press.

Yasmin Jiwani. (1999). Erasing race: The story of Reena Virk. *Canadian Woman Studies/les cahiers de la femme*, 19.3, 178–84. Reprinted with permission of the author and *Canadian Woman Studies/Les Cahiers de la femme.*

Cassandra Lord. (2001). The silencing of sexuality. In Allyson Mitchell, Lisa Bryn Rundle and Lara Karaian, (Eds.), *Turbo chicks: Talking young feminisms* (pp. 207–212). Toronto, ON: Sumach Press.

Lee Maracle. (1988, 1996). Isn't love a given? *I am a Woman: A Native perspective on sociology and feminism* (pp. 20–30). Vancouver, BC: Press Gang Publishers.

Joanne Minaker and Laureen Snider. (2006). Husband abuse: Equality with a vengeance? *Canadian Journal of Criminology and Criminal Justice*, 48:5, 753–780. Reprinted with permission from the *Canadian Journal of Criminology and Criminal Justice.*

Patricia Monture. (2007). Confronting power: Aboriginal women and justice reform. *Canadian Woman Studies/les cahiers de la femme*, 25:3–4, 25–32. Reprinted with permission by the author with the specific purpose of republishing edition version and *Canadian Woman Studies/Les Cahiers de la femme.*

Jean Bobby Noble. (2004). Sons of the movement: Feminism, female masculinity and female to male (FTM) transexual men. *Atlantis*, 29:1, 21–28. Excerpted from an article in *Atlantis*, 29.1, 2004. www.msvu.ca/atlantis.

Christine Overall. (1990). Heterosexuality and feminist theory. *Canadian Journal of Philosophy*, 20:1, 9–17.

Natasha Pinterics. (2001). Riding the feminist waves: In with the thirds. *Canadian Woman Studies/les cahiers de la femme*, 20/21:4/1, 15–21. Reprinted with permission by the author and *Canadian Woman Studies/Les Cahiers de la femme*.

Jennifer Plyler. (2006). Rooting out injustice: Discussions with radical young women in Toronto, Canada. In Shamilla Wilson, Anasuya Sengupta and Kristy Evans (Eds.), *Defending our dreams: Global feminist voices for a new generation* (pp. 136–149). London: Zed.

Sherene H. Razack. (2000). Gendered racial violence and spatialized justice: The murder of Pamela George. *Canadian Journal of Law and Society*, 15:2, 91–130. Reprinted with permission from the publisher.

Carla Rice. (2002). Between body and culture: Beauty, ability, and growing up female. In Vanaja Dhruvarajan, and Jill Vickers. (Eds.), *Gender, race, and nation: A global perspective* (pp. 205–221). Toronto, ON: University of Toronto Press. Reprinted by permission of University of Toronto Press Incorporated.

Rakhi Ruparelia. (2006). Does no "no" mean reasonable doubt? Assessing the impact of *Ewanchuk* on determinations of consent. *Canadian Woman Studies/les cahiers de la femme*, 25:1–2, 167–172. Reprinted with permission by the author and *Canadian Woman Studies/Les Cahiers de la femme*.

Kim Sawchuk. (2007). Feminism in waves: re-imagining a watery metaphor. Solicited for this collection.

Leslie Regan Shade. (2006). Feminizing the mobile: Gender scripting of mobiles in North America. *Continuum: Journal of Media and Cultural Studies*, 20:3, 177–187. Reprinted by permission of the publisher (Taylor & Francis Ltd, (http://www.informaworld.com).

Status of Women Canada. (2005). Assessing gender equality: Trends in the situation of women and men in Canada. Ottawa, ON: Secretary of State. Her Majesty the Queen in Right of Canada. All rights reserved. Source: Status of Women Canada 2005, http://www.swc-cfc.gc.ca/resources/consultations/ges09-2005/assessing_e.pdf. Reproduced with the permission of the Minister of Public Works and Government Services, Canada, 2007.

Sunera Thobani. (2003). War and the politics of truth-making in Canada. *International Journal of Qualitative Studies in Education*, 16:3, 399–414. Reprinted by permission of the publisher (Taylor & Francis Ltd, (http://www.informaworld.com).

Marianne Valverde. (2006). The respectable same-sex couple: A new entity in the history of sexuality. *Feminist Studies*, 32:1,155–162. Reprinted by permission of the publisher, *Feminist Studies, Inc*.

Susan Wendell. (1996). Abortion. *The rejected body: Feminist philosophical reflections on disability.* New York, NY: Routledge, pp. 151–155. Copyright 1996. From Abortion. *The rejected body: Feminist philosophical reflections on disability* by Susan Wendell. Reproduced by permission of Routledge, a division of Informa pic.

Susan Wendell. (1996). The flight from the rejected body. *The rejected body: Feminist philosophical reflections on disability.* New York, NY: Routledge, pp. 85–93. Copyright 1996. From The flight from the rejected body. *The rejected body: Feminist philosophical reflections on disability* by Susan Wendell. Reproduced by permission of Routledge, a division of Informa pic.

Claire Young and Susan Boyd. (2006). Losing the feminist voice? Debates on the legal recognition of same-sex partnerships in Canada, *Feminist Legal Studies,* 14, 213–240. Reprinted with permission from *Feminist Legal Studies*.

Introduction: What Is Women's Studies?

Lise Gotell and Barbara A. Crow

Women's Studies is a field of study that developed out of a critique of phallocentric knowledge which treats masculinity as central and representative of the universal. Definitions of this field are temporal, shifting and political, and as a recent Canadian volume on the state of Women's Studies has emphasized, often unstable and ambiguous (Braithwaite et. al. 2004). Until recently, Women's Studies has been defined as an academic project that "places women's experiences at the centre of inquiry" (Hunter College Women's Studies Collective 1995); this definition, however, has been challenged as too narrow. Feminist anti-racist, lesbian and disability scholars have confronted the exclusiveness of a Women's Studies that is primarily focused upon gender, emphasizing the importance of complicating categories of women and gender by understanding their implication in other forms of alterity. It is no longer enough to centre women, as we stress in this text; the contemporary project of Women's Studies involves questioning how systems of power based upon race, class, sexuality and ability interact with gender. In the current context, the category "women" has emerged as a conceptual window for interrogating interlocking systems of power, including race, class, ability and sexuality.

An emphasis on social justice and transformation underpins Women's Studies (Pryse 2000, p. 112). In fact, Women's Studies has often been described as the institutional arm of the women's movement. In the 1970s, when many students and faculty became active in social movements, including the students', civil rights, gay rights, antiwar and women's movements, women started to demand space for themselves within higher education (Boxer 1998). These activist academics fundamentally challenged prevailing canons by asking critical questions about what constituted knowledge and whose knowledge was legitimated and valued (Bird 2001). It was from these political roots that the first Women's Studies programs emerged in Canadian universities more than three decades ago. Women's Studies as a field of scholarly endeavour may be marked by deep diversity, and this is something we highlight in this reader, but its common features are its commitments to interrogating power relations, to fostering social change and to breaking down the boundaries between the personal and political.

Although feminist practice and Women's Studies scholarship are entwined, academic feminism has often been charged with diverting focus away from feminist political struggles. Feminist academics have been critiqued for producing theory rather than focusing on real life conditions, for being elitist and inaccessible (Nussbaum 1999). In this collection, however, we take the view that it is not theorizing and academic practice per se that are problematic; it is instead particular theories and practices. There are exciting possibilities for critical and exploratory thought outside the constraints of the everyday. Indeed, much contemporary feminist debate occurs in academia; the strength of this work is the critical distance academia provides, creating opportunities for theorizing and renegotiating gender relations (Kemp and Squires 1997, p. 6). Women's Studies must be viewed as an element of wider feminist endeavours, and conversations between activists and scholars must be encouraged. This productive relationship between politics and academia has been a vital part of the Canadian Women's Studies project.

In 1990, Margrit Eichler found that 93% of Women's Studies faculty members combine scholarship with feminist activism (1990, p. 7). Rather than retreating into the academy, Women's Studies has continued to be a politically informed activity. Canadian feminist scholars routinely engage in public policy debates. Women's Studies faculty have produced research studies for feminist movement organizations that have generated new demands and strategies. Feminist academics have worked together with feminist litigators to construct legal arguments that have advanced substantive equality on a number of fronts. Feminist researchers and grassroots activists have engaged in collaborative research projects that question hierarchies between academic and activist knowledge, producing synthetic and innovative results. In a context marked by the elimination of governmental funding for community-based feminist activism and research, such active collaborations assume a renewed importance.

Many students, excited by the questions raised in their Women's Studies courses, have been propelled into a variety of campus- and community-based feminist activisms. Routinely, this activism is carried back into the classroom and becomes a basis for challenges to professors and course materials. There is an ongoing conversation, sometimes tense, often productive, between feminist activism and Canadian Women's Studies scholarship. There is a vital interrelationship between feminist politics on the street and in the academy.

DIVERSITY IN FOCUS: OUR APPROACH IN THIS READER

Academic feminism in the early 21st century is marked by diversity of method, motivation and focus. In its earlier days, feminism, newly institutionalized in Women's Studies programs, adopted a posture of defensiveness by necessity. Attempting to legitimize their place in the university where the study of women had never been seen as scholarly or worthwhile, Women's Studies practitioners emphasized the unity or potential unity of feminism and its challenge to patriarchal scholarship. More than three decades after the establishment of the first Canadian Women's Studies programs, we are fortunate to be the beneficiaries of that first wave of academic feminist struggle. The development of Women's Studies programs has contributed to the creation of a space in which the differences that constitute feminism can find their fullest expression.

It is our intention in this text to provide an overview of some key debates that have marked the evolution of Women's Studies in Canada. We are second-generation feminist scholars; the struggles and achievements of our academic foremothers have enabled us to inhabit our classrooms as places of respectful debate and challenge. One of the critical insights of feminism has been the claim that knowledge is always situated and engaged (Haraway 1988). In this way feminism challenges the very claim that knowledge is objective. The "view from nowhere gaze" that has been the centre of post-Enlightenment Western thought has been dethroned and revealed as masking the specific perspective and interests of dominant social groups. With this insight comes the necessary realization that the creation of feminist "Truth" cannot be the aim of Women's Studies scholarship. Instead, as graduate student Eva Karpinski (1998) has emphasized, the notion of community that we create must "accommodate critique and questioning" and the right to "dissent and disagreement"; it must be "specific, situated, self-critical" (p. 139). The unsettling of foundations that has characterized feminism's relationship with traditional academic disciplines must be brought into the very heart of Women's Studies (Braithwaite et. al. 2004). Offering competing answers to an ever-changing set of questions and providing students with the critical tools to assess contending perspectives is how we see the role of academic Women's Studies practitioners.

We compiled this reader with this approach to teaching Women's Studies in mind. While there have been some fine Canadian introductory texts, a text, or even a collection of overview articles, cannot always illuminate the rich contours and distinctive edges that comprise Women's Studies scholarship. It is for this reason that many instructors have supplemented texts with course kits designed to bring a multiplicity of voices to students. This collection, focusing on Canadian Women's Studies scholarship in English, grew out of our own efforts to map for our students the diverse contributions of Canadian scholars. It is our hope that this reader will reveal the dynamic nature of Canadian feminist debates, the genuine diversity within current feminist theory and some of the central issues at stake in the differing approaches to feminist activism.

THE INSTITUTIONALIZATION OF CANADIAN WOMEN'S STUDIES

The first undergraduate course in Women's Studies in Canada was offered by Professor Marlene Dixon at McGill University and the first program was initiated at the University of Toronto in 1974. Since these beginnings, most Canadian universities have established undergraduate degree programs in Women's Studies (34 by 2007). Initial programs borrowed and cross-listed courses from various disciplines. Some of these courses focused on "women and" or "women in," such as "Women and Politics" and "Women in Canadian Literature," with an emphasis on making women visible where they had once been absent. Since the 1970s, there has been a dramatic proliferation of courses and new curricular emphases, with programs developing and mounting their own core courses that surpass this earlier "women and" focus. Courses now interrogate the production of gender and its intersection with race, class and sexuality, and include such titles as "Queer Theory," "Gender, Race and Class," "Transnational Feminisms," "From Silence to Song: Voices of Women with a Disability," "Feminisms: Anti- and Third Wave" and "Feminist Culture/Popular Culture."

We have witnessed profound shifts in Women's Studies curriculum and greater institutional commitments to programs. At the beginning of the 21st century, some Canadian Women's Studies programs are expanding with the hiring of young scholars and the introduction of new courses and graduate degrees.[1] Nevertheless, most programs remain marginalized in their universities: many confront unstable funding and few dedicated Women's Studies faculty positions. Some Canadian programs exist because of the goodwill of feminist faculty, who perform a "second shift" of service to Women's Studies once their disciplinary obligations in their home departments are fulfilled. This is a practice that Dale Bauer (2002) has labelled "academic housework." Moreover, we have seen an increasing trend for new hires in Women's Studies to start their careers with heavy administrative responsibilities (such as chairing and coordinating their programs) at the same time that they face rigorous pre-tenure requirements to publish. Because of inadequate resources, most Canadian programs continue to rely heavily on the practice of cross-listing courses. Cross-listing has contradictory implications. On the one hand, it enables the interdisciplinary work that is a critical dimension of Women's Studies. On the other hand, however, curricular development and cohesion are impeded when programs are unable to mount their own core courses.

Accompanying the development of Women's Studies and women's increased participation in post-secondary institutions,[2] there has also been a growth of services designed for and by this constituency. These services include the creation of women's centres and sexual harassment offices, the support of feminist scholarship through various awards, the formation of women's committees as offshoots of larger university representative bodies,[3] the establishment of special library collections,[4] and the implementation of various university policy initiatives, including pay and employment equity and childcare. These developments reflect not only the increased presence of women in post-secondary education, but also the political role of Women's Studies faculty, who have often been at the forefront of struggles for the kinds of institutional changes that are required to make universities more equitable for all students, staff and faculty.

The phenomenal growth in feminist scholarship that has occurred over the past 35 years is reflected in ongoing Canadian feminist journals, presses and associations. When Women's Studies first emerged, it was possible for feminist scholars to read every new book or article that appeared. Since then, there has been a veritable knowledge revolution and feminist scholarship has grown remarkably both in quality and complexity. As Christina Gabriel and Katherine Scott (1993) highlight, feminist publishing has had a crucial role in the rapid acceleration of feminist knowledge:

> Women have struggled long and hard to find a place in public discourse. The lack of access to critical material resources such as printing and publishing has been a significant barrier to efforts to create and disseminate a counter-hegemonic discourse against the dominant patriarchal, racist and homophobic mechanisms of capitalist society. Feminist publishing [has] worked to recover women's history, provided women with alternative political views and generally been part of the organized expression of the movement (p. 26).

From its beginnings, Canadian academic feminism has confronted disciplinary journals and other scholarly forums resistant to the insights offered by feminist approaches. This resistance lingers on. For example, Jane Arscott and Manon Tremblay found that in the 30-year history of the *Canadian Journal of Political Science*, only 3.5% of its articles have focused on women (1999, pp. 128–129). In this context, the continued existence of Canadian feminist journals, associations and presses has proven essential for the creation of research and theory. Publications such as *Resources for Feminist Research* (1972), *Atlantis* (1974), *Canadian Woman Studies les cahiers de lafemme* (1978), and *Canadian Journal of Women and the Law* (1985) have become internationally recognized scholarly journals. Feminist presses include the Toronto Women's Press (1972), Sister Vision Press (1984), Ianna and Sumach Press (2000).

As a final mark of its institutionalization, academic associations have emerged to foster Women's Studies scholarship and research, creating the possibility of conversations among diverse researchers. Crucially, the Canadian Women's Studies Association/L'association canadienne des études sur les femmes was founded in 1982 to build a feminist scholarly network and to promote Women's Studies as an interdisciplinary field within the academic community. Over the past several years, the Association has made a tremendous effort to integrate new media as a means of nurturing a cross-Canada Women's Studies community among its several hundred members (see CWSA website at www.yorku.ca/cwsaacef). Other associations devoted to feminist research include: the Canadian Research Institute for the Advancement of Women (CRIAW) (1976), the Canadian Women's Movement Archives (CWMA) (1976), the Canadian Congress for Learning Opportunities for Women (CCLOW) (1978), the National Association of Women and the Law (NAWL) (1980) and the establishment of five regional Women's Studies chairs (1985).

National extra-academic associations such as CRIAW, the CCLOW and NAWL have played a crucial role in raising difficult issues that impact on women's lives, proposing concrete policy responses and holding governments accountable for respecting and promoting women's rights. And these associations have provided forums for active collaborations between feminist academics and activists. In 2006, the Harper Conservative government cut the budget of Status of Women Canada (SWC) by 40%, removed the word "equality" from its mandate and fundamentally altered the funding criteria for women's organizations, making research and activities related to advocacy ineligible for funding (Canada, 2007). The continued existence of organizations such as CRIAW, the CCLOW and NAWL has been threatened by these cutbacks. Feminist research and critique within the academy assumes greater importance in a political context in which community voices are being increasingly silenced.

Despite the lack of resources and institutional support that plagues many programs, Women's Studies as an academic endeavour continues to survive and often thrive, providing a site for sustaining feminist research and knowledge production. A special issue of the U.S. journal *differences* entitled "Women's Studies on the Edge" (1997) captures the contradictory state of contemporary Women's Studies. Underlying diverse perspectives on the state of the field, the articles together emphasize how Women's Studies' intellectual work remains on the critical "edge," asking difficult questions and taking theoretical perspectives that enliven its continued challenge to masculinist and hegemonic scholarship; yet at the same time Women's Studies is on the "edge" in another sense, as it remains struggling on the institutional margins of the university. As Shirley Yee contends, it may be that Women's Studies "occupies an embattled position on campuses" precisely because it makes "women and feminism visible in the academies" (1997, p. 50).

CANADIAN WOMEN'S STUDIES: ANALYTIC TOOLS AND CHANGING DIRECTIONS

The analytic tools of Women's Studies are feminism, sex, gender, race, sexuality and class. Definitions of feminism as both a practice and an academic endeavour now proliferate. Most introductory Women's Studies courses present a typology of feminist theories, and these feminisms are modified by other theoretical positions—for example, liberal feminism, Marxist feminism, psychoanalytic feminism, postmodernist feminism, anti-racist feminism and third wave feminism. What many professors and students find in this typology is that feminist theories overlap and that any attempt to define feminism narrowly or categorically, without multiplicity, will inevitably be problematic. Nonetheless, it is important to understand the divergent approaches feminist scholars have employed in their efforts to analyze systems of domination. Much of this reader represents a conversation among competing feminist perspectives.

Patricia Elliot and Nancy Mandell (1998) define the project of feminist theory in the following broad terms:

> First, feminist theorists seek to understand the gendered nature of virtually all social and institutional relations . . . . Second, gender relations are constructed as problematic and as related to other inequities and contradictions in social life . . . . Third, gender relations are not viewed as either natural or immutable but as historical and socio-cultural productions, subject to reconstitution. Fourth, feminist theories tend to be explicitly political in their advocacy for social change. (p. 4)

In keeping with our focus on Women's Studies as a field of academic inquiry marked by diverse voices, we emphasize that feminist theory must move beyond an exclusive and primary focus on gender relations. In advocating for egalitarian social changes, feminist scholars have been forced to recognize that, as bell hooks (1997, p. 26) argues, if "feminism is a movement to end sexist oppression, then it must not focus exclusively on any specific group of women, any particular race or class of women." Attention to the construction, formation and articulation of gender by many of the contributions to this reader reveals that gender is made in specific ways. To understand the content poured into the category "women," we need to recognize the racial construction of that category; we need to recognize that the material conditions of middle-class professional women and women living in poverty differ in fundamental ways; and we need to acknowledge that compulsory heterosexuality and norms of gender conformity have an impact on how lesbians, bisexuals and transgendered people relate to the category "woman." Disentangling the complex relationships, discourses and material structures that intersect on the very bodies of contemporary Canadian women is a preoccupation of contemporary Women's Studies.

If feminist theorizing is the first analytic tool of Women's Studies, interdisciplinarity is its companion. The commitments to social justice that motivated the emergence of Women's Studies carried with them strong challenges to the disciplinary organization of knowledge. Women's Studies scholars embraced a particular kind of interdisciplinarity, one that began with questioning how conventional disciplinary frameworks have been resistant and often blind to gender analysis (Blee 2002, p. 177). The form of critical interdisciplinarity embraced by Women's Studies is problem-based. As we will see in the pages of *Open Boundaries,* Third Edition, exploring such enduring and pervasive problems as gendered violence involves not only moving across and synthesizing the insights of diverse disciplines (for example, law, sociology, political science, psychology, sociology), it also involves interrogating how disciplinary knowledges can operate as barriers to understanding and change. Moreover, as Marjorie Pryse (2000, p. 109) has argued, Women's Studies interdisciplinarity produces a flexibility and mobility that is conducive to self-reflexivity. Understanding the complexities of gendered violence involves transcending gender-focused approaches in order to analyze the contextual intersections of race, gender, class, ability and sexuality. In moving across disciplinary lines, Women's Studies students and scholars gain practice in intellectual border-crossing that can also promote thinking, theorizing and listening across vectors of race, class, ability and sexuality. Labelling this form of boundary-crossing "transversal method," Pryse contends that it enables Women's Studies scholars to construct research that emerges from women's lives, while at the same time getting specific about differences between women.

It is difficult to pin down the distinctive characteristics of Women's Studies in Canada, mainly because of the plurality of voices in this forum and the manner in which these voices contest the meaning of Canadian nationhood. Contemporary Canadian feminism is shaped by the maternal feminist legacy of the "first wave" and by the organizations and activists that struggled on after the vote was won. It has also been shaped by our colonial history and by the cultural and economic dominance of the United States. Nevertheless, some feminist scholars have sought to articulate the specific configuration of Canadian Women's Studies.

The emphases on diversity and boundary-crossing that are so central to the thrust of *Open Boundaries,* Third Edition, demand that we interrogate and disrupt the place of "nation" and "Canadian" in Women's Studies, especially in the contemporary global context of the rise of ethnic nationalism. Canada is a country where feminist organizing has been divided by national identity and where scholarly conversation is often difficult because of linguistic duality. Given the close association between Quebec feminism, the Quebec state and the project of Quebec nationalism, most scholars now recognize that there is a fundamental division between Quebec feminism and feminism in the "rest of Canada" (Lamoureux 1987). Apart from a provocative essay on the meaning of feminism in a context of backlash by the renowned Quebecoise lesbian novelist, poet and essayist Nicole Brossard, our collection does not include any selections in French addressing the different trajectories and voices that constitute Quebec feminism. However, we chose not to modify "Canadian" with the adjective English in the title of this volume in order to encompass the national identities of First Nations' women, whose scholarship has greatly influenced Canadian feminist thought, and the contributions of immigrant women with diverse ethnic and linguistic identities. Much scholarship by immigrant women and racialized women has been concerned with identifying the racist, classist and sexist dimensions of Canadian nation-building and construction. Many contributions to *Open Boundaries,* Third Edition, provide us with ways to identify problems, thereby revealing how "Canada" invokes certain exclusionary assumptions and values. Indeed, as Dua (this volume) argues, anti-racist feminism has both a long history and an active engagement in Canadian feminist scholarship and Women's Studies. Moreover, as Joyce Green has recently argued, Canadian Aboriginal women have been at the forefront of the development of indigenous feminisms, bringing together feminist and postcolonial critiques to theorize the historical and contemporary intersections of patriarchy, racism and colonialism.

Maroney and Luxton (1987, p. 8) emphasize the overwhelming contributions that Canadian socialist feminists have made to Women's Studies scholarship. This tradition can be understood as the result of feminist involvements in Marxist-influenced social movements in the 1960s and in the social democratic traditions that maintained an openness to socialist politics in Canada. The legacy of this materialist feminism for Women's Studies, including its careful analysis of work and its attention to political economy, is evident in many contributions to this reader. It is also the case that most contemporary Women's Studies instructors have been critically influenced by this tradition, both as its creators and students.

Another distinctive feature of Canadian Women's Studies scholarship grows out of the particular character of feminist politics after World War II. Whereas it could be argued that only a minimalist welfare state emerged in the United States, in postwar Canada the state underwent massive expansion, taking on new roles and engaging in the project of ensuring social citizenship. Women's movement activisms have thus focused on the state, and (with the exception of Quebec) on the federal state, given its central role as the initiator of social programs and the guarantor of national standards. This focus has resulted in a rich literature within Canadian Women's Studies that interrogates the role of the state vis-à-vis women. As the threads of the Canadian welfare state have been dismantled over the past 25 years, an equally rich literature has emerged disentangling the impacts of neoliberalism on feminism. Many contributions to this reader are concerned with analyzing contemporary feminist issues and struggles within the context of neoliberalism—a governmental ideology that erases structural disadvantage, pathologizes dependence on the state and constructs equality-seeking movements as antithetical to a new public good defined in terms of individual responsibility.

While these analytic traditions and concerns have marked the field, it would be a great simplification to define anti-racist feminism, indigenous feminism, materialist feminism and feminist state theory as the distinctive features of Canadian Women's Studies. Women's Studies everywhere has become the site of multiple inquiries and new kinds of questions. Many initial contributions to Canadian Women's Studies stressed the sociological and the material, and while this rich tradition continues to have a strong presence, some scholars have shifted their attention to the interaction between images and social representation, culture and the production of identity. The critical insights of radical social constructionism are represented most clearly in this volume, including contributions dealing with sexuality, reproduction and the body and violence. This literature calls attention to the ways in which masculinity, femininity, race and sexuality are continually produced and reproduced in language and in discourse. American feminist Judith Butler, for example, calls attention to gender as "performance," to the rigid binary that divides masculine from feminine and to the necessity of deconstruction, that is, the erosion of gender as dichotomy (1990). For Butler, identity always excludes just as it includes, and, given that "women" are constructed, our experience and identity provide no stable ground from which to build theory and politics. Challenging the idea that "women" represents a fixed category, this literature calls attention to the multiple ways in which women are constructed in language and in discourse, including within feminist theory itself.

Some scholars have drawn upon Butler's insights to argue that just as we must "trouble gender," so too must we "trouble Women's Studies" (Braithwaite et. al. 2004; Brown 1997). As Ann Bratihwaite, Susan Heald, Susanne Luhmann and Sharon Rosenberg contend, Women's Studies has been rendered unstable by the loss of the category "woman" as a foundation. Rather than attempting to shore up a singular meaning of Women's Studies in defence against such profound challenges, they argue that we must embrace the ambiguities of our intellectual project and accept that our field is a site of contestation that should not remain bound to its origins. In *Open Boundaries*, Third Edition, we embrace this call for complexity and self-reflection. But at the same time, we see such critical interventions on the "state of Women's Studies" as signifying not a crisis of the field, but instead its maturity.

Women's Studies is a field of critical intellectual inquiry and debate at almost every Canadian university, whose scope, methods and theoretical commitments must be subject to ongoing debate and revision. Its direction continues to be challenged and contested, most recently by third wave feminist scholars emphasizing: the embrace of contradictions within feminism; the importance of sexual expression; the defiance of rigid binary constructions of gender and sexuality; the centrality of anti-racism and inclusive forms of feminist activism; and the importance of culture as a site of politics (Pintareks, this volume). We have tried to capture the thrust of these challenges in diverse contributions to *Open Boundaries*, Third Edition. At the same time, however, and along with Kim Sawchuk (this volume) we emphasize the importance of critical conversations between second and third wave feminisms, highlighting the ways in which the metaphor of "waves" operates as a force of division and one that may hide the complexities within and among generations of feminists.

What makes Women's Studies most exciting to us is that it is both a dynamic theoretical framework and practice, elastic enough to be a site of these kinds of important debates and challenges. Women's Studies keeps "gender" on the table as a visible, yet contested and complex, category of analysis entwined with race, class, sexuality and ability. Feminism takes on the monumental challenge of interrogating the relationship between systems of domination, exploring and making concrete their interconnections and highlighting the necessity of diverse forms of social, cultural and political change. Sometimes this approach has the effect of making feminism seem "messy." We believe, however, that this appearance is a reflection of the complexity of feminist theories and practices. To paraphrase Audre Lorde (1984), *while surely the master's tools cannot dismantle the master's house, such dismantling will involve the simultaneous uses of different kinds of feminist tools.* We hope that this reader contributes to this complex and contested project.

Endnotes

1. There are currently eight Canadian MA Programs: York University; Simon Fraser University; Saint Mary's University/Mount Saint Vincent University (joint program); University of British Columbia (Women's and Gender Studies); University of Toronto (Women's and Gender Studies); University of Northern British Columbia (Gender Studies); Memorial University; and Western University (Women's and Feminist Studies). In addition, three universities have collaborative MA Programs (where students pursuing an MA in another field can designate to complete a combined MA in Women's Studies and another field): University of Ottawa; Lakehead University; and Ontario Institute for Studies in Education (Women's Studies/Feminist Studies). There are Ph.D. programs at Simon Fraser University, York University, University of British Columbia (Women's and Gender Studies) and a collaborative program at the Ontario Institute for Studies in Education (Women's Studies/Feminist Studies).
2. Women's participation rates in undergraduate programs have increased from 43% in 1972 to 58% in 2004; in master's programs from 27% in 1972 to 51% in 2004; and in doctoral programs from 19% in 1972 to 46% in 2004 (CAUT Almanac of Post-Secondary Education in Canada, Ottawa, 2007).
3. Examples would be the Canadian Association of University Teachers (CAUT) Status of Women Committee, and the Canadian Federation for the Humanities and Social Sciences (CFHSS).
4. Special library collections include the Nellie Langford Rowell Library at York University and the housing of the Canadian Women's Movement Archives (CWMA) at the University of Ottawa.

CHAPTER 1

Who Is the "Woman" of Canadian Women's Studies? Theoretical Interventions

Students frequently want to run away at the very mention of "theory." Our students will often tell us that they find feminist theory difficult and detached from the everyday. But theory is simply about constructing informed interpretations of the world in which we live. If our goal as feminists is to invent new futures, then it is necessary for us to critique the status quo; theory-making is essential to this task. Theory itself should not be rejected. Instead, particular kinds of theories need to be interrogated and displaced from their powerful position in shaping how we see the world and how we seek to act within it. As Chris Weedon argues, "To dismiss all theory as an elitist attempt to tell women what their experience really means is not helpful, but it does serve as a reminder of making theory accessible and of the political importance of transforming the material conditions of knowledge production and women's access to knowledge" (Weedon, 1997, p. 7).

Feminist theory emerged as a critique of the patriarchal values and interests embedded within existing social theories. Indeed, as feminists have pointed out from a variety of perspectives, "malestream" theory has not only tended to exclude women and their experiences; it has also been involved in justifying and rationalizing oppression and in privileging the masculine over the feminine. Feminist theorizing, while remaining attentive to the gendering of knowledge claims, has, by the dawn of the 21st century, been propelled to explore exclusionary, racialized, ableist, classist and heterosexist presumptions of its own growing body of texts. Indeed, as Chandra Mohanty argued over a decade ago, "Histories of feminism also document theories of domination. No non-contradictory or pure feminism is possible" (Mohanty, 1991, p. 20). Like the project of feminist theory, the project of Women's Studies must be critically self-reflexive about its own knowledge claims.

When Women's Studies first emerged into the academy in the 1970s, it was described through the language of identity—the study of women, by women and for women (Wiegman, 2002, p. 108). This approach focused on one dimension of power—sex/gender—as primary and structuring. The question "Who is the 'woman' of Women's Studies?" was also seen to have a self-evident answer. Second wave feminist theorists powerfully insisted that all women shared an experience of gender oppression, and that these experiences provided the foundation of feminist theory and the object of Women's Studies. This is not to suggest that all second wave feminist theorists constructed women's experiences in homogenous terms. As we argued in the first edition of *Open Boundaries*, socialist feminist theory has been a dominant presence within Canadian feminism. Canadian socialist feminists interrogated the material realities of production and reproduction and analyzed the social relations of the sexual division of labour in late capitalism. Nonetheless, even if attentive to classed relations, many second wave Canadian theorists held on to a conception of women's experience that erased racialization, sexuality and ability. Moreover experience, once interpreted, was seen to provide the basis of feminist knowledge.

Standpoint feminism—that is, the insistence that the experience of gender oppression can provide a foundation for theory—is a project that assumes that correctly produced knowledge will add up to an answer to the question, "What should we do?" This assumption, some feminists argue, is no longer tenable in an increasingly complex, postmodern world. Theorists such as Judith Butler and Joan Scott contend that experience provides no stable ground for knowledge; experience itself acquires meaning only through construction in discourse (1992). In other words, from a postmodern feminist perspective, there is no stable "I" and no fixed collectivity "women." Subjects and groups are shaped by language, and reality does not stand apart from the concepts used to describe it. Consistent with the view that feminist "Truth" is itself constructed, postmodern feminism challenges us to be self-critical about our own knowledge claims.

It is in this spirit of self-reflexivity that we begin this reader with a set of theoretical reflections that challenge us to think through the question, "Who is the woman of contemporary Women's Studies?" The readings in this chapter present a range of positions on gender essentialism—that is, the assertion that women's experience can be isolated and described independently of race, class, sexuality and other social relations. For some feminist theorists, the feminine is a site for the subversion of patriarchal knowledge that must be sustained. For others, attention to differences and power relations among women, especially racial differences, have produced a re-articulation of feminist understandings of gender, contesting overarching concepts such as women's oppression and patriarchy as inadequate descriptions of social worlds that are marked by multiple axes of power (Wiegman, 2002, p. 108). From philosophical and literary reflections, to the rich Canadian literature on anti-racist feminism, to the post-colonial critiques of Native women, to a consideration of new waves of feminism, this chapter reconsiders the very foundations of Canadian Women's Studies.

TAKING THE RISK OF ESSENTIALISM

The "woman" who had stood at the centre of second wave feminist theory and who had been installed as the subject of the first Women's Studies programs in the 1970s came under attack in the 1980s and 1990s with the emergence of feminist critiques of essentialism. In a key expression of anti-essentialist feminist critique, Elizabeth Spelman argued that much feminist theory had confused the condition of one group of women with the condition of all; in this way, the identities of privileged women became representative of all women, thereby erasing differences, especially differences of race and class (Spelman 1988). Obscuring diversity and power relations within the category "women," essentialist forms of feminist theory reduced the experience of those subject to multiple forms of oppression to addition problems (for example, racism + sexism = black women's experience). Not only did this additive formula forcibly fragment identities, it also functioned to affirm that all women shared a primary core of "unmodified" womanhood (Harris, 1990).

While highlighting the crucial significance of diversity and power relations among women as a central concern of feminist theory, anti-essentialist critiques sometimes signalled a slide into an imprisoning form of identity policies in which only each group is authorized to speak from its own experiences. Is it possible to speak of women? Is it necessary for feminist thought to take the risk of essentialism?

As **Nicole Brossard ("To Write Society: Adrift on the Edge of Reality and Fiction")** writes, "To write *I am a woman* is full of consequences" (2005, p. 241) These consequences are, for her, the very terrain of feminism and also of Women's Studies. Brossard is a Quebecoise novelist, poet and essayist; her work has been translated into many languages and she has won many prestigious literary prizes. Susan Rudy (2005) describes Brossard's focus as being "on women: women thinking, reading, writing, loving, desiring" (p.11). For Brossard, the feminine is a colonized terrain within patriarchal thought. The feminist project is to reclaim and reinvent what has been denied and objectified. In an essay published in 1985, Brossard introduced the concept of the "integral women" which she described in the following terms: "if patriarchy can take what exists and make it not, surely we can take what exists and make it be" (Rudy, 2005, p.10). This idea has continued to be the basis of her feminist theoretical interventions and her experimental fictional and poetic writings. For her, feminism is a project of becoming, of overflow and invention.

In the piece included here, Brossard provides us with a concise formulation of feminist thought. She argues that the feminist posture is that of reclaiming the "Other" and that this posture is only possible through holding on to the extreme margins. For Brossard, this space on the edge is a site of creativity; but it is also necessarily founded upon a relation between women. Brossard contends that the gaze of women is necessary if we are to disrupt a worldview where women and men are trained to direct their eyes on the capital M of man. Yet this focus is simultaneously difficult to maintain because of our marginalization. Brossard sees lesbian desire as enabling this focus on women. Brossard's feminism can certainly be described as "lesbian feminism;" elsewhere she argues that lesbian feminism is a site of challenge to the dominant position of white middle class heterosexual feminists, analogous to the challenge posed by African American feminists (2005, p.235). Her intervention can, in this way, be seen in relation to the challenges of anti-racist and Native feminists that follow. But at the same time, Brossard's work can be read as an insistence on the necessity of "essentialism" for feminism. At one level, this "essentialism" is the simple recognition of women's continued subordination. Yet, on another level, for Brossard feminism means the creation of new forms of consciousness, new ways of being—a project that can only be accomplished through reinventing language and imagining women anew. As she has argued elsewhere, "there is a distinction between an essentialism that would refer to biological determinism and as the projection of a mythic space freed of inferiorizing patriarchal images" (Huffer, 1995, p.118). For Brossard, this form of "essentialism" gestures towards a future of possibilities and diversity, rather than the imposition of rigid boundaries or hierarchies.

While Brossard's feminism insists upon the risk of essentialism, **Cressida Heyes ("Philosophical Investigations [in a Feminist Voice]")**, engages in a philosophical analysis of how and on what terms it may be defensible to draw a line around the category "woman". Is there a space between the deployment of exclusive generalizations and an acute gender skepticism where we can never invoke the sign "woman"? Heyes deploys the philosopher Wittengenstein in an effort to develop a position that is both self-conscious and self-critical about the basis of classifications, a practice she sees as being a necessary part of feminist consciousness-raising in the current political climate. Her use of Wittgenstein's injunction to "look and see" coalesces with postmodern feminist concerns about the constructedness of our categories. There is no single characteristic defining of womanhood, and when we use the term "women" we invoke a group who share a set of resemblances. Heyes argues powerfully that where we draw the line around "women" constitutes a political act, and this line may shift according to both context and politics. Engaging in a discussion of sex and gender, she contends that biology cannot be seen as creating a stable basis for line-drawing. Heyes insists that the experiences of transsexuals and the insights of transgender theory provide opportunities for feminists to think through the effects of binary conceptions of sex/gender. Indeed the question of transsexual access to women-only space has been very fraught in recent years. Heyes contends that male-to-female transsexuals bear family resemblances to "women-born-women" and that there is no mistake in calling them women. Yet the question of inclusion or exclusion depends upon strategy and context. Heyes's approach to the question of "Who is the woman of Women's Studies?" then, is one which invites us to be both reflexive about, and responsible for, how we designate our object of study.

ANTI-RACIST FEMINIST THEORY

Perhaps more forcefully than any other set of feminist interventions, anti-racist feminism placed the question of the exclusive nature of feminist theorizing on the table. The necessity of interrogating Canada as a "white settler society" and charting complex interrelations of race, gender and society broadly describes the project of Canadian anti-racist feminist thought. As defined by **Enakshi Dua** in this chapter **("Canadian Anti-Racist Feminist Thought: Scratching the Surface")**, anti-racist feminist thought interrogates the way race and gender function together in structuring social inequality. As she contends, anti-racist feminist thought has both a long history and an active engagement in contemporary feminist theory.

Crucially, anti-racist feminism has been a powerful force in revealing how Women's Studies itself is a site of regulation. Anti-racist feminist thought is marked not only by critiques of Women's Studies' narrow focus on "women," but also by the insistence on how this primary focus reflects white and racialized women's uneven relationship to the mode in which they are produced in Women's Studies. This unevenness is not simply a function of differences, but differences that are ranked. **Himani Bannerji's** 1987 piece in this chapter **("Introducing Racism: Notes Towards an Anti-Racist Feminism")** is a now-classic text that emphasizes the erasure of women of colour, "Third World" and southern European women, from what has constituted the mainstream of Canadian feminist theory. Racism becomes invisible, she argues, because it is part of our historically constructed everyday life and way of seeing. Bannerji draws a distinction between "overt" and common sense racism and she demonstrates how common sense racism has been a structuring presence in Canadian Women's Studies. The silences and gaps that attend the elaboration of a homogenous women's experience not only erase racialized women's experiences, they also support the hegemony of a feminism that is fundamentally white and middle class. In this very important article, Bannerji calls for feminist theorists to recognize that all women's experiences are shaped by racism, producing power relations among women that work to inhibit the critical analysis of Canada as simultaneously marked by complex interrelations of patriarchy, capitalism and racism.

Dua underlines the diversity and complexity of contemporary Canadian anti-racist feminist thought. As she demonstrates in her careful elaboration of the divergent strains of anti-racist feminism, the thrust of this body of theory is emphatically not the simple insistence on "differences" among women. Instead, anti-racist feminism inquires into the social relations that produce both identity groupings and power relations among women. It is the production of "differences" and social, economic and political implications of "differences" that defines the project of Canadian anti-racist feminist thought. Anti-racist feminist theorists have interrogated the manner in which mainstream feminist theory and activism have perpetuated and reinforced racism. Dua emphasizes that, while joined together in a theoretical project of analyzing the interconnections of race and gender, anti-racist feminist writers have been divided about whether to employ standpoint methodology or a reformulated political economy approach. Standpoint theorists, such as Bannerji, highlight the significance of the "outsider within" status of women of colour, occupying a structural position that overlaps the margins of race, class and gender. Analyzing this positioning provides an analytic lens for tracing how race, class and gender have been constituted historically. Political economists deploy a different analytic lens, focusing on how a racialized political economy differentiates women according to race, class and sexuality. Anti-racist feminists have used these methodological frameworks and others to interrogate the role of culture in producing racism, the racialization of work and the role of immigration and other state policies in producing racialized differences.

In locating racialization as integral to feminist scholarship and activism, anti-racist feminism issues a powerful challenge to the practice of Women's Studies teaching and scholarship. This challenge, as Dua laments, has yet to fundamentally reshape the object of this field of study. Dua emphasizes how the critical insights of anti-racist feminist scholarship have been met with resistance, ranging from silencing to tokenistic accommodation to dismissal. Contesting the view that the analysis of difference has gone too far, Dua challenges Women's Studies students and scholars to embrace a politics of accountability and anti-subordination.

NATIVE WOMEN AND COLONIZATION

While the "experience" of Canadian Native women has often been appropriated by feminist thinkers in their efforts to reflect "difference," this gesture itself very often embeds an essentialized and abstracted view of indigenous women. As Bonita Lawrence and Kim Anderson have argued, it is not an easy task to express the diverse experiences of Native women that spans the lives of "reserve residents and urban women, those with Indian status and those without, those who identify themselves as mixed-bloods, those who call themselves Métis and those who identify unequivocally as 'Indian' and do it in a way that shows the organic connections between these experiences." (Lawrence and Anderson, 2003, p. 11–12). Yet as Lawrence and Anderson contend, if the sign of the "Native woman" must be recognized as encompassing great diversity, the voices of Native women together express a critique of colonization and the challenge to rebuild.

Anti-racist feminist thinkers have revealed and critiqued the whiteness of the woman at the heart of feminist theory. Native women thinkers have simultaneously revealed how the woman of Women's Studies is also Western and European—her experiences and struggles defined through dominant Western theoretical frameworks that very often embed a nature/culture dichotomy and rest upon a world view emphasizing conflict and competition. Native women have critiqued this world view from the perspective of Aboriginal cultural beliefs that have been subjugated and undermined through the colonization of Aboriginal peoples.

As **Jeannette Armstrong ("Invocation: The Real Power of Aboriginal Women")** argues powerfully in this chapter, colonization has not only suppressed Aboriginal cultural beliefs and forms of government, it has also dramatically undermined the place and value of women in Aboriginal cultures. As she demonstrates, violence (both inside and outside Aboriginal communities), dispossession, the erosion of family structures and mothering through the residential schools policy and the seizure of children by child welfare authorities have left Native women dehumanized and in despair. Colonization has quite literally taken place on the bodies of Native women, eroding their central roles as the keepers of the next generation. And yet Armstrong paints a powerful picture of Aboriginal women as survivors, nurturers and agents for restoring that which colonization has eroded.

Armstrong's invocation of the strength of Native women and the importance of rescuing suppressed traditions that value harmony challenges Women's Studies scholars and students to think beyond Euro-Canadian frameworks. Crucially, Canadian Women's Studies must interrogate the history of Canada as a history of the colonization of Aboriginal peoples. The world view that Armstrong draws upon informs the diverse politics of Aboriginal women's political activism.

WOMEN'S STUDIES: NEW WAVES

As some second wave feminist theorists have asked, if we dispense with "women" as the subject of feminism, what then can be the ground of feminist activism? If we acknowledge that women's experience is constructed and infused with power relations, does this signal then the end of feminism and the end of Women's Studies as an intellectual project?

Some contemporary Canadian Women's Studies scholars contend that we must embrace the instabilities that these questions imply. **Ann Braithwaite** ("**Origin Stories and Magical Signs for and in Women's Studies**") encourages us to question the necessary links between the past, present and future of Women's Studies. As she argues, the rapid changes in the field since its inception must be viewed as exciting developments and signs of growth rather than as dangerous to Women's Studies' stability, meaning, role and identity. Here she questions the understanding of Women's Studies as the academic arm of the women's movement and interrogates how this narrative is being used in the present to tie the future of the field to some mythic past. While not questioning the links between Women's Studies as a scholarly endeavour and feminist activisms, she argues that contemporary laments that the field has strayed from its political origins work to foreclose intellectual debate and self-reflexivity. In effect, Braithwaite argues for a new wave of Women's Studies scholarship, one in which there can be a division between feminist politics and feminist intellectual work, so that the latter is freed to ask difficult questions and imagine new possibilities.

There is a relationship between Bratihwaite's argument that we must decouple the past from the future and the arguments of third wave feminists. Third wave feminists view the embrace of difference, anti-essentialism and multi-vocality, not as the death knell of feminism, but instead as the very condition of feminism's possibilities and futures. As **Natasha Pinterics ("Riding the Feminist Waves: In with the Thirds")** insists, there is a fundamental difference between post-feminist claims about the end of feminism and third wave feminism's claims about the necessity of reconfiguring the project of feminism. Whereas post-feminism contends that the goals of feminist movements have been achieved and thus feminism is now obsolete, third wave feminism must be seen as an act of strategic defiance that insists on the continuity and movement of feminism.

Pinterics wrote this 2001 article when she was an undergraduate student in Women's Studies. In elaborating the contours of third wave feminism, she situates its emergence within the context of anti-essentialist and anti-racist feminism. Indeed, as Heywood and Drake (1997) have argued, the definitional moment of third wave feminism took place on the terrain of race. Third wave feminism can be seen as taking up the anti-racist feminist call for a new feminist subjectivity in what has been a white and middle-class movement. In challenging the exclusiveness of the feminist "we," as Pinterics contends, third wave feminists also push towards a more complex politics of sexuality, insisting on the importance of sexual pluralism and challenging dominant feminist frameworks that have normalized some forms of sexual expression, while vilifying others. In focusing on political activism based upon coalitions, grassroots organizing and cyberfeminism, third wave feminism embraces a concept of theory fused with action, one that emphasizes accessibility and seeks to move theory beyond the academy.

Third wave feminism, emphasizing central concerns with race and sexuality, produces an interrogation of the orthodoxies that are perceived to reside within second wave feminist theorizing. Third wave feminism is often constructed as a generational rebellion against the symbolic second wave feminist "mother." **Kim Sawchuk ("Feminism in Waves: Re-imagining a Watery Metaphor")** contends that the conceptualization of feminism in waves does signal legitimate generational grievances; but it also presupposes the necessity of a distancing the old from the new in order to go forward. In this piece, she argues for a careful reconsideration of the wave metaphor and what it implies. Sawchuk delineates the origins of the wave metaphor within second wave feminism. As she contends, implicit in the conceptualization of feminism in waves is a kind of intellectual matricide. Despite the fact that the metaphor of waves carries the message that new waves are linked to past waves, ever flowing forward, the narrative simultaneously implies a necessary break with the past. As Sawchuk contends, this produces a highly caricatured view of past waves. In the present, this leads third wave feminists to erase the complexities of second wave feminism and its attention to the concerns that mark contemporary feminism—including debates on transsexuality, race, lesbianism and the politics of international feminism. Sawchuk does not argue for a rejection of the wave metaphor, but instead its reconceptualization. Waves, as she reminds us, transmit energy, do not come from a singular source and produce complex patterns. She urges us to be attentive to how this dynamic movement conveys ripples from the past that contribute to the future momentum of feminism and Women's Studies.

To Write Society: Adrift on the Edge of Reality and Fiction

Nicole Brossard

Nicole Brossard has published more than 30 books since 1965 and has twice won the Governor General's Award for her poetry. Many of her books have been translated into English, including Mauve Desert, The Aerial Letter, Lovers, Museum of Bone and Water, Intimate Journal *and, most recently,* Yesterday, at the Hotel Clarendon. *In 1991 she was awarded le Prix Athanase-David, the highest literary recognition in Quebec. She lives in Montreal.*

Feminist discourse is inspired by women's lives and testimonies and is nourished by feminist thought. Where women express their confusion, where feminist thought reveals the inner workings of the patriarchy, feminist discourse draws conclusions and takes action. Where women blame a husband, a lover, a father or an employer, where feminist thought incriminates the patriarchal system, feminist discourse *accuses* men. Where feminist thought discovers the laws that perpetuate women's alienation, where women reveal the drama of the female condition, feminist discourse *denounces* the institutions that contribute to the domination and exploitation of women. It analyzes their effects, proposes changes. Feminist discourse "objectivizes" women's subjectivity and it politicizes the assertions of feminist thought. It dares pass judgment. It assumes the right to generalize.

It harnesses women's anger, revolt, tears, hopes, humour and utopias. It points fingers. It polarizes. *It exacerbates differences, divides, creates solidarities.* All at once it is normative, iconoclastic, catalytic and responsible. It changes the rules of the game, roles, representation. It parties. It pontificates. It is multiple.

So we understand why it is accused of being irrational. Why it is so disturbing. Why it is often the object of suspicion on the part of women and how it is always the object of enormous resistance, if not an hysterical opposition, on the part of men.

Feminist discourse maintains a social and psychic tension by placing at the forefront and in everyone's full view that which divides economically, separates culturally, "disunites" men and women. It is astonishing that feminism has been accused of contributing to the discord between men and women when, in showing what divides them, it applies itself to giving women back their humanity. In fact, feminist discourse maintains a debate in the public forum without which (and this is demonstrated by history) the subjugation of women goes back to being common currency.

What has not been forgiven in feminist discourse is having politicized the most intimate and everyday. Having introduced the notion of power in relationships that were previously considered as following from a "natural" order. Having attacked an ideological consensus and a social order by going directly through the individual, that is to say by asking the latter to change its habits but also its way of imagining sexualized relationships. In addition to this, feminist discourse is perceived as moralizing, as an intrusion at the heart of what is most intimate to us all.

But, as opposed to most political discourses that aim to come into actual political power, feminist discourse aims to redistribute the power between men and women. For this, it must inevitably take on macho and phallocentric power. To give back to women power over their lives and bodies, it must interrogate all forms of activities where male power has installed itself. Feminist discourse would call into question the holy institution of marriage where love, domestic work, sexuality, economy, affectivity, maternity and the care and education of children are tossed in a random heap. Obviously, women's power over themselves cannot be recuperated without directly antagonizing those who believe it to be theirs by divine right, and I would go so far as to say antagonizing those women who live in the certainty that they already possess this power.

Feminist discourse goes directly to the heart of women and men. It touches the most sensitive fibres of our emotions, of our affectivity; it touches the image that every man and woman creates for themselves by belonging to a gender.

Yet, feminist discourse is partisan, that is to say that in addition to siding with women against violent and dominating men, it interrogates and virtually accuses those men that refuse to call into question illegitimately acquired power and privilege. Thus it provokes in men a gamut of troubling feelings that oscillate between incomprehension, guilt, anger and a loss of identity.

Because it is partisan, feminist discourse exacerbates the differences, creates solidarities.

Basing itself on the testimonies of women and on the initial findings of feminist thought, feminist discourse was first of all able to show the differences; then it exacerbated them by revaluing the feminine and everything related to it as well as by discrediting the masculine and that which is generally associated with it. For a relatively simplistic formula, it still has the advantage of weaving new ties between members of the dominated group and hence creating a solidarity in the face of a common "enemy," a solidarity that engenders energy and projects that allow for action to be taken.

Yet, despite women's subjectivity becoming the objective through feminist discourse around a common project (fighting against sexism, the patriarchy, misogyny), women have not ceased to question themselves on the objective conditions of their lives, on their emotions and their relationship to power. Once again, women will resort to the expression of their lived experience to bear witness to the position they occupy in the social hierarchy.

Thus will they name the disparities and the differences that, this time, follow from their belonging to a social group that is oppressed and discriminated against. Some of these differences will be debated ideologically through the masculine-conceived filters of Marxism, psychoanalysis and nationalism. But others—the most important ones, for they call into play the body, sexuality and self-image—will be debated viscerally. It is thus that lesbian feminists and African-American feminists, by calling into question the discourse of the white heterosexual feminists of the upper middle class, will exacerbate another series of differences, create new solidarities, diversify feminist discourse and its field of action and nourish new tensions that, in the United States and in Canada, would find partial resolution in the creation of the concept of "politically correct."

These days this concept, recent to appear in the political configuration of French-speaking Quebec, is readily mocked. People are amused by confusing it with a form of egalitarian morality that would level desires, imagination and fantasies, that would forbid any overflow, any deviation. And yet, the concept of "politically correct" essentially aims to increase the participation and the development of the individuals belonging to inferiorized and marginalized groups. It is a concept that allows for the development of minority and marginalized discourses but also allows that history be re-read from different angles. It engenders a new dynamic in power relations whose effects we do not yet know: Babel, hybridity, or a new territory for identification? There again, we do not know what will be left for women of this new concept developed by feminists.

Will feminist work serve once more as a bridge between white, black, First Nations and ethnic minority men? In principle, we would have reason to rejoice at having such influence, but can we really speak of cultural change if the only cultures coming together are misogynistic and sexist? Not easy coming out of marginality, is it?

The problem is one of size: each time feminism succeeds in disseminating in society propositions founded on respecting the Other and difference, these propositions, first initiated according to sexual difference, transform themselves bit by bit into common occurrences from which the feminine is eliminated in the mid-term.

If we can affirm that each time the patriarchal system integrates feminine values, men and women benefit, we can thus ask ourselves whether feminism is irremediably condemned to opening doors on the field of relational possibilities, that is to say playing a mediating role. Thus, we could say that, dominated, women served as trade currency between men; their wits about them, they can aspire only to being high-ranking, competent and influential civil servants without decision-making powers, which is not without recalling the traditional position of the strong woman, who, so they say, always hides herself behind a great man.

Politically, we could thus affirm that, amid men, women are invisible; beside men, they are marginalized; as separatists (in the lesbian sense of the term), they are ignored; opposed to sexist politics, that is to say feminist, they are threatened with retaliation. Thus we understand why feminist discourse is simultaneously normative, iconoclastic, catalytic and responsible. Because feminist discourse is nourished by the question of identity, which constantly questions reference, difference and environment, this discourse remains an open space. I would also say that like every discourse that proceeds from an interrogation of reality and the imaginary, feminist discourse also needs poetry. There is nothing immoral in feminist discourse being, at times, more surreal than a Breton poem, more baroque than a Bernini sculpture, more repetitive than the music of Steve Reich, more turbulent than a choreography by *La La La Human Steps,* more pieced together than a Gaston Miron poem. Emotion matters to me.

Philosophical Investigations (in a Feminist Voice)

Cressida Heyes

Cressida Heyes is Canada Research Chair in Philosophy of Gender and Sexuality at the University of Alberta. She is the author of Line Drawings: Defining Women through Feminist Practice *and* Self-Transformations: Foucault, Ethics, and Normalized Bodies. *She is currently co-editing a volume of essays on feminist perspectives on cosmetic surgery.*

1. Let us consider the construct that we call "women." I don't just mean white, middle-class, heterosexual, able-bodied, young, attractive, Western women, but all women. What is common to them all? Don't say: *"There must be something in common or they wouldn't be called 'women.'"* Likewise, don't say: *"If women have nothing in common, then how can feminism form a political movement?"* Look and see what the construct of women consists of, and what women might have in common. For, if you look, you will not see something that is common to all, but similarities, relationships and a whole series of them at that. Look, for example, at heterosexual women. They are attracted to, and may form sexual relationships with, men. Now pass to bisexual women: some features drop out and others appear! Think now of a woman of colour (if you haven't already). How is she like a white woman? . . .

2. And the result of this examination is: we see a complicated network of similarities overlapping and crisscrossing: sometimes overall similarities, sometimes similarities of detail (Wittgenstein [1953], *Philosophical Investigations* [PI]–66).

Furthermore, even when I talk about one woman it is not correct to find the logical sum of these individual interrelated concepts: if I am white, anglophone, middle class, young . . . then the concept of "me" is not an additive analysis of these different parts (PI–68). I cannot abstract from the rest that part of me that is race, that which is sexuality and so on. (Yet obviously I can still *use* the concept of myself.) Likewise, when I compare myself to a woman of colour, whom I resemble in many other respects, I cannot say "add some colour, and we are the same."

3. *"So how can you talk about women at all?"* Well, when I talk about them, I give examples that I intend to be taken in a particular way, so that the examples may be *used* (in the game of politics perhaps). The danger of this is that we may not recognize that these are just examples and not an ideal, an inexpressible common thing that represents all women. For what does the mental picture of a woman look like when it does not show us any particular image, but what is common to all women? I think that if you see "women" in a cer-

tain light you will use the term in a certain way, and because your account does not apply to all women, but only to those you are thinking of, in using an ideal you will be guilty of a generalization that is quite unjustified . . . .

4. *"So what is the purpose of this ideal, if it is not found in reality?"* In this case, the ideal comes to serve a political purpose for you, as my examples serve my political purposes. The ideal woman can be held up as a metaphysical necessity that comes to legislate my identity. So when we identify similarities and differences, we must be quite clear that this is a pragmatic exercise . . . .

5. *"But if you are a feminist, then you need to make generalizations about women, for this is the essence of feminist politics!"* Exactly. I have never denied that. When I look around a classroom, for example, I see women having common experiences of being excluded and trivialized. But that is not to say that even we are all the same. I can draw a boundary around us, for a special purpose . . . .

6. The ideal becomes an empty notion, which muddles me, and prevents me from seeing what I have to do. What feminist action should I take if I am in pursuit of a chimera? We have taken out all the substance of "women" and are left with a vacuous concept: "We have got onto slippery ice where there is no friction and so in a certain sense the conditions are ideal, but also, just because of that, we are unable to walk. We want to walk: so we need *friction.* Back to the rough ground!" (PI–107).

7. Sometimes you draw a boundary around concepts to use them yourself. (This may be called a stereotype.) What matters is that you look and see whether or not you have drawn the boundary self-consciously. Sometimes the boundary is oppressive; sometimes it acts as an object of comparison . . . .

8. But now you will say: *"This is nonsense. All women do have something in common; namely, their bodies. Do you want to deny that?"* All right, the concept of "women" is bounded for you by the physical reality of sexed existence. It need not be so. You have given the physical character of "women" particular limits, but I can use the term so that its extension is not closed by the same frontier.

9. This much I will allow you: some aspects of some male and female bodies are different. But why have we drawn the most important boundaries there? Why do we not draw them around other differences between us? Certainly it matters that some women menstruate, have breasts, vaginas, bear children. But do all women share these features? And how will we describe them? The physical boundaries of sex are elective foundations, supported by the walls of social practice . . . .

10. So now you agree: *"bodies don't matter"* (on this I am still only partly in agreement) and ask again, *"If bodies aren't exactly real, how is the social construct of 'women' bounded?"* It is bounded by a set of rules that regulate it very well, yet which leave some gaps.

11. "*Essence* is expressed by grammar." (PI–371). The category of "women" has been confirmed by language—such as the gendered pronouns some languages use to divide the world in two. This obscures the contingency of that division and leads us to assign it more importance than we otherwise might: "Philosophy is a battle against the bewitchment of our intelligence by means of language." (PI–109).

12. The category of sex is created and defined by a fluid boundary. For what matters about being a woman? Look and see. We can claim things in common, like perhaps motherhood, or sexuality, or emotional sensibilities, but that is not to say that we will all, always, have these things in common. I use my own experience to find out what the women I know have

in common. The construction of gender identity is a complex thing, and it varies among people; that is to say, it is mutable. (We have approached the problem from the other side, and now we know our way about!)

> One might say that the concept "game" is a concept with blurred edges. *"But is a blurred concept a concept at all?"* Is an indistinct photograph a picture of a person at all? Is it even always an advantage to replace an indistinct picture by a sharp one? Isn't the indistinct one often exactly what we need? (PI–71).

13. So, perhaps we do not need to specify what the concept "women" is at all. In fact, specifying might not be to our advantage. Rather we need to take the longer path toward discovering who we are and who we are not.

14. We extend our concept of women as in spinning a thread we twist fibre on fibre. And the strength of the thread does not reside in the fact that some one fibre runs through its whole length, but in the overlapping of many fibres.

What does the preceding Wittgensteinian conversation tell us about feminist theory? First, it elaborates a familiar stalemate: namely, that any feminist theory that tries to incorporate the multiplicity of differences among women will not be able to make the generalizations required for feminist politics. This leaves feminist theory trapped between an acute gender skepticism and the use of crude and exclusive generalizations. These polar accounts are sometimes presented as the only options for feminists, yet by enquiring both into meaning and into feminist method, a Wittgensteinian feminist critique of essentialism helps us to locate ourselves outside the terms of the dichotomy. . . .

. . . [A family resemblance account avoids] a misleading ontology that sets up mutually exclusive, bounded categories.

. . . There need be no definitive set of characteristics that all women share, but rather we can understand ourselves as connected to each other by a network of overlapping similarities, some of which may be biologically real—like breasts, a vagina, a uterus, the capacity to conceive and bear a child, XX chromosomes; others of which may be more obviously constructed—like a particular relation to one's mother, ethical attitudes, experiences of subordination, and so on. But no *single* characteristic is necessary to make an individual a woman, and none is sufficient. Thus, on this view, it is perfectly possible to make sense of the fact that two "distantly related" individuals can both be women and share none of the same characteristics except that they are called "women." A male-to-female (MTF) transsexual woman, for example, might have XY chromosomes; experience of being raised as a boy in a white, urban, bourgeois, nuclear family and conventionally feminine self-presentation. A butch woman might have XX chromosomes, experience of being raised as a girl by lesbian parents in a small Northern community and conventionally masculine self-presentation. On my Wittgensteinian-feminist view, it is not "wrong" to call them both "women" even though they do not share any common features potentially definitive of womanhood. . . .

Wittgenstein anticipates several objections to these considerations, all helpful for my anti-essentialist feminism. First, he argues that all instances of concepts like "game" (or, we might add, "women") do not have a disjunctive shared property—some characteristic(s) we can identify as being common to all games—but rather the common term gathers together multiple instances that have overlapping similarities. Our attempts to find common properties are examples of our being led astray by the single word that links these family resemblances. Second, a concept is not the logical sum of sub-concepts, each of which can be rigidly defined—board games, card games, Olympic games, etc.—since we can, and often do, use it in a way that is not bounded. That is, we invent new games, or make the case that something not previously thought of as a game should be included in that concept. Wittgenstein rejects the idea that a concept without rigid boundaries is useless, and he shows us a variety of ways in which we use concepts despite the openness of their frontiers. Thus explanation of a particular phenomenon by example is not necessarily subsequent to explanations that posit essences, but rather may be a better strategy for articulating the use of a particular term.

This attack on linguistic essentialism has important implications for methodological essentialism. It provides an alternative ontology that sidesteps the view that there is an essential womanness, separable from class, race and other contexts, that all women share. This approach also sidesteps the ontological (if not the political) need to have people pass through classifications of the sort Spelman describes. However, we can still use the term "women," make generalizations about women and engage in feminist politics. Wittgenstein's notion of family resemblances offers not only a supplementary ontological critique of essentialist practices, but also a solution—a new way of thinking about the similarities and differences among people. Of course, to describe women as bearing family resemblances to each other only constitutes an ontological therapy, or a way of freeing ourselves from the misleading philosophical picture that holds us captive, not necessarily a riposte to those (myself included) who see political reasons for positing gender commonality. It does, however, reveal these reasons as purposive rather than predetermined, and therefore as carrying a concomitant demand for justification. The practice of becoming self-conscious and self-critical about the bases of one's own classifications is, I think, a crucial part of feminist consciousness-raising in the current political climate.

Rather than considering language as revealing truths about the world, we are urged to examine linguistic usage. Thus instead of assuming a quintessential "womanness" that all women share because they are called "women," we should look more closely at the applications of the term. Then, to understand what "women" means, we would have to give examples of different people called "women," and if feminists wanted to describe a particular social phenomenon as, for example, "a women's issue," we would have to justify that label by pointing to the ways it affects (and sometimes, constructs) people we call "women" and stipulate the women to whom it applies. In addition to preventing some women from simply ignoring the experiences of others, this method would also de-legitimate the claim that the experiences of nondominant women do not actually count as "women's experience" . . . .

LINE DRAWINGS

. . . In locating feminist theorists between methodological essentialism and principled anti-essentialism, a Wittgensteinian approach gives us reason to see the decisions we make about definitions as deeply political. In Wittgenstein's remarks on the possibilities of setting the boundary of a concept in many different places, and further on the need to set a boundary at all, I see radical possibilities for feminism. It might initially seem as if I am . . . using philosophy to obscure biological difference, if the word "women" actually corresponds to the category of women bounded by the physical reality of the female body. Indeed we do need to recognize the reality and significance of biology, not as pre-social or extra-linguistic "facts" about chromosomes or genitalia, but as lived experience of embodiment with politically significant cultural meaning . . . [B]oth feminist and non-feminist discourses make uncritical assumptions about the natural reality and necessity of sexual dimorphism. Simultaneously afraid that our bodies would be erased, that we would be reduced to our bodies, or that our bodies would over-determine our selves, we have struggled with how to locate the sexed body in feminist philosophy.

The specific contribution of a Wittgensteinian feminism to these debates lies in the argument that where we draw the boundary around the category "women" constitutes a political act, and one that should be scrutinized for its particular purpose, no less when biological characteristics feature on one side or the other of the boundary. "To repeat, we can draw a boundary—for a special purpose. Does it take that to make the concept usable? Not at all! (Except for that special purpose.)" (PI–69). Thus feminists can aim for semantic influence over the category "women" and redefine its boundaries with the explicit acknowledgment that this is a political activity (not an unproblematically "objective" scientific or medical one) within which power differentials affect the semantic authority of the participants, including different women . . . . If we posit "women" as that bounded group of people held in place . . . by various popular, medical and scientific discourses, not fixed in the sense that a pre-existing reality "holds it fast," we can also see how adding feminist challenges to "the movement around" women might lead to further displacement of those who are accepted as women, by way of an alteration in the meaning of that term.

Such methodological possibilities for the subversion of sex and gender identities form a key part of undermining simplistic and rigidly imposed binary definitions of "women" and "men"—an integral part of the task of any feminist theory. It is also a task that makes especially apparent the necessary connections between feminism and queer theorizing and activism: any feminism that fails to understand itself as deeply implicated in the struggles of all those who are oppressed by normative heterosexuality—not only lesbians and not only women—will miss a key facet of gender oppression. So how can feminists allied with queer activists challenge oppressive sex and gender binarisms while justifying strategic line drawing around particular groups of people for the purposes of oppositional politics? The notion that male and female bodies create two discrete groups that are biologically bounded and exist prior to any use of category labels is both empirically inaccurate, and obscures the fact that the terms "man" or "woman," "female" or "male," and "boy" or "girl" are not attributed by unequivocal reference to primary or even secondary sexual characteristics. In fact, to the extent that physical sex cues are real, they can be overridden to a remarkable degree by social context. The crucial exception here is, of course, the classic delivery room question, "Is it a boy or a girl?," an attribution that obscures the existence of intersexed infants, who cause discursive chaos for medical practitioners and others intent on imposing and constructing human sexual dimorphism.

Thus some of the deepest challenges to the boundary of the term "women" in Western societies come from those whose gender presentation does not conform to their birth sex (or perhaps to any commonly understood category), who alter the physical sex of their bodies, or those who have sexual characteristics that fall outside the terms of the conventional binary. While an obsession with genital status can serve merely to reinforce the myth that gender collapses into sex, critical histories and theories of transsexuality and intersexuality are important. They offer openings to dialogue for all feminists thinking through the political effects of binary conceptual schemes, and opportunities for building political coalitions with those who have related but not identical experiences of sex-gender oppression. The extreme reactions of confusion, distaste and violence toward those whose bodies do not accommodate sexual dimorphism, or whose gender identity deviates from their sex assignment, demonstrate the deep psychological and political dependence within dominant Western cultures on sex-gender conformity . . . .

For example, non-transsexed feminists have had ambivalent attitudes toward the inclusion of MTF transsexuals in feminist community that deserve further political scrutiny. Janice Raymond's classic hostile analysis of the politics of transsexuality, along with highly publicized essentialist transsexual memoirs (of which Jan Morris's *Conundrum* is perhaps the most highbrow), has contributed to a thread of feminist skepticism about the politics of transsexuality. One major source of this skepticism has been the deployment of essentialist accounts of sex and gender in theories of transsexuality. Raymond, for example, stresses the conservatism of the then-dominant medical model and makes the case that transsexuality (and, by default, transsexuals themselves) reinscribes oppressive patriarchal sex and gender binarisms, and both reflects and generates popular support for metaphysical and biological essentialisms.

Likewise popular discourse around transsexuality in modern Western cultures has clung to a metaphysical essentialism both historically specific and in denial of its own historicity. For example, Morris remarks at the beginning of her autobiographical narrative: "I was three or perhaps four years old when I realized that I had been born into the wrong body and should really be a girl." And later: "I believe [the 'conundrum' of 'transsexualism'] to have some higher origin or meaning. I equate it with the idea of soul, or self, and I think of it not just as a sexual enigma, but as a quest for unity . . . in my mind it is a subject far wider than sex: I recognize no pruriency to it, and I see it above all as a dilemma neither of the body nor of the brain, but of the spirit." Here in its most extreme form is the idea that one's soul is sexed and must conform to its sexed body. Biologically essentialist claims have also been embedded in medicalized understandings of transsexuality as a "disease" caused by, for example, hormonal imbalance.

Thus feminists such as Raymond point to the essentialisms implicit in medical and popular models of transsexuality, and have constructed MTF transsexuals in particular as reinforcing a politically suspect line drawing between female and male. Raymond's interpretation of transsexuals' testimony reinforces an understanding of MTFs as mimicking and reinscribing a patriarchal construct of femininity. Thus, the argument runs, dominant accounts of transsexuality reify a binarism that should properly—in the interests of both adequate explanation and effective political strategy—be deconstructed. The paradox of this position is that similarly located feminists have also been critical of transsexuals for the latter's failure to recognize the *inflexibility* of gender boundaries. Arguing that MTF transsexuals are not "real women," many radical feminists have resisted including MTFs in the category. Border wars over the admission of MTF transsexuals to women-only festivals and organizations, for example, continue to divide feminist communities. Such arguments for the exclusion of MTFs shy away from explicitly essentialist claims about the biological basis of femininity, claiming instead that they do not have the experience of childhood female socialization in a patriarchal society, or that transsexuals will contaminate women's hard-won separate space with their "male energy" or desire to appropriate. Nonetheless, the use of the euphemism "womyn-born-womyn" to characterize those who *are* counted seems to belie this claim. (One cannot, surely, since Beauvoir, be "born" a woman?)

This contradictory feminist position relies on a partial account of transsexed identities that is rarely in keeping with transsexuals' own understandings . . . . [T]here exist numerous dominant essentializing models of femininity—each endorsed by some anti-feminist women—alongside diverse feminist alternatives. Likewise in transsexual theorizing, the conservatism of a Morris can be juxtaposed with more radical and politically astute accounts of trans-subjectivity, such as those offered by Kate Bornstein, Leslie Feinberg, Jay Prosser and Susan Stryker. Many of these theorists are themselves critical of the essentialisms in medical discourses, but they point out that conformity to medical gatekeepers' expectations is a central criterion for gaining access to surgeries or hormone treatments. Surgeons, physicians and psychiatrists persistently reinscribe oppressive gender scripts and construct normative heterosexuality when they insist on pre-op transsexuals living *as a man,* or *as a woman,* in their most patriarchal and essentialist senses, or demand that MTF transsexuals endure more pain or surgical intervention in the interests of, for example, acquiring a vagina "deep enough" for penile penetration. These treatments are important in a culture that demands that one's sexed body minimally conform to one's gender presentation not least for personal safety and legal purposes. Changing information technology has made critiques of medical practices more accessible and thus more widely integrated into transsexuals' constructions of their own needs, and some are organizing against certain medical and psychiatric norms. Again, different trans-theorists have different attitudes to body modification, and a growing movement among transgendered men in particular argues against it, partly in light of the poor aesthetic and functional quality of phalloplasties, but also on political grounds.

The arguments I have put forward against the reduction of the category "women" to any set of necessary and sufficient conditions provide compelling philosophical reasons against the methodologically essentialist view that MTFs cannot count. The appeal to "womyn-born-womyn" first fails as a biological criterion: it seems also to exclude intersexuals who have been surgically constructed as female perinatally and lived their lives as girls and women, while including FTM transsexuals who are living as men. Politically speaking, too, the exclusion of MTFs from women-only space relies on a blanket characterization of the motivations and histories of a diverse group. Furthermore, this is a group whose members are systematically stigmatized and harassed for gender transgressions and who struggle for recognition as "women" in a culture that insists on a conformity that for most will only ever be partly achieved. MTF transsexual narratives frequently dispute the presumed trajectory of a male-privileged life prior to transition, instead positing a turbulent and silenced experience of gender ambivalence, accompanied by attempts at gender discipline and abuse from others. These experiences of gender oppression seem to provide a useful basis for alliance with non-trans-feminists. That some MTFs do not have feminist consciousness, or have self-understandings with which some radical feminists disagree, hardly distinguishes them from "womyn-born-womyn" . . . .

. . . I want to indicate, first, the connections between trans-theory and critiques of essentialism; second, I want to endorse the extension of the border of the concept "women" to include MTF transsexuals, suggesting that this move is supported by my Wittgensteinian feminist approach. The question "Are MTF transsexuals women?" is not well-formed in the absence of a fixed set of criteria of womanhood to which we can appeal. I suggest that MTF transsexuals bear family resemblances to those people conventionally labelled "women" and that there is no mistake entailed in calling them women. This endorsement, however, need not imply that all claimants to the title "woman" need be uncritically embraced by any coalition of feminists struggling to carve out a space of resistance. The term does not lose all meaning merely because a novel contested use has won the battle for acceptance. Again, which uses should be accepted by any marginalized group is a contextual and strategic question. The criteria of difference offered by some feminists (for example, the experience of what Naomi Scheman calls "perinatal pinking"—that is, "having been named female around the time of birth") may mean that in some contexts there are good political reasons for stressing that transsexed women are distant rather than close relations of the women making the judgment about inclusion or exclusion. Thus part of the challenge of my analysis comes from its insistence that deciding whom to exclude (or include) in a given political context is a power struggle, in which the dominant members of an existing group vie with the peripheral members, rather than an exercise in ontological correctness.

To make this clear, let me give another example in which my judgment is that *exclusion* is the most politically appropriate move. Jacquelyn Zita, in her widely cited article, "Male Lesbians and the Postmodernist Body," poses the question "Can men be lesbians?" Zita asks whether a theory of the post-modern body might allow men to occupy the subject-position of women-loving-women. If this subject-position is an historical construction, a placeholder in a range of identities rather than a natural kind, then a given body may merely occupy that space rather than define it . . . .

The central drawback to this suggestion is that the theory works to its logical conclusions by focusing on subjectivity as a linguistic space rather than on the politics of the bodily experience of the agent and how she is located in a material context of oppression. There are reasons for drawing the line around the concept "lesbian" in such a way that it includes those who have lived experience of desiring women while occupying a female-coded body, given the deeply significant social and political ramifications of this experience. Furthermore, the appropriation of the term "lesbian" by male-bodied, male-gendered men—not all of whom, in my experience and as my prediction, are or would be even minimally well-intentioned or politically astute—would result in tangible political losses: less "female lesbian"-only space, a fading of the distinct character of lesbian communities, or a weakening of the ability powerfully to name oneself "lesbian," for example. The central difference between this case and the MTF transsexual example is that the use of the term "lesbian" to apply to men fails deeply to challenge conventional understandings of sex and gender boundaries: a person with a male body who changes her gender presentation to female, feminist caveats notwithstanding, is disturbing an established frontier around the concepts "women" and "men." She will likely struggle for a recognition that will never be comfortably attained in a trans-phobic and essentialist culture, and will often be punished for her transgressions. The straight man dating women who suddenly renames himself "lesbian," no matter how astutely he reworks his own subjectivity, however, is unlikely to be recognized as a gender outlaw unless he also modifies his gender presentation. Lesbianism is not only a state of mind. The more radical move for the woman-identified man, it seems to me, would be to remain nominally heterosexual, but to show by example the (admittedly constrained) progressive possibilities for that subject-position.

Thus it is often the case that, even as we accept the radical ontological consequences of an anti-essentialist Wittgensteinian approach, we must pay careful attention to the political consequences of where we draw lines around terms. Zita's discussion points not to an affirmative answer to the question "Can men be lesbians?" but to the need for justificatory strategies that emphasize the material political gains and losses of line drawing in specific contexts. Ambiguously sexed bodies, trans-identities, the case of the male lesbian and other examples illuminate the politically salient, as well as the variously constructed, qualities of sex and gender boundaries. These examples highlight the fluidity of the boundary around the concept "women," and the possibilities for challenge to conventional usages. While our ontological concerns give us some freedom in leaving terms open, however, the strategic imperatives of politics require objects of comparison; they demand that we draw boundaries around terms to use them as "measuring rods." As Linda Zerilli says,

> Politics consists precisely in the making of claims, which being claims, are inevitably partial and thus exclusive . . . . That the claim "we women demand x" excludes some women turns not on the theoretical insight (in the study) into the exclusionary character of the category of women but rather on the political character of making claims (in a public space).

Making a concept comparatively useful might entail that its boundary be firmly, albeit not immutably, fixed. Wittgenstein recognizes the need for some conceptual delimiting; however, he urges us to acknowledge the contingent nature of our terms, and to view them as purposive tools rather than "a preconceived idea to which reality must correspond."

None of the foregoing implies that all categories are oppressive and that women should therefore cease to lay claim to gender as an explanatory element of social theory. The excessive reluctance to draw lines around terms can be just as ontologically misguided and politically unhelpful as essentialism, not least because I sometimes suspect that this kind of theory is written by those who can afford to let their philosophical imaginations run away with them, leaving more prosaic politics behind for the less privileged. Some anti-essentialist philosophical strategies give the impression that their exponents toy with, or are titillated by, the kind of examples that make an anti-essentialist case, rather than examining how, in the light of anti-essentialism, we can move on and construct useful feminist theory. To claim, for example, that "woman can never be defined" may constitute a valuable critical contention within an existing philosophical discourse yet does not obviously further feminist projects that must draw on the notion of specific groups of women, united in some identifiable set of experiences or political objectives.

I have come up against a familiar paradox: namely, that at the same time as feminists try to subvert the stereotypical categories established by patriarchy, we may wish to defend the conceptual limits of the categories women create for ourselves. Otherwise everything becomes available for co-optation, and in the process feminist claims lose their political saliency. Overcoming the "bewitchment of our intelligence by means of language" is not simply a matter of opening every conceptual boundary and inviting everybody in. It consists in careful attention to the political and ethical implications of where we draw lines around terms, not on philosophical well-wishing.

Between the poles of radical deconstruction and rigid essentialism lies a large philosophical terrain, and it is here that Wittgenstein sets us down. His choice is plain: we can leave a concept open (using it in the knowledge that its constituents have no common disjunctive property), or we can draw a line around it for a purpose. Here there is a case for taking very seriously the possibly negative political implications of that boundary, yet even a concept with "blurred edges" is identifiable. In some cases refusing to allow any politically motivated limits of meaning might have negative political connotations, as I showed above. Some commentaries on categories like "women" and "lesbians" seem excessively reluctant to draw boundaries, and in leaving terms gaping risk political vacuity and ineptitude. There are good political reasons for being inexact about what we mean in many cases, yet at other times philosophy must not be allowed to run ahead of the political reality with which it contends, lest it participate in the creation of deconstructive theories that are as far from usage and experience as the metaphysics they seek to undermine.

Introducing Racism: Notes Towards an Anti-Racist Feminism

Himani Bannerji

Himani Bannerji is a professor in the Department of Sociology at York University and teaches in the areas of anti-racist feminism, Marxist cultural theories, gender, colonialism and imperialism. Her recent publications include Of Property and Propriety: The Role of Gender and Class in Imperialism and Nationalism *(edited and co-authored with S. Mojab and J. Whitehead, 2001)*, Inventing Subjects: Studies in Hegemony, Patriarchy and Colonialism *(2001),* The Dark Side of the Nation: Essays on Multiculturalism, Nationalism and Racism *(2000). A new book,* Projects of Hegemony and Projects of Knowledge: Essays on Nationalism, Gender, Ethnicity and Ideology, *will be published by Orient Longman in 2008.*

From its very early phase the word "silence" has been important in the vocabulary of feminist writing. It spoke of being *silent* or having been *silenced*—of two distinct but related themes. In a cluster with "silence" there are other words speaking of gaps, absences, being "hidden in history," of being organized *out* of social space or discourse, or *into apathy*, and of "a problem without a name." Not exceptionally, therefore, there also appeared other expressions—signifying women's struggles—about gaining or giving a voice, a direct assumption of our subjectivity, creating a version of the world from "our" own standpoint, and thus speaking from our own "self" or "centre" or experience.

For many years now I have read and taught this literature. I have spoken of it as combatting sexism internally within ourselves and externally in relation to a sexist world. I did this for years and in a way it had a resonance for me, and gave me the feeling that finally I had a way of interpreting what I felt since my early childhood. But very soon I began to develop a discomfort and sometimes even a feeling of antagonism towards this type of feminist writing, for reasons initially unclear to me. Of course, this was accompanied by feelings of guilt and worries that perhaps my politics were not feminist after all. Needless to say, I did not encounter feminists in the university who experienced any basic and fundamental sense of insufficiency with this feminism, which passes as *the* feminism. I had heard of old struggles between feminists on the ground of class, but when I came into the scene the talk of class, if it ever existed in Canada, had ceased to have any serious content. With the exception of isolated instances, class was paid mere lip-service, and the discourse of gender, professionalism and mobility had asserted itself in the university. Lacking colleagues, I spoke to my students and other women in the city who, like me, also happened to be non-white, or so-called "immigrants" from the less industrialized parts of Europe and Latin America. It was speaking with these women that saved my sanity, because this feeling of discomfort that I had with feminist currency or discourse seemed to be something other than paranoia or reactive politics on my part. In editing "Women of Colour," Issue 16 of the feminist magazine *Fireweed*, some of us tried to grope towards a formulation of what felt wrong and of some of the reasons for our entry at a wrong angle into the feminist world of Toronto.

In time I began to understand better what was going on in my classroom. The truth was that neither I nor many of my students with a Third World or southern European background were participating in our own capacities as "persons" in that classroom: rather we were "personas," characters called "students" and "teacher" in a Canadian university, learning the "feminist framework" which in the end turned out to be the story of the European bourgeois family. At the end of some of the books we used a section on "women of colour" was included, but this topic was not integrated into the book's overall perspective. Similarly, in some of the university's courses a section or two was taught on the topic of "women of colour" or "immigrant women," but again the issues were not integrated into the course material as a whole. I began to toy with the idea of designing a course on "Women of Colour" or "Immigrant Women . . . and Racism!"

So this was the issue—that once more there were gaps or silences, that people like us were never present in what we taught and read. In volumes of material produced in the West on women, with all the talk of "herland" and "herstory," our absences have not ceased: our voices, if we have any, are very small ones. I have rarely, while doing work in Women's Studies proper, come across a framework or methodology which addresses or legitimizes the existence and concerns of women like us, or helps give our voices strength and authenticity. How then can we speak of "gaining voices," "shattering silences," of sharing experiences, being empowered, and so on? The great bulk of Canadian literature on women and what passes for Women's Studies curriculum leaves the reader with the impression that women from the Third World and southern Europe are a very negligible part of the living and labouring population in Canada. Furthermore, the silences in this literature would seem to imply that nothing much is to be learned about the nature of economic, social and political organization of Canada by studying lives or concerns of women of colour. Not even most of the works of feminist women writers claiming to be interested in "class" in Canada contain full-length chapters on such a population. One might ask what produces this phenomenon, which simultaneously expresses a lack of consciousness as well as a false consciousness? And this happens in a country with the history of a settler colonial state and economy, where "reserves" exist in large numbers for the indigenous peoples, where a working class is still being created through racist immigration policies and segmentation of the labour market, and where a U.S.-dependent capitalism has long ago entered an imperialist phase?

The full answer to my question of how we got here is complex and not fully visible to me. But I do have these notes towards an answer, which offer us a possibility of explanation as well as a basis for moving towards an anti-racist feminism. It is this possibility rather than the urge for sharing experiences that impels me to this writing. The answer begins in the history of colonial and imperialist economic, social and political practices that have in the past and now continue to construct Canada. It also lies in certain habits or ways of thinking and seeing that have emerged in the course of history, as well as clearly developed ideologies and methods for constructing social and political discourse—feminist or any other.

For my exploration I will rely to some extent on Antonio Gramsci's notion of common sense, which, put simply, might be seen as the submerged part of the iceberg which is visible to us as ideology. Writers such as Fredric Jameson have phrased it in terms of the political unconscious. Its efficacy for understanding the situation of non-white people living in the West is clearly demonstrated by a volume produced in Britain about race and racism in the 1970s, entitled *The Empire Strikes Back.* In this volume Errol Lawrence paraphrases Gramsci in a way that is useful for me. He writes:

> The term "common sense" is generally used to denote a down-to-earth "good sense." It is thought to represent the distilled truths of centuries of practical experience: so much so that to say of an idea or practice that it is only common sense, is to appeal over the logic and argumentation of intellectuals to what all reasonable people have known in their "heart of hearts" to be right and proper. Such an appeal can act at one and the same time to foreclose any discussion about certain ideas and practices and to legitimate them. (Empire Strikes Back, 48)

What is more, common sense is accretional, and being unthought out it leaves plenty of room for contradictions, myths, guesses and rumours. It is therefore by no means a unified body of knowledge, and as a form of our everyday way of being it is deeply practical in nature. The general direction of its movement as such comes from common socio-economic and cultural practices, which, in turn, common sense helps to organize. From this point of view the history, ontology and ongoing practice of an imperialist capitalist society appears to me to find its epistemology in the common sense of racism. Whereas clearly stated racism definitely exists, the more problematic aspect for us is this common sense racism, which holds the norms and forms thrown up by a few hundred years of pillage, extermination, slavery, colonization and neo-colonization. It is in these diffused normalized sets of assumptions, knowledge and so-called cultural practices that we come across racism in its most powerful, because pervasive, form.

These norms and forms are so much a daily currency, they have been around for so long in different incarnations, that they are not mostly (even for an anti-racist person) objects of investigation, for they are not even visible. They produce silences or absences, creating gaps and fissures through which non-white women, for example, disappear from the social surface. Racism becomes an everyday life and "normal" way of seeing. Its banality and invisibility is such that it is quite likely that there may be entirely "politically correct" white individuals who have a deeply racist perception of the world. It is entirely possible to be critical of racism at the level of ideology, politics and institutions—do Southern Africa solidarity work, or work with "women of colour" for example—and yet possess a great quantity of common sense racism. This may coexist, for example, with a passively racist aesthetic. Outside of the area which is considered to be "political" or workplace—i.e., public life—this same white activist (feminist or solidarity worker) probably associates mainly or solely with white middle-class people. That fine line which divides pleasure and comfort from politics is constituted with the desire of being with "people like us."

While white obviously racist individuals are avoided, the elements of everyday life—family forms, food, sport, etc.—are shot through with racism. Non-white people associating with them will/do feel oppressed by their very way of "being" rather than by what they say or do "politically." These white progressive activists may have dealt with the overtly political, ideological dimension of their own racism, but not with their common sense racism. It is perhaps for this reason that the racism of the left feminists is almost always of omission rather than that of commission. They probably truly cannot *see* us or why it is that racism and "ethnicity" are integral to the study of women in Canada—even when they study the area of labour/capital relations, i.e., class. And those feminists who do see us, or that racism is an issue, very often deal with it in the spirit of Christian humanism, on the ground of morality and doing good, or in the spirit of bourgeois democracy, which "includes" or adds on representatives from the "minority" communities.

The fact of the matter is that it is almost impossible for European societies as they are to eliminate racism in a thoroughgoing way. Racism is not simply a set of attitudes and practices that they level towards us, their socially constructed "other," but it is the very principle of self-definition of European/Western societies. It could be said that what is otherwise known as European civilization—as manifested in the realm of arts and ideas and in daily life—is a sublimated, formalized, or simply a practiced version of racism. In his book *Orientalism*, Edward Said (1979) draws our attention to this as he points out that the "Orient was almost a European invention" and "one of its deepest and most recurring images of the other"—but additionally " . . . the Orient has helped to define Europe (or the West) as its contrasting image, ideal, personality and experience." What he says of "orientalism" can be said of racism as well, that it is " . . . a style of thought based upon an ontological and epistemological distinction made between 'the Orient' and (most of the time) the 'occident'."

If we substitute the two terms with black and white, or better still with a comprehensive binary of white and non-white, European (including the U.S. and Canada) and non-European—we get the picture. Europe or America created (and continues to create) myths of imperialism, of barbarism/savagery, a general inferiority of the conquered, enslaved and colonized peoples and also created myths of exoticism at the same instant as it defined itself also as an "other" of these. The negative determinations of Europe's or America's/Canada's racism manifest themselves everywhere. Some of the humblest to the most cerebral/aesthetic dimensions of white people's lives are informed with racism. Its notion of female beauty, for example, which is so inextricably meshed with eroticism (sexuality) is fundamentally racist—not only sexist—not to mention some of the obviously "social" practices, such as mothering, "good housekeeping," etc. The racist assumptions about "the black family," as manifested in the works of U.S. sociologists such as Daniel Moynahan, constitute the negative dialectic of a "good American (white) home (family)." This is taken up very clearly in the essays of Pratibha Parmar, Hazel Carby, Errol Lawrence, et al. in *The Empire Strikes Back*, where the racism of British middle-class social assumptions are fully bared by being put next to the white/European "civilized" ideals of the family. As many black writers point out—most importantly Frantz Fanon in *The Wretched of the Earth* and Aime Cesaire in *Discourse on Colonialism*—the colonizer (slaver or imperialist or whatever) not only reorganized the identity and social space of the colonized, but also at the same instant, through the same process, his own. Europe was not only substantively itself, but also non-Africa, non-India.

It is not surprising then that both in its omissions and commissions racism is an essential organizing device of European (white) feminist discourse—as much as of any other type of discourse. If this were to be effectively challenged it would need the turning of every stone of imperialism. White feminists would have to re-examine the very ground of their historical-social identity, their own subjectivity, their ways of being and seeing—every bit of what passes for "culture" or art. In short, it would be a process of re-making themselves, and their society, in totality. This would of course have to take place in the world, not in their heads, since common sense, as I said before, is a very practical matter. In the world, as practices, it would have to be a kind of anti-imperialist anti-capitalism that tries not only to undo ideologies, institutions, economies and state powers as they presently exist, but also to reconstruct the most mundane aspects of social life, and to re-think class—that wellspring of struggles and changes.

So we have a sense now of what may be some of the reasons for the fact that in the annals of feminist history, or "herstory," in Canada, there are only fleeting glimpses of us. A few allusions to "slavery," a few numbers indicating a statistical state of being in the records of government agencies, some reference to an entity called the "immigrant woman" or the "visible minority" woman, are what we have so far. The result is that for a few years I stood next to a blackboard and in the name of women—*all* women—taught a one-dimensional theory of gender and patriarchy, which primarily reveals the concerns and preoccupations of white middle-class women. And I sense among many of my women students a disinterest, a withdrawal and a patient resignation to the irrelevancies of an institutional education. Now I no longer do that kind of teaching, and instead try to raise the issues I raised in the paragraphs above to question those methods of social analysis current among us, which are by and large liberal-empiricist or idealist (ideological) ones. I also try to show how these methods, in the end, serve the interest of the status quo—a white imperialist hegemonic discourse. This cannot but serve the interests of white middle-class women.

While reading feminist writing a reader cannot but be aware of the particular connotation the word "woman" takes on, which extends way beyond description into the realm of power and politics. Gendered divisions of labour and accompanying relations of power are connotatively inseparable from this word nowadays. But as it gains a political nuance, so it also takes on a quality of universality and an overridingness. As the word becomes in some ways political/actionable on one ground—that of gender and patriarchy—so it also becomes an abstraction. How does this happen? And what does it have to do with not attending to racism?

In this method of operating, the abstraction is created when the different social moments which constitute the "concrete" being of any social organization and existence are pulled apart, and each part assumed to have a substantive, self-regulating structure. This becomes apparent when we see gender, race and class each considered as a separate issue—as ground for separate oppressions. The social whole—albeit fraught with contradictions—is then constructed by an aggregative exercise. According to this, I, as a South Asian woman, then have a double oppression to deal with, first on the count of gender, and second on the count of race. I am thus segmented into different social moments, made a victim of discrete determinations. So it is with the moment of gender, when it is seen as a piece by itself, rupturing its constitutive relationship with race and class. Needless to say, race and class could also be meted the same treatment. What this does is to empty out gender relations of their general social context, content and dynamism. This, along with the primacy that gender gains (since the primary, social determinant is perceived as patriarchy), subsumes all other social relations, indeed renders them often invisible. The particular—i.e., one moment—begins to stand in for the whole.

This process is fully at work in the method and social analysis of much of the feminist literature we read. What seems to happen is that the word "woman" takes on a conceptual/categorical status encoding patriarchal social relations, which are viewed as substantive structures. So issues pertaining to "women" would be discussed largely without locating them in a historical, social organization context, such as that of race and class (in the case of Canada). In fact, the notion "women" in plurality is substituted with that of *Woman*—a singular yet universal entity. So it becomes possible for a feminist journal to call itself

"*Canadian Woman Studies*." The assumption is, of course, that all women are one, and this is inescapable since the logic of such a method of decontextualizing, or dehistoricizing, can only lead to this conclusion since the aspect of gender is not constitutively related to other social and formative relations.

Having established this pseudo-universality which confers a legitimacy and an interpretive and organizing status to this notion of "woman"—the actual pieces of writing, however, go on to speak of some very concrete existing problems and experiences of particular groups of women, and not to do philosophy. They are in fact specific problems and experiences of the woman who is writing, or of people like herself, that are peculiarly oppressive for her. There is, of course, nothing wrong with that—as long as we know it—and are not presented with it as "Everywoman's problems" and concerns. This is of course not done since to speak in the name of all confers a legitimacy without which such a stand of authority could not have been constructed. Nor are problems of race and class emphasized or seen as related to gender issues, because such a thing would break down the homogeneity and even reveal the class location of the theorist/writer. The result of course is that with which I started at the very beginning—my/our experience—a new political and academic field in which we are marked by absence, subsumption and, if we are noticed at all, we are given an interpreted status by those who are in a position to control and generate forms of discourse. As at the level of method, one moment stands in for others in a controlling, hegemonic relation to the rest, so that in the actual writing, one group of women's interests (however valid for them) is smuggled in, masquerading as the interests of all women.

Both the method and the politics implied in it are old. It is the fact that they are employed in an oppositional political context—namely feminism—that makes it initially hard to recognize them. In *The German Ideology*, Marx talked about this very method of extrapolation, universalization, establishing "mystical" connections and eventually interpretive schema "theories." This is his critique of ideology. In his "introduction" to what has come to be called *The Grundrisse*, he further critiques this ideological method when he makes an attempt to create a method of social analysis in which the different social moments can retain both their specificity and reveal their implication and constitutive relation to all other specific social relations.

The advantage of this ideological procedure is well brought out in the context of the bourgeoisie's assumption of political power. We see in several texts—beginning with the most explicit *Communist Manifesto* to *The Eighteenth Brumaire of Louis Bonaparte*—Marx speaks of how it benefits a particular class to speak of itself/its interests, etc. as the universal class/interests. It is a way to gaining power and keeping power. As Gramsci put it years later in the context of Italy, to gain and keep leadership one must exert a moral and social hegemony. If the middle-class women's interests are those of all of us, then we must drown ourselves in their version of the world and their politics. This gives them a solid base to wage their own hegemonic fractional conflict with bourgeois males, while we intensify our own oppression. If we were actually to advance our own position, we could not but show that organization by race (or racism) is a fundamental way of forming class in Canada, and that this formation of class is a fully gendered one. Far from being our "sisters," these middle-class women are complicit in our domination. Being class members of a middle class created on the terrain of imperialism and capitalism—hiding it (even from themselves perhaps) behind ideological methods constructed for ruling—they cannot but be part of our problem, not the solution.

This version that I have offered of the mainstream feminist theories, or even of those socialist feminists who are colour-blind or leave out the determinations of class, is also arrived at by being sensitized by the work of Dorothy E. Smith. In her work on Marx's method, attempts at creating a sociology from a woman's standpoint, and enquiry into how the work of sociologists (academics in general) in the process of ruling holds an exploitive system in place, Smith gives us an extremely valuable insight into the production and practice of ideology. Also valuable has been the work of Michel Foucault, who bared for us the role of power in constructing/defining what constitutes knowledge and thus in constituting the "other" in the course of, or for the purpose of, domination. It must also be mentioned that the liberal empiricist method of thinking in terms of single issues, so current in North American academia and politics, is also particularly favourable to this ideological way of thinking about (and subsequently acting in) the world. And all this fits right in with the racist common sense of a people, whose self-definition and social organization, not to mention economic organization, has been fundamentally based on racism and imperialism.

The ground of discourse as much as the ground of everyday living are contested grounds. Class struggle in Canada goes on—even in the name of extending a helping hand. Class rule solidifies itself in an oppositional guise, where bourgeois men and women wrestle for power but form a solid body vis-à-vis us. Maybe one should re-read Mao Tsetung—and figure out where the contradictions lie—and where they are genuinely antagonistic or non-antagonistic. The poor in the French Revolution did get to storm the Bastille, but Napoleon came to power. Here we—the other women—haven't even stormed the Bastille, but a Napoleon is already in the wings.

Canadian Anti-Racist Feminist Thought: Scratching the Surface

Enakshi Dua

Enakshi Dua is an Associate Professor in the School of Women's Studies at York University. She teaches critical race theory, anti-racist feminist theory, post-colonial studies and transnational feminist theory. She has extensively published on racism and anti-racism, immigration processes, women and health, equity policies, globalization and biodiversity. Her publications include Scratching the Surface: Canadian Anti-Racist Feminist Thought. *She is currently working on several research projects. One focuses on the historical construction of the categories of nation, race and gender in Canada. She has more than 30 years of experience in anti-racist work in the community as well as within the academy.*

Recently, a twelve-year-old friend asked his parents if I was Canadian or Indian. After discussing the question for a couple of minutes, one of his parents, jokingly referring to childhood years spent in the United States, replied that I was neither—I was American. While this excursion into national identity drew humorously on notions of hybridity, fluidity and dislocation, it also illuminates the structures that organize race and gender in Canada. As anti-racist feminists have pointed out, the social and political definitions of who is defined as Canadian reflect the race and gender underpinnings of Canadian society. Underlying this question is the image of a Canadian as someone who is white. This stereotype works to determine who belongs to Canada, who is from elsewhere, who is a hyphenated-Canadian and who is normal.

The question of whether a person of colour is a Canadian hides the complex history through which Canada became a white settler society. As, historically, the notion of who could be legally eligible for Canadian citizenship was tied to race, skin colour became a central (though not the only) marker of who could belong to the Canadian national formation. In the words of John A. Macdonald, Canada was to be a "white man's country." Today, the stereotype of who is and is not a Canadian works to reinforce the historical process by which indigenous, mixed race, African-Canadians, Asian-Canadians, Arab-Canadians, and others[1] have been marginalized from Canadian society, as it obscures the history of colonialism, settlement, immigration and citizenship policies that ensured the racialization and gendering of 20th century Canada. . . .

. . . [A]nti-racist feminists have concentrated on analyzing the forces that have shaped the historically specific pattern of racialization in Canada. It is their focus on the process of racialization that differentiates their writing from other kinds of feminist theorizing.[2] This body of thought illustrates the process by which racialization produces differences among women, challenging the idea that a common experience with gender exists. In addition, by bringing an analysis of race to feminist theorizing, this work offers a different feminist epistemology—a distinctive method of analyzing gender, nation, state, economy and society. . . .

ANTI-RACIST FEMINIST THOUGHT: CONNECTING RACE AND GENDER

Within Canadian feminist literature, a collection of writing exists that we have labelled anti-racist feminist thought. Notably, these writers have often been excluded from Canadian feminist historiographies. While this body of thought is part of the history of Canadian feminist theorizing, to date, there has been little documentation of the work and ideas of these writers (for an exception, see Bristow 1994). In particular, the writings of those who wrote on race and gender before the 1960s have been unrecorded. Such omissions in feminist historiography are especially problematic as the vast majority of those who are part of this body of work are women of colour. The failure to record anti-racist feminist work has facilitated the impression that women of colour have been historically absent from feminist and anti-racist theorizing and organizing.

Not only has there been little documentation of this body of work, but an analysis of its underlying epistemological and ontological assumptions is also missing (for an exception, see Stasiulis 1990). As Canadian anti-racist feminist thought is premised on offering a different epistemological and ontological approach to the study of gender, the failure to undertake such an analysis makes it difficult to assess the usefulness of its central tenet: that an analysis of race needs to be integrated into feminist theorizing.

Evaluating a distinct body of thought involves delineating its parameters. However, defining what constitutes anti-racist feminist thought is a contentious task. While anti-racist feminist thought is generally defined as an attempt to theorize the interconnections between race, class and gender, there are different interpretations on how to go about this. As the vast majority of those who write on these topics are women of colour, there are those who would narrow this body of work to the writings of "black feminists" (for example, Hill Collins 1990; in Canada see Stasiulis 1990, 282). For others, anti-racist thought is the body of literature that positions the lives and experiences of women of colour as the starting point for a feminist analysis (Brand 1988; Dua 1992; Agnew 1996). And for some, anti-racist thought is the body of literature that examines the "multiplicity of experiences" (Stasiulis 1990; Khayatt 1995). . . .

The history of Canadian anti-racist feminist work can be traced through three phases of development, which I have identified as first, second and third wave. Since the 19th century, anti-racist feminists have pointed to the importance of racism, and questioned a universal politics of gender. . . . [I]n Canada, anti-racist feminism stems from women of colour's willingness to strive for equality within a racialized society and feminist movement. These writers have consistently illustrated how the workings of race and gender need to be located in a particular history—the history of a post-colonial, white settler formation. Significantly, in each phase writers have focused on similar questions, and offered remarkably similar epistemological approaches to the interconnections of race and gender.

Despite a long legacy of illustrating the ways in which a racialized society impacted on women of colour, two significant epistemological differences have recently emerged among anti-racist feminists. The first is what to prioritize in the study of interconnections. As Satzewich (1998) notes, there are considerable differences among writers about how to conceptualize the interrelationship between race and gender: "there are class approaches to race and gender, gender approaches to race and class, and race approaches to class and gender" (Satzewich 1998, 41). Secondly, anti-racist feminist writers are divided between employing a reformulated political economy approach or a standpoint methodology.

These epistemological differences have led to important debates among anti-racist writers, such as, what are the implications of employing the term "women of colour"? While the term arises from an attempt to disrupt the universalist and essentialist notion of gender in Canadian feminist theorizing, does it replace the concept of a woman with an equally universalist and essentialist concept of a woman of colour? Does it homogenize experiences of racism? Does it hide class difference? Does the acknowledgement of a diversity of experiences with racism mean that we need to identify different kinds of racism? Does analyzing a women-of-colour outsider-within status allow for different insights? Does a standpoint epistemology challenge simplistic accounts of identity and inequality, or replace these accounts with an essentialist one?

THE THIRD WAVE, 1990–1999: THEORIZING RACIAL DIFFERENCES IN AN INCREASINGLY FRAGMENTED WORLD

By the end of the 1980s Canadian anti-racist feminist thought represented a new way of feminist theorizing, a project of integrating race and gender that offered exciting possibilities for feminist thinking and organizing. . . . The recognition that Canadian social institutions perpetuate racism would lead several writers to reject the epistemology underlying socialist feminist and Canadian political economy traditions. As a consequence, in the past decade two different epistemological approaches to the study of race and gender have emerged. The literature in this period can be categorized as having three broad parameters: interrogating mainstream feminist theory and praxis for the ways in which it perpetuated racism, raising epistemological questions of how to theorize the interconnection between race and gender and continuing to document how racial differences are created between women.

The third wave of anti-racist feminist writing has concentrated on interrogating mainstream feminism, both theory and praxis, for its role in perpetuating racial difference between women. Several writers illustrated the ways in which middle-class women's standpoint historically came to configure the contours of liberal, radical and socialist-feminist theory (Dua 1992; Mukerjee 1992; Simms 1992; Monture-Okanee 1992, 1995; Agnew 1996). These writers pointed out that women of colour's experiences with all aspects of gender—femininity, sexuality, marriage, family and work—varied substantially from that of middle-class white women. Such differences raised the question of whether a universal experience with gender exists (Mukerjee 1992; Monture-Okanee 1992). This led others to argue that by marginalizing the study of race in feminist analyses, mainstream feminists continue to marginalize women of colour from feminist organizations (Simms 1992; Bannerji 1995). Writers also noted that underlying the feminist movement has been a commitment to a racialized nation-state, a commitment that has contributed to positioning women differentially within the political economy. . . .

Ironically, despite an increasing awareness of the ways in which mainstream feminist praxis created divisions among women, transforming feminist organizations and theory was not an easy task. Attempts to alter shelters, crisis lines, immigrant women's services and cultural institutions were met with resistance and hostility, struggles that often were well-covered by Canadian newspapers (for a report of such cases see Cayenne 1988; Kohli 1993; Crean 1991; Gabriel and Scott 1993; Agnew 1996). While efforts to make the National Action Committee on the Status of Women (NAC) inclusive resulted in the election of two women of colour as presidents, this was accompanied by a loss of support. As Beverley Bains, who worked for NAC during these years, stated: "We do hear from some white women their perception that suddenly black women's or non-white women's issues are becoming important. These women . . . are not seeing the connections between black women and white women's issues" (quoted in Gottlieb 1993, 382). The result of such resistance has been to entrench coalition and identity politics within these organizations (Bannerji 1995; Robertson 1999).

Anti-racist feminist academics found it equally difficult to challenge the pedagogical paradigms and canons of various disciplines, including feminist theory (Carry 1991; Millar 1993 Bannerji et al. 1995; Das Gupta 1996). As many writers have repeatedly pointed out, most disciplines, including women's studies, have largely ignored anti-racist feminist thought (Mukerjee 1992; Carty 1993; Stevenson 1992, 1995; Jhappan 1996). . . .

Anti-racist feminists tied their critique of feminist praxis to an analysis of the ways in which Canadian academia constructed knowledge about race. Starting from the perspective that the social relations of production of knowledge in institutional settings privilege perspectives that encompass systematic ideological stances, several writers argued that canons of various disciplines worked to maintain the ideological frameworks through which racial differences among women are maintained (Bannerji 1995; Monture-Okanee 1995; LaRocque 1996). These writers pointed out that when it came to racialization, it was not only conservative and liberal frameworks that contributed to a discursive understanding of race. Importantly, critical paradigms, particularly the Canadian political economy approach[3] and socialist feminist analysis, also perpetuated the discursive understanding of race. . . .

. . . Others, such as Bannerji (1995) and Henry et al. (1995), have called for new paradigms with which to analyze Canadian society. . . .

Given these different projects, it is not surprising that anti-racist feminists have put forward two very different approaches to the study of race and gender—one approach located in a standpoint epistemology and another approach located in a reformulation of Canadian political economy. These two approaches offer two very different epistemological frameworks for how to integrate race into a gender and class analysis. Moreover, such differences lead to differences on several key questions: whether the focus should be on the differences between white women and women of colour; how to analyze class differences between women of colour; and how to theorize the role of race in Canadian society. . . .

The clearest exposition of the standpoint approach has been put forward by Himani Bannerji in *Thinking Through* (1995). Bannerji begins by identifying an epistemological site in which a new paradigm can be formulated. As she asked: "Where are we to turn? Where are we to find interpretive frameworks and methods that are more than alternative and would go beyond inclusion? How can we gain insight into the social relations and culture of advanced capitalism which allows for direct representation and a revolutionary political agency?" (1995, 63). The answer to this question was to begin with the lived experiences of women of colour: "Once again I must begin from myself. From my body as a political signifier" (1995, 61). . . .

For Bannerji and others (for example, Brand 1988; Carty 1992; Nourbese Philip 1992), the strength of employing a standpoint methodology is located in women of colour's "outsider-within" status. Anticipating Homi Bhabha's concept of a "third space," these writers have pointed out that women of colour occupy a structural position within the Canadian political economy that overlaps the margins of race, gender and class. They argue that by tracing how women of colour are positioned within Canadian society, we can simultaneously trace how race, class and gender have been constituted in Canadian history. . . .

The strength of a standpoint epistemology is that it allows for a more sophisticated understanding of the ways in which the discourse of race shaped the contingent character of colonialism, imperialism and capitalism. Underlying this approach is the premise that racialized regimes of power and knowledge were as important in determining the historical specific path of Canadian colonial and capitalist development as was the imperative for profits. . . .

However, the use of a standpoint methodology has not been without criticisms (Stasiulis 1990; Khayatt 1995; Jhappan 1996). Several writers have pointed out that women's experiences with racialization vary according to class location, the different ways different groups have been racialized, sexuality and personal history (Mahtani 1995; Ahmad 1995). This led Jhappan (1996) to question whether a standpoint methodology replaced "gender essentialism" with an equally problematic "race essentialism." Others noted that an additional danger in such a methodology was that it did not allow for the fluid character of social identities. . . .

The degree to which experiences with racism among women of colour are shared raises important methodological issues regarding how to integrate a race, gender and class analyses, whether the aim of anti-racist feminism should be to explain differences between white women and women of colour and whether a standpoint approach conflates race and class. . . .

The clearest exposition of the political economy approach has been put forward by Stasiulis (1990) in *Theorising Connections.* Referring mainly to the work of second wave writers, Stasiulis questioned the analytical use of skin colour as a demarcation of racism. She argues that such an approach limited the study of race, class and gender to an "implicit black/white dichotomy that is frequently assumed to structure the racist and gendered oppression of women" (290). She suggests that such a dichotomy poses a number of limitations: it fails to deal with other "immigrant" women; it links racism to skin colour rather than structural location of the particular groups of women in concrete social relations; it ignores different kinds of racism—especially those built on language, religion and other cultural markers; and it treats women of colour as a homogenous category, thereby failing to account for the fact that women of colour are located in a variety of class positions. She concludes that "black feminism" does not allow for the task of understanding the complex processes through which race, class and gender are constructed for specific groups of racial and ethnic-minority women. In contrast, Stasiulis advocates an epistemology that focuses on "the structural location of particular groups of women in concrete and historically specific social relations and to the accompanying discourses that aid in the processes of denigration, subordination and exploitation" (1990, 290). Through this, anti-racist feminism is better able to produce "a more complex mapping of oppression, inequality and resistance" (Stasiulis 1994, 6).

These two approaches offer very different ways of studying the interconnections between race and gender. Importantly, they differ on what should constitute the subject of study, on what central question needs to be investigated. For those who employ a standpoint methodology, the central question is: how are racial differences between women created and maintained? For those who work within the broad framework of political economy, the central question is to explain how women come into and experience multiple locations and identities. These are two different, but not contradictory, questions.

The two approaches also adopt very different implicit epistemological assumptions on how to theorize racism. For those who work within a political economy epistemology it is crucial to study racism as relational and contradictory (Stasiulis and Crease 1996, 8). These writers posit racism as a phenomenon which differs according to one's structural location. . . .

In contrast, those who employ a standpoint epistemology conceptualize race, racism, racialization and social structures differently. For them it is not sufficient to focus on how the process of racialization creates differences among women, for such a focus leaves the systems of oppression unexplained, raising the danger of taking them for granted. . . .

. . . [T]hese writers conceptualize race as discourse, which is constituted in multiple ways, through knowledge, culture, the imperatives of imperialism and capitalism, as well as through power and agency. For these writers, the discourse of race becomes the starting point for analyzing institutional mechanisms that locate women in differential positions and social relations. Moreover, it is through discursive operations that racialized structures are created. . . . This does not deny that such discursive operations are not historically contingent, that they operate through different signifiers (language, immigration status) and differently for different groups of racialized women (including white women) and vary according to class location. It does suggest that the discourse of race is as "foundational" to the creation and maintenance of the Canadian political economy as are capitalist relations and patriarchy.

While these are two different approaches to the study of racism, I would point out that again these writers are asking different questions. For those who work within a standpoint epistemology, the central question is to show how the discourse of race shapes and maintains a racialized political economy. For those who work within the broad framework of political economy, the central question is to explain how the process of racialization differentiates between women, according to race, ethnicity, class and sexuality. . . . This leads to the third parameter of anti-racist feminist writing in this period, studies that examine the impact of a discourse of race on women of colour.

Drawing on the anti-racist work in the second wave, writers have continued to document the ways in which Canadian "culture" and institutions create and maintain racial differences. Nourbese Philip (1992) pointed out that culture is the central mechanism through which "whiteness" is asserted. Through cultural images in stories, narratives and photographs, Canadians are divided into a normalized group and "others." Others illustrated the prevalence of racialized images of femininities: the dutiful Asian or Islamic wife and daughter, the happy and grateful female immigrant worker, the sexually available First Nations woman, the controlling black mother, the unassimilated immigrant women unable to adequately socialize her children, the ignorant and oppressed third world women (see for examples, Douglas 1988; Hoodfar 1993; James and Shadd 1994; Bannerji 1995). . . .

Others pointed out that these notions were tied to the maintenance of white hegemony. Brand (1988), Hoodfar (1993) and Bannerji (1995) point out that these images are located in imperial regimes of power—as the racialization of colonized women legitimated colonial and capitalist domination. Dua (2000) illustrates how the racialization of South-Asian Canadian women normalized white femininity and masculinity, and allowed for the construction of a Canadian national identity. The hegemonic role of "culture" in reproducing racism has led to several struggles over the access that people of colour have to Canadian cultural institutions and over cultural appropriation—struggles over who has the power to define whom, and when, and how (Crean 1991; Nourbese Philip 1992; Gabriel and Scott 1993; Henry 1995).

Another focus of the research has been to continue to elaborate on the ways in which employment practices reproduce racialized labour markets. Statistical analyses suggested that the colour of one's skin translated into advantage or discrimination in the labour market. Li (1998) found that the Canadian economy places a market value on skin colour, such that people of colour suffer an income penalty while white Canadians receive an income premium. This did not imply that women of colour are positioned similarily within income and occupational structures. Boyd, employing 1986 data, illustrated the "split" character of women of colour's labour force participation—that women of colour occupy both some of the better jobs in Canadian society as well as many of the poorly paid jobs in Canadian society (Boyd 1992). . . . The implications for such differential location with the labour market remains to be explored. Others noted that gender-based equity policies failed to include women of colour, reproducing racial difference between women (Stasiulis 1989; Boyd 1992; Joanne St. Lewis 1997).

Writers also elaborated on how state policies produce racial differences. While postwar immigration policies have tied immigration to labour market needs, these policies have incorporated Canadian state and public concerns that "new" immigrants do not alter the "foundations" of Canada (Stafford 1992). These policies continue to deny some categories of migrants, such as domestic workers, rights such as residency and family unification (Arat-Koc 1992; Bakan and Stasiulis 1997). . . .

For First Nations women, the impact of dominant culture in maintaining race and gender became a divisive issue, leading to radically different positions on the issue of First Nations self-government. Most writers have illustrated that the Department of Indian Affairs, empowered by a number of legislative *Acts,* placed indigenous women in subordinate positions, in First Nations communities as well as in Canadian society (see McIvor and Stevenson in Dua and Robertson 1999). However, given the entrenchment of patriarchal relations, First Nations women differed on how to view self-government. The Native Women's Association of Canada argued that given the entrenchment of male power in First

Nations communities, self-government would not allow First Nations women to deal with sexism and violence. Rather, the Canadian Charter offered First Nations women the most influential mechanism with which to challenge gender inequality within First Nations communities (Nahanee 1997). In contrast, Monture-Angus (1995) and Turpel (1989–90, 1990) point out that not only are these gender (and other) inequalities the consequence of European discourses and social patterns, these discourses are continually being reproduced through the legal apparatus. Given these conditions, Monture-Angus (1995) and Turpel (1990) argue that it is only through "traditional" gender, social and legal practices that differences within First Nations communities can be eradicated.

This body of work does point to the importance of discourses of race for how women of colour are positioned within Canadian society. These writers illustrate the ways in which notions of insiders and outsiders are crucial for the production of racial differences. They also suggest that these notions have an impact on how an individual is economically and socially located within Canadian society. On the other hand, they tell us little about the processes through which these ideas came to be hegemonic in the Canadian context. . . .

SYNTHESIZING CANADIAN ANTI-RACIST FEMINIST THOUGHT

Despite the diversity and richness of Canadian anti-racist feminist thought, much of this work remains fragmented, as many writers have often focused on a particular aspect of state, nation, economy, society or culture. There is no synthesis of the processes through which racialization has taken place in Canada. . . .

Notes

1. Hereafter, I will use the term "women of colour" to refer to indigenous, mixed race, African-Canadians, Asian-Canadians, Arab-Canadians and Central and South American-Canadians.
2. Hereafter, I will use the term "mainstream feminism" to refer to liberal, radical and socialist feminist paradigms.
3. By the Canadian political economy approach, I refer to the analyses of the development of Canadian capitalism and state (see for examples, Laxer 1973, 1989; Naylor 1975; Panich 1994). While it is beyond the scope of this chapter to document the ideas within Canadian political economy, for my purposes, I would like to draw attention to two of its characteristics. First, because of its focus on Canada's peripheral position within British and American capitalist development, the Canadian tradition of political economy has underemphasized the role Canada has played in facilitating imperialist and neo-imperialist expansion. Second, is the reduction of race to class. Bolaria and Li (1988), for example, argue that the Canadian capitalist class' "functional" need for a reserve army of labour explains the emergence and persistence of racism. For Bolaria and Li, it is the process of accumulation that has led to racialized immigration policies, discourses and practices.

References

Adachi, Ken. *The Enemy that Never Was.* Toronto: McClelland and Stewart, 1976.

Aggarwal, Pramila. "Business as Usual in the Factory." *Resources for Feminist Research/Documentation sur la recherche feministe,* vol. 16, no. 1 (1987): 42–4.

Agnew, Vijay. *Resisting Discrimination: Women from Asia, Africa, and the Caribbean and the Women's Movement in Canada.* Toronto: University of Toronto Press, 1996.

Ahmad, Fawzia. "Reflections of an African Woman." *Canadian Woman Studies,* vol. 14, no. 2 (1995): 25–8.

Amos, Valerie, and Pratibha Parmar. "Challenging Imperial Feminism." *Feminist Review,* vol. 17 (1984): 3–19.

Andrew, Caroline, and Sandra Rodgers. *Women and the Canadian State/Les Femmes et l'etat Canadien.* Montreal and Kingston: McGill-Queen's University Press, 1997.

Arat-Koc, Sedef. "Immigration Policies, Migrant Domestic Workers and the Definition of Citizenship in Canada." In *Deconstructing a Nation: Immigration, Multiculturalism and Racism in '90s Canada,* ed. Vic Satzewich. Saskatoon: University of Saskatchewan Press, 1992.

Bacchi, Carol. *Liberation Deferred? The Idea of the English-Canadian Suffragists, 1877–1918.* Toronto: University of Toronto Press, 1983.

Backhouse, Constance. "'I Was Unable to Identify with Topsy': Carrie Best's Struggle against Racial Segregation in Nova Scotia, 1942." *Atlantis,* vol. 22, no. 2 (Spring/Summer 1998): 16–27.

Bakan, Abigail, and Davia Stasiulis. *Not in the Family: Foreign Domestic Workers in Canada.* Toronto: University of Toronto Press, 1997.

Bannerji, Himani. "Introducing Racism: Notes towards an Anti-Racist Feminism." *Resources for Feminine* [sic] *Research/Documentation sur la recherche feministe,* vol. 16, no. 1 (1987): 10–13.

——. *Thinking Through: Essays on Feminism, Marxism, and Anti-Racism.* Toronto: Women's Press, 1995.

Bolaria, B. Singh, and Peter S. Lee, eds. *Racial Oppression in Canada.* Toronto: Garamond Press, 1988.

Bourgeault, Ron. "Race and Class under Mercantilism: Indigenous People in Nineteenth-Century Canada." In *Racial Oppression in Canada,* eds. Singh Bolaria and Peter Li. Toronto: Garamond Press, 1988.

——. "Race, Class, and Gender." In *Racism in Canada,* ed. Ormond McKague. Saskatoon: Fifth House Publishers, 1991.

Boyd, Monica. "Gender, Visible Minority and Immigrant Earnings Inequality: Reassessing an Employment Equity Premise." In *Deconstructing a Nation: Immigration, Multiculturalism and Racism in '90s Canada,* ed. Vic Satzewich. Saskatoon: University of Saskatchewan Press, 1992.

——. "Immigrant Women: Language, Socio-economic Inequalities and Policy Issues." In *Ethnic Demography: Canadian Immigrant, Racial, and Cultural Variations,* eds. S. Halli, F. Trovato, and L. Driedger. Ottawa: Carleton University Press, 1990.

Brand, Dionne. "Black Women in Toronto: Gender, Race, and Class." *Fireweed* (Summer/Fall 1984): 26–43.

Brand, Dionne, and Krisantha Sri Bhaggiya Datta. *Rivers Have Sources, Trees Have Roots: Speaking of Racism.* Toronto: Cross-Cultural Communication Centre, 1986.

Brand, Dionne. *A Conceptual Analysis of How Gender Roles Are Racially Constructed: Black Women.* Master's Thesis, University of Toronto, 1988.

Bristow, Peggy, ed. *We're Rooted Here and They Can't Pull Us Up: Essays in African Canadian Women's History.* Toronto: University of Toronto Press, 1994.

——. "Introduction." In *We're Rooted Here and They Can't Pull Us Up: Essays in African Canadian Women's History,* ed. Peggy Bristow. Toronto: University of Toronto Press, 1994.

——. "'Whatever you raise in the ground you can sell it in Chatham': Black Women in Buxton." In *We're Rooted Here and They Can't Pull Us Up: Essays in African Canadian Women's History,* ed. Peggy Bristow. Toronto: University of Toronto Press, 1994.

——. "The Hour-a-Day Study Club." In *And Still We Rise: Feminist Political Mobilizing in Contemporary Canada,* ed. Linda Carty. Toronto: Women's Press, 1997.

Burton, Antoinette. *Burdens of History: British Feminists, Indian Women, and Imperial Culture, 1865–1915.* Chapel Hill: University of North Carolina Press, 1994.

Calliste, Agnes. "Canada's Immigration Policy and Domestics from the Caribbean: The Second Domestic Scheme." In *Race, Class, and Gender: Bonds and Barriers,* eds. J. Vorst, et al. Toronto: Between the Lines Press, 1989.

Carby, Hazel. "White Woman Listen! Black Feminism and the Boundaries of Sisterhood." In *The Empire Strikes Back: Race and Racism in 70s Britain.* London: Centre for Contemporary Culture Studies, 1986.

Carter, Sarah. "First Nations Women of Prairie Canada in the Early Reserve Years, the 1870s to the 1920s: A Preliminary Inquiry." In *Women of the First Nations: Power, Wisdom and Strength,* eds. Christine Miller and Patricia Churchryk. Winnipeg: University of Manitoba Press, 1996.

Carty, Linda. "Black Women in Academia: A Statement from the Periphery." In *Unsettling Relations: The University as a Site of Feminist Struggles,* H. Bannerji et al. Toronto: Women's Press, 1991.

——. "Combining Our Efforts: Making Feminism Relevant." In *And Still We Rise: Feminist Political Mobilizing in Contemporary Canada,* ed. Linda Carty. Toronto: Women's Press, 1997.

Carty, Linda, and Dionne Brand, " 'Visible Minority' Women: A Creation of the Canadian State." *Resources for Feminist Research,* vol. 17, no. 3 (1989): 39–40.

Cayenne. "Racism and International Women's Day in Toronto." *Cayenne,* vol. 12, nos. 2/3 (1986): 25–45.

Collins, Patricia Hill. *Black Feminist Thought: Knowledge, Consciousness, and the Politics of Empowerment.* New York and London: Routledge, 1991.

Cooper, A. "Black Women and Work in Nineteenth-Century Canada." In *We're Rooted Here and They Can't Pull Us Up: Essays in African Canadian Woman's History,* ed. Peggy Bristow. Toronto: University of Toronto Press, 1994.

Crean, Susan. "Taking the Missionary Position." In *Racism in Canada,* ed. Ormond McKague. Saskatoon: Fifth House Publishers, 1991.

Creese, Gillian. "Exclusion of Solidarity? Vancouver Workers Confront the 'Oriental Problem.'" *BC Studies,* no. 80 (Winter 1988–89): 24–51.

Creese, Gillian, and Daiva Stasiulis. "Introduction: Intersections of Gender, Race, Class and Sexuality." In *Studies in Political Economy,* vol. 51 (Fall 1996): 15–64.

Das Gupta, Tania. "Unraveling the Web of History." *Resources for Feminist Research/Documentation sur la recherche feministe,* vol. 16, no. 1 (1987): 13–15.

——. *Learning from Our History: Community Development by Immigrant Women in Ontario 1958–1986.* Toronto: Cross-Cultural Communication Centre, 1986.

——. "Involving Immigrant Women: A Case of Participatory Research." *Canadian Woman Studies,* vol. 8 (1987): 14–15.

Dickason, Olive Patricia. *Canada's First Nations: A History of Founding Peoples from Earliest Times.* Toronto: McClelland and Stewart, 1993.

Douglas, Debbie. "Young Black Women Speak." *Resources for Feminist Research,* vol. 16, no. 1 (1989): 23–8.

Dua, Enakshi. "The Hindu Woman's Question: Canadian Nation-Building and the Social Construction of Gender for South Asian Women." In *Canadian Reader on Anti-Racism,* eds. George Dei and Agnes Calliste. Toronto: University of Toronto Press, 2000.

——. "Racism or Gender: Understanding Oppression of South-Asian Canadian Women." *Canadian Woman Studies,* vol. 13, no. 1 (1992): 6–10.

Estable, Alma. "Immigration Policy and Regulations." *Resources for Feminine Research/ Documentation sur la recherche feministe,* vol. 16, no. 1 (1987): 28–9.

Fanon, Franz. *Black Skin, White Masks.* New York: Grove Press, 1986.

Gabriel, Chris, and Katherine Scott. "Women's Press at Twenty: The Politics of Feminist Publishing." In *And Still We Rise: Feminist Political Mobilizing in Contemporary Canada,* ed. Linda Carty. Toronto: Women's Press, 1997.

Giles, Winona. "Language Rights are Women's Rights: Discrimination against Immigrant Women in Canadian Language Training Policies." In *Resources for Feminist Research/Documentation sur la recherche feministe,* vol. 17, no. 3 (1988): 13–15.

Gilroy, Paul. "Steppin' out of Babylon: Race, Class and Autonomy." In *The Empire Strikes Back: Race and Racism in 70s Britain.* London: Hutchinson, The Centre for Contemporary Studies, 1982.

Go, Amy Teng-Teng. *Discussion Paper on E.S.L. Funding for Submission to the OCASI Board of Directors.* Toronto: OCASI, 1987.

Gottlieb, Amy. "What about Us? Organizing Inclusively in the National Action Committee on the Status of Women." In *And Still We Rise: Feminist Political Mobilizing in Contemporary Canada,* ed. Linda Carty. Toronto: Women's Press, 1997.

Guillaumin, C. *Racism, Sexism, Power and Ideology.* London: Routledge, 1995.

Hall, Stuart. "Racism and Reaction." In *Five Views of Multi-Racial Britain.* London: Commission for Racial Equality, 1978.

Hall, Stuart. "New Ethnicities." In *'Race', Culture and Difference,* eds. James Donald and Ali Rattansi. London: Sage, 1941.

Hamilton, Sylvia. "Naming Names, Naming Ourselves: A Survey of Early Black Women in Nova Scotia." In *We're Rooted Here and They Can't Pull Us Up: Essays in African Canadian Women's History,* ed. Peggy Bristow. Toronto: University of Toronto Press, 1994.

——. "The Women at the Well: African Baptist Women Organize." In *And Still We Rise: Feminist Political Mobilizing in Contemporary Canada,* ed. Linda Carty. Toronto: Women's Press, 1993.

Harstock, Nancy. "The Feminist Standpoint: Developing the Ground for a Specifically Feminist Historical Materialism." In *Discovering Reality,* ed. Sandra Harding. Boston: D. Reidel, 1983.

Henry, Frances, C. Tator, W. Mattis, and T. Rees. *The Colour of Democracy: Racism in Canadian Society.* Toronto: Harcourt Brace, 1995.

Hoodfar, Homa. "The Veil in Their Minds and on Our Heads: The Persistence of Colonial Images of Muslim Women." *Resources for Feminist Research/Documentation sur la recherche feministe,* vol. 22, nos. 3/4 (1993): 5–19.

hooks, bell. *Ain't I a Woman. Black Women and Feminism.* Boston: South End Press, 1981.

——. *From Margin to Center.* Boston: South End Press, 1984.

——. *Talking Back: Thinking Feminist, Thinking Black.* Boston: South End Press, 1989.

Iacovetta, Franca, and Mariana Valverde. "Introduction." In *Gender Conflicts,* eds. Franca Iacovetta and Mariana Valverde. Toronto: University of Toronto Press, 1992.

James, Carl B., and Adrienne Shadd. *Talking about Difference: Encounters in Culture, Language and Identity.* Toronto: Between the Lines, 1994.

Jayawardina, Kumart. *The White Woman's Other Burden: Western Women and South Asia during British Rule.* London: Routledge, 1995.

Jhappan, Radha. "Post-Modern Race and Gender Essentialism or a Post-Mortem of Scholarship." *Studies in Political Economy,* vol. 51, (Fall 1996): 15–64.

Khayatt, Didi. "The Boundaries of Identity at the Intersections of Race and Gender." *Canadian Woman Studies,* vol. 14, no. 2 (1994): 6–14.

Kitagawa, Muriel. *This is My Own: Letters to Wes and Other Writings on Japanese Canadians, 1941–1948.* Vancouver: Talon, 1981.

Kobayashi, Audrey, and Linda Peake. "Unnatural Discourse, 'Race' and Gender in Geography." *Gender, Place and Culture,* vol. 1, no. 2 (1994): 225–43.

Kogawa, Joy. *Obasan.* Toronto: Lester and Orpen Denneys, 1981.

Kohli, Rita. "Power or Empowerment: Questions of Agency in the Shelter Movement." In *And Still We Rise: Feminist Political Mobilizing in Contemporary Canada.* Toronto: Women's Press, 1993.

LaRocque, Emma. "The Colonization of a Native Woman Scholar." In *Women of the First Nations: Power, Wisdom and Strength,* eds. Christine Miller and Patricia Churchryk. Winnipeg: University of Manitoba Press, 1997.

Law Union of Canada, *Immigrant Women's Handbook.* Montreal: Black Rose, 1981.

Laxer, Gordon. *Open for Business: The Routes of Foreign Ownership in Canada.* Toronto: Oxford University Press, 1989.

Laxer, Robert. *(Canada) Limited: The Political Economy of Dependency.* Toronto: McClelland and Stewart, 1973.

Leah, Ronnie, and Gwen Morgan. "Immigrant Women Fight Back: The Case of the Seven Jamaican Women." *Resources for Feminist Research,* vol. 8, no. 3 (1979): 23–4.

Li, Peter S. "The Economics of Brain Drain: Recruitment of Skilled Labour to Canada, 1954–1986." In *Deconstructing a Nation: Immigration, Multiculturalism and Racism in '90s Canada,* ed. Vic Satzewich. Saskatoon: University of Saskatchewan, 1992.

——. "The Market Value and Social Value of Race." In *Racism and Social Inequality in Canada: Concepts, Controversies and Strategies of Resistance,* ed. Vic Satzewich. Toronto: Thompson Educational Publishing, 1998.

Mahtani, Minelle. "Polarity versus Plurality: Confessions of an Ambivalent Woman of Colour." *Canadian Woman Studies,* vol. 14, no. 2 (1994): 14–18.

McClintock, Anne. *Imperial Leather: Race, Gender and Sexuality in the Colonial Conquest.* London: Routledge, 1995.

McIvor, Sharon. "Self-Government and Aboriginal Women." In *Scratching the Surface: Canadian Anti-Racist Feminist Thought,* eds. Enakshi Dua and Angela Robertson. Toronto: Women's Press, 1999.

Miles, Robert. *Racism.* London: Routledge, 1989.

Mirza, Heidi Safia. *Black British Feminism.* London and New York: Routledge, 1997.

Monture-Angus, Patricia. *Thunder in My Soul: A Mohawk Woman Speaks.* Halifax: Fernwood, 1995.

Monture-Okanee, Patricia, "The Violence We Women Do: A First Nations View." In *Challenging Times: The Women's Movement in Canada and the United States.* Montreal and Kingston: McGill-Queen's Press, 1992.

Mukherjee, Arun. "A House Divided: Women of Colour and American Feminist Theory." In *Challenging Times: The Women's Movement in Canada and the United States,* eds., Constance Backhouse and David Flaherty. Montreal and Kingston: McGill-Queen's University Press, 1992.

Nahanee, Theresa. "Indian Women, Sex Equality, and the Charter." In *Women and the Canadian State,* eds. Caroline Andrews and Sandra Rodgers. Kingston: McGill-Queen's University Press, 1997.

Naylor, Tom. *The History of Canadian Business, 1867–1914.* 2nd ed. Toronto: McClelland and Stewart, 1975.

Ng, Roxana, and Alma Estable, "Immigrant Women in the Labour Force: An Overview of Present Knowledge and Research Gaps." *Resources for Feminist Research/Documentation sur la recherche feministe,* vol. 16, no. 1 (1987): 29–34.

Ng, Roxana. "Immigrant Women in Canada: A Socially Constructed Category." *Resources for Feminist Research*, vol. 15, no. 1 (1986): 13–14.

——. *The Politics of Community Service.* Toronto: Garamond, 1988a.

——. "Immigrant Women and Institutionalized Racism." In *Changing Patterns: Women in Canada,* eds. Sandra Burt, Lorraine Code, and Lindsay Dorney. Toronto: McClelland and Stewart, 1988b.

Nip, Dora. *Canada-Bound: An Exploratory Study of Pioneer Chinese Women in Western Canada.* Master's thesis, University of Toronto, 1983.

Nourbese Philip, Marlene. "Distortions and Liberal Intentions: Pandering to the Unwitting Subtleties of Racism." In *Racism in Canada,* ed. Ormund McKague. Saskatoon: Fifth House Publishers, 1991.

——. *Frontiers: Essays and Writings on Racism and Culture.* Stratford: The Mercury Press, 1992.

Panich, Leo. *The Canadian State, Political Economy and Political Power.* Toronto: University of Toronto Press, 1977.

Parades, Milagros. "Immigrant Women and Second-Language Education." *Resources for Feminist Research,* vol. 16, no. 1 (1989): 23–8.

Parmar, Pratibha. "Gender, Race, and Class: Asian Women in Resistance." In *The Empire Strikes Back: Race and Racism in 70s Britain.* London: Hutchinson, The Centre for Contemporary Studies, 1985.

Payment, Diane. "La Vie en Rose?" In *Women of the First Nations: Power, Wisdom and Strength,* eds. Christine Miller and Patricia Churchryk. Winnipeg: University of Manitoba Press, 1996.

Ramazanaglu, Caroline. *Feminism and the Contradictions of Oppression.* London: Routledge, 1989.

Rattansi, Ali. "Changing the Subject? Racism, Culture and Education." In *'Race,' Culture and Difference,* eds. James Donald and Ali Rattansi. London: Sage, 1992.

Razack, Sherene. *Looking White People in the Eye.* Toronto: University of Toronto Press, 1998.

Roberts, Barbara. "Ladies, Women and the State: Managing Female Immigration, 1880–1920." In *Community Organization and the Canadian State,* eds. R. Ng, O. Walker, and J. Muller. Toronto: Garamond, 1990.

Robertson, Angela. "Continuing on the Ground: Feminists of Colour Discuss Organizing." In *Scratching the Surface: Canadian Anti-Racist Feminist Thought,* eds. Enakshi Dua and Angela Robertson. Toronto: Women's Press, 1999.

Satzewich, Vic. "Racisms: The Reactions to Chinese Migrants in Canada at the Turn of the Century." *International Sociology,* vol. 4, no. 3, 321–27.

——. ed. *Racists and Social Inequality in Canada.* Toronto: Thompson Educational Press Inc., 1998.

Shepard, Bruce. "Plain Racism: The Reaction against Oklahoma Black Immigration to the Canadian Plains." In *Racism in Canada,* ed. Ormond McKague. Saskatoon: Fifth House Publishers, 1991.

Silvera, Makeda. *Silenced.* Toronto: Williams-Wallace, 1983.

Simms, Glenda. "Beyond the White Veil," In *Challenging Times: The Women's Movement in Canada and the United States,* eds. Constance Backhouse and David Flaherty. Montreal and Kingston: McGill-Queen's Press, 1992.

Spivak, Gayatri. "Can the Subaltern Speak." In *Marxism and the Interpretations of Culture,* eds. C. Nelson and L. Grossberg. London: MacMillan, 1988.

St. Lewis, Joanne. "The Entire Woman: Immigrant and Visible Minority Women." In *Women and the Canadian State,* eds. Caroline Andrew and Sandra Rodgers. Kingston: McGill-Queen's Press, 1997.

Stafford, James. "The Impact of the New Immigration Policy on Racism in Canada." In *Deconstructing a Nation: Immigration, Multiculturalism and Racism in '90s Canada,* ed. Vic Satzewich. Saskatoon: University of Saskatchewan, 1992.

Stasiulis, Daiva and Radha Jhappan. "The Fractious Politics of a Settler Society: Canada." In *Unsettling Settler Societies,* eds. Daiva Stasiulis and Nira Yuval-Davis. London: Sage, 1995.

Stasiulis, Daiva. "Theorizing Connections: Gender, Race, Ethnicity, and Class." In *Race and Ethnic Relations in Canada,* ed. Peter Li. Toronto: Oxford University Press, 1990.

Stepan, Nancy. "Race and Gender: The Role of Anatomy in Science." In *The Anatomy of Racism,* ed. David Goldberg. Minneapolis: University of Minnesota Press, 1990.

Stevenson, Winona. "Colonialism and First Nations Women in Canada." In *Scratching the Surface: Canadian Anti-Racist Feminist Thought,* eds. Enakshi Dua and Angela Robertson. Toronto: Women's Press, 1999.

Stoler, Ann Laura. *Race and the Education of Desire.* Durham: Duke University Press, 1995.

Thornhill, Esmerelda. "Focus on Black Women." In *Race, Class, and Gender: Bonds and Barriers,* eds. J. Vorst et al. Toronto: Between the Lines Press, 1989.

Turpel, Mary Ellen. "Aboriginal People and the Canadian Charter: Interpretive Monopolies, Cultural Differences." *Canadian Human Rights Yearbook,* vol. 6, no. 3 (1989–90): 3–45.

——. "Women on the Rekindling of Spirit at the Wake for the Meech Lake Accord." *Queen's Law Journal,* vol. 15 (nd): 345–59.

Valverde, Mariana. *The Age of Light, Soap and Water: Moral Reform in English Canada, 1885–1925.* Toronto: McClelland and Stewart Press, 1991.

——. "'When the Mother of the Race is Free': Race, Reproduction, and Sexuality in First-Wave Feminism." In *Gender Conflicts,* eds. Franca Iacovetta and Mariana Valverde. Toronto: University of Toronto Press, 1992.

Walker, James W. *"Race," Rights and the Law in the Supreme Court of Canada: Historical Case Studies.* Waterloo: The Osgoode Society for Canadian Legal History and Wilfrid Laurier University Press, 1997.

Ware, Vron. *Beyond the Pale: White Women, Racism and History.* London: Verso, 1992.

Wotherspoon, Terry. "From Assimilation to Self-Government: Towards a Political Economy of Canada's Aboriginal Policies." In *Deconstructing a Nation: Immigration, Multiculturalism and Racism in '90s Canada,* ed. Vic Satzewich. Saskatoon: University of Saskatchewan Press, 1992.

The Women's Book Committee, Chinese Canadian National Council. *Jin Guo: Voices of Chinese Canadian Women.* Toronto: Women's Press, 1992.

Invocation

Jeanette Armstrong

Jeannette Armstrong is a renowned visual artist, activist, educator and author from the Penticton Indian Reserve of the Okanagan Nation. She is the founder/director of the En'owkin International School of Writing and a highly sought-after speaker on issues related to indigenous rights. Her books include Slash, Native Creative Process, Breathtracks, *and her most recent novel,* Whispering in Shadows.

We are all very much aware of the history of the colonization process, which has systematically achieved, through various well-known measures, a breakdown in the structures upon which the well-being and health of our peoples depended. Our present social conditions bear this out.

What is not as well known is that the influences of patriarchal and imperialistic culture upon a people whose systems were fundamentally co-operative units have been not only devastating, but dehumanizing to an unimaginable degree. I speak in particular of the damage to the family-clan systems as the base units of social order in Aboriginal societies of North America. I speak in specific of the severe and irreversible effects on Aboriginal women, and the resultant effect on our nations.

The role of Aboriginal women in the health of family systems from one generation to the next was one of immense power. The immensity of the responsibility of bearer of life and nourisher of all generations is just becoming clear in its relationship to all societal functioning.

In traditional Aboriginal society, it was woman who shaped the thinking of all its members in a loving, nurturing atmosphere within the base family unit. In such societies, the earliest instruments of governance and law to ensure social order came from quality mothering of children.

In our instruments of teaching, the use of non-gendered figures, such as animals, provided a focus for instructions based on human worth. Our languages contained no words for *he* or *she* because of the high elevation of human dignity and personal recognition in our culture. The concept of colonization of one group or people by another group of people lies outside the understanding of those of us whose language and philosophy strive for co-operation and harmony wherever possible with all things, as a *necessary* means to survival. It is impossible to dominate or coerce another when these basic principles are childhood requisites in the learning of a social order. Traditionally, it was woman who controlled and shaped that societal order to a state of harmony, which in this time of extreme disorder seems nearly impossible.

Let me tell you that upon European contact our societies required no prisons, armies, police, judges or lawyers. Prostitution, rape, mental illness, suicide, homicide, child sexual abuse and family violence were all unheard of. Upon contact, physical diseases were so rare among us that our bodies had no immunities to even simple endemic diseases.

It is through the attack on the power of Aboriginal woman that disempowerment of our peoples has been achieved, in a dehumanizing process that is one of the cruellest on the face of this earth. In the attack on the core family system, in the direct attack on the role of Aboriginal woman, the disintegration of our peoples towards genocide has been achieved.

It is a fundamental human right for parents to nurture, to protect and to love their children. It is a fundamental and basic human right that parents raise their own children. It is a fundamental right that parents determine their children's culture and heritage, and what their children learn.

These fundamental human rights were seized, and still are being seized, from Aboriginal people in this country. Aboriginal children were taken from their homes and forcibly placed in sterile, military-like, hostile institutions called residential schools. These places of horror were invariably run by people who, themselves, never had children, and whose only goal was to "civilize." This process took place during the child's most essential stages of development. The resultant breakdown in our communities emerged from helpless parents left with nothing to live for and children raised in racist hostility and dispassion.

The ensuing nightmare of the effect of residential schooling on our communities has been what those "Indian problem" statistics are all about. The placement of our children in residential schools has been the single most devastating factor in the breakdown of our society. It is at the core of the damage, beyond all the other mechanisms cleverly fashioned to subjugate, assimilate and annihilate.

Throughout the dehumanizing years that followed those residential-school years, the struggle of Aboriginal woman has simply been to survive, under the onslaught of a people steeped in a tradition of hostile cultural supremacy. The struggle has been to survive, to be able to give protection, food and love to our children. The struggle has been just to keep our children with us. And the struggle has been intense for those of us whose residential-school experience deprived us of essential parenting skills, parenting skills that could have been learned only through quality parenting of ourselves. The struggle has been to keep families together and functioning with nothing but the worst patriarchal, dictatorial models on which to base relationships. The struggle has been to try, when the males stopped struggling, to provide the essentials for our children in an employment atmosphere hostile to all Natives and to all women. The struggle has been intense, too, because we have found ourselves stripped of our basic rights to family and community support systems through loss of status. The struggle has been to nurture, to protect, to provide and to heal in an environment in which we, as Aboriginal women, have been trodden to the edge of total despair—and in a country boasting its high standards.

Therefore, when I see my sisters in the prisons, on the streets and in their walking coffins, I see where the battle has taken its greatest toll. I see the scars. I see that these women, my sisters, have fought the cruellest of battles on earth. I see them through eyes of love and compassion. Never disgust. My utter disgust is for those who feed on the wounded. Who abuse them further with their bodies, their eyes and their unclean minds. Who dare to think that they are somehow better. I see that, when women of our nations are dying thus, it is we who are all in danger.

Through all the horror, it has been the struggle of those women who somehow survived against all odds to bring healing where they could to their families and nations. It has been through the struggle of these women that we have maintained some balance, so that our children could survive and contribute to our peoples. It has always been the women, the mothers, who have provided that chance.

We find our strength and our power in our ability to be what our grandmothers were to us: keepers of the next generation in every sense of that word—physically, intellectually and spiritually. We strive to retain our power and interpret it into all aspects of survival on this earth in the midst of chaos.

It is the fierce love at the centre of our power that is the weapon our grandmothers gave us, to protect and to nurture against all odds. Compassion and strength are what we are, and we have translated these into every area of our existence because we have had to. And we must continue to do so. It is a matter of the right of females to be what we fundamentally are—insurers of the next generation. It is a matter of survival where genocide is an everyday reality.

It is our compassion and strength that have been at the forefront of change in our communications. It is the power to adapt to all situations that has enabled us to ensure health and therefore survival of the young. It is the spirit to infiltrate into and learn all the systems around us in a balanced way that has enabled us to engender compassion and understanding in our children. Only those who know the true nature of despair and suffering can express compassion and understanding in all we do. It is the spirit of the female, holding in balance the spirit of the male, in a powerful co-operative force, that is at the core of family and community.

It is the strength of this female force that holds all nations and families together in health. It is the bridge to the next generation. It is this female power that is the key to the survival of us all, in an environment that is becoming increasingly damaged and unfit for all life forms. It is woman who holds this power and becomes powerful only when catalyzing co-operation and harmony, and therefore health, at all levels—from the individual, outward to the family, to the community and to the environment. Without it, all becomes chaos, despair, hostility and death. That is immense power.

Let this be known as the truth to all, so that we might all come through to a world once more in balance and harmony. I pray for that and struggle for that, for my great-grandchildren to come.

To you Aboriginal women out there, to you survivors, I congratulate you, I encourage you, I support you and I love you.

Origin Stories and Magical Signs in Women's Studies

Ann Braithwaite

Ann Braithwaite is Associate Professor in Women's Studies at the University of Prince Edward Island. She is the co-author of Troubling Women's Studies: Pasts, Presents, and Possibilities, *(Sumach Press, 2004) and her articles have appeared in journals such as* Feminist Theory: An International Interdisciplinary Journal *and the* Journal of International Women's Studies. *She has been active on the Executive of the Canadian Women's Studies Association/l'association canadienne des études sur les femmes for many years, including serving as President from 2004–06.*

> "Origin stories are . . . interested stories, all of them. They construct the present moment, and a political position in it, by invoking a point in time out of which that present moment unfolds—if not inevitably, then at least with a certain coherence." (King, 124)

The importance of examining "origin stories" for and in Women's Studies has gained particular relevance in the past ten years, especially in the wake of the publication of a range of histories and memoirs of both Women's Studies and "the women's movement" that purport to explain both "where we've been" and to ruminate on "where we're going." While fascinating for the very different stories they tell, as I read through this range of texts a few years ago, I also found myself getting increasingly intrigued—and troubled—by the numerous questions raised in this idea of telling, or constructing, stories about origins. What, I found myself asking about so many of these texts, were the stakes in or consequences of the kinds of narratives being told? Why, even given their many differences, did so many of these texts construct what seemed ultimately like quite similar stories about the past and its relationship to the present and the future, and about the connection between "the women's movement" and contemporary Women's Studies? As I read through many of these texts, I became increasingly worried by what I kept seeing as a kind of nostalgia that permeated so many of their accounts of both Women's Studies and "the women's movement," as well as by how they so often assumed these two were and must be inevitably connected. What both fascinated and troubled me then, and still does now, about so many of these texts is that in their range of memories and musings, so many of them seem to end up seeing the contemporary moment as a moment of loss, a moment where both Women's Studies and women's movements have strayed from their origins, and thus lost their way in the present and, by extension, for the future. These were perceptions of both Women's Studies and social movements that I could not agree with, and that I thought in turn needed their own troubling, in order to unpack their consequences, and construct other possibilities, other narratives, other futures.

Central to my re-examining of the "origin stories" and "magical signs" being set up in these texts is the contention that *how* we remember something is just as important, perhaps more important, than *what* we remember. How we come to know something, how we construct narratives about either a social movement or an academic field, is as important as what is then included in those narratives—because how a story is told always signals a particular understanding of what is important to tell, what must be included and what can be excluded, and for whom, under what circumstances, and, especially, to what ends. To ask *how* something is remembered forces us to account for what animates that remembering to begin with, and to self-reflexively acknowledge what too often remains taken for granted—that all narratives, even histories and memoirs, are told from a particular point of view and for particular purposes. My concern with many of these texts is thus not so much with "correcting" what is included or not as the details of their various narratives; rather, it is in exploring how they never step back to reflect on the reflections they're producing, how they never reflect on what's at stake in or what the consequences are (and for whom) of the details they do select to include in their narratives—in short, it is with how they never think about *how* they are constructing their various narratives about either "the women's movement" or Women's Studies. In never troubling the stories they tell themselves—or us, the readers—though, in never also thinking of why they are telling particular kinds of stories over others or what is at stake in the stories they construct, they can also never account for why they all tell such similar kinds of stories about the past that see the present—and by extension the future—as a place of loss and even betrayal. In short, what troubled me, and what I found myself wanting to trouble in turn, was that they never seemed to think very much about how the stories they told both enabled and delimited or shut down possibilities for Women's Studies both in the present and for the future. Memoirs and histories, then, whether about "the women's movement" or about Women's Studies more specifically, are not inconsequential; in framing what their authors see as important observations, issues, concepts and theories, they in turn inform and construct the field's identity and that of its practitioners, becoming part of the everyday practices in and perceptions about that field or movement. And thus, I am arguing, much is at stake in re-visiting what kinds of origin stories are being told, and how they are being constructed, about and in Women's Studies.

As mentioned above, two issues in particular struck me repeatedly about many of these texts: i) they all continually linked their perceptions of the past as existing in a linear relationship to the present and for the future, but often in ways that were unacknowledged; and ii) they almost all consistently linked those time frames through a repeated and largely unquestioned yoking together of activities in a past "women's movement" with contemporary academic Women's Studies. In many of these memoirs and histories, then, the result of the narratives of the past being told, and especially of the authors' involvements in what they repeatedly refer to as "the women's movement," is to consistently attempt to secure a particular kind of focus and future for Women's Studies through recalling a particular version of the past as an "origin story" or a founding or beginning point for the field. While there are many examples of this tendency throughout these texts, it is perhaps best reflected in the title of one of them: *The Politics of Women's Studies: Testimony from 30 Founding Mothers*, where the memories of a number of early practitioners are consistently held up as correctives to what the editor calls the current "amnesia afflicting most of those teaching or studying about women" (xiii). The texts under examination here not only understand the relationship between past, present and future as only a one-way trajectory—where the past inevitably leads to the present leads to the future (in a recurring teleology of ongoing progress or "things always getting better"), but they also set up the present and the future as accountable to that past, and as having to continually repeat that past. As one writer in *The Feminist Memoir Project* articulated in her vision of how the present needs to look to the past and repeat what it did right: "young women, especially, must take in these lessons so that instead of being intimidated by the activism of the 1960s, they will realize that *they are basically like us* . . . If youth learns to build on the knowledge that lies in our history, they can go even further than we have" (Hanisch, 201–202; emphasis mine). Here, in an especially characteristic example of this kind of trajectory, the present is seen as lacking the purpose and vision of the past—a purpose and vision that can only be regained by returning to one's origins in the past.

Stories about the past and one's beginnings, however, are never simple or unproblematic. As Elizabeth Grosz notes, this kind of articulation can only work by assuming that "the past is fundamentally like the present," where "the more and better we understand the past, the more well-armed we are to face a future that is to a large extent a copy or reformulation—the variation on a theme—of historical events" (Grosz, 29). Even more provocative, though, is the idea that "origin stories" are always "contests" or struggles for meaning, and, as King argues, "contested meanings tell us how we are interested and how we are politically positioned and positioning. Our erasure and creation of historical memory constructs who we are, our . . . identity" (136)—an understanding of how meaning is always both contested and contestable that is absent from the majority of these texts. The past is never simply remembered, but rather, is always *re-membered*—that is, the parts or members are put together into one particular kind of story; and one could take the same elements and put them together into a completely different kind of story too. Looking at contested moments, King goes on, "tells us something about what we have at stake in our history, what different groups have at stake in our history, and how we erase and/or create our own historical memories" (126); how the parts or elements are linked, then, highlights a particular vision of the field and structures its identity.

One way so many of these texts create this unproblematic link from past to present to future, and by extension offer a commentary on their perceptions of contemporary Women's Studies, is through consistently yoking Women's Studies in the present (and future) to some version of "the women's movement" in the past. Thus, in many of these texts, the authors' involvements in what they call "the women's movement" (always mentioned in the singular) are continually invoked as an origin story or founding moment for contemporary Women's Studies. Buhle, for example, notes that "the first programs in women's studies bore the distinctive imprint of women's liberation" and, even more to the point, "for many of the first teachers and students, women's studies and women's liberation were one and the same" (xix–xx), while Rothschild quotes a pamphlet (from the late 1970s, but articulating a sentiment still widely espoused) that argued "we propose that the principal function of university Women's Studies is to serve the Women's Movement" (22). The "women's movement" here, though, too often simply becomes a kind of "magical sign"—a term that marks a place of both the condensation and displacement of meaning, a place where a range of different possible meanings gets condensed and simplified into one, and comes to have a powerful signification. For King, this reduction and displacement is not just a curious phenomena, but one with significant political, ideological and theoretical consequences. Magical signs work to stabilize and anchor one particular meaning; they arise out of a multiplicity of possible meanings (for example, whose women's movements are being talked about, which group of women's experiences are being included in that term), that are then erased as the meaning of a term comes to be seen as singular and stable. Even more than just simplifying multiple different meanings into one assumed one, though, "the women's movement" in these texts also comes to operate as a signifier without either a referent or a denotative signified. It never really refers to any specific or shared set of issues or approaches, so much as it comes to connote an emotional relationship to a re-membered past, an affect that is largely nostalgic and that is always to a past that is no longer, and that we in the present seem to have forgotten and strayed from. And of course the issue with this kind of nostalgia about the past is that one can never live up to it . . . and hence the present is always a place of loss, precisely because it is not—and it can never be—like that re-membered past.

Narratives about, or re-memberings of, the past, though, are always told from the point of view of the present. How one thinks about the past, and the narratives one tells about that past, demonstrate also how one thinks about the present and what one hopes for the future. What is remembered, what is forgotten, what is included and what is excluded are all framed by contemporary concerns and interests, and thus inform how the parts being re-membered are to be understood. The texts under examination here, then, in addition to being fascinating memoirs and histories in their own right, also, I am arguing, offer a window onto perceptions of the present and the future—and onto what their authors evidently interpret as a moment of instability, even crisis, in and for contemporary Women's Studies. Through this window, the rapid and multiple changes in the field since its inception in academe almost four decades ago—in terms of its content, focus, concepts, approaches, theories (and even the name of the field itself)—are, rather than being seen as exciting developments and signs of growth in the field, instead consistently understood as dangerous to the field's stability, meaning, role and identity. The re-memberings here thus become origin stories in precisely King's sense of the term—they are "interested" versions of a past that always denote particular points of view about the present and particular visions of the future. What concerns me about these two interrelated stories of Women's Studies and "the women's movement," then, is precisely that they also reflect perceptions about and construct their versions of an appropriate identity of and for Women's Studies and its practitioners—an identity to be found solidly within the terms of re-membering set out by these authors. And in these versions, the meaning of Women's Studies in the present, and for the future, is located in very particular versions of its beginnings in the past, and the current *raison d'être* of Women's Studies continues to be located in "the women's movement."

To harness Women's Studies to "the women's movement," (or to any version of feminist social action), however, to make it simply and only an offshoot of that movement and keep it ultimately answerable to that movement—as in oft-heard clichés like "Women's Studies is the academic arm of the women's movement"—is to elide the differences between these two endeavours, especially so many years later. Not only does it depend on and perpetuate a delimited notion of "the women's movement"—as an always vaguely defined and nostalgic enterprise—but it also shuts down the possibilities for and in Women's Studies itself, with the result that it makes Women's Studies only identical to particular definitions of politics and activism and demands that it remain faithful to those understandings. The result of this pairing is that it anchors and legitimates Women's Studies only in relation to some pre-given definition of what constitutes appropriate feminist work or politics in academia—politics that always occur, "really," outside of academia. But what gets lost in this formulation is the possibility of thinking of Women's Studies as a different institutional and political site, where different kinds of questions can be (and have been) potentially—and productively—asked and explored.

None of this is to suggest that there is not a long relationship between feminist social movements and academic Women's Studies, nor that the latter did not initially arise from the former's understanding that academia was as in need of change as other social institutions. Nor is it to argue that all of this work does not still go on on many campuses, and that many people involved in Women's Studies, as well as across the campus community, might not be animated by its undertaking. (Nor is it at all to suggest that universities aren't in need of many kinds of transformations.) All of this certainly has been and continues to be the case for many of us working in Women's Studies. But my argument here is that the long history and oft-repeated narrative that makes the connection between these kinds of social transformation projects and Women's Studies an *automatic* one is problematic, and that the relationship between feminism as a social movement and academic Women's Studies can, must and has changed, especially as Women's Studies has become so much a part of contemporary academe—and that this is not a loss for the field. As Robyn Wiegman so succinctly puts it in her commentary on this supposed relationship, "any attempt to write movement subjectivity as the field's origin and reproductive goal is not simply wrong-headed but counterproductive precisely because it generates *as a disciplinary imperative* a certain understanding of the political" (20). It is precisely the continued insistence on—or at least the unquestioned acceptance of—this relationship as a *necessary* connection, though, which leads so many of these texts to (usually not consciously) bemoan the current state of Women's Studies, to see academic feminism (in any discipline) as that which has brought "the women's movement" to an end, and to see the correctives to this state of affairs in a return to that past—

because the past came first, was headed in the right direction, but we, in the present, have forgotten and betrayed it, and in order to get the future right, we now need to line ourselves up again with the past.

Acquiescing to this relationship and trajectory, though, forecloses any future for Women's Studies except as always replaying the past—and a very particular past at that. It perpetuates a notion that the present and the future are/should be like the past—except that, as I've already said, that past is itself a magical sign. It leaves no room for the kinds of contemplations of Women's Studies as a site of critical and intellectual work, of thinking about the intersections between power, knowledge and knowledge production, or of Women's Studies as a site that "resists closure, invites conversation, and promotes a reflexive capacity for 'ongoing reinterpretation' and accountability for those reinterpretations" (134–135), as Vivian May so compellingly articulates it. And it certainly leaves no room for any kind of accountability or self-reflexivity that could examine what's at stake—with all of its attendant questions about for whom and to what end—in any imagining or story of the current and future intellectual projects of Women's Studies. And thus it is not only this search for "origin stories," but more centrally all the problems generated by not recognizing that origin stories are contests for meaning, are struggles over which meanings will dominate, that troubled me then—that troubles me still—about so many narratives about women's movements and Women's Studies.

King's compelling arguments about the construction of origin stories and their dependence on unacknowledged magical signs are thus especially relevant ideas to bring to this examination of the recent genre of reflections on Women's Studies and "the women's movement." Because origin stories are not just partial stories or incomplete histories; they are narratives with a purpose, and they rest on equally unrecognized magical signs that write out complexity and multiplicity of meaning. To say that all of these recent texts tell an unacknowledged origin story in an attempt to secure or stabilize what they think Women's Studies should mean is certainly not to say that they all tell the same story. As I am arguing here, however, many of them nonetheless share a more than coincidental "interest" in passing on particular kinds of stories about the past and about the relationship of Women's Studies to "the women's movement" that are not innocent, but that reflect a particular set of concerns about the present and the future of the field. To re-think the kinds of "origin stories" and "magical signs" being produced about contemporary Women's Studies, then, is to both demand an accountability for the narratives being produced and to in turn produce other possibilities, other imaginings, for and of the field's presents and futures.

Endnotes

1. The following is adapted from "'Where We've Been' and 'Where We're Going': Reflecting on Reflections of Women's Studies and 'the Women's Movement'" in Braithwaite, Ann, Susan Heald, Susanne Luhmann, and Sharon Rosenberg. *Troubling Women's Studies: Pasts, Presents, and Possibilities.* Toronto, ON: Sumach Press, 2004.

2. Readers will notice that I use the term "the women's movement" in quotation marks throughout this paper. While I contend that this term must always be used in the plural — as women's movements — in order to signal both that there were and are a multiplicity of social movements organized around this "identity," and that paying attention to this necessitates always interrogating "whose movement" and "which women," its use with

quotation marks and in the singular throughout this paper reflects its common invocation in these texts. Indeed, one of my "troubles" with these texts is precisely with the constant unexamined use of this term in the singular.

3. Some of the texts I'm referring to here include: Rachel Blau DuPlessis and Ann Snitow's collection *The Feminist Memoir Project;* Florence Howe's edited text *The Politics of Women's Studies: Testimony from 30 Founding Mothers;* Ruth Rosen's *The World Split Open;* Susan Brownmiller's *In Our Time;* Marilyn Boxer's *When Women Ask the Questions;* Joan Mandle's *Can We Wear Our Pearls and Still be Feminists?;* Ellen Messer-Davidow's *Disciplining Feminism;* and Phyllis Chesler's *Letters to a Young Feminist.* Additionally, there have been a number of special journal issues on the current and future state of WS (i.e. in *Signs,* in *Feminist Studies* and in *NWSA Journal*), and even on PAR-L, the Canadian feminist listserv which recently produced a "Chronology of the History of Women's Studies in Canada," charting Women's Studies programs in Canadian universities since the 1970s. While I certainly don't want to imply that these are all doing the same kinds of things (indeed, they are not!), taken as a whole they illustrate that there has been a lot of thinking about feminisms' and Women's Studies' past(s) going on since the mid-1990s, and a lot of stories being produced about the field's founding, its trajectory, and its changes over the past almost 40 years. For a more detailed reading of some of these texts, see my essay in *Troubling Women's Studies.* Here, for brevity's sake, I focus on some of the broad observations and conclusions I make in more detail there about what is at stake in constructing these kinds of origin stories.

4. Both of these terms are borrowed from Katie King's influential article, "Lesbianism as Feminism's Magical Sign: Contests for Meaning and U.S. Women's Movements, 1968-1972," in her *Theory in Its Feminist Travels: Conversations in U.S. Women's Movements.* Bloomington: Indiana University Press, 1994. While her article addresses a very different issue than mine does here, these two concepts are especially useful for exploring these current and popular ways of perceiving Women's Studies.

5. King's use of this term circulated around her elucidation of the word "lesbianism" in feminist circles between 1968 and 1972, exploring how a range of often contested understandings of the politics of that term were very quickly erased and instead condensed into one simplified — and thus too simplistic — meaning that has come to dominate what she calls "feminist taxonomic identities" ever since.

6. Some of these changes and developments in the field include: questions of disciplinarity and the institutionalization of Women's Studies in academia; ongoing concerns about the inevitable and much bemoaned separation between theory and practice — that is, between academic feminism/Women's Studies, especially in its taking up of postmodern and poststructuralist languages, and feminism more broadly constituted as activist and thus as more "real," more "political" and "more important"; debates about "differences between women" — and the movement from an earlier focus on identities and identity politics to the more recent anti-identitarian emphasis; the reworking of taken for granted assumptions about sisterhood, power, experience, activism and the "personal as political"; definitional conflicts over post- and third-wave feminisms and over distinctions between generations and waves of feminisms; and doubt over the definition and stability of the very term "woman" itself — all current points of much debate and contention, but even more, I believe, exciting exploration, in Women's Studies. In the longer piece in *Troubling Women's Studies,* I go on to explore in more detail some of the complexities of how differences between women — of race and class in particular — are problematically addressed — and not — in these texts.

References

Braithwaite, Ann, Susan Heald, Susanne Luhmann, and Sharon Rosenberg. *Troubling Women's Studies: Pasts, Presents, and Possibilities*. Toronto: Sumach Press, 2004.

Buhle, Mary, "Introduction." In Florence Howe, ed., *The Politics of Women's Studies: Testimony from 30 Founding Mothers*. New York: The Feminist Press, 2000.

DuPlessis, Rachel Blau and Ann Snitow, eds. *The Feminist Memoir Project: Voices from Women's Liberation. New York:* Three Rivers Press, 1998.

Grosz, Elizabeth. "Histories of a Feminist Future." In Judith A. Howard and Carolyn Allen, eds., *Feminisms at the Millennium*. Chicago: University of Chicago Press, 2000.

Hanisch, Carol. "Two Letters from the Women's Liberation Movement." In Rachel Blau DuPlessis and Ann Snitow, eds., *The Feminist Memoir Project: Voices from Women's Liberation*. New York: Three Rivers Press, 1998.

Howe, Florence, ed. *The Politics of Women's Studies*: *Testimony from 30 Founding Mothers*. New York: The Feminist Press, 2000.

King, Katie. "Lesbianism as Feminism's Magical Sign: Contests for Meaning and U.S. Women's Movements, 1968-1972." In *Theory in Its Feminist Travels: Conversations in U.S. Women's Movements*. Bloomington: Indiana University Press, 1994.

May, Vivian M. "Disciplinary Desires and Undisciplined Daughters: Negotiating the Politics of a Women's Studies Doctoral Education." *NWSA Journal* 14, no. 1 (Spring 2002): 134–159.

Rothschild, Joan. "NEWSA25: In the Beginning." *NWSA Journal* 14, no. 1 (Spring 2002): 22–28.

Wiegman, Robyn. "Academic Feminism Against Itself." *NWSA Journal* 14, no. 2 (Summer 2002): 18–37.

Feminism in Waves: Re-Imagining a Watery Metaphor

Kim Sawchuk

Kim Sawchuk is an associate professor in the Department of Communication Studies at Concordia University in Montreal, where she teaches courses in research methodologies, communications theory and feminist media studies. For the past two years she has been a member of the Mobile Digital Commons Network, a research consortium investigating and inventing wireless mobile technologies for artistic practices and public usage. She is a founding editor of wi: a journal of mobile digital culture *and is the current editor of the* Canadian Journal of Communication.

The past, present, and future are composed not only of dates but also, in a more complex and incalculable way, of events. How we understand the relations between past and present has direct implications for whatever conceptions of the future, the new, creation, and production we may develop.

Elizabeth Grosz, "Histories of a Feminist Future"

In the past five years I have noticed more and more of a preoccupation and investment in the terms first, second and third wave feminism amongst my students. In many of these discussions I have found myself being questioned about what wave I belong to and at times ascribed, uncomfortably, with a label of belonging to either the second or the third wave of feminism. The older I get, the more I am assumed to be a card-carrying member of the second wave. The wave is a trope that troubles me.

Posing this question, and deploying this image, conveys a tacit acceptance of a historical narrative that goes something like this. The primary goals of this first wave are described as a struggle to grant the vote to middle-class women (DuBois,1971). This long period of battle, and its subsequent waning, is marked by the return of feminism in the 1960s with the rise of other protest movements, including the civil rights movement in the United States (Baxandall and Gordon, 2000; Nicholson, 1997). A third wave of feminism returned in the late 1980s as a response to claims of post-feminism (Braithwaite), to media declarations of the death of feminism and to perceived absences and gaps within the second wave (Walker). While most accounts of the wave end with the third wave, others argue that in the wake of 9/11, a fourth wave is being established that is more international in scope (Woodhull, Kaplan).

This is a simplified version of the standard narrative of feminism in waves. It has several variations and has stimulated debate on its ideological content, its proper periodization, the inclusion of different scholars and the merits and shortcomings of each wave. The focus of the debates may vary, but what remains consistent is the image of a wave as a wall of water that gathers momentum, peaks and dissipates. Only a handful of articles question the performativity of the metaphor itself (Bailey, 1997; Garrison, 2000; Purvis, 2004; Spigel, 2004). Many have embraced the notion of the wave to signal that the torch of feminism is re-ignited by each successive generation. However, the dominant metaphor of the wave carries with it significant amounts of flotsam and jetsam that we need to query, lest they douse the flame.

In my attempt to re-imagine feminism in waves, I will examine the first uses of the term by feminists and by the media in the late 1960s, a scattered origin that is rarely discussed. I will then discuss how the wave reduces the complexity of a variegated social movement to a teleological cycle of accelerated momentum, followed by a brief spectacular climax and an inevitable decline. Finally, I will discuss how this narrative of succession closes down the metaphoric potential of waves, and of feminism, as the transference of energy. If we are to retain the wave *for* feminism, then our image of its shape needs to shift, accommodate and promote the complex currents and flows of water *and* of feminism.

When did feminism begin to construct its history and politics through the image of the wave? Catherine M. Orr comments in a footnote that "'Wave' is a term coined during the 1970s to emphasize the contemporary movement's (second wave) connection and indebtedness to the Woman's Rights movement of the nineteenth century (first wave)", but she furnishes no further details (43). This narrative has, as far as I can tell, its origins in the late 1960s and early 1970s. Kate Millet sanctified the wave in her groundbreaking 1970 book, *Sexual Politics*: "It may be that a second wave of sexual revolution might at last accomplish its aim of freeing half the race from its immemorial subordination and in the process bring us all a great deal closer to humanity." In a short article "Feminism Old Wave and New Wave" Ellen Dubois asserted: "There have been two major feminist waves in this country, one running from about 1835 to 1920 (it took that long to win its major demand—the vote); the other beginning some time in the middle of the sixties and ending who knows when . . . " (1971). The wave was promoted by specific feminists, such as Dubois and Millet, and gained use within the feminist media at this time. Millet's words, for example, inspired a locally produced Boston feminist magazine entitled *The Second Wave: a magazine of the new feminism* (1971–1984) who used this very quote to affirm their editorial scope on their masthead.

In these early discussions the wave is used to introduce the idea of feminism as a potent postwar force of social change. Looking back on the *Second Wave* for an article in the *Nation* (2001), Rosalyn Baxandall and Linda Gordon stake a claim for feminism's primordial influence on the political landscape of America.

> The women's liberation movement, as it was called in the sixties and seventies, was the largest social movement in the history of the United States—and probably in the world. Its impact has been felt in every home, school and workplace, in every form of art, entertainment and sport, in all aspects of personal and public life in the United States. Like a river overflowing its banks and seeking a new course, it permanently altered the landscape.

The specificity and shortfall of this U.S.-centred vision of feminism has been critiqued by activists and writers from within America and around the globe (Graff; Taylor; Woodhull). Yet what is carried forward, as well, in this retrospective invocation of this watery terminology?

Return for a minute to the subtitle of the *Second Wave* as "the magazine of the new feminism" and to the title of DuBois' article. The pointed use of the term "new" presumes an "old feminism" indicating one of the key problems with the standard image of the wave as it emerges in the late 1960s. Despite the putative desire to connect the present with the past, implied in the emphasis on the new is that something has disappeared, is dated, or is washed up. This idea has been carried over, like so much flotsam, from the past into the present. Allyson Mitchell (2002), for one, comments: "I was concerned by some of the sentiments that 'older' feminists were voicing about young women like me. My experiences contradicted their accusations of apathy." I am not denying that there may be generational differences or genuine grievances that need to be put on the table for debate. However, my larger point is that the image of the wave presupposes the necessity of a distancing between old and new in order to go forward. This creates, as Jennifer Purvis (2004) argues, a host of intergenerational anxieties.

What is assumed in this argument for a continuity, is an essential core of shared values at the centre of each wave and that these cores are incompatible. Amanda Lotz puts it this way: "Third-wave feminism departs from what was the core of second-wave liberal feminism on a key ideological issue. Where second-wave liberal and cultural approaches sought to unify diverse women by appealing to a universal sisterhood, third-wave activists recognize the racist, heterosexist, classist and other implications of the erasure of difference" (2003, 5–6). Commenting upon this, Purvis (2004) writes that third wave feminists see the second wave as rigid, monolithic and tyrannical, then second wave feminists accuse the "third-wave or third generation feminisms as apolitical, postfeminist and inherently incompatible with the issues and political agendas characteristic of second wave or second

Lab Grading Sheet: Executive Function Lab

Name(s): Silvi Lavoie, Jenna Decaire **Grade:** 28.5 **/50**

Introduction 6 /10

- Formatting/readability issues
- Flow issues
- key parts are here, 3 sources, hypotheses (& data analysis in methods)
  - but needs more synthesis

Method

Participants 4 /4

Materials 3 /5

organization issues but key info included

Procedure 2.5/5

- data analysis lacking specifics
+ mixed in with materials/measures

Results

- missing a lot of detail
- unclear what each is referring to
- need to name tests & explain variables
- correlation?

Discussion 5 /10

- what you've included is clear, but lacking key info/implications

APA (Including in report and references) 2 /4

- running head moved (pg 10)
- formatting stats & reporting
- formatting references

Appendices/attachments 2 /2

generation feminism" (2004, 95). Such acrimony and anxiety is, I contend, made possible because the image of the wave leads to a kind of intellectual matricide despite the avowed intention of each successive self-identified generation to create a link to the past.

Lynn Spigel, likewise, questions the "slippery" historical assumptions embedded in the term, commenting that with " . . . both its oceanic and avant-garde connotations, the waves thesis works to place old feminists on the beach—washed up like fish on the shore. Meanwhile, as in all teleological narratives, the 'new' feminist (regardless of her age) is taken to be an immersive body, fully refreshed by sea change and outfitted in new feminist swimsuit styles" (2004). Indeed, the tendency is problematic in two other respects: first, the past is homogenized while distinctions in the present are often finely parsed; second, the numerical ordering into first, second, third and fourth creates a fiction that these moments have a solidity and irrefutable numerical facticity. This listing practice leaves little space for the in-between despite the feeling of many that they are "lost between the waves" (Graff, 2003, 103).

Presumed core distinctions are ascribed to successive waves based on a neat linear notion of the divisibility of time and space. This tendency towards a sense of certainty has echoes in debates between second, third and fourth wave feminists. As Winnie Woodhull (2003) has written, "If anything can be said with certainty about third wave feminism, it is that it is mainly a first-world phenomenon generated by women who, like their second wave counterparts have limited interest in women's struggles elsewhere on the planet"(1). In these incarnations this image and the figure of feminism that may accompany it unfortunately signifies the idea that those within a period and a place embrace a singular vision of feminism's goals, that feminism is generational, that depending on when one was born, one is part of a particular world view (see Steenbergen).

Are any one of us either a singular age, of a generation, and as a generation only of this particular time? While Emma Goldmann's marvelous essay "The Traffic in Women" clearly addresses Victorian morays of sexuality it is an essay that I read over and over again because its radical class and sexual politics continues to resonate in our own period (1917). It is of *her* time, yet it is also of *our* time. Debates on core issues are at the very heart and history of feminism and are never resolved with finality, precisely because the terms of debate may change *through* time. The magazine the *Second Wave* that existed between 1971–1984, at the height of the so-called second wave demonstrates this point. Ironically, the content of the magazine does not live up to the clichés of the second wave as exuding wishy-washy liberal values or as essentialist in its understanding of a unified womanhood, captured in phrases like "sisterhood." Past issues of the *Second Wave* included debates on transsexuality, lesbianism, motherhood, poverty, childcare, the family and the politics of international feminism. It included interviews and coverage on the condition of women in the Sudan and in Vietnam. It did not demand a singular position, but was a lively and heated forum on the very meaning and agenda of feminism.

Here it is worth recalling that the wave was not only used by feminists in the late 1960s and early 1970s. At the same time that feminists were beginning to use the wave to self-describe, the mainstream print media used the wave in their descriptions of the revolutionary power of "women's liberation." *Globe and Mail* journalist William Johnson, for example, excitedly reported in 1969 "that a new wave of feminism is breaking out over Toronto" (w5). In 1970 a strike by teachers in Ontario was discussed as supported by the wave of feminism sweeping the country (11) accompanied by another report on feminist activities in Australia whose headline conveyed the warning that "feminism spreads" (11).

In this latter media account, in particular, we see that the wave connotes that those participating in the movement are simply being carried along by a force that is outside of rational thought or a willful, conscious assessment of inequity. Within this media discourse on feminism as a wave, women are denied agency within the political process. It raises the specter of a mob mentality that brainwashes ordinary women. This discourse on the wave as a threat from irrational forces is similar to the use of the term "wave" within media discussions of immigration or terrorism in our present context.

What is shared in both feminist and the media discourses on the wave in this period, despite their clear ideological differences and values, is the idea that feminism is an unstoppable, powerful unified social force. I want to be clear; my critique is not of a particular wave of feminism, be it first, second, third or fourth. My critique is of the standard image of the wave that frames the trajectory of feminist history and politics. There is nothing natural about this image of the wave. It has a definite history, a history that is often forgotten, a history that influences how we conceptualize our relationship to the past and how we imagine the future. Is it time to wave good-bye to the wave? Can we?

The problem with rejecting the wave is that a whole generation of self-identified feminists, in particular those working as the third wave, have adopted the language of the wave from their second wave foremothers. The danger is that in repudiating the wave that these contributions would be erased from the lively history of feminism. I propose in this final section that if we are to retain the wave, then we must re-conceptualize it to break away from the dominant image of a wave as a monolithic wall of water that comes crashing onto shore.

And here I turn to the physical sciences, which offers a description of the activities of water that suggests that a wave is an energy, and what we witness when we see a wave move is the transference of energy. "The significance of all waves is that whether they are sound waves, light waves, or water waves is that they carry energy from one place to another" (Muller and Oberlander, 1984, 493). This understanding of feminism as an energy, albeit a specific type, is found in the writing of feminists who would most likely be classified as second wave, such as Luce Irigaray, but it is also present in a variety of feminist perspectives from the second and third waves. Jennifer Baumgardener and Amy Richards describe their *Third Wave ManifestA*, as "an attempt to open people's eyes to the power of everyday feminism right in front of our noses. We must see its reality if we are to corral that energy into attacking the inequalities that still exist" (49). Waves create very little forward displacement of water. What is being transmitted is energy, through the water, not the water itself. Water is a medium.

Waves do not come from a singular source. They may be created by the action of wind, by an earthquake, or through the pull of gravity down a river creating rapids. The swells we see move to the shore from different directions, and they often interfere with each other, thereby producing wave patterns of varying complexity. This description of complexity has echoes in Laura Karaian's eloquent defense of feminism: "Any criticism that rejects complexity in favour of simplification is the real threat to the real power of feminism. I see the 'anything goes' retort as a way to dismiss a generation of feminists who embrace complexity and fight oppressions in multiple, unique and creative ways."

Water, like feminism, contains many kinds of motion that isn't only apparent on the surface: there are undercurrents that move at different speeds and velocities and all may be necessary to maintain or consider. Seismic shock waves, tsunamis are dangerous because while they are spectacular, they are in fact, barely discernable, reaching heights of only a meter. It is their ability to carry energy at incredible speeds that makes them dangerous, destructive and deadly as we have so recently witnessed. A swell of moderate size is capable of traveling halfway across the world before all of its energy is absorbed. If it is these moderate swells that most often make it to shore, then this is a reminder for feminism that it is the everyday quiet struggles of thousands, visible to only a few, which may have the greatest and most enduring power.

Feminism re-conceptualized in these ways is not "a wave" but a plethora of waves. The flexible core of this energy is captured in the words of Joan Grant Cummings who puts it this way: "Feminism is the full participation of women in the political, economic, social, civil, cultural, intellectual, spiritual and sexual spheres of life. Feminism works with race equality, sexual rights, disability rights, economic, social and education equality, age rights and gender equality at its centre" (311). These waves have the power to move, create disturbances and sculpt new formations from what already exists. "The future is the domain of what endures" ruminates Liz Grosz (2000). Thought of in this way, feminism as a series of confluent waves that transfer energies of this dynamic movement conveys how ripples from the past may contribute to feminism's ongoing future momentum.

Acknowledgments

I thank Candis Steenbergen and Neil Barratt for their assistance with this paper.

References

Bailey, Cathryn. (1997). "Making Waves and Drawing Lines: The Politics of Defining the Vicissitudes of Feminism." *Hypatia*. 12.3: 17–28.

Baumgardner, Jennifer and Amy Richards. (2000). *ManifestA: Young women, feminism and the future.* New York: Farrar Strauss and Giroux.

Baxandall and Linda Gordon (2000). Second-wave Soundings. The nation. Posted at *July 3, 2000 issue* www.thenation.com/doc/20000703/Gordon.

Braithwaite, Ann. (2002). "The Personal, the Political, Third Wave, and Post Feminism," *Feminist Theory: An International Interdisciplinary Journal,* 3:3, 335–344.

DuBois, Ellen. (1971). "Feminism Old Wave and New Wave." www.cwluherstory.com/CWLUArchive/wave.html.

Freeman, Jo. (1996). "Waves of Feminism." H-Women in May of 1996. www.jofreeman.com/feminism/waves.htm.

Garrison, Ednie Kaeh. (2000) "Are We on a Wavelength Yet? On Feminist Oceanography, Radios and Third Wave Feminism." Conclusion to *The Third Wave and the Cultural Predicament of Feminist Consciousness in the United States*. Doctoral Thesis, Washington State University.

The Globe and Mail (1970). "Feminism Spreads" (Reuters). August 31, 11.

Goldmann, Emma. (1917; 1970). "The Traffic in Women," in Emma Goldmann, *The Traffic in Women and other essays on Feminism*. California: Times Change Press. (Originally printed in 1917 in Mother Earth Publishing, New York City.)

Cummings, Joan Grant. (2001). "From Natty Dreads to Grey Ponytails: The Revolution is Multigenerational." (309–314). *Turbochicks: Talking Young Feminisms*. Allyson Mitchell, Lisa Bryn Rundle and Lara Karaian. Toronto: Sumach Press.

Graff, Agnieszka. (2003). Lost Between the Waves? The Paradoxes of Feminist Chronology and Activism in Contemporary Poland. *Journal of International Women's Studies*, Vol. 4: 2, 103–116.

Grosz, Elizabeth. (2000). "Histories of a Feminist Future." *Signs: Journal of Women in Culture and Society*. 25:4, 1017–1021.

Irigaray, Luce. (1977). "The Mechanics of Fluids." This Sex Which is Not One trans Katherine Porter. (106–118). Ithaca: Cornell University Press.

Johnson, William. (1969). "The wave of feminism opposes motherhood, marriage: traditional role rejected." *The Globe and Mail*, Thursday, May 1, 1969, w 5.

Johnson, William. (1970). "Can Ontario teachers federation meet challenge of reforming negotiations?" *The Globe and Mail,* Monday, Aug. 31, 11.

Kaplan, E. Ann. (2003). "Feminist Futures: Trauma, the Post-9/11 World and a Fourth Feminism?" *Journal of International Women's Studies*, 4;2, 46–59. www.bridgew.edu/soas/jiws/April03/index.htm.

Karaian, Lara. (2002). "talkin' 'bout my generation" *herizons magazine*. www.herizons.ca/magazine/backissues/fal02/index.html.

Lotz, Amanda D. (2003). "Communicating Third-Wave Feminism and New Social Movements: Challenges for the next century of feminist endeavor." *Women and Language*, vol. XXVI, 1, 2–9.

Millett, Kate. (1970). *Sexual Politics*. New York: Doubleday.

Mitchell, Alyson. (2002). "talkin' 'bout my generation" *herizons magazine*. www.herizons.ca/magazine/backissues/fal02/index.html.

Muller, Robert A. and Theodore M. Oberlander. (1984). New York: McGraw-Hill College.

Nicholson, Linda ed. (1997). *The Second Wave: A reader in feminist theory*. New York: Routledge.

Orr, Catherine M. (1997). "Charting the Currents of the Third Wave." *Hypatia*. 12:3, 29–45.

Purvis, Jennifer. (2004). "Grrrls and Women Together in the Third Wave: Embracing the Challenges of Intergenerational Feminism(s)." *NWSA Journal*. 16: 3, 93–123.

Spigel, Lynn. (2004). "Theorizing the Bachelorette: 'Waves' of Feminist Media Studies." *Signs: Journal of Women in Culture and Society,* 30:1, 1209–1221.

Steenbergen, Candis(2001). "Talkin' 'Bout Whose Generation?" (256–271). *Turbochicks: talking young feminisms*. Allyson Mitchell, Lisa Bryn Rundle and Lara Karaian eds. Toronto: Sumach Press.

Taylor, Ula Y. (1998). "Making Waves: The Theory and Practice of Black Feminism." *The Black Scholar,* 28:2, 185–195.

Walker, Rebecca, ed. (1995). *To Be Real: Telling the Truth and Changing the Face of Feminism.* New York: Anchor Books.

Winnie Woodhull. (2003). "Global Feminisms, Transnational Political Economies, and Third World Cultural Production." *Journal of International Women's Studies,* vol.4, 2, www.bridgew.edu/soas/jiws/April03/index.htm.

Riding the Feminist Waves: In with the Thirds

Natasha Pinterics

Natasha Pinterics recently completed her master's thesis, Big & Bawdy Bodies: A Feminist/Cultural Studies Analysis of Fat & Frisky Performances *at St. Mary's University.*

I set out to research third wave feminism with a fairly broad mandate; to discover and relay the theory and practice of third wave feminism, and the critiques made by and against third wave feminism. . . Many argue that the third wave of feminism began in the 1990s with a new wave of anti-racist feminists who thoroughly deconstructed white mainstream feminism's maintenance of racist and classist oppression. Others maintain that the third wave of feminism is a generational phenomenon, comprised of generation Xers dissatisfied with what they perceived to be the rigidity of morals espoused by second wave feminism. Others still insist that the third wave of feminism is one and the same with the anti-feminist movement. I will argue that third wave feminism is an amalgamation of many different streams of theorizing—including that of women of colour and younger women disillusioned with what they perceive to make up the body of "second wave" feminism—in intrinsically different formulations than the theorizing coming from anti-feminists.

THE PREMISES, IDEAS AND INFLUENCES THAT INFORM THIRD WAVE FEMINISM(S)

Underlying the theory espoused by many third wave feminist thinkers is the premise that the experiences leading women and men to feminism in the 1990s are significantly different from those that led previous generations to feminism. . . . [C]hanges have meant that young women have had greater freedoms than did our predecessors and have taken them, to some degree, for granted. They have meant that many young women (myself included) were raised with the propensity to question what we were given as "truths," be they feminist, mainstream or otherwise. It must also be noted that our generation, as with all generations, has been shaped by unparalleled historical circumstances and happenings.

. . . [Y]oung women today experience sexism, racism, homophobia and classism that is more underground, more insidious, and much more difficult to pinpoint than its previous incarnations.

Young women are questioning second wave feminist theory, and pushing the boundaries of who and what constitutes feminist community and defines feminist theorizing. What seems to have arisen through this questioning are new forms of feminist ideological frameworks. Within the body of third wave feminist thinking, there exist strains and influences of other feminist epistemologies, including standpoint theory, queer theory, postmodernist, poststructuralist feminist thought and anti-essentialism . . .

Much of the third wave theorizing . . . emphasizes above all else the need for greater acceptance of complexities, ambiguities and multiple locations, and highlights the dangers of reduction into dichotomous thinking. . . .

Many third wave thinkers have criticized the second wave feminist movement heavily for essentializing notions of "women" and "sisterhood," and for organizing and theorizing around women's "sameness," at the expense of our differences. The theorizing of "sameness," and perceived essentialism of second wave feminist thinkers have also been criticized by many woman of colour theorists, including Enakshi Dua, Sherene Razack, bell hooks, Himani Bannerji, and Ien Ang, among others. These writers have raised concerns about the fact that women of colour's experiences of gender in all aspects, including femininity, marriage, conceptualizations of family and relationships to paid labour varied immensely from those of middle-class, white women: "such differences raised the question of whether a universal experience with gender exists" (Dua 16). . . .

THIRD WAVE THEORIES

Although it remains true that third wave feminist theorists rely heavily on the feminist tool of critique, it must be made clear that third wave theorizing consists of a great deal more than simply criticizing their predecessors. As mentioned previously, much of third wave theory rests upon embracing and utilizing multi-vocality/locality. The use of often divergent personal narratives in anthologies, cyberspace and zines are indicative of this theoretical basis, and of the third wave theoretical insistence on taking on feminist politics as they exist at individual, personal levels. . . .

There is much emphasis on synthesis, coalition building and networking within the frameworks of third wave theorizing. Synthesis refers to examining what works or doesn't from pre-existing feminist theories and combining these elements with new theories. . . . Coalition building in the third wave analysis is meant to happen without the aid of larger umbrella organizational structuring, that is to say, smaller organizations would retain their own standings and mandates, and would co-operate with each other when prudent to do so, but only in the sense of using each other as resource bases (Carlson et al.). Occasionally, attempts by anti-racist feminists to bring such changes into existing organization have been met with backlash and resistance from white feminists, as exampled aptly by the withdrawal of support by many white feminists from the National Action Committee on the Status of Women (NAC) when two women of colour were consecutively chosen to head the organization (Dua). "The result of such resistance has been to entrench coalition and identity politics within these organizations" (Dua 17).

Another exceptionally important aspect of third wave feminist theorizing involves pushing the boundaries and limitations of gender definition, sexuality definition, race and class definitions. In pushing these boundaries, it is essential not only to explore the various ways in which we are oppressed by some of these identities, but also the ways we are privileged by them. The lack of self-inquiry into the ways in which privileges and oppressions go hand in hand has been a source of criticism of white mainstream feminism by feminist theorists of colour, and is echoed by the new strains of third wave feminism. . . .

THIRD WAVE ACTIONS

Evidence of third wave feminist actions can be found in a variety of areas: zines, hybrid magazines, cyberspace and anthologies where theory and action are tightly bound together, but also in various forms of grassroots organizing, as illustrated by a myriad of grassroots organizations. . . .

Zines are a way for young feminists to share political views and keep each other informed about a variety of feminist actions. A grassroots phenomenon, zines are usually handwritten or typed, and then photocopied for a limited distribution, largely through informal networks. Often a practice ascribed to the Riot Grrrl generation, zines can include poetry, essays, interviews, rants, manifestos and articles ranging from how to make your own pads and tampons, to information about date rape resources. Zines are accessible to a wide range of people, largely because they are often given away instead of sold for profit. The production of zines, often by financially struggling young women, has also inspired other kinds of activism. . . .

Hybrid magazines, such as *BUST* and *Fat Girl: A Magazine for Fat Dykes and the Women Who Love Them,* have also emerged from the space between established feminist journals such as *Ms.* and *Herizons* and the more informal zine networks.

Cyberspace has been a prime site to find information about third wave feminist theory and narratives, as well as to dig up facts about various organizations and actions taking place in different communities. Perhaps most importantly, it is also a forum for community building across a variety of boundaries, geographical, cultural, racial and sexual. . . .

THIRD WAVE CRITICISMS OF SECOND WAVE FEMINISM

. . . [M]any of the third wave critical writings . . . argue that distance-normalizing language prevents many people from understanding or caring about feminist theory:

> *I have serious problems about the difficult, specialized, jargonistic language in which much recent feminist philosophy is being presented . . . [t]his type of language perpetuates elitist power relations associated with who gets to speak of oppression. (Alfonso and Triglio 10)*

This also invariably affects who gets to participate in the eradication of oppression, as feminist theory is often considered an integral part of performing feminist acts of resistance, and feminist actions. Another criticism is the perceived move away from the concrete realities of women towards increasingly complex issues stemming from academic discourse. . . .

An issue that comes up in much of third wave feminist thinking is who has the power to define and conceptualize what exactly comprises "theory" in the feminist realm. Many feel that the creation of feminist theory and discourse has largely been the prerogative of feminists within academia, and that correspondingly has led to too narrow a framework. . . .

. . . Third wave feminists, particularly anti-racist feminists, argue that academic feminism . . . needs to be engaging in more self-reflection and self-criticism: "Anti-racist feminists found it equally difficult to challenge the pedagogical paradigms and canons of various disciplines, including feminist theory" (Dua 17).

The second wave of feminism took on the daunting task of deconstructing the regulation of women's sexuality, and put forth extremely successful and important challenges to male-centred and controlled sexuality and compulsory heterosexuality. These challenges and their outcomes have been incredibly important in establishing discourse about the right of all women to sexual autonomy: putting the widespread problem of sexual assault into dominant discourse, greater access to birth control and abortion, and gay and lesbian rights. However third wave feminists seek to build upon the changes brought about by second wave feminists, and argue that alternative forms of sexuality and sexual expression need to be allowed into more accepting feminist frameworks, and that feminist theorizing needs to stop normalizing and essentializing some forms of sexual expression (i.e., lesbianism) and vilifying others (i.e., pornography, S/M, or sex trade work).

There has also been a concerted critical effort by third wave theorists regarding the relationship between second wave feminism and sexuality. . . .

Many younger feminists are now balking at what they perceive to be the anti-sex, anti-porn and anti-S/M stance of many feminist communities. During the 1970s and 1980s there were immense and huge debates, also dubbed "the lesbian sex wars," about the political correctness of various forms of lesbian sexuality, including S/M, pornography and butch/femme relationships. The effects of these confrontations are still lingering in many feminist communities today, particularly the lesbian feminist communities. . . .

SECOND WAVE CRITICISMS OF THIRD WAVE FEMINISM

While third wave theorists have had ample criticisms for those feminist theorists and theories that have gone before them, second wave theorists have not been silent in their critique of third wave theories. . . .

[Some argue] that third wave feminists are forgetting the incredible battles it took to get the second wave achievements that women enjoy today.

Another criticism regularly levelled at third wave feminists is that they oversimplify ideologies presented by the second wave of feminism. . . .

Others feel that third wave feminists, in their ardent espousal of individualism, are lacking the basis of organization and theory required of movements for social change. . . .

In researching this article online, I ran across an abstract for a paper to be given at a conference called "Just a Stage: The Rhetoric of Third Wave Feminism." The abstract was particularly critical (and I would argue offensively critical) of third wave ideologies, claiming that themes espoused by third wavers, such as sexuality and identity were a part of "growing up" and not something to base a feminist movement on: "These writers are young adults, and the common themes they espouse—sexuality and identity—are themes unique to a period of development known as young adulthood" (Ruffino 2). . . .

POST/ANTI FEMINISM AND THE THIRD WAVE

Many second wave theorists have equated the up cropping of third wave feminism with that of anti-feminism, partially because of the timing, one surmises, but also because third wave feminists have been rather critical of many aspects of second wave approaches to feminist actions and theory. However, there are also some differences between anti-feminism and third wave feminism. . . . [T]hird wave feminists are very much active and vocal on a number of feminist issues, such as rape, violence against women, economic equality and other forms of the exploitation of women.

. . . They do not accept the idea that feminism has already "eradicated institutional sexism, or that the lines between privilege and exploitation based on race, ethnicity, religion, sexuality, physical ability and body shape have disappeared. Nor do they disregard the need for organized feminist responses to oppressive institutions" (Orr 34). . . .

WHERE DO WE GO FROM HERE?

I must admit, I rather dislike the metaphor of feminism happening in waves. . . . Despite the minor glitch in word choice, it seems to me that something very exciting is happening: feminism is going through yet another growth spurt, taking another great leap along the continuum of change . . . . Without conflict, such growth and change would be impossible. In the words of one of my all-time favourite "second wavers," Audre Lorde:

> *The creative strength in women lies in recognizing the differences between us as creative and in standing to those distortions which we inherited without blame, but are now ours to alter. The angers of women can transform difference through insight into power. For anger between peers births change, not destruction, and the discomfort and sense of loss it often causes is not fatal, but a sign of growth. (1984, 131)*

References

Alfonso, Rita, and Jo Triglio. "Surfing the Third Wave: A Dialogue between Two Third Wave Feminists." *Hypatia.* 12(3) (Summer 1997): 7–15.

Allen, Kim. "Birth of a Third Wave Feminist," www.io.com~wwwave/second_third/index.html. Accessed February 28, 2000.

Ang, Ien. "I'm a Feminist but . . . : 'Other' Women and Postnational Feminism." *Transitions: New Australian Feminisms.* Eds. Barbara Caine and Rosemary Pringle. Sydney: Allen and Unwin, 1995. 57–73.

Bailey, Catherine. "Making Waves and Drawing Lines: The Politics of Defining the Vicissitudes of Feminism." *Hypatia.* 12(3) (Summer 1997): 16–27.

Bannerji, Himani. Ed. *Returning the Gaze: Essays on Racism, Feminism, and Politics.* Toronto: SisterVision Press, 1993.

Carlson, Julie, Kathryn Starace, and Alexandra Villano. "The Third Wave Shift," www.Feminist.com/third.htm. Accessed March 2, 2000.

Davis, Angela. "Afterword." *To Be Real: Telling the Truth and Changing the Face of Feminism.* Ed. Rebecca Walker. Toronto: Anchor Books, 1995. 279–284.

Denfield, Rene. *The New Victorians: A Young Women's Response to the Old Feminist Order.* Australia: Unwin & Allen, 1995.

Dent, Gina. "Missionary Position." *To Be Real: Telling the Truth and Changing the Face of Feminism.* Ed. Rebecca Walker. Toronto: Anchor Books, 1995. 61–75.

Detloff, Madelyn. "Mean Spirits: The Politics of Contempt between Feminist Generations." *Hypatia.* 12(3) (Summer 1997): 76–93.

Drake, Jennifer. "Third Wave Feminisms." *Feminist Studies* 23 (1) (Spring 1997): 97–104.

Dua, Enakshi. "Canadian Anti-Racist Feminist Thought: Scratching the Surface of Racism." *Scratching the Surface: Canadian Anti-Racist Feminist Thought.* Eds. Angela Robertson and Enakshi Dua. Toronto: The Women's Press, 1999. 7–34.

Ferguson, Ann. "Moral Responsibility and Social Change: A New Theory of Self." *Hypatia* 12 (3) (Summer 1997): 116–137.

Hoff Sommers, Christine. *Who Stole Feminism?: How Women Have Betrayed Women.* New York: Touchstone Press, 1995.

hooks, bell. *Black Looks: Race and Representation.* Toronto: Between the Lines Press, 1992.

Lorde, Audre. "The Uses of Anger: Women Responding to Racism." *Sister Outsider: Essays and Speeches.* Freedom, CA: The Crossing Press, 1984. 124–133.

Mann, Susan A., and Lori R. Kelley. "Standing at the Crossroads of Modernist Thought: Collins, Smith, and the New Feminist Epistemologies." *Gender and Society* 11(4) (August 1997): 391–402.

Orr, Catherine M. "Charting the Currents of the Third Wave." *Hypatia.* 12 (3) (Summer 1997): 28–46.

Overall, Christine. *A Feminist I: Reflections from Academia.* Toronto: Broadview Press, 1998.

Razack, Sherene, *Looking White People in the Eye: Gender, Race and Culture in Courtrooms and Classrooms.* Toronto: University of Toronto Press, 1998.

Revolution Girl Style Collective. *Fireweed: Revolution Girl Style.* 59/60 (Fall/Winter 1997).

Ruffino, Joan. "Just a Stage: The Rhetoric of Third Wave Feminism," www.femrhet.cla.umn.edu.prosal/g8.htm. Accessed March 3, 2000.

Schrof, Joannie M. "Feminism's Daughters: Their Agenda is a Sea of Cultural Change." *U.S. News and World Report.* 115(12) (September 27, 1993): 68–73.

Siegel, Deborah L. "The Legacy of the Personal: Generating Theory in Feminism's Third Wave." *Hypatia.* 12 (3) (Summer 1997): 47–71.

Stein, Arelene, Ed. *Sisters, Sexperts, Queers: Beyond the Lesbian Nation.* New York: Penguin Books, 1993.

Steinem, Gloria. "Foreward." *To Be Real: Telling the Truth and Changing the Face of Feminism.* Ed. Rebecca Walker. Toronto: Anchor, 1995. xiv–xxvii.

Thomas, Trish. "36 Strokes." *Click: Becoming Feminists.* Ed. Lynn Crosbie. Toronto: Macfarlane, Walter and Ross, 1997. 83–91.

Walker, Rebecca. "Being Real: An Introduction." *To Be Real: Telling the Truth and Changing the Face of Feminism.* Ed. Rebecca Walker. Toronto: Anchor, 1995. xxx–xi.

Vitale, Sidra M.S. "Feminist History, or the Lack Thereof, or Young Women Who Don't Call Themselves Feminists, and the Older Women Who Are Pissed Off About It," www.io.com~wwwave/second_third/index.html. Accessed February 28, 2000.

Zita, Jacquelyn N. "Introduction." *Hypatia* 12 (3) (Summer 1997): 1–7.

CHAPTER 2

The Changing Context of Activisms

In the current context of neoliberal and neoconservative politics, women's movements in Canada have experienced a decline in political influence. Because feminist organizations continue to push governments to ensure social equality through greater expenditures and new and more effective social programs, they have increasingly been cast as "special" interest groups—antithetical to the public good as defined by deficit reduction and the market (Brodie 1995). Moreover, the discourse of post-feminism circulates in the media (Bromley and Ahmad 2006). This discourse promotes the view that equality has now been substantially achieved and that feminism is passé. In 2006, the federal government cut the budget of Status of Women Canada (SWC) by 40%, removed the word equality from its mandate and announced that women's organizations would no longer be able to receive grants for projects that involved advocacy work, lobbying or research (O'Grady 2006). Some have suggested that this move was ideologically motivated and that the clear intent is to silence feminist organizations who criticize government policies.

Collectively, the readings in this chapter interrogate the profound transformations in feminist activisms in Canada that have occurred in the past 20 years. In the 1970s and 1980s, feminist organizations enjoyed state funding, political influence and legitimacy. The National Action Committee on the Status of Women (NAC) formed in 1972, was a cross-Canada coalition of women's groups that at one time boasted more than two million members. NAC was considered a legitimate lobby group with entitlement to consultation in the policy-making process, gender-designated funding and special points of access within the federal bureaucracy (see Vickers et. al. 1993). But since the mid-1980s much has changed. With the embrace of neo-liberalism and the erosion of governmental commitments to ensuring social equality, the women's movement was placed on the defensive. Feminist organizations were marginalized and their funding cut. As a result, national feminist organizing has experienced a rapid decline. As contributions to this chapter suggest, however, this story does not confirm the now ascendant discourse of post-feminism. The delegitimization of feminist activism needs to be understood in relation to the emergence of a neoliberal state form. The current context is one in which feminist and social change movements face incredible constraints. And yet, new forms of organizing and activism are emerging in the present context, as feminists both continue to struggle around the enduring concerns of the second wave and at the same time, engage in new forms of political organizing.

NEOLIBERALISM AND FEMINISM

As **Janine Brodie** (**"The Great Undoing: State Formation, Gender Politics and Social Policy in Canada"**) argues, gender and the equality agenda have been virtually erased from policy and political discourse. But what Brodie labels a "magical disappearing act" does not signal a victory over gender-based inequality. In fact, studies continue to demonstrate the persistence and even the intensification of the gender-, race- and class-based disadvantages that second wave Canadian feminists identified and struggled against.

Given the dominance of the post-feminist and neoliberal insistence on the "myth of equality," we thought it was important to begin this chapter with a statistical picture of the contemporary status of women. In 2005, **Status of Women Canada** published a report entitled "**Assessing Gender Equality**," gathering recent statistics on gender (in)equality. As this report demonstrates, the status of Canadian women has changed dramatically in some respects. There have been striking increases in women's labour force participation and Canadian women now outnumber men in post-secondary institutions.

Despite these significant changes, the report conclusively demonstrates the persistence of systemic inequality. The wage gap between men and women has remained stable since 1990, fluctuating around 70%. Women still remain responsible for the bulk of unpaid caring work and domestic labour. Poverty remains a women's issue with race, disability and single parent status intensifying women's economic insecurity. And as the report documents, and as we emphasize in the following chapter, violence against women continues to be pervasive, with Aboriginal women subject to dramatic rates of spousal violence and sexual assault.

Given such clear evidence of systemic inequalities, how is it possible for the "myth of equality" to carry such weight? As Brodie argues, in order to understand how and why disadvantage has been written out of government policy frameworks, we need to engage in a careful and critical feminist interrogation of the emergence of the neoliberal state. The postwar Canadian welfare state, while gendered, did encompass a notion of social citizenship, allowing for those who experienced inequality to make legitimate claims upon the state. It was within this context that the second wave women's movement emerged and flourished. The ascendance of neoliberalism, beginning with the election of the Mulroney Conservatives in 1984, placed the women's movement on a collision course with Canadian governments. The dominant current of the women's movement in the postwar years consistently linked the achievement of women's equality with economic intervention and social policy. The dominant tenets of neoliberalism, by contrast, emphasize the importance of removing the government from the economy, reducing government expenditure and decreasing reliance on the state. As Brodie outlines in this important article, the philosophy of the neoliberal state rests on three fundamental pillars—privatization, decentralization and individivualization—that act to intensify gender inequalities, while denying the political relevance of gender.

Christina Gabriel and Laura MacDonald ("Managing Trade Agreements? Mapping the Contours of State Feminism and Women's Political Activism") also explore the implications of changing governance practices and of new conceptions of citizenship for feminist activism. They add to Brodie's analysis by drawing attention to how neoliberal ideals were embraced in response to the pressures of globalization; crucially, they interrogate trade liberalization as a centrepiece of the neoliberal agenda. Gabriel and MacDonald trace the emergence of a women's policy machinery in the federal state in the 1970s and early 1980s and detail how, during this period, state funding and privileged points of access within the bureaucracy enabled women's movement influence. From the mid-1980s to the mid-1990s, by contrast, the Canadian state embraced economic rationalism, bringing it into conflict with women's groups. At this time, as Gabriel and MacDonald contend, the women's movement became increasingly radical, challenging cuts to social policy and engaging in a campaign against the government's free trade agenda. As women's groups, such as NAC, moved to challenge the government's trade agenda, they found themselves under attack and increasingly marginalized within the policy process.

This is an important argument. The declining influence of organizations like NAC has been attributed to struggles around differences that occurred within the English Canadian women's movement in the 1990s. Debates around race and class within feminist organizations at this time led key movement organizations to incorporate anti-racist and intersectional work into their agendas. As this occurred, NAC was increasingly constructed in the media as being weakened by internal divisions. But, as Gabriel and MacDonald emphasize, these difficult struggles occurred at a time when feminist actors were being recast as unrepresentative special interests and when women's groups were being targeted for funding cutbacks. As the women's movement influence declined, the women's policy machinery within the state was sidelined and its connections with grassroots activists severed. In these ways, trade liberalization was insulated from gender-based analysis and feminist critique.

POLITICAL REPRESENTATION AND DEMOCRATIC RENEWAL

Alongside autonomous feminist organizing and the promotion of a gender-based policy machinery within the state, second wave feminists struggled to improve women's representation within liberal democratic institutions. In 1984, only 10% of federal Members of Parliament were women. While increasing to 20% by 1997, women's representation has stagnated at both the federal and provincial levels. Moreover, political scientists have identified a growing political malaise in which citizens, and especially young people, are increasingly alienated and disaffected from electoral politics, signified by extremely low voter turnouts.

Alexandra Dobrowolsky (**"Intersecting Identities and Inclusive Institutions: Women and the Future of Transformative Politics"**) contends that current democratic practices are inadequate for dealing with women's political exclusion. Dobrowolsky engages in an important critique of conventional reform projects such as the implementation of gender parity rules or of a proportional representation electoral system. These strategies, she acknowledges, have been successful in other countries in increasing women's numerical representation in electoral politics. Yet, as Dobrowolsky insists, there is a distinction between increasing the number of women politicians and what she labels "substantive representation." Numbers of women may rise, but this can occur in neoliberal governments that ignore or are hostile to women's issues. Moreover, Dobrowolsky contends that conventional reform strategies reify "women" as a group, give priority to a single identity and fail to acknowledge differences and power relations among women.

Dobrowolsky is insisting on the importance of democratic revitalization and reform as an important site of feminist struggle in the present. Her arguments are prescriptive, rather than descriptive—that is, rather than describing current feminist activisms, she is defining an agenda for activism that might be seen as a "third wave" approach for enhancing democratic representation. As she contends, feminists must go beyond proposals for the reform of electoral and partisan politics to build new political sites. She recommends the creation of citizens' fora built upon group representation in which women's organizations, alongside other groups, could collaborate to formulate policy alternatives. These new political spaces would be based upon heterogeny and coalition building, thereby surpassing the essentialist thrust of conventional reform proposals for increasing women's representation.

THE GENDERED DIVISION OF LABOUR AND CARING WORK: ORGANIZING INTERNATIONALLY AND DOMESTICALLY

As Brodie emphasizes, individualization is a central tenet of neoliberalism. In a shift away from notions of collective values and social responsibility that had underpinned the postwar Canadian state, social problems are increasingly depoliticized and individuals are held blameworthy for their experiences of inequality and poverty. In addition, as states back away from social provision, individuals and families are compelled to take on increasing responsibility for the care of others. Feminist critics argue that we are witnessing the privatization of social reproduction.

As **Pat Armstrong and Hugh Armstrong ("Thinking it Through: Women, Work and Caring")** remind us here, caring work is gendered work and the privatization of social reproduction, therefore, means an intensification of women's labour. All societies throughout recorded history have been marked by a gendered division of labour. Women's assumed responsibility for caring work, including domestic labour and the care of children, the sick and the elderly, has influenced both unpaid work and the structure of the labour market. While a gendered division of labour is universal, it is not natural; both its specific form and its generalized features need to be understood as an effect of ever-shifting power relationships. While Armstrong and Armstrong draw attention to continuities in the gendered division of labour, what they refer to as "lumping," they are equally attentive to its complexities and changing character, what they refer to as "slicing." Paying attention to "slicing" alerts us to significant differences among women related to class, race, age, marital status and sexual orientation. If "slicing" highlights how a gendered division of labour is experienced differently by women, it also reveals important contextual features of changes in the division of labour.

Armstrong and Armstrong's contribution is particularly useful in situating the gendered division of labour in an era of globalization and in drawing out its meanings and implications for women in both Western industrialized countries and in the so-called Third World. Describing globalization as an outcome of complex forces, institutions and actors, including transnational corporations, international organizations such as the World Bank and the International Monetary Fund, and trade agreements between First World countries, the authors argue that we are witnessing a decline of democratic control of the economy and growing gaps between men and women and amongst women themselves. Crucially, however, Armstrong and Armstrong insist that we need to pierce through an economic ideology viewing globalization as the outcome of an inevitable logic and recognize that it is instead the result of decisions and practices. Such recognition opens up the possibility of feminist resistance, and Armstrong and Armstrong highlight the importance of anti-globalization protests and international feminist organizing as a means of holding the international economy accountable and promoting social equality.

At a domestic level, the struggle for a national publicly funded childcare program is crucial for resolving the tensions between women's paid and unpaid work. As **Martha Friendly** ("**Why Women Still Ain't Satisfied: Politics and Activism in Canadian Childcare**") points out, it has now been more than 35 years since the Royal Commission on the Status of Women recommended a national childcare program. Given women's unequal responsibility for the care of children in a context where most women with young children engage in paid work, childcare remains an important feminist issue. Despite extensive second wave feminist activism, the promise of a national childcare strategy has appeared in electoral platforms, only to be dropped from political agendas after elections. The failure to establish a national childcare program has been accompanied by measures such as enhanced tax deductions, (inadequate) funding for the creation of new spaces and subsidization of costs for low-income women. Underpinning this piecemeal strategy was the construction of childcare as a series of privatized arrangements to be negotiated by individuals. In 2004, the Martin Liberal government finally followed through with an election promise to improve childcare at a national level, committing $5 billion dollars and negotiating agreements with all provinces.

Friendly describes the emergence of a cross-Canada coalition led by feminist and childcare activists in response to the Harper Conservative government's decision to cancel the Liberal childcare program. The Harper government is firmly committed to a neoliberal agenda and it is also influenced by social conservatism. Responding to right-wing claims that government funding for childcare disadvantages "traditional families" with stay-at-home mothers, the Conservative government implemented a "Choice in Childcare" allowance of $1200 per year for each child under 6. As Friendly insists, this allowance does nothing to improve the crisis in access to quality, affordable childcare, nor will it address the low wages paid to women who are childcare workers. The Harper childcare "solution" has politicized and galvanized Canadian women. Code Blue, a coalition of childcare organizations, feminist, labour and social justice groups, demonstrates the continued vibrancy of feminist activism in the present. Challenging the dominant portrayal of the women's movement as either dead or irrelevant, childcare has re-emerged as a site of national feminist organizing.

ABORIGINAL WOMEN AND RESISTANCE TO COLONIZATION

Aboriginal feminism combines feminist and anti-colonial critiques to show how Aboriginal women are affected by colonialism and by patriarchy. Linking together racism and sexism, Aboriginal feminist organizing has challenged the marginalization of women within Aboriginal organizations and indigenous governance practices and the vulnerabilities and oppression that Aboriginal women continue to experience as an effect of colonization (Green 2007, 23). At a time when mainstream Canadian women's groups were being challenged and marginalized, Aboriginal women continued to mobilize through organizations such as the Native Women's Association of Canada (NWAC) to: ensure women's human rights and their full membership within indigenous communities; address the treatment of Aboriginal women as victims and as offenders within the criminal justice system; and to combat the specifically gendered effects of colonization that have left Aboriginal women poor and extremely vulnerable to racist and sexist violence. The continued visibility and vibrancy of Aboriginal feminist organizing contests post-feminist narratives about the decline of feminist politics.

In Chapter 3 of *Open Boundaries*, Anita Olsen Harper describes NWAC's Sisters in Spirit campaign—a grassroots effort to combat the epidemic of racist, sexist violence against Aboriginal women, providing support to families of the missing and murdered women and demanding state action. In this chapter, **Patricia Monture ("Aboriginal Women and Justice Reform")** analyzes Aboriginal women's activism on behalf of criminalized and incarcerated women. As Monture argues, criminalization of indigenous populations is a strategy of colonization and Aboriginal women and men are dramatically overrepresented within Canadian prison populations. "The prison," she writes, "is a total institution that relies on isolation as the essential means of control over the prisoner in the same way that reserves isolated Aboriginal peoples." In this article, Monture reflects upon efforts to bring the lived experiences of Aboriginal women prisoners to bear on the *Task Force on Federally Sentenced Women,* resulting in a report that did acknowledge the links between women, prison and colonialism. Yet Monture is highly critical of the reforms that emerged out of the report. As she argues, the thrust of the reform effort, the empowerment of women, was reconstructed in a highly individualized manner through the concept of "individual responsibility," decontextualizing feminist and Aboriginal constructions of systemic oppression. Moreover, despite the involvement of organizations such as NWAC in the establishment of Aboriginal-specific initiatives, their transformative potential has also been contained. Monture calls attention to the ongoing necessity of Aboriginal feminist challenges to correctional practices and also to the role of the prison in contemporary colonization.

FEMINIST RESISTANCE AND THE WAR ON TERROR

It is quite ironic that Canadian feminist organizations were constructed as unrepresentative "special interests" at the very moment when previously silenced groups of women were gaining a greater voice and assuming leadership positions. In 1993, **Sunera Thobani** was the first woman of colour to be elected as NAC's president. This elicited a range of criticism both from within the organization and from anti-feminist politicians and political commentators. One Tory MP even suggested in the House of Commons that Thobani, a Tanzanian Canadian, was an illegal immigrant and should be deported. Almost a decade later, Thobani's address to a Canadian Association of Sexual Assault Centres' conference, one month after September 11th, 2001, created a national controversy. In this speech, Thobani mounted a feminist and post-colonial critique of U.S. foreign policy and called for solidarity with women's organizations in Afghanistan. In response to her hard-hitting speech, Thobani's citizenship status was invoked again; she was challenged for being anti-American and told to "go home." Thobani received hate mail and death threats and there were demands that she be fired from her position as a Women's Studies professor at the University of British Columbia.

In "**War and the Politics of Truth-Making in Canada**," Thobani uses this experience to reflect on the politics of truth-making in Canada in the post 9/11 context. As several contributions to this chapter have emphasized, feminist voices are increasingly delegitmized in a context of neoliberalism. Under the shadow of the U.S.-led War on Terror, there has also been a closing down of public space for informed debate on the realities of U.S. foreign policy. Thobani's feminist and anti-imperialist critique and her call for the women's movement to mobilize against the War on Terror had the effect of positioning her outside dominant consensus, underlining the dangers of voicing dissent in present day Canada. Yet Thobani's point is to highlight the particularly precarious status of immigrant people of colour in the post 9/11 atmosphere of racial profiling and the targeting of immigrants and refugees as threats to national security. The attacks on Thobani emphasized her status as an immigrant outsider, invoking a highly racialized discourse of who "belongs" to the Canadian nation, and who has a right to "speak" to it. Thobani calls attention to the politics of "truth-making" and engagement in anti-imperialist struggles as important sites of contemporary feminist activism. Crucially, such struggles must be waged in coalition with organizations representing immigrant people of colour in Canada and in connection with international women's organizations.

THIRD WAVE FEMINISM AND YOUNGER WOMEN'S ACTIVISM

Third wave feminist activism emphasizes inclusivity, embracing a complex understanding of identity that includes class, race, sexuality and ability, as well as engagement in anti-globalization and other social justice struggles. As Bromely and Ahmad have noted, most third wavers do not deny the need to continue mobilizing around core issues defined by second wave feminists; recent campaigns such as Code Blue have involved alliances between younger and older feminists (2006, p.67). At the same time, third wave feminists have emphasized the importance of rethinking activism in the present. Perhaps most importantly, third wave feminists depart from the state-centred forms of feminism that proliferated in Canada in the 1970s, 1980s and 1990s, emphasizing instead cultural subversion and a "do it yourself" (DIY) philosophy. Third wave feminism may appear less cohesive and ad hoc than the national and highly visible organizing that defined Canadian feminism's earlier years. Yet third wave feminism defines flexibility and collaboration among diverse groups as strengths, rather than weaknesses. The Miss G. Project, a campaign initiated by Women's Studies graduates from the University of Western Ontario, can be seen as an example of third wave feminism in action. The project goal is to incorporate Women's Studies into the Ontario high school curriculum, using cyberspace mobilization and parody (for example, a beauty pageant at the Ontario legislature where contestants wore sashes inscribed "Miss Education (miseducation)") as tools (see Bromley and Ahmad 2006, pp.67–68).

Brandi Leigh-Ann Bell ("**Riding the Third Wave: Women Produced Zines and Feminism**") and **Jennifer Plyler** ("**Rooting Out Injustice: Discussions with Radical Young Women in Toronto, Canada**") reflect on new strategies of organizing being embraced by young feminists. As noted earlier, the mainstream media has played a key role in disseminating the post-feminist message that feminism is now irrelevant. While second wave feminism sought to engage the mainstream media, third wave feminism has sought alternatives to popular media representations. Bell analyzes the role of zines as a form of cultural production by women that is unconstrained by corporate or institutional interests. Zines, small circulation, underground publications often associated with the Riot Grrrl movement, construct a space for the articulation of young feminists' realities. While Bell acknowledges important critiques of zines, (their limited circulation and their focus on personal experience), she emphasizes their political and critical significance. Zine production is connected with the contemporary mobilization of young feminists in cyberspace, where third wavers are deploying blogs and websites as forums for collaboration, debate, feminist organizing and subversion.

Plyler writes against what she sees as a tendency for second wave feminists to dismiss the insights of younger feminists. In this article, she describes radical young women's involvement in social justice struggles against imperialism, colonialism, racism, sexism and poverty. All of the young women described by Plyler hold a commitment to an intersectional analysis of oppression, emphasizing the connections between racism, colonialism, ableism, heterosexism, patriarchy and poverty. Rather than organizing solely on the basis of gender, they bring feminist politics and analysis into social justice movements concerned with poverty, imperialism and globalization. The activisms described by Plyler are consistent with third wave feminist commitments to coalition building and to confronting oppression in all of its forms. Plyler argues that the ability of feminism to remain relevant to social change depends upon this vital work and she insists that older feminists respect the visions, perspectives and leadership of young women.

Assessing Gender Equality: Trends in the Situation of Women and Men in Canada

Status of Women Canada

This background paper has been prepared by Status of Women Canada (SWC) based on a framework for assessing the state of gender equality initiated in 2004 in collaboration with several federal departments. It is a work in progress and at this point focuses on six main categories—economic security, education, work, health, immigration and justice. It compares the situation between women and men as well as among them, based on factors such as age, family status, disability, Aboriginal origin, visible minority and immigrant status. Making comparisons among women is especially important as their patterns of education, work for pay or profit, work in the household and other activities tend to be more varied than men's, whether on a day-to-day basis or over a lifetime.

The framework is intended as a diagnostic tool to aid in assessing change over time—to show progress and to improve understanding of gender equality gaps so that they can be better addressed. Within this diagnostic framework, a great deal of population-based data has been compiled showing areas of change and progress for women, areas of similarity between women and men and areas of inequality. This paper summarizes some of the key trends. Moreover, because SWC is in the process of consulting on potential ways to move forward on gender equality, this paper, while providing some context, tends to focus on gender equality gaps. Comprehensive information is available in Statistics Canada's *Women In Canada: A gender-based statistical report.*

We recognize that various sources of information are important in assessing where and how best to move forward. For example, in a few places in this paper we use results information from federal programs. This is a source that we hope to build upon in a long-term gender equality strategy. Hand-in-hand with our efforts to establish an ongoing statistical or quantitative basis for assessing gender equality, SWC also continues to support and value qualitative work that goes beyond the numbers and enables Canadians to have their voices heard.

DEMOGRAPHIC TRENDS

Currently, women over the age of 65 account for 7% and men for 5.5% of the population. It is important to note that among Aboriginal people in Canada trends are quite different with higher fertility rates and a younger population. Immigrants made up 18.4% of the population in 2001 and will continue to be a main source of population growth.

Changing trends and increasing diversity in the composition of families also have implications for gender equality. For example, there has been a dramatic increase in the number of families with children that are headed by lone parents. In 1962, only 9% of all families with children were headed by a female lone parent, numbers that increased to

16.4% in 1991 and 20.1% in 2001, rates that are much higher than among men.[1] Moreover, lone parenthood is also more likely to occur within certain populations. In 2001, 8.7% of all Canadian women were lone parents (compared to 2.1% of men). These rates are marginally higher for immigrants (9.4% of women, 2.1% of men) and visible minority communities (10.4% of women, 2% of men), dramatically higher for Aboriginal women (19.4%) and significantly higher for Aboriginal men (4.8%).

Changes in living and work arrangements are resulting in greater work-family stress. This has implications for the work that women do for pay or profit and for their care-giving responsibilities. Being the primary caregivers of children continues to be reflected in women's lower incomes, even with their increased labour force participation. Given an aging population, and the large share of informal caregiving for seniors[2] done by women, maintaining positive trends in gender equality presents new challenges. Increased demands on women to care for aging relatives, for example, may reduce their ability to meet their own care and financial needs by the time they are seniors themselves.

EDUCATION TRENDS

There has been a dramatic increase in the proportion of the female population with a university degree in the past several decades. In 2001, the percentage of women and men who had earned a university certificate, diploma, or degree was almost the same (17.8% of women and 18.1% of men).[3] This positive trend is likely to continue.

While gains in educational attainment have been made in general, access and affordability remain issues for some women. For example, data from the Canada Student Loans Program indicates that every year from 1996 to 2002, the percentage of student loans negotiated by women has increased (53% in 1996 to 58.3% in 2002) and decreased among men (47% in 1996 and 41.7% in 2002).[4]

Despite advances in education, Table 2-1 shows that for every age group, the employment income gap between male and female university graduates who work full time has widened between 1995 and 2000.[5]

TABLE 2-1 Women to men's average employment

Income (University Graduates)

Age Group	1995 (%)	2000 (%)
15–24	87.3	84.3
25–34	81.4	76.7
35–44	74.2	70.3
45–54	69.3	67.7
55–64	63.1	59.7

FIGURE 2.1 **Hourly Wage Rate for Full-time Employees**

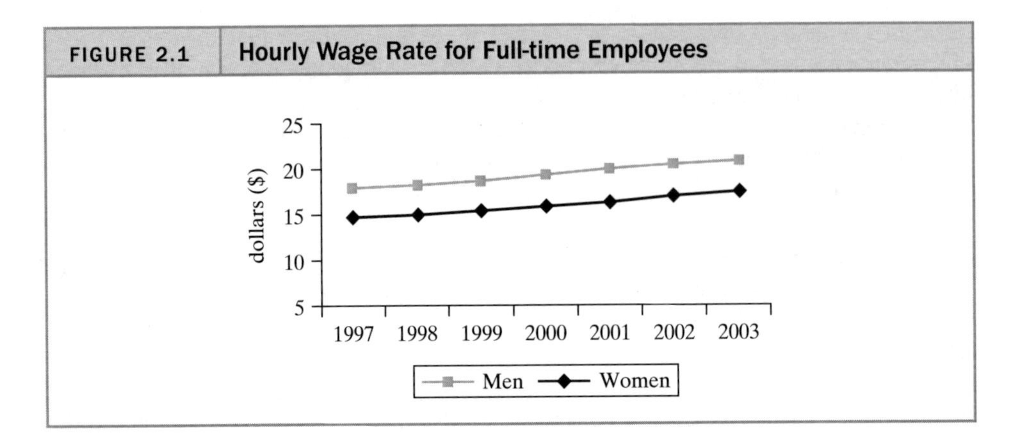

PAID WORK TRENDS

Women's increased participation in the labour market has been one of the most significant trends in the last few decades.

While part-time and other non-standard employment can be a strategy to balance work and family demands, it also generally means lower earnings and less access to benefits, and for some this type of work is involuntary.

Although women have made strides in terms of labour market experience and attachment, they continue to face obstacles. For example, among full-time employees, women have consistently lower hourly wages than men, as shown in Figure 2.1.

The wage differentials can be partially explained by the fact that women still face some occupational segregation and job undervaluation.

UNPAID WORK TRENDS

As Figure 2.2 indicates, the balance between women and men in sharing paid and unpaid work shows signs of improvement.

In 1993, 16% of women and 12% of men reported being time stressed, increasing to 21% and 16%, respectively, in 1998.[6] Time-stress is also more pronounced among women

FIGURE 2.2 **Women's Share of Time Spent on Paid and Unpaid Work Compared to Men**

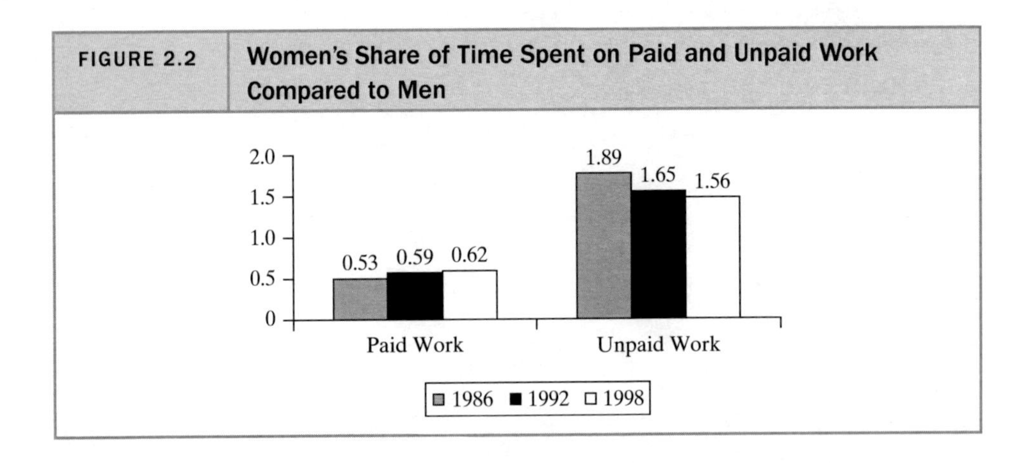

FIGURE 2.3 **Total Earnings for Women and Men**

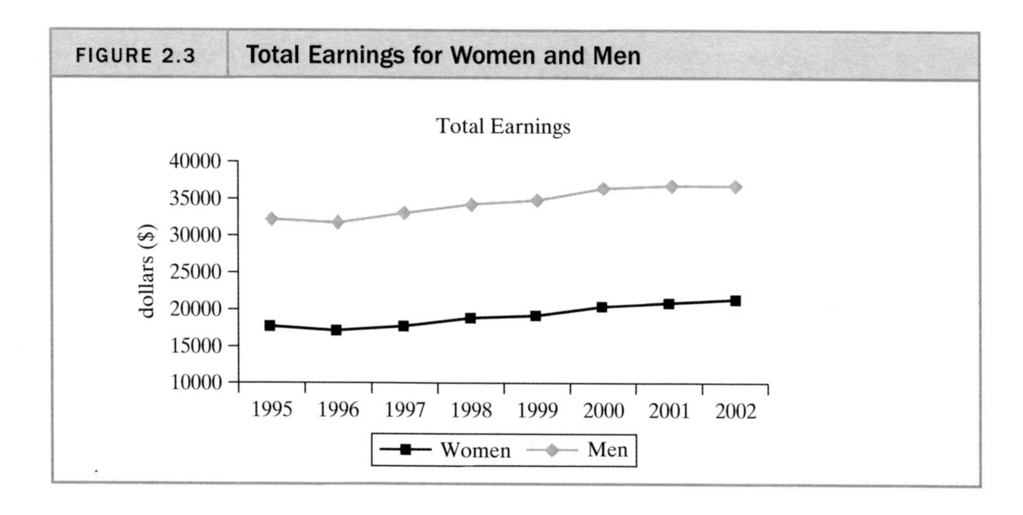

and it appears to be increasing for both women and men. Underlying the averages for all women and men, there are considerable differences depending on family type, age, and number of children and other factors that affect how well individuals and families are faring. For example, between 1986 and 1992, in households where there was a child under six and mothers were employed full-time, women's share of paid work time and unpaid child-oriented time both increased. These mothers significantly reduced their share of unpaid work for themselves and the household and dramatically reduced their share of unpaid work for other relatives and friends.[7]

EARNINGS AND INCOME TRENDS

Women's earnings are gradually increasing but are still well below men's. Figure 2.3 shows that between 1995 and 2002 the relative gap between women and men remained sizeable.

Average male earnings in 1995 were $32,312, compared to $17,788 for women (about 55% of men's).

While earnings make up the largest share of total income for men and women, other sources of income, such as child support payments, maternity benefits, child benefits paid to the mother, social assistance and old age security are relatively more important to women. Many people view after-tax income as a better reflection of how much money people actually have to spend. In addition, because our tax system is generally progressive, those with less income pay relatively less tax. Using this measure, the gender gap narrows further, with women's relative after-tax income at 66% of men's, also shown in Figure 2.4.[8]

POVERTY

As the earnings and income figures above would suggest, Canada does not have an official poverty rate but Statistics Canada has for many years produced low-income cut-offs and we use those, after tax, in this paper. As the earnings and income figures above would suggest, women are more at risk of living in poverty than men. Overall, women continue to be overrepresented among people living in low income, as Figure 2.5 shows, although the gap has narrowed.

FIGURE 2.4 Total Before- and After-Tax Income for Women and Men

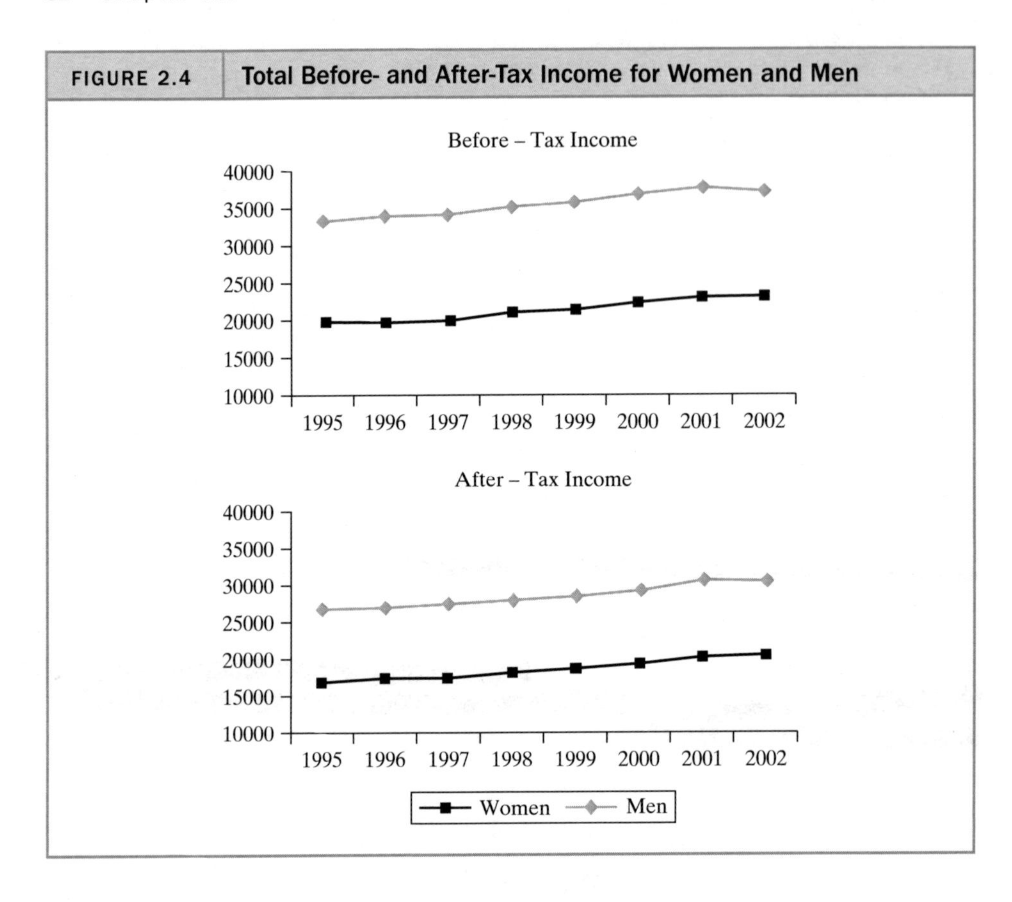

As with other overall trends, however, underlying the averages there can be significant differences among women and men. One of the most significant is seen in the incidence of low income. The earnings and income data presented earlier were based on individuals but low-income cut-offs are based on household size. Because most women live in male-female couples, women's rates of low income are the same as men's in these households. In fact, women's income helps prevent more households from being in a low-income situation. For other women, the picture is quite different.

Figure 2.6 shows low-income rates for selected populations compared to the general rate in 2002. In each case, women face far higher rates of low income than men in a comparable situation. In addition to the high rate of 34.8% for lone parents, 39% of children in female-headed lone parent families were living in low-income situations as well.

Figure 2.7 presents the information in a different way to focus on the size of the gender gap—the additional risk of poverty that women face compared to men in each group. This added risk is several percentage points higher for unattached individuals and dramatically higher for lone parents. Many female lone parents have incomes far below the cut-offs and they tend to stay in poverty longer than other Canadians. Also, because women move out of lone parenthood as children become adults, or new marriages or common-law relationships are formed, lone parenthood and its risk of poverty affects more Canadians than those counted in a given year.[9]

Women are also affected by factors in addition to age and family or relationship status, as Figure 2.8 illustrates. While Figure 2.8 uses before-tax income based on 2001 Census data and cannot be compared directly to the data in Figure 2.6, similar gendered patterns are revealed.[10] As indicated earlier, some of these groups of women are also more likely to be lone parents than the average. Because of the diversity of Canada's population, working towards gender equality in our particular context requires attention to the combination of gender and other factors.[11]

FIGURE 2.5 **Women and Men in Low Incomes (After-Tax)**

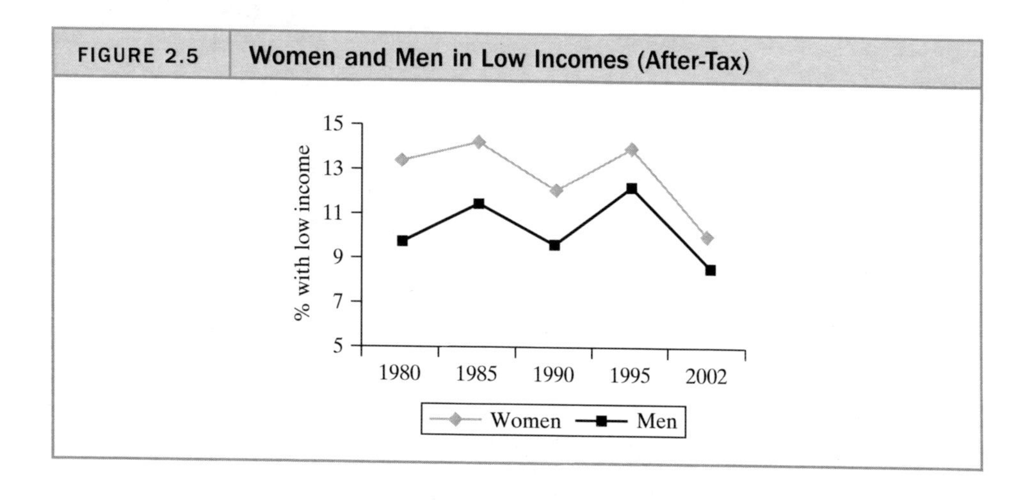

FIGURE 2.6 **Percentage of Selected Groups with Low After-Tax Income (2002)**

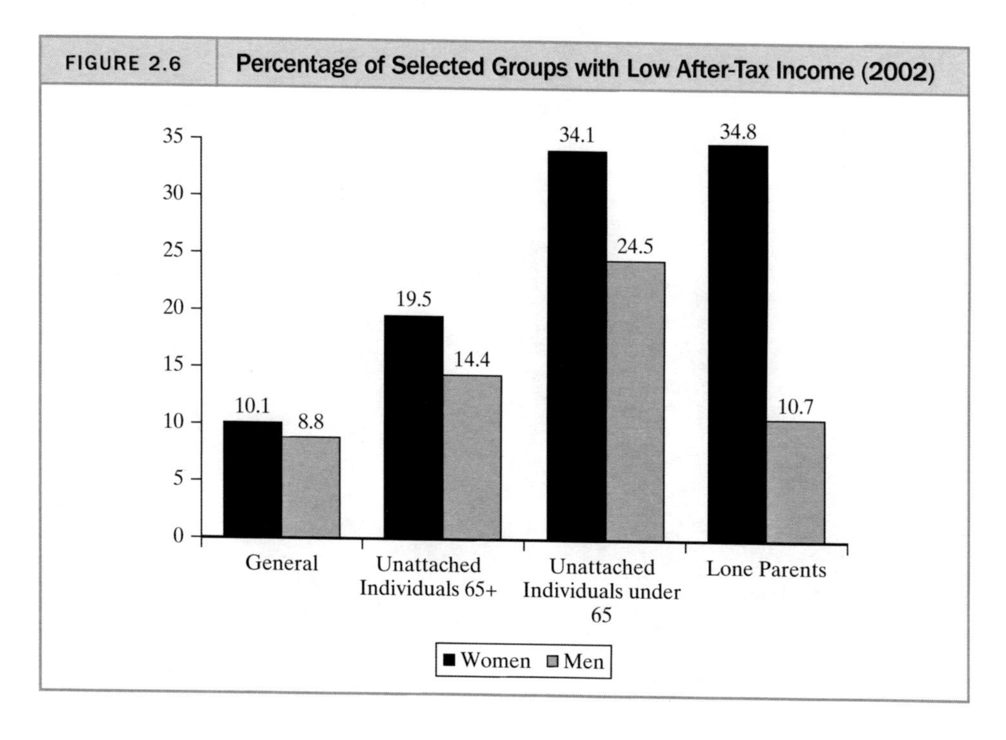

FIGURE 2.7 Size of Gender Gap for Women Among Selected Groups with Low After-Tax Income (in percentage points)

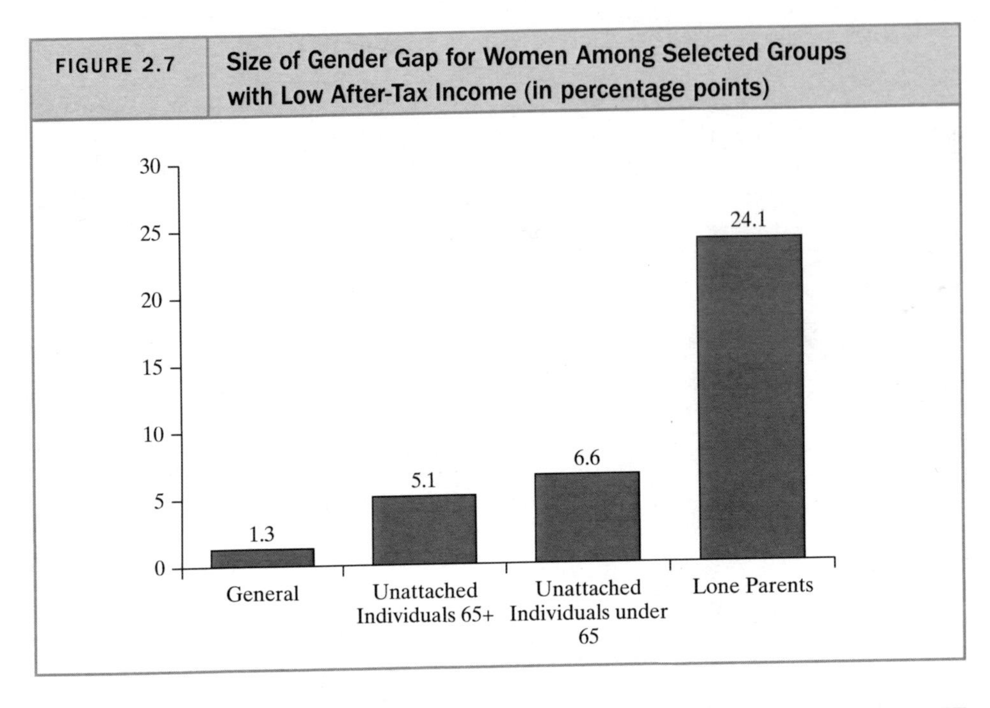

FIGURE 2.8 Low-Income Status (%) of Certain Populations of Women and Men (2001)

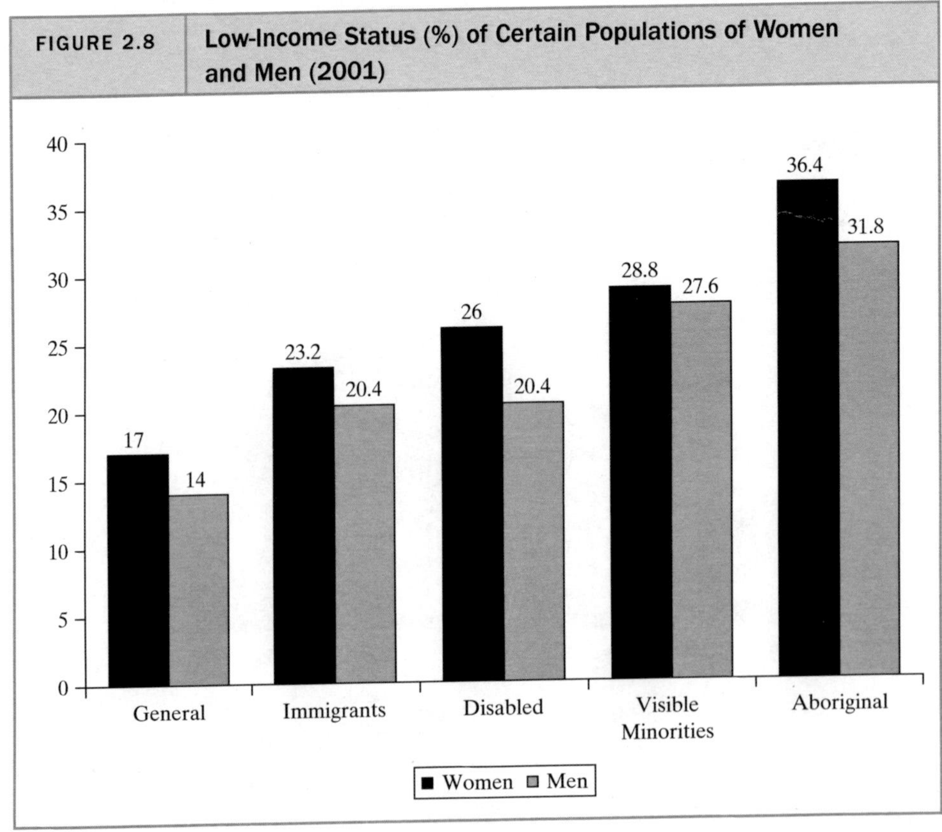

HEALTH

Life expectancy at birth is a key indicator of a population's health status. In 2002 it reached highs for both women and men in Canada. Life expectancy for women is 82.1 years. Men, on average, can expect to live 77.2 years. Women, however, experience more years of disability and have more co-morbidities than men.[12] Women also are more likely than men to die due to sex-specific causes such as breast cancer, ovarian cancer and pregnancy-related complications. On the other hand, there is evidence that men are more likely to die from external causes such as accidents and injury.

For Aboriginal peoples, examination of life expectancy shows a very different experience. Although life expectancy has improved, it is still lower than the national average. Life expectancy at birth among the status Indian population, for example, has gone up for males from 59.2 years in 1975 to 68.9 years in 2000, and for females from 65.9 years to 76.3.[13]

Poverty, economic insecurity, and lack of access to benefits and services can also have a harmful impact on women's health. In this regard, women with low levels of education, income and control over their work environment are at higher risk of heart disease than other women. For example, Aboriginal women have higher rates of poverty, unemployment and poor housing and have lower life expectancy, higher rates of a range of health conditions and experience higher mortality due to violence.[14]

VIOLENCE AND CRIME

Violence against women is another issue that profoundly affects women's health, and also affects and is affected by their socio-economic status. For example, women may be forced to stay in abusive relationships in order to avoid living in poverty as lone mothers.[15]

Between 1974 and 2003, the rate of spousal homicide against females has typically been four to five times higher than the rate of male spousal homicide.[16] Between 1994 and 2003, females aged 15 to 24 had the highest rate of spousal homicide—nearly three times the overall rate of spousal homicide for female victims during the same period and nearly three times the rate of males aged 15 to 24.

Close to four out of ten senior female victims are assaulted by a family member, while this is the case for 20% of senior male victims.

With regard to criminal harassment and stalking, 80% of victims were stalked by men, regardless of the sex of the victim. The most common gender pattern in stalking is one of male offender and female victim (53%) followed by male-male (28%).[17]

Moreover, results of the 2004 General Social Survey on victimization indicate that Aboriginal people are twice as likely as non-Aboriginal people to have reported experiencing in the previous five years some form of stalking that caused them to fear for their life (17% versus 9%).

CONCLUSION

Moving forward on gender equality will continue to require an analysis of the situation of women and men that takes many diverse factors into account. Moreover, gender equality is not an end that can be achieved once and for all. It is a goal that exists in a dynamic world—society and the economy will continue to evolve and will bring new opportunities and challenges.

Endnotes

1. Statistics Canada, 2001 Census of Canada
2. Statistics Canada, Gender Social Survey, 2002
3. Statistics Canada, Census of Canada, 2001
4. Canada Student Loans Program, HRSDC
5. Statistics Canada, 2001 Census of Canada
6. Statistics Canada, General Social Survey
7. Economic Gender Equality Indicators, F/P/T Ministers Responsible for the Status of Women, 1997
8. Statistics Canada Labour Force Survey and Survey of Labour and Income Dynamics.
9. National Council of Welfare (2002). *The Cost of Poverty.*
10. Data on after-tax income for these groups is not available.
11. For information on Canada's situation relative to other countries, see for example, Picot, G., &; Myles, J. (2005). *Income inequality and low income in Canada: An international perspective.* Ottawa: Statistics Canada.
12. Statistics Canada, Participation and Activity Limitation Survey.
13. Statistics Canada, Census of Canada.
14. Lin (2004).
15. Scott, E., London, A., &; Myers, N. (2002). Dangerous Dependencies: The Intersection of Welfare Reform and Domestic Violence. *Gender & Society, 16,* 878–897. See also: Purvin, D. (2003). Weaving a Tangled Safety Net. *Violence Against Women,* 9, 1263–1277.
16. Family Violence in Canada, 2005.
17. *Family Violence in Canada: A Statistical Profile 2005,* Canadian Centre for Justice Statistics, Statistics Canada.

Thinking It Through: Women, Work and Caring in the New Millennium

Pat Armstrong

Hugh Armstrong

Hugh Armstrong is a Professor in the School of Social Work and the Institute of Political Economy at Carleton University in Ottawa. With Dr. Pat Armstrong, he has written extensively on health care and on women and work. He currently serves as an elected member of the Board of Directors for the Ottawa-Carleton Community Care Access Centre (CCAC), and as coordinator of the editorial board for the academic journal Studies in Political Economy.

Pat Armstrong is co-author of such books as Wasting Away: The Undermining of Canadian Health Care; Universal Health Care: What the United States Can Learn From Canada; Vital Signs: Nursing in Transition*; and* Take Care: Warning Signals for Canada's Health System. *She has also published on a wide variety of issues related to women's work and to social policy. She has served as Chair of the Department of Sociology at York University and Director of the School of Canadian Studies at Carleton University. She is a partner in the National Network on Environments and Women's Health, and is currently chairing a working group on health reform that crosses the Centres of Excellence for Women's Health.*

The American feminist Deborah Stone, an eloquent analyst of women's caring, talks about being a "'lumper' rather than a 'splitter'" (91). For "lumpers," the emphasis is on what is common about women's work, on what women share. At the same time, there remains in her publications a clear recognition of tensions and differences. Miriam Glucksmann's revealing analyses of British women's work speaks of "slicing" data, theory and concepts to create multiple and complex pictures of particular peoples in particular places (16). Her purpose is to look at the various ways work is divided up within what she calls the "total social organization of labour."

This paper is about both lumping and slicing. It attempts to explore what is common, not only among women but also across time and space. At the same time, it seeks to examine different slices of the same questions. Such slices are meant to help expose the complex and contradictory nature of the concepts we use in considering women's work and of the current state of women's work. It assumes that contexts and locations matter, and that while women face considerable pressure from forces outside their immediate control, they also are active participants in shaping their own lives.

WHY LUMP?

Everywhere throughout recorded time there has been a division of labour by gender. Every society we know about has defined some work as men's and some as women's. And every society we know about has made distinctions between what women can and should do. Women have primary daily responsibilities for children and for the sick or disabled, as well as for much of the other work in domestic domains. They do most of the cooking, washing, cleaning, toileting, bathing, feeding, comforting, training for daily living, shopping and planning for domestic consumption and care. And it is women who bear the children.

This division of labour is combined with a gap between average male and female wages. Jobs mainly done by men pay more than those mainly done by women. Women are much more likely than men to work part-time or part-year and to have interrupted career patterns or casual, temporary jobs. When self-employed, they are much less likely than men to employ others. And much of the work women do pays no wage at all.

Feminists have long been struggling to make the full range of women's work both visible and valued. Lumping has allowed them to do this. They began in the early 1960s by focussing on domestic labour, understood as the unpaid work women do in households, and by revealing the institutional and social arrangements that combine to produce systemic discrimination in the paid workforce. Initially, the emphasis was on what was termed the reproduction of labour power on a daily and generational basis. This meant having babies and providing for their needs, along with those of their breadwinning fathers. As the research on women's work expanded, the picture of this work became both more refined and more complex. More categories of work, such as care for the elderly, the sick and the disabled, appeared in literature. Then this care category, too, was further refined to include care management, assistance with daily living and personal as well as medical care, and it came to be seen as a relationship rather than simply as a work category. Similarly, the picture of women's work in the labour force was further developed to encompass the detailed division of labour found within occupations and industries and the nature of workplace relationships. Within the formal economy outside the home, working in the public sector was distinguished from the private sector, and then this private sector itself divided between the for-profit and the not-for-profit, or what came to be called the third sector.

Within this not-for-profit sector, women's work as volunteers was distinguished from their paid employment. Locations in the underground economy, where women worked for pay as cleaners, prostitutes, babysitters and secretaries, and in formal economy jobs that they did in their own homes, also have been exposed.

Lumping also allows us to explore the social, economic and institutional arrangements as well as the policies and practices that contribute to these patterns in women's work. But lumping is not only about processes remote from the individual lives of most women, about abstract concepts or far-away decision-makers. It is also about how women's work is shaped at the level of the hospital, day-care, community centre, clinic, home and office; about the fine divisions of labour; the ways policies are played out in daily lives and the ways women act to create spaces in their own lives or to limit those spaces. So, for example, lumping allows us to ask what kinds of caring work women and men do, and what kinds of government funding support or undermine this work.

Lumping, then, is appropriate because there are so many common patterns in women's work. Lumping allows us to see what women, as women, share, in terms of the nature of both the work and the work relationship. It also helps us to expose the forces that keep these patterns in place and change them.

WHY SLICE?

Although there is a division of labour by sex everywhere, there is also no common division of labour across time and space and often not even within countries during a particular period. What is defined and practiced as men's work or women's work varies enormously, and most cultures have at least some women who do men's work. Moreover, the actual division of labour can contradict the prescriptions or accepted practices. Equally important, there are significant differences among women related to class, race, culture, age, marital status, sexual orientation and spatial locations, as well as for the same women over time.

Once, those paid to do secretarial and teaching work were mainly men; now, most are women. Those paid as chefs are mainly men, while women do most of the unpaid cooking. However, in Canada at least, if the unpaid cooking is done outside on the barbeque, it is men who do the work, but the unpaid kitchen jobs are still done primarily by the women. In the USSR, most doctors were women at the same time as North American medicine was dominated by men. The care provided by women in a Bosnian refugee camp differs fundamentally from that provided in a household in Ottawa's exclusive Rockcliffe neighbourhood. While care work is women's work, there are multiple forms of women's paid and unpaid caring. There are also considerable variations in what is defined as women's caring work. Our grandmothers, for example, did not clean catheters, insert needles, or adjust oxygen masks as part of the care work they did at home.

There may also be large gaps in both places between what women and men think they should do and what they are able to do. There is, in other words, often a gap between practices and ideas about appropriate practices. For example, while most Canadian and British men think they should equally share the domestic labour, there is little evidence that such sharing actually happens in practice. Yet many men who think care is women's work find themselves providing care for ill and aging partners. Many women who provide care do not necessarily think that it is their job, nor do they necessarily have the skills to do the work. At the same time, many women who think they should provide care cannot do so because they have too many other demands on their time, because they do not have the skills, because they do not have the other necessary resources or because they do not have the physical capacity. Many who do provide care, providing services such as meal preparation, comforting and cleaning, may not even see this as care because it is so much a part of their daily lives.

Not only within countries at particular times, but also within workplaces, there may be significant differences among women. A hospital, for example, may have women working as managers and women working as housekeepers. The managers are more likely to be white, Canadian-born, with English or French as a first language and relatively young, while the housekeepers are more likely to have migrated to this country, to have neither English or French as their mother tongue and may be older than the female managers. And, of course, there are significant differences between these groups in terms of power, pay and ideas about work, and in their political, material and symbolic resources related not only to their positions in the paid workforce, but also to their positions in their households and neighbourhoods.

But slicing is not only necessary to draw out the differences related to women's various spatial, physical, social, psychological, economic, work and age locations, it is also necessary in order to see the different ways of understanding the evidence, different ways of developing evidence and different views on the same processes. It is, for example, possible to look at care from the perspective of the care provider or from that of those with care needs, or to examine care as a relationship. Furthermore, the family as a group may see care issues one way, and the government, the agencies and the paid providers in other ways. Indeed, each household member may have a specific way of slicing the situation. Equally important, the tensions among these may not be possible to resolve but possible only to recognize and handle. By beginning with a recognition of contradiction, by taking this slice, it is possible to base and develop policies and practices that seek to accommodate such tensions rather than setting out single solutions based on notions of harmony.

Analysis can begin from a number of different questions: asking, for example, what does this mean in the short term and what does it mean in the long term? What does it mean for those immediately involved, and what does it mean for the country or the world? It can also begin by acknowledging that some practices, conditions and situations are contradictory. Women, for example, may at one and the same time want to provide care and find it impossible to do so. They may love the person for whom they provide care but, precisely because of this love, hate to provide care.

Slicing can expose the different kinds of care work involved in providing for children with and without disabilities, for teenagers who join gangs and for those unable to attend university because there is no money, for adult neighbours with chronic illness and for those with marital problems, for healthy elderly and severely ill old people. It can also reveal what it means to provide this care at home or in an institution and what different kinds of institutions and homes there are.

It is also possible to begin with quite different purposes. For example, most policies are about helping households and families adapt to the demands of paid work and services. It is also possible, as some Norwegian policy analysts make clear, to start by figuring out how paid work can adapt to family lives (Brandth and Kvande). Instead of asking what resources the growing number of elderly require, the questions could be about the resources they bring and the services they provide. Rather than asking how care can be made an individual responsibility, we can ask what conditions make it possible to care without conscripting women into caregiving. Rather than assuming, as we do in Canada, that public care is what supplements family care done mainly by women, we could assume that families supplement public care.

Slicing adds both a recognition of difference and the possibility of developing different views of the same issues, circumstances and evidence.

WHY WOMEN?

On the one hand, we have a universal pattern in terms of a division of labour by sex and women embracing caring work. On the other hand, we have an incredible range of labour done by women and defined as women's work. We also have women resisting caring work. Indeed, American historian Emily Abel argues that some 19th century women "complained bitterly that caregiving confined them to the home, caused serious physical and emotional health problems and added to domestic labour, which was gruelling even in the best of times" (Abel 5). What factors, ideas, structures and processes contribute to this universality and difference, this embracing and resistance? More specifically, why do women provide the care but in so many different ways? There are no simple answers to these questions. Rather there are a number of answers that help contribute to a better understanding of care as women's responsibility.

We do know that only women have babies. But we also know that the meaning, experience and consequences of having babies varies enormously, not only across time and with location and culture, but also for individual women from one baby to another. Having a baby is fundamentally different for Celine Dion than it is for an Aboriginal woman who must leave her northern Quebec community if she is to receive medical assistance. Moreover, there is no necessary connection between having babies and rearing them; that is, to providing care. Bodies, then, are a factor in all of women's lives, but these bodies themselves are embedded in social, economic and political structures that are continually influencing how bodies work, as well as how they are defined and valued. They cannot provide much of the explanation for why women provide most of the care, not only for the babies they bear, but for other people as well.

Although there is plenty of evidence to suggest that women are more likely than men to identify with the emotional aspects of caring, there is very little evidence to suggest that this is connected to the way women's bodies or minds are physiologically constructed or that men are physiologically incapable of such caring emotions. There is also evidence to suggest that girls are taught and expected to exhibit such caring, and they are also more likely than their brothers to be assigned the caring jobs in the home. What sociologists call early socialization obviously contributes to women's skills in and attitudes about care, as well as to their brothers' notions of who is responsible for care and knows how to care. However, the pressures on women to provide care do not end and perhaps are not primarily created by early learning. Just as children are born and formed within a social context, so too are women carers daily created and shaped within social relationships, processes and structures. At the same time, women are active in creating these same relationships, processes and structures, albeit often from a weaker position than that of men.

These relationships, processes and structures are about power, not only in the sense that governments, employers, community organizations and husbands have specific powers and protect specific rights, but also in the more general sense of whose preferences, ways of acting and ideas prevail in daily practices. And they are about resources and the principles, as well as the mechanisms for their distribution. Power and resources in the formal and underground economies, in community organizations and households are often mutually reinforcing and are definitely linked. They are also unequally distributed, not only between women and men, but also among women. Women do have resources and are active participants in creating caring work. However, most women have fewer resources than most men, and the resources, as well as the means of participating they have, are frequently different from those of men.

There is, then, very little that is "natural" about women's work in general or their caring work in particular. Contexts matter much more than bodies in creating and maintaining women's caring work. Caring can be understood only as women's work within unequal relationships, structures and processes that help create women as carers and undervalue this caring work.

THINKING GLOBALLY: THE LARGEST CONTEXT

Globalization has become a familiar term in recent years. While familiar, though, teasing out its meanings and its implications for women in different locations is a complicated task.

Globalization implies a process that is drawing the world and its occupants closer together on what is often seen as an inevitable and undirected path. At the core of this process are giant corporations centred in one, usually northern, country but operating throughout the globe. These transnational corporations (TNCs) helped create the technologies that have themselves contributed both to the corporation's multinational form and their power. Such technologies make it possible to move money rapidly around the globe, thus allowing these corporations to avoid or at least threaten to avoid any particular government's taxes and regulations by moving their investments. The technologies also make it possible to move work around the world, thus allowing the corporations to avoid or threaten to avoid demands from workers or restrictions on the use of labour imposed by governments. In order to facilitate this movement of goods, money and work, the giant corporations have been central in promoting what is often called free trade. Free trade is far from new, and traders have always enjoyed considerable freedoms as well as considerable power. It may well be, however, that the speed of transactions has altered along with the size of the corporations directing them. As a result, their power may be greater than ever before.

Instead of combining to resist this pressure, many governments have come together to support the process of achieving greater and easier movement of goods, services and money. At the international level, the First World countries (also called northern, developed or industrial countries) in particular, have worked through the International Monetary Fund, the World Bank and the World Trade Organization to promote the removal of restrictions on trade, a process that entails both de-regulation and re-regulation. Countries owing enormous debts have been required to introduce structural adjustment programs that involve the removal of many restrictions on foreign investment and labour practices, as well as the sale of public corporations to private ones, cutbacks in public services and the adoption of market strategies within the public sector that remains. The impact on women has been mixed and contradictory, both within and across nations.

Some women have been able to get new jobs on the "global assembly line," producing goods and even services previously produced mainly by women in the highly industrialized countries. Precisely because firms have relocated in these countries in order to avoid high wages and restrictions on working condition, these jobs for women have rarely been good jobs. But they have offered some new possibilities for work, income, shared locations and minimal protections. More common has been the expansion of paid work for women outside the factory walls within the underground or informal economy where few, if any, rules apply. Women have been drawn into small-sale retail and service work, into domestic and homework, or simply into semiclandestine enterprises (see Ward). Here the boundaries between household and formal economy, between public and private space, and between employment time and non-employment time are blurred and protection visibility absent. At the same time, the withdrawal of public services has meant that women have had to do more of this work without pay or support within the confines of their private worlds, where the work is less visible and less available. For many women within these countries, there is no paid work at all. The poverty and unemployment that follow in the wake of structural adjustment policies push many to search for jobs in those First World countries that have created these policies. Women, in particular, have sought work as what Grace Chang calls "disposable domestics." Separated in time and space from their children, these women often do the domestic and caring work for First World women under conditions supported in the First World by the combination of government regulations, women's working conditions and the failure to provide care services. Like free trade, the movement of women to do such work is not new, but the scale has altered. The result is a growing gap among women within and between countries, a gap that is frequently linked to racialized categories as well.

In addition to imposing structural adjustment programs on Third World countries (or what are often called southern or developing countries), First World countries have entered into trade agreements that promise to support the movement of goods, services, money and, to a lesser extent, people across borders. This has not necessarily meant less government, but it has meant more measures to allow corporations to operate with less regard to national practices and preferences and fewer taxes or other contributions to national economies. It has also meant less local and democratic control as more decisions are being made by these international trading groups. Facing debt pressures themselves, these countries have adopted strategies similar to those imposed on the Third World. First World countries have acted more like entrepreneurs at the same time as they have handed over more of the services previously provided by governments to private, for-profit firms.

These shifts have had critical consequences for women. The expansion of the public sector had provided many, and often quite good, jobs for women. Indeed, in 1981, between 65 and 75% of college-educated women in Germany, Sweden and the U.S. were employed in the "socal welfare industries" (Pierson 130). Many of these jobs disappeared or their character changed in the wake of the global reforms. Trade agreements did allow some women to move to other countries in search of work. Registered nurses, for example, left Canada in large numbers when hospitals closed, acquiring jobs in the United States. But those women from Third World countries seeking work in Canada found it more difficult to gain full citizenship status, providing just one example of how free trade has not worked in the same way for everyone.

As public services have declined, more of the services have been provided for sale in the market.

This process, often described as commodification, determines access primarily on the ability to pay rather than on need. More of the women in First World countries, as compared to those in the Third World, have had the means to pay for commodified services. However, women in both Worlds have continued to earn less than men, and women have continued to bear primary responsibility for care and domestic work. Faced with fewer public services and relatively low pay, but still in need of income to purchase these services, women in the First World have sought the cheapest means of paying for care or other supports. These means have often involved the even poorer women from the Third World. This is not to suggest that most First World women have completely escaped unpaid work or that the majority of women could afford to pay for services. Indeed, the reduction in public services has meant that a considerable amount of this work, formerly done by women for pay in the market, is now done by women without pay in the home. In other words, it has been decommodified but not eliminated. Rather, it is to stress the linkages among women created by globalization and the growing gaps among women that these linkages often entailed.

Globalization does not simply refer to economics, however. It also refers to the ways people, ideas and cultures are brought closer together around the world. This has, in many ways, meant the spread of First World, and especially U.S. practices. Along with music, movies, fashions and food have come ideas about all aspects of social life, including women's work. This dissemination of ideas is also linked in many ways to the corporations, both through their ownership of companies that produce these goods and through their influence over the media. In these global sources, the emphasis is increasingly on the individual as a consumer with choices being based on the capacity to purchase. Like the relocation of jobs, the spread of ideas is a mixed blessing. On the one hand, feminist ideas have spread rapidly around the world. On the other hand, the First World version of feminism is what has spread most rapidly, and this version too often fails to take context and difference into account.

This notion of shared international perspectives is not particularly new. Indeed, after the Second World War there was much talk of a postwar consensus. This consensus was based on a commitment to expanded government-provided services to a mixed economy that combined public and private enterprise, and to policies of full employment along with sustained economic growth (Pierson 125). Redistribution of goods and services was part of the package, as were collective responsibility and shared risk. Now, this consensus seems to have fallen apart, only to be replaced by a new, and quite different, one. Public rights are replaced by private ones, with markets rather than states as the preferred means of allocating jobs, goods and services. But markets are unable to respond to many human needs and are especially ill-equipped to promote equity and full employment or to avoid long-term problems like pollution or other health consequences. Instead, they result in greater inequality, especially for women. As British theorist Ian Gough puts it, "Markets paradoxically require altruistic, collective behaviour on the part of women in the household in order to enable men to act individualistically in the market" (16).

Globalization has allowed much more than money, people, goods and services to move quickly around the world. Diseases, too, face more permeable borders. New epidemics, such as HIV/AIDS, are transported along with old ones, like tuberculosis and hepatitis, around the globe with relative ease, transported in and by airplanes, as well as by service workers. Increasing inequality, not only in the Third World but also in the First, encourages their development and prevents their treatment. Diabetes has become much more common, especially among marginalized groups in large urban centres and on reservations. At the same time, protections under free trade rules for pharmaceutical patents frequently leave treatments beyond the reach of many.

One way, then, to slice globalization is to reveal the increasing dominance of transnational corporations, the converging of governments around market strategies, the declining democratic controls and the growing gap for and among women. Another way to slice it is to expose the counter tendencies. The same technologies that support corporate power allow various kinds of social and labour movements to organize around their interests. We see evidence of this not only in the "battle of Seattle" and in the streets of Quebec, but also in the Beijing Conference on Women that reached a consensus around means of promoting women's equality and in the attempts to protect sweatshop workers encouraged by the success of Naomi Klein's book *No Logo*. The movement of people around the globe has meant that many of us are more familiar with other cultures and practices.

We also see counter tendencies in the escalation and power of terrorism. Although many governments have adopted strategies taken from the for-profit sector, there is still an incredible variety in the ways these governments operate. Important public programs that reflect a continuing commitment to social rights and collective responsibility remain in many countries. Others have taken a route that emphasizes family values while still others have turned to religion and ethnicity. Moreover, the trade alliance among members of the European Union has served to improve working conditions for many women and help improve services for others. Instead of de-regulation, we see on occasion the extension of regulation. Britain, for example, has been required to provide protections for part-time workers and to introduce both minimum wage and equal pay legislation, all of which improve women's market jobs. Several countries are resisting the high drug prices that prevent them from treating mothers with HIV/AIDS, a sign that not all countries are willing to put property rights above people's right to life. And perhaps most importantly, there is ample evidence to demonstrate that spending on social programs can enhance rather than prevent trade, and that gender-based analysis linked to effective programs is essential to economic development.

Contradictions within global developments, as well as those among particular kinds of developments, are important in understanding where and how change may occur or is occurring. It is equally important to examine the details of how global agreements and patterns are played out within specific locations, because practices may well defy or transform intentions. In short, globalization is about processes that result from actual decisions and practices rather than about forces beyond human control. While there is strong evidence to demonstrate that corporations are powerful players that are often supported by governments, there is also evidence to suggest that there are both limits on this power and contradictory patterns. There are choices to be made. These choices can have important consequences for women and their work and have to be considered in developing strategies for care.

References

Abel, Emily K. "A Historical Perspective on Care." *Care Work: Gender Labour and the Welfare State.* Ed. Madonna Harrington Meyer. London: Routledge, 2000.

Brandth, Berit, and Elm Kvande. "Flexible Work and Flexible Fathers." Paper presented to the conference on "Rethinking Gender, Work and Organization." Keele University, England, June 2001.

Chang, Grace. *Disposable Domestics: Immigrant Women Workers in the Global Economy.* Cambridge, MA: South End Press, 2000.

Glucksmann, Miriam. *Cottons and Casuals: The Gendered Organization of Labour in Time and Space.* London: British Sociological Association, 2000.

Gough, Ian. *Global Capital, Human Needs and Social Policy.* New York: Palgrave, 2000.

Klein, Naomi. *No Logo: Taking Aim at the Brand Bullies*. Toronto: Knopf Canada, 2000.

Pierson, Christopher. *Beyond the Welfare State: The New Political Economy of Welfare.* Second Edition. Oxford: Blackwell, 1999.

Stone, Deborah. "Caring by the Book." *Care Work: Gender, Labour and the Welfare State.* Ed., Madonna Harrington Meyer. London: Routledge, 2000.

Ward, Kathryn, Ed. *Women Workers and Global Restructuring.* Ithaca, NY: Cornell University Press, 1990.

The Great Undoing: State Formation, Gender Politics and Social Policy in Canada

Janine Brodie

Janine Brodie is a Professor of Political Science at the University of Alberta, where she served as Chair from 1997-2003. In 2004, she assumed a Canada Research Chair in Political Economy and Social Policy. Her research foci include Canadian political economy and politics, gender and politics, and social theory and policy.

. . . As Canadians enter the 21st century, they, like their counterparts throughout the Western world, have been ushered through a paradigmatic shift in the dominant philosophy of governance. The latter term is meant to capture the historically shifting and politically negotiated (and enforced) relationships among the three principal domains of a liberal-democratic polity—the state, civil society and the market—as well as the ways in which citizens understand themselves, articulate their interests, exercise their rights and obligations and mediate their differences (UNDP 1997:11). Philosophies of governance, if well conceived and widely supported, tend to have long shelf lives. For example, the consensus underlying the postwar years, variously described as "the postwar compromise," "embedded liberalism" and "the welfare state," shaped Canada's political geography for thirty years. Since the early 1980s, it has been gradually and progressively replaced with a new set of assumptions of governance. This new philosophy of governance—neoliberalism—represents an amalgamation of policy postures including decentralization, privatization, individualization and the elevation of the market over the public sector. . . .

GOVERNMENTS, GOVERNANCE AND GENDER

The emergence of the neoliberal state in Canada and elsewhere has been marked by a growing income polarization between the rich and the poor (both within countries and between the North and the South), an acceleration and intensification of the feminization of poverty and the marginalization of already marginalized groups, especially single mothers, persons with disabilities and visible minority women, to the fringes of the labour market and of society. At the same time, the political muscle and tangible accomplishments of the second wave of Canadian feminism during the 1970s and 1980s have all but disappeared. In only a few years, gender and the equality agenda generally have been virtually erased from public discourse and public policy. This magical disappearing act does not signal a victory over gender-based inequality in Canada. Indeed, almost every measure of economic and social well-being demonstrates the opposite. Instead, the undoing of the gender equality policy agenda in Canada (indeed, all structurally based equality claims) reflects the way in which the concepts of gender and group equality have been de/reconstructed within the neoliberal governing paradigm. This becomes apparent when this paradigm is contrasted with the assumptions underpinning the postwar welfare state.

LIBERAL PROGRESSIVISM AND THE WELFARE STATE

. . . Feminist interpretations of the welfare state have consistently pointed out that its liberal-progressivist discourse of universality, unconditionality, equality and neutrality was decidedly gendered. Social citizenship rights were premised largely on full-time employment. This definition of citizen-worker, combined with the postwar construction of the appropriate gender order as male breadwinner and dependent wife and children, meant that men gained the *entitlements* of social citizenship. They could claim social security as a right. Women, in contrast, were cast as dependent citizens—dependent either on individual men, family or state-funded and delivered social welfare, which involved surveillance, conditionality, social stigma and lower levels of compensation (Bakker 1994a; Young 1990b). In other words, social rights were neither universal nor unconditional but, instead, highly gendered, casting the male breadwinner as the social citizen and women as dependents or clients of the state. . . . Public policy included women under the umbrella of the state primarily as wives and mothers.

Although accurate and appropriate, this popular assessment of the gendered underpinning of the welfare state does not tell the whole story. Liberal-progressive discourse also provided for women and a nascent women's movement to pronounce themselves as something different from and more than dependents, wives and mothers. This new governing philosophy, especially the priority it attached to social rights, equality, democracy, social planning and progress, provided a different political space for women, which was outside the confines of the home. Women were encouraged and, indeed, empowered by the state to make claims on the state as *citizens* who had been actively denied the promise of equality and progress, although all too frequently it was white middle-class women who had the loudest voice (Brodie 1995). . . . Liberal progressivism held out the promise that the many strains of structural and systemic disadvantage rooted in the postwar world could be minimized through social planning and public policy.

The second wave of the Canadian women's movement grew up beside and, in many ways, was shaped by the welfare state and its liberal-progressivist governing philosophy. Central to this relationship was the federal government's acquiescence in 1966 to the demands of a small group of influential women to appointment of a Royal Commission on the Status of Women (RCSW). Its mandate was to identify the major impediments to the achievement of gender equality in almost all walks of Canadian life and to recommend policy responses that would break down these barriers. Reporting in 1970, the RCSW made over 150 recommendations for federal government action. One unintended outcome of the Royal Commission was the consolidation of a growing and increasingly politicized women's movement, especially in English Canada, which fixed its eyes firmly on the federal state and its promise of planning and progress. In 1972, the National Action

Committee on the Status of Women (NAC), second wave feminism's key frontline organization, was launched for the precise purpose of monitoring the federal government and pressuring it to implement the recommendations of the RCSW. . . .

The 1970s and early 1980s were empowering days for the women's movement. The goal of women's equality crept up the ladder of policy priorities, especially after the United Nations declared 1975 the International Year of Women. It was followed by the Decade of Women (1976–85) when governments of all countries were encouraged to put sexism and gender inequality squarely at the centre of national and international policy agendas. These years saw the proliferation of strategic sites for women within the federal state—among them, the Women's Bureau in the Department of Labour, the Office of Equal Opportunity in the Public Service Commission, the Status of Women branch of the Privy Council Office, a minister responsible for the Status of Women within the federal cabinet, and, most important, the Women's Program in the citizenship branch of the Secretary of State. The placement of the latter was not accidental. It reflected the linkage drawn by liberal-progressivist discourse between democracy, equality and inclusion. The Women's Program was specifically mandated to pursue "the development of a society in which the *full potential of women as citizens* is recognized and utilized" (Burt 1994:216). To this end, federal funding for the Women's Program mushroomed from a meager $223,000 in 1973 to a peak of $12.4 million in 1985.

The mid-1980s marked the apex of political influence for the second wave of the Canadian women's movement. In only a few short years, it had witnessed an exponential growth in the number of women in elective office, a proliferation of provincial and federal policy initiatives aimed at the elusive goal of gender equality, the entrenchment of a sexual equality clause in the new Charter of Rights and Freedoms, unprecedented attention from the major political parties both in speech and in platform, a televised federal leadership debate devoted exclusively to women's issues, and, in the early 1980s, the emergence of a gender gap which suggested that ordinary Canadian women were prepared to choose among political parties on the basis of what they were saying about and doing for women, especially in the social policy field. Throughout this period, indeed currently, pollsters found that women were much more likely than men to support social programs and an activist state.

Yet, these victories proved both vulnerable and short-lived. The mid-1980s also witnessed the election of the first overtly neoliberal government, which promised, albeit with characteristic Canadian moderation, to chart the federal state along the path already carved by Margaret Thatcher and Ronald Reagan. Since the election of Brian Mulroney's Conservative government, Canadians have witnessed political parties of all stripes systematically undo the very foundations of the welfare state and replace it with a leaner and meaner neoliberal alternative. This transformation in governing philosophies is now essentially complete. What vestiges of the postwar welfare state that remain have been so undermined and altered that they would be unrecognizable to their creators. The proportion of federal spending currently directed to social programs is lower than in 1949, before the welfare state was set in place. The vast majority of Canada's unemployed no longer qualify for benefits while the federal government funnels the growing surpluses generated by the employee-funded program into general revenues. The gap between the rich and the poor has widened, the poor have grown poorer and are increasingly isolated in urban ghettos, and poverty is now more often the fate of select groups of Canadians. "High risk" groups, in the federal government's current terminology, primarily consist of lone parent families, families headed by a disabled person, immigrants arriving during the past decade, Aboriginals and senior women living alone (Canada Privy Council Office 1999). Deepening poverty and other measures of social exclusion are increasingly gendered at the same time as the goal of gender equality has been erased from public discourse and the formation of public policy. The next section of this chapter, which explores the foundational premises of neoliberal governance, fleshes out this paradox.

PERFORMATIVITY AND THE NEOLIBERAL STATE

. . . From the mid-1980s onward . . . the women's movement, in coalition with other progressive groups, fought against the implementation of what they termed the "Mulroney" or "Tory" agenda. The women's movement was a frontline opponent of the Free Trade Agreement with the United States (FTA, 1988), the extension of this agreement to include Mexico (the North American Free Trade Agreement, NAFTA, 1994) and two failed attempts to constitutionally recognize Quebec's unique position in the Canadian confederation and realize greater autonomy in areas of provincial jurisdiction (the Meech Lake Accord, 1987, and the Charlottetown Accord, 1992). In each case, the objections of the women's movement centred around both preserving the gains that had already been achieved and defending the power of the federal state to fund and shape social policy and enforce minimum national standards. Not surprisingly, the women's movement was increasingly reviled, by the federal government and neoliberal ideologues generally, as a selfish coalition of "special interests" that threatened Canadian consensus. At the time, journalists commonly joked that feminism had become the new "f-word" on Parliament Hill.

The collision between the federal government and the women's movement during the Mulroney years (1984–93) increasingly became centred on the federal government's growing embrace of the principle axioms of neoliberalism. In simple terms, this philosophy of governance emphasizes the importance of removing government from the economy, especially with respect to regulating business. Indeed, this fundamental tenet is encoded in NAFTA, which effectively exercises quasi-constitutional authority over the Canadian state and its electorate in important policy areas. Neoliberalism also downplays the importance of expending public funds to promote social well-being and equality agendas and it was precisely on this terrain that the government's repudiation of the women's movement centred. The dominant current of the second wave of the Canadian women's movement in the postwar years, responding to liberal-progressivist discourse and practice, consistently linked the achievement of women's equality to state intervention in the economy whether through social policy, the courts or through the regulation of the private sector. Key feminist policy demands, constitutive elements of the postwar women's movement in Canada, such as universal and affordable childcare, income security for sole mothers and elderly women, affirmative action and pay and employment equity, all called for more government, not less government. The undoing of the welfare state obviously threatened both the identity and the strategic agenda of the dominant current in the women's movement. These diametrically opposed world views leave little room for political compromise.

The governing philosophy of the neoliberal state has been termed *performativity* (Yeatman 1994). This term points to the increasing tendency for the state to fashion itself as a market player rather than as the embodiment of the public sphere, the source of public goods, the greater equalizer of structural inequalities and the expression of democratic consensus. . . . Public goods are privatized while the public sphere embraces as its governing logic market principles and measurements (Brodie 1997).

. . . The idea of performativity marks the ascendancy of the market *over* the state and *inside* the state. This embrace of the logic of the market atrophies the public, closes political spaces and further marginalizes the economically and socially marginalized who depend on the state to redress the most adverse consequences of the capitalist economy. A performative philosophy of governance engages with those who do not fit neatly into a market model in one of two ways: either they are treated as inadequate or dysfunctional market players or they are completely erased from the public agenda.

Performativity, being grounded in the assumptions and language of neoclassical economics and laissez-faire liberalism, also explicitly rejects the policy relevance of gender or any other systemic barrier to equality . . . Moreover, neoclassical economics brackets out women's reproductive and caring labour because it has no market value. As Isabella Bakker reminds us, "markets operate without recognizing that the unpaid work of reproduction and maintenance of human resources contributes to the realization of formal market relations" (1994a:2). . . .

Liberalism, in turn, asks individuals to bracket out their particular social location such as those structured by gender, race and class. This formula blinds us to the daily realities of living in gendered, raced and classed bodies and to the fact that these bodies are treated differently and unequally across the entire spectrum of social relations. Within this barren discursive terrain, performativity sees only one social agent—one good citizen—the atomized market player who recognizes the limits and liabilities of state provision and embraces his/her obligation to work longer and harder to become self-reliant. . . .

. . . In stark contrast to liberal progressivism, performativity provides little discursive or institutional space to make claims on the state on the basis of morality, fairness, collective difference or structural inequality.

. . . The performativity philosophy of the neoliberal state rests on three fundamental pillars—privatization, decentralization and individualization—all of which act simultaneously to intensify gender inequality and to erode the political relevance of gender.

PRIVATIZATION

Privatization (and its ideological handmaiden, deregulation) is a key governing instrument of the neoliberal state that serves both to valorize market mechanisms over the public sector and to diminish the terrain of democratic accountability. . . .

Privatization involves much more than simply removing things from one sector and placing them in another. It is a profoundly cultural process in which the thing moved is itself transformed into something quite different. Objects become differently understood and regulated. The deinstitutionalized (privatized) schizophrenic becomes a street person and is more often attended to by the police than by mental health professionals. Citizens become gender-neutral shareholders and are asked to assess their government in terms of its credit ratings and fiscal bottom lines rather than how it promotes collective well-being and democratic decision-making. . . . Of course, government downsizing, privatization and deregulation all have gendered underpinnings as the examples of health care and pay equity demonstrate.

The crowning achievement of the Canadian welfare state was the implementation of a universal public health-care system in the mid-1960s. It also represents a formidable hurdle for a complete conversion to neoliberal performativity in Canada. Health care consumes a significant proportion of both provincial and federal expenditures. It also represents a potential gold mine for the private sector as the profit margins of American private health-care providers readily attest. At the same time, Canadians have made it abundantly clear to government that its obsession with the market does not and will not extend to public health care. . . .

Privatization nonetheless has crept into the public system incrementally and imperceptibly. . . . Systematic cuts to health care, however, have intensified the privatization of the health-care system in a number of ways, including:

- privatizing costs of health care by shifting the burden of payments onto individuals (for example, refusal to recognize an illness or treatment as insured by the public system);
- shifting the burden from public institutions to community-based organizations and private households (for example, cost-cutting has resulted in shorter hospital stays which, in turn, shifts the cost of patient recuperation to the home and most often to the unpaid caring work of women);
- privatizing care work from public health-care workers to the growing for-profit caring industry; and
- privatizing management practices within the health-care system by adopting systems developed for the private sector (for example, the "efficiency" of nursing staff is now measured in terms of time allocation per patient rather than in terms of quality of care, trust and interpersonal contact) (Scott, Horne and Thurston 2000:1).

Each of these privatizing gestures has disproportionately affected women insomuch as they are less able to buy drugs or for-profit services and more likely to assume the role of caregiver, either informally in the home and community or formally as health-care workers. . . .

The negative impact of privatization on women also can be viewed from the perspective of privatizing employment opportunities that were once the purview of the public sector. The welfare state was of critical importance to women as an employer and as a regulator of gender relations and employment practices in the workplace. The federal government was and remains the largest single employer of women in Canada and, in the postwar years, took upon itself the task of being a leader in setting standards for women's employment. Government downsizing and the privatization of public sector jobs obviously closes career options for women, especially young minority women, in an era of persistently high un- and underemployment. . . .

DECENTRALIZATION

In its simplest terms, decentralization is a governing instrument that transfers power, responsibility and accountability from a single centre to smaller units. Some of these units are more easily identified than others and some may not be subject to direct democratic control. Decentralization is generally applauded on the grounds that it enhances democratic accountability and corrects for the worst bureaucratic excesses of the welfare state. This was the case advanced by equality-seeking groups in the 1960s and 1970s. Decentralization, they argued, allowed for more control in the design and delivery of social services and for more integrated community-based and administered programs. Presumably, too, local administrators would be more easily held accountable by the objects of social programs.

This depiction of the benefits of decentralization, however, was premised on . . . assumptions that quickly lost validity in the 1990s. . . .

The Canadian experience, however, is that the democratic potential of decentralization can be quickly offset by fiscal constraints. The rhetoric of decentralization, in fact, has masked a demolition derby—a scurry of fiscal off-loading onto newly designated "shock absorbers". . . .

By the end of the 1990s, the predictable effects of the neoliberal assault on social programs was clearly evident in the daily lives of Canadians and in official government statistics. The homeless and food banks have become a familiar part of the social fabric when only twenty years ago they would have been exceptional. The income gap between the rich and the poor has widened while the poor have become poorer. The poor are also more likely than a decade ago to be concentrated in urban ghettos. According to a report of the Canadian Council on Social Development released in 2000, the number of poor people living in cities increased by 34% between 1990 and 1995. One third of the children living in Montreal and Toronto are now classified as poor (*Globe and Mail,* April 17, 2000, A5). Moreover, poverty is increasingly the fate of a few identifiable groups. Women are more likely to be poor than men and visible minority women are more likely to be poor than the "invisible" majority of Canadian women. One quarter of the former group is classified as poor compared to 13% of the latter. The federal government has recently identified five groups which, the government suggests, are at "high risk" for a life of poverty—single mothers, disabled persons, recent immigrants (predominately persons of colour), Aboriginal peoples and elderly women living alone. This notion of "high risk" conjures up medical images which stigmatize and decontextualize poverty in the same way that, for example, medical officials talk of gay men as being a high-risk group with respect to HIV infection or Aboriginal peoples as a high-risk group with respect to alcoholism. Again, this contrasts sharply with liberal progressivism's underlying moral code that everyone is at risk and everyone is responsible for everyone else.

The rates of poverty among these groups are startling by any measure. In 1997, a full 43% of families headed either by lone parents (80% of whom are women), recent immigrants, or persons with disabilities were, according to official measures, poor, compared to 9% of other families (HRDC 2000:1). Single mothers and their children are especially vulnerable to poverty as the following statistics amply demonstrate:

- 61% of single mothers live in poverty;
- 83% of single mothers under the age of twenty-five live in poverty;
- 45% of all children living in poverty are in lone parent families; and
- 33% of social assistance recipients are single parents (Canada Privy Council Office 1999:27–29).

The experience of Canada and other advanced industrial countries that have embraced neoliberal governance is that wealth trickles down to some and not others. The growing gulf between the rich and the poor is partly attributable to changes in the global economy and the labour market, to the persistence of structural barriers rooted in class, race and gender and to the undoing of the welfare state. In Canada, the residualization of social policy and the abandonment of the idea of collective responsibility for the structurally disadvantaged has been intensified by decentralization and governing instruments that discourage even minimum public provision for the disadvantaged. . . .

INDIVIDUALIZATION

At the heart of the new governing philosophy is a tidal shift away from notions of collective values and shared fate to those of family and individual responsibility. The central operating principle here is that it is up to families to look after their own and it is up to the government to make sure that they do. In a sense, the affirmation of family and individual responsibility is simply another manifestation of privatization and decentralization. But it is also more than this. First, it is an attempt to recast both the individual and the citizen in the abstract and decontextualized language of neoclassical economics and classic liberalism. Individualism valorizes the rational economic actor and market relations, which, as we know, have particularly insidious consequences for women, children and other marginalized groups. Women are assumed to take up the slack in the new order, particularly with respect to caring activities (Bakker 1996). The rebirth of abstract individualism represents the systematic erasure of structural factors in the formation of social policy. The poor become responsible for their own plight while the state becomes preoccupied with using its powers to enforce the individualization of the social costs associated with neoliberal public management and economic globalization more generally. . . .

The Canadian experience is replete with examples of this shift in thinking about social policy. The new "active" welfare model, which informed the federal social policy review in 1994 and is now being implemented by the provinces, is premised on a human resources model that sees poverty as an individual defect rather than as a product of social structures which, by definition, create winners and losers. Instead, poverty is attributed to individual skill or motivational deficits that lead to dependence on the state. The idea that social assistance recipients are dependent on welfare carries with it a barrage of negative images that stigmatize the poor and make them appear to be personally to blame for their condition. Welfare dependency, similar to drug dependence, is a mark of individual weakness, irresponsibility and immaturity and, most of all, is avoidable (Fraser and Gordon 1994).

. . . One obvious disciplinary measure is to cut welfare benefits to a level below minimum subsistence; another is to force welfare recipients to work for their benefits. The most populous province, Ontario, has adopted workfare and has passed legislation to ensure that workfare will not be subject to the minimum protections provided other workers by employment standards legislation. Workfare, snitch-lines and extraordinary surveillance are all affronts to the basic civil rights of welfare recipients. Obviously, too, these disciplinary practices are focused on some groups more than others. The systemic bases of poverty in Canada mean that women, persons with disabilities, visible minorities and Aboriginal people have become the primary objects of the individualization in social policy.

At the same time, neoliberal governments are busy crafting legislation that attempts to reconstruct the patriarchal nuclear family and its distinct lines of responsibility and power relations. Youth have been cut from welfare rolls under the assumption that they will be cared for by their families. Disregarding the reason why children leave home in the first place, among them, physical, emotional and sexual abuse, the result is often street kids, juvenile prostitution, addiction, disease, crime and despair. Women's shelters have been closed, thereby forcing abused women to stay in or return to abusive homes. Perhaps the most obvious example of the reconstruction of the patriarchal family is the federal government's new child support legislation designed to discipline the so-called deadbeat dad—the father who refuses to support the children he has left. Although long a reviled figure in feminist discourse, the deadbeat dad's centrality to the neoliberal state has been more recent. The federal government has passed legislation that standardizes child support payments and sets penalties for parents who fail to make them. While few would disagree with the intent of the legislation, it fails to address the realities of child poverty in Canada. The federal government's own research, for example, indicates that few separated fathers fit the stereotypical image of the deadbeat dad. A great many separated and divorced fathers recouple and remarry and simply do not have the income to support two families. This policy also marks single mothers who can or will name fathers (deserving) and those who cannot or will not (undeserving).

The single or sole mother provides a more vexing case for neoliberal policymakers because often she cannot be wedged into the heteropatriarchal model of privatized social provision. Under the welfare state, single mothers were primarily seen as mothers who were unemployable, at least until their children entered school. These mothers are now framed in policy as potential employables who need surveillance and discipline in order to make them take personal responsibility for their children or find a man who will. To this end, the Ontario government has revived the "spouse in the house" rule, which dictates that single mothers lose their benefits when they live with a man. . . .

The idea that the single mother should take care of herself and her children at the same time as the government is systematically withdrawing support for her to do so would seem to be, at best, counterintuitive. However, neoliberal policymakers seem unconcerned about realities of sole parenting or the material conditions of women and children caught in the distortion of extreme poverty in a highly unbalanced gender order. Single mothers, as we have seen, are the poorest among the poor in Canada. Nevertheless, they have been erased in the poverty debate through the federal government's child poverty initiative, which constructs children as deserving independent of their family or community condition. Poor children just float out there completely decontextualized from the circumstances that surround and shape them. . . .

CONCLUSION

In 2000 the federal government boasted that for eight consecutive years the United Nations named Canada the best country in the world to live by placing it first on the Human Development Index (HDI), which combines measures of life expectancy, education and income. Policy-makers were less vocal about the fact that Canada ranked eighth on the gender empowerment index and slid to eighth on the human poverty index. The government was decidedly silent about the fact that Canada would have been lodged among developing nations if the UN only took account of Canada's Aboriginal peoples (UNDP 2000). These, nevertheless, should be worrying trends for social policy-makers.

. . . The past two decades have witnessed the reinvention of the Canadian state and the implementation of a new philosophy of governance. Neither of these processes can be divorced from gender (or race or class). In contrast to the era of the welfare state, which spoke to and helped form an undifferentiated category of women and advanced a state-driven gender equality agenda, the politics of gender is far more complex under the neoliberal state. Poverty has become increasingly feminized but it is not borne by all Canadian women. There is also increasing income polarization among Canadian women themselves, enabling some Canadian women, usually white middle-class professionals, to buy caring work from other Canadian women who are marked by economic, racial and ethnic disadvantage. Women and men who have benefited from the new economic and political order, moreover, are increasingly likely to interpret both their prosperity and others' poverty as a measure of the individual rather than as resulting from a fissure in the social fabric. The systematic erasure of structural considerations in popular understandings as well as in the formation of social policy has profound implications for the formation of political identities and alliances under the umbrella of the neoliberal state. Blinkered by the requisites of performativity, "the economic fates of citizens are uncoupled from one another and are now understood and governed as a function of their own particular levels of enterprise, skill, inventiveness and flexibility" (Rose 1996b:339). This individualized and distorted vision of ourselves, our families and our communities both erases recognition of the systemic underpinnings of gender inequality (as well as that of race and class) and intensifies its manifestations because systemic solutions to these inequalities are discounted as irrelevant. This is the fundamental paradox confronting all equality seeking groups in the new millennium. It is a paradox that, if left unchallenged, will continue to marginalize and stigmatize many "different" women and, ultimately, exact great costs to all.

Intersecting Identities and Inclusive Institutions: Women and the Future of Transformative Politics

Alexandra Dobrowolsky

Alexandra Dobrowolsky is Professor and Chair of the Political Science Department at Saint Mary's University. She teaches and writes in the areas of Canadian, Comparative, and Woman and Politics. She has published widely, written the book The Politics of Pragmatism: Women, Representation, and Constitutionalism in Canada *(2000), and co-edited* Women Making Constitutions, New Politics and Comparative Perspectives *(2003) with Vivien Hart, as well as* Women, Migration and Citizenship: Making Local, National, and Transnational Connections *(2006) with Evangelia Tastsoglou.*

When addressing the issue of under-representation of women, one invariably hears that change has come about incrementally, but that gender imbalances will, none the less, slowly but surely right themselves. There is no doubt that the number of women in conventional politics has increased. From journalist Barbara Frum's comment that there were more whooping cranes (a virtually extinct species) in Canada than women in Parliament in the 1960s, to the reality of the 1980s and 1990s, where the percentage of women in the House of Commons inched forward from 13% in 1988 to 18% in 1993, and 20% in 1997, the steady climb in women's numbers could be used to justify such complacency. Moreover, the proliferation of women "firsts"—first female Canadian Prime Minister, Kim Campbell (if only for five months); first woman Chief Justice of the Supreme Court,

Beverley McLachlin; and first woman of a minority background as Governor General, Adrienne Clarkson—all could be invoked to illustrate that gaps in female representation were finally being filled.

While women's participation rates can go up, however, they most certainly can also go down. This became glaringly obvious with the collapse of communism in Eastern Europe. Closer to home, in the November 2000 Canadian election, the number of female candidates running for most parties, except the New Democratic Party (NDP) and the Bloc Québécois (BQ), dropped. In addition, witness the half-hearted efforts to break down the barriers facing women in political parties, such as the modest funds set aside for women candidates (for example, the Ellen Fairclough/Judy LaMarsh/Agnes McPhail Funds for Progressive Conservative (PC)/Liberal and NDP, respectively) or the top down powers given to the Liberal leader enabling him or her to parachute women and minorities into ridings.

Also there are the discrepancies between numerical and substantive representation. The proportion of women may rise, but this can occur in a government that ignores or is hostile to women's issues, as with the Mulroney government of the 1980s and early 1990s (Bashevkin), or in a party that is ideologically opposed to feminism.

The neoliberal state operates as if equality exists, despite a socio-economic context in which the gap between the rich and the poor is widening. When these harsh realities, and ironies, are taken into account, any ostensible gains in women's numerical representation become obscured. What does becomes clear, as Lisa Young comments, is that "[i]n substantive terms, issues of importance to women have all but disappeared from the policy agenda of government" (182). As a result, at a time in Canadian history when there are more women than ever in prominent political positions, inequalities are growing rather than subsiding, and thus huge shortfalls in the aggregation and articulation of various women's interests and identities remain. While feminists discuss whether women should seek access to traditional political structures, rather than change them, it is evident that obstacles still exist to conventional participation for women from many social groups. Thus, the basic presuppositions of liberal democracy, from equality to the impartiality of the state and the law, are more about rhetoric than reality.

What can be done to make the future brighter, to provide better, more substantive representation for women, and for women of differing identities and with different needs? The aim of this article is to try to answer this rather large question by looking at a much bigger picture beyond the current myths of liberal representative democracy. Although dominant political institutions in Canada can be reformed, and some suggestions to this end will be made, this would have only limited results. Because totally dispensing with conventional political forms in Canada is extremely unlikely, however, I suggest an alternative of radical interventionism and synthesis.

Despite a host of ills, their chronically un- and under-representative nature among them, our liberal democratic institutions continue to exist, but appear to do so artificially, in the face of mounting scepticism, cynicism, dissatisfaction and alienation (Canada, Royal Commission on Electoral Reform; Canada, *The Citizens' Forum*; Dalton 271–79). Conventional political structures, in my view, can only be given new life through a sizeable infusion of radical democracy. Put simply, we need to hazard not only more, but also *different kinds* of democracy.

Democratic expansionism will require experimentation and long-term risk taking, which will involve clearing new terrain. That is, we need to break ground in a forest of existing (and perhaps some dead) political institutions in order to sow the seeds of unconventional politics. The time is ripe for new kinds of non-institutional politics premised on collective engagement and reflective of diverse communities. Unlike conventional political processes, these would not propagate individualism, exclusivity, obfuscation, adversarialism and confrontation. Rather, they would cultivate collective mobilization, inclusivity, openness, collaboration and coordination. They would be designed to share planning and decision-making with traditional institutions, but they would also send offshoots into various communities that, in turn, would sprout networks of political communication and action. Thus, they would include women and under-represented groups in ways that were mindful of the danger of de-radicalization through partial incorporation, for they would be oriented towards various communities' political struggles. Thus liberal and radical democracy could coincide, providing opportunities for diverse voices to be heard and to be acted upon. In sum, fostering a more welcoming environment for the women's movement and for other social movements is necessary to give diverse actors more legitimacy in the traditional political process (in policy, and in decision-making), as well as to encourage broader interactions that defy conventional political proclivities.

PROBLEMATIZING WOMEN AS A GROUP

Volumes have been written to both sustain and refute the argument that: "women are often best represented by other women, as they have an understanding of what equality means for them that is not available to men" (Williams 13).

What is more, feminist theorists in the 1980s and 1990s grappled with the fallout of having conceptualized women as a group. As they drew attention to inequalities or differences between men and women, the inequalities and differences among women tended to be disregarded (Collins; Spellman; Mohanty). The invocation of "woman" often universalized women and failed to consider that the realities of a white, Western, English-speaking, able-bodied, middle-class woman, for instance, were far removed from those of many other women. This not only had a significant impact on feminist thinking, but also on feminist mobilization. The Canadian women's movement was chastened, as women of colour (among others) criticized pan-Canadian feminist organizations for pursuing the priorities of white, straight, able-bodied, middle-class women (Agnew; Driedger; Stone).

This consideration of "woman" is not just about word play. Affirmative action programmes and other measures geared towards redressing under-representation have been spurned on this basis by both the right and the left. They also befuddle poststructuralists, who question how such representational remedies can ever encompass women and other collective identities in all their diversity. It is argued that such propositions will ultimately close off categories like gender, race and so on (Butler; Brown; Squires) and fail to respond to their fluidity and mutability. Yet as Evelyn Nakano Glenn points out, "unfortunately, not paying attention to race and gender does not make gender-race inequalities go away, precisely because these inequalities are institutionalized and not just ideas in people's heads" (12). So there are practical political reasons for considering women as a group.

Here and elsewhere, it has been persuasively argued that we can strategically use identity to think about, and act on behalf of, women and other collective identities in ways that are not necessarily essentialist, universalizing and unchanging (Jhappan; Bernstein). The goal, then, is to foster a practical, open-ended identity politics that reflects contingencies and multiplicity, affinities as well as difference.

REFORMING THE INSTITUTIONAL POLITICAL: SHORING UP LIBERAL DEMOCRACY?

Conventional reform suggestions seldom go far enough. For instance, copious amounts of ink have been spilled on the topic of changing our electoral system to make every vote count, and to produce fairer representation (Milner). Proportional representation (PR) is often touted as a better option for women than our current first-past-the-post (FPTP) system, with proponents citing the high proportion of women in politics in Scandinavian countries with PR as proof (Norris 280). Yet what tends to be overlooked is that with PR the onus still falls on the political party. For instance, in list systems, if parties are not interested in putting women high on their lists, women are not liable to be elected. Moreover, PR advocates often fail to recognize that in countries with more women politicians, there may be other contributing factors beyond PR at play. The activism of the women's movement in concert with the state and political parties is a crucial consideration (Skjele). Forging connections between the formal and informal political may produce a more conducive environment for under-represented groups than simply a change in electoral system that leaves party pre-eminence intact.

Political parties have not been paragons of democratic restructuring, though some have put nominal reforms in place—given that most people agree that under-representation of women and people of racial and ethnic minorities is regrettable (Howe and Northrup). When "the stakes are raised, however, to include more decisive guarantees of political presence, the potential backing often drops away" (A. Phillips 22).

For those women politicians who manage to get elected and wish to make change, it becomes all too apparent that bucking longstanding political trends is not easy. As Linda Trimble reminds us,

> *Research conducted in the United States, Norway and Canada indicates that female legislators are more likely than their male counterparts to support the women's movement and tend to have different policy preferences. . . . Yet, in all three countries it seems that female legislators are at times unwilling or unable to translate these preferences into action because their choices are inhibited by ideological and institutional factors such as party positions on gender-equality goals, support for (or antipathy toward) women in the institutional environment, and the mechanics of the legislative process itself. (130)*

A numerically representative legislature does not guarantee more substantive representation of interests and identities. Political theorists and activists alike have come to recognize that standing for is not acting for.

Lisa Young submits that in Canada one could only begin to act for women if the party system were substantially recast in relation to gender. She suggests not only securing gender parity in upper echelons of political parties (through bringing down barriers to women's participation or through representational quotas) but also ensuring that half the parliamentary or legislative caucus be female (204). Yet the problem persists that the presence of women does not guarantee that they would be able to influence policy changes to benefit women, or guarantee that women's diverse interests and identities would be represented. Young recognizes that the system would only be transformed by *including feminist stances on policy issues in its electoral platform, where they would figure prominently, not merely as an afterthought or addendum. As the party developed new policies on a range of issues, their gendered dimensions would be considered and incorporated . . . [and if] elected the party would move to enact these policies with . . . speed and diligence. (204)*

But how would this happen if increased numbers of women representatives holds no guarantees? More women will just have to work within the same old strictures and structures. How can radical alternative visions, like those of feminism, be integrated into conventional institutions or parties that tend to shy away from controversial policies and demands?

The foregoing recommendations are simply not far-reaching enough, for they revolve around the current institutional political and liberal democratic constructs. Citizens are increasingly calling for something more than the traditional institutions of democratic governance. According to Clarke et al., there is "a serious thirst among Canadians" for not just maintaining but "extending the spaces of democratic politics" (411). One option would be to give greater legitimacy to political groups that have operated more on the "outside" than the "inside" of conventional politics. This is not simply a call for liberal pluralism, rather, it would be a radical democratic project incorporating collective action and interaction. It would require a formal response to social movement politics and the enlistment of a broad spectrum of special interests and identities.

As we face the new century, a more formalized, legitimate yet non-partisan, space that reinforces collective identity and aspirations is necessary. This would be, paradoxically, an institutional response to the non-institutional, an authentic and structured response that features the unconventional political and various forms of community activism. Only through the incorporation of alternate forms of representation, particularly via social movement organizations, can the old-style, opaque, elitist, individualistic and adversarial politics of the present be challenged.

This would not involve replacing one system with another by supplanting liberal democracy with radical democracy, rather, it would transcend dichotomous political understandings and behaviour and develop a new political synthesis.

AN INFUSION OF THE NON-INSTITUTIONAL POLITICAL: INCLUDING RADICAL DEMOCRATIC POTENTIAL

Given women's limited substantive gains in official politics, it is not surprising that women's movements in Canada have been ambivalent about liberal democracy and the political party system. Whereas Canadian women, and women around the world, have been under-represented in conventional politics, they have been over-represented in the unconventional (Vickers). So, rather than reforming existing institutions where women have been weak, why not build on those forms of politics where women have been strong; working not just within traditional liberal democratic institutions but also from without. To ensure that women are no longer excluded, however, there must be a radical democratic impetus, fundamental accommodations inside to make space for movements typically on the outside. Moreover, these new and expansive political premises should be open not just to women, but to other heretofore neglected identity groups. This would mean more than a politics of recognition, then, but a politics of transformation, nudged forward via formal and informal political alliances.

While subordinate groups would still need to deliberate free from the surveillance of traditional institutions of democratic governance, in order for the concerns of the former to be accepted and acted upon, there must be a degree of connection to the latter. With this comes the ever present danger that "organizational hierarchies and specialised representational roles [may] reinforce the subordination which women's groups [and other collective identities] are seeking to redress" (Sawer 7). If the new arrangements are constructed to circumvent such obstacles, however, the risks may be minimized, for it is precisely at the juncture of representative and participatory democracy that my suggestion lies: creating new political spaces in old political places. The objective is "to reconnect politics to needs, interests and collective attachments" (Krieger 173). Negotiating binary political structures will not be easy, but the proposition is to construct leverage points in institutional politics for non-institutional politics. Assemblies or fora that are context dependent are sites for critical contestation where women and other actors could challenge liberal individualism, but also collaborate and consult to formulate workable political alternatives. Fostering alliance building, encouraging creative exchanges and being exposed to changing relationships would address Iris Marion Young's concerns about frozen identities and normalization. By being grounded in, and keeping lines of communication open with, various communities through continuous networking locally and globally, the hope is that these assemblies would pre-empt individualist and universalist tendencies.

The main responsibility of these fora would be to gather, produce and share knowledge of many interconnected forms of oppression, gender among them. Initially, efforts would be directed inward, with information gathering and having input into conventional political decision-making processes a priority. These new bodies would collect information to form legislation and plan policy directives that are grounded and dialogical, as opposed to decontextualized and promotional. They would not be secondary, remote from the seat of primary political power. On the contrary, their very presence presumes that traditional political decision-making would have improved through the integration of diverse, traditionally marginalized groups.

These fora would work at building productive relationships between formal and informal political structures. They would be "iterative, ongoing, open-ended, co-decisional in nature" (Mendelsohn 264), alternative conduits to conventional political decision-makers providing more imaginative and substantive policy options. With principles of accountability and transparency, participants would toil together with political officials to arrive at solutions to vexing issues. Collaborative projects would entail deliberation and intensive negotiations to provide antidotes to quick fixes and politically expedient short-term policy thinking. Equally significant, the work of participants in these new assemblies would be directed outward, getting input and information from diverse communities and dispersing political potential. They would include a changing array of participants with extensive grassroots contacts. There would be a recognition that no single person or group is fully representative but, rather, are "subjects of activity...constituted in relation to one another" (Jakobsen 147). Participants' work in and between various communities would be their credentials.

Heterogeneity, not homogeneity, would form the nucleus of these new political spaces. Their *modus operandi* would be connecting with others, articulating others' needs and promoting other understandings. While working on consensus and striving for compromise, they would acknowledge that unanimity is not always possible, that complexity and contradiction exist, and so, they would act as incubators for experimentation and creativity. They would allow for fallibility and fungibility, admitting that through trial and error growth can occur. All these elements are necessary given that the ultimate goal is to produce inclusive, imaginative, grounded programmes oriented towards comprehensive problem solving, as well as to transforming politics and cultures.

It could be said that this approach amounts to attaching simply more desirable qualities to preferred actors and locales, but, consider the unique political potential of social movements. In their aspirations and in their political struggles, social movements constitute an alternative, often creative, force in politics. As Susan Phillips writes, "By definition, social movements are unconventional, that is, they are engaged in political and cultural conflicts that question the status quo and prevailing world views, challenge privilege, and offer new meaning systems" (377). Representation and participation lie at the heart of social movements, their existence hinges on constructing, deconstructing, reconstructing, responding to, as well as challenging, collective identities. Their aim is not just to democratize standard political forms, but to democratize everyday life (Melucci), to do which they deploy a range of tactics (Dobrowolsky "Of Special Interest"; *The Politics*). Positive outcomes are not inevitable, mistakes have been made and hard lessons have been learned. For example, the women's movement has become aware that "an important starting point must be a recognition of the diversity of women's experiences and the specificity of oppressions that particular women face. This is essential if marginalized groups are to become visible and develop their own perspectives, rather than being added to existing frameworks" (Bryson 66). The claim here is that creating a more conducive political environment for the women's movement and for other social movements will deepen and widen democracy and fundamentally challenge liberal assumptions.

LESSONS FROM REAL LIFE

Canada has flirted with elements of the foregoing proposals. Judy Rebick reminds us of the existence of citizen fora in the 1920s, 1930s and 1940s in Nova Scotia, Saskatchewan and federally (83). Prior to the Charlottetown Accord of 1992, a series of constitutional conferences across the country brought together politicians, citizens and group representatives. Participants moved beyond individual and/or vested interests, dispensed with preconceived notions and seriously negotiated commitments and compromises (Dobrowolsky, *The Politics*; Mendelsohn). The process failed when political officials did not respond to the conference recommendations and, in the end, the Accord was defeated by popular referendum.

There have been efforts to forge social partnerships, given that without collaboration among individuals and groups, effective policies and programmes would not exist. The consultations around Bill C-49 provide one example. After the Supreme Court struck down the rape shield law (which limited the questioning of a complainant's past sexual history in sexual assault trials) a coalition of diverse women's groups (Canadian Advisory Council on the Status of Women; Disabled Women's Network; National Action Committee on the Status of Women; National Association of Women and the Law; National Organization of Immigrant and Visible Minority Women; Native Women's Association of Canada; Prostitutes and Other Women for Equal Rights; Canadian Association of Sexual Assault Centres; Canadian Nurses' Association; and Women's Legal Education and Action Fund) advised the Minister of Justice, Kim Campbell. The minister and her staff caucused with certain groups and followed this with further consultations with a wider array of women including "black women, lesbians, sex trade workers" (McIntyre 309). This helped to produce legislation to mitigate some of the law's harm to women.

What explains such political enterprises, and what accounts for their non-extension or their demise? The pre-Charlottetown Accord conferences in part reflected the willingness of Tory Constitutional Affairs Minister, Joe Clark, to experiment in the unenviable, apparently no-win, task of negotiating a post-Meech Lake deal. The case of Bill C-49 may be attributed to the priorities of a woman Justice minister. Although Kim Campbell's party's record in relation to women was patchy, she was a self-described feminist and professed a commitment to consultation and a willingness to court new kinds of politics.

The demise of such initiatives can be explained by various factors from cost benefit analyses (too much time, effort, resources involved) to the lack of sustained political support in a neoliberal era. Brian Mulroney did not expect his Constitutional Affairs minister to succeed (Russell 196), and when Joe Clark made progress the prime minister took over and pushed ahead with more customary executive federalist-style constitutional negotiations. Since then, democratic experiments like constitutional conferences have been dismissed as too expensive, time consuming, complicated and, ultimately, ineffectual (Lusztig; Ajzenstat). After becoming party leader and then Prime Minister, Kim Campbell's efforts to do politics differently were quashed, in part through internal party machinations reminiscent of the deterrents described above by Linda Trimble.

But socio-economic forces do change and they need not be all determining. Political actors can make different political choices and create new political opportunities (Dobrowolsky, "Political Parties"). Developments in the United Kingdom (UK) are particularly apt, given that Canada and the UK share similar institutions (liberal, representative, parliamentary, single member plurality systems). Through concerted mobilization from women's movements, the Labour Party has been swayed to a certain extent. The results have been mixed with a Women's Unit, established by the Labour government upon its election in 1997, not meeting expectations, for it proved to be too far removed from the Labour government's policy-making priorities (Perkins); nonetheless, the British have committed some resources to building a "femocratic" network, while the Canadian government has been dismantling the "woman's state." In the UK there have been some noteworthy political openings given various pressures on the party to commit to political modernization.

There seems to be real potential for new kinds of politics advocated in other parts of the UK. In Scotland, for instance, with the advent of a Scottish Parliament, women not only mobilized for improved numerical representation, with a 50/50 male/female legislature (missing this threshold, but nonetheless doubling Westminster levels with 37% women, mainly through twinning), but it was also recognized that more substantive representation required new and distinctive political arrangements (W. Brown). This meant advocating a "woman-friendly" Parliament by trying to mitigate adversarialism and partisanship, and introducing practical measures such as avoiding after school sessions and not sitting during school holidays. It all resulted in commitments to various consultative mechanisms, including a Civic Forum and a Scottish Women's Consultative Network, creating space for civil society in the Scottish Parliament, and making community networks a priority.

CONCLUDING COMMENTS AND CAUTIONS

Where does this leave the Canadian context now and in the future? In the short term, parliamentarians should begin to appreciate and access, not denigrate or dismiss, the potential contributions of social movements. This means re-instituting and increasing funding to women's organizations and to other collective groups. Intra- and inter-movement networking organizations must be encouraged and subsidized, so that groups can share material and resources, instead of spending their time raising, or competing for, scarce funds.

In the longer term, the goal should be a response to various collective identities through institutions that work on creating more of a synthesis between liberal and radical democracy. This means not only refurbishing existing institutions, reforming committees and the like, but building new political sites. These would include not only state-tied bodies like women's units and equality committees, but also organizations that transcend typical representational forms. Bodies like the CACSW should be restored, but this time ensuring that they are closer to policy-makers *and* more connected to women's movements. New ways to inject radical democracy into existing structures should be created, like the Civic Fora experiments in the UK.

These changes are not without major challenges. For instance, as Mendelsohn acknowledges, they can be passed off as mere "gimmicks" or "entertainment" that merely "legitimize prior decisions, or [act] as nothing more than interesting academic exercises with no public policy implications" (269). But the widely based agreement that current political activities and outcomes are deficient, and the fact that citizens' faith in them has plunged to new lows, may provide the incentive to make serious commitments to change, though in our results-oriented climate, such enterprises might be ruled out as being inefficient, or not worth risking given indeterminate, unquantifiable outcomes. Russell Dalton urges,

We should remember that democratic politics is not designed to maximize government efficiency and increase the autonomy of political elites. Just the opposite. Efficiency is partially sacrificed to ensure a more important goal: popular control of elites. Expanding participation is not a problem but an opportunity to come closer to matching...democratic ideals. (283)

Some feminists might caution that an approach based on multiple identities, coalitions and alliances may water down women's demands. This is a valid concern, but working with others can help to develop more comprehensive analyses of oppression, how forms of oppression intersect and how to counteract them (Morrow 253). There are also the critiques of identity politics, that they promote exclusionary and fragmented identities. But, again, efforts to interact with diverse groups, acknowledging interdependence given the interrelated nature of structural inequalities, and being open to changing relationships will help to attenuate these problems.

In conclusion, current liberal democratic practices and discourses are inadequate means for dealing with women's political exclusion. Given the norms of institutional politics, the fact that they have been constructed and are dominated by white men and reflect equality myths and entrenched individualistic values, conventional political reforms will not suffice. They operate in a circumscribed framework of cutthroat partisan politics, and an adversarial, executive-dominated, elitist parliamentary system. Instead, what is required is the promotion of alternative political spaces that open up political ideas and institutions to more diverse collective identities. Canada's political future should reflect a synthesis of democratic forms where the exclusions of each are addressed, and the inclusion of each can be mutually reinforcing. Connections and complementarity should be valued. Promoting this democratic medley would not be problem-free, but it provides the most heartening scenario for, in the final analysis, as bell hooks wisely observed, visionary politics will only emerge from those with knowledge of both margin and centre.

References

Agnew, Vijay. *Resisting Discrimination: Women From Asia, Africa, and the Caribbean and the Women's Movement in Canada.* Toronto: University of Toronto Press, 1996.

Bashevkin, Sylvia. *Women on the Defensive.* Toronto: University of Toronto Press, 1998.

Bernstein, Mary. "Celebration and Suppression: The Strategic Uses of Identity by the Lesbian and Gay Movement." *American Journal of Sociology* 103.3 (1997): 435–44.

Brown, Wendy. *States of Injury: Power and Freedom in Late Modernity.* Princeton: Princeton University Press, 1995.

Bryson, Valerie. *Feminist Debates: Issues of Theory and Political Practice.* New York: New York University Press, 1999.

Butler, Judith. *Gender Trouble: Feminism and the Subversion of Identity.* New York: Routledge, 1990.

Canada. Royal Commission on Electoral Reform and Party Financing. *Reforming Electoral Democracy.* Ottawa: Supply and Services, 1991.

Clarke, Harold D. and Jane Jenson, Lawrence Leduc and Jon H. Pammett. "Absent Mandate: Canadian Electoral Politics in an Era of Restructuring." *Party Politics in Canada.* Eds. Hugh G. Thorburn and Alan Whitehorn. Toronto: Prentice Hall, 2001. 398–412.

Collins, Patricia Hill. *Black Feminist Thought: Knowledge, Consciousness and the Politics of Empowerment.* New York: Routledge, Chapman &; Hall, 1990.

Dalton, Russel. *Citizen Politics: Public Opinion and Political Parties in Advanced Western Democracies,* 2nd. ed. Chatham: Chatham House, 1998.

Dobrowolsky, Alexandra. "Political Parties: Teletubby Politics, the Third Way and Democratic Challenge(r)s." *Canadian Politics in the 21st Century.* Eds. Michael Whittington and Glen Williams. Scarborough: Nelson, 2000. 131–58.

——. "Shifting States: Women's Constitutional Organizing Across Space and Time." *Women's Movements Facing the Reconfigured State.* Eds. Lee Anne Banaszak, Karen Beckwith and Dieter Rucht. Princeton: Princeton University Press, forthcoming.

——. *The Politics of Pragmatism: Women, Representation and Constitutionalism in Canada.* Toronto: Oxford University Press, 2000.

Drieger, Diane, Irene Feika and Eileen Girón Batres. *Across Borders: Women with Disabilities Working Together.* Charlottetown: Gynergy Books, 1996.

Howe, Paul and David Northrup. "Strengthening Canadian Democracy: The Views of Canadians." *Policy Matters Institute for Research on Public Policy* 1.5 (2000): 3–104.

Jakobsen, Janet R. *Working Alliances and the Politics of Difference: Diversity and Feminist Ethics.* Bloomington: Indiana University Press, 1998.

Jenson, Jane. "Understanding Politics: Concepts of Identity in Political Science." *Canadian Politics.* Eds. James Bickerton and Alain G. Gagnon. Peterborough: Broadview, 1999. 39–56.

Jhappan, Radha. "Post-Modern Race and Gender Essentialism or a Post-Mortem of Scholarship." *Studies in Political Economy* 51 (1996): 15–63.

Krieger. Joel. *British Politics in the Global Age: Can Social Democracy Survive?* New York: Oxford University Press, 1999.

Kymlicka, Will. *Multicultural Citizenship.* Oxford: Oxford University Press, 1995.

McIntyre, Sheila. "Redefining Reformism: The Consultations that Shaped Bill C-49." *Confronting Sexual Assault: A Decade of Legal and Social Change.* Eds. Julian V. Roberts and Renate M. Mohr. Toronto: University of Toronto Press, 1994. 293–326.

Melucci, Alberto. "Social Movements and the Democratization of Everyday Life." *Civil Society and the State.* Ed. John Keane. London: Verso, 1988. 245–60.

Mendelsohn, Matthew. "Public Brokerage: Constitutional Reform and the Accommodation of Mass Publics." *Canadian Journal of Political Science* 33.2 (2000): 245–72.

Mohanty, Chandra Talpade "Under Western Eyes: Feminist Scholarship and Colonial Discourses." *Third World Women and the Politics of Feminism.* Eds. Chandra T. Mohanty, Anne Russo and Lourdes Torres. Bloomington: Indiana University Press, 1991. 51–80.

Morrow, Marina Helen. "Feminist Anti-Violence Activism: Organizing for Change." *Reclaiming the Future: Women's Strategies for the 21st Century.* Ed. Somer Brodribb. Charlottetown: Gynergy Books, 1999. 237–57.

Nakano Glenn, Evelyn. The Social Construction and Institutionalization of Gender and Race: An Integrative Framework. *Revisioning Gender.* Eds. Myra Marx Ferree, Judith Lorber and Beth Hess. London: Sage, 1999. 3–43.

Perkins, A. "Take Two." *The Guardian* [London] 1 June 1999: 6.

Phelan, Shane. "The Space of Justice: Lesbians and Democratic Politics." *Social Postmodernism: Beyond Identity Politics.* Eds. Linda Nicholson and Steven Seidman. Cambridge: Cambridge University Press, 1999. 332–56.

Phillips, Anne. *The Politics of Presence.* Oxford: Clarendon Press, 1995.

Phillips, Susan. "Social Movements in Canadian Politics: Past Their Apex? *Canadian Politics.* Eds. James Bickerton and Alain G. Gagnon. Peterborough: Broadview Press 1999. 371–91

Rebick, Judy. *Imagine Democracy.* Toronto: Stoddart, 2000.

Sawer, Marian. "Representation of Women: Questions of Accountability." Paper for IPSA Conference, Quebec, 1–5 August 2000.

Spellman, Elizabeth. *Inessential Woman.* Boston: Beacon Press, 1988.

Squires, Judith. "Quotas for Women: Fair Representation?" *Parliamentary Affairs* 49.1 (1996): 71–88.

Stone, Sharon Dale. "From Stereotypes to Visible Diversity: Lesbian Political Organizing." *Organizing Dissent Contemporary Social Movements in Theory and Practice."* Ed. William Carroll. Toronto: Garamond, 1997. 171–96.

Taylor, Charles. "Shared and Divergent Values." *Options for a New Canada.* Eds. Ronald L. Warts and Douglas M. Brown. Toronto: University of Toronto Press, 1991. 53–76.

Trimble, Linda. "Feminist Politics in the Alberta Legislature." *In the Presence of Women: Representation in Canadian Governments.* Eds. Jane Arscott and Linda Trimble. Toronto: Harcourt Brace, 1997 128–53.

Vickers, Jill. *Reinventing Political Science.* Halifax: Fernwood, 1997.

Williams, Melissa. *Voice, Trust, and Memory: Marginalized Groups and the Failings of Liberal Representation.* Princeton: Princeton University Press, 1998.

Young, Lisa. *Feminists and Party Politics.* Vancouver: UBC Press, 2000.

Managing Trade Engagements?: Mapping the Contours of State Feminism and Women's Political Activism

Christina Gabriel and Laura Macdonald

Christina Gabriel's specific research interests focus on gender, citizenship and migration, North American regional integration and globalization. She has co-authored (with Yasmeen Abu-Laban) Selling Diversity: Immigration, Multiculturalism, Employment Equity, and Globalization *(2002). She currently holds a three-year SSHRC grant (2006–2009) with Dr. Laura Macdonald and Dr. Rianne Mahon for a joint study, "Social Citizenship in North America."*

Laura Macdonald is a Professor and Chair in the Department of Political Science and the Institute of Political Economy at Carleton University. She publishes in the area of the role of non-governmental organizations in development, global civil society, citizenship struggles in Latin America and the political impact of the North American Free Trade Agreement (NAFTA) on human rights and democracy in the three member states.

INTRODUCTION

In recent years, women's groups both in Canada and abroad have highlighted the importance of changing trade relations for gender equality. Feminist economists and others have argued that changing trade relations are not gender neutral, but have a differential impact on men and women based on their access to resources, education and market opportunities, among other factors (Macdonald 1999; 2004). At the same time, feminist activism has been successful in pressuring many Western democratic states, including Canada, to develop women's policy machinery and gender-based policy analysis. In this article, we analyze the failure of official Canadian commitments to adopting gender-equity policies to have an impact on Canadian trade policy. We argue that this failure must be understood within the context of broader restructuring of the Canadian state and state–society relations within the context of neoliberal globalization. As Jane Jenson and Susan Phillips (1996) have argued, the Canadian "citizenship regime" has undergone dramatic changes in recent years. Their analysis of regime shift is primarily directed to changes in the domestic realm. However, in this article, we argue that neoliberal globalization destabilizes pre-existing divisions between the national and the international, and puts strain on domestic practices of citizenship and representation. In this environment, changes in the citizenship regime in part ensure that state policies related to international economic policy are increasingly insulated from domestic pressures and particularly impervious to critiques from women's movements and others. This argument is illustrated with reference to women's political activism around the Canadian trade agenda.

CITIZENSHIP REGIMES, STATE FEMINISM AND THE LIBERAL DEMOCRATIC STATE IN CANADA

Our assessment of women's political activism around the Canadian trade agenda takes as its starting point a consideration of the liberal democratic state as a key space of feminist political engagement. Following recent feminist theory, we see the state "not [as] a unitary structure but a differentiated set of institutions, agencies and discourses, and the product of a particular historical and political conjuncture" (Waylen 1998: 7). This understanding allows us to consider the opportunities and constraints that the phenomenon of state feminism in Canada presents for women's activism around trade issues.

The concept of citizenship regime further elucidates the way in which state forms and discourses are changing within the context of neoliberal globalization. In their influential article, *Regime Shift: New Citizenship Practices in Canada*, Jenson and Phillips (1996: 113) argue that citizenship regimes "exist as the concretization in a particular place of a general model of citizenship." Citizenship is a social construct that establishes a system of inclusion and exclusion that has two key dimensions: "citizenship as the conferring of rights, and citizenship as grounding for feelings of identification with a particular community" (Ibid: 114). Citizenship regimes help order social relationships, and define the relationship between the state and society, and forms of legitimate representation of citizens.

Jenson and Philips argue that there has been a broad change in state-society relations associated with a shift from the postwar citizenship regime to the current, neoliberal model, involving not just a change in the relationship between states and markets but also a fundamental restructuring of citizens' relationship with the state. They suggest that the postwar regime in Canada recognized citizens as individuals and as members of particular groups. In fact, government departments provided funding to advocacy groups, such as women's groups. Consequently, as Jenson and Phillips (1996: 118–119) state: "achieving social justice and equity were legitimate goals, and therefore groups which made claims, and programs which responded to such claims, were in the political mainstream." The second wave of the women's movement, which emerged in the mid-1960s, operated within this social environment.

Jenson and Phillips (1996: 114) further emphasize that state institutions are engaged in a "politics of recognition" that recognizes some groups and their claims as part of the ongoing process of "stabilizing or altering the citizenship regime." Women and women's advocacy groups were constructed as legitimate actors within the postwar citizenship regime. The recognition of their particular needs "for access to the state provided a protected institutional space for claims-making" (Ibid: 119). An aspect of this recognition was the establishment of internal mechanisms within the Canadian state to represent women's interests. These internal state mechanisms have been characterized as a form of state feminism, and have been the subject of scrutiny by feminist scholars. State feminism "refers to the activities of government structures that are formally charged with furthering women's status and rights. At issue is the extent to which these agencies are effective in helping women as a group and in undermining patterns of gender-based inequities in society" (Stetson and Mazur 1995: 1–2).

Today, as we discuss below, both women's groups and the organizations that represent them within the state find themselves on the margins. This is related, according to Jenson and Phillips, to the transformation of the citizenship regime in the 1990s. As a result, group action and the espousal of social justice are giving way to new individualized conceptions of citizenship (Jenson and Phillips 1996: 119–120). Thus both grassroots activists and "femocrats" within the state itself have to negotiate within an environment where not just social justice and equity goals are vociferously debated, but the very notion of collective group disadvantage is rejected. This has important implications in terms of whose claims are rendered legitimate and whose are sidelined, and regarding the ability of women's groups to influence the decision-making process in certain policy areas, such as international trade, that are central to neoliberal reform.

Jenson and Phillips (1996: 120–121) argue that these neoliberal policies were linked to a restructuring of the Canadian postwar citizenship regime. This restructuring involved three key elements:

1. the restructuring of state institutions to lower the visibility of certain categories of citizens, like women;
2. an attack on the credibility of advocacy groups; and
3. the delivery of state services under a rubric of partnerships.

Below, we discuss how these changes negatively affected the capacity of women's groups to inject gender issues into trade debates.

The shift from the assumptions that underwrote the Keynesian postwar welfare state in Canada, as Jenson and Phillips' framework suggests, to current neoliberal understandings that structure the leaner state, have had profound implications for both the grassroots women's movement in Canada and for those women working within the state to advance a women's agenda. Canada, like many other countries in the North, embraced neoliberal ideas in response to processes of globalization. Through the 1980s and 1990s, both Progressive Conservative and Liberal governments moved to address deficits by cutting public programs, retrenching the state and privatizing public goods. Additionally, market-oriented solutions were valorized as the means to address problems in society and economy (Gabriel 1999).

However, the centrepiece of the neoliberal agenda was the emphasis on promoting an export-led growth strategy through trade liberalization. Accordingly, Canada entered the Canada–U.S. Free Trade Agreement in 1988 and subsequently the North American Free Trade Agreement (NAFTA) in 1994. It is beyond the scope of this paper to detail the gender impacts of neoliberal policy rationales and trade liberalization here (see Cohen 1997; Macdonald 1999). However, the policy discourse emphasizing trade liberalization and pro-market policies entailed a number of changes within the national state that had gendered consequences. Australian feminist scholar Marian Sawer captures some aspects of this change when she talks about the increasingly influential role played by economic rationalists, "ecorats". Officials working under this label, she points out, see the welfare state as an impediment to competitiveness and champion market-based solutions. In doing so, they reject the social citizenship norms associated with the postwar welfare state. Yet, as femocrats recognize, women as a group are more dependent on the welfare state than men. Consequently, the dominant rationales of ecorats bring them up against femocrats, whose position often necessitates a defense of welfare state provisions and equity agendas. Increasingly, Sawer argues, "femocrats had to shift from social justice discourse to market discourse (stressing human resource and efficiency arguments for gender equity) in order to be 'heard'" (Sawer 1996: 3). The triumph of economic rationalism and the subsequent move toward further liberalization of international trade and investment rules has important implications for the women's state in Canada and women's activism.

To sum up, we argue that the failure until now of women's activism to influence Canada's trade agenda has to be interpreted in the light of broader changes in the nature of the state and citizenship regimes in Canada, and changes related to globalization.

MAPPING GRASSROOTS MOVEMENTS, WOMEN'S POLICY MACHINERY AND STATE FEMINISM

1972–1984—CONSTRUCTION OF WOMEN'S POLICY MACHINERY

In the first period examined here, 1972 to 1984, the state reached out to women's organizations and encouraged the formal representation of women's interests within the postwar citizenship regime, both inside and outside the state. One of the key landmarks in the state's recognition of women's interests and claims was the Royal Commission on the Status of Women (RCSW), established in 1967. The government was prompted to establish a commission as a result of women's activism in both English- and French-speaking Canada along with developments abroad. The RCSW ultimately produced 167 recommendations that in effect provided a blueprint for government action (cf. Bégin 1992; Andrew and Rodgers 1997).

In the wake of the Royal Commission's Report, women's groups met in 1972 and pledged to monitor the government's implementation of the report's recommendations. This meeting resulted in the birth of the National Action Committee on the Status of Women (NAC). This umbrella group would provide one of the most significant challenges to the neoliberal free trade agenda in subsequent years. In its initial period, however, it functioned more as a lobby group (Vickers et. al. 1993: 66). At the same time, however, the Canadian women's movement and NAC's own membership contained a variety of other orientations and strategies. In addition to the liberal feminists who in the beginning dominated the public face of the movement, socialist feminists worked on a number of fronts. They debated and organized around the value of housework, and many of them were engaged in "working class feminism" within and outside the unions (Maroney 1987). Ultimately, it would be the latter group of activists, as we discuss below, who would play an influential role in confronting the government's proposals for free trade.

Overall, in this initial period Canadian women in the movement had not yet directed their energies towards macro-economic policy. Indeed, for most of the 1970s, "women's confrontation with the federal government over national economic policy was muted" (Cohen 1993b: 265). This was related, Cohen suggests, to pragmatic decisions about where to focus limited energies and resources. Cohen is careful to point out that women's groups did not neglect economic issues. The RCSW detailed numerous recommendations directed at women and work issues. The grassroots movement itself was engaged in struggles around the workplace, including employment equity, pay equity and unemployment insurance reform. However, these were largely single-issue campaigns. Through them, she argues, " . . . the significance of overall economic policy (or what economists refer to as macro-economic policy) became apparent. Women might spend years, for example, struggling for legal changes related to equal pay, but ultimately achieving equal pay legislation could be subverted by economic policies that were eliminating jobs altogether" (Cohen 1993b: 266). In many ways, then, these single-issue struggles were the precursor for women's activism around neoliberal trade policy.

In trying to address women's economic status through the use of single-issue campaigns, women activists looked to potential allies and points of access within the state. The creation of women's policy machinery, a development linked to the RCSW's recommendations, provided such a space. This machinery included the Canadian Advisory Council on the Status of Women (CACSW), a Women's Program within the Department of the Secretary of State (1973) and Status of Women Canada (1971) (O'Neil and Sutherland 1998: 210–211). In this respect, this machinery became one mechanism for women as a group to achieve representation and make citizenship claims (Jenson and Phillips 1996: 121).

It should be noted that the Women's Program within the Department of Secretary of State was particularly important to grassroots women's groups in Canada. Its mandate was to promote "the development of a society in which the full potential of women as citizens is recognized and utilized", (Pal cited by Burt 1999: 404) and it did so by providing grants to women's organizations for core and project funding. Its budget in 1973 was $223 000. By 1987 this had grown to $12.4 million (Burt 1999: 404). During this period NAC drew most of its funds from government grants (Geller-Schwartz 1995: 55).

The other key structure, Status of Women Canada (SWC), was much more closely linked to the government through the Minister Responsible for the Status of Women. Initially its role was designed as a coordinating one between government departments, but in 1976 its mandate was broadened to "include 'analyzing policies, programs and legislation for their impact on women' and 'recommending changes' as well as 'initiating' policies to 'advance women's equality'" (SWC cited by Geller-Schwartz 1995: 47). While this mandate is laudable, assessments of SWC have outlined a number of structural constraints. First, SWC staff has to negotiate the tension between being part of the formal bureaucracy while representing the concerns of the women's movement outside the state. In doing so, they come up against the conventions governing the bureaucracy, such as public service neutrality, and suspicions of the grassroots movements. In terms of the former, for example, "the idea that civil servants should adopt the role of internal lobbyists for women as a definable group was an anathema" (Geller-Schwartz, 1995: 49).

More significantly, the positioning of SWC within the state and its limited resources has meant that it was unable to fulfill its mandate effectively. SWC is designated as a "stand alone agency" and, as such, does not occupy a very influential institutional position within the state. This initial weak institutional positioning coupled with a small budget remains the same today. It has significant implications because SWC has emerged today as the one key department to represent women's interests—however defined—within what Rianne Mahon (1977) has termed an "unequal structure of representation." That is, it has to contend with more entrenched well-established departments, Finance and Trade for example, which represent particularly powerful interests.

1984–1995—WOMEN AS "SPECIAL INTERESTS"

The election of the Progressive Conservative Party under the leadership of Brian Mulroney marked the beginning of a decided shift from the practices and policies that characterized the postwar citizenship regime. In the period from the mid-1980s to the mid-1990s, the Canadian state wholeheartedly embraced economic rationalism, bringing it into conflict with Canadian women's groups. Many of the goals of the mainstream movement, such as universal daycare and employment equity, required both greater public spending and government regulation in the labour market and society, not less. This social agenda was at odds with the government's focus on the deficit and market-based solutions. Women's groups began to actively organize to confront the government and challenge cuts in a host of social services. NAC, for example, was at the forefront of this activism.

It was during this period that grassroots women's movements also began to pay greater attention to macro-economic issues. The federal government's decision to negotiate a Canada–U.S. Free Trade Agreement proved to be a decisive point in the government's increasingly conflictual relationship with NAC. NAC raised concerns about the gender impact of the proposed agreement not just in terms of job loss but also in terms of its possible impact on social services. It also spearheaded a broadly based social justice coalition, Coalition Against Free Trade (later the ProCanada Network), which challenged free trade (Cohen 1993b: 278). It played a similarly active role in the debate around NAFTA and forged and developed links with women's groups in United States and Mexico (Gabriel and Macdonald 1994).

Throughout this entire period as NAC criticized the federal government's "core economic priority", it was still funded through the Women's Program of the Secretary of State. Ironically, the Canadian state itself provided the resources that gave NAC the capacity to criticize the government of the day. This anomalous situation came to a quick end when the Progressive Conservatives cut NAC's funding in half between 1990 and 1992 (Sawer 1996: 16).

Despite the gendered criticisms of the free trade agreements that NAC and other grassroots women's groups were raising, SWC kept a low profile on the issue of free trade in this period. This was not surprising, given the fact that the federal government was actively espousing trade liberalization.

Despite the fact that there appeared to be a disjuncture between the position of activists and those women working within the state in terms of their position on the government's trade agenda, the fate of both was implicitly tied together. That is, they were all working within an environment that was increasingly hostile to women's issues, and to women's representatives within and outside of the state. As Jenson and Phillips argue, in this period of restructuring of the postwar citizenship regime, the Canadian state undertook a series of measures of great importance to the Canadian women's movement. First, mechanisms that existed earlier that promoted the representation of the interests of certain categories of citizens were eroded or removed. This is epitomized, as they point out, by the dismantling of the "women's state" that took place in the early 1990s. In short order, Jean Chrétien's Liberal government, which succeeded the Tories in 1993, abolished the Canadian Advisory Council on the Status of Women and integrated the Women's Program into Status of Women Canada. Additionally, the position of Minister Responsible for Women's Issues was downgraded to Secretary of State Responsible for the Status of Women. These measures were rationalized by the government as both cost cutting measures and as a consolidation of women's programs. However, Jenson and Phillips challenge this justification and write: "Thus the surviving institution of the former Women's State can be most easily controlled by its 'political masters' with less capacity to act as an internal advocate for women. The signal is clear. Groups should be self-supporting and voluntary. The state experiment to facilitate and even promote the collective voice of women and its representation within the state is gone" (Jenson and Phillips 1996: 123). Additionally, they note that the government also enacted a series of direct cutbacks in respect to social group funding. This had significant repercussions on the operations of many Canadian women's groups, NAC included. Furthermore, as Jenson and Phillips suggest, funding cutbacks are only part of a broader based attack on the credibility of advocacy groups (1996: 123–124). Brodie refers to this as "the politics of marginalization," whereby women's groups, for example, are discursively constructed as "special interests." Within this construct, women's groups are cast as unrepresentative of the majority of Canadian women and, by extension, a threat to democracy. Further, they are accused of promoting a particular or partial viewpoint (Brodie 1995: 68–70). Consequently, at one and the same time as women's groups, such as NAC, moved to challenge the government's trade agenda and the state's embrace of economic rationalism, they found themselves under attack and increasingly marginalized as legitimate players in a policy process. Similarly, within the Canadian state, women's policy machinery has been scaled back, but more significantly, the ability of femocrats to advance a gender assessment of policies and programs or raise gender issues is compromised by the attack on the credibility of their constituency—the grassroots movement itself.

THE EMERGENCE OF GENDER BASED ANALYSIS—1995

In the final period examined here, the shifts in Canada's citizenship regime were marked, in part, by new approaches to policy-making on issues related to gender. During this period, international trade moved to the centre of the state's economic development strategy at a time when the government was actively dismantling women's policy machinery within the state and disorganizing many women's groups in civil society. Ironically, it was also at this time that the federal government, as part of its international commitments to gender equality, adopted the principle of Gender Based Analysis (GBA) in the policy process.

The Canadian government released *Setting the Stage for the Next Century: The Federal Plan for Gender Equality* at the Fourth United Nations World Conference on Women, in Beijing in 1995. In it, GBA was defined as integral to policy analysis: "Gender analysis is based on the standpoint that policy cannot be separated from the social context, and that social issues are an integral part of economic issues. Social impact analysis, including gender analysis, is not just an add-on, to be considered after costs and benefits have been assessed, but an integral part of good policy analysis. GBA identifies how public policies differentially affect women and men" (SWC 1995: 16). The government pledged to implement GBA throughout all federal departments and agencies. This led to a variety of initiatives and approaches across the federal government, with different departments attempting to form new gender units and/or engage in the process of gender mainstreaming (Rankin and Wilcox 2004: 55). Consequently, GBA does have the potential to address how various policy choices like trade liberalization produce differential outcomes for different groups of men and women. However, as we will see in the case of trade policy, whether this potential will be realized rests both on the manner in which the internal contradictions of the approach are resolved and the degree to which it is actually implemented.

SWC was to provide the lead role in implementing the GBA commitment. To this end, it appointed a Director, Gender Based Analysis to coordinate an Interdepartmental Committee on GBA (SWC 2000: 4–5). However, as SWC itself acknowledges, "while SWC can and does influence other departments, it seldom possesses the direct authority to lead policy development" (SWC 2000: 22). Rankin and Wilcox have also pointed out that the capacity of SWC to assume the coordinating role is further compromised by its lack of resources and low visibility within the state. Increasingly, the focus is internal and procedural—how to do gender analysis—as opposed to looking on the outputs of government. This development has led to the further marginalization of the women's movement as a legitimate policy actor in the process (Rankin and Wilcox 2004: 55–57).

A number of assessments have suggested that GBA can be problematic for other reasons (Burt and Hardman 2001; Rankin and Wilcox 2004). "GBA risks slipping into a status quo approach that represents the perceptions of well-educated, well-paid, predominantly white women as if they were the perceptions of all women, particularly as the analytic focus of gender mainstreaming rests squarely on comparing the situation of women against that of men" (Rankin and Wilcox 2004: 58).

To the extent that internal gender expertise tends to be insulated from grassroots advocacy, there is a danger that differences between and among women will be neglected. The mainstream women's movement in Canada, through the 1980s and 1990s, struggled around issues of identity and difference (see Pierson 1993) and this prompted many groups to develop intersectional analysis. Debates took place within Canadian women's movement organizations but also internationally in UN forums. They underscored a key recognition that groups of women in Canada and women abroad do not experience neoliberal globalization in the same way.

The ongoing struggle with differences within the Canadian women's movement is too frequently blamed for marginalization of the movement in English Canada from national politics in the 1990s. Such accounts neglect to consider the impact of changes in state-society relations, outlined above, that actively disorganized the movement and its claims. Advocacy groups such as NAC, for example, no longer play the role they once did. Yet, as Judy Rebick astutely points out: "Feminism would have betrayed its vision and therefore lost its purpose, if it had continued to marginalize the poorest and most oppressed women to favour those more privileged. As neoliberal globalization increased the gap between rich and poor, the challenge of maintaining a common vision among women became much greater" (2005: 254). Within this context, she goes on to say, the broader backlash against feminism and cutbacks to women's organizations, "made dealing with these difficulties much harder" (2005: 255).

Yet even within this environment, the grassroots movement continues to organize, albeit in new ways. Feminists are actively involved in movements against corporate globalization.

The 2000 World March Against Poverty and Violence Against Women was a global action instigated by the Federation des Femmes du Québec. It encouraged women to organize both at a local level and internationally. In Canada, the Canadian Women's March Committee (CWMC) a broad based coalition of 24 national organizations mobilized 50 000 women to march to Ottawa. Among its "13 Immediate Demands to the Federal Government to End Poverty and Violence Against Women" were:

- Support women's organizing for equality and democracy
- Fund consultations with a wide range of women's equality-seeking organizations prior to all legislative reform of relevance to women's security and equality rights (Cited in Canadian Woman Studies 2000: 23).

In other words, as part of its broad based agenda, it was demanding that the Canadian government live up to its existing gender equality commitments.

In sum, we suggest that the shift from the assumptions that characterized the postwar citizenship regime, in which women's groups were encouraged, empowered and represented, to neoliberal understandings that currently characterize state-society relations and citizenship, in which state support for advocacy groups declined, was problematic. This shift did not mean that women's interests were suddenly ignored, but rather that the responsibility for ensuring that women's interests were met was delegated to certain rather weak state agencies, while the state, to some extent, insulated itself from outside pressures.

CONFRONTING THE TRADE AGENDA: STATUS OF WOMEN CANADA AND DEPARTMENT OF FOREIGN AFFAIRS AND INTERNATIONAL TRADE (DFAIT)

Canadian women's organizations have continued, since the FTA and NAFTA, to view organizing around globalization generally and trade agreements specifically, as a high priority. Concern has shifted somewhat from the labour market effects of free trade on women workers (particularly women of colour) to concern about the implications of free trade agreements like NAFTA and proposed agreements like the Multilateral Agreement on Investment (MAI) on social services and the state's capacity to regulate in such areas as the environment, and on the undemocratic nature of decision-making around trade policy (Cohen et al 2002). For example, in February 1999 40 Canadian women's equality-seeking organizations came together in a new coalition, the Canadian Feminist Alliance for International Action (FAFIA). FAFIA's goals are:

- to develop the capacity of women's organizations to work at the international level;
- to make links between international instruments and agreements and domestic policy-making; and
- to hold Canadian governments accountable to the commitments they have made under international human rights treaties and agreements, including the [Beijing] Platform for Action (FAFIA 2000: 4).

The groups involved in FAFIA identified trade policy as one of their core concerns. FAFIA received support from the SWC, and the member groups encouraged SWC to take on a role around Canadian trade policy.

Despite the growing national and international mobilization of women's organizations, including workshops around gender and trade issues at the Seattle WTO demonstrations and the subsequent formation of a global International Gender and Trade Network, (Macdonald 2004) Canadian Foreign Affairs and Trade ministries have remained apparently oblivious to the demands of these groups.

As Claire Turenne Sjolander (2003) states, "... the Canadian government as a whole, and the Department of Foreign Affairs and International Trade in particular, has been largely unable, and often unwilling, to consider the ways in which the global economy has a fundamentally gendered nature, and that global economic restructuring has a consequential gendered impact."

As Turenne Sjolander documents, the only area in which (individual) women do figure explicitly within the Canadian government's trade agenda is as entrepreneurs, primarily within the small and medium enterprise (SME) sector. This confirms the concern highlighted by Rankin and Wilcox that gender mainstreaming, in the absence of grassroots pressure, may result in policies that benefit a small group of affluent white women, at the expense of less privileged women. For example, on the DFAIT website, there is a "Businesswomen in Trade" site, designed to "meet the special information and assistance needs of women entrepreneurs who lead small- and medium-sized enterprises." The site is explicitly targeted at encouraging women entrepreneurs to begin exporting or to help them improve their current export performance.

Turenne Sjolander traces DFAIT's unwillingness to respond to broader gender critiques to the "discursive representations of the global economy echoed by Canadian policy makers." Within this discourse, "The gendered logic of globalization is obscured by the logic of competition, winners and losers, and the rules of the game, which reinforces the bias toward the analysis of individual circumstance at the expense of the whole—of an analysis of globalization as a series of processes which depend upon gender to function" (Turenne Sjolander 2003: 107). However, our analysis also suggests that the problem of the discursive framework promoted by globalization is compounded by institutional issues—the unequal structure of representation within the state. As we outlined above, this has involved the sidelining of the women's policy machinery within the state and, simultaneously, the cutbacks in state support to autonomous women's organizations.

In this context, the women's policy machinery has limited capacity to intervene in debates around trade policy. As Soraya Hassanali, (2000: 10) a SWC official working in the trade area, notes, "Generally, Status of Women Canada (SWC) is not viewed as an important voice within trade negotiation discussions or committees, and is not consulted on trade policy." The fact that the federal Ministry Responsible for the Status of Women, as well as Women's Bureaus within other government departments, are not players in the trade policy-making process is one of the key obstacles to integrating a gender perspective in trade policy." As Hassanali discusses, DFAIT has responded to increasing public pressure for transparency and public participation in the formulation of Canadian trade policy by establishing a series of mechanisms to facilitate consultation with civil society. Nevertheless, critics charge that fundamental biases result in an uneven playing field in which some players have a greater power than others to shape the consultation process and, ultimately, to influence Canada's trade negotiating positions (Hassanali 2000: 9; see also Macdonald and Schwartz 2002).

CONCLUSION

Contestations around gender and trade provide an interesting window into policy dynamics within neoliberal states in the context of globalization. Globalization does not eliminate state's policy autonomy, nor does it necessarily preclude achievements for women's demands in some areas—for example, Canada has recently adopted progressive measures around parental leave and childcare. As well, it is important to recognize that globalization does not operate as an implacable external force, but is internalized both discursively and in policy terms by states, and mediated through domestic state institutions, which exist in dialogue with powerful domestic interests. Nevertheless, this case study of the absence of a gender-sensitive analysis of trade policy within the Canadian government highlights the challenges faced by feminists, both inside and outside the state, in attempting to contest some of the most central elements of the government's neoliberal agenda.

Specifically, Canadian women concerned with the gender implications of trade agreements have faced the central dilemma of globalization: on the one hand, international advocacy and organizing resulted in national states adopting gender-based analysis across all policy areas, and creating policy machinery, where it did not exist, to promote women's interests. On the other hand, women's capacity to take advantage of the new spaces opened up by these international agreements has been severely limited. We attribute these limitations to two main factors: cutbacks in state support to women's groups that evolved during the Keynesian era, as well as the discursive devaluation of the broader women's movement as representing "special interests," have reduced the capacity of women's advocacy organizations to influence public policy. Simultaneously, while women's policy machinery has been created within many government departments, and SWC has been assigned the role of monitoring the government's commitments at Beijing and elsewhere, SWC's capacity to gain access to and influence public policy is also severely limited. Moreover, several key government departments that are central to the process of neoliberal restructuring, including the trade ministry, have resisted adopting a gender-based analysis and have been impervious to women's demands to open up the policy process, both to women's demands and broader public consultation. This case thus illustrates the way in which changing structures of representation of citizens' rights constrain the capacity of women's rights advocates, both inside and outside of the state, to effectively influence state policy in an area as central to the neoliberal agenda as trade policy.

References

Brodie, Janine (1995). *Politics on the Margins. Restructuring and the Canadian Women's Movement*. Halifax: Fernwood.

Burt, Sandra (1997). "Canadian Women's Movements: Revisiting Historical Patterns and Considering Present Development." In James Bickerton and Main Gagnon (eds.) *Canadian Politics* 3rd Edition. Peterborough: Broadview Press.

Burt, Sandra and Sonya Hardman (2001). "The Case of Disappearing Targets: The Liberals and Gender Equality". In Leslie Pal (ed.) *How Ottawa Spends*. 2001–2002. Toronto: Oxford University Press.

Cohen, Marjorie (1997). "From Welfare State to Vampire Capitalism." In Patricia Evans and Gerda R. Wekerle (eds.) *Women and the Canadian Welfare State*. Toronto: University of Toronto Press.

Cohen, Marjorie (1993b). "Feminism's Effects on Economic Policy." In Ruth Roach Pierson and Marjorie Cohen (eds.) *Canadian Women's Issues: Bold Visions*. (Vol. II) Toronto: Lorimer.

Cohen, Marjorie Griffin et al (2002). "Globalization: Some implications and strategies for women." *Canadian Woman Studies* (Spring/Summer) 21/22(4/1): 6–14.

FAFIA (2000). *2000 Alternative Report on Canada—Toward Women's Equality: Canada's Failed Commitment*. Prepared by Shelagh Day, Canadian Feminist Alliance for International Action, for the Special Session of the United Nations General Assembly, to review progress in implementing the Beijing Platform for Action, June. www.fafia.org/Bplus5/altrep_e.htm (February 14, 2003).

Gabriel, Christina and Laura Macdonald (1994). "NAFTA, women and organizing in Canada and Mexico: Forging a feminist internationality." *Millennium* 23(3): 535–62.

Geller-Schwartz, Linda (1995). "An Array of Agencies: Feminism and State Institutions in Canada." In Dorothy McBride Stetson and Amy Mazur (eds.) *Comparative State Feminism*. London: Sage.

Hassanali, Soraya (2000). *International Trade: Putting Gender into the Process—Initiatives and Lessons Learned*. Ottawa: Status of Women Canada. www.swc.cfc.gc.ca/pubs/0662661974/200012_0662661974_2_e.html (May 23, 2005).

Jenson, Jane and Susan D. Phillips (1996). "Regime Shift: New Citizenship Practices in Canada." *International Journal of Canadian Studies* (Autumn) 14: 111–135.

Macdonald, Laura (2004). "Gendering Transnational Social Movement Analysis: Women's Groups Contest Free Trade in the Americas." In Joe Bandy and Jackie Smith (eds.) *Coalitions Across Borders: Transnational Protest and the Neo-Liberal Order*. Lanham: Rowman and Littlefield.

Macdonald, Laura (1999). "Trade with a Female Face: Women and the New International Trade Agenda." In Annie Taylor and Caroline Thomas (eds.) *Global Trade and Global Social Issues*. London: Routledge.

Macdonald, Laura and Mildred A. Schwartz (2002). "Political Parties and NGOs in the Creation of New Trading Blocs in the Americas." *International Political Science Review* (April) 23(2): 135–158.

Mahon, Rianne (1977). "Canadian Public Policy: The Unequal Structure of Representation." In Leo Panitch (ed.) *The Canadian State: Political Economy and Political Power*. Toronto: University of Toronto Press.

Maroney, Heather Jon (1987). "Feminism at Work." In Heather Jon Maroney and Meg Luxton (eds.) *Feminism and Political Economy*. Women's Work, Women's Struggles. Toronto: Methuen.

O'Neil, Maureen and Sharon Sutherland (1997). "The Machinery of Women's Policy: Implementing the RCSW." In Caroline Andrew and Sanda Rodgers (eds.) *Women and the Canadian State*. Montreal-Kingston: McGill-Queen's Press.

Rankin, Pauline and Krista Wilcox (2004). "De-gendering Engagement? Gender Mainstreaming, Women's Movements and the Canadian Federal State." *Atlantis* (Fall/Winter) 29(1): 52–58.

Rebick, Judy (2005). *Ten Thousand Roses. The Making of a Feminist Revolution*. Toronto: Penguin.

SWC (2000). *Canadian Experience in Gender Mainstreaming*. Paper prepared by the Status of Women Canada for the Sixth Meeting of Commonwealth Women's Affairs Ministers, April, New Delhi, India.

SWC (1995). *Setting the Stage for the Next Century: The Federal Plan for Gender Equity*. Ottawa: Status of Women Canada.

Stetson, Dorothy McBride and Amy Mazur eds. (1995). *Comparative State Feminism*. California: Sage Publications.

Turenne Sjolander, Claire (2003). "Of playing fields, competitiveness and the will to win: representations of gender and globalization." In Claire Turenne Sjolander, Heather Smith and Deborah Stienstra (eds.) *Gendered Discourses/Gendered Practices*. Toronto: Oxford University Press.

Vickers, Jill, Pauline Rankin and Christine Appelle (1993). *Politics as if Women Mattered*. Toronto: University of Toronto Press.

Waylen, Georgina (1998). "Gender, feminism and the state: An overview." In Vicky Randall and Georgina Waylen (eds.) *Gender, Politics and the State*. London: Routledge.

Why Women Still Ain't Satisfied: Politics and Activism in Canadian Childcare

Martha Friendly

Martha Friendly is Coordinator of the Childcare Resource and Research Unit (CRRUO), Canada's primary childcare policy research facility. She has authored many popular and scholarly works and works closely with community and advocacy groups and with other researchers, international groups and policy makers, supporting a universal system of early learning and childcare.

It's now more than 35 years since the Royal Commission on the Status of Women first recommended a National Day Care Act (1970) and more than 20 years after Judge Rosalie Abella called childcare "the ramp that provides equal access to the workforce for mothers" (Royal Commission on Equality in Employment). Sixty years have passed since women organized to fight closure of Toronto's wartime day nurseries (Prentice 1996) and more than two decades since the inspired day care activism of the 1970s and 1980s put childcare on Canada's political map to stay (Rebick).

Yet Canada has not achieved the "free, non-compulsory, publicly-funded, non-profit, 24-hour national day care system" promoted by Toronto's Action Day Care in the 1970s and 1980s. Indeed, although in most modern countries the idea that high quality childcare and early childhood education are synonymous and a benefit to young children is well accepted (OECD 2006; UNESCO), the very idea of early learning and childcare is under attack by the religious right in Canada (McDonald) and by the federal government. In the words of the Honourable Diane Finley, federal minister responsible for childcare: "There have been many studies that show that the best people to raise children are the parents" (*CTV News*).

At the same time, the idea that childcare is an issue of special interest to women is disparaged by the right, as, for example,

Childcare, caregiving and poverty are not just women's concerns but the problems of the Canadian family. To ghettoize them...does a disservice to others in the game including men, children and extended family members. (Kheiriddin)

This suggestion that today "women's priorities are everybody's priorities" and that gender wars over issues like childcare are "old wars" is consistent with the statement of the

Honourable Bev Oda, Conservative Minister responsible for women's issues, who contends that "We don't need to separate the men from the women in this country" (qtd. in "An agency well pruned").

Nevertheless, research shows that while both mothers (including employed mothers) and fathers devote more time to their children than previously (Gauthier, Smeeding and Furstenberg Jr.), women still carry the major responsibility for children in a variety of ways—taking parental leave (available to either parent) at a considerably higher rate (Friendly and Beach), working a "double day" (Gauthier, Smeeding and Furstenburg Jr.) and—if they are lone parents—claiming the very lowest incomes among family types (Statistics Canada).

Most early childhood educators and childcare workers—a notoriously underpaid group—are women as well (Beach, Bertrand, Forer, Michal and Tougas). And over the years, organizing and activism for childcare has been primarily by women (Prentice 2001). While now there are undoubtedly more men—fathers, childcare workers, trade unionists, politicians, economists—who are essential and dedicated players in the Canadian fight for childcare, by and large, the childcare movement is still mostly made up of women.

THE CURRENT CHILDCARE SITUATION IN CANADA

In 1986, the federal Task Force on Childcare concluded that sound childcare and parental leave programs can no longer be considered a frill but are, rather, fundamental support services needed by all families in Canada today (Cooke, London, Edwards and Rose-Lizée iii). But Canada has made little or no progress towards this system at the national level or outside Quebec—in any of the provinces.

Canadian women with young children have joined the paid labour force in ever-increasing numbers for the past three decades. By 2003, their labour force participation rate had risen from 61% (1995) to 66% for mothers whose youngest child was zero to three years, 75% for those whose youngest was three to five years and 82% with a child six to 15 years (Friendly and Beach). Canadian mothers' employment rates are high among the Organization for Economic Co-operation and Development (OECD) countries, higher than those in France, Denmark, Hungary, the U.S., the UK and others (Friendly).

In its review of Canada undertaken as part of its 20-nation comparative study of early learning and childcare, the OECD commented that:

> *national and provincial policy for the early education and care of young children in Canada is still in its initial stages. Care and education are still treated separately and coverage is low compared to other OECD countries. (2004: 6)*

Canada's childcare lags not only when compared to Western Europe but also to the Anglo-American nations and even in some developing countries (OECD 2006; UNESCO). As the OECD's 2006 analysis showed, Canada was the lowest spender in the OECD at 0.25% of GDP (compared to Denmark, the highest spender, at 2% of GDP). Canada also had very high costs to parents relative to most other OECD countries and had very low rates of access both for children aged zero to three and aged three to six years (Friendly, 2006a).

No province/territory provides space for anywhere close to a majority of young children. There are no national standards or approach and while each province/territory has regulated childcare centres, part-day nursery schools, regulated family day care (in private homes) and public kindergarten, the range, quality and access to early learning and childcare programs varies considerably by region and circumstance. Funding in all provinces except Quebec still relies heavily on a residual welfare model—fee subsidies for eligible low-income families—which by no means suggests that all low-income families can access a subsidized place. As a result, high user fees for regulated childcare—required to support most of the cost of program operations—are a main barrier to access for modest and middle-income families.

THE POLITICS OF CHILDCARE: 2003–2006

Following the activism for childcare throughout the 1980s, childcare mostly remained off national policy agendas until 2003 when the Multilateral Framework on Early Learning and Childcare was put in place by Federal Human Resources Minister Jane Stewart who called it "the beginning of a very solid national day-care program for Canadians" (Lawton). Then, in the 2004 election campaign, the federal Liberals under Paul Martin promised to build on this commitment to begin developing national early learning and childcare system based on four principles—Quality; Universality; Accessibility and Developmental [programming] (QUAD). After the Liberals won the 2004 election with a minority government, they committed $5 billion over five years (new dollars) to begin to build the system. In 2005, the federal government came to agreements-in-principle with all provinces based on only one condition—that the federal funds be used for regulated early learning and childcare programs.

This marked the first time that a Canadian government had followed through with an election commitment to improve childcare at the national level. While there was considerable variation in the provinces' directions, in coming to agreements-in-principle with the federal government, provinces committed to detailed action plans specifying how the federal transfer funds would be spent. On the federal side, in signing the agreements-in-principle, the federal government promised five-year funding upon production of the action plan. Three provinces, Manitoba, Quebec and Ontario, had completed and publicly released their action plans, and concluded five-year funding agreements with the Government of Canada in November 2005.

In the 2006 election campaign, the Conservatives under Stephen Harper made childcare one of their five priority election issues, vowing to reverse the processes set in motion by the Liberals. The Conservatives' intention was to cancel the agreements; to send all families a monthly check for $100 (taxable) to promote "choice in childcare"; and to set out capital financial incentives to encourage employers to establish childcare (Conservative Party). Following the January 2006 election of a minority Conservative government, the new government's first announcement after officially taking office was that the agreements would be terminated. They announced that all jurisdictions—the three provinces with five-year funding agreements (Quebec, Ontario and Manitoba), the seven provinces that had not yet released their action plans and the three territories (who had not yet finished negotiations) would get federal funding for just one year. Thus, all federal funds for the nascent national childcare program would end March 31, 2007.

Instead the Conservative government promised an individual cash payment to parents—the "Choice in Childcare Allowance"—a payment to all parents with children under age six of $1,200 a year, taxed in the hands of the lower-income spouse. In addition, the Conservatives said that they would initiate a capital funding program to "help employers and communities create childcare spaces in the workplace or through cooperative or community associations by establishing a tax credit" of $10,000 per space (Conservative Party, 2006).

LA LUTTE CONTINUE: CODE BLUE FOR CHILDCARE

The federal election of 2006 is over. As a result, childcare is at risk as never before. After 30 years of hard work, the foundation of Canada's newest social program is on the chopping block with cuts of almost $4 billion on the line. Families, communities, providers and advocates will not stand by and watch this happen.

The election of the Conservative government of Stephen Harper in January 2006 brought to power (albeit with a minority) a federal government that was the first in modern Canada with a stated position of opposition to regulated childcare. With a goal of keeping the national childcare program on the public agenda, women from across Canada who had long advocated for a universal national childcare program formed Code Blue for Child Care, a loose national coalition with goals dedicated to putting the national childcare program back on track.

Code Blue for Child Care is a Canada-wide campaign to protect the progress we've made on childcare. The membership is broad, cross-Canada and cross-sectoral. It includes women's groups such as the YWCA and Feminist Alliance for International Action (FAFIA), labour groups like the Canadian Labour Congress (CLC), childcare advocacy and professional groups from across Canada, teachers' groups and the Ontario Public School Boards Association, social planning councils, Aboriginal and antipoverty groups, Canadian Association of Food Banks, and many others. Code Blue will speak for the 64% of Canadians who voted for a childcare system to meet the needs of Canada's children, families and communities (Code Blue for Child Care).

Even before the childcare agreements were cancelled, the group's steering committee developed goals and a work plan and implemented a series of activities designed to keep childcare on the political agenda.

Code Blue's Goals

(1) Saving existing federal-provincial agreements on childcare.
(2) Building on the foundation of the agreements to press all levels of government to build the system that Canada's children and families deserve and need.
(3) Supporting families: Comprehensive family policy must address families' income needs *and* support expansion and operation of early learning and childcare.

ARE WE THERE YET?

The woman-led childcare activism of the 21st century exemplified by Code Blue for Child Care is quite multi-faceted, encompassing organizing, lobbying, research, public education, policy development and direct action and involves a wide range of sectors and players in all regions of Canada.

Women in Canada are still struggling to balance work, family and personal lives without the support of a well-developed accessible system of childcare. Although the percent of children for whom childcare is accessible has crept up over the years, the situation isn't fundamentally better than it was in the 1980s when a much smaller proportion of women with young children were in the paid labour force. The 2006 election of the Harper government eliminated even the better-late-than-never first steps that were being taken. But at the end of 2006, a federal election is on the near horizon and the childcare movement is well positioned to ensure that childcare will be at the top of political agendas.

References

"An agency well pruned." Editorial. *The Globe and Mail* 1 December 2006: A26.

Beach, J., J. Bertrand, B. Forer, D. Michal, and J. Tougas. *Working for Change: Canada's Child Care Workforce. Labour Market Update Study*. Ottawa: Child care Human Resources Sector Council, 2004.

Code Blue for Child Care. Online at www.childcareadvocacy.a/action/codeBlue/index.html. Retrieved December 2, 2006.

Conservative Party. *A New $1,200 Choice in Child Care Allowance for Pre-school Kids*. December 6, 2006. Online: www.conservative.ca/EN/1091/33693. Retrieved December 6, 2006.

Cooke, K., J. London, R. Edwards, and R. Rose-Lizée. *Report of the Task Force on Child Care.* Ottawa: Status of Women Canada, 1986.

CTVNews. The Honourable Diane Finley. Federal Minister Responsible for Child Care. February 24, 2006.

Environics Research Group. *Canadians Attitudes Towards National Child Care Policy*. Toronto: Author, 2006.

Friendly, M. *Early Learning and Child Care: How Does Canada Measure Up? International Comparisons Using Data from Starting Strong II (OECD)*. Toronto: Child Care Resource and Research Unit, University of Toronto, 2006a. Online: www.childcarecanada.org/pubs/bn/early learningo6.html.

Friendly, M. *Looking Beyond Our Borders: Early Learning and Child in Quebec, Canada and in the OECD.* Powerpoint for a presentation at Politiques familiales et bien-être des enfants. Conseil de développement de la recherche sur la famille du Québec. Université du Québec a Trois-Rivières, 2006b.

Friendly, M. and J. Beach. *Early Childhood Education and Care in Canada 2004*. Toronto: Child Care Resource and Research Unit, University of Toronto, 2005. Online at www.childcarecanada.org/ECEC2004/index.html.

Friendly, M. and L. White. *From Multilateralism to Bilateralism to Unilaterism in Three Short Years: Child Care in Canadian Federalism 2003–2006*. Oxford University Press (in press).

Gauthier, A. H., T M. Smeeding and F. Furstenberg, Jr. "Are Parents Investing Less Time in Children? Trends in Selected Industrialized Countries. *Population and Development Review* 30 (4) (2004): 647–661.

Kheiriddin, T. "Colour in the Liberal Ghetto Pink." *The Globe and Mail* December 1, 2006: A27.

Lawton, V. "Ottawa, Provinces Sign Day-care Deal; 50,000 New Spots over Five Years $900M Program 'essential first step'." *Toronto Star* 14 March 2003: Al.

McDonald, M. "Steven Harper and the theo-cons. The Rising Clout of Canada's Religious Right." *The Walrus* October 2006. Online: www.walrusmagazine.com/articles/politics-stephen-harperand-the-theocons/. Retrieved December 2, 2006.

Organization for Economic Co-operation and Development. (OECD). *Starting Strong II. Early Childhood Education and Care*. Paris: Author, 2006.

Organization for Economic Co-operation and Development (OECD). *Thematic Review of Early Childhood Education and Care. Canada Country Note*. Paris: Author, 2004.

Prentice, S. *Changing Child Care: Five Decades of Child Care Advocacy and Policy in Canada*. Halifax: Fernwood Publishing, 2001.

Prentice, S. *Theorizing Political Difference in Toronto's Postwar Child Care Movement*. Occasional Paper #8. Child Care Resource and Research Unit. Toronto: University of Toronto, 1996.

Rebick, J. *Ten Thousand Roses: The Making of a Feminist Revolution*. Toronto: Penguin Books, 2005.

Royal Commission on Equality in Employment. Ottawa: Minister of Supply and Services Canada, 1984.

Royal Commission on the Status of Women in Canada. *The Status of Women in Canada*. Ottawa: Minister of Supply and Services Canada, 1970.

Statistics Canada. *Women in Canada: Work Chapter Updates*. Ottawa: Author, 2003.

United Nations Educational, Scientific and Cultural Organization (UNESCO). *Strong Foundations: Early Childhood Care and Education. Education for All Monitoring Report*. New York: Author, 2006.

Confronting Power: Aboriginal Women and Justice Reform

Patricia A. Monture

Patricia Monture is a citizen of the Mohawk Nation, Grand River Territory (near Brantford, Ontario). She is mother, sister, auntie. Trisha was educated as a lawyer in Ontario and has graduated from the University of Western Ontario, Queen's University and Osgoode Hall Law School. From 1989 to 1994, she taught in Canadian law schools. In 1994, Trisha joined the Department of Native Studies at the University of Saskatchewan as an associate professor. She was granted tenure in 1998 and promoted to full professor in 1999. From 2001 to 2004 in addition to her teaching responsibilities, she was Special Advisor to the Dean of the College of Arts and Science on Indigenous Initiatives. Presently, she is a Professor in the Department of Sociology and active teaching in the area of Aboriginal justice.

This is my story about women and justice, about activism and reform. It is a story about speaking to power. Power not only of race but the power of the prison to resist reform and continually reinvent itself as a place of coercion, power and punishment (Rothman 1971). I share with imprisoned Aboriginal women many of the experiences of oppression on account of our race and gender. I hold privilege as a Haudenosaunee woman who is both free (not sentenced) and no longer living in poverty. I am not an expert on prison, never having been sentenced or incarcerated. Such an assertion of expertise on my part would violate the tenets of the Haudenosaunee knowledge system, which requires lived experience and reflection to be the basis of knowing. I do have an idea or two about activism learned from my experiences working toward reform of the Canadian criminal justice system and the sometimes harsh impacts it has had on the lives of Aboriginal women who are imprisoned federally.[1]

Any story I tell must reflect on gender and be grounded by women as knowledge among my people, the Haudenosaunee, is gendered. Teachings, shared through story, create a complex structure of knowledge. There are men's teachings and women's teachings as well as teachings for all people. As an experience-based knowledge system, most often Aboriginal systems rely on reflection with self-interpretation at the core as the grounding methodological practice. And as such, an experience-based knowledge system[2] is also necessarily about a gendered system of knowing because I can only live the experience of woman.

Criminalization of Indigenous populations, which results in the present rates of over-representation, is in fact a strategy of colonialism and it is therefore seen globally. And as rates of Aboriginal over-representation continue to increase it perhaps reflects that the colonial trajectory continues to increase in impact as well.

In 1990 the *Task Force on Federally Sentenced Women* was created in an effort aimed at addressing the impacts of discrimination carried by female federal prisoners. Participating in the *Task Force on Federally Sentenced Women,* the Aboriginal women confronted not only the power of prisons to control prisoners and to re-invent themselves as places of punishment, and the power of the bureaucracy to entrench itself, but also the ability of civil servants to locate themselves in that power[3] of bureaucracy. It was also understood that each of these powers is overlain with colonial impacts including the oppression of women. A number of scholars have noted this association between colonialism and the oppression of women, but no rigorous analysis of that connection to colonialism presently exists in the Canadian literature (Acoose; Jaimes; McCaskill; Monture-Angus 1999; Smith; *TFFSW*).

Confronting the power of colonialism is one of the central challenges the Aboriginal women brought to the *Task Force* discussions as lived experiences of the Aboriginal women who are federal prisoners. And the report that was produced did force correctional officials to confront those understandings of that lived experience. As it brought colonial history to the centre of the analysis of gender (Hayman), the report may in fact be the only government report to begin to speak inclusively to Aboriginal women's experiences in the way Aboriginal women see the issues.[4] Although the report is only 16 years old, the analysis of women, prison and colonialism was at its best rudimentary. In those intervening years, the scholarship that considers Aboriginal women's experience of law, power, gender and legal force has been enriched significantly. Sherene Razack writes:

> *Colonizers at first claim the land of the colonized as their own through a process of violent eviction, justified by notions that the land was empty or populated by peoples who had to be saved and civilized.*

To understand the transformative potential the energy of Aboriginal reformers put into the *Task Force,* the degree to which colonial impacts were overlooked for female prisoners requires consideration. To date, feminist scholars have not examined the work of the *Task Force* or the subsequent building of the new women's facilities from this position. In fact, much of the work is silent on race (see, for example, Hannah-Moffat) or fails to consider that the six Aboriginal women who worked on the two committees did not share a singular vision of the politics of the *Task Force* or the prison as a coercive institution (see, for example, Hayman). In particular, not all of the Aboriginal women who participated were abolitionists. The inability to recognize this fact vanishes the very real differences of Aboriginal women and places an additional pressure on Aboriginal women to be seen to agree with one another. It, as well, fosters stereotypes of Aboriginal women and pan-Indian understandings (which are often inaccurate).

What is unique about the work of the *Task Force on Federally Sentenced Women* is the way in which the voices of Aboriginal women, both prisoners and advocates, were included in the report. Those voices spoke clearly to the power of colonialism that continues to this day to impact on the lives of Aboriginal women. The *Task Force* was not the first time that the state elected to study the situation of federally sentenced female prisoners. In fact, the Prison for Women was the subject of inquiries and commissions almost since the time the first prisoners were admitted (*TFFSW* 35–41). What is remarkable is that it is the first time that Aboriginal women were an integral part of the body doing the studying and this is the result of efforts of both the Canadian Association of Elizabeth Fry Societies and the Native Women's Association of Canada. There were two First Nations women on the working group of the *Task Force.*[5] On the steering committee, there were four Aboriginal women, two of whom were federally-sentenced prisoners on community release.

The innovative research completed by the *Task Force* at the insistence of Aboriginal women is one of the positive outcomes of the work reformers invested. It accomplished more than providing skills and income to two formerly federally sentenced women. It set a new standard, in my view, for other researchers conducting studies in this area by seeing colonialism as a central factor in the analysis of present day social problems. The members of the *Task Force* believed that this piece of work was necessary in our efforts to find answers to the complex policy questions before us. It is one of the lasting contributions and, because truth and knowledge operate to thwart the continuation of colonialism, it is an important contribution.

Until very recently in Canadian history, Aboriginal people, but particularly Aboriginal women, have not had the opportunity to read our truth and thereby have it affirmed. The total impact of this aspect of the *Task Force* has never been the focus of study. Nor has its impact on the lives of the Aboriginal women who were (and in too many cases, remain) the prisoners been studied. It is ironic that the analysis of the *Task Force* and the new women's facilities is critical of the outcomes of the *Task Force's* recommendations, often concluding that it is the women prisoners who paid the price while neither returning to speak to those women nor placing colonialism at the centre of the analysis. This is an ultimate irony in that the analysis of the "success" or "failure" as one of the goals of the *Task Force,* reflected in the structure of the report, which begins with the voices of the women who are prisoners, is discussed without the very voices that the *Task Force* tried to centre.

Prison is also a particular kind of place, which also serves a particular, albeit not always acknowledged, social function. It is equally an identity-making space, for the prisoners but not just for the prisoners. First, the fact that the prisoners also produce the prison should not be forgotten (Gaucher 43). Second, "we," those of us who are not labeled as in violation of the criminal law and are, therefore, not criminals, have our identities as respectable citizens affirmed. Criminals are wrongdoers (that is, not respectable and civilized) and it is therefore right and just to punish them. Thus, the prison is about a particular social function in which respectability and the accompanying social power is distributed in Canadian society.

Recognizing the parallel between the social function of the prison and its impact on Aboriginal peoples and colonialism, provided lessons I would not have learned if I had not been directly involved with prisons and prisoners. Visiting prison, seeing the control and relations of power, was an early step for me in understanding the complexity of colonialism. Power, control and isolation are all visible in the prison. Uniforms distinguish prisoners from guards. The quality of the tailoring of the guards uniforms distinguish them from the prisoners as well as the keys on their belts clanking with their footsteps. Bars, control posts and locked doors make the message about who has power and who does not very clear. Power, control and isolation are key components in not only maintaining the "good order" of the institutions but were key components of colonialism. But in this country, in this century, many of these colonial vestiges are no longer visible as the oppression of residential schools once was to Aboriginal eyes. They are now embedded.

The *Task Force* attempted to re-create the kind of physical space that women would serve their sentences in and as such it is an interesting study because it connects space to power, isolation and control.[6] Because many of us felt we could not "get to" the power of the prison and its officials, we took a step back and tried to minimize the ability for exercises of power and control that result in coercion, resistance, violence and isolation. For the Aboriginal women involved, most of us had never had such an opportunity before and were willing to take risks with the hope that we could make positive changes in the experience of incarceration. The title of the report, *Creating Choices*, reflects the philosophical attempt to shift the gaze from a system that corrects to one that collectively empowers women. This was an attempt to move women's corrections to a place that constructed women's criminal offending as a mere reflection of gender oppression in Canadian society (*TFFSW* 16, 25). It was an attempt to relocate the power to make choices in their lives back to the women themselves and out of the hands of prison officials. As noted in the preface, the consensus process engaged by the *Task Force* was often a painful process but through this commitment we learned that "only if people are treated with respect, only when they are empowered, can they take responsibility for their actions and make meaningful choices" (2). The report did not contain a finished plan but rather the authors urged that it be seen "as only a beginning to a much longer process of change in our justice system, and in society as a whole" (2). To obtain these goals, the *Task Force* attempted to reconfigure a space known as the women's prison. Whether the reconfigured spaces change women's experiences generally, or specifically if the healing lodge does, remains an unexamined question. Perhaps, given the degree to which the implementation of the report reconfigured the vision, it may be a question that is unnecessary to examine.

It is precisely this re-focusing on empowerment as an individual responsibility that has interfered with the transformative[7] potential of the vision of *Creating Choices* and resulted in consequences often unforeseen by those of us involved with the preparation of that report. Kelly Hannah-Moffat notes that Correctional Service of Canada (CSC) has taken the feminist notion of empowerment and attached a notion of self-responsibility to it that transforms the idea of "empowering women" into something less than satisfactory (170). CSC's actions ignore the way empowerment was located at the very beginning of the report. Empowerment follows respect and only when both conditions are present can women make choices that they should be held accountable to.

It is the individualization of the concept "empowerment" that is the problem as well as its detachment from both the other five principles the *Task Force* articulated as well as from the historical analysis that acknowledges systemic patterns of colonization, gender discrimination and unequal wealth distribution. By ignoring systemic patterns the transformative potential of *Creating Choices* is impaired. As a tool to thwart colonialism, the *Task Force's* work at least partially and perhaps significantly was stripped of its power to offer opportunities to decolonize.

The five "principles for change" are: empowerment; meaningful and responsible choices; respect and dignity; supportive environment; and shared responsibility (*TFFSW* 128–135). The principles were not drafted as a checklist but are complementary and must operate in an interlocking pattern of commitment to the women who are prisoners. One of the difficulties I often experience in justice reform efforts is that I forget to be mindful enough of the different cultural contexts—forgetting that non-Aboriginal peoples do not share the same view of the world or the same understanding of knowledge. It means never forgetting that you are different and think differently than non-Aboriginal people (and this is almost an impossible requirement to fulfill as it requires you to analyze each and every thought that passes through your mind or every word that crosses your lips). And who is doing the double thinking is a fact that should not escape our attention. Explaining Aboriginal traditions, world views and knowledge systems is insufficient to guarantee respect, understanding or reaching a shared meaning. This has been one of my hardest lessons and it indeed remains a conundrum. It is a conundrum faced every time I work in a non-Aboriginal institution from the prison to the university.

More disturbingly, the result of what reformers intended to be a transformation of women's prison has instead been shifted to a recharacterization of women prisoners as dangerous. The shift can be seen in the enhanced security measures such as the "eye in the sky" surveillance camera, fences and razor wire. This recharacterization is substantiated in some instances with stereotypes of Aboriginal peoples. It is important to acknowledge that in 1990, one of the cornerstones of the *TFFSW* (and one of its strategies) was the acknowledgement that women prisoners were not as dangerous as men in prison. Coupled with this was an agreement among the majority of the *Task Force* that the security rating scales were not valid and some of us thought we had secured a promise that these scales were not to be used any longer at least until they had been demonstrated to be valid. Women were to be treated as women and not as a particular kind of security risk.

This consequence born so heavily by women prisoners may be explained as a response to a report which demanded that female prisoners be treated with respect in the post-Charter era and indeed would result in the deprisoning of female corrections. As a government report on prisoners has never before attempted this challenge to the construction of the assumed dangerousness of prisoners, a challenge that goes to the heart of the legitimacy of the prison to punish, coerce and restrain human beings, the *Task Force* could not have known what the government's response would be. What is learned then, is to not challenge the legitimacy of the prison (no matter how much sense it makes) without the resources necessary to ensure that there is an opportunity for reforms to respond to the backlash as there indeed will be backlash from the prison bureaucracy.

Never before had the Correctional Service of Canada relinquished so much power to a community to be involved in correctional decision-making and no mechanisms were in place to ensure that community members or organizations continued to hold some power. And this is the fatal flaw in our abilities to secure meaningful and long-term reform. Insufficient power over the long term sat and sits in the hands of the reformers.

It was the advocates of women prisoners who so strongly asserted that the voices of the women had to come first. Failing to continue to include the community has jeopardized the continuity of that acknowledgement and the commitment to listen to the women who are imprisoned has continued to be lost over the years.

Reflecting on the silencing of the women prisoners' voices (and those in the community who advocate for them) is an important aspect of understanding what went wrong. It is important to recognize that during the life of the *Task Force*, the working environment was a women's, maybe even a feminist, environment. This made it easy to retain the feminist principles we agreed were foundational to our work. Once the *Task Force's* work was completed, many of the civil servants returned to the male-dominated bureaucracy of corrections where feminist values, principles and beliefs are not respected or well-regarded. This was another structural pressure well beyond the control of any individual *Task Force* member that diminished the reformist vision.

Despite the involvement of the Native Women's Association of Canada in the establishment of Aboriginal specific initiatives, the transformative potential here has also been contained. The report of the *Task Force on Federally Sentenced Women* contains a specific focus on Aboriginal women that is maintained throughout the report. The recommendations are both inclusive and separate as appropriate. The most transformative of the ideas resulted in the building of the Healing Lodge at the Nekaneet First Nation (ironically on land surrendered for the purpose of building the Lodge). This was an attempt to create Aboriginal space for women to serve their sentences in.[8]

On a visit to the Ochimaw Ochi Healing Lodge several years ago, I had occasion to sit with the Elders in the Spiritual Lodge. One of the Elders expressed to me that "there was not enough Aboriginal programming at the Lodge." This statement encapsulates the degree to which those involved with the *Task Force* and those charged with implementing it have been successful (or not) in creating Aboriginal space. The prison was to be in its entirety an Aboriginal "program" (or Aboriginal space). It was not to rely on discrete Aboriginal programs to supplement the core programs of CSC. Those few words from the Elder "unmapped" for me the success (or the lack thereof) of this endeavour. A word of caution is essential around this point. There is no doubt that the Healing Lodge is not all that I have imagined it to be. I, however, base my analysis on an outsider position, granted one who is vested in the building of the Lodge. It is clear to me that individual women (both Aboriginal and non) who have served their sentences at the Lodge have benefited by being there as some of us originally envisioned.[9]

There are a number of questions I continue to ponder. The *Task Force,* its implementation and the new women's facility will never be experienced as something that is either a success or failure, however you define those terms. For me, I think it will always be both. And as a woman who is not serving time, I recognize the privilege in that statement. In prisons, physical space is an important organizational quality. Compare the visual image of a maximum-security facility (and often what we conjure up reflects the reality at male prisons)—rolls and rolls of razor wire, fences or limestone walls and highly controlled offender movement. A minimum-security facility may look more like a resort than a penal institution. Although institutional-looking, the new regional facilities for women did not look like prisons prior to the enhancement of security measures in the first year of their operations. This exposes an interesting research question: how does the look of the new facilities change the experience of doing time? Or does it? What is the transformative value in changing the physical space of prisons if indeed there is one?

The relationship between the colonial legacy, the portrayal of women as violent and increasingly as dangerous, and the racialization of Aboriginal women are interwoven strategies used by correctional systems. This emphasizes how important the broader context of power, while recognizing the many forms power takes, is to understanding the experiences of women who are prisoners.

When we reflect on our experiences and not just react to them, we create our stories. And those stories "are power, create people and author tribes" (Howe 29). And the land we now call Canada supports layers and layers of these Indigenous stories. Our actions, our trickster lessons, and our stories have the power to turn colonialism over and our people will reclaim our power and our freedom. It is in this way that I offer my thoughts on reforming prisons and the lessons I have learned thus far. This is my small offering to that process of reclaiming just relations as prison is just one small part of a much larger problem for Aboriginal people around the world.

Endnotes

1. In Canada, the constitution establishes that there are both federally and provincially sentenced prisoners. Federal prisoners are distinguished from provincial because their sentences are longer than two years.
2. I am not trying to diminish the learning that comes from books although I do want to note that my time spent learning in university-based systems of knowledge are also lived experience. As such, then, it is for me always about balancing learning in two very differently structured systems of knowledge (for a fuller discussion of my experience in the university please see Patricia Monture in "On Being Homeless: One Aboriginal Woman's Conquest of Canadian Universities, 1989-1998").
3. This power takes several forms. At the time of the *Task Force,* many of the community members of the *Task Force* did not have access to email. Our long distance calls, facsimiles and other expenses came directly out of our pockets and were eventually reimbursed. The civil servants had unlimited resources at their immediate disposal. They had the ability to caucus on the government's dime and many worked in the same geographic area. Community members did not have this ability to caucus other than at meetings. This imbalance in resources and power impacts on the ability of the community sector to participate and results in a documentary record, such as the recording of minutes, that was really more firmly in the hands of the bureaucrats. These are significant issues that impact on the ability of reformers to see their views equally recorded.
4. Compare this to the report of the *Royal Commission on Aboriginal People (RCAP)* where the discussion of gender is little more than the discussion of loss of status under former section 12(1)(b) of the Indian Act despite the fact the RCAP reported six years after the *Task Force on Federally Sentenced Women.*
5. The author of this paper was one of those two women.
6. Many of these negotiations were not easy ones but ones made under the pressure of the consequences for prisoners if we did not agree as the civil servants often reminded us. I remember long, hard discussions about segregation units. I remember opining that locking me in a penthouse suite of the luxurious Royal York Hotel was still dehumanizing and a fancy place was still segregation (even if you called it something else). These are the kinds of heated discussions that were never reflected in the minutes.
7. Laureen Snider writes: "Indeed, criminal justice systems are probably the least effective institutions to look for transformative change. Even the staunchest advocates of incarceration do not argue that prisons are successful institutions, only that they punish well" (11).
8. This was the first of the healing lodges built by the government in Canada. There are now eight lodges that are federally funded including those that are still in the development phase with the Okimaw Ochi Healing Lodge being the only female facility; These are Waseskun House in Quebec; Ochichakasipi (Crane River) in Manitoba; Willow Cree Healing Lodge in Saskatchewan, Wapatin in Saskatchewan; Stan Daniels Healing Centre in Alberta; Pe Sakawtew in Hobbema, Alberta and Kwe Kwe Kwelp in British Columbia.
9. The birth of the healing lodge was not a well-thought out plan but more of a coincidence. It was a reaction to yet another suicide at the Prison for Women. It was a spur of the moment comment about not needing another prison to warehouse Aboriginal women as my sisters kept coming home to us in boxes. It was this abolition point I was making. But I followed it with a comment about Aboriginal women needing a place to heal, a lodge. The civil servants at the table immediately embraced this

idea of a healing lodge. They started to question me what such a lodge would look like. It left us stunned and I felt like I had made a mistake sharing our dream about a healing place.

References

Acoose, Janice. *Iskewewak kah'Ki Yaw Ni Wahkoma Kaak: Neither Indian Princesses nor Easy Squaws*. Toronto: Women's Press, 1995.

Canadian Human Rights Commission. *Protecting Their Rights: A Systemic Review of Human Rights in Correctional Services for Federally Sentenced Women*. Ottawa: Canadian Human Rights Commission, 2003.

Correctional Investigator. *Annual Report of the Office of the Correctional Investigator 2005–2006*. Ottawa: Minister of Public Works and Government Services, 2006.

Faith, Karlene and Kim Pate. "Personal and Political Musing on Activism: A Two Way Interview." *Ideal Prisons? Critical Essays on Women's Imprisonment in Canada*. Eds. Kelly Hannah-Moffat and Margaret Shaw. Halifax: Fernwood Publishing, 2000. 136–147.

Gaucher, Bob, ed. *Writing as Resistance: The Journal of Prisoners on Prisons Anthology (1988–2002)*. Toronto: Canadian Scholars Press, 2002.

Griffith, Curt T. and Simon N. Verdun Jones. *Canadian Criminal Justice*. 2nd Ed. Toronto: Harcourt Brace, 1994.

Hamilton, A. C and C. M. Sinclair. *The Report of the Aboriginal Justice Inquiry of Manitoba: The Justice System and Aboriginal People*. Winnipeg: Queen's Printer, 1991.

Hannah-Moffat, Kelly. *Punishment in Disguise: Penal Governance and Federal Imprisonment of Women in Canada*. Toronto: University of Toronto Press, 2001.

Hannah-Moffat, Kelly and Margaret Shaw, eds. *An Ideal Prison? Critical Essays on Women's. Imprisonment in Canada*. Halifax: Fernwood Publishing, 2000.

Hayman, Stephanie. *Imprisoning Our Sisters: The New Federal Women's Prisons in Canada*. Montreal: McGill-Queen's University Press, 2006.

Horii, Gayle K. "Processing Humans." *Ideal Prisons? Critical Essays on Women's Imprisonment in Canada*. Eds. Kelly Hannah-Moffat and Margaret Shaw. Halifax: Fernwood Publishing, 2000. 104–116.

Howe, LeAnne. "The Story of America: A Tribalography." *Clearing a Path: Theorizing the Past in Native American Studies*. Ed. Nancy Shoemaker. New York: Routledge, 2002. 29–48.

Jaimes, M. Annette, ed. *The State of Native America: Genocide, Colonization and Resistance*. Boston: South End Press, 1992.

McCaskill, Don. "Native People and the Justice System." *As Long as the Sun Shines and the Water Flows: A Reader in Canadian Native Studies*. Eds. Ian Ghetty and Antoine Lussier. Vancouver: University of British Columbia Press, 1983. 288–298.

McCaslin, Wanda, ed. *Justice as Healing: Indigenous Ways*. St. Paul, Minnesota: Living Justice Press, 2005.

Monture, Patricia. "On Being Homeless: One Aboriginal Woman's Conquest of Canadian Universities, 1989–1998." *Crossroads, Directions and a New Critical Race Theory*. Eds. Franscisco Valdes, Jerome McCristal Culp and Angela P. Harris. Philadelphia: Temple University Press, 2002. 274–287.

Monture, Patricia. "Aboriginal Women and Correctional Practice: Reflections on the Task Force on Federally Sentenced Women." *Ideal Prisons? Critical Essays on Women's Imprisonment in Canada*. Eds. Kelly Hannah-Moffat and Margaret Shaw. Halifax: Fernwood Publishing, 2000. 52–60.

Monture-Angus, Patricia. "Considering Colonialism and Oppression: Aboriginal Women and the 'Theory' of Decolonization." *Native Studies Review* 12 (2) (1999): 63–94.

Razack, Sherene. "Gendered Racial Violence and Spatialized Justice: The Murder of Pamela George." *Race, Space and the Law: Unmapping a White Settler Society*. Ed. Sherene Razack. Toronto: Between the Lines, 2002. 121–156.

Ross, Luana. "Race, Gender, and Social Control: Voices of Imprisoned Native American and White Women." *Wicazo Sa Review* 10 (2) (1994): 17–37.

Rothman, David J. *The Discovery of the Asylum: Social Order and Disorder in the New Republic*. Boston: Little Brown and Company, 1971.

Sinclair, Roberta Lynn and Roger Boe. *Canadian Federal Women Offender Profiles: Trends from 1981 to 2002 (Revised)*. Ottawa: Research Branch, Correctional Service of Canada, 2002.

Smith, Andrea. *Conquest: Sexual Violence and American Indian Genocide*. Cambridge: Southend Press, 2005.

Snider, Laureen. "Towards Safer Societies: Punishment, Masculinities and Violence Against Women," *British Journal of Criminology* 38 (1) (1998): 1–39.

Sugar, Fran and Lana Fox. "Nistum Peyako Séht'wawin Iskewewak: Breaking Chains." *Canadian Journal of Women and the Law* 3 (2) (1989–90): 465–482.

Task Force on Federally Sentenced Women (TFFSW). *Creating Choices: The Report of the Task Force on Federally Sentenced Women*. Ottawa: Correctional Service of Canada, 1990.

War and the Politics of Truth-Making in Canada

Sunera Thobani

Sunera Thobani teaches Women's Studies at the University of British Columbia. Her research interests include race and gender relations, globalization, migration and citizenship, and media and the war on terror. She is a past president of the National Action Committee on the Status of Women and a founding member of Researchers and Academics of Colour for Equity.

INTRODUCTION

The politics of knowledge production and truth claims have become a major concern of the social sciences in the face of challenges from anti-racist, feminist and postcolonial studies. Contesting notions of objective "truths," theorists from these various traditions have directed our attention to their socially constructed nature, pointing out that power relations are deeply imbricated in respective processes of truth "making" about the nature of the social world. Contrary to the claims of colonizers bringing "civilization" to the colonized world, Frantz Fanon, for instance, argued that colonial relations were predicated upon the violent enslavement of black peoples and on the racialized dehumanization of both colonizer and the colonized (1963, 1986). In a different vein, the feminist sociologist Dorothy Smith has pointed out that sociology's use of abstract categories to uncover "objective" forms of knowledge removes knowledge producers from the particularities of their "everyday/every night" localized experiences and reflects a dominant male standpoint (1987, 1990). Gayatri Spivak has argued for the critical necessity of interrogating elitist knowledge production by recognizing the experiences of the subaltern subject positions that such elitism seeks to silence (1996).

The politics of contesting elite truth claims has been highlighted recently in a controversy generated by political and media elites in Canada following a speech I made to a women's movement conference. In the aftermath of the September 11 attacks on the World Trade Centre and the Pentagon, the Bush administration launched America's "War on Terrorism." Rejecting a significant role for the United Nations in formulating a response to the attacks, as well as the need to abide by international law, the administration initiated the forming of an international coalition to justify its unilateral military action against Afghanistan. One of its early partners was the Canadian government, committing its unequivocal support for whatever forms of assistance the United States might request. Challenging the claim that military aggression was the only reasonable and understandable response to the September 11 attacks, I spoke at the *Critical Resistance* conference in a bid to mobilize the women's movement against supporting this "new war."

Situating the current political crisis within the context of the ongoing North/South relations rooted in colonialism and the increasingly unilateral expansive claims of sovereignty by the U.S. wherever it decides its interests are being challenged, the speech criticized American foreign policy and President Bush's racialized construction of the American nation in mobilizing it for war. I argued that women's groups should oppose the Canadian government's support for military action and call on it to withdraw support for U.S. foreign policy. I argued instead for building solidarity with Afghan women's organizations.

In this paper, I draw upon materialist, anti-racist and postcolonial feminist theories to examine the racialized and gendered politics of knowledge production and "truth-making" in contemporary Canada through an analysis of the public controversy following the speech. Situating the very public attacks on the speech in this context, I will argue that the media coverage worked to dehistoricize the attacks of September 11, to close off public space for debate by refusing to engage in a substantive discussion of the effects of U.S. foreign policy, and to thus enable claims of American innocence to be publicly upheld.

Further, I will argue that by repeatedly reconstructing my status as a non-white, immigrant woman, the media reiterated—in a highly intensified manner—the historically racialized discourse of who "belongs" to the Canadian nation, and hence has a right to "speak" to it. This racialized discourse constructed me as an outsider to the nation, part of the "enemy" within its territorial boundaries, against which the ideological borders of the nation had to be defended. Repeated calls for me to be fired from my teaching position, and to have me "go back to where I come from" (and in a good number of cases for me to "go back" to Afghanistan!) reconstituted—in a moment of crisis—the vulnerable and constantly "under surveillance" status of Third World immigrants in Canada. While a small number of columnists did attempt a more balanced coverage of my speech, the overwhelming media response was to resort to vicious personal attacks, casting me in the role of a hostile and irresponsible immigrant woman. This intensely racialized/gendered discourse played no insignificant role in recuperating the colonial stereotype of the irrational native, albeit in its current gendered version, that of the *angry woman of colour*. Through these rhetorical strategies, a critique of U.S. foreign policy, informed by well-documented and perfectly respectable sources, was turned into the ranting and raving of a "nutty" professor. The attacks on me also sent a very direct and clear message to others about the costs of challenging elite "truth" claims and of the dangers of voicing dissent in present-day Canada.

ON SPEAKING OUT

Given that the Canadian government had pledged its support for America's new war, my speech urged women's groups to examine the record of U.S. foreign policy, arguing that this record is alarming. For instance, in Chile the CIA-backed coup against the democratically elected Allende government led to the deaths of over 30,000 people. In El Salvador, the U.S.-backed regime used death squads to kill about 75,000 people. In Nicaragua, the U.S.-sponsored terrorist contra war led to the deaths of over 30,000 people. The initial bombing of Iraq left over 200,000 dead, and the bombings have continued for the last 10 years. UNICEF estimates that over one million Iraqis have died, and that 5,000 more die every month as a result of the U.N.-imposed sanctions, enforced in their harshest form by U.S. power. In order to support its economic interests, the U.S. pattern of foreign intervention has been to overthrow leftist governments and to impose right-wing regimes which, in turn, support U.S. interests, even if this requires the training and use of death squads and the assassinating of progressive leftist politicians and activists (Chomsky, 1985; Landau, 1993; Johnson, 2000). To this end, the U.S. government has a record of treating civilians as entirely expendable. Indeed, some commentators have argued that the U.S. has a policy of deliberately targeting civilians in order to terrorize them into withdrawing support for progressive movements. The United States is therefore the largest and most dangerous global force, unleashing horrific levels of violence around the world, and U.S. foreign policy is soaked in blood.

Further, I pointed out that in order to legitimize the military aggression being undertaken by the United States against Afghanistan, President Bush was invoking an American "nation" and its "enemy" in clearly racialized civilizational terms.

In examining how this nation was being mobilized for the war, I asked the conference to consider the language used by President Bush, other senior U.S. Administration officials, their Western allies such as British Prime Minister Tony Blair and the Italian Prime Minister Silvio Berlusconi, as well as major figures in the media. If we do this, we encounter the following language: launching a "crusade" to "defend freedom at any cost;" the need to summon among Americans "hatred" and "rage" and the need for a "policy of focused brutality;" "Operation 'Infinite Justice;'" fighting the "barbarians;" a commitment to "hunt down" and "smoke [terrorists] out of their holes;" warnings that the Taliban "face[d] the full wrath of the United States of America."

The use of this highly charged colonial discourse at that particular moment of crisis revealed the nature of the absolutist racialized Western ideology being mobilized to rally the troops, and to build a national and international consensus in defense of the "West" and its civilization. It suggested implicitly that anyone who hesitated to join the war was likewise "evil" and "uncivilized." It is a crude Manichean remapping of the colonial divide in the current age of Empire, articulated once again through the discourse of the civilized West and the barbaric Islamic world.

I also pointed out that the institutionalization of racial profiling in the wake of September 11, and the targeting of immigrants and refugees within Canada and the United States as a threat to the nation's security, especially of those who "look" like Muslims, inevitably followed from this logic. The women's movement had to disrupt this racialized discourse and challenge the notion that the War on Terrorism was a reasonable, just, or righteous response, and instead insist upon naming it the imperialist venture that it was. Finally, I addressed how the treatment of women by the Taliban regime was being used to further legitimize the war. The military attack on Afghanistan was being represented as necessary and welcome in bringing about the liberation of Afghan women. While there could be little disagreement about defining the Taliban regime as misogynist, I argued there would certainly be no emancipation for women anywhere until Western domination of the planet is ended.

ON BEING HEARD

For articulating the position outlined above, I was immediately attacked in the media, by the Canadian Prime Minister in the House of Commons, by the leaders of all the major opposition parties and by the Premier of British Columbia. This was followed by similar attacks from other politicians, editorialists and media columnists across the country in the days following the initial reports of the speech. I began to receive hate mail, harassing phone calls and death threats. Numerous calls were made for me to be fired from my teaching position at the University of British Columbia, both publicly and privately, in phone calls and letters. In this climate, the Royal Canadian Mounted Police (RCMP) chose to make public, through an announcement in the media, that I was the subject of a "hate-crime" investigation, an offence under the criminal code. A complaint had apparently been made to them alleging that my speech amounted to a "hate crime" against Americans.

The attacks on my speech were led by political leaders and by key figures in the mainstream media, who turned these into a public spectacle played out on the front pages of newspapers and on prime-time television and radio programs.

The fury generated by the media reporting of my comments has been instructive and reveals several interesting patterns. Accusations were immediately made that I was an academic impostor, morally bankrupt and was engaging in hate mongering. My comments, informed by well-documented and numerous sources whose accuracy cannot be faulted, were categorized simplistically as "hateful." The media reports can largely be characterized as follows. First, a number of phrases, such as the one describing the U.S. as being the "most dangerous global force unleashing horrific levels of violence" and the one arguing that U.S. foreign policy was "soaked in blood" were taken out of the context of the entire speech and were sensationally repeated. The airing of these comments, in isolation from the analysis informing them, inevitably gave rise to misrepresentations about their full meaning. The words "horrific violence" and "blood-stained" were singled out as particularly offensive. Second, and predictably enough, the media reports—and the public criticisms they generated and subsequently reported upon extensively—did not address the veracity of the speech's assessment of the U.S. historical record. Third, instead of engaging with the substance of my comments, most commentators directed public attention to my tone of voice and choice of words (i.e., shrill, inflammatory, disgraceful, outrageous, insensitive, angry, excessive, inelegant and unacademic, etc.), elevating a form they attributed to the speech above its contents. These rhetorical maneuvers served at least two purposes: first, they contributed to a dehistoricizing of the attacks of September 11 and the subsequent U.S. response, thereby enabling claims of American innocence to be upheld; and second, they directed personalized attention towards me, rather than to the substance of my speech, thereby enabling the construction of me personally (and other immigrants by association) as treacherous outsiders-to-the-nation, its "enemy" within, against whom the nation had to remain on guard.

DEHISTORICIZING SEPTEMBER 11

In the immediate aftermath of the collapse of the Twin Towers, the trauma triggered by the attacks seemed to find collective voice in the question, why? Why had the attacks taken place? This was a question echoing across the United States, becoming the most intense articulation of the trauma that people seemed to experience. Concurrently with the question why, one also heard an equally intense anger being expressed at the attacks, as well as a demand for some kind of immediate response to them. The answer to the question why was provided by the President and other "experts": the American nation, its "freedoms" and its "way of life" were fiercely hated abroad and it was for this reason that the United States had become the target of a terrorist campaign of murderous envy. It was not the specific foreign policy of the U.S. in the Middle East or Central Asia, or in other parts of the global South, which was being attacked, but the nation's love of freedom and democracy. This answer was to become a key plank in the mobilizing of public support for the war in the United States and at the international level, and to further fuel demands for military retaliation. The war was represented as nothing less than a fight for democracy and freedom in the world.

As Sherene Razack has convincingly argued, demands made by oppressed groups for justice are often met by dominant groups with a denial of their responsibility for, and complicity in, the oppression of marginalized others (1998). Such denials are accompanied by claims of their own innocence, which enable members of dominant groups to instead construct themselves as the victims of those whom they are complicit in oppressing. The mainstream media's refusal to engage with the substance of the speech sought to accomplish such a dehistoricizing of September 11, and of the U.S. state's role in oppressing and exploiting peoples around the world, thereby enabling the construction of American innocence. Instead, the focus on my tone of voice, choice of words, speaking style and (lack of) intelligence became the most salient point for most commentators. The form of the speech was elevated in order to override its content, undermining the "truth" of the historical record I was referring to, and in the process I became constructed as hateful and aggressive.

Name-calling and personalized accusations then, as well as allegations that my comments were untimely (five days *before* the bombing of Afghanistan began!), were deemed sufficient enough to suppress discussions of the historical record of U.S. foreign policy. Caricatured as angry and insensitive, the "truths" of the historical experiences I referred to were implicitly avoided, and the "truth" of U.S.-backed coups, death squads, bombings and mass terror were left unacknowledged and unaddressed in the public discussion. In this, the majority of media commentators, journalists and editors alike made the perspective of the Bush administration and its supporters the only possible rational, intelligent, sane and informed perspective.

DIS-EMBODYING OTHERS

Examining the collective outrage expressed regarding my tone of voice and choice of words has also been instructive. The use of the words *horrific violence* and *soaked in blood* in the speech, singled out for particular derision, was indeed deliberate. To successive U.S. administrations and their supporters, the deaths resulting from its policies have been just so many statistics, just so much collateral damage, regrettable inevitabilities of what have been essentially just policies. This rendering invisible of the lives and humanity of the peoples targeted for attack is an old strategy used to mask the impact of colonialist and imperialist interventions. Perhaps there is no more potent a strategy of dehumanization than to proudly proclaim the accuracy and efficiency of "smart" weapons systems, and of surgical and technological precision, while rendering invisible the suffering and broken bodies of the peoples under siege, to be registered, if at all, only as disembodied statistics and mere "collateral damage." My use of embodied language, grounded in the recognition of the actual life-blood running through these bodies, was an attempt to humanize the victims of U.S. aggression in profoundly graphic terms.

A number of scholars have argued that if we were to centre in our analysis of the social world the experiences of those who are oppressed and marginalized, we would have to radically redefine dominant perspectives on the nature of the social world (Collins, 1998; Devi, 1997; hooks, 1981; Morrison, 1994; Maracle, 1996; Spivak, 1996; Williams, 1991). These feminists, and others, have forcefully drawn our attention to what is actually done to women's bodies in the course of mapping out racialized colonial/imperialist relations. Frantz Fanon, one of the foremost analysts of decolonization, studied and theorized the role of violence in colonial social organization and the psychology of oppression; but he described just as readily the bloodied, violated black bodies and the "searing bullets" and "blood-stained knives" which were the order of the day in the colonial world he was living in and studying (1963, 1986). If our analysis is to centre the experiences of the targets and victims of U.S. aggression and their allied local elites, as Ms. Menchú sought to accomplish in her testimonial, the impact of U.S. foreign policy has to be ascertained and redefined from the perspective of their experiences. Our analysis then expands to "see" not just sanitized, disembodied policies and cold statistics, but the murderous practices that work to maintain the role of the U.S. as the world's hegemon. Anti-colonial and anti-imperialist movements and theorists have long insisted on placing the bodies and experiences of marginalized Others at the centre of our analysis of the social world, and to fail to do so at such a critical moment would have been unconscionable.

The United States was using the events of September 11 to claim unilaterally the right to intervene anywhere on the planet where it deems its interests to be under threat, despite its signing of the U.N. Charter. According to political theorists Michael Hardt and Antonio Negri, such an assertion points to a radically new form of globalized sovereignty, consistent with similar economic patterns of expanding sovereignty in the activities of the World Bank, International Monetary Fund, World Trade Organization, etc. (2000). I would argue that this new globalized sovereignty of the U.S. and its allies is highly racialized. The words "bloodthirsty" and "vengeful" are designations which have, with a certain degree of comfort, been attributed to "savages" and to the "uncivilized" by defenders of the West, while the West itself is self-represented as the beacon of democracy and civilization. To name the practices of the U.S. administration as "bloodthirsty" and "vengeful," to force a recognition of the actual bloodletting that upholds Empire, is to confront the nature of the racialized ideological justification for the War on Terrorism, as well as its historical roots, unsettling and discomforting as that might be.

RESURRECTING THE IRRATIONAL NATIVE

Predictably enough, there was no discussion in the media about the racialized discursive practices being used by the Bush Administration and the Canadian state, which the speech sought to draw attention to. The constant referencing of Americans as living in a higher state of civilization and of the enemy as barbarians who nurse a primal rage towards the West, recuperated racially coded constructs of the colonizer and the colonized. Significantly, the form in which the media response to the speech was shaped itself used similarly racialized discursive practices. The speech was seized upon as part of the forging of a national "Canadian" consensus in support of the war, in this case through the public attacks on me as an immigrant-outsider-to-the-nation and as thus allied with the "enemy." The category "immigrant" is a racially coded one that has come to be a referent for all people of colour within Canada, regardless of their citizenship or actual legal status in the country (Bannerji, 2000; Thobani, 2000). Himani Bannerji has spoken specifically about the paradox of "both belonging and non-belonging simultaneously" that shapes the lives of immigrants (2000, p. 65): living within the nation's geographical boundaries, labouring within its economy, subject to its legal systems, immigrants are nevertheless racialized as outsiders, as not being "real" Canadians. Account after account in the media pointed to my "un-Canadian" origins, stressing that I was an immigrant, that I had been born in Tanzania and for those readers who might still miss the point, that I am "non-white." Many columnists asked in all seriousness why I did not "go back to where I come from." One columnist asked, "Why does she not flee back to enlightened Tanzania . . . ? Or to Afghanistan . . . ?"

In the context of the United States, Chandra Mohanty has discussed experiencing a similar, and constant, questioning of her presence in the country by the seemingly innocent query: "When are you going home?" (1993, p. 352). This everyday questioning of the presence of immigrants in North America that both Bannerji and Mohanty have discussed became highly intensified in the personal attacks and the questioning of my presence in the country—as an outsider-within—a challenge that was turned into a "national" public spectacle. Whereas the everyday forms of exclusion described by Mohanty and Bannerji seek to keep immigrants in their place at multiple sites in their everyday lives, these everyday forms became highly magnified at this moment, working as the terrain for the (re)articulation, and thus (re)assertion of the nation's identity and of its national cohesion. The attacks assumed the perspective of a patriotic "Canadian" sensibility that had come under attack. Establishing and repeatedly stressing my outsider-to-the-nation status, these media reports and columns came to crystallize the articulation of a "Canadian" national perspective, *by* and *through* these attacks.

Here, dissent itself became constructed as "un-Canadian" and foreign, a strategy particularly effective in this instance because, as a woman of colour, I could readily be (re)constructed as already suspect within the ongoing legacy of the historically racialized practices of Canadian nation-building.

The sustained focus on the tone of my voice can also be read as a resurrection of the stereotype of the irrational—to the point of lunacy—"angry" women of colour. A woman with a chip on her shoulder. This is a stereotype deeply rooted in the colonial trope of the "irrational" and "angry" native, brought into History, Reason and Civilization under the auspices of the West, yet who remains stubbornly unwilling to recognize the benefits to him/herself of this benevolence. The "angry" woman of colour can be read as a contemporary gendered version of this colonial construct, and it played a key role in the shaping of this controversy. It is intriguing that in the construction of my comments as bordering on lunacy, an utter incredulity and incomprehension was expressed regarding my comments about the bombing of Afghanistan being detrimental to the interests of women in Afghanistan, and also as having a negative impact on women's status within North America. As Razack has noted, "Oppressed Third World women, particularly the passive, downtrodden Indian woman and the veiled Muslim one, are recurring and familiar images in Canadian public discourse" (1998, p. 100). These images were being circulated in full force as legitimizing devices for the attacks on Afghanistan, and the construction of me as a lunatic for daring to disrupt this familiar public discourse is a reminder of just how heavily invested Canadian elites are in racialized/gendered discourses about Muslim, and other Third World, women. It was the American state's economic and political interests that led to its initial support for, and arming of, Gulbadin Hekmatyar's Hezb i Islami and its support for Pakistan's collaboration in, and organization of, the Taliban regime in the mid-1990s. We have witnessed the horrendous consequences this initial support for the Taliban has had for women in Afghanistan. During that period, Afghan women's groups were calling attention to the American and Pakistani support as a major factor in the Taliban regime's coming to power, but most people in North America chose not to heed them. Nor did they recognize in the aftermath of September 11 that Afghan women's groups were, and had been, in the front line of resistance to the Taliban and its Islamist predecessors, including the present militias of the Northern Alliance. Instead, they chose to see them only as "victims" of a timeless, a historical Islamic culture, to be pitied and "saved" by the West.

Third World feminists have pointed to the pitfalls of rendering invisible the agency and resistance of Third World women, and of the racialized reduction of women's oppression to various "backward" and timeless Third World "cultures" which are defined as irremediably misogynist (Ahmed, 1992; Amos & Parmer, 1984; Mohanty, 1991; Razack, 1998). In the case of Afghanistan, repeated media attention was directed to the misogynist practices of the Taliban. But the truth that the U.S. bombings were displacing hundreds of thousands, if not millions, of Afghan women and their children, turning them into destitute refugees, was conveniently overlooked by the media. Humanitarian agencies reported that over three million Afghan refugees were on the move in the wake of the U.S. attacks, and to raise questions about the costs of this in human terms, to disrupt the representation of the U.S. as "saving" these women and children, as I tried to do, was considered utter blasphemy.

Even more ferocious were the attacks on me for daring to suggest that it was equally important to recognize that the globalization of Western sovereignty and militarism would not further women's liberation in the countries of the West either. The struggles of feminist movements in these countries attest to how widespread women's oppression is in these countries, ranging from the rape, sexual assault and murder of women to their sexual objectification, their inequalities in the workplace and their growing poverty. In the specific case of the War on Terrorism, women were being brought into line to support racist imperialist practices and goals. It is these women who will also have to live with the men who go to serve in the war, and who themselves become brutalized in its waging. These are hardly the conditions in which women's freedoms can be furthered, either in the United States, Canada or the countries of their European allies. Indeed, in their alleged commitment to Afghan women's liberation, and through their claims of being more enlightened on questions of gender than the barbaric Others, the U.S. administration and its Western allied states have made the War on Terrorism a key site for the reconstitution of the supremacy of the West, and of the supremacy of individual Western men and women who have come to the "rescue" of Afghan women. So readily and completely is the supremacy of the West assumed to be in mainstream public discussions of questions of gender that any questioning of this common sense "truth" is dismissed as utterly incomprehensible. An analysis of gender relations at the global level, which claims that women's oppression in the Third World is deeply shaped—and greatly exacerbated—by the domination of the global South by imperialist powers, is reviled as idiotic.

CONCLUSION

People in Canada were being asked by political leaders and most public commentators to accept the United States military aggression against "evil-doers" as natural, understandable and even reasonable, given the September 11 attacks. My speech sought to rupture this discourse of the power elites who prefer to claim only that the American "war" is necessary, that there are no other alternatives to fighting "terrorism" than dropping bombs. My speech rejected this position, arguing that it would be just as understandable a response to reexamine U.S. foreign policy, to address the root causes of the September 11 attacks, and for the U.S. to make a commitment to abide by international law. I urged the women's movement in Canada to disrupt the discourses naturalizing and normalizing military aggression, and to recognize the war for what it is: vengeful retribution and an opportunity for a crude display of American military might and dominance. I likewise urged them to reject the notion that the United States can singlehandedly, and based solely upon its own economic and strategic interests, claim the right to define entire countries and "nations" as being terrorists, outlaws and murderers. Women need to ask: Who will make the decision regarding which "nations" are to be labelled as "murderers" and "outlaws"? Which notions of "justice" are to be upheld? Will the Bush administration set the standard, even as it is overtly institutionalizing racial profiling across the United States?

References

Ahmed, L. (1992). *Women and gender in Islam: Historical roots of a modern debate*. New Haven: Yale University Press.

Amos, V. &; Parmer, P. (1984). Challenging imperial feminism. *Feminist Review* No. 17, 3–20.

Bannerji, H. (2000). *The dark side of the nation: Essays on multiculturalism, nationalism and gender*. Toronto: Canadian Scholar's Press.

Chomsky, N. (1985). *Turning the tide: U.S. intervention in Central America and the struggle for peace*. Boston, MA: South End Press.

Collins, P. H. (1998). *Fighting words: Black women & the search for justice*. Minneapolis: University of Minnesota Press.

Devi, M. (1997). *Rudali: From fact to performance* (A. Katyal, Trans.). Calcutta: Seagull Books.

Fanon, F. (1963). *The wretched of the earth*. New York: Grove Press.

Fanon, F. (1986). *Black skin, white masks*. London: Pluto Press.

hooks, b. (1981). *Ain't I a woman: Black women and feminism*. Boston: South End Press.

Johnson, C. (2000). *Blowback: The costs and consequences of American empire*. New York: Henry Holt.

Landau, S. (1993). *The Guerilla Wars of Central America: Nicaragua, El Salvador and Guatemala.* London: Weiderfeld and Nicholson.

Maracle, L. (1996). *I am woman.* Vancouver: Press Gang Publishers.

Mohanty, C. T. (1991). Cartographies of struggle: Third World women and the politics of feminism. In C.T. Mohanty et al. (Eds.), *Third World women and the politics of feminism* (pp. 51–80). Bloomington: Indiana University Press.

Mohanty, C. T. (1993). Defining genealogies: Feminist reflections on being South Asian in North America, the Women of South Asian Descent Collective. In *Our feet walk the sky: Women of the South Asian diaspora* (pp. 351–358). San Francisco: Aunt Lute Books.

Morrison, T. (1994). *Beloved.* New York: Alfred A. Knopf.

Razack, S. (1998). *Looking white people in the eye: Gender, race and culture in courtrooms and classrooms.* Toronto: University of Toronto Press.

Spivak, G. C. (1996). *The post-colonial critic: Interviews, strategies, dialogues* (S. Harasym, Ed.). New York: Routledge.

Thobani, S. (2000). Nationalizing Canadians, bordering immigrant women in late twentieth century Canada. *Canadian Journal of Women and the Law, 12*(2), 279–312.

Williams, P. J. (1991) *The alchemy of race and rights.* Cambridge, MA: Harvard University Press.

Rooting Out Injustice: Discussions with Radical Young Women in Toronto, Canada

Jennifer Plyler

Jennifer Plyler is a Toronto-based activist in grassroots organizations challenging poverty, occupation, colonialism and violence against women. She also works in community health on issues of harm reduction and sex workers' rights. Her passion is in the struggle for housing rights, and she believes a safe and sustainable home for everyone is worth fighting for.

A few years ago, while at a women's rights conference, I attended a workshop entitled "Taking on the WTO." I was excited at first to be participating in an explicitly feminist discussion on how to challenge more effectively the global powers forcing neoliberalism and imperialism on us, but my enthusiasm quickly dwindled. As each panellist spoke, it became clear that their focus was more on how to increase the number of women in positions of power within the WTO than to formulate strategies on how to dismantle it. This was disappointing since, as a young woman engaged in struggle against imperialist globalization, I knew that simply gaining power within capitalist superpowers would never satisfy me.

When the question period began, I approached the microphone and directed my question to the person I felt was the most radical speaker on the panel. "Wouldn't it be more strategic to unify our efforts to tear the WTO down rather than divide our efforts between reformist and radical camps?" The panellist answered my question with a chuckle, "Well, when I was 20 I had no problem with running around in the streets and getting arrested, but I have different priorities now." Numerous older women in the audience laughed. This response did not answer my question, nor did it even begin to address whether efforts to reform dominant institutions are effective or whether it is simply easier to work within them because it requires less sacrifice. What it did do was embarrass me in front of a lot of older feminists and make me feel isolated and unwanted. The existence of a divide among women's rights activists seemed threatening and real. Unless action is taken to recognize and show solidarity with the visions, analysis and actions of young radical women on the frontline of struggles, we may start finding ourselves not only on opposite sides of the fence at anti-globalization protests but also on opposite sides of the fence within our efforts to transform our own communities.

In Toronto, Canada, there are young women building radical movements of action and solidarity that challenge injustice head on. These young women, who epitomize the slogan "think global, act local," are leading new and militant struggles against the forces of imperialism, colonialism, racism, sexism and poverty. They are organizing within their communities not only for justice and rights but also for survival. This article aims to introduce you to a few of these women, the organizations they lead and their perspectives on social change. It also aims to document their struggles, their sacrifices and their raging spirits.

Lilsa, Farrah, Rachel and Rafeef are all young women activists and community organizers in Toronto, fighting back against the injustices taking place in our city. Their community work is diverse and intersecting, addressing issues of occupation, political prisoners, poverty, capitalism, anti-racism and immigrants' rights. I met with each of these young women to hear about their journeys to activism, the groups they work with, the action they take, the challenges they face and the wins they've had in defending rights and contributing to change. I also asked them about feminism: how they define it and how it has influenced their ideas and actions.

LILSA: THE 30 JUNE COMMITTEE

Lilsa, a student activist at York University in Toronto, is a leading organizer around issues of occupation and war. She describes her upbringing and explains how it politicized her and defined her relationship with the state.

Lilsa: I grew up with my mom and my brother after my mom left my father, who was abusive. My mom has a permanent disability. And so surviving was a constant financial struggle because she couldn't work full-time. Eventually she had to go on Ontario disability support. We grew up in poverty with a single mother who was constantly trying to make ends meet, constantly coming up against the Ontario government not giving us enough to buy winter boots, groceries or pay the rent. I became politicized at a young age, as I was exposed to what it's like for a woman trying to get away from an abusive situation and then trying to survive economically without enough support from the Ontario government.

Beginning in her teenage years, Lilsa became active in advocating on behalf of her mother's case to gain disability benefits from the Canadian government. She describes trying to get enough support to survive from the government as "a huge battle" and says, "I think that's when I stopped having any faith in electoral politics or any faith in the government as it stands." She was also inspired to become politically active through the strength that her mother, and other survivors of abuse, demonstrated to her.

For the past several years, Lilsa has been active on her campus around anti-war and human rights issues. Last spring she became involved in a coalition that brought together activists working against the occupations in Iraq, Palestine and Afghanistan to organize a demonstration marking the day that U.S. forces were supposedly going to hand over power to the interim Iraqi government. This coalition named itself The June 30th Committee. With the goal of achieving more than symbolic actions against U.S. foreign policy, The June 30th Committee aims to raise awareness about Canadian involvement in the occupation of Iraq.

Lilsa: It was definitely a different anti-occupation organizing experience than I've had in a long time because we started off with having a very anti-imperialist and anti-capitalist analysis. We wanted to draw out Canada's role in imperialism and Canada's role in the occupations.

The June 30th Committee organized a day of action in response to the Canadian government's indirect involvement in the Iraq war. This day drew attention to the fact that although the Canadian government had publicly declared that it would not send troops to the U.S.-led invasion of Iraq, this has not stopped Canadian corporations from profiting from the war through military contracts and weapons manufacturing at the expense of lives and autonomy in Iraq.[1] The action included setting up pickets and an aggressive march through Toronto's financial district. The day was notable in that young women were both the primary organizers and the primary decision-makers.

Lilsa: The day challenged both the state and our own structures at the same time. I think confronting the state in such a harsh way and being able to do it with young women was a really inspiring and empowering moment.

The June 30th Committee has been a strong (re)mobilizing force among anti-war and anti-occupation activists in Toronto. It has opened a space for increasing radical analysis and action. It continues to organize direct action against war-profiteers throughout the city.

FARRAH: PROJECT THREADBARE

Farrah was active in the anti-globalization movement when she was in high school. When she started university, she knew she wanted to become politically involved in the university setting but, as a young woman of colour, found few opportunities to do so.

Farrah: The only groups that were politically active on campus were mostly white-dominated spaces that were organizing within a Christian framework. This work wasn't really based on systemic change or actions against the state; it was more service-type stuff that was available to become involved with at the time, and I felt very frustrated.

Since September 11, 2001, Islamophobia[2] and xenophobia have been on the rise throughout Canada, including Toronto. On August 14, 2003, a joint investigation by the Royal Canadian Mounted Police (RCMP) and Citizenship and Immigration Canada (CIC), called "Project Thread," led to a predawn raid targeting 24 South Asian Muslim men who were held without charges and on unsubstantiated terrorist allegations that were later dropped. The targeting of these men, and the damage done to their lives and reputations as a result of the accusations, has had a paralyzing effect on South Asian and Muslim communities in Toronto. Everyone is wondering, "Who could be targeted next?"

When Farrah came across a poster advertising a public forum that read: "Being Pakistani is not a crime," she decided to attend. The forum was organized by a group called "Project Threadbare," a joint initiative of mainly South Asian men and women whose aim is to expose the injustices done to the 24 victims of the Project Thread investigation and win their release from detention. Farrah began organizing with this group. She and numerous other young activists of colour began providing legal and jail support to the detainees. They were able to secure the bonds and release of many of the detainees, but many others had been pressured by detention authorities to sign consent forms authorizing their deportation and were subsequently deported back to Pakistan straight from jail. As part of their campaign, Project Threadbare also undertook educational and awareness-raising initiatives, such as pickets, delegations and letter-writing campaigns, to educate the Canadian public about the victims of Project Thread and about the targeting of South Asians and Muslims in general.

The campaign reached a point where one of the ex-detainees, Fahim Kayani (a man who had become active in the Project Threadbare campaign since his release from detention), was informed by CIC that he was going to be deported. This was despite the grave risk of persecution he would face in Pakistan as a result of the unfounded Canadian terrorist allegation, and despite Canada's international responsibility to provide protection to those at risk of torture. Faced with the news of Fahim's pending deportation, members of Project Threadbare decided to intensify their actions.

Farrah: We were at a point in our campaign where we were going to lose the heart of the coalition—we were going to lose our leading organizer—and we were absolutely furious. In a meeting, we decided that we had to step up our action, and though we realized that we wouldn't necessarily be able to stop Fahim's deportation, we were determined to send a message to CIC that it would not be "business as usual" at their offices while they continued to deport these men without apology and without any kind of compensation for the trauma they were put through. A group of us, acting outside of the coalition, organized an occupation at the minister of citizenship and immigration Canada's office. This action was a very emotional response to the minister, who had been attacking not just the men targeted by Project Thread but also other leading nonstatus organizers working to challenge Canadian immigration policies.[3] The people who participated in the occupation were all young women and men of colour in the city: of Arab, South Asian, First Nations, West Indian and Iranian decent. It was the first action of its kind, where young people of colour challenged the state in such a direct way.

Despite their efforts, Fahim was deported to Pakistan, and all the young activists who participated in the action were arrested and are now facing criminal charges. However, those involved have set an example of how young activists of colour can work together to gain power and push for radical change.

Farrah: The action built trust, understanding and commitment within the group of people that participated in the occupation, and we continue to work with other young activists of colour around issues of immigration. We have since developed a commitment to working in our own communities trying to mobilize other young people to get involved in the same kind of work. Through this, we aim to start raising these issues and making people see how it affects not only their communities, and non-status people in those communities, but also how we can concretely challenge racist attacks through our ongoing activism.

RACHEL: ONTARIO COALITION AGAINST POVERTY

Rachel is a 20-year-old woman who has lived in Toronto her entire life. She describes her parents' involvement in union organizing as central to helping her understand how people can resist injustice in Canada.

Rachel: I grew up in downtown Toronto in a very mixed neighbourhood in terms of class and race. This has had a huge impact on the way that I see things. One would have to have blinders on not to notice that there is a lot of injustice going on in both Toronto and the rest of the world.

Neoliberal welfare reform has been a rising trend in Canada for several decades. The eight years of Conservative rule in Ontario (from 1995 to 2003), led by Premier Mike Harris, and the social service funding cuts that his government enacted, have contributed to an ever-widening gap between rich and poor. With promises to decrease the budget deficit and lower taxes, the Harris government slashed social welfare programmes, including health care, education, social assistance and housing (among many others) to a state where they are shadows of their former selves. In the face of the destruction of social welfare programmes, increased levels of resistance and popular mobilization arose and many Canadians began making the connections between what was happening in Ontario and the impact of capitalism and neoliberalism in the rest of the world.

In 1990, a group called the Ontario Coalition Against Poverty (OCAP) emerged to defend poor and working-class people against the violence of capitalism and welfare reform. Since then, OCAP has carved out a reputation across North America for its aggressive and radical actions in support of poor communities. Although best known for organizing militant demonstrations against government spending cuts, the bulk of OCAP's work revolves around providing direct-action casework to poor individuals, resisting the institutions that keep them poor. This work includes preventing evictions, gaining social assistance money and fighting deportations.

Rachel became involved in OCAP while she was still in high school and explains that "since then that's where my heart and days have been." Rachel explains that OCAP believes in the power of poor people to organize themselves and sees its role as providing support to these communities in whatever way is necessary. Unlike many other groups that identify themselves as anti-capitalist, Rachel explains, "OCAP shows through its actions where it stands, how corrupt the system is and how the system breaks people's backs and then throws them in the trash, instead of just talking about it."

The casework that Rachel does with poor women highlights the intersectionality between sexism and poverty in Toronto.

Rachel: I was working on a case with a woman who had been abused and beaten by her husband. She left her husband and was living in a government-subsidized social housing project. However, her husband found out where she was living and broke in several times, threatening her and her children. The housing provider who was in charge of the housing project she lived in refused to move her to another location, even though both the break-ins and threats she had received from him were well documented. She was in a position where she was being forced to choose between living in fear for her life or living on the streets to avoid her husband, as she couldn't afford to pay rent at a place that wasn't subsidized. We corresponded with the housing office several times but they refused to do anything about the situation. So we took a delegation to the office of the housing provider, laid the facts of the situation out for them and demanded she be accommodated. A couple of weeks later, the woman was transferred to another apartment.

RAFEEF: SUMOUD, A POLITICAL PRISONER SOLIDARITY GROUP

Rafeef is a Palestinian refugee who grew up in the refugee camps of Lebanon. For her, being politically conscious, particularly around the Palestinian struggle for self-determination, was not a choice, but a given, due to the politically charged environment she was raised in. What was more complicated for her to grasp was the dichotomy that existed within her family and her community in relation to the revolutionary struggle and women's roles.

Rafeef: I think my first feminist moment, when I thought "something is wrong with this picture," was when I realized that even though I was raised to idolize the women revolutionary fighters, I was never meant to become like them. I was meant to get married, have kids, be a good wife and support my husband. I was taught that these women were important components of the Palestinian resistance, but I was not meant to become one of them because that would mean that I was not a "good Arab woman."

Rafeef recalls that after the signing of the Oslo Accord with Israel, there was a sense among Palestinians that their fight was over and people felt "that there was peace now, and all we had to do was go back to Palestine and build a capitalist economy." When Rafeef's family moved back to Palestine, she was shocked at the poverty and corruption that was taking root, as well as the conservative elements that were starting to restrict women's freedoms so much more so than had been the case during the first Intifada. It was from this shock that her class-based politics developed and her concept of revolutionary change was altered. She refused to believe that the Palestinian struggle for self-determination could be about the wealth and power of a few select men.

Rafeef decided to come to North America to study, first in the U.S. and then in Toronto. In the past year she has co-founded a political prisoner solidarity group called Sumoud, which means "steadfastness" in Arabic.

Rafeef: Sumoud wanted to bring out the issue of not only political imprisonment of Palestinians but also the imprisonment of indigenous communities and people of colour in North America. Our aim was to raise awareness about the racism and criminalization of poverty that exists within the prison system. The group envisioned working on issues of how colonialism and imperialism manifest worldwide, not only in Palestine.

One of Sumoud's primary focuses has been a pressure campaign against the International Red Cross. The Red Cross is responsible for overseeing the treatment of political prisoners in numerous conflict zones including Palestine, where, having not taken a public stand against Israel's human rights violations, they have become complicit in them. When Palestinian political prisoners staged a nationwide hunger strike to demand better treatment in Israeli jails, Sumoud members and supporters organized, in solidarity, a hunger strike across from the Red Cross offices in Toronto.

CHALLENGES AND STRENGTHS

The organizing that Lilsa, Rafeef, Farrah and Rachel are involved with provides examples of dynamic community-based activism. Their insight, leadership and commitment provide a glimpse into the power that young women possess to create radical social change. That being said, it is also important to recognize some of the real challenges politically active young women in Toronto face. All of the local groups discussed above stay afloat on bare-bones budgets collected mainly through fundraising events. None of these groups receives any government or private funding. Lilsa, Rafeef, Farrah and Rachel are not paid for the activism that they engage in; they balance their time between community work and finding the means of survival (either through waged employment, scholarships or social assistance), which is a constant concern for them and many other young activists.

The radical nature of their work, and the ways in which it directly challenges the powers that be, is threatening to those who benefit and profit from maintaining the status quo and the inequality and exploitation inherent in it. In addition to being arrested, tear-gassed, pepper-sprayed and beaten by state authorities through the course of their political work, young women activists also face threats and violence from men in far-right political groups. Last year during an anti-occupation rally at York University to commemorate the one-year anniversary of the death of U.S. activist Rachel Corrie,[4] several young Arab women were spat on, kicked and threatened with rape by white men belonging to right-wing pro-Zionist groups.

The organizations that these young women work within are not necessarily safe spaces either. As within our city and communities, sexism is often present within the groups we work with and in the communities where we live; it constantly needs to be rooted out and addressed. To do this, numerous groups have created "women's caucuses" within their organizations; however, these caucuses have often created more work for women members and reinforce misconceptions that sexism is a "women's issue" rather than leading to a stronger feminist analysis of the group as a whole. Each of the young women interviewed offered other ideas and strategies for addressing sexism, heterosexism and patriarchy within our activist circles. Within Project Threadbare, Farrah says an important starting point has been educating young men within the group about their responsibility to confront the sexism they witness—be it disregarding women's ideas and opinions or talking too much and taking up too much space. Rafeef calls for procedures to be put in place so that organizations know how to address sexist behaviour collectively, instead of letting the responsibility fall on the victims. Rachel points out that women have played very central roles in OCAP's organizational and campaign development; this has helped to ensure that the organization addresses the ways in which poverty impacts women specifically. The need to make more space to address these challenges and develop strategies, as well as learn from women who have faced similar struggles before us, is very much acknowledged.

In the long run, our ability to dismantle inequality and challenge injustice will depend on our collective ability to confront oppression in all its forms. For older feminists, supporting young women does not only mean making space for them in already existing organizations and movements, nor does it only include efforts to mentor or share knowledge and experience (although these things are both essential and appreciated). Solidarity with young women activists also means giving time, energy and support to the initiatives and actions they are leading—whether they are taking place in local community centres, on campuses or in the streets. The ability of feminist organizations to remain relevant to social change will depend on their efforts to support this vital work. Only when the visions, perspectives and leadership of young women are given respect and solidarity will we be able to create movements that are truly transformative.

Endnotes

1. June 30th Committee (2004), 'A guide to Toronto's war profiteers', see www.fr.freeshell.org/june30th_factsheets.pdf.
2. Islamophobia refers to discriminatory attitudes, stereotypes and fear of Muslims.

3. The term "nonstatus" refers to anyone without full legal citizenship or permanent residence status in Canada.
4. Rachel Corrie was a U.S. citizen and a member of the International Solidarity Movement. She was crushed to death by an Israeli bulldozer while attempting to prevent the demolition of Palestinian homes in the Gaza Strip on March 16, 2003.

Riding the Third Wave: Women-Produced Zines and Feminisms

Brandi Bell

Brandi Bell is a doctoral candidate in the Joint PhD program in Communication Studies at Concordia University. Her academic and research interests are broadly encompassed within youth, citizenship and technology studies and her doctoral work is focused on examining representations of Canadian youth as social and political actors.

ZINES AND ZINE HISTORY

Defining zines has been a difficult and highly problematic task. Both scholars and zine creators have struggled in their attempts to define what a zine is, often failing to arrive at a consensus on the issue. Problems arise concerning what characteristics define a zine and differentiate it from a magazine. Typical definitions of zines focus on their tendency to be noncommercial and amateur, and to have a small range of influence. Other definitions, however, focus on the reasons behind creating a zine, arguing that zines are created out of a pure desire or need to communicate, as opposed to magazines, which may be created in order to make a profit. . .

Similar to defining zines, scholars and zine creators have difficulty agreeing on the details of the history of zines. Accounts of the history of zines vary in many ways, including what constitutes the first zine and to what extent non-zine cultural activities affected today's zines. What is made clear through an examination of the history of zines is that they are not simply the antithesis of magazines, but are closely related to independent publishing ventures such as pamphlets, newsletters and fanzines. In the 1970s, punk fanzines appeared and added new elements to zine culture, most importantly the do-it-yourself ethic. Other forms of punk culture and music called upon individuals to reject the culture produced for them and make their own culture with whatever resources were available. In terms of format, the increased availability of the photocopier and desktop publishing have expanded zines beyond cut-and-paste methods, sometimes to more professional-looking styles. The content of zines also continues to expand to include almost anything imaginable, such as personal stories, writing, religion and fringe culture.[1] Despite this diversity, there are common elements among zines and their creators that connect them and help to produce a particular culture.

Zines are part of what Duncombe calls the "Scene": "the loose confederation of self-consciously 'alternative' publications, bands, shows, radio stations, cafes, bookstores and people that make up modern bohemia" (Duncombe, 1997, p. 53). These elements of underground culture often criticize mainstream culture and advocate an alternative, or ideal, world of production and consumption. While the content of zines often highlights their opposition to mainstream culture and the discussion of alternatives, it is the very existence of zines that provides the best argument for the possibility of alternatives to the mainstream. Zines are "politics by example" (Duncombe, 1997, p. 196). Not only do zine creators advocate cultural alternatives in their zines, but the fact that they create a zine is, in itself, an act in opposition to mainstream culture.

In *A Girl's Guide to Taking Over the World: Writings from the Girl Zine Revolution*, Karen Green and Tristan Taormino argue that one of the most important reasons for zines is that they "are sites for communication, education, community, revolution, celebration and self-expression" (Green and Taormino, 1997, p. xiv). Zines are one of the ways that the underground community is bound together. Since zines regularly discuss and review other zines, "every zine is a community institution in itself, as each draws links between itself and others" (Duncombe, 1997, p. 48). Not only is the underground community built through the referencing of zines by others, but the common practice of trading zines and encouraging others to produce them also connects zine creators. This networking aspect of zine culture is so important that Friedman refers to it as "the lifeblood of the zine community" (1997, p. 9).

It is important to understand who is involved in this network and who is excluded in order to understand the limitations of zine culture and possible issues for feminist zine creators. Once again, because zines are part of the underground, it is difficult to determine who exactly creates zines in any concrete sense. However, there are some general characteristics of zine creators that are known and these will provide an idea of who makes up zine culture.

Zines produced by women and girls are not a new phenomenon, but part of a long tradition of information sharing among women. It is in this context that women-produced zines should be understood, and this paper defines women-produced zines as those that are created "primarily by and for girls and women" (Green and Taormino, 1997, p. xi). References to women-produced zines should be understood to include female producers of all ages, since women of all ages produce zines; however, it should be remembered that it is young women (in their teens to their thirties) who seem to produce most women's zines.

While women and girls of all types participate in zine culture, "Riot Grrrl" zines are generally understood to have greatly influenced women's zine culture. It is important to remember, however, that not all women-produced zines are Riot Grrrl zines and not all female zine producers would necessarily identify with the movement. Riot Grrrl was a social movement, located primarily in North America, comprised of "a network of young women linked by zines and bands" (Duncombe, 1997, p. 8).[2] Like zine culture, most of the girls involved in Riot Grrrl were white and middle class. Riot Grrrl is generally believed to have begun in Washington, D.C. in 1991, with the intent "to make girls and women more involved in D.C.'s predominantly white, male punk scene" (Rosenberg and Garofalo, 1998, p. 809). It is unclear whether girls used zines to create the network, or if it was created through bands and concerts, but what is clear is that zines became a central element of the movement. Riot Grrrl is only one facet of what is often called third wave feminism.

THIRD WAVE FEMINISM

Feminism is constantly changing and shifting, attempting to incorporate numerous views and survive differences. In recent years, the concept of a third wave of feminism has gained attention from both feminists and the mass media. An exact definition of third wave feminism does not exist, but there are some characteristics of this new feminism that help to identify it and distinguish it from the previous wave.[3]

In their introduction to *Third Wave Agenda: Being Feminist, Doing Feminism*, Leslie Heywood and Jennifer Drake define that third wave feminism as "a generational perspective, gathering the voices of young feminists struggling to come to terms with the historical specificity of our feminisms and with the times in which we came of age (the late 1970s through the late 1980s)" (1997, p. 2). The third wave is generally understood to be a feminist movement of young women who did not have the same experiences as second wave feminists; third wave feminists have spent most of their lives surrounded by feminism and its ideas. They have grown up with various real-life experiences of feminism and with representations of it, neither of which always lived up to their own feminist ideals.

As a result of living with both feminism and the cultural backlash against it, "navigating feminism's contradictions—historical, cultural, psychological—is a primary theme of third wave feminism" (Orr, 1997, p.31). There is a departure from previous feminist work that in some respects focused on political action. Third wave feminists, according to Heywood and Drake, "often take cultural production and sexual politics as key sites of struggle, seeking to use desire and pleasure as well as anger to fuel struggles for justice" (p. 4). Cultural production is one of the central methods of engagement. The act of producing cultural products serves to incorporate and introduce new ideas into public discussion and link women together to explore new issues. Zines are one aspect of third wave feminist activity and this paper explores some of the possibilities and limitations of this medium for feminist action.

EXAMINATION OF ZINES

The zines discussed here were collected through mail order and women's bookstores between November 1999 and March 2000. The criteria for selecting zines was that they were produced by women, or groups of women, and that their content dealt somewhat with women's and girls' issues.

The style and content of the zines collected are extremely varied and it is impossible to explain the characteristics of each one here. My analysis is meant to demonstrate what opportunities and limitations women-produced zines hold for feminism. The analysis is divided into themes reflecting a number of the elements of third wave feminism, including cultural production, autobiography, reclamation of language and culture and critique of mainstream culture. It attempts to draw out some of the more salient examples of how the women-produced zines collected reflect third wave feminism.[4]

Editors of women-produced zines help to encourage cultural production by reviewing and discussing work done by other women in their zines. In her zine *Queen of the Universe*, Jeannette Ordas interviews independent filmmaker Sarah Jacobson and reviews other zines produced by women—a common element of the zines collected. Another version of this encouragement to produce occurs when zine editors thank others for their help with the zine. For example, *Mystery Date* editor Lynn Peril thanks readers for sending her the information she uses to create her zine, such as books and other publications. Other zines such as *FanGirl* and *Beautiful Bras* and *Bodyhair* include short biographies of their contributors.

Legionella's Manifesto: Strange Attractor directly discusses cultural production. The zine is a collection of 13 statements on various issues. Statement #5 argues, "we R culture breakers and culture makers we will remix their myths and follow our bliss," and statement #10 encourages readers to create cultural products in order to ensure history is not lost: "we will document & archive our stories—so our histories can never be lost again—so that each succeeding generation does not have to start from scratch in an indifferent world."

Some of the zines collected were very heavily autobiographical. The best example of this is *The East Village INKY*, which is described by editor Ayun Halliday as "the continuing adventures of a 34-year-old mother and a 3-thumbed 2-year-old in New York City's EAST VILLAGE." The zine contains short stories, comics and anecdotes about the editor and her child. In the "High Horse" section of the zine, Halliday openly enters into political space and discusses her parenting philosophy (she writes that she has become aware that she is the "2nd most permissive mother" in her neighbourhood) and her views on breast-feeding toddlers.

The producer of zines such as *Liliane in Anti-Porn Fanatic* and *The adventuresome and action-packed life of Butler Biggest!!,* Leanne Franson openly admits that her comics are partially autobiographical: "Yes, this is based on Butler's life but incidents have been fictionalized." Unlike Halliday in *The East Village INKY*, Franson does not have a section of her zine that is openly political. However, in *Liliane in Anti-Porn Fanatic*, the main character Liliane struggles with feminist politics concerning pornography. While no conclusions are reached, simply creating this space in her zine allows Franson to explain some of the conflicting feelings women have on the issue.

Autobiography is a central element of the zine *FanGirl*, produced by Sarah Kuhn. *FanGirl* is, in Kuhn's words, "a publication meant to celebrate bonding over our shared geekiness and to champion sci-fi / fantasy's current plethora of kickass chicks." Kuhn's zine is full of stories by herself and contributors about their experiences of being fans. For example, contributor Megan Connolly describes her experiences at a fan convention in "Joxer and the Xenites."

Third wave feminists often work to reclaim language and activities that are elements of women's and girls' culture. *FanGirl* and *Mystery Date* are the best examples of zines that celebrate girls' culture. *FanGirl* writers use words such as "girl," "sisters," "geek," and "chick" in their articles and discuss various female science fiction characters, from Jane Fonda's character Barbarella in the film *Barbarella, Queen of the Galaxy*, to the more contemporary Sarah Michelle Gellar as Buffy in the television show *Buffy the Vampire Slayer*. *Mystery Date* also reclaims women's and girls' culture, but does not focus so heavily on popular culture. Instead, *Mystery Date*'s editor, Peril, discusses elements of women's culture such as bras and feminine hygiene.

Others also attempt to reclaim some of the messy parts of women's and girls' culture. In *Wive's Tales* and *Hot Pantz*, the editors discuss women's health issues including menstruation, vaginal infections and sexually transmitted diseases—topics often considered taboo. *C.U.N.T.* is another zine that reclaims a part of women's and girls' culture that is often ignored by the mainstream. It is a zine about women who cycle and also has articles about female skateboarders, including a comic on the subject of women trying to find a place in the male-dominated world of skateboarding.

In *The Search for the Meaning of Life*, editor M. Stanton criticizes the comic industry for being "created by and for men." By making this criticism in her own cultural production, she demonstrates that zines are a viable alternative to mainstream culture and a place where women comic artists can have their work published. Many of the zines collected criticize mainstream culture in review sections or discussions about cultural products. For example, in *The East Village INKY*, Halliday reviews a book on midwives and criticizes it for its portrayal of women: "it really yanks my chain that it's aimed at female readers & all the female characters seem so fake & humorless & far off the mark."

Other zine editors, such as Ordas of *Queen of the Universe*, and Kuhn of *FanGirl*, criticize mainstream culture aimed at women and girls while also celebrating it. These editors highlight another element of third wave feminism: contradiction. In *Queen of the Universe*, Ordas comments on the television program *The View*. In "When the Personal Isn't Political," she wonders, "Why am I so fascinated by *The View*?" She realizes that it is "soul-sucking, standardized trash," but admits that she still enjoys watching it. In a *FanGirl* article, "Blast From the Past," a contributor discusses her love of science fiction television shows, but also reveals her dissatisfaction with the lack of characters who are girlfriends.

Some of the zines do not broach the subject of popular culture specifically, but criticize the organization and structure of the society at large. *Wive's Tales* and *Hot Pantz* are the best examples of this. These two zines are women's health resources. They contain information on herbal treatments and remedies for various women's health issues such as menstruation, infections and contraception. The editors of both zines argue that the medical establishment has too much power over women's bodies.

ANALYSIS AND CONCLUSION

Perhaps the most important characteristic of zines for feminism is their ability to make women and girls cultural producers. Women-produced zines provide an alternative to mainstream culture, and their existence demonstrates to other girls and women that they can also produce culture rather than just consume it. According to Duncombe, "what is so radical about zines is not the writing, but the form. A form that says to anyone who picks it up: You can Do-It-Yourself, stop buying culture made for you and make your own" (Duncombe, quoted in Bigge, 2000, p. 17).

By creating their own cultural products, women and girls are creating their own space—a space that can be used not only to explore women's lives, but also to criticize mainstream culture and raise political awareness. Cathryn Bailey argues that the fact that zine producers and younger feminists "focus so much on cultural images may not represent a retreat from reality as much as an appreciation for how much of our reality is mediated through such images" (Bailey, on-line, n.p.).

Feminists can use zines to share their experiences of political awareness and to connect with other women who have similar concerns and beliefs. As Jen Smith argues, processes of cultural production by feminists "construct both a physical and psychic space for articulating our realities. By connecting with one another in these different spaces, we both create and participate in the making of our identities and our community" (Smith, 1997, p. 238).

Another possibility zines offer to feminists is their ability to reach women and girls outside of academia. Zines are typically created and read by younger women who may not identify with second wave feminism and/or be interested in Women's Studies programs. Zines may provide opportunities for second and third wave feminists (or older and younger feminists) to share information and communicate their ideas, since younger feminists may be reluctant to enter the institutions of second wave feminism but may be more likely to read zines.

Despite the many possibilities zines provide for feminism, their format also creates some limitations for feminist activity. Perhaps the most obvious and important limitation of zines is their inability to reach a large audience. For the most part, zines have very small print runs and are not read by very many people. This limits the impact they can have on society, since most people will never be aware of a zine's existence let alone go through the process of obtaining and reading it. While zines are theoretically an effective way to communicate with others, the underground culture in which they most often exist places restrictions on them and limits the possibilities they have for effectively communicating ideas between large numbers of people. Since the overarching goal of feminism is to affect social change, this is a major limitation of using zines for feminist activity.

There are some women-produced zines that have started to make the transition to become more mainstream publications. Magazines such as *BUST* and *Bitch* (both formerly zines) have been able to expand their readership, demonstrating the possibility of overcoming the problem of the small reach of zines through mainstreaming the publication. While mainstreaming zines introduces new challenges and limitations for feminist activity, such as the conflict between maintaining an underground mentality and accepting advertising, it is still too early in the process of mainstreaming to determine its overall effects.

Another important limitation of zines for feminist activity is the type of political activity they represent and encourage. Third wave feminists and zine producers mainly approach cultural production and criticism by individuals as political action. Bailey openly critiques this form of political activism:

> *Although there is tremendous variety among third wave material, one of the most worrisome features of the music and zines is the tendency to focus on a narrowly construed type of individual expression without drawing out deeper political implications. It is one of the most insidious strategies of patriarchy to acknowledge feminist insights only to reinscribe them as individual women's problems to solve rather than as societal ones. (Bailey, online, n.p.)*

As discussed before, both third wave feminists and women zine producers incorporate many autobiographical elements into their work. While this characteristic of zines provides opportunities for women to reflect on and share their experiences with others, the focus on the personal may overshadow the political. While some women zine producers use their personal experiences to encourage broad political activity, many producers overwhelmingly focus on the personal and fail to connect those personal experiences with characteristics of the larger society.

Critiquing mainstream cultural images and creating alternatives cannot substitute for political activism that is directly aimed at changing social structures and inequalities on a broader level. While the failure of many zines to reach the level of broad political activity is an important limitation to acknowledge, it is unwise to assume that zines and zine production cannot lead to, and influence, political activity. Further study, including research incorporating the voices of women zine producers and readers, will be necessary to determine how effective zines are in encouraging political activism. More research also needs to be done concerning the women who produce zines and their experiences as cultural producers.

And more in-depth studies of the role zines play in feminism is required. The current trend towards mainstreaming some women-produced zines, and the growing phenomenon of ezines, should also be monitored to determine what possibilities they may offer for feminist activism.

Endnotes

1. See Stephen Duncombe, *Notes From Underground: Zines and the Politics of Alternative Culture* (London: Verso, 1997), pp. 9–13, for a categorization and explanation of various types of zines.
2. For more information about the history and politics of Riot Grrrl, see Melissa Klein, "Duality and Redefinition: Young Feminism and the Alternative Music Community," in *Third Wave Agenda: Being Feminist, Doing Feminism*, Leslie Heywood and Jennifer Drake, eds. (Minneapolis: University of Minnesota Press, 1997), pp. 207–225, and Jessica Rosenberg and Gitana Garofalo, "Riot Grrrl: Revolutions from Within," *Signs: Journal of Women in Culture and Society* vol. 23, no. 3 (Spring 1998), pp. 804–841.
3. For examples of published third wave feminist work, see Barbara Findlen, ed., *Listen Up: Voices From the Next Feminist Generation* (Seattle: Seal Press, 1995), Rebecca Walker, ed., *To Be Real: Telling the Truth and Changing the Face of Feminism* (Toronto: Anchor Books, 1995), and Leslie Heywood and Jennifer Drake, eds., *Third Wave Agenda: Being Feminist, Doing Feminism* (Minneapolis: University of Minnesota Press, 1997).
4. Please note that no citations will be used in this section due to the nature of the material being referenced. Most zines do not contain page numbers and those that do often do not follow a logical order. For these reasons, only the zine names will be used to reference content.

References

Bailey, Cathryn. "When Girls Just Wanna Have Fun: Third Wave Cultural Engagement as Political Activism." Internet. November 23, 1999. Available: www.krypton.mankato.msus.edu/bailec/thirdwave.htm.

Bigge, Ryan. "Notes from Underground: Reassessing the State of Zinery with Prof. Stephen Duncombe." *Broken Pencil* vol. 12 (Spring 2000), pp. 16–17.

Chu, Julie. "Navigating the Media Environment: How Youth Claim a Place Through Zines." *Social Justice* vol. 24, no. 3 (Fall 1997), pp. 71–85.

Duncombe, Stephen. *Notes From Underground: Zines and the Politics of Alternative Culture.* London: Verso, 1997.

Findlen, Barbara, ed. *Listen Up: Voices From the Next Feminist Generation*. Seattle: Seal Press, 1995.

Friedman, R. Seth, ed. *The Factsheet Five Zine Reader: The Best Writing from the Underground World of Zines.* New York: Three Rivers Press, 1997.

Green, Karen and Tristan Taormino, eds. *A Girl's Guide to Taking Over the World: Writings from the Girl Zine Revolution*. New York: St. Martin's Griffin, 1997.

Heywood, Leslie and Jennifer Drake. "Introduction," in *Third Wave Agenda*, Heywood and Drake, eds., pp. 1–20.

Heywood, Leslie and Jennifer Drake, eds. *Third Wave Agenda: Being Feminist, Doing Feminism.* Minneapolis: University of Minnesota Press, 1997.

Kearney, Mary Celeste. "Producing Girls: Rethinking the Study of Female Youth Culture." In *Delinquents and Debutantes: Twentieth-Century American Girls' Cultures.* Sherrie A. Inness, ed. New York: New York University Press, 1998, pp. 285–310.

Klein, Melissa. "Duality and Redefinition: Young Feminism and the Alternative Music Community." In *Third Wave Agenda*, Heywood and Drake, eds., pp. 207–225.

Orr, Catherine M. "Charting the Currents of the Third Wave." *Hypatia* vol. 12, no. 3 (Summer 1997), pp. 29–45.

Rosenberg, Jessica and Gitana Garofalo. "Riot Grrrl: Revolutions from Within." *Signs* vol. 23, no. 3 (Spring 1998), pp. 804–841.

Scott-Dixon, Krista. "Ezines and Feminist Activism: Building a Community." Resources for Feminist Research/Documentation sur la recherche feministe vol. 27, nos. 1/2 (Spring/Summer 1999), pp. 127–132.

Smith, Jen. "Doin' It for the Ladies—Youth Feminism: Cultural Productions/Cultural Activism." In *Third Wave Agenda*, Heywood and Drake, eds. pp. 226–238.

Walker, Rebecca, ed. *To Be Real: Telling the Truth and Changing the Face of Feminism*. Toronto: Anchor Books, 1995.

CHAPTER 3

Engendering Violence

For more than 35 years, Canadian feminists have theorized, documented, pressured governments and constructed independent responses to violence against women. Against the dominant understanding of gendered violence as a series of uncommon events perpetuated by deviant criminals, feminist analysts have illuminated its widespread incidence and structural nature. Yet, as the contributions in this section emphasize, political and public recognition of violence against women has had complex consequences. In fact, many analysts suggest that the current period is one of backlash, in which feminist insights have been resisted and are increasingly displaced through decontextualized and depoliticized analytic and policy frameworks. The predominant construction of gendered violence as a problem of criminal law ignores the power relations producing violence, drawing us into a law-and-order agenda. Political responses to violence focused on criminalization and "victim services" have been accompanied by the incremental de-funding of grassroots and frontline feminist anti-violence work, silencing feminist knowledge and critique. At the same time, feminists have had to confront the limitations of the gender-focused models that framed earlier activism and scholarship. These essentialist frameworks, ignoring race, class, ability and sexuality, have revealed themselves as insufficient to explore the complex power relations through which violence is enacted and legitimized.

The articles in this section are engaged in the project of coming to terms with this complicated legacy and developing analyses with which to confront the persistence and complexities of gendered violence.

RESPONDING TO BACKLASH

The trajectory of public response to feminist anti-violence work has moved from outright denial to recognition to backlash and re-privatization. One discursive strategy that has emerged in reaction to feminist power-sensitive analyses of violence is "degendering." In the 1970s and 1980s, Canadian feminists were successful in drawing attention to "wife abuse" as a serious and widespread social problem, located within and reinforcing women's subordination. Feminist efforts to challenge men's violence in the context of intimate relationships challenged normative heterosexuality and the dominant image of the family as a haven. Frontline activists politicized "wife abuse," leading to important criminal justice reforms, such as mandatory charging policies, and increased governmental resources for transition houses and services for women and children leaving violent men. In the present context, however, feminist activists and scholars are forced into defensive postures to prevent the erosion of policy gains. As **Joanne Minaker and Laureen Snider ("Husband Abuse: Equality with a Vengence")**, demonstrate, power-sensitive frameworks have been replaced with a new "common sense" understanding of intimate violence, one that denies its gendered realities and challenges decades of feminist research and activism. In this important contribution, Minaker and Snider confront the myth of "husband abuse," demonstrating how the claim that women have now achieved gender parity in intimate violence is increasingly becoming the dominant lens used by policy makers, media and interest groups.

In an effort to contest the myth of gender parity in violence, Minaker and Snider call attention to the faulty empirical evidence on which this claim is based. While the 2004 General Social Survey found that 7% of women and 6% of men had experienced "spousal abuse" in the past five years, it also demonstrated that the severity of spousal violence is far greater for women, with far more women than men reporting beatings, injuries and chronic, ongoing assaults (Johnson 2006: 19). Why, then, does the myth of gender parity have such a purchase? Minaker and Snider contend that the rise of degendered understandings of violence needs to be understood in a context marked by anti-feminist backlash, neoliberal governance and the increased power of men's rights movements. And when a new degendered discourse of family violence seizes the public imagination and dominates policy agendas, it becomes possible to avoid dealing with the causes and consequences of the still pervasive reality of violence against women.

Minaker and Snider do not deny the fact that women can be violent, nor do they seek to minimize the suffering of men who are victimized in the context of intimate relationships. Instead, they call attention to the consequences of a new focus on "female aggressors," arguing that this focus obscures the pervasive realities of violence against women and undermines the ideological climate that feminists struggled to create, where male dominance, gendered inequality and systemic violence are problematized and challenged. **Yasmin Jiwani's ("Erasing Race: The Story of Reena Virk")** point of departure is similar. Jiwani interrogates the recent media fixation on "girl on girl" violence, using the high profile murder of Reena Virk to analyze the individualization of violence and the erasure of systemic sexism and racism that marks the contemporary framing of violence.

In 1997, a group of six girls and one boy brutally attacked Virk, a 14-year-old girl, of South Asian origin. As she tried to escape, she was caught, beaten and drowned by a girl and a boy who were part of the initial attack. The media seized on this act of extreme violence as a demonstration of the reality of female aggression. Jiwani's analysis reinforces Minaker and Snider's contention that the amplification of female violence functions in a context of backlash to deny systemic realities and to reinforce "equality with a vengeance." Yet Jiwani shifts our attention towards how the cultural obsession with "girl on girl" violence accomplishes the erasure of systemic racist violence against racialized women and girls. As she details, immigrant and refugee girls experience higher rates of violence because of dislocation, racism and sexism from both within their own communities and the external society. Yet in dominant framings, the vulnerabilities of racialized young women are often reduced to an effect of "traditional cultures," constituted as inferior to dominant white and Western values. Jiwani is challenging an essentialist feminist framing of violence against women, decrying the inattention to the intersections of racism and sexism that have marked feminist analyses of violence against women. In this way, she moves towards a third wave feminist analysis of systemic violence, calling attention to the intersections of racism and sexism that produce specific forms of gendered/racialized violence.

At the same time, however, her analysis points toward the necessity of interrogating the systemic conditions that marginalize racialized girls and women, rendering them vulnerable to racist and sexist violence. The dominant media framing of the murder of Reena Virk, stressing the escalation of "girl on girl" violence, focused on Virk's inability to "fit in." Her size and weight became explanations for the bullying to which she was subjected, while the white specificity of normative beauty standards was never interrogated. As Jiwani argues, the murder of Reena Virk was constructed in a way that individualized both her marginalization and her murder, while the nature of racism as a system of domination informing everyday life remained relegated to the margins. Along with other contributors to this section, Jiwani emphasizes the importance of sustaining a contextualized, intersectional feminist analysis and politics to counter the effects of depoliticized frameworks that ignore the systemic causes and consequences of violence.

SEXUAL ASSAULT AND LAW

Since the 1970s, Canadian feminists, activists and scholars have challenged sexual coercion, drawing attention to the pervasiveness of rape in the lives of women and girls and contesting the law's role in sustaining rape mythology. Beginning with the founding of Vancouver Rape Relief in 1973, activists built a national network of rape crisis centres to respond to and empower women and children who had experienced sexual violence. Feminists framed sexualized coercion as a systemic problem deeply rooted in gendered and racialized inequalities, and demanded state action on a number of fronts, including social policy, public education and crucially, the provision of a stable funding base for independent, women-controlled, frontline work and activism. Yet governments have contained this broad equality agenda, framing the problem of sexual violence as a problem of crime control and offering up law reform as the principal means of responding to sexual assault. Both **Rakhi Ruparelia ("Does No 'No' Mean Reasonable Doubt?: Assessing the Impact of Ewanchuk on Determinations of Consent")** and **Jane Doe ("The Ultimate Rape Victim")** interrogate the shortcomings of criminal law reforms, the manner in which they have been resisted through the practices of legal actors and the failure of governments to address the persistent inequalities enabling male violence.

In 1992, and emerging out of a series of national consultations with women's groups, the federal government enacted a set of important revisions to Criminal Code provisions on sexual assault that attempted to reduce the sway of rape mythology in law and encourage police reporting. These amendments restricted the use of complainants' sexual histories in trials. The reforms also explicitly defined consent as voluntary agreement and limited the use of "mistaken belief in consent" defence, requiring defendants to have taken reasonable steps to secure consent and barring the use of this defence when an accused person is reckless or willfully blind to the absence of agreement to engage in or continue with sexual contact.

While Canadian provisions on consent have been held up internationally as a model of feminist law reform, Ruparelia draws our attention to inconsistent applications of the consent standard and to the persistence of rape mythology in judicial decision-making. Her analysis begins with the important Canadian Supreme Court decision in *R. v. Ewanchuk* (1999), clarifying the meaning of consent in Canadian law. As Ruparelia insists, *Ewanchuk* clearly articulated an explicit consent standard, standing for the proposition that "only yes means yes." Yet by exploring several recent decisions, she shows us how judges continue to base their determinations on a "no means no" standard, a standard that is especially problematic in cases where complainants are silent or ambiguous.

Ruparelia's analysis points to the incompleteness of criminal law reform as a feminist strategy and to the manner in which progressive reforms can be resisted through the practices of legal actors. Jane Doe also critiques criminal justice responses to rape, though from a vastly different perspective than Ruparelia. Jane Doe writes from the standpoint of a raped woman determined not to be a victim. In 1986, a serial rapist who had been stalking her downtown Toronto neighbourhood attacked Jane Doe in her own apartment. Despite the fact that the police knew what he was doing and were tracking his path, women in the neighbourhood were not warned. Drawing upon her own feminist politics and her connections in the women's movement, Jane Doe enacted a profound act of resistance. In a landmark case, she successfully sued the Metro Toronto Police

Department for negligence in their failure to protect, and of Charter violations in the subsequent investigation of the rape.

Jane Doe's contribution is a selection from her powerful book *The Story of Jane Doe: A Book About Rape* (2004). In a cultural context in which raped women are always spoken for (by legal actors, therapists, the media) but never speak, this book stands as a powerful example of the resistant potential of survivor discourse. In the selection reproduced here, Jane Doe confronts the ways in which raped women are constructed as broken, as "victims," as incapable of being agents of social and political change. She highlights the ways in which law enforcement continues to devote enormous resources to the investigation of violent stranger rapes, when 80% of women and children know their aggressors and when the most common sexual violence is intimate violence and so-called "date rape." A distinction between "ideal victims" and unworthy complainants frames legal responses to sexual assault, and women and children's claims are routinely discounted when they fail to approximate the characteristics of good victims. As Doe powerfully argues, the strategies used to discount claims of sexual violation mean that women continue to distrust the criminal justice system and overwhelmingly choose not to report their assaults. Doe's insights are backed by recent statistics confirming that 3% of Canadian women were sexually assaulted in 2004, only 8% reported to the police (Johnson 2006: 24-25).

Jane Doe is asking us to think beyond criminal justice solutions. She argues that the myth of "stranger danger" functions to limit and control women, making their behaviour and diligent adherence to safety rules the focus of rape prevention. Instead, and echoing a theme that resounds in the contributions to this unit, she urges us to think about the power structures that hold sexual violence in place. Rather than feeding a law-and-order agenda that focuses on punishment and that constructs women as passive victims, effective political responses to violence should draw on the leadership of feminist anti-violence activism, provide funding for frontline work and enact social policies challenging gendered power relations.

GENDERED RACIALIZED VIOLENCE AND ABORIGINAL WOMEN

Most second wave feminist antiviolence and activism was framed by a gender essentialist analysis of male violence. The claim that all women are potential victims of male violence operated as a powerful mobilizing call, one that firmly situated the pervasiveness of violence within an analysis of patriarchy. As many of the contributions in this section underline, feminist activists and scholars face a hostile political climate in which earlier feminist critiques have been silenced through de-gendered policy approaches and individualistic constructions. This is also a time in which feminist frameworks have been challenged for failing to account for the complexities and specificities of gender violence. Analyses of the causes and consequences of gendered violence cannot proceed without careful attention to the intersections of race, colonization, class and sexuality. **Sherene Razack ("Gendered Racial Violence and Spatialized Justice: The Murder of Pamela George")** and **Anita Olsen Harper ("Is Canada Peaceful and Safe for Aboriginal Women?")** each forge a contextualized and critical analysis of gendered racialized violence that profoundly challenges earlier feminist claims.

Razack explores gendered racialized violence and the continued colonization of Aboriginal people through an analysis of the trial of two white university students for the murder of an Aboriginal woman who worked as a sex trade worker. This case was highlighted by Amnesty International (2004) in a report that condemns Canadian governments' inattention to a national crisis of missing and murdered Aboriginal women. The Native Women's Association of Canada estimates that as many as 500 Aboriginal women have been killed or reported missing in the last 20 years. Moreover, empirical studies demonstrate the depressing and pervasive realities of all forms of violence in the lives of Aboriginal women: Aboriginal women are subjected to intimate violence at more than three times the incidence rate for other women and statistics suggest that rates of sexual assault are many times greater (Johnson 2006: 64–69).

Razack writes against a de-raced analysis of violence against Aboriginal women under the rubric of "patriarchal violence against women." As she powerfully contends, while patriarchy produces men who gain identity through brutalizing women, both the murderers' and the criminal justice system's ability to dehumanize Pamela George was rooted in their understanding of her as a gendered racial "Other" whose degradation confirmed their own identities as white. In contextualizing the murder of George, Razack draws our attention to the colonization of Aboriginal peoples and the manner in which sexual violence has operated as a technology of domination. Gendered racialized violence is related to the continued sway of the 19th century perception of the Aboriginal woman as a dehumanized "squaw," and the brutalization of Pamela George can be interpreted as an act of colonization, bringing her assailants together in a shared sense of whiteness and masculinity. Razack details the mechanisms through which Aboriginal women come to be seen as rightful targets for gendered violence, limiting the extent to which this can be recognized in law and those responsible made accountable for it. Crucially, in telling the story of George, Razack is not simply arguing that we must analyze race in interrogating the extremely high rates of violence against Aboriginal women. Instead, as she insists, racialization and attention to the ongoing legacy of colonization must be made integral to feminist analyses of gendered violence.

The Sisters in Spirit Coalition, spearheaded by the Native Women's Association of Canada, stands as a model of new politics of resistance against violence. Olsen moves from Razack's focus on the murder of Pamela George as exemplary of gendered practices of colonization, violence and denial, to a focus on the political strategies that have arisen to contest racialized violence against Aboriginal women. Like Razack, Olsen locates violence against Aboriginal women within colonial practices that have eroded their political power and in the social conditions of economic and social marginalization that are the legacy of this history. Yet as she demonstrates, in the face of governmental intransigence, Aboriginal women have organized to raise awareness of gendered racialized violence and to demand action.

At a time in which systemic and politicized feminist analyses of gendered violence are being silenced beneath gender-neutral policy discourses, it is tempting to forcefully proclaim the continued and dramatic reality of "violence against women." Yet, as Razack and Olsen remind us, we cannot move ahead with analytic models and political platforms that obscure the complexities of gendered violence. Race and sexuality, along with ability and class, deepen our analyses of gendered violence and constitute bases for our strategies of resistance.

References

Amnesty International, *Stolen Sisters: A Human Rights Response to Discrimination and Violence Against Indigenous Women in Canada*, 2004, online: www.amnesty.ca/resource_centre/reports/view.php?load=arcview&article=1895&c=Resource+Centre+Reports.

Johnson, Holly. "Measuring Violence Against Women: Statistical Trends." *Statistics Canada Catalogue no. 85-570-XIE* (2006).www.statcan.ca/english/research/85-570-XIE/85-570-XIE2006001.pdf.

Husband Abuse: Equality with a Vengeance?

Joanne C. Minaker

Laureen Snider

Dr. Joanne C. Minaker teaches in the Sociology Department at MacEwan College in Edmonton, Alberta. Her research centres on questions of social justice and gender. She is working on two major projects: first, an exploration of the experiences and perspectives of young people involved in the youth justice system, and second, an examination of the contradictions, controversies and challenges of combining career/work and motherhood and its impact on women's identity.

Laureen Snider is a Professor in the Department of Sociology at Queen's University in Kingston, Ontario. She has interrogated feminism and "the punitive turn" in numerous publications. Recent publications include "Constituting the Punishable Woman: Atavistic Man Incarcerates Postmodern Woman", British Journal of Criminology, *V43, No.2, 2003: 354–78; "Making Change in Neo-Liberal Times" in G. Balfour & E. Comack, eds.,* Criminalizing Women: Gender and (In)justice in Neo-liberal Times. *Halifax: Fernwood, 2006:322–343; and "Female Punishment: From Patriarchy to Backlash", in C. Sumner, ed.,* The Blackwell Companion to Criminology. *Malden, Mass.: Blackwell, 2004: 228–252.*

INTRODUCTION

The most recurrent backlash against women's safety is the myth that men are battered as often as women . . . Of course we must have compassion for those relatively few men who are harmed by their wives and partners, but it makes logical sense to focus our attention and work on the vast problem of male violence . . . and not get sidetracked by the relatively tiny problem of male victimization. (Straton 1994: 79–80)

This article employs the phenomenon of "husband abuse" to analyze feminist initiatives to ameliorate and empower women through criminal-law reform.

"Wife battering"—the original problem constituted by 1970s feminists—has morphed into "domestic violence" and then into "husband abuse." The husband-abuse argument runs counter to decades of feminist research, theory and activism. One of the battered women's movement's key goals was to challenge the silence over woman abuse and decrease public tolerance of it. With the proliferation of "husband abuse" discourse, feminist assumptions, research evidence and claims—that women are more likely to be injured, that women are murdered at three times the rate of men, and that, when separated, they are eight times as likely to be killed (Jiwani 2000; Statistics Canada 2005)—are under attack. As we shall show, the claim that spousal abuse is a gender-neutral phenomenon has become the new "common sense," the dominant lens used by policy makers, media and influential interest groups. To understand how and why this has happened, "husband abuse" must be situated in the social, economic and political milieu that produced it and that reinforces it to this day. This article demonstrates how the very successes of feminism, combined with neoliberal governance, the burgeoning power of men's movements and new communication media, have given rise to new subjects, mentalities and practices.

1. A CASE OF BACKLASH: MALE VICTIMS AND FEMALE ABUSERS

Rationale and Claims: Domestic Violence as Gender Neutral

The claim/myth that domestic violence is an equal-opportunity activity—that is, women are as violent as men, women initiate violence as often as men and male victims are as likely to be harmed as female victims—is a striking example of feminist backlash (see Cook 1997; Macchettio 1992; Straus 1993). The creation of a "female aggressor" to match male aggressors suggests mutual battering as well as an even playing field inside and outside the family. In other words, Canada has a husband-battering problem, but it remains hidden because of cultural scripts that keep men silent and because powerful women's groups overstate male-against-female violence. We do not challenge the fact that some men are victimized in the context of intimate relationships, nor do we seek to minimize their suffering. Rather, we assert that focusing on "female aggressors" ignores the damaging violence men inflict on other men and on women, obscures who is doing what to whom and undermines the ideological climate feminists struggle to create, wherein instances of male domination, gender inequality and systemic violence are called into question.

The first question to ask, then, is whether men really are highly vulnerable to attacks from their wives and girlfriends. Are patriarchy and sexism obsolete, no longer ongoing realities in women's lives?

In 1999 social work professor Leslie Tutty published a government-commissioned study summarizing this work. Titled *Husband Abuse: An Overview of Research and Perspectives*, Tutty's report drew attention to a new "problem." Tutty asks why "it is rare to hear" stories of men abused by their wives. She relies on three sources of evidence: community studies, a summary of two small studies of abused men and conversations with representatives of 40 family-violence treatment programs and men's groups. Tutty reports "many" tales of male victimization, but the family violence intervention practitioners in her sample reported that they saw few or no male victims. For Tutty, this shortage of victims can be explained only by examining the *lack* of societal recognition of husband abuse as a problem. The reasoning is tautological: men won't come forward without more services available, but governments will only provide services if men come forward. Five years later, Health Canada commissioned another controversial report on male victimization, *Intimate Partner Violence Against Men*, authored by Eugen Lupri and Elaine Grandin (2004). Lupri and Grandin view Tutty's claims as too "feminist" and strongly criticize the government's attempt to take husband abuse seriously. They vehemently argue that there are far too many services for women, which has served to eclipse the very real problem of husband abuse.

The argument is a prototypical illustration of claims making, showing the mechanisms whereby husband abuse is discursively constructed as a real phenomenon and a pervasive social problem, thereby challenging feminist claims that asymmetrical violence within the home is the norm. Although some men are emotionally, psychologically or physically mistreated by their intimate partners, the bulk of the empirical evidence (Rodgers 1994; Johnson 1996; Fitzgerald 1999) indicates that female partners are abused more frequently and suffer more serious injuries (Comack, Chopyk and Wood 2000). But as articles in scholarly journals, newspaper reports and websites present "evidence" purportedly showing that husband abuse is a serious social problem, and as more and more stories of the plight of abused male victims attract disproportionate publicity, the "problem" becomes more deeply entrenched into the public mind.

To expose this tautology, public discourse, specifically print and Internet media, must be more closely examined. Our search of Canada Newsstand, a database of events as reported in major Canadian newspapers, revealed more than 100 articles on the topic "husband abuse," indicating its wide dissemination.

They make "sense" because they are inserted into a larger symbolic structure where equality is assumed to exist and differences between men and women have disappeared. The argument reproduces rather than challenges male domination, as well as obscuring structural inequalities. It is very much about silencing feminist claims. Abuse in the home is no longer a woman's or feminist issue but a "human issue," with men and women equally affected (McNeely and Mann 1990). Under the guise of "completing the picture," the reality of power, control and conflict in heterosexual intimate relationships is masked; the very essence of the problem of violence against women disappears. Advocates use terms like "partner conflict," "mutuality of abuse" and "family violence" to make the problem of male battery real through tautology (Fontes 2003).

The prominence of the social problem of husband abuse indicates something else—a countermovement led by pro-men's rights groups and anti-feminist women's groups aimed at re-appropriating male power and privilege lost to second wave feminism. In an attempt to reclaim lost ideological power, husband-abuse discourse denies that the familial home is patriarchal. Gender parity validates gender-neutral policies that result in a focus on individual cases of violence, ignoring the systemic reality of male violence against women. In short, the social construction of the problem of "husband abuse" not only calls for, but has largely brought about, a resurgence of gender-neutral politics.

EMPIRICAL EVIDENCE: WHAT'S JUSTIFYING THESE CLAIMS?

On July 14, 2005, Statistics Canada posted a statistical profile of family violence in Canada which asserts that "an estimated 7% of women and 6% of men in a current or previous spousal relationship encountered spousal violence during the five years up to and including 2004" (Statistics Canada 2005). Based on data from the 2004 General Social Survey, the report also notes that the severity of spousal violence is greater for women: 23% of female victims reported the most serious forms of violence (being beaten, choked, or threatened by a gun or knife), compared to 15% of men. Only 19% of men indicated they suffered injuries, compared to 44% of women. Proof positive of gender parity?

The "canon" or "edict" supporting these claims is a bibliography published by psychologist Martin Fiebert in 1997 and updated in 2001. Fiebert's bibliography is often taken as gospel and used to convey the impression that there is solid empirical grounding for husband-abuse claims. His "extensive bibliography" has frequently been called on to demonstrate that women are as violent as men, that women initiate violence as often as men and that male victims are as likely to be harmed as female victims.

To interrogate these claims, we went straight to the source—Martin Fiebert's *References Examining Assaults by Women on Their Spouses or Male Intimate Partners: An Annotated Bibliography* (2005), and what we found was revealing.

Of the 176 sources listed, at least 80 employed the Conflict Tactics Scale, noted for equating physical with psychological violence. Another 50 sampled only college or university students in dating relationships. Nineteen sampled selective groups (e.g., only women identified as "aggressive," only males, or military couples), and of these 11 studied high school students and youth (some as young as 10 years old). Twenty-four were review studies, many citing sources included on the primary list. Many studies cited were flawed or outdated. Three of the studies cited (Feather 1996; Gonzalez 1997; Milardo 1998) used hypothetical scenarios. For example, N.T. Feather (1996) presented participants with a hypothetical scenario in which either a husband or wife had perpetrated domestic violence and evaluated participants' reactions. The study found that most participants were more sympathetic to the wife and viewed husbands as deserving of harsher penalties.

Despite these weaknesses, Fiebert's (2001) bibliography carries impressive scholarly weight. The "empirical evidence" he has compiled, and studies published by reputable, respected sources such as Statistics Canada, are seized, publicized and celebrated by anti-feminist journalists and conservative men's groups.

One does not have to look far to see the results. Statistics Canada has retreated to gender-neutral "family violence research" (DeKeseredy and Kelly 1993; DeKeseredy and Schwartz 2003), eschewing gender-specific definitions of violence in intimate relationships employed earlier (in the Violence Against Women Survey and the Canadian National Survey on Woman Abuse in University and College Dating). As we will argue below, husband-abuse claims are used as a rationale to further reduce resources for women's groups, shelters and other social-support services for female victims of male violence (Jiwani 2000).

2. SITUATING HUSBAND ABUSE: ANALYSIS AND IMPLICATIONS

Removing Male Privilege—The Successes of Feminist Movements

To understand why Canada in particular (and Anglo-American democracies overall) has been so ready to accept claims that spousal abuse is gender neutral, we must go back to 1970 and examine not the failures of feminism but its real and enduring successes. Over the past 35 years, feminists throughout the developed world have achieved remarkable victories, revolutionizing dominant institutions, laws, tolerance levels and subjectivities.

Women's opportunities for jobs, education, benefits, affluence and independence increased. So did women's expectations of men, and their/our unwillingness to accept or excuse bad (male) behaviour. Rape and domestic-assault laws were revised; policies banning sexual and workplace harassment became common. One predictable, indeed inevitable, response to this very successful bid for power was the emergence of resistance (Foucault 1977; Faludi 1991). Voices in media and government began proclaiming that the pendulum had swung too far. Men, it was claimed, were now the disadvantaged and oppressed sex.

MAKING LIVES HARDER—DISMANTLING THE WELFARE STATE

Resistance and resentment were reinforced by concomitant economic changes, changes that destroyed much of the social safety net and removed many of the benefits associated with the Keynesian welfare state (Fudge and Cossman 2002). Starting in the 1980s, powerful economic elites persuaded state actors to embark on wide-ranging programs of neoliberal "reform."

Neoliberal governance required the constitution of a new subject, the responsibilized individual. The goal of government was no longer to deliver social justice or full employment or to guarantee minimum standards of living to those on the bottom. Social safety nets, it was argued, discourage people from making prudent investments in their future. The result has been extensive privatization, the fraying of the social safety net and sharply heightened levels of inequality (Cossman and Fudge 2002; Schrecker 2001).

While these policy shifts affected all men, women and children, groups were differentially affected. The virtues of neoliberalism—self-reliance, independence, marketing oneself as a product—are difficult to realize if you are poor, young, female, single, uneducated, disabled or marginalized by race or ethnicity. When governments turn responsibilities for day care, elder care and healthcare over to the private sector, those unable to pay for services are punished.

But many men were also hard hit. Neoliberal changes produced "a sharp deterioration in the labour market position of young men" (Fudge and Cossman 2002: 25). Throughout the 1980s and 1990s, unionized, well-paid, secure jobs disappeared, and young working-class men suffered—they lost earning potential, income, security, status and power.

RESULTS: ANTI-FEMINIST BACKLASH

Women's successes and male economic, political and ideological losses, then, have provided fuel for widespread resistance and what has been called anti-feminist backlash (Faludi 1989). Many institutions today are questioning, if not reversing, feminist-inspired initiatives: in education, boys are now portrayed as disadvantaged; in the workplace, claims of female sexual harassment are seen as out of control. The identity labelled "feminist" has been transformed from badge of honour to stigma (Masuch 2004). In 1998 Canada's federal government, the body that established the inquiries and commissions that put feminism on the policy map in the first place, eliminated all subsidies to the National Action Committee on the Status of Women (Fudge 2002). Women and girls are depicted as the equals of men: equally violent, aggressive and sadistic (Pearson 1995, 1997; Dutton 1994; Laframboise 1996, 1998). Stories that reflect unfavourably on "feminists" receive massive primetime media coverage.

Thus it is not surprising that husband abuse is widely accepted as real, or that women today are constructed as equally violent. These claims are made in the prestigious languages of science; they resonate with well-established, powerful discourses of equality and risk. Such factors facilitate their cultural penetration and make them appear both salient and relevant. As social problem and claim, husband abuse reflects and simultaneously reinforces the "mentalities and sensibilities" of our time (Garland 1990, 2001). Seeing the world through lenses of equality has become simple common sense. However, its effects are neither simple nor benign. Discourses of equality and risk transmit important gender-neutralizing, gender-denying messages, messages with real, often deleterious effects.

Today the compulsion to (re)discover and (re)assert equality between men and women permeates cultural, political, economic and social life, particularly in English-language capitalist democracies. Virtually every social problem and issue has been reinterpreted in terms of gender equality. If fathers are the prime culprits in child sexual abuse, mothers must be equally likely to offend. If boys bully, so do girls. In Canada moral panics centred on sadistic antisocial women and violent thrill-seeking girl gangs are common, fuelled by the notorious real-life examples of Karla Homolka and the murderous assault on teenager Reena Virk. And now, in the area of domestic abuse, the logic that the existence of battered wives "proves" the existence of battered husbands, and the allied assumption that women inflict equally serious injuries and psychological damage, permeates dominant culture. However few battered husbands there actually are, they will be "found," publicized and hailed as examples of a reality formerly obscured by man-hating feminists.

The effect is an ongoing cultural denial of the reality of unequal victimization. Portraying spousal violence as gender neutral sends powerful political messages, messages that justify "an ideological and moral retreat" by professionals and policy makers (Worrall 2002: 48). Denying the victimization of women is not merely politically and culturally attractive; it is a potential money-saver. If men and women are equally likely to batter, why should governments provide specialized counsellors for rape victims or costly gender-specific programs and institutions?

However, portraying reality this way requires a highly selective reading of extant empirical literatures. Numerous studies document the long-established fact that the percentage of female batterers, child sex abusers and violent girls is much lower than that of males; in most offences, the sex ratio discrepancy is close to 10:1 (Chesney-Lind 1987; Daly and Chesney-Lind 1988; DeKeseredy 2000; Belknap 2001). A similar Canadian study found that 80% of spousal violence, 75% of physical child abuse and 100% of child sexual abuse involves male perpetrators (Mann 2000: 31). Those studies of domestic violence that present evidence of gender equivalence (Straus 1993; Straus and Gelles 1986; Straus et al. 1980; Kennedy and Dutton 1989) turn out, on closer analysis, to tell a very different story. Conflict scales that equate verbal and physical violence hide the fact that female violence against men is usually defensive and fail to mention that women are usually the help-seeking party (Comack et al. 2000). The fact that women victims of spousal violence are much more likely to be injured, and much more likely to suffer serial assaults, also disappears (Statistics Canada 2005).

IMPLICATIONS AND CONCLUSION

This study has shown how a new de-gendered consciousness of family violence has seized the public imagination and come to dominate policy agendas.

The claim that male and female partners are equally prone to violence is made by powerful groups, resonates with discourses of equality and reinforces constituencies promoting criminal justice "solutions" to all social problems. Men's movements and pro-status-quo women's groups ensure public prominence for such claims, while social-science experts confer legitimacy. The quest to discover, document and publicize the hypothesized "missing" male victim (and to criminalize the hypothesized female offender) can thus be situated in the social, political and cultural conditions that produced it.

The consequences for women, particularly those disadvantaged by class and ethnicity have been more negative than positive. The invention and celebration of "husband abuse" makes it more difficult to deal with real power imbalances between male and female partners and easier to ignore or explain away empirical evidence showing that family violence usually means wife abuse. For men and men's groups, if women are really "just as bad as men," it becomes acceptable—even legitimate—to avoid dealing with the causes and consequences of the still ubiquitous reality of male violence against women. When policy makers take husband-abuse claims at face value, resources allocated to rape crisis centres, shelters and services for battered women can be reduced or eliminated. Feminist scholars are forced into defensive postures to prevent the erosion of gains already won (or so it was believed) and away from gender analyses that help us to understand and respond constructively to the realities of intimate violence. The social and cultural conditions that reinforce violent solutions create more desperate citizens, and ever more desperate social orders are ignored, silenced or obscured. And the struggle to build safer societies becomes a battle over which sex should be punished more (Snider 1998).

References

Belknap, Joan. 2001. *The Invisible Woman: Gender, Crime and Justice*, 2nd ed. Belmont, CA: Wadsworth.

Carlen, Pat, ed. 2002. *Women and Punishment The Struggle for Justice*. Collumpton, U.K.: Willan Publishing.

Chesney-Lind, Meda. 1987. "Girls and violence: An exploration of the gender gap in serious delinquent behaviour." In D. Corwell, I. Evans, and C. O'Donnell (eds.), *Childhood Aggression and Violence*. New York: Plenum.

Comack, Elizabeth, ed. 1999. *Locating Law: Race/Class/Gender Connections*. Halifax: Fernwood Publishing.

Comack, Elizabeth, Vanessa Chopyk, and Linda Wood. 2000. *Mean Streets? The Social Locations, Gender Dynamics, and Patterns of Violent Crime in Winnipeg*. Ottawa: Canadian Centre for Policy Alternatives.www.policyalternatives.ca/documents/Manitoba_Pubs/meanstreets.pdf

Common questions about domestic abuse against men. n.d. Men's Activism News Network.www.mensactivism.org/activism.files/q_and_a_flyer.pdf

Condon, Mary. 2002. "Privatizing pension risk: Gender, law and financial markets". In Brenda Cossman and Judy Fudge (eds.), *Privatization, Law, and the Challenge to Feminism*. Toronto: University of Toronto Press.

Cook, Philip. 1997. *Abused Men: The Hidden Side of Domestic Violence*. Westport, CT: Praeger.

Cony Charles E., Martin S. Fiebert, and Erin Pizzey. 2002. "Controlling domestic violence against men".http://www.familytx.org/research/Control_DV_against_men.pdf

Daly, Kathleen and Meda Chesney-Lind. 1988. "Feminism and criminology". *Justice Quarterly* 5(4): 101–143.

DeKeseredy, Walter. 2000. *Women, Crime and the Canadian Criminal Justice System*. Cincinnati: Anderson.

DeKeseredy, Walter and Martin O. Schwartz. 2003. "Backlash and whiplash: A critique of Statistics Canada's 1999 General Social Survey on Victimization". *Online Journal of Justice Studies* 1(1).http://ojjs.icaap.org/issues/l.l/dekeseredy-schwartz.html

Dutton, Donald. 1994. "Patriarchy and wife assault: The ecological fallacy". *Violence and Victims* 9: 125–140.

Evans, Patricia. 1996. *The Verbally Abusive Relationship: How to Recognize It and How to Respond*. Avon, MA: Adams Media.

Evenson, Brad and Carol Milstone. 1999. "Women emerge as aggressors in Alberta survey". *National Post*, July 10: Al.

Faludi, Susan. 1991. *Backlash: The Undeclared War against American Women*. New York: Crown.

Feather, N.T. 1996. "Domestic violence, gender and perceptions of justice". *Sex Roles* 35: 507–509.

Fiebert, Martin S. 2001. "References examining assaults by women on their spouses or male partners: An annotated bibliography".http://www.batteredrnen. com/fiebert.htm

Fitzgerald, Robin. 1999. *Family Violence in Canada: A Statistical Profile*. Ottawa: Statistics Canada.

Foucault, Michel. 1977. *Discipline and Punish: The Birth of the Prison. Trans. Alan Sheridan*. New York: Pantheon.

Fudge, Judy. 2002. "From segregation to privatization: Equality, the law and women public servants 1908–2001". In Brenda Cossman and Judy Fudge (eds.), *Privatization, Law, and the Challenge to Feminism*. Toronto: University of Toronto Press.

Fudge, Judy and Brenda Cossman. 2002. "Introduction: Privatization, law and the challenge to feminism". In Brenda Cossman and Judy Fudge (eds.), *Privatization, Law, and the Challenge to Feminism*. Toronto: University of Toronto Press.

Garland, David. 1990. *Punishment and Modern Society*. Chicago: University of Chicago Press.

Garland, David. 2001. *The Culture of Control*. Oxford: Oxford University Press.

Gilmore, Jane. 2002. "Creeping privatization in health care: Implications for women as the state redraws its role". In Brenda Cossman and Judy Fudge (eds.), *Privatization, Law, and the Challenge to Feminism*. Toronto: University of Toronto Press.

Gonzalez, Denise. 1997. "Why females initiate violence: A study examining the reasons behind assaults on men." Master's thesis, California State University, Long Beach.

Hammer, Rhonda. 2002. *Antifeminism and Family Terrorism: A Critical Feminist Perspective*. Lanham, MD: Rowman & Littlefield.

Hannah-Moffat, Kelly. 2001. *Punishment in Disguise: Penal Governance and Canadian Federal Women's Imprisonment*. Toronto: University of Toronto Press.

Hannah-Moffat, Kelly and Margaret Shaw, eds. 2000. *An Ideal Prison? Critical Essays on Women's Imprisonment in Canada*. Halifax: Fernwood Publishing.

Jiwani, Yasmine. 2000. "The 1999 General Social Survey on Spousal Violence: An Analysis".http://www.harbour.sfu.ca/freda/reports/gssol.htm

Kennedy, Lesley and Donald Dutton. 1989. "The incidence of wife assault in Alberta". *Canadian Journal of Behavioural Sciences* 21: 40–54.

Johnson, Holly. 1996. "Violent Crime In Canada". *Juristat* 16.6.

Laframboise, Donna. 1996. *The Princess at the Window: A New Gender Morality.* Toronto: Penguin Books.

——. 1998. "Battered shelters". *National Post*, November 14: B1.

——. 1999. "Men and women are equals in violence". *National Post*, July 10: Al.

Lupri, Eugen and Elaine Grandin. 2004. *Intimate Partner Violence against Men*. Ottawa: Minister of Health.

Macchettio, John. 1992. "Aspects of male victimization and female aggression: Implications for counselling men". *Journal of Mental Health Counseling* 14: 375–392.

Mackiln, Audrey. 2002. "Public entrance/private member". In Brenda Cossman and Judy Fudge (eds.), *Privatization, Law, and the Challenge to Feminism*. Toronto: University of Toronto Press.

Mann, Ruth. 2000. *Who Owns Domestic Abuse? The Local Politics of a Social Problem.* Toronto: University of Toronto Press.

——. 2002. "Emotionality and social activism". *Journal of Contemporary Ethnography* 31: 251–284.

Martin, Diane. 2002. "Both pitied and scorned: Child prostitution in an era of privatization". In Brenda Cossman and Judy Fudge (eds.), *Privatization, Law, and the Challenge to Feminism.* Toronto: University of Toronto Press.

Masuch, Christie. 2004. "Man-Haters, Militants and Aggressive Women: Young Women, Media Representations and Feminist Identity". Master's thesis, Queen's University, Kingston, ON.

McNeely, R.L. and C.R. Mann. 1990. "Domestic violence is a human issue". *Journal of Interpersonal Violence* 5: 129–132.

MENWEB. n.d. MenWeb—Domestic Violence (home page).www. batteredmen.com

Milardo, R.M. 1998. "Gender asymmetry in common couple violence". *Personal Relationships* 5: 423–443.

Pearson, Patricia. 1995. "Behind every successful psychopath". *Saturday Night* (October): 50–63.

——. 1997. *When She Was Bad: Women's Violence and the Myth of Innocence*. Toronto: Random House.

Peterson, Karen S. 2003. "Studies shatter myth about abuse". *USA Today*, June 22.www.usatoday.com/news/health/2003-06-22-abuseusat_x.htm

Philips, Lynn. 2002. "Tax law and social reproduction: The gender of fiscal policy in an age of privatization". In Brenda Cossman and Judy Fudge (eds.), *Privatization, Law, and the Challenge to Feminism*. Toronto: University of Toronto Press.

Rodgers, Karen. 1994. "Wife Assault: The Findings of a National Survey". *Juristat* 14.9.

Sacks, Glenn. 2003. "Battered husbands' injuries no jokes: Men as well as women deserve shelter from domestic violence".www.ifeminists.net/introduction/editorials/2003/0617sacks.html

Saenger, Gerhart. 1955. "Male and female relations in the American comic strip". *Public Opinion Quarterly* 19: 195–205.

Sarantakos, Sotorios. 1999. "Husband abuse: Fact or fiction?" *Australian Journal of Social Issues* 34: 231–252.

Schrecker, Ted. 2001. "From the welfare state to the no-second-chances state". In Susan Boyd, Dorothy Chunn, and Robert Menzies (eds.), *(Ab)Using Power: The Canadian Experience*. Halifax: Fernwood Publishing.

Smart, Carol. 1959. *Feminism and the Power of the Law*. London: Routledge.

——. 1995. *Law, Crime and Sexuality: Essays in Feminism*. London: Sage.

Snider, Laureen. 1955. "Legal reform and social control: The dangers of abolishing rape". *International Journal of Sociology of Law* 13: 337–356.

——. 1994. "Feminism, punishment and the potential of empowerment". *Canadian Journal of Law and Society* 9(1): 75–104.

——. 1998. "Towards safer societies: Punishment, masculinities and violence against women". *British Journal of Criminology* 38: 1–39.

——. 2000. "The sociology of corporate crime: An obituary Theoretical Criminology" 4: 169–206.

Stanko, Elizabeth. 2001. "The day to count: Reflections on a methodology to raise awareness about the impact of domestic violence in the UK". *Criminal Justice* 1: 215–226.

Statistics Canada. 2005. *Family violence in Canada: A statistical profile, 2005*. The Daily, July 14.www.statcan.ca/Daily/English/050714/td050714.htm

Steinmetz, Suzanne. 1977. *The Cycle of Violence: Assertive, Aggressive and Abusive Family Interaction*. New York: Praeger.

Steinmetz, Suzanne. 1978. "The battered husband syndrome". *Victimology* 2: 499–509.

Straton, Jack. 1994. "The myth of the 'battered husband syndrome.'" *Masculinities* 2: 79–82.

Straus, Murray. 1993. "Physical assaults by wives: A major social problem". In Richard Gelles and David Loseke (eds.), *Current Controversies on Family Violence*. London: Sage.

Straus, Murray and Richard Gelles. 1986. "Societal changes and change in family violence from 1975 to 1985 as revealed by two national surveys". *Journal of Marriage and the Family* 48: 465–480.

Straus, Murray, Richard Gelles, and Suzanne Steinmetz. 1980. *Behind closed doors: Violence in the American family*. New York: Doubleday.

Tutty, Leslie. 1999. *Husband Abuse: An Overview of Research and Perspectives*. Ottawa: National Clearinghouse on Family Violence.

Welldon, Elizabeth. 1988. *Mother, Madonna, Whore: The Idealization and Denigration of Motherhood*. London: Free Association Books.

Wolf, Naomi. 1993. *Fire with Fire*. Toronto: Random House.

Worrall, Anne. 2002. "Rendering women punishable: The making of a penal crisis". In Pat Carlen (ed.), *Women and Punishment The Struggle for Justice.* Cullompton. U.K.: Willan Publishing.

Vosko, Leah. 2004. *Confronting the Norm: Gender and the International Regulation of Precarious Work*. Ottawa: Law Commission of Canada.

Erasing Race: The Story of Reena Virk

Yasmin Jiwani

Yasmin Jiwani is an Associate Professor in the Department of Communication Studies at Concordia University, Montreal. Her recent publications include: Discourses of Denial: Mediations of Race, Gender and Violence. *Vancouver: University of British Columbia Press, 2006; and a co-edited anthology titled:* Girlhood, Redefining the Limits. *Montreal: Black Rose Books, 2006.*

On November 14, 1997, 14-year-old Reena Virk, a girl of South Asian origin, was brutally murdered in a suburb of Victoria, British Columbia. Reena was first beaten by a group of seven girls and one boy between the ages of 14 and 16. She was accused of stealing one of the girls' boyfriend and spreading rumours. Her beating was framed as retaliation to these alleged actions. According to journalistic accounts, the attack began when one of the girls attempted to stub out a cigarette on her forehead. As she tried to flee, the group swarmed her, kicked her in the head and body numerous times, attempted to set her hair on fire and brutalized her to the point where she was severely injured and bruised. During the beating, Reena reportedly cried out "I'm sorry" (*The Vancouver Sun* A10). Battered, Reena staggered across a bridge, trying to flee her abusers, but was followed by two of them—Warren Glowatski and Kelly Ellard. The two then continued to beat her, smashing her head against a tree and kicking her to the point of unconsciousness. They then allegedly dragged her body into the water and forcibly drowned her. Reena's body was subsequently found eight days later on November 22, 1997, with very little clothing on it. The pathologist who conducted the autopsy noted that Virk had been kicked 18 times in the head and her internal injuries were so severe as to result in tissues being crushed between the abdomen and backbone. She also noted that the injuries were similar to those that would result from a car being driven over a body. The pathologist concluded that Reena would likely have died even if she had not drowned.[1]

This chilling murder of a 14-year-old girl was singled out by the news media and heavily reported in the local, national and international press. The media's initial framing of the murder focused largely on "girl-on-girl" violence. The issue of racism, sexism, pressures of assimilation and the social construction of Reena Virk as an outcast were rarely addressed. When they were addressed, it was always in the language of appearance—that she weighed 200 pounds and was five feet, eight inches tall. According to media accounts, her heaviness and height precluded her from being accepted. The assumptions regarding the validity of normative standards of beauty and appearance were significantly absent in all accounts of the story. Rather, as with dominant frameworks of meaning that are utilized to cover stories of racialized immigrant and refugee communities—Reena's difference was underscored and inferiorized.

This article focuses on the framing of the Reena Virk murder in media accounts. The aim is to draw attention to the lack of coverage and critical analysis of racism as a form of violence communicated by exclusion, scapegoating and targeting of "others," and underpinned by the inferiorization of difference as well as its framing as deviance. Additionally, this article argues that the absence of any discussion of racism as a motivating factor in the murder is symbolic of the denial of racism as a systemic phenomenon in Canada. The absence of any mention of racism in the judicial decision concerning the murder is echoed in the news coverage of the decision, thereby privileging a particular interpretation of the case as one involving physical gang violence. Finally, the erasure of race in the discourse of the news media is made evident by the complete denial of Virk's appearance and racialized identity and its significance in terms of her vulnerability to violence. By not referencing "race" in this context, the media were able to negate and omit any substantive discussion of racism, and at the same time, to reinforce hegemonic notions of racism—as behaviour which is simply confined to hate groups.

RACIALIZED GIRLS AND THEIR VULNERABILITY TO VIOLENCE

A recent study conducted by the Alliance of Five Research Centres on Violence underscores the vulnerability of girls and young women to male violence. It has been found, for instance, that girls comprise 84% of the reported victims of sexual abuse, 60% of the physical child abuse cases and 52% of cases of reported neglect (Department of Justice). Girls are also victims in 80% of the cases of sexual assaults reported to police (Fitzgerald). Many flee abusive homes and end up on the streets where they are subjected to further abuse (Alliance). The situation is compounded for marginalized girls who have to deal with the interlocking effects of racism, homophobia, classism, ableism and sexism (Jiwani 1998b; Razack).

The Working Groups on Girls (WGG) noted in its report that immigrant and refugee girls experience higher rates of violence because of dislocation, racism and sexism from both within their own communities and the external society (Friedman). Caught between two cultures, where their own is devalued and constructed as inferior, and where cultural scripts in both worlds encode patriarchal values, these girls face a tremendous struggle in trying to "fit." When they don't, they suffer intense backlash. In effect, what these girls experience is a double dose of patriarchy—the patriarchal values encoded in the dominant society, which resonates with the patriarchal values encoded in their own cultural backgrounds.

At the core of the diversity of experiences that shape the lives and realities of girls from marginalized groups is the intensity of rejection and exclusion mediated by the mainstream of society. Faced by racism, and the double dose of sexism, girls from racialized immigrant and refugee communities have few avenues of recourse available to them.[2] The obverse side of this rejection is the overwhelming pressure to conform and assimilate into the dominant normative framework and thereby strive for at least conditional acceptance. However, the internalization of the dominant culture often leads to an inferiorization, negation and hatred of the self and their communities.

CULTURAL IDENTITY AND CONFLICT

Rather than focusing on girls' experiences of racism and sexism, many studies have tended to concentrate on issues of cultural and intergenerational conflict within racialized immigrant communities. To some extent, these studies have emerged in response to prevailing occupations in the area of ethnicity and identity retention cohering around the debate of whether such identity is primordially rooted (Geertz; Isaacs) or situationally constructed (Keyes; Lyman and Douglass). Further, the prevalence of these identity-oriented studies suggests a greater degree of comfort in looking at "cultural" issues of co-existence, conflict and exchange, or assimilation and acculturation (Drury; Jabbra; Kim; Rosenthal et al.), although more recently, this trend has shifted (see, for example, Matthews).

Despite the use of culture as the focal point of inquiry, many of these studies reveal that girls within racialized immigrant cultures experience a greater degree of dissatisfaction and strain with the normative values imposed by their own culture (Hutnik; Miller; Onder; Rosenthal et al.). The contextual factors influencing and shaping this dissatisfaction tend not to be examined in structural terms, i.e., as emanating from the subordinate position of the cultural group in relation to the dominant society, and the construction of racialized immigrant communities as deviant Others (Bannerji 1993; Thobani; Tsolidas as cited in Turnbull 163). Nor has the complex interaction of sexism and racism shaping the lives and choices of young women been examined in great detail in Canadian studies (see Bourne et al.; Vertinsky et al.). Thus, rather than focusing on how racialized girls are inferiorized and how they internalize dominant values, which embody a rejection of the self and their cultural communities, many of the existing studies tend to frame these "Other" communities as being problematic insofar as clinging to traditional, non-liberatory and patriarchal cultures (Alicea).

Within the context of the violence of racism, girls from marginalized communities are often faced with systemic barriers around which they must negotiate their survival. They may choose to try to conform and assimilate, although this choice is often not available to them due to the exclusionary impact of racism and/or homophobia. On the other hand, the deviant characterization of their communities by the mainstream often forces them into silence as they are afraid to report experiences of violence for the fear of betraying their own communities (Burns; Razack). As Burns notes, our abuse has been hidden in our communities' refusal to acknowledge the pervasiveness of violence in our lives. This refusal is not maliciousness but a protective measure born of the legitimate fear that such information would be used as a weapon by the dominant culture. Our abuse has been hidden behind bravado and denials. The result is the creation of a climate of tolerance.

Yet, it is critical to form a space whereby the specific kinds of violence that racialized girls experience can be discussed and analyzed. It is not enough to universalize their experiences within the category of "girls" or "women" (Tipper; Russell), or alternatively "youth" and "children." At the same time, focusing on culture fails to capture the structural forces of oppression that shape the lives of racialized and marginalized girls. A central issue here is the subtlety with which racism is communicated and naturalized, and how it intersects with sexism to influence the lived reality and strategies of survival of racialized girls. As Kimberle Crenshaw notes, "Race and gender are two of the primary sites for the particular distribution of social resources that ends up with observable class differences" (97).

An analysis of how racism interlocks with other systems of domination to influence the life chances and reality of racialized girls requires acknowledging racism as a form of violence that is endemic and pervasive. Nevertheless, while it has become increasingly common to accept the structured inequality produced and reproduced by sexism, the same does not hold true for racism. Thus, rather than accepting racism as a structure of domination, similar to sexism, and as arising from a legacy of colonialism, the reality of racism has to be "proven" continually (Bannerji 1987; 1993). In part, this denial of racism is formed and informed by the dominant mediated discourses on race and racism, which are powerfully communicated through the mass media.

THE MASS MEDIA, "RACE," AND RACISM

The media play a critical role in communicating notions of "race" and racism. In effect, they help define these terms and locate them within the public imagination (Hall 1990; van Dijk 1993). In the production and reproduction of social knowledge, the mainstream mass media are crucial vehicles in reinforcing hegemonic interpretations and interests (Cottle, 1992). Thus, how they frame race and racism is both derived from and informed by social life, and reproduced in everyday talk and thought (Smitherman-Donaldson and van Dijk; van Dijk 1987).

Previous research has documented the ways in which Canadian mainstream media communicate notions of "race" and forward particular definitions of racism (Bannerji, 1986; Indra; Jiwani, 1993; Scanlon). These definitions explain racism as arising from ignorance, increasing immigration and economic downturns (Jiwani 1993; see also van Dijk 1993). Such explanations are privileged through various discursive means so that they appear to be meaningful and resonate with everyday social reality. "Racists" are then defined as ignorant, uneducated and usually rural-based individuals who at times are organized into hate groups (Jiwani, 1993). At the same time, "race" is represented by allusions to cultural differences and phenotypic differences where these can be readily observed (i.e., through film footage and pictures), and through Manichean oppositions that underscore these differences within the footage itself or in the presentation of the story (see also Jan Mohamed; Jiwani, 1998). It has been argued that the Canadian news media communicate race and racism by "omission and commission"—at times in a deliberate manner, and at other times, through strategic absence (Jiwani 1993).

MEDIA FRAMES—THE ERASURE OF RACE/RACISM

As the events leading to Virk's murder unfolded in the daily papers and television newscasts, the horror of what "girls do to other girls" was highlighted and quickly overshadowed the issue of male violence. In contrast to the numerous deaths of women by their spouses and ex-spouses, Reena's death was held up as a symbol of how girls are not immune to committing acts of violence. Story after story in the daily papers covered the issue of teen girl violence, quoting research to support the main contention that girls are just as dangerous as boys.[3] Even though existing research clearly links the issue of teen girl violence to the internalization of a dominant, patriarchal culture that values sex and power, this connection was trivialized if not side-stepped altogether (Artz; Joe and Chesney Lind). Additionally, counter-evidence, which demonstrates that only 3.83% of violent crimes are committed by girls (Schramm, 1998), failed to hit the headlines in the same manner or intensity.

Headlines from *The Vancouver Sun* during this early period (November 1997) framed the story in the following way: "Teenage girls and violence: The B.C. reality"; "Girls fighting marked by insults, rumours, gangs"; "Bullies: Dealing with threats in a child's life"; "Girls killing girls a sign of angry, empty lives." This last headline suggests that had girls followed a traditional (gender-based) lifestyle, their lives would not be so empty and frustrating.

Throughout the coverage, the media dwelt with puzzlement on the increasing violence of teenage girls at a time when they were supposedly enjoying greater equality. Statistics indicating the growing number of girls graduating with honours, as compared to boys, were used to demonstrate this perplexing contradiction. Implicit throughout the news coverage was the sense that girls do not deserve to be violent because of the privileges they are now enjoying, and further, that girls are not used to the demands inherent in these privileges and therefore can not cope, a disturbing echo of late 19th century ideology.

At no time did the media provide any in-depth analysis of the violent nature of the dominant culture, or examine ways in which violent behaviour is internalized as a function of coping with a violent society. Nor did the media report on the kinds of violence to which girls are generally subjected, or the differential impact of violence on girls and boys from different backgrounds. In fact, this kind of coverage only surfaced with the school murders in Littleton, U.S.A., and the subsequent copycat murder in Taber, Alberta (see for instance, *The Vancouver Sun* Special Issue on Teen Violence), where suddenly, boys who were considered marginalized became the objects of public sympathy and reporting.

While the dominant filter became one of girl-on-girl violence, this subsequently shifted, albeit slightly, towards a sustained coverage of schoolyard bullies, sprinkled with some sympathetic coverage of children who are marginalized in school because they do not fit peer-group normative standards. Aside from opinion pieces written by individuals, mostly South Asian, none of the news articles discussed the issue of racialization as it impacts on girls who are physically different by virtue of their skin colour, or the pressures of assimilation that racialized girls experience in attempting to fit within their peer group culture. Interestingly, in contrast to previous patterns of coverage observed in the news accounts of the stories of young racialized women, accounts which tended to focus on issues of cultural and intergenerational conflict (Jiwani 1992), the coverage of the Reena Virk murder did neither. Instead, the coverage continued to focus on girl-on-girl violence in the immediate aftermath of the murder.

Subsequent coverage of the court appearances and sentencing of the six girls who were charged, focused on Virk's inability to find acceptance in her peer culture, and once again, emphasized her weight and height as the major contributing factors. Despite her physical difference—as a racialized girl—there was no mention, save one, of the possible motive being racism. Instead, the stories repeatedly stressed her lack of "fit" and her overweight appearance. The implication was that had Reena Virk fit the normative standards, she would have been acceptable. Normative standards in this society imply a body which is thin, white, (or exotic and beautiful), able-bodied, heterosexual and which conforms to accepted notions of female teenage behaviour.[4] In essence, the victim is held responsible for her own fate. The issue of racism as a motive is significantly absent in early media coverage and only surfaced two years later in the coverage of the trial of one of her attackers (Hall 1999a).

A brief interlude in the construction of the story occurred with the revelation that Virk had allegedly been sexually abused by a close family member. This underlined once again, her lack of "fit"—both within her familial culture and the external, dominant culture of her peers. The allegations were immediately denied in the detailed coverage of the eulogy delivered by an elder of the Jehovah's Witness church at her funeral. The denial was underscored by her mother's comments to reporters suggesting that Reena had been a troubled child. Journalistic accounts that stressed her inability to conform to her family's ethnic values, combined with the strict beliefs of the Jehovah's Witness church, reinforced her mother's statements and helped locate the issue as one of intergenerational conflict, youth rebellion and cultural conflict (Beatty and Pemberton; Dirk). However, despite this obvious location and familiar terrain, these lines of inquiry were never investigated in subsequent stories. The allegations were reported again in a subsequent article that focused on a friend's disclosure of Virk's sexual abuse by a family member, but were not contextualized in reference to existing statistics on child sexual abuse and the links between violence in the home and running away from home (Kinnon and Hanvey).[5] Aside from these subdominant motifs, the framework of the story remained that of the escalating girl-on-girl violence.

Not only was Virk's racialized identity erased, but there was a significant lack of attention paid to even the possibility that her death was racially motivated. Almost two years later, at the trial of one of her alleged murderers, Warren Glowatski, the issue of racism was brought up by one witness—Syreeta Hartley, his girlfriend (Hall 1999a). However, aside from the brief reporting of her testimony in the daily coverage of the trial, the issue itself was neither investigated by the media nor considered to be of importance by Justice Macaulay in his decision (*R. v Warren Paul Glowatski*, 1999). This absence occurred despite the hate crimes legislation available to the courts; existing documentation of the activity of hate groups in schools and college campuses (Prutzman; Sidel); existing studies that highlight the vulnerability of racialized girls to violence; or the racial connotations imbuing the acts of brutality to which Virk was subjected, as for example, the stubbing of a cigarette on her forehead—the place usually used to put a bindi, which is a common practice among various South Asian cultures.

The significant absence of any discussion or investigation of racism as a motive reflects not only a minimization of the violence of racism, but also its sheer taken-for-granted character as a non-problematic and unrecognizable element. As Hall (1990) and Essed point out, everyday racism is ingrained in the daily interactions of people of colour with the dominant society—it structures common sense reality and is thereby naturalized in an insidious way. Part of its naturalization arises from its taken-for-granted nature and embeddedness. The media's denial of racism corresponds with hegemonic definitions of racism as an activity confined to extreme hate groups, rather than as a system and structure of domination inherent in the very fabric of society and its institutions. Thus, even though Syreeta Hartley's testimony was explicit in highlighting the racial motivations of the murder, its import was minimized both by the media and the judge. As one journalist stated, "Syreeta Hartley said her former boyfriend told her that his involvement was partly motivated by racism. Virk was Indo-Canadian" (Hall 1999a: A5). The media also reported that Glowatski did not know Reena Virk and had never spoken to her.

At no time did the local or national media dwell upon or investigate the fact that Warren Glowatski had first bragged about picking a fight with a Native man (Hall 1999b). The issue of why he would first select a Native man as the target for his aggression remained unexamined and yet suggests the vulnerability of marginalized groups and the hierarchy in which they are positioned. The reporting implies that it is much easier to beat a Native man and get away with it, than it is to beat up a white male. The value of difference is thus communicated by allusion and association.

The dominant framing of "Other" cultures as deviant is naturalized and taken for granted by the dominant media, and tends to be used strategically to underline the "unassimilable character" of immigrant communities (Jiwani 1992). However, in the case of Reena Virk, there was a significant absence of any kind of cultural framing. It could be argued that the dominant media have become more sensitized to issues of cultural representations. Alternatively, the media's reluctance to use a cultural frame may be derived from the possibility that some of the girls involved in the first fight were themselves of South Asian origin. This in itself does not negate the reality that many members of a racialized community internalize the normative values and behaviours of the dominant society and reject identifiers and people of their communities. In fact, the cultural frame would have allowed the media to continue a noted tradition—that of portraying racialized communities as being sites of conflict and disturbance created by their own members (Entman; Indra). It can be argued that in this particular instance, the construction of girl-on-girl violence became a dominant filter as it better served masculinist hegemonic interests within a contextual climate of backlash against women. For the media to have focused on culture at this point would, by necessity, have involved an examination of racism as predicated on Virk's exclusion from and marginalization by her peer group, as well as the defining characteristics which resulted in her "lack of fit." Organizing and translating information within this frame would thus have resulted in a confrontation with the reality of racism and its prevalence in Canadian society, as well as the vulnerability of racialized people to racially motivated violence.

As an elite institution, the media reproduces hegemonic values, and often does so by reporting on the decisions and perspectives of other elites (van Dijk 1993). In the case of Reena Virk, the accounts that were reported on a sustained basis—each story referenced the other thereby resulting in a cumulative stock of knowledge—tended to be based on the reports or announcements of other elites. These included academics, police and judges. Alternative interpretations based on the views of advocates were significantly absent, the exception being those cases where individuals wrote opinion pieces that were subsequently published. Thus, the complete absence of any mention of racism in Judge Macaulay's sentencing decision was echoed in the news coverage and served to secure his view of the case as the dominant and preferred interpretation—that the murder was the result of violent intent, but an intent that was unconnected to racism, sexism, or a combination thereof.

CONCLUSION

From the above analysis, it can be seen that the Canadian print media continue to favour and forward interpretations of race and racism that resonate with elite definitions and that reinforce hegemonic interests. In the case of Reena Virk, the critical issues facing racialized girls were never examined by the media, nor was the issue of racism dealt with in any substantive manner. Rather, as with issues concerning child abuse, racism was relegated to the background and overshadowed by stories regarding the increasing levels of girl-on-girl violence, and the inability of Reena Virk to "fit." Thus, the issue of racism was erased from the dominant discourse, and Reena Virk's identity as a racialized young woman has been similarly erased in terms of its significance and contribution to her vulnerability and marginality. As a young woman of colour, she was visibly different, yet her difference was only understood in terms of her weight and height and her general "inability to fit." The issue of what she needed to "fit into" was never explored, nor were the assumptions underlying normative standards of beauty and behaviour for teenage girls interrogated. Yet these issues are central to highlighting the particular ways in which racism and sexism interact in shaping the lives of racialized girls, and in contributing to their marginalization and vulnerability to violence—both as girls and as racialized others. The erasure of race and racism in this story reinforced the accepted stock of knowledge that racism is confined to the acts of organized hate groups. Thus, the structured nature of racism as a system of domination that informs everyday life and constrains the life chances of racialized peoples remains outside the dominant discourse, relegated to the margins.

Endnotes

1. This composite is derived from the accounts presented in various newspapers and magazines over a two-year period (1997–1999).
2. For a discussion of racism and sexism within the school system, see Bourne et al.
3. This analysis of news coverage is based on articles on the story of Reena Virk that were published in *The Vancouver Sun* during November and December in 1997. In addition, an electronic search of all articles appearing in Canadian newspapers pertaining to the decision in the Warren Glowatski trial were also examined.
4. In their examination of girls' critique of schooling, Bourne et al. note that the South Asian girls in their focus groups commented on how their appearance is exoticized, suggesting that this is one of the ways in which they are considered acceptable.
5. In their review of the literature on violence against women, Kinnon and Hanvey note that, "60 to 70% of runaways and 98% of child prostitutes have a history of child abuse."

References

Alicea, Marixsa. "'A Chambered Nautilus,' The Contradictory Nature of Puerto Rican Women's Role in the Social Construction of a Transnational Community." Gender and Society 11 (5) (1997): 597–626.

Alliance of Five Research Centres on Violence. Final Report on Phase I, Violence Prevention and the Girl Child. 1998. Research funded by the Status of Women Canada. Available online:www.harbour.sfu.ca/freda/

Artz, Sibylle. Sex, Power, and the Violent School Girl. Toronto: Trifolium Books, 1998.

Bannerji, Himani. "Now You See Us/Now You Don't." Video Guide 8 (40) (1986): 5.

Bannerji, Himani. "Introducing Racism: Notes Towards an Anti-Racist Feminism," Resources for Feminist Research 16 (1) (May 1987): 10–12.

Bannerji, Himani, ed. Returning the Gaze: Essays on Racism, Feminism and Politics. Toronto: Sister Vision Press, 1993.

Beatty, Jim and Kim Pemberton. "Teen Recanted Claims of Abuse Says Church Elder." The Vancouver Sun. November 29, 1997. A3.

Bourne, Paula, Liza McCoy and Dorothy Smith. "Girls and Schooling: Their Own Critique." Resources for Feminist Research 26 (1/2) (Spring 1998): 55–68.

Burns, Mary Violet C., ed. The Speaking Profits Us: Violence in the Lives of Women of Colour. Seattle, WA: Centre for the Prevention of Sexual and Domestic Violence, 1986.

Cottle, Simon. "'Race,' Racialization and the Media: a Review and Update of Research." Sage Race Relations Abstracts 17:2 (1992): 3–57.

Crenshaw, Kimberle Williams. "Mapping the Margins: Intersectionality, Identity Politics, and Violence Against Women of Color." The Public Nature of Private Violence, The Discovery of

Domestic Abuse. Eds. Martha Fineman and Roxanne Mykitiuk. New York: Routledge, 1994. 93–118.

Drury, Beatrice. "Sikh Girls and the Maintenance of an Ethnic Culture." New Community 17 (3) (1991): 387–399.

Entman. "Modern Racism and the Images of Blacks in Local Television News." Critical Studies in Mass Communication 7 (1990): 332–345.

Essed, Philomena. Everyday Racism. Reports from Women of Two Cultures. Translated by Cynthia Jaffe. Claremont, CA: Hunter House, 1990.

Fitzgerald, Robin. "Assaults Against Children and Youth in the Family, 1996." Juristat 17 (11) Ottawa: Canadian Centre for Justice Statistics, Statistics Canada, November 1997.

Friedman, Sara Ann with Courtney Cook. Girls, A Presence at Beijing. New York: ngo wgg (Working Groups on Girls), 1995.

Geertz, Clifford. "The Integrative Revolution: Primordial Sentiments and Civil Politics in New States." Old Societies and New States. Ed. Clifford Geertz. New York: Free Press, 1963. 105–57.

Hall, Neal. "Virk's Killing Motivated by Racism, Witness Says," The Vancouver Sun. April 15, 1999a: A5.

Hall, Neal. "Accused Changed Bloody Clothes on the Night Virk Dies, Court Told." The Vancouver Sun. Tuesday April 20, 1999b: A6c.

Hall, Stuart. "The Whites of Their Eyes." The Media Reader. Eds. Manuel Alvarado and John O. Thompson. London: British Film Institute, 1990.

Hutnik, Nimmi. "Patterns of Ethnic Minority Identification and Modes of Adaptation," Ethnic and Racial Studies 9 (2) (April 1986): 150–167.

Indra, Doreen. "South Asian Stereotypes in the Vancouver Press." Ethnic and Racial Studies 2 (2) (1979):166–189.

Isaacs, Harold. Idols of the Tribe, Group Identity and Political Change. New York: Harper and Row, 1975.

Jabbra, Nancy. "Assimilation and Acculturation of Lebanese Extended Families in Nova Scotia." Canadian Ethnic Studies 15 (1) (1983): 54–72.

Jan Mohamed, Abdul R. "The Economy of Manichean Allegory: The Function of Racial Difference in Colonialist Literature." Critical Inquiry 12 (1) (1985): 59–87.

Jiwani, Yasmin. "To Be or Not to Be: South Asians as Victims and Oppressors in the Vancouver Sun." Sanvad 5 (45) (1992):13–15.

Jiwani, Yasmin. "By Omission and Commission: Race and Representation in Canadian Television News." Unpublished doctoral dissertation, School of Communications, Simon Fraser University, 1993.

Jiwani, Yasmin. "On the Outskirts of Empire: Race and Gender in Canadian Television News." Painting the Maple: Essays on Race, Gender, and the Construction of Canada. Eds. V. Strong-Boag, S. Grave, A. Eisenberg, and J. Anderson. Vancouver: University of British Columbia Press, 1998. 53–68.

Jiwani, Yasmin. Violence Against Marginalized Girls: A Review of the Literature. Vancouver: FREDA, 1998b.

Joe, Karen A. and Meda Chesney-Lind. "'Just Every Mother's Angel': An Analysis of Gender and Ethnic Variations in Youth Gang Membership." Gender and Society 9 (4) (August 1995): 408–431.

Keyes, Charles F. "The Dialectics of Ethnic Change." Ethnic Change. Ed. Charles F. Keyes. Seattle: University of Washington Press, 1981.4–30.

Kim, Jin K. "Explaining Acculturation in a Communication Framework: An Empirical Test." Communication Monographs 47 (August 1980): 155–179.

Kinnon, Diane and Louise Hanvey. "Health Aspects of Violence Against Women." Available online:www.hwcweb.hwc.ca/canusa/papers/english/violent.htm

Lyman, Stanford M. and William A. Douglass. "Ethnicity: Strategies of Collective and Individual Impression Management." Social Research 40 (1973): 344–365.

Macaulay, J. "Reasons for Judgment in R v. Warren Paul Glowatski." Supreme Court of British Columbia, Docket 95773. June 2, 1999.

Matthews, Julie Mariko. "A Vietnamese Flag and a Bowl of Australian Flowers: Recomposing Racism and Sexism." Gender, Place and Culture 4 (1) (March 1997): 5–18.

Meissner, Dirk. "Murdered Girl Was Turning Her Life Around, Mother Says." The Vancouver Sun. Monday April 19, 1999. B6c

Miller, Barbara D. "Precepts and Practices: Researching Identity Formation among Indian Hindu Adolescents in the United States." New Directions for Child Development 67 (1995): 71–85.

Onder, Zehra. "Muslim-Turkish Children in Germany: Socio-cultural Problems." Migration World Magazine 24 (5) (1996):18–24.

Prutzman, Priscilla. "Bias-Related Incidents, Hate Crimes, and Conflict Resolution." Education and Urban Society. 27 (1) (November 1994): 71–81.

Razack, Sherene H. Looking White People in the Eye, Gender, Race, and Culture in Courtrooms and Classrooms. Toronto: University of Toronto Press, 1998.

Rosenthal, Doreen, Nadia Ranieri, and Steven Klimidis. "Vietnamese Adolescents in Australia: Relationships between Perceptions of Self and Parental Values, Intergenerational Conflict, and Gender Dissatisfaction." International Journal of Psychology. 31 (2) (April 1996): 81–91.

Russell, Susan with the Canadian Federation of University Women. Take Action for Equality, Development and Peace: A Canadian Follow-up Guide to Beijing '95. Eds. Linda Souter and Betty Bayless. Ottawa: criaw, Canadian Beijing Facilitating Committee, 1996.

Scanlon, Joseph. "The Sikhs of Vancouver." Ethnicity and the Media. Paris: Unesco, 1977.

Schramm, Heather. Young Women Who Use Violence: Myths and Facts. Calgary: Elizabeth Fry Society of Calgary, 1998.

Sidel, Ruth. "Battling Bias: College Students Speak Out." Educational Record 76 (2, 3) (Spring-Summer 1995): 45–52.

Smitherman-Donaldson, Geneva and Teun van Dijk. Discourse and Discrimination. Detroit: Wayne State University Press, 1988.

Thobani, Sunera. "Culture isn't the Cause of Violence." The Vancouver Sun. September 26, 1992:A12.

Tipper, Jennifer. The Canadian Girl Child: Determinants of the Health and Well-Being of Girls and Young Women. Ottawa: Canadian Institute of Child Health, September 1997.

Turnbull, Sue. "The Media: Moral Lessons and Moral Careers." Australian Journal of Education 37 (2) (1993): 153–168.

Van Dijk, Teun A. Communicating Racism, Ethnic Prejudice in Thought and Talk. United States: Sage, 1987.

Van Dijk, Teun A. Elite Discourse and Racism. Sage series on Race and Ethnic Relations, Volume 6. California: Sage, 1993.

The Vancouver Sun. May 8, 1999: A10

The Vancouver Sun. Special issue on Teen Violence. May 14, 1999

Vertinsky, Patricia, Indy Batth and Mita Naidu. "Racism in Motion: Sport, Physical Activity and the Indo-Canadian Female." Avante 2 (3) (1996): 1–23.

Gendered Racial Violence and Spatialized Justice: The Murder of Pamela George

Sherene Razack

Sherene Razack is a Professor of Sociology and Equity Studies in Education at the Ontario Institute for Studies in Education of the University of Toronto. Her research and teaching interests lie in the area of race and gender issues in the law. Her most recent book Dark Threats and White Knights: The Somalia Affair, Peacekeeping and the New Imperialism *(University of Toronto Press, 2004) is an examination of the violence of Canadian peacekeepers in Somalia and an exploration of the role of law in violence enacted on racialized bodies in the new world order.*

To unmap literally is to denaturalize geography, hence to undermine world views that rest upon it.

Richard Phillips[1]

*I would like to thank Mona Oikawa, Leslie Thielen-Wilson and, especially, Sheila Gill, for outstanding research assistance, insight and dedication, Barbara Buckman for her help in thinking through these ideas, the students of the OISE/UT Race and Space graduate course, and the works-in-progress group of the Western Law Professors of Colour Conference, Hawaii 2000 (especially Adrienne Davis and John Calmore) for useful critical feedback.

INTRODUCTION

On Easter weekend, April 17, 1995, Pamela George, a woman of the Saulteaux (Ojibway) nation and a mother of two young children, was brutally murdered in Regina, a small Canadian prairie city. Beyond the fact that Pamela George came from the Sakimay reserve on the outskirts of the city, and that she occasionally worked as a prostitute, something she was doing that Easter weekend, court records of the trial of the two white men accused of her murder and media coverage of the event reveal few details of her life or the life of her community. More is known about her two murderers, young, white, middle-class men. Easter marked the first weekend since the end of their university exams. There was a week or so of freedom before summer jobs began. Nineteen-year-old university athletes Steven Kummerfield and Alex Ternowetsky set out to celebrate the end of term. They went out drinking in isolated areas under bridges and behind hockey arenas, and then cruised "the Stroll," the city's streets of prostitution. Eventually, after failing to persuade one Aboriginal woman working as a prostitute to join them in the car, one man hid in the trunk. Approaching her twice and being refused twice, they finally succeeded in persuading another Aboriginal woman, Pamela George, who was working as a prostitute that night, to enter the car. The two men drove George to an isolated area outside the city, a place littered with bullet casings and condoms. Following oral sex, they took turns brutally beating her and left her lying with her face in the mud. They then drove to a fast food restaurant and later to a cabin on Saskatchewan Beach that belonged to one of their grandfathers. The next morning, upon returning to town, they heard a radio report describing a body found outside the city. After both first confided their involvement in the murder to a number of friends and to one of their parents, one man left town to take up his summer job planting trees in the Northern forests of British Columbia. The other man flew to the mountain resort of Banff, Alberta, where he joined other white male university athletes celebrating the end of term. In early May, nearly one month after the murder, after following a tip and having exhausted the list of suspects who were mostly Aboriginal and/or of the "streets" of the Stroll, the Royal Canadian Mounted Police (RCMP) arrested both men for the murder of Pamela George. The arrest of two young, white, middle-class men for the murder of an Aboriginal woman working as a prostitute sent shock waves through the white population of this small prairie city.

At the trial two years later, the Defence at first tried to argue that Pamela George managed to walk away from the isolated field and was killed by someone else, an Aboriginal man. They also argued that since both men were highly intoxicated, they bore diminished responsibility for the beating. The boys did "pretty darn stupid things,"[2] but they did not commit murder. Both the Crown and the Defence maintained that the fact that Pamela George was a prostitute was something to be considered in the case.[3] The judge sparked a public furor when he instructed the jury to bear this in mind in their deliberations. The men were convicted of manslaughter and sentenced to six and a half years in prison, having already spent twenty months in prison. The objections of the Native community and some members of the white community stemmed from their belief that the crime was at the very least one of second degree murder and that the judge acted improperly in directing the jury to a finding of manslaughter.[4]

Why write about this trial as spatialized justice and this murder as gendered racial or colonial violence? Some readers of early versions of this article have commented that the prison sentences for manslaughter meted out to the two accused were not highly unusual and therefore not indicative of the court's leniency. Others noted that a finding of murder would have required more evidence than was available. In agreement with this latter view, in 1998, the Saskatchewan Court of Appeal rejected an appeal by the Crown that the trial judge had failed to fairly present the Crown's position that the two men had murdered Pamela George. The Appeal Court concluded that Mr. Justice Malone had made it clear to the jury that a finding of murder, whether first or second degree, would require evidence that the accused intended to commit murder or knew that their actions would result in Pamela George's death. . . .

I propose to show that a number of factors contributed to masking the violence of the two accused and thus diminishing their culpability and legal responsibility for the death of Pamela George. Primarily, I claim that because Pamela George was considered to belong to a space in which violence routinely occurs, and to have a body that is routinely violated, while her killers were presumed to be far removed from this zone, the enormity of what was done to her remained largely unacknowledged. My argument is in the first instance an argument about race, space and the law. I deliberately write against those who would agree that this case is about an injustice but who would de-race the violence and the law's response to it and label it more generically as patriarchal violence against women, violence that the law routinely minimizes. While it is certainly patriarchy that produces men whose sense of identity is achieved through the brutalizing of a woman, the men's and the court's capacity to dehumanize Pamela George derived from their understanding of her as the (gendered) racial Other whose degradation confirmed their own identities as white—that is, as men entitled to the land and the full benefits of citizenship. . . .

[Natives represent] approximately 8% of the population [of Regina].[5] Regina is estimated to have a higher urban Aboriginal population per capita than all other major Canadian cities. The city's Aboriginal population is also the youngest one in Canada with 43% of it 15 years old or younger.[6] However, the presence of a significant Aboriginal population in an urban centre is a relatively recent historical development. Canada's colonizing endeavours confined the majority of Aboriginal peoples to reserves by the second half of the 19th century, establishing in the process the geographical configuration of Regina today as a primarily white city in the midst of the reserves of the Qu'appelle Valley. This 19th century spatial containment of a subject population was never secure and often required brutal policing and settler violence. Fearful of Native rebellions, for example, in 1885 white settlers of Regina organized a home guard and pressed vigorously for the North West Mounted Police (NWMP) to police Natives and to hang Native leaders arrested after the Riel rebellion.[7]

Sexual violence towards Aboriginal women was an integral part of 19th century settler technologies of domination. In her research on the appearance during this time of captivity narratives (stories about the abduction of white women and children by Aboriginal peoples), Sarah Carter documents the important role that stereotypical representations of Aboriginal women played in maintaining the spatial and symbolic boundaries between settlers and natives. While prior to 1885 there had been relative co-existence between fur traders and Aboriginal peoples, the rebellion of the Metis and general Aboriginal resistance to their spatial confinement, as well as the increasing presence of white women on the prairies, led to powerful negative images of Aboriginal women. The negative images of these women, portrayed as licentious and bloodthirsty, helped to justify the increasing legal regulation of Aboriginal women's movement and their confinement to reserves. As Carter demonstrates, "the squalid and immoral 'squaw'" helped to deflect criticism away from the brutal behaviour of government officials and the NWMP, and it enabled government officials to claim that the dissolute character of Aboriginal women and the laziness of the men explained why reserve land was not used to capacity and were pockets of poverty. . . .

Newspaper records of the 19th century indicate that there was a near universal conflation of Aboriginal woman and prostitute and an accompanying belief that when they encountered violence, Aboriginal women simply got what they deserved. Police seldom intervened even when the victim's cries could be clearly heard. . . .[8]

[Such an attitude] continues to prevail. The Aboriginal Justice Inquiry's discussion of the 1971 murder of Helen Betty Osborne in The Pas, Manitoba, elaborates on its prevalence. Brutally murdered by two white men, Osborne, an Aboriginal student who was walking down a downtown street, was picked up in town and driven to a more secluded spot where she was assaulted and killed. As the Commissioners of the Aboriginal Justice Inquiry concluded, Osborne's attackers "seemed to be operating on the assumption that Aboriginal women were promiscuous and open to enticement through alcohol or violence. It is evident that the men who abducted Osborne believed that young Aboriginal women were objects with no human value beyond [their own] sexual gratification. . . ."[9] Such assumptions often appear to be operating when the police fail to respond to the disappearance of Aboriginal women, citing their involvement in prostitution and their practices of moving from place to place. In the early 1990's, John Crawford, a white man, was convicted of murdering three Aboriginal women, Calinda Waterhen, Shelley Napope and Eva Taysup. In each case, Crawford and another white friend began by drinking and having sex with the woman in question who was possibly working as a prostitute. The women's disappearance attracted little attention. When their families reported them missing, police appeared to assume that such women were simply transients on the move. As police sergeant Dave Kovach told a reporter, the police don't look for transient adults because such individuals often go missing and often don't want to be found.[10] Crawford's victims were indeed, as Denise McConney has written, "caught up in the ongoing displacement, relocation, and search for a safe place that is a consistent theme in the lives of most Native women."[11] Ironically, it is their very dispossession that is held against them when Aboriginal women encounter violence on the streets.

THE MAKING OF WHITE MEN: THE TWO ACCUSED

European empires and European masculinities were imagined in geographies of adventure.

Richard Phillips[12]

Alex Ternowetsky and Steven Kummerfield's histories begin in the colonial practices described above. In their everyday life, they would have had almost no chance of encountering an Aboriginal person. Absent from the university, the ordered suburbs of their families, the chalets and cottages, spaces that come into existence through the violent dispossession of Aboriginal peoples, Aboriginal bodies must be sought out in those marginal spaces of the city. Why would white men seek out these bodies? Why would they leave their own spaces of privilege? How do young white men such as Alex Ternowetsky and Steven Kummerfield come to know themselves as beings for whom the definition of a good time is to travel to the parts of the city inhabited by poor and mostly Aboriginal peoples and there to purchase sexual services from an Aboriginal woman? In this section, I offer the argument that the subject who must cross the line between respectability and degeneracy and, significantly, return unscathed, is first and foremost a colonial subject seeking to establish that he is indeed in control and lives in a world where a solid line marks the boundary between himself and racial/gendered others. For this subject, violence establishes the boundary between who he is and who he is not. It is the surest indicator that he is a subject in control.

I have argued elsewhere[13] that the spatial boundaries and transgressions that enable the white, middle-class male to gain mastery and self-possession, are generally evident in a man's use of a woman in prostitution. When they purchase the right of access to the body of a prostitute, men, whether white and middle-class or not, have an opportunity to assert mastery and control, achieving in the process a subjectivity that is intrinsically colonial as well as patriarchal. Naturalized as necessary for men with excess sexual energy, prostitution is seldom considered to be a practice of domination that enables men to experience themselves as colonisers and patriarchs, that is, as men with the unquestioned right to go anywhere and to do anything to the bodies of women and subject populations they have conquered (or purchased). Instead, the liberal idea that we are autonomous individuals who contract with each other is used to annul the idea that prostitution is non-reciprocal sex and thus a violation of the personhood of the prostitute. The contract cancels the violence, although we readily recognize the violence of other financial transactions (such as Third World youth who sell their corneas to First World buyers). The space of prostitution, which Malek Alloula describes as *"the very space of orgy:* the one that the soldier and the coloniser obsessively dream of establishing on the territory of the colony,"[14] is the space of license to do as one pleases, regardless of its impact on the personhood of others.

How did the two men enact their colonial histories? Race is not at first glance as evident as gender although neither exists independently. . . . Drawing on the work of scholars researching sports and masculinity, notably Peggy Reeves Sanday, Robinson suggests that sexual violence collectively enacted enables the men to get as close to each other as they can without endangering their sense of themselves as heterosexuals. To debase and degrade a woman in the presence of other men secures the masculinity that must be aggressive and that must disavow sexual feelings for other men. . . .[15] The players resorted to a variety of violent practices to "distance themselves from the feminine," continually reminding one another what masculinity is.[16] Donnelly and Young also note "the fragility of reputations" in sports subcultures, that is, the need to make and remake masculine identity and the constitutive role that violence plays in this cycle.[17] Wenner describes the male adolescent for whom excessive public drinking (as well as buying thc services of a prostitute) is a rite of passage into manhood, an exposure of oneself to a dangerous situation from which one emerges triumphant. Sport, Wenner suggests, works in a similar way, enabling men to establish their reputations with other men and to mark off the distinction between themselves and women.[18] As I show below, such practices also enable men to mark themselves as different from and superior to racial Others.

Kummerfield and Ternowetsky inhabited a world in which the homo-social bonding, drinking and aggression described by scholars of sports masculinities were important features. . . .

Of the dozen or so male friends of the accused who testified, all were white male athletes attending university. In this remarkably homogeneous shared world of young, white, athletic, middle-class men (some of whom even had the same first Christian names), drinking and socializing occurred in isolated spaces mainly outside of their respectable homes. . . .

The sense of identity that both accused gained from their activities with other men was premised on a shared whiteness. Their sports activities cement white settler identity in ways I do not explore here,[19] but evidence of their shared whiteness is most apparent in their own and their friends' and families' responses to Pamela George and to the Stroll. The men told several of their friends about the events the night of the murder and received considerable support and advice. Alex Ternowetsky told at least four of his friends. One of these, Rodney McLeod, with whom he had been drinking at Massey Pool and whose fleece jacket he was wearing the night of the murder reassured him that no one would find out.[20]To another, Tyler Harlton, he confided that he had killed "an Indian hooker".[21] Ryan Leier, with whom Ternowetsky had been in trouble before and to whom he confided the full details of the night while both were in a hot tub at a chalet in Banff, reassured his friend with the advice "you shouldn't assume you killed her."[22] Finally, Ternowetsky told his friend Eric Willrich, whose jeans he was wearing the night of the murder and at whose house he is alleged to have washed the blood stains off. Steven Kummerfield confided to his best friend Tyler Stuart, with whom he had once gone to the area of prostitution, that "we beat the shit out of an Indian hooker."[23] In Tyler Stuart's account, Kummerfield also elaborated that he said to Pamela George "If you don't give us head, we're going to kill you."[24] Stuart, apparently mostly concerned about the transmission of disease to Kummerfield's white girlfriend, advised his friend to break up with her if he hadn't worn a condom the night of the murder.[25] In none of these conversations was there any indication that the men acknowledged that a woman had been brutally murdered; her death seemed almost incidental and simply inconvenient. The men seemed to possess a collective understanding of Pamela George as a thing, an objectification that their exclusively white worlds would have given them little opportunity to disrupt. . . .

In addition to their own isolated spaces, the men also inhabited those of middle-class respectability. They inhabited the spaces of the university, which Carol Schick demonstrates to be so clearly white space on the Canadian prairies,[26] and sports arenas, again white space as Laura Robinson demonstrates with respect to hockey. . . .[27]

In this all-white masculine world of privilege, the Stroll, the area of prostitution described in the trial as encompassing St. John and Ottawa streets and involving a specific set of streets and hotels in between,[28] represented the dangerous world of racial Others, a frontier on the edge of civilization. Police described the Stroll as a world of drugs and prostitution, and most of all, as a space of Aboriginality. Steven Kummerfield and his friends visited the Stroll "out of curiosity."[29] Alex Ternowetsky and his friends took their girlfriends on an adventure to the Stroll, "sort of seeing who was there," as his lawyer put it.[30] The young women hid under blankets while the young men negotiated for the services of an Aboriginal prostitute: a thrilling excursion to the slums that would have helped these young white people to know their own place in the world.

When young white men enter racialized urban spaces their skin-privilege clearly marks them as out of place. They are immediately read as johns, and as rich white men who have come "slumming." In this respect, they experience an unfamiliar racial marking. . . . It is perhaps the men's perception that they were marked and at risk on the Stroll that prompted them to drive Pamela George outside of the city to a borderland between the country and the city, a no-man's-land that offers greater anonymity. . . .[31]

It is difficult to avoid both the historical and contemporary racial and spatial parallels between the murders of Helen Betty Osborne and Pamela George. Equally, newspaper reports in 1999 calling attention to cases of Aboriginal men found frozen to death after Saskatoon police apparently dropped them outside the city limits in the dead of winter, outline the tremendous violence of the eviction of Aboriginal peoples from urban space.[32] In each instance, white men forcibly and fatally removed Aboriginal bodies from the city space, a literal cleansing of the white zone. The violence is itself cleansing, enabling white men to triumph over their own internal fears that they may not be men in control. The evictions are to areas where white men are able to evade responsibility for their violent acts, areas where there are few witnesses and where, significantly, the norms of civility are suspended and violence by contract is known to occur. . . .

During the trial, the murder scene and the Stroll were described as spaces somehow innately given to illicit and sexual activity. The bodies of Charlene Rosebluff, Pamela George and a number of Aboriginal men were represented variously as bodies that naturally belonged to these spaces of prostitution, crime, sex and violence. This degenerate space, into which Kummerfield and Ternowetsky ventured temporarily, was juxtaposed to the spaces of respectability. Each space required a different legal response. In racialized space, I argue below, violence may occur with impunity. Bodies from respectable spaces may also violate with impunity, particularly if the violence takes place in the spaces of prostitution, racial spaces. . . .

. . . [D]uring the trial, Pamela George came to be seen as a rightful target of the gendered violence inflicted by Kummerfield and Ternowetsky. Put another way, her murder was characterized as a natural by-product of the space and thus of the social context in which it occurred, an event that is routine when the bodies in question are Aboriginal. This naturalizing of violence is sustained by the legal idea of contract, an agreement between consenting and autonomous individuals. Because she consented to provide sexual services, the violence became more permissible. The moment of violence is contained within the moment of the contract and there can be no history or context, for example the constraints on her choice and the historical conditions under which the bargain was made. Trapped in the moment in time of the contract, during the trial, Pamela George remained simply "the prostitute" or the "Indian." In the absence of details about George's life and critical scrutiny of the details of the lives of the accused, a number of subject positions remained uninterrogated. Thus, not only did George remain the "hooker" but Ternowetsky and Kummerfield remained boys who "did pretty darn stupid things"; their respective spaces, the places of white respectability and the Stroll, simply stood in opposition to each other, dehistoricized and decontextualized. If Pamela George was a victim of violence, it was simply because she was of the Stroll/reserve, Aboriginal and engaging in prostitution. No one could then be really held accountable for her death, at least not to the extent that there would have been accountability had she been of spaces within the domain of justice. . . .

Apart from a few moments, such as when Charlene Rosebluff remembered her as a nice person and a mother with two children,[33] and when her mother and sister recalled that she liked doing crafts, could cook anything and was a good mother to her ten- and five-year-old, Pamela George never left the racially bounded space of prostitution and degeneracy during the trial, a space that marked her as a body to be violated. We never learn of the Sakimay reserve and the extensive familial networks of her life there, nor do we learn anything about why she resorted to prostitution a few times a month, and why she left the reserve in the first place. It is only in newspaper articles that we learn that she helped her father through his crisis with alcohol abuse, supporting him in his journey to become an addictions counselor.[34]

When details of her life emerged, such as the fact that Pamela George had a cousin in prison, and her father had himself been falsely accused of a crime,[35] they only confirmed the equation of Aboriginality with violence, a state of affairs that remained unconnected to the violence of the colonizers. In place of details that might have given her personhood, there were a myriad of other details that instead reassured the Court of her belonging to spaces of violence. The needle marks on her arm,[36] the tattoos on her body with the words "Ed" and "I love mom,"[37] the stories of her ripping off clients (stories the police report they heard from Lenny Hall),[38] the mention of her sister who was also a prostitute[39] and the detailed descriptions of how prostitutes conducted their business (but not how clients participate) leave a powerful image of degeneracy. This degeneracy was clearly racial. . . .

Ultimately, it was Pamela George's status as a prostitute, hence not as a human being, and her belonging to spaces beyond universal justice, that limited the extent to which the violence done to her body could be recognized and the accused made accountable for it. Although it was central to the Defence to spatialize accountability in this way, neither the Crown attorney nor the judge contested these relations between space and justice. The Defence naturalized the violence by framing it as merely something that happens in prostitution and in those spaces. Describing the murder scene as a "quiet" rather than isolated location in which to have sex,[40] Defence attorney Kovach suggested at sentencing: "They were out in the country doing what happens apparently on that road on a regular basis. . . . This is a fairly common area for that type of activity to be taking place. . . . She wasn't stabbed forty times. There wasn't a hammer used."[41] In perhaps the most convoluted but revealing of arguments that prostitution lies beyond the space of universal justice, the Defence lawyer for Alex Ternowetsky suggested that if the Court was going to ignore that Pamela George was working as a prostitute (and thus consider the beating and murder as one would any other), then the same consideration must be extended to his client:

> *But I think the same consideration has to apply when you look at the evidence as it applies to Alex Ternowetsky. Alex admits that he drank excessively, that he picked up a prostitute, that he hit her and he left her out in the country to walk back to the city on her own, and no one can blame you if you look at that and say that's disgusting behaviour. But the issue that you have to consider is whether or not he's guilty of murder. . . .*[42]

Although it is difficult to follow his logic, Defence lawyer Aaron Fox appeared here to be suggesting that if the court ignored that the violence occurred within the context of prostitution (and is thus a lesser violence), then it must also ignore that his client drove George to a place of prostitution and inflicted the violence that caused her death. The social meaning of places and bodies must all be studiously ignored even as the law depends on these meanings to evaluate the violence. Presumably, his client would then be guilty of disgusting behaviour but not of murder. A parallel was being made between [George's] engaging in prostitution and his client's drinking, both being examples of risky and ill-advised behaviour. Prostitution in particular "may not be pleasant but that's the reality."[43] Further, Pamela's alleged drug addiction can be equated to their client's drunkenness.[44] It was indeed central to the Defence's arguments that the accused were simply young men who went out drinking. . . . For the Defence, if there was a problem to be named in this trial, it is "substance abuse,"[45] and not racial or sexual violence that ended in murder. . . .

In his summation, after noting that Pamela George worked as a prostitute, the Crown attorney reminded the court that everyone was entitled to the protection of the law.[46] He nevertheless concluded in his summary remarks, after sympathizing with the families of the accused, that "Pamela George obviously lived a lifestyle far removed, probably from yours and mine. . . . The fact that she was a prostitute obviously is a fact, and you have to consider that as part of the case."[47] In his address to the jury, the judge directed the jury as follows:

> *Now, if you should find that Pamela George consented to the sexual activity of the two accused, notwithstanding Kummerfield's remark about killing her if she did not give them head, or if you should have a reasonable doubt as to whether the accused consented or not, bearing in mind that the evidence indicates that she indeed was a prostitute, then the Crown has not made out its case with respect to first-degree murder occurring during a sexual assault, and you must find the accused not guilty of first-degree murder but guilty of second-degree murder.*[48]

He then clarified that forcible confinement was a separate and distinct issue from confinement for sexual assault. For there to be forcible confinement, Pamela George would have to be shown to have been dragged to the car and held against her wishes; she cannot simply have been forced to have sex.[49] He directed the jury to remember that George consented to perform sexual acts and that the accused were within their rights to hire her. Even Kummerfield's remark that he would kill her if she did not perform the sexual acts had to be considered in light of the fact that he had in fact hired her to perform these acts.[50] While George was to be judged for engaging in prostitution, the men were not to be judged for having purchased her services. Put more plainly, her activity was a crime that carried the risks of violence, while theirs was a contract. Taking her out to the country should then have no bearing on how the intentions of the accused were understood.[51] Presumably, this was all within the purview of the contract Pamela George made to sell her sexual service and within the limits of her lifestyle.

I suggest that it was difficult for the Crown to disturb the argument of drunkenness and disorderly conduct (as opposed to murder), primarily because of an implicit spatial underpinning that was never challenged and was indeed shared by the Crown. While Pamela George remained stuck in the racial space of prostitution where violence is innate, the men were considered to be far removed from the spaces of violence. She was of the space where murders happen; they were not. They received support from several white people and were praised for their accomplishments. The RCMP reported that they got along well with the accused[52] and a correctional officer conveyed that he related to Alex Ternowetsky like a father.[53] Counsel received an anonymous note claiming that a juror flirted with the boys.[54] Steven Kummerfield's lawyer reminded the court at sentencing that Kummerfield had often been the most valuable player of the week and that his sports record "is some indication of who he is and more important who he is now and hopefully who he'll be able to become after he pays his debt."[55] At the trial's end, the judge defended his remarks to the jury by noting that the media did not report evidence that was favourable to the accused.[56] As Robinson shows in her review of cases involving hockey players accused of sexual assault, such evidence need hardly be mentioned since white male judges and lawyers alike often share the view that the loss of the young men's hockey career is a greater tragedy than the young women's loss of her life. . . .[57]

It is no small irony that racism, so rarely named during the trial, only emerged explicitly during sentencing. The Defence reported that Alex Ternowetsky had taken a course on Native literature while in prison and had written a paper on Aboriginal/white relations that proved that he had "no clear motive of hatred towards someone of a particular racial origin."[58] Racelessness was pursued to the bitter end, however. When there were complaints made against him after the trial, Mr. Justice Malone confirmed (in a letter to Chief Justice Allan McEachern) that race overdetermined the trial, but noted that only a strategy of racelessness (ignoring everyone's race) countered it:

> *I suspect the real basis for most of the complaints, including the two that I have dealt with, is the underlying feeling that because the two accused were white and the victim was a First Nations person they received special treatment and the jury's verdict [of manslaughter and not murder] was based on racism. This was certainly the reaction of several First Nations spokesmen and extensive media coverage was given in [sic] their remarks in this regard. Furthermore, both accused came from financially secure homes and enjoyed the material benefits associated therewith. Their position in life was in striking contrast to the position of the victim. Every effort was made during the trial by counsel and myself to deal with the case strictly on the basis of relevant evidence and not on the financial and social positions of the accused and their victim or their race.*[59]

Here, colour-blindness as a legal approach, the belief that justice can only be achieved by treating all individuals as though they were the same, held full sway.

Race, social position and, I would add, gender, were indeed made to disappear during the trial and in sentencing. The social meaning of spaces and bodies was deliberately excluded as evidence that would contaminate the otherwise pure processes of law, evidence that was not relevant. It was not then possible to interrogate what white men thought they were doing in journeying to the Stroll to buy the services of an Aboriginal prostitute. It was also not possible to interrogate the meaning of consent and violence in the space of prostitution and between white and Aboriginal bodies. Since bodies had no race, class, or gender, the constructs that ruled the day, heavily inflected with these social relations, coded rather than revealed them explicitly. Thus, "prostitute," and people of "the street" came to signify the racial Other and the spaces of violence. . . .

Endnotes

1. R. Phillips, *Mapping Men and Empire: A Geography of Adventure* (New York: Routledge, 1997) at 147 [hereinafter *Phillips*].
2. *R. v. Kummerfield & Ternowetsky,* "Transcript of 12–15, 18–22, 25–28 November, and 2–5, 9–12, and 17–20 December 1996" [1997] (Regina, Sask. Prov. Ct. [Crim. Div.]) at 3469 [hereinafter "Transcript"].
3. *Ibid. at* 4755.
4. B. Pacholik, "Relief, and Anger: Aboriginal Spokesman Demands Appeal" *Regina Leader Post* (21 December 1996) Al.
5. Canada, *Profile of Census Tracts in Regina and Saskatoon* (Ottawa: Statistics Canada, 1999). Regina's total population for 1996 was 193,652. Of that total 14,565 persons identified as Aboriginal. *Ibid.* at 4–6. On the problems associated with Aboriginal census data, see J. Saku, "Aboriginal Census Data in Canada: A Research Note" (1999) 19:2 Can. J. Nat. Stud. 365. In coming years Saskatchewan is expected to have a greater proportion of population with Aboriginal identity: 13% by 2016. Statistics Canada and Population Projections Section, Demography Division, *Projections of the Population with Aboriginal identity, Canada, 1991–2016* by M. J. Norris, D. Kerr & F. Nault (Ottawa: Statistics Canada, 1996).

6. D. Anaquod & V. Khaladkar, "Case Study: The First Nations Economy in the City of Regina," CD-ROM: *For Seven Generations: An Information Legacy of the Royal Commission on Aboriginal Peoples* (Ottawa: Libraxus, 1997) at 6 [hereinafter *For Seven Generations*].
7. J. W. Brennan, *Regina, An Illustrated History* (Toronto: Lorimer & Canadian Museum of Civilization with the Secretary of State, 1989) at 37; S. Carter, *Capturing Women: The Manipulation of Cultural Imagery in Canada's Prairie West* (Montreal & Kingston: McGill-Queens' Press, 1997) at 20–21. The brutality of the NWMP and the RCMP towards Aboriginal peoples, and their sexual brutality towards Aboriginal women is described in L. Brown & C. Brown, *An Unauthorized History of the RCMP* (Toronto: James Lewis & Samuel, 1973) at 143–181.
8. Carter, *Ibid.* at 181.
9. Manitoba, *Report of the Aboriginal Justice Inquiry of Manitoba: The Deaths of Helen Betty Osborne and John Joseph Harper,* vol. 2 (Winnipeg: Queen's Printer, 1991) at 52.
10. J. L. Sheane, "Life and Death on the Edge of Nowhere" *[Saskatoon] Star Phoenix* (8 June 1996) C3.
11. McConney, *supra* note 10 at 212.
12. Phillips, *supra* note 1 at 3.
13. Razack, *supra* note 7.
14. M. Alloula, *The Colonial Harem,* (Minneapolis: University of Minnesota Press, 1986) cited in R. Bishop and L. S. Robinson, *Night Market: Sexual Cultures and the Thai Economic Miracle* (New York & London: Routledge. 1998) at 151.
15. L. Robinson, *Crossing the Line: Violence and Sexual Assault in Canada's National Sport* (Toronto: McClelland & Stewart, 1998) at 151–52.
16. S. P. Schacht. "Misogyny On and Off the 'Pitch': The Gendered World of Male Rugby Players" (1996) 10:5 *Gender & Soc.* at 557–558
17. P. Donnelly & K. Young, "The Construction and Confirmation of Identity in Sport Subcultures" (1988) 5 *Soc. Sport J.* 223 at 235.
18. L. A. Wenner, "In Search of the Sports Bar: Masculinity, Alcohol, Sports, and the Mediation of Public Space" in G. Rail, ed., *Sport and Postmodern Times* (Albany: SUNY Press, 1998) 301.
19. Although few scholars of sports masculinity discuss the role that race plays in the making of the white male athlete in the contemporary context, several scholars have noted the connections between sport masculinities and empire. See *e.g.* R. Morrell, "Forging a Ruling Race: Rugby and Masculinity in Colonial Natal, c. 1870–1910" in J. Navright & T. J. L. Chandler, eds., *Making Men: Rugby and Masculine Identity* (London: Frank Cass, 1996) 91; J. Rutherford, *Forever England: Reflections on Masculinity and Empire* (London: Lawrence & Wishart, 1997). Related Canadian work on sport and national identity has not been explicitly about race and the forging of identities in a white settler society. See *e.g.* K. B. Wamsley, "The Public Importance of Men and the Importance of Public Men" in P. White & K. Young, eds., *Sport and Gender in Canada* (Don Mills, ON: Oxford University Press, 1999) 24 at 34; A. Bélanger, "The Last Game? Hockey and the Experience of Masculinity in Quebec" in P. White & K. Young, eds., *Sport and Gender in Canada* (Don Mills, ON: Oxford University Press, 1999) 293–309.
20. "Transcript", *supra* note 2 at 315–324.
21. *Ibid.* at 457.
22. *Ibid.* at 595–615.
23. *Ibid.* at 858.
24. *Ibid.* at 846–910.
25. *Ibid.* at 871.
26. Schick describes how white teacher-training candidates whom she interviewed about their responses to a mandatory course on Aboriginal issues experienced the university as elite space,

into which Aboriginal bodies entered as interlopers, contaminating the space by representing everything that was not rational. C. Schick, "Keeping the Ivory Tower White: Discourses of Racial Domination."

27. *Crossing the Line, supra* note 15 at 226.
28. "Transcript," *supra* note 2 at 2921.
29. *Ibid.* at 3760.
30. *Ibid.* at 892.
31. This interpretation was suggested to me by Carol Schick.
32. Following press coverage of this incident, the Assembly of First Nations for the prairie region received nearly 600 calls from Aboriginal men and women describing similar acts of violence towards them. M. O'Hanlon, "RCMP Investigate Deaths of Saskatoon Aboriginals" [*Toronto*] *Star* (17 February 2000) A3.
33. "Transcript," *supra* note 2 at 811.
34. T. Sutter, "She Was My Baby" [*Regina*] *Leader Post* (13 May 1995, Saturday Magazine) at 1.
35. *Ibid.*
36. "Transcript", *supra* note 2 at 1113.
37. *Ibid.* at 33, 132.
38. *Ibid.* at 4248.
39. *Ibid.* at 2993.
40. "Transcript," *supra* note 2 at 2139.
41. *R v. Kummerfield & Ternowetsky,* "Transcript of Sentencing 30 January 1997" [1997] (Regina, Sask. Prov. Ct. [Crim. Div.]) at 37.
42. "Transcript," *supra* note 2 at 3480.
43. *Ibid.* at 4632.
44. *Ibid.* at 4633.
45. *Ibid.* at 4633.
46. "Transcript of Sentencing," *supra* note 41 at 69.
47. "Transcript," *supra* note 2 at 4755.
48. *Ibid.* at 4825.
49. *Ibid.* at 4344.
50. *Ibid.* at 4809, 4824.
51. *Ibid* at 4795.
52. *Ibid.* at 406.
53. *Ibid.* at 1409.
54. *Ibid.* at 3205.
55. "Transcript of Sentencing," *supra* note 41 at 47.
56. Justice Malone, "Response to the Honourable Chief Justice Allan McEachern to Complaints by Ms. Sharon Ferguson-Hood and Ms. Ailsa Watkinson and Others, February 6, 1997" [1997] (Regina, Sask. Prov. Ct. [Crim. Div.]).
57. *Crossing the Line. supra* note 15 at 44.
58. "Transcript of Sentencing," *supra* note 41 at 40.
59. Justice Malone, *supra* note 56.

Does No "No" Mean Reasonable Doubt? Assessing the Impact of *Ewanchuk* on Determinations of Consent

Rakhi Ruparelia

Rakhi Ruparelia is an Assistant Professor of Common Law at the University of Ottawa. She also has a background in social work, a perspective that she brings to her research, which focuses on race and gender issues in the law. She has conducted judicial training sessions on sexual assault.

To the delight of the feminist community, the Supreme Court of Canada released its decision in the case of *R. v. Ewanchuk* in 1999, which clarified the defence of honest but mistaken belief in consent in sexual assault cases and emphatically rejected a defence of implied consent. This decision was widely heralded as confirming, once and for all, that No Means No. Considered radical in this sense, the judgment also attracted considerable criticism from those who claimed that it burdened men who would otherwise face the possibility of a criminal conviction, with the onerous task of explicitly seeking consent before each sexual act. Many grumbled that consent requirements would become so stringent as a result of the decision that men, in effect, would need signed contracts before sex to prove that consent was in fact given.

Given predictions made by both supporters and opponents about the significance of *Ewanchuk*, I will explore how the decision has actually impacted on the resolution of sexual assault cases over the approximately seven years since it was released. First, I will briefly overview the *Ewanchuk* case and explain how it more accurately stands for the proposition that "only yes means yes" rather than "no means no" as is commonly asserted. With this clarification in mind, I will discuss a number of sexual assault cases to consider how *Ewanchuk* has affected the determination of consent. Although a number of cases that I refer to involve adolescent complainants, the concerns raised are not limited to younger women as these decisions resemble those involving adult women as well. I will argue that *Ewanchuk* has been most clearly and consistently applied in cases in which the complainant expressly communicated her lack of consent. In circumstances where the complainant was silent or her conduct was passive or ambiguous, judges have been less consistent in their application of *Ewanchuk*. Essentially, many judges determine consent on the basis of "no means no" rather than "only yes means yes." Moreover, even where courts have properly applied *Ewanchuk*, stereotypical assumptions about women as complainants continue to inform their analysis of the facts and the applicable law.

EWANCHUK

Before *Ewanchuk*, the case law on sexual assault was haphazard, despite legislative attempts to offer direction. Judicial determination of consent was inconsistent, unpredictable and unprincipled. Many judges relied heavily on stereotypical assumptions about women as complainants to find that male perpetrators had an honest but mistaken belief in consent, even when a complainant had clearly refused.[5] *Ewanchuk* has undoubtedly helped to clarify the law of consent and has offered a useful framework for adjudicating guilt in sexual assault cases.

In *Ewanchuk*, the accused interviewed the 17-year-old complainant in his van for a job. After the interview, he invited the complainant to see some of his work that was in a trailer behind the van. The complainant left the trailer door open and became frightened when the accused shut the door in a way that suggested he had locked it. The accused initiated a number of increasingly intimate incidents involving touching, notwithstanding the fact that the complainant plainly said no on each occasion. He stopped his assaults after each "no," only to resume shortly afterwards with a more serious assault. The trial judge acquitted the accused on the basis that there had been implied consent, even though he believed that the complainant did not want the touching to take place and that she was afraid.

The Supreme Court unanimously rejected the availability of an implied consent defence in sexual assault cases. In addition, the Court laid out a framework for assessing both the *actus reus* and *mens rea* of sexual assault. The *actus reus* should be determined from the perspective of the complainant, and particularly through a consideration of whether the complainant, in her mind, wanted the sexual touching to take place. If there is reasonable doubt as to consent or if the complainant participated (or was passive or ambiguous in her conduct), "the courts must ask whether the complainant consented because of force, fear, threats, fraud or the exercise of authority as enumerated in s. 265(3) of the *Criminal Code*.

The *mens rea*, on the other hand should be determined from the perspective of the accused: did the accused honestly believe that the complainant communicated consent through her words and/or actions? If yes, the trier of fact must consider whether the accused's belief was reckless, wilfully blind or tainted by an awareness of any of the factors enumerated in ss. 273.1(2) and 273.2 of the *Criminal Code*. The trier of fact should also consider whether the accused took reasonable steps in the circumstances known to the accused at the time, to ascertain that the complainant was consenting. If the complainant at any point expressed a lack of agreement to engage in sexual activity, it is incumbent on the accused to point to evidence that supported his belief that consent had been unequivocally communicated before he had proceeded. Quoting the concurring decision of Justice L'Heureux-Dubé in the case of *Parks*, Justice Major reiterated one of the most important clarifications of the law of sexual assault in the *Ewanchuk* decision:

> *. . . the* mens rea *of sexual assault is not only satisfied when it is shown that the accused knew that the complainant was essentially saying "no," but it is also satisfied when it is shown that the accused knew that the complainant was essentially not saying "yes."*

In other words, only yes means yes.

CASES FOLLOWING *EWANCHUK*

The Ontario Court of Appeal encountered one of the earliest opportunities to interpret *Ewanchuk* in *R. v. O.(M.)*. The Court had to determine whether the trial judgment was consistent with the principles articulated in *Ewanchuk*, even though the trial decision writs released before the judge had the benefit of the Supreme Court's directions.

In this case, the complainant, a 15-year-old ward of the Children's Aid Society, met the 23-year-old accused at a bus stop. They chatted and agreed to go to the accused's apartment, where they drank beer. The complainant testified that she had said "no" when the accused tried to remove her pants. However, the accused testified that the complainant removed her own pants. He acknowledged that at some point, the complainant had said "no," but he took that as meaning "no" without a condom. The trial judge found that it was common ground that the complainant did say "no" at one stage, although on the evidence it was unclear when she said it and under what circumstances.

The trial held that the complainant was not an active participant in the sexual activity and that in her mind, she did not want to have sexual relations with the accused. However, the trial judge acquitted the accused because the complainant had not expressed by words or conduct a lack of agreement to engage in such activity. Therefore, the accused had an honest, if mistaken, belief that the complainant was consenting.

The majority decision at the Court of Appeal, written by Justice Finlayson, held that although the trial judge did not express the correct criterion given that his decision preceded *Ewanchuk*, his findings were compatible with the standard articulated in *Ewanchuk*. In his view, there was ample evidence on which the trial judge could have based a finding that the complainant had affirmatively communicated her consent as required by *Ewanchuk*. The trial judge's finding that the accused honestly believed that the complainant consented coupled with his finding that she did not express a lack of agreement to engage in such activity substantially complied with *Ewanchuk*, such that a new trial was not warranted. The majority opinion demonstrates the difficulty in, or perhaps resistance to, interpreting *Ewanchuk* as intended, and exemplifies the types of application issues that subsequent decisions have encountered as well.

On the other hand, the insightful dissenting opinion of Justice Rosenberg, whose reasons were later accepted by the Supreme Court, offers further clarification on the proper application of *Ewanchuk*. Justice Rosenberg asserted that recent cases of the Supreme Court have made it clear that "neutral conduct on the part of the complainant cannot on its own serve as a basis for the defence of mistake. Moreover, the accused must have a belief in the way that consent was manifested: "The accused must believe that either by actions or words the complainant said 'yes'." Applying these principles to the *O.(M.)* case, Justice Rosenberg stated the following:

> *In my view, the trial judge in this case asked himself the wrong question. He asked whether it was apparent to the respondent from the complainant's words or actions that she was not consenting. He answered that question in the negative. He was unable to conclude that "she expressed by words or conduct, a lack of agreement to engage in such activity" and therefore found that the defence of mistake was established. However, that was not sufficient to establish the defence.*

Applying *Ewanchuk*, the question was whether the accused honestly believed that the complainant had communicated consent.

The confusion evident in the majority decision of *O.(M.)* is not unusual. Many subsequent decisions that have attempted to interpret and apply *Ewanchuk* have also been muddled. In some cases, the judge has recognized the relevance of *Ewanchuk* but has failed to apply it in a meaningful way.

For example, in *R. v. S.D.P.*, Justice Wayne Gorman quoted extensively from the *Ewanchuk* decision. However, *Ewanchuk*'s analysis was not applied to the facts at hand. In fact, *Ewanchuk* was never mentioned in the decision again. In *S.D.P.*, Justice Gorman recognized that the 16-year-old complainant had expressed her lack of consent to sexual touching by the accused, which had escalated over the course of the evening. Although the trial judge found the complainant to be a credible witness for the most part, he remained unconvinced by some aspects of her version of events. He remarked that although the complainant had left the impression that she had resisted all of the accused's attempts at sexual contact, she had willingly unzipped part of the hooded sweatshirt she was wearing. Moreover, she "should have easily been able to frustrate any attempts by S.D.P. to unhook her brazier [sic] by simply moving a small bit." In the end, the trial judge was left with reasonable doubt about whether an assault had taken place and thus entered an acquittal.

The trial judge had discretion to make determinations of credibility based on the evidence before him, which in this case involved finding parts of the complainant's testimony to be inconsistent with her account of resisting the sexual advances of the accused. However, his token recognition of *Ewanchuk*, without application, suggests that he was not clear on how to apply the case. *Ewanchuk* does not require a complainant to actively resist as an indication of non-consent to establish the accused's culpable state of mind. Even if the trial judge was concerned about the truthfulness of the complainant's resistance, there was no evidence that the accused believed the complainant had actually communicated consent to his sexual touching. That she said "no" at some point should make this finding even more difficult. To complicate things further, the trial judge did not distinguish between his analysis of her non-consent and the accused's culpable awareness of her non-consent, which would have been helpful in pinpointing at what stage he thought the prosecution had failed. I assume that he was not convinced that the requirements of *mens rea* had been met.

A particularly shocking example of resistance to the principle in *Ewanchuk* was evident in a Quebec case involving an Inuit complainant and an Inuit accused in Kuujjuaq, who, along with two other Inuit friends, was accused of sexually assaulting the complainant. The accused suggested that the sexual contact between the complainant and the three men had been consensual, the version preferred by the trial judge. Interestingly, the trial judge was willing to overlook the inconsistencies in the testimonies between the three accused as being a result of the nearly four-year time lapse before trial. He was less forgiving of inaccuracies and inconsistencies in the complainant's testimony (including details as petty as her claim that they were drinking Labatt Blue beer and not Budweiser as reported by the men). The judge noted the complainant's delay in bringing forth a complaint, her crush on one of the accused, the fact that the accused were more than mere acquaintances of the complainant and her incentive to reconceptualize a consensual sexual encounter as a rape to avoid further blame by her spouse for being with three men. In addition, the judge noted that the "assault from the three individuals would be completely incompatible with the reputation and image they project in the community."

In finding the complainant's version of events to be irrational, Justice Denis Lavergne made the following statement about the application of *Ewanchuk*:

> *Even when applying the statement of the Supreme Court in the Ewanchuk case, cited before about the notion of consent in sexual assault, one cannot, with due respect, give any credit to this sequence of her testimony where she states not having protested, resisted or expressed her refusal in any way, out of fear. Now, nothing in the evidence attributes to any of the three men, in any way possible, whatever gesture of a hostile or threatening nature, whether direct or indirect, used so as to induce her consent to sexual relations. Furthermore, Mrs. Adams states without hesitation that neither one treated her harshly, threatened or forced her in any way. Quite on the contrary, all three were quite nice. In short, the three individuals are persons she knows well enough to accept to go for a ride with; neither one of them has the reputation of being violent, even less of being a woman abuser; neither one of them acts towards*

her in any reprehensible manner so as to force her into having intercourse. Actually, if she was afraid, we do not know why. We do not know why, for example, as she mentions, it could have been worse if she would have attempted something. . . .

Besides displaying reprehensible stereotypical assumptions about complainants and perpetrators of sexual assault, and implicitly suggesting Inuit women to be promiscuous, the decision reveals an alarming misapprehension about the meaning of *Ewanchuk*. For this woman to prove she had been raped, she needed to convince the judge that she had protested the assault. Again, this is not what *Ewanchuk* requires. The judge disbelieved her claim that she did not resist out of fear because there was clearly no reason, in his view, to fear these "nice" men. *Ewanchuk* will undoubtedly have less impact when the accused's version varies greatly with that of the complainant; credibility will continue to be the defining factor in these cases. However, for an accused's version to be credible, *Ewanchuk* makes it clear that a man's belief in consent cannot be based on the complainant's lack of resistance.

Even when courts have correctly applied *Ewanchuk* and rendered convictions, stereotypical assumptions continue to inform the discussion for many judges. These decisions remind us that although *Ewanchuk* has helped to protect the interests of complainants, work in judicial and public education continues to be necessary.

For example, in *R. v. C.R.N.*, the 16-year-old complainant alleged that she had been raped twice at a party by the 20-year-old accused. The accused claimed that the first act was consensual, but admitted that he figured she did not want to have sexual intercourse with him the second time. The judge questioned the complainant's judgment in putting herself in a potentially dangerous situation by accompanying her friend to a party at the residence of five young men and sleeping over. However, the judge noted that this fact did not reflect upon her credibility directly and had no bearing on whether she consented. He went on to wonder, however, whether a 16-year-old girl might, "in guilt and hindsight place blame on someone to take condemnation away from herself."

Although Justice Ian M. Gordon applied *Ewanchuk* properly in finding that there was no consent communicated by the complainant in the second incident, which was around 30 seconds after the first, he was not persuaded beyond a reasonable doubt that the complainant had not consented to the first incident. While the accused was convicted for the second incident based on an application of *Ewanchuk*, the judge was clearly uncomfortable with the law he felt compelled to apply. He stated:

Though not specifically at issue here, I must say this application of the law gives me some concern. The practical reality of a sexual incident becoming nonconsensual within a short period of time, some 30 seconds, requiring immediate control of a hormonal urge which in some cases has been jointly nurtured seems objectively somewhat idealistic.

This characterization of the sexual assault in biological terms, as hormonal, is disturbing. It ignores that sexual assault is an exercise of power and control over a woman. It also echoes the highly criticized comments of Justice John McClung of the Alberta Court of Appeal in *Ewanchuk*, in which he stated that the "clumsy passes" of the accused were "far less criminal than hormonal." In *C.R.N.*, the accused admitted that he knew that the complainant was not interested in participating in the second sexual act. Essentially, Justice Gordon suggested that once men are "turned on," it is unrealistic to expect them to "turn it off" instantaneously.

Whereas some decisions have relied on stereotypes *despite Ewanchuk*, more encouragingly, others have referred to Justice L'Heureux-Dubé's concurring judgment to explicitly counter myths about sexual assault. For example, Justice Mary-Ellen Turpel-Lafond criticized an accused's suggestion that not paying a sex worker as agreed upon before sex was fraud, but not sexual assault. In her view, accepting this position in sexual assault would be tantamount to resurrecting the rape myth that a prostitute's consent to sex is less worthy of legal protection than it is for other women. This approach to consent, she noted, was rejected by the concurring opinions of Justices L'Heureux-Dubé and McLachlin in *Ewanchuk*.

Similarly, Justice K. Leslie Jackson rejected the accused's claim that the complainant greeted his unannounced visit at 4:00 a.m., where the complainant was babysitting, with requests for money in exchange for sexual favours. Although the judge found that *Ewanchuk* was not applicable in the circumstances given that no consent was given or alleged to have been given, he noted that the accused's evidence relied on an acceptance of myths and stereotypes about women. Referring to Chief Justice Fraser's comments in the dissenting opinion in *Ewanchuk* for the Alberta Court of Appeal, which were later cited with approval by Justice L'Heureux-Dubé, Justice Jackson noted that, "this attitude or myth implies that women are "walking around this country in a state of constant consent to sexual activity."

CONCLUSION

Ewanchuk has brought us a long way in protecting a woman's right to be free of unwanted sexual intrusions. It has given more teeth to the requirement that an accused must have honestly and reasonably believed that consent was expressly communicated in order to raise it as a defence. Despite progress, ingrained stereotypes about complainants will be slow to disappear altogether. These myths and stereotypes continue to appear in many sexual assault decisions, regardless of the ultimate verdict rendered, and seem to impact decision-making most directly when the complainant's conduct is viewed as neutral, passive or ambiguous. In many of these cases, judges misapply *Ewanchuk* in finding that the complainant did not explicitly communicate non-consent rather than considering whether the accused had any basis to believe that the complainant had positively communicated her voluntary agreement.

We must continue to hold our courts accountable and ensure that *Ewanchuk* is applied in an accurate and responsible manner. Even when convictions are entered, we need to draw attention to stereotypical assumptions about women who have been raped that creep into decisions. We cannot depend on appellate courts to correct the mistakes of trial judges given that the majority of sexual assault acquittals will not be appealed by the Crown, even when incorrect in law.

Although the controversy surrounding *Ewanchuk* has died down in the years following its release, its message must continue to be heard loud and clear: Only Yes Means Yes.

Is Canada Peaceful and Safe for Aboriginal Women?

Anita Olsen Harper

Anita Olsen Harper is Ojibwa from the Lac Seul First Nation. Her undergraduate degree is in adult education from the University of Alberta, and she has a graduate degree in Heritage Conservation from Carleton. As lead researcher in a project of the National

Aboriginal Circle Against Family Violence, her research over several years focused on violence against Aboriginal women.

Aboriginal women in Canada are the victims of very serious human rights violations. One blatant example is the legislative gap in both federal and provincial law in protecting a spouse's right to equal division of matrimonial real property on-reserve. All other Canadians are protected by provincial laws regarding this matter, but the same laws are not applicable on-reserve because only the federal government has jurisdiction over "lands reserved for Indians" and this includes real property on-reserve. There has never been a law enacted by the Canadian Parliament to address how real property, including matrimonial homes, will be divided when a marriage or common-law relationship breaks down. Aboriginal women and their children who reside on-reserve directly bear the brunt of this serious legislative gap. Further, because almost all reserves in Canada suffer from a severe lack of adequate housing, women who cannot remain in the family home are forced to go elsewhere with their children. *This is only one example of the rights of on-reserve women remaining unprotected; a parallel situation concerning non-Aboriginal women does not exist in Canada.*

These facts remain in spite of the fact that for most of the decade up to the year 2001, Canada was ranked number one among 175 countries in the world as being the best country in which to live. The United Nations' Human Development Index (HDI) makes this determination through its Quality of Life survey, which examines the health, education and wealth of a country's citizens by measuring life expectancy, educational achievement, secondary and tertiary enrolment and standard of living.[1]

These findings would make one think that almost all Canadian citizens do quite well, and perhaps this is the case. For the Aboriginal people who have been living *ab initio* on these lands, this is simply not true. The disparity in health, educational attainment, accumulation of wealth, life expectancy and standard of living is a noticeably wide gap in comparison with the life experiences of most Canadians. Aboriginal women, in particular, suffer from inequality of status compared to both Aboriginal men and, especially, their non-Aboriginal counterparts.

In this and other respects, and mostly because Canada as a nation does not make it a priority to address issues such as these, it cannot "look in the mirror" and see a truly civilized and liberated nation.

Other countries in the world might have a difficult time comprehending that Canada hosts serious human rights problems. These beliefs and perspectives, though, do not take away from, or diminish the reality faced by many Aboriginal women in this country because of these violations. For example, Aboriginal women in Canada are subject to high rates of violence in all forms. In particular, racialized violence targeting Aboriginal women is especially disturbing because these experiences are passed on intergenerationally to children and youth in other violence-related forms such as through involvement in street gangs and other "street" misbehaviours. In far too many instances, extreme racialized violence against Aboriginal women leads to their disappearances and even murder. The life destroyed in these circumstances is not only the victim's, but those whom she has left behind: grandmothers, parents, sisters, aunts, children, other relatives and friends. Could the long-standing general lack of awareness within Canada about the extreme violence against Aboriginal women mean that the public simply does not want to know? Does the public think that these "uncomfortable" issues will perhaps just somehow "go away?"

REPRESENTATION OF ABORIGINAL PEOPLE IN CANADIAN HISTORY

The way Aboriginal people have been represented in Canadian history plays an important part in how Aboriginal people, including Aboriginal women, are perceived in today's Canadian society. In these times of rapid technological and other change, any statements about the importance of history seem almost naïve; modern Western societies appear to self-define according to their future plans, not from their past or history. Nonetheless, such perceptions do not take away from the validity of understanding the past in order to understand the present. Only by thoroughly comprehending the paths that have been leading to the present can appropriate and timely steps be taken to solve long-term problems, such as those faced by Aboriginal women in Canada. Incidentally, Aboriginal tradition places a high importance on expending time and effort in teaching youngsters their family and tribal history because they believe that a youth with a solid understanding of the past is a youth that values its own individual and collective identity.

There are many examples that demonstrate the reality that historical representation and its subsequent presentation is not necessarily trustworthy. In Canada, most recordings of the European-Aboriginal relationships have been preserved, presented and accepted according to the values, perceptions and general life philosophies of the prevailing Euro-Canadian society. Even within the relatively short span of that society, historiography points out an interesting phenomenon: narrations over time are recorded, shaped and fixed according to prevailing Eurocentric societal attitudes (Blaut 10). Paralleling any change in the view of the present is a change in the view of the past.

Historical presentations then, have many serious limitations. One of their sanctions is as a tool for propaganda to encourage thought and motivation into predetermined outcomes. The "battleground for the public mind" has always had many different fronts to serve certain specific purposes. For example, within their own societies at the time of contact, the roles of Aboriginal women were vastly different from those of European women. The latter held a status that was shared with minors and wards of the Crown; they were perceived as property—in their early lives, their father's property, and later when they married, the property of their husbands. Aboriginal women, on the other hand, headed family line,[2] exerted a great deal of power such as the authority to choose and oust their nation's chiefs, and were a vital part of consensus decision-making. Nevertheless, Canadian history presents these Aboriginal traditions in a negative light; the Indian Act of 1876 created the elected chief and council system thereby removing Aboriginal women's political powers by stipulating that only men could be elected as chiefs and councilors.

Canadian history shows that stereotypical images were serving a purpose for those who endorsed them. The primary overall opinion of the first Europeans was cautiously optimistic for they relied on the First Peoples for all their basic livelihood needs. They condescendingly acknowledged that these "primitive" peoples needed civilizing, but were fully confident that this could be accomplished through educational processes that they themselves would predicate. Times began to change. The true imperialist ambitions of the colonialist powers began to emerge, and the fairly balanced early relationship began to crumble to give way to the birth of the interpretation of Aboriginal people as wretched and barbaric, even demonic. Many history and children's books of the 19th century were based on this imagery (Francis 159–164).

Settlement in Canada's "wild west" increased, but not from invitation by the First Nations themselves, who due to decimation from foreign diseases increasingly found themselves on the fringes of their own territories. These times saw rampant theories of Native racial inferiority for these provided a rationale to the Europeans for indiscriminately taking lands that were not rightfully theirs (Hawkins 62). Newcomers willingly listened to academics who predicted the disappearance of the entire Indigenous peoples as God's way of using nature to weed out an inferior group in favour of a superior one (Le Conte 359–361). In the meantime, the First Peoples were being further marginalized into the undesired hinterlands and their suffering, if it was known at all, was treated with indifference by both the Canadian government and general public who were too busy and apathetic to involve themselves in any meaningful way.

INEQUALITIES LEAD TO THE "SISTERS IN SPIRIT" INITIATIVE

People treated with inequality by government are fair game for societal discrimination, and racism if they belong to a different ethnic group. Aboriginal people, meeting these conditions, are both discriminated against and suffer the consequences of racism. Further, because of the patriarchy of Canadian society, Aboriginal women are subject to even more inequality than Aboriginal men. There are many different arenas in "everyday Canadian life" in which Aboriginal women do not fare well at all.

Looking at Canada's Aboriginal women from an economic perspective, we see that, in one province (Manitoba), 42.7% off-reserve live in poverty (Donner, Busch and Fontaine). The corresponding figure for non-Aboriginal women is half that number. Aboriginal women's average annual income was $13,300; Aboriginal men's was $18,200 whereas that of non-Aboriginal women was $19,350 (NAPO 2). This synopsis is a prime example of Aboriginal women's inequality in relation to both Aboriginal men and non-Aboriginal women in the area of earning power for meeting basic livelihood needs.

Canada's child welfare system continues to be disastrous for Aboriginal families. Provincial government policies target Aboriginal children for transition into various agencies and adoption into non-Native families. While these practices are now being lobbied against by Native women's and other groups, policy changes are painfully slow. A significant but undesirable result is that, very often, the traditions and practices of most of these children, as grown adults, are not recognizable as Aboriginal and their connections to birth families tends to be weak at best. In 2004, a large proportion—30,000 out of a total of 76,000 children in care—is Aboriginal; this is an astonishing 39.5% (Blackstock and Trocme 1). More disturbingly, this large number of children has all but lost its true identity; searching out family roots and ties is problematic and traumatic for most.

In the area of education, there is a particularly large gap between the rates of non- and Aboriginal women with university degrees: in 2001, 7% of Aboriginal women over 25 years of age had a university degree, compared with 17% for non-Aboriginal women within the same age group (Statistics Canada). While two-thirds of Aboriginal graduates are women, equal access to employment opportunities is still lagging; this is because gendered racism obstructs Aboriginal women's access to a fair share of the labour market (Jacobs). In the same year, 40% of Aboriginal women over the age of 25 had not graduated from high school compared with 29% among non-Aboriginal women (Women in Canada 2005 196).

Federal, provincial and territorial justice systems are other areas that discriminate against Aboriginal women on the basis of their race, gender and class. The systemic racism of all police forces albeit some "better" than others, and not applicable to every single member, is one way of explaining this. For example, most police officers need a fair and open attitude towards those working in the sex trade and must learn to treat street people as human beings—with dignity and respect. Another area that needs serious revision is the Court system. Court personnel often fail to either recognize or acknowledge the unique forms of injury that Aboriginal women suffer when they report being sexually assaulted or raped or any number of violations. Many Aboriginal women and girls are ostracized by their families or reserves when they go through with criminal charges; often, they themselves are blamed for their situations. This is especially harmful when so many live in the northern, more isolated areas of the country; a general lack of counseling and support services in many reserve communities does little to help and encourage these women.

The "Stolen Sisters" report by Amnesty International (Canada) made the following statements about the way in which police treat or relate to Aboriginal people:

- Most disturbingly, the inquiry concluded that police had long been aware of white men sexually preying on Indigenous women and girls in The Pas but "did not feel that the practice necessitated any particular vigilance." (1)
- The inquiry explained that many police have come to view Indigenous people not as a community deserving protection, but a community from which the rest of society must be protected. (30)
- Many Indigenous families told Amnesty International that police did little when they reported a sister or daughter missing and seemed to be waiting for the woman to be found. (32)
- . . . few police forces have specific protocols on actions to be taken when Indigenous women and girls are reported missing. (33)

Amnesty International's report concluded that Canadian authorities and most police forces do not protect Aboriginal women from violent attacks (including murder) but, instead, tend to disregard these violations when they occur and are reported.

These long-standing realities, faced by all Aboriginal women in Canada, remain mostly unaddressed and given a low priority for change by governments. The *status quo* continues to place Aboriginal women at a much greater risk of social and economic marginalization, laying fertile ground for higher risks of victimization from all types of crimes—but most likely physical and sexual crime at the forefront. So far, all levels of government have not implemented the necessary legislative action and policy direction to decrease the risks that would help protect Aboriginal women from being targets of violence and other related criminal activity.

THE SISTERS IN SPIRIT INITIATIVE

In the meantime, not awaiting government policy and legislative change to address what became known as "racialized, sexualized" violence[3] against Aboriginal women, many began working with unrelenting perseverance in lobbying and involved advocacy efforts. This was taking place at both the grassroots and organizational levels in the Native community; one of those was the Native Women's Association of Canada (NWAC) and its

Board of Directors who were Provincial/Territorial Member Associations (PTMAs). Many others were Aboriginal families and women themselves; they were helped by non-Aboriginal women's groups and individuals. Some of these were Amnesty International (Canada), KAIROS Canadian Ecumenical Justice Initiatives, the Canadian Association of Elizabeth Frye Societies, and the United, Anglican and other churches.

The year 2002 saw national momentum building up. Those involved pooled their efforts to raise awareness of the racially motivated attacks on Aboriginal women. This group was known as the "National Coalition for our Stolen Sisters" and adopted a red heart-shaped logo with an inscription commemorating February 14 for "a day of love and hope and memory for our Stolen Sisters." This was the beginning of Aboriginal women's voices being heard at the national level in an area that for so long was a source of trauma for them.

The Coalition, spearheaded by NWAC, was simultaneously working to cultivate federal government allies; these were Indian and Northern Affairs Canada, the Department of Justice Canadian International Development Agency, Public Safety and Emergency Preparedness Canada (part of which is the Royal Canadian Mounted Police), Foreign Affairs Canada and Status of Women Canada (SWC). Only one department made a formal agreement with NWAC. In November 2005, SWC committed five-year[4] funding for Sisters in Spirit and this moved the campaign into a full research, education, national-awareness and policy initiative. Qualitative research in the form of life histories will be undertaken with the victims' family members and friends in order to gain a better understanding of the circumstances, root causes and trends that surround these cases. The terms of the funding agreement provide NWAC with the fiscal and human resources to work in collaboration with other non- and Aboriginal women's organizations and with various federal government departments to improve the human rights of Aboriginal women in Canada, and to target the racialized and/or sexualized violence directed at this particular group.

Sisters in Spirit's update includes an exegesis of the recent history of violence against Aboriginal women. From the 1980s through to the 2000s, concern for the safety of Aboriginal women was steadily increasing and posters of missing women were becoming a common sight anywhere Aboriginal people congregated—in community halls, stores and band offices, for example. Websites began to appear, listing the names of missing women, many being Aboriginal. Families of those missing and/or found murdered were starting to voice the pain, isolation and trauma they were experiencing, and talked about the lack of support from police and other authorities when they tried to report on the status of their loved ones.

In the early 1990s, sex trade workers in Vancouver's downtown east-side were noticing that, for at least the past decade, many of their peers were simply vanishing, never heard from again. For those friends and family members trying to get help from police, interactions were generally not fruitful. For example, in April 1999, there was a move to get police to offer a reward for information on the missing women, but instead the City of Vancouver[5] suggested offering $5 000 to any of the missing women to come forward. This offer reveals that authorities did not believe that the women were indeed missing, but had perhaps simply gone off somewhere. Then, the media became knowledgeable, curious and involved. Journalists began to ask the same questions that family members had been asking for years. The eventual result was the formation of a joint Vancouver City Police/RCMP Taskforce. More than 70 women were listed as missing. An arrest was made in early 2002 and Robert Pickton was charged with 27 murders. It is believed that at least one-third of his victims were Aboriginal.

Statistically, Vancouver's Aboriginal population is about 7% (Vancouver/Richmond Health Board 7). There is a high prevalence of prostitution in the city's downtown east-side where many Aboriginal women go missing. Aboriginal women are significantly overrepresented in Vancouver's sex trade and this "reflects not only their poverty but also their marginalized and devalued status as Canadians" (Fancy, Lynne and Cotton 256). Victoria, the capital of B.C., reports a similar overrepresentation: 15% of women in escort prostitution are Aboriginal, although the Aboriginal population is only around 2% (Benoit and Millar 18).

Vancouver is not the only "hot spot" in the province, however. Another area is now known as the "Highway of Tears" because of the large number of missing and/or murdered Aboriginal women along this nearly 500-mile stretch between Prince Rupert and Prince George. These murders started coming to light around 1994/1995 when three 15-year-old Aboriginal girls were found, in three separate instances, murdered in Prince George and Smithers. In March 2006, concerned community and family members held the "Highway of Tears Symposium" to address the urgent issue of the missing and murdered women along this highway. Nine families were officially listed as having members go missing—including an entire family. Only one young woman was non-Aboriginal.

The Symposium made four broad recommendations:[6]

- Emergency readiness must include an enhanced "amber alert" program, which fast-tracks a public alert when someone goes missing, and preparation of an inventory of violent offenders for release into communities.
- Prevention programs must involve both families and communities as advocates for policy change in the area of regulations regarding missing persons; installing well-lit emergency telephones along this stretch of highway; creation of a hitchhiker tracking system that would work somewhat like a block watch program; and, development of youth awareness programs such as "street smarts" and "stranger danger."
- Community development to address racism and oppression; identify "safe homes" along Highway 16; and, placing coordinators in Prince George and Terrace to move identified action plans.
- Counseling and support services that offer an Aboriginal focus on spirituality; advocates working with the RCMP in victim services.

Sisters in Spirit works to support initiatives like the Highway of Tears Symposium. NWAC President, Beverley Jacobs, speaking at various functions, articulates the integral connection of colonization to the displacement of Aboriginal women in this country, and that an undeniably strong example is the missing/murdered in this region. She also mentions the need for collaboration among all those working to draw national, regional and local attention to the missing women and how awareness itself can help guard against further disappearances and murders. Ms. Jacobs always speaks of hope and adds words of encouragement to all those families who suffer from the loss of loved ones.

The Sisters in Spirit initiative has other related objectives that are directed at cultivating strength and support for Aboriginal families and entire communities. These include helping to mobilize the caring power of the family and community; providing tools accessible by Internet to help the families of victims familiarize themselves with the justice and other related systems; and providing links to community organizations for frontline delivery service (such as grief counseling, therapy, Legal Aid and discussion circles).

The strategic outcome for Sisters in Spirit is gender equality for all Aboriginal women in Canada, and their full participation in the economic, social, cultural and political arenas that are available to all other citizens in this country.

CONCLUSION

The Sisters in Spirit initiative works to reduce the risks and increase the safety and security of all Aboriginal women in Canada, regardless of where they work or where they live. The initiative also works to draw attention, recognition and dignity to those Aboriginal women and girls who are still missing and those already found murdered. While the actual number is still unknown, most Aboriginal people, both men and women, would say that they know at least one person who simply disappeared from sight; some would know at least one who was murdered.

It is not hard to make the connection between being socially, economically and politically marginalized to being targets of hatred and violence. This is exactly the plight of Aboriginal people in Canada, particularly Aboriginal women. The effects of Canada's historical grounding are proving to be, without a doubt, disastrous for Aboriginal women. The way and means of Canadian history being interpreted and presented in educational and other fundamental institutions portrays a "logical rationale," convoluted and pejorative as it is, that allows and perpetuates Aboriginal women continuing as targets of violence and death just because of their gender and racial identity.

Clearly, Aboriginal women's self-interpreted concerns must be allowed in all modalities of expression within Canadian society. Aboriginal women need their distinct voices heard in re-defining a better society in which they are included in positive and meaningful ways, ones that elevate their historic positions as significant decision-makers, choosers of chiefs, and landowners. Indigenous truths, as a whole, need to be communicated everywhere in this country; world views and cosmologies must be known in educational institutions and political establishments, for example; no longer should room be made for the kind of cultural bigotry that sees Aboriginal women's thoughts and concerns as unsophisticated, undeveloped or simply unapplicable in a contemporary highly technological global society. Historically, the "Fathers of Confederation" deliberately excluded Aboriginal people, both men and women, from vital nation-building processes, and now there is a crucial need to restore the contributions of Indigenous people to an honourable and rightful place, and to recognize the enormous challenges they still face because of Canada's continuing discriminatory laws and practices.

Sisters in Spirit, striving to eliminate the objectification and dehumanizing activities that Aboriginal women have been subjected to since European contact, has a definite and significant role in helping to change the attitudes, practices, policies and awareness levels of everyday Canadians. Undoubtedly, Canada still manages to maintain a relatively high global image—but for this country's Aboriginal women, continuing to suffer from large-scale inequalities, this has little meaning and no relevance.

Endnotes

1. Real Gross Domestic Product per capita based on Purchasing Power Parity exchange rates (PPPs are the ratios of the prices in national currencies of the same goods or services in different countries).
2. They were matrilineal and matriarchal, generally speaking.

3. This is violence directed at a person because of their gender and race.
4. The initiative ends in 2010.
5. Vancouver, meanwhile, was being placed high on the annual Quality of Life survey. Other major Canadian cities were honoured for high levels of "personal safety and security" ("Vancouver 3rd in world in quality of life survey").
6. The broad recommendations were fleshed out on the second day of the Symposium. The full report was released to the public on June 21, 2006.

References

Amnesty International (Canada). *Stolen Sisters: A Human Rights Response to Discrimination and Violence Against Aboriginal Women in Canada*. Ottawa: Amnesty International (Canada), 2004.

Benoit, C. and A. Millar. "Dispelling Myths and Understanding Realities: Working Conditions, Health Status and Exiting Experiences of Sex Workers." 2001. Online: www.web.uvic.ca/~cbenoit/papers/DispMyths.pdf. Accessed May 13, 2006.

Blackstock, Cindy and Nko Trocme. *Community Based Child Welfare for Aboriginal Children: Supporting Resilience through Structural change*. First Nations Child and Family Caring Society and Centre of Excellence for Child Welfare, University of Toronto, Oct. 9, 2004.

Blaut, I.M. *The Colonizer's Model of the World: Geographical Diffusionism and Eurocentric History*. New York: Guilford Press, 1993.

Donner, Lissa, Angela Busch and Nahanni Fontaine. "Women, Income and Health in Manitoba: An Overview and Ideas for Action." Women's Health Clinic website, 2002. www.womens healthclinic.org/resources/wih/wth.html. Accessed June 2, 2006.

Francis, Daniel. *The Imaginary Indian: The Image of the Indian in Canadian Culture*. Vancouver: Arsenal Pulp Press, 1995.

Hawkins, M. *Social Darwinism in European and American Thought*. Cambridge: Cambridge University Press, 1997.

"Highway of Tears" Symposium Broad Recommendations. Online:www.highwayoftears.ca/recommendations.htm

Jacobs, Beverley. "Review of Beijing from an Indigenous Perspective: Secretariat Permanent Forum on Indigenous Issues." Paper presented at the Secretariat Permanent Forum on Indigenous Issues. New York, March 3, 2005.

Le Conte, J. "The Race Problem in the South." *Evolution Series No, 29: Man and the State*. New York: Appleton and Co, 1982.

National Anti-Poverty Organization. (NAPO) *The Face of Poverty in Canada: An Overview* (updated January 2006). Online: www.napo-onap.ca/en/issues/2006POVERTYinCANADA.pdf

Parley, Melissa, Jacqueline Lynne and Ann J. Cotton. "Prostitution in Vancouver: Violence and the Colonization of First Nations Women." *Transcultural Psychiatry* 42(2) June 2005: 242–271.

Statistics Canada. "Aboriginal Women in Canada." *Women in Canada 2005*. Catalogue No. 89-503-XE. Ottawa: Statistics Canada, 2005.

"Vancouver 3rd in world in quality of life survey." CBC News, Sun. 13 March 2005, 17:56:35 EST.

Vancouver/Richmond Health Board. *Healing Ways: Aboriginal Health and Service Review*. October 1999.

The Ultimate Rape Victim

Jane Doe

The woman known as Jane Doe is a teacher and an arts and culture worker who lectures extensively about her case. Her civil trial in 1998 was the focal point of headline coverage in national newspapers. CBC aired a TV movie about her experience called The Many Trials of One Jane Doe *in 2004. Jane Doe's case is now cited in law textbooks and studied in law schools internationally.*

It just so happens that I grew up in a Roman Catholic parish that was dedicated to the veneration of St. Maria Goretti. My grade school was also named after her. She was our patron saint. Maria Goretti was a 12-year-old devout Italian girl who was stabbed to death in 1902 when she refused to succumb to the man who tried to rape her. The miracles required for her canonization were testified to in the years following her death. They included her appearance in the prison cell of her murderer and his subsequent spiritual redemption (and early parole).

She was beatified, and attained sainthood in 1950. One of the best things about a Catholic childhood is the stories of the lives of the martyrs and saints. They are romantic and horrific both, laced with sexual innuendo, braced by bloody murder, torture and vengeance. Good lord, the saints were crucified upside down, burned alive, ventilated with arrows, eaten by lions, ripped apart by juggernauts! Their blood was slowly drained, their skin flayed. And they got to die for a larger good. They died for God, to uphold his one true faith. Upon their grisly deaths they were delivered immediately and whole unto heaven and in rapture. It was all fabulous and Grimm. Often much more than a young soul could bear.

Maria Goretti's story was a little different. It contained the requisite bloodletting (she was stabbed repeatedly), but the truth that her resistance to her rape was the motive for her murder (and canonization) could not be spoken aloud. That part was too horrific even for Catholic ears. Instead we were introduced to the codification of female purity as holy, and female sexuality as sinful. We were taught through her example that it was better to die in a state of purity and resistance than to live defiled as a raped woman. The spinning of her murder upheld the religious doctrine common to all denominations that female sexuality is problematic, a sinful lure that few men can resist and that must be cloaked in oppressive tradition and law.

Unlike the stories of the former saints George and Christopher, whose lives and saintly deeds (dragon-slaying and marine navigation) were erased by 12th-century papal decrees, the real story of Maria Goretti is more firmly located in human rather than heavenly design.[1] The man who murdered Maria was, in fact, just a boy, who was well known to her family. After 30 years in prison, he claimed that Maria had appeared and forgiven him. He entered a Catholic order of monks and lived out the rest of his life in the protective custody of the Church. Maria was not rewarded for her purity or goodness by deliverance into a position of power or respect in the religion she died for. She lives on rather as the ultimate rape victim. Her canonization occurred at a time when women in the West had achieved increased economic status and liberation but under a pope whose motives and morals continue to be the subject of public debate. Pope Pius XII did not elect to situate Maria in a powerful position within the faith after her death, as happened with Paul, who hated women, or John the Baptist, who thought women impure. These guys are bigger than saints. Bigger than life. Instead, the pope extolled Maria as a girl whose sexual identity precipitated her death and who was better dead than raped. Amen.

I have never allowed anyone to refer to me as a "rape victim." Certainly for the time that buddy held a knife to my throat I was his victim and I cannot deny that. But every time that term is used to define me, I feel I am returned to that moment, that night of terror and helplessness. Nor am I fond of the label "survivor." Like everyone else, I was already surviving the normal pain and hardships of life before I was raped, thank you very much. "Okay. So what do we call you?" you ask. Call me a woman. Call me a woman who has been raped. Call me a woman who has been raped by a man.

Rape victims are supposed to be helpless. We require assistance and must play a passive role while the good men, the police, lawyers and judges, punish the one, isolated bad man who committed the crime. Mass media reflect on and report their version of the raped or beaten woman as victim. Rape victims are othered, viewed as less than normal, unraped people. The term, its use and purpose, is not particular to the legal system and its players or the media. It is commonly used by members of the medical and helping professions as well, and by feminists. A more appropriate language to describe these crimes of violence was developed by feminists during the seventies and eighties but has been all but forgotten. Look at terms like "wife assault," "partner assault," "domestic violence" and "family abuse." Statistics overwhelmingly support the fact that these crimes are committed by men against women and children. And yet the language we use is gender-neutral. Listening to it, one could logically assume that the wife or partner had assaulted herself, that the children of the family were fighting with or abusing each other and that the violence referred to was homegrown as opposed to imported.

Not so long ago, women working in rape crisis centres and shelters developed language that identified the nature and perpetrator of the crime. Meaning men. Rape is about men. "Male violence" and "violence against women" were the terms we used. After a few years of this, and as we began to work with legal, social and government systems in the hope of effecting change, after we accepted their money to pay our wages and signed on the dotted line of institutional bureaucracy, we were requested to alter our language, to cut back on the perceived "rhetoric" so as not to alienate or hurt the feelings of the men who were sensitive to our issues (and signed our cheques). The long-term effect has been the un-gendering of sexual assault. But what is its cause? What are its other components? How does it end? Who benefits? Why do men rape?

If rape hadn't existed by now, we would have invented it. The rape of women has immense economic, social and legal advantages that are seldom articulated. Put plainly, rape works. It is a tool of sexism, and like racism, it exists because it "works." Stay with me, don't go away, this gets interesting. As a white woman who is anti-racist, I work hard to understand the causes and effects of racism. I understand that I benefit socially and economically from racism, especially the systemic, institutionalized, polite form that Canada has perfected.

As a white woman, I am more employable, better paid and less fetishized than Native women or women of colour. My menfolk are not incarcerated or stopped by police at the same rate. My children are not taunted, bullied or subjected to discriminatory treatment based solely on their skin colour. I can move a little more freely, hold my head a little higher, because I am not a visible container for racial intolerance. In these ways I enjoy privilege based on my racial origin. This acknowledgement does not by itself make me a racist. It helps me to understand racism and how it works.

Similarly, men benefit in systemic and obvious ways from a society that is inherently sexist. Men earn more than women, hold more positions of power, are not responsible for the unpaid work of mothering, walk freely and are free to walk alone. They need not worry about unwanted pregnancies, body image, aging and financial security with anywhere near the same intensity as women. They do not consciously fear the stranger rapist or feel compelled to monitor the actions of strange women around them. They are not taught at a very early age that there is a damned good chance they will experience a form of male violence staved off only by their lifelong vigilance and the curtailing of certain actions, pleasures and freedoms they might otherwise enjoy.[2] In Canada, the government statistics are that one in four men would rape if given the opportunity. This is unacceptable, frightening, outrageously high. But let's flip that stat for a moment and look at the inverse proposition: three out of four men would not rape. Indeed there are many more good men than bad. Where are they? What are they doing to address the rapes of their mothers, daughters, sisters and wives? How do I differentiate them from the bad guys? Sure, they're against rape, but do they understand the ways in which it maintains their privileged status as males? If rape is an extreme tool of sexism used to maintain the male status quo, doesn't it work for all men? In lectures I have given, this is where good men redden, their brows furrow and they start to disengage. They don't understand and they ask what they can do, what they should do, but mostly they want to go home. At another time—and appropriately so—I might have said, "Read a book. Don't expect me to take responsibility for your consciousness-raising."

But this is what I say here: It's hard to be a man. I shouldn't like to try it. Men are still socialized from a very young age that to be emotional, delicate or tender is to be a girl, and that that is the worst they can be. They must not cry or play with nurture-based toys or wear pastels. They are overwhelmed with male images that drive cars, leave the house for the majority of the day, and return only to mete out discipline and to enjoy the labour of the more home-based female parent. Traditional family values do not require that men prepare food, clean, organize, schedule or provide health care at the same level as women or at all. Their leisure pursuits are sports or technology-based, their literacy level is lower than girls', their demonstrative signs of affection limited. Our baby boys, whom we love and cherish and who are born to us free from malice or ill will, are conditioned to understand human sexuality as singular to their individual wants and needs, to translate "bitch" and "ho" as labels of both affection and contempt, to mistrust anything that "bleeds for five days every month and doesn't die," and to appreciate "gay," "faggot" and "queer" as variations of the greatest, most final insult of all.

A good friend of mine, a man who is sweet, smart and pro-feminist, has pointed out in more than one conversation about the meaning of life that his instinct, his motivation, is to follow his dick. To be true to it. I have challenged him on this, suggested that perhaps these are not quite the words he is reaching for when he discusses his life. But he stands firm, and I retreat, fearful that he really means what I think he means. Fearful that I really do—or don't—understand men and the cultural divide that distances them from me.

Every few decades and recently so, the tired sociological saw that men are biologically predetermined to rape is dressed up and trotted out to explain the eternal and rising incidence of the crime.[3] Women are cautioned to govern themselves accordingly given that the boys simply can't help it. The books, articles, columns that tooth the saw are well received and become the subject of circular logic and debate. What I cannot understand, am fascinated by, is that men themselves do not rebel against such a limited definition of their ethos and are not insulted by their group equation to molluscs and amphibian life. *Good men don't do it. Our men don't do it.* What to make of the fact that 75 to 80% of reported rapes are committed by men known to the women involved. The woman has no problem making an identification. The lighting is fine. She can provide you with her rapist's address and any other identifying information you could imagine. Some you could not. There is no need for a profile, criminal, geographic or artistic. Computer experts, criminologists, DNA and forensic scientists are not called in. They will not be part of the investigation into a crime that escalates yearly and has the lowest reporting rate of all violent crimes. That job goes to the uniformed officer who catches the 911 call or takes the report at the station. That officer has received a maximum of five days' training in a workshop called Family Violence, which blends the rape and sexual assault of adult women with similar crimes of violence committed against youth and children.

The training is delivered by other police officers. A rape victim may talk about how well her assault was investigated, she might chide (never challenge) or horrify the cadets to attention with her story. The necessity for adequate diversity training to assist these young men in sexual-assault investigation—which cops themselves will tell you is the most murky and difficult crime to investigate—is ignored. Directives to increase the numbers of women and non-white police force applicants have failed or fallen far short of their projected marks. Instead, increasingly significant portions of police budgets are designated for the purchase, maintenance and upgrading of computer technology to investigate and solve crime. VICAP and VICLAS, the systems used in Canada and the United States, are compatible with European and other international policing instruments. They are effective in dealing with international espionage, corporate and white-collar crimes, and auto, credit card or jewellery theft rings. And that's a good thing. Their efficacy in infiltrating prostitution, sex trade, pornography and child abuse networks is heralded by law enforcement officers. I'm sure they have been helpful in other violent crimes. But if you have not been raped by a stranger or an "anger retaliatory rapist" (who constitute only 25% of the rapist population), your crime will not be compatible with computer technology. These tools and the information they store are based on faulty conclusions about empirical evidence. Which means they can be as racist and as sexist as the agents who design and interpret them. Only now they get to call profiling "science," so it acquires a whole new, if undeserved, credibility. In the majority of rape cases, consent is the issue. The accused has agreed that there was sexual intercourse but it was, he swears, consensual. If the woman involved has prior activity that registers on the VICLAS system, it is used against her in a court of law. For instance, if the woman involved was raped before or if she did time for a crime she did or did not commit. If in the past she was apprehended by police under the *Mental Health Act*,[4] if she was hospitalized for postpartum depression or protested against government policies resulting in police apprehension, or if she whored to pay for college or drugs, fled her country of origin because of police abuse or was part of a Native roadblock, it will show up in a VICLAS search. (If you don't believe that this kind of information is collected and stored and available for some to access, take the time to file an Access to

Information Act application on yourself. There is probably a file with your name on it.) Next, an "expert" witness will be hired to testify that you are a slut, addict, terrorist, deviant or other form of miscreant, and your rapist is free to rape you again or otherwise complicate your life.

Actually, it probably won't even get as far as the expert-witness scenario because the rapist's lawyer can ask questions to elicit the information himself, or he can get it through his own computer search and not even have to pay for expert medical testimony. One of the things we need if we are to encourage women to report is increased and ongoing training and education on rape and other crimes of violence committed against women by men, delivered by women who are professionals in the area, meaning women who work in shelters and rape crisis centres. This will only happen through police policy and operational changes in law enforcement practices. Changes that will also benefit policing. Changes that women have been suggesting globally. For decades.

Women who work in anti-violence, who write about it and educate others and have first-hand experience of it, are the experts in the field of rape—not some Eliot Ness clone or computer nerd with a Ph.D. Hire us. And by the way, we will expect to be paid for our work.[5] The escalating focus on "stranger danger" by police through the media and with the assistance of so-called victims' rights groups has worked to maintain a climate of fear that ensures a large degree of control over how and where women live. Current warnings issued by police to alert communities of a serial rapist are fear-based and hysterical in language and nature. Instead of factual warnings that give us information about the dangerous men in our midst, they issue "don'ts" directed toward women, the people most at risk: The don'ts include:

Don't go out alone. Don't go out alone at night. Don't go out alone or at night unless accompanied by someone (male). Don't open the windows. Don't open the doors. Lock the windows and doors. Don't talk to strangers (men). Don't assist strangers (men). Don't take shortcuts. Alternate your daily routine and routes to work or school. Don't take elevators by yourself (or with strange men). Monitor the motions of the men around you. Don't ride the bus alone. Don't get off the bus alone. Leave your lights on. Don't use underground parking. Don't park on the street. Walk in pairs. Walk on the road. Walk down the middle of the road. Carry a cell phone. Don't struggle. Don't resist. Don't fight back. Don't arm yourself. Eat grass.

Hey! We already don't do those things! Tell us something we don't know. Give us adequate information that does not interfere with your investigation. Give us dates, times, locations, any description you might have, and let us work in the community to craft solutions and to support you and each other. And stop using the fear of strange men to deflect the bigger problems of sexual assault, beatings and other inhumane atrocities committed against us by men we know.

A lot of women have told me that they think it would be "worse" to be raped by a stranger than by a man you know. Personally, I think that in the larger sexual-assault lottery, I lucked out by being raped by a stranger. For one thing, I was not assaulted by someone I loved or trusted or otherwise chose to let into my life. I did not have to deal with that level of emotional betrayal. For another, there was never any question of consent or introducing my past sexual history during the rapist's trial. Oh, his lawyer would have done it—in fact, there is even a pamphlet called "Whack the Sexual Assault Complainant at Preliminary Hearing," which advises defence lawyers on how to get women's past sexual history introduced at trial. Defence lawyer Michael Edelson wrote (originally in an article published in a professional journal called *Lawyers Weekly* in May 1988):

You have to go in there as defence counsel and whack the complainant hard . . . get all the medical evidence; get the Children's Aid Society records and you've got to attack with all you've got so that he or she will say, 'I'm not coming back.'

The fact that I was raped by a stranger who was a serial offender with a history of identical crimes actually worked in my favour in court. It predisposed the police and the courts to believe that I was telling the truth and not making a false allegation. As a result, there was no legal basis to introduce my sexual history. (I did not dream that it or my medical and family histories would become issues in my civil trial twelve years later. In fact, if I had known it would come to that, I probably would not have proceeded.) It is easier (but not a foregone conclusion) for the courts to establish lack of consent if the rapist is a stranger. The justice system is less likely to think or believe that you agreed to sex and then changed your mind or just made the whole thing up to get attention. It should be relatively safe to assume that if a strange guy has a knife at your throat, the issue of consent is not to be debated.[6]

Mind you, if you change the picture just a bit and make the man with the knife at your throat your husband, boyfriend or date, well maybe he thought you liked it that way because he'd done it before and you didn't call the police that time, or it was just a little fantasy so he's not guilty. Not really. If he doesn't have a weapon but hurts you with his hands or threatens to, drops something in your drink or withholds money or food or shelter unless you succumb, then your consent does become the issue. The only issue that matters. The fact that you had prior sexual relations with him (or others), had been sexually assaulted before, consumed drinks or drugs that night (or ever), the very fact that you knew him can be used against you in a court of law to raise doubt about your consent and to determine that he is not guilty. And they wonder why more women don't report . . .

Endnotes

1. In 1969 the Church decreed that George, who killed dragons and rescued beautiful women, and Christopher, who carried the child Jesus across a swollen river, were no longer saints and that their deeds are mythical.
2. Again, the incidence of male-on-male violence is high and rising. Young men today, especially youth of colour, think twice about walking alone at night. Their mothers certainly worry about it. The subject I am addressing, however, is the rape and sexual assault of adult women by adult men, and how that works as a tool of sexism.
3. *A Natural History of Rape: Biological Basis of Sexual Coercion*, by Randy Thornhill and Craig T. Palmer (2000), is the most recent manifesto of this sort.
4. The *Mental Health Act* gives police the authority to arrest and incarcerate individuals they deem to be mentally ill who are held (but not charged) until the diagnosis is confirmed. The record of the arrest is permanent.
5. The point of payment for work done by professional women who consult with police departments on rape or wife assault is one of the hottest hot-button issues I have encountered in my work as Jane Doe. Even other women working in the area take issue with it, claiming it will further alienate police. Since 1975 anti-violence workers in Toronto have left their paid work to sit on panels and committees or go

to meetings with police without financial reimbursement for wages and time lost. And to no effect. Would consultants on helicopter use and purchase or stun-gun efficacy in crime fighting work for free? Should they? The practice of not paying people for their work results in that work being undervalued or ignored. Not to mention poverty.

6. The film *The Accused*, starring Jodie Foster and based on a true story, is an example of the courts believing that a woman consented to a gang rape by strangers, even though she was sure she did not. We need not go as far as Hollywood to find examples. In Canada see *Regina v. Wald, Hockett and Gin,* Alberta Court of Appeal and *Regina n. Sansregret*, Supreme Court of Canada.

CHAPTER 4

The Body: Reproduction and Femininity

Feminist critics have revealed how the mind/body dualism is gendered and how women's subordination is linked with the reduction of women to "the body." As Susan Bordo (1993, p. 17) writes, ". . . for women, associated with the body and confined largely to a life centered on the body (both the beautification of one's own body and the reproduction, care and maintenance of the bodies of others), culture's grip on the body is a constant intimate fact of everyday life." The readings in this chapter represent a range of recent Canadian writings confronting dominant constructions of the female body, focused on two critical themes: the struggle for reproductive control and the struggle against normalizing standards of femininity. Following from the concerns guiding this reader, contributions in this chapter interrogate the body with careful attention to differences of race, class, ability and sexuality. Moving away from the essentialist arguments that dominated second wave feminist analyses of reproductive control and normative femininity, these readings both broaden the agenda and engage in new complexities.

ABORTION

The demand for bodily agency has been clearly expressed in Canadian women's continued struggles over abortion. The struggle to decriminalize abortion and to ensure women's control over fertility was central to the politics of second wave Canadian feminism. The first reading in this section highlights the incompleteness of this struggle and the need for continued vigilance. The Canadian Supreme Court's decision in *R. v. Morgentaler* (1988) is popularly understood as a watershed victory in the long battle for reproductive control. For many students in today's Women's Studies classrooms, the struggle for abortion "rights" is viewed historically, as a battle already won. Yet **Canadian Abortion Rights Action League (CARAL) ("A Special Report to Celebrate the 15th Anniversary of the Decriminalization of Abortion: Protecting Abortion Rights in Canada")** emphasizes, Canadian women's access to abortion remains severely circumscribed.

The *Morgentaler* decision struck down Criminal Code restrictions on abortion as a violation of women's Charter rights to "security of the person." Until 1988, abortion was criminalized in Canada unless numerous conditions could be met, including determination by a hospital-based "therapeutic abortion committee" that continuation of a pregnancy would endanger a woman's "life" or "health." In removing these obstacles and effectively decriminalizing abortion, the *Morgentaler* decision was indeed an important symbolic victory and a step towards enhanced reproductive control. Yet at the same time the decision was both limited and ambiguous. Most importantly, the decision failed to establish a positive right to abortion, leading to a series of restrictive provincial funding practices around abortion.

The wide chasm between decriminalization and access is starkly underscored by CARAL. Despite decriminalization, abortion is still difficult or impossible to obtain in some provinces and many rural areas and the "right to life movement" has increased its surveillance of doctors performing abortions. Undertaken on the 15th anniversary of the *Morgentaler* decision, the CARAL study canvassed the availability of abortion services in Canada. Included here is a brief section of the comprehensive study with the startling finding that only 17.8% of hospitals provide abortion services. As CARAL documents, each year more and more Canadian women seek abortion services from an ever-shrinking number of hospitals prepared to treat them, resulting in long waiting lists, the need to travel long distances and unnecessary costs. CARAL's conclusions highlight class-based inequities—low-income women who live in provinces and regions lacking hospital services and who are unable to pay private clinic and/or travel costs face extreme barriers in accessing abortion. The report demands decisive action from federal and provincial governments to ensure public provision and cross-Canada access to abortion. Just as importantly, however, the CARAL study functions as a call to Canadian feminists to continue in broad-based struggles for women's reproductive control, working towards the goal of equitable, public provision of abortion services.

If the feminist contributions to reproductive control included in this section underline the incompleteness of past strategies, so too do they interrogate crucial questions of differences among women. Recent feminist scholarship has revealed the racist, ableist and classist assumptions informing past struggles for reproductive control. It may well be that achieving decriminalization has allowed feminists to grapple with the deep tensions and complexities that mark the politics of reproduction. In the section on abortion taken from **Susan Wendell**'s important book *The Rejected Body* (**"Abortion"**), we encounter the challenging ethical and moral questions raised by feminist disability analyses of reproductive control. As Wendell contends, feminist disability perspectives "have deepened the debates on the morality and politics of abortion by questioning the consequences of reproductive technologies and abortion policies for everyone with a disability." Wendell draws our attention to the consequences of developments in genetic and prenatal screening. Through the normalizing practices of contemporary reproductive technologies, some women are discouraged from becoming pregnant at all, while others are encouraged to terminate their pregnancies. Feminist disability theorists acknowledge that, under current conditions, the care of others is both privatized and deeply gendered; for this reason, many support women's right not to give birth to a fetus with a disability. At the same time, however, Wendell critiques the eugenic implications of reproductive screening and the devaluation of people with disabilities that results.

THE CONSTRUCTION OF FEMININITY AND THE BODY

The final four contributions to this section shift our attention to cultural constructions of femininity through the idealization, objectification and demands for control of the female body. Earlier feminist interrogations of "beauty norms" conceptualized the female body as a socially shaped and colonized territory, contained and controlled by dominant ideologies that were imposed externally by men (Dworkin 1974). Such a perspective ignores how multiple power relations, including racism and ableism, are inscribed on the female body. Furthermore, in constructing women as passive victims of male dominance, this approach obscures how normative standards of femininity are not only externally imposed, but sustained through women's self-surveillance (Bordo 1993, p. 27; Bartky 1990, p. 65). It is for this reason that many contemporary analysts have embraced an approach attentive to construction of femininity through "disciplinary practices." As described by **Wendell ("The Flight from the Rejected Body")** such disciplinary practices, ". . . [including], among other things, dieting, exercise, control of facial expression and careful constraint of movements, removal of body hair, application of skin-care preparations, hairdressing, and the 'correct' application of cosmetics, are not forced upon anyone in particular (indeed, they are often self-imposed, although there are also several external sanctions)[;] they appear to be natural or voluntary while they wield tremendous power in women's lives."

Carla Rice ("Between Body and Culture: Beauty, Ability and Growing Up Female") analyzes young women's relationship to these disciplinary practices, exploring the challenges that diverse groups of women face concerning their developing bodies as they grow up female. Rice identifies the period between childhood and adulthood as a time of intense pressure, during which young women face the greatest internal challenges to their body images. The educational and medical systems and the media reinforce socializing practices concerning weight and beauty, and, as Rice documents, many young women internalize destructive images regarding their bodies. This results in (among other disturbing trends) a preoccupation with thinness and an epidemic of dieting. In addition, Rice illustrates how dominant standards of feminine appearance are racially specific, creating hierarchies based upon approximating a global beauty norm defined by fair skin and European features. The great strength of Rice's contribution, however, is its demonstration of young women's agency and of wide-ranging strategies for resisting dominant beauty ideals.

Leslie Regan Shade ("Feminizing the Mobile: Gender Scripting of Mobiles in North America") affirms, yet again, how despite being modified by "new" technologies mobile phones continue to rely on gendered and racialized notions of femininity and masculinity. In an extensive survey of advertisements for mobile technologies, particularly cell phones, Shade reveals how telecommunication industries market these products by representing young girls and women as communicators, taking care of social relations. These young girls and women are almost always shown in groups while most representations of men in this context are largely white, young to middle-age men. They are generally alone and mostly being represented in some kind of paid work context. Despite the possibilities mobile technologies promise, they continue to tie women to the private and social realms and men to the public and paid work.

Wendell ("The Flight from the Rejected Body") interrogates normative standards of the body from a feminist disability perspective, charting the connections between disciplinary practices of femininity and disciplinary practices of bodily normality. Importantly, she situates the contemporary idealization of the body within forces of consumer capitalism; as she contends, profit drives the construction of an increasingly narrow bodily ideal, suppressing the enormous diversity of actual bodies. The ideal of the "normal body," defined by strength, health, appearance and performance, rests on a devaluation of the "rejected body," marked by illness or disability. Like Rice, Wendell is concerned with ways of resisting the disciplinary grip of cultural constructions of the body. She suggests that the creation of disability cultures and the revaluing of disabled bodies could provide sites of resistance. Crucially, Wendell cautions feminists about the exclusionary implications of celebrating strength and bodily control as a means of contesting dominant constructions of femininity. These feminist body ideals reinforce the devaluation of disability.

The theme of control and mastery of the body is also critically interrogated in the final contribution to this section **(Darling-Wolf, "From Airbrushing to Liposuction: The Technological Reconstruction of the Female Body")**. Fabienne Darling-Wolf identifies the belief that we can escape from the body and its natural processes as the central contemporary ideology of the body. Through science, medicine and media representations, actual female bodies are increasingly pathologized and reconfigured as raw material for technological interventions, ranging from exercise machines to plastic surgeries. Failure to submit to technological intervention is constructed as moral weakness. Darling-Wolf analyzes the role of technology in reinforcing racist and sexist ideologies, with consequences that are physically and psychologically damaging to most women. But, as she argues, while dominant ideologies of the body are powerful, we must not construct women as colonized or controlled by them.

Darling-Wolf's emphasis on agency provides an appropriate conclusion to this chapter of the text. As she contends, feminists need to recognize the complex ways that women survive, resist and challenge culture's grip on the body. Female bodies are not simply passive targets of regulation. Feminist re-appropriations of female bodies and explorations of embodiment can provide powerful resources for challenging both the regulation of reproduction and the disciplinary practices of femininity.

A Special Report to Celebrate the 15th Anniversary of the Decriminalization of Abortion: Protecting Abortion Rights in Canada

The Canadian Abortion Rights Action League (CARAL)

CARAL, the Canadian Abortion Rights Action League, is Canada's pro-choice, volunteer organization working exclusively to ensure that all women have total reproductive freedom to exercise the right to safe, accessible abortion. www.caral.ca

In January 1988 the Supreme Court of Canada made an historic decision that, at the time, made our country the envy of the world, because it clearly articulated the essence of what many had been arguing for years: any law that restricted a woman's right to life, liberty and security of person—as guaranteed under the *Canadian Charter of Rights and Freedoms*—was unconstitutional. This was the "Morgentaler Decision."

The Morgentaler Decision struck down Bill C-150 (passed in 1969), which had "legalized" abortion, but only upon the approval of a Therapeutic Abortion Committee (TAC). For nearly 20 years, this requirement had had the effect of denying abortion access to millions of Canadian women.

Three years after the historic Morgentaler Decision of 1988, the Conservative government of Brian Mulroney attempted to pass a regressive bill designed to, yet again, restrict access to abortion. The bill stated that unless a medical practitioner deemed that the health or life of a woman was threatened by her continued pregnancy, abortion was to be an *indictable offence,* thus potentially criminalizing thousands of women and their doctors. In their wisdom, Canada's Senate defeated this bill. Abortion had now been acknowledged by Canada's Supreme Court and government for what it was, is and always has been: a medical procedure. As such, abortion was to be covered under the *Canada Health Act* (CHA, 1984), and all women, regardless of age, economic status or place of residence, were to have access to the procedure based on the Canada Health Act's five principles of accessibility, comprehensiveness, public administration, portability and universality.

Finally it seemed the air had been cleared, and that women could exercise their constitutional right, free from the moral manipulations and legal and political stonewalling that had coloured the debate for so long.

Sadly, in 2003, fifteen years later, this is still not the case.

How do we know? We sent out written questionnaires to hospitals, asking them about the abortion services they provide. We also sent a survey to Planned Parenthood affiliates across the country. But how do we *really* know? We put ourselves in the place of the thousands of women every year who call their local hospital seeking an abortion. A CARAL researcher, representing a young woman with a not uncommon profile (20 years old, 10 weeks pregnant, recently moved to the area, no current family doctor, a Canadian citizen with health care) called local hospitals across the country and tried to schedule an appointment for an abortion.

DECLINE IN SERVICES

Nationally, an average of only 17.8% of hospitals provide abortion services. Women in Prince Edward Island and Nunavut have no access to abortion, while women in Newfoundland, New Brunswick, Manitoba and Saskatchewan have extremely limited services: only two hospitals in each of these provinces could confirm access. Since the completion of this survey the Moncton Hospital in New Brunswick has ceased providing abortions, thereby forcing women to seek care from the very restricted services of one remaining hospital in the province doing abortions, or, alternatively, women must pay for the abortion themselves at the Fredericton clinic. In Nova Scotia, the CARAL caller could confirm only three hospitals providing abortion services. These statistics provide the quantitative data behind the stories related by Planned Parenthood affiliates and documented by the caller from CARAL. Figure 1, below, provides documented evidence of the critical lack of hospital abortion services across Canada.

FIGURE 1 Hospital Access to Abortion Service: Province by Province

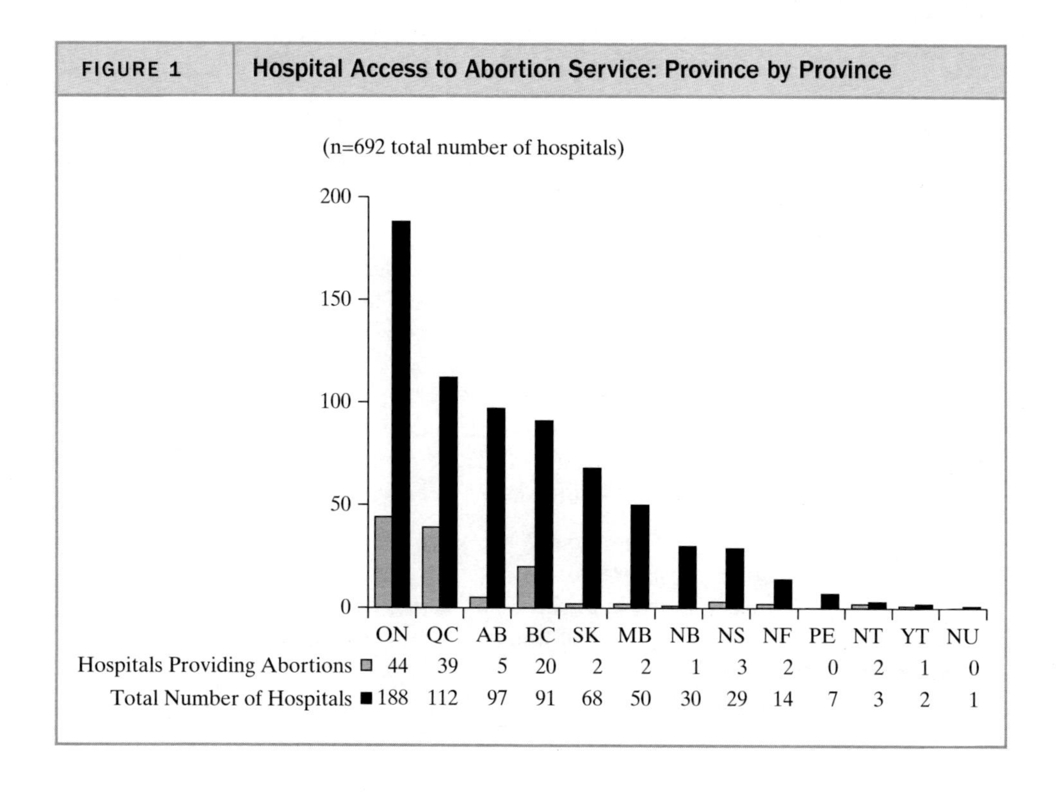

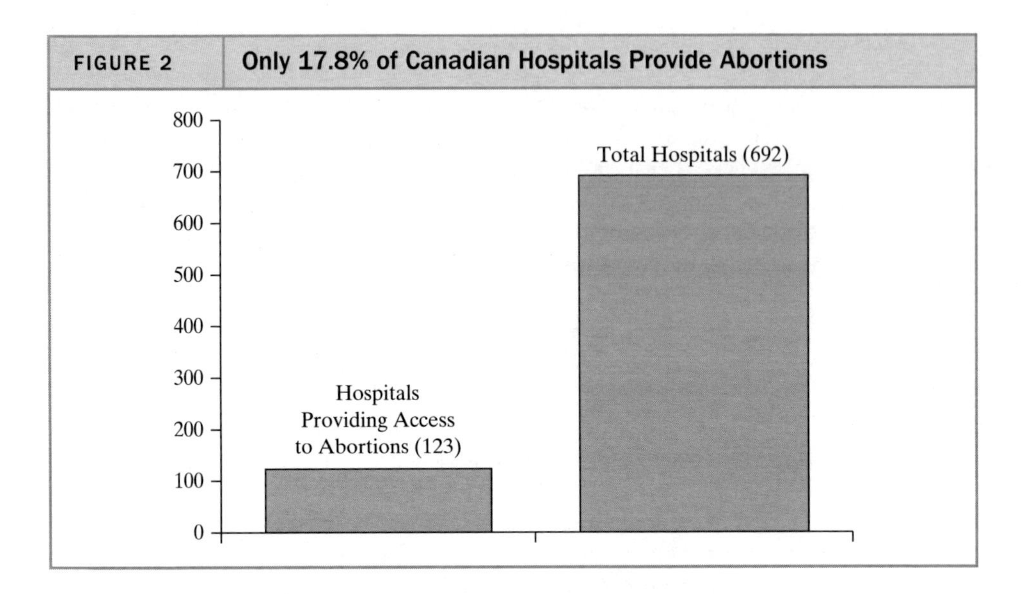

Figure 2, above, provides a graphic representation of the national situation: 692 hospitals with only 123, or 17.8%, providing access.

Abortion

Susan Wendell

Susan Wendell is Professor Emerita in Philosophy and Women's Studies at Simon Fraser University. Her research interests include feminist social and political theory, feminist ethics, feminist epistemology and women and disability. Since 1997, she has been interested in studying the influence of gender, race and class on psychosomatic diagnosis.

In "Shared Dreams: A Left Perspective on Disability Rights and Reproductive Rights," Adrienne Asch and Michelle Fine argue that women have "the right to abortion for any reason they deem appropriate," and that newborns with disabilities have "the right to medical treatment whether or not their parent(s) wishes them to be treated" (Fine and Asch 1988, 297). They affirm the value of the lives of people with disabilities, while defending women's "unequivocal" right to choose abortion, by drawing the moral line between the fetus residing inside and the infant living outside the mother's body. They say this about aborting fetuses with potential disabilities:

> *When a woman decides that she wants to abort, rather than carry to term, a fetus with Down's syndrome, this represents a statement about how she perceives such a child would affect her life and what she wants from rearing a child. Every woman has the right to make this decision in whatever way she needs, but the more information she has, the better her decision can be. Genetic counsellors, physicians and all others involved with assisting women during amniocentesis should gain and*

provide far more and very different information about life with disabilities than is customarily available. Given proper information about how disabled children and adults live, many women might not choose to abort. And many will still choose to abort. While a fetus resides within her, a woman has the right to decide about her body and her life and to terminate a pregnancy for this or any other reason (Fine and Asch 1988, 302).

In contrast, Jenny Morris says that women with disabilities who support non-disabled women's right to choose abortion while wishing that they would not choose to "deny existence to a disabled child" (Morris 1991, 81) are avoiding the issue.

There is no absolute right to choose whether to have a disabled child or not. An acceptance of such an absolute right belongs within an individualistic tradition, which, in the last analysis, gives all rights and responsibilities to individuals with no recognition of the collective rights and responsibilities of society. It is not in the interests of either women or disabled people to rely on liberal individualism for the furtherance of our rights (Morris 1991, 81).

Morris believes that the extensive use of genetic screening for the purpose of aborting potentially disabled fetuses questions the right of all people with disabilities to exist. It devalues people with disabilities; it implies that people who were born with disabilities should never have been born and that the existence of others like them should be prevented. It is also likely, Morris predicts, that genetic screening will increase the pressure on women with genetic disabilities not to have children.

Ultimately Morris supports a woman's "having some power" (82) to abort a potentially disabled fetus, but she insists that this power must be balanced against "the extent to which the fetus has rights as a human being" (82). Her solution is to say that a fetus that is viable outside the mother's body has a greater right to live than the mother's right to refuse to give birth to it. Given the fact that much prenatal diagnosis takes place near or after fetal viability, this solution, which Morris chooses on moral grounds, would in fact allow many infants with disabilities to be born. But if the rapid development of technology for genetic screening and prenatal diagnosis makes it possible to detect most potentially disabling physical conditions before viability, the conflicts between women's rights to choose abortion and the harms threatened to people with disabilities by selective abortion of potentially disabled fetuses will not be easily resolved.

Positions on abortion among people with disabilities, even among feminists with disabilities, vary widely from Asch and Fine's pro-choice-with-better-information position to alliance with anti-choice activists. The issues that people who do not devalue disability have raised have deepened the debates on the morality and politics of abortion by questioning the consequences of reproductive technologies and abortion policies for everyone with a disability. Rather than attempting to cover the extensive literature on the subject, I shall try here to summarize some major points, with references that the reader can pursue further:

1. The development of increasingly sophisticated genetic screening and prenatal diagnostic techniques holds out the "hope" of eliminating many inherited and prenatal potentially disabling conditions by selective abortion. Nevertheless, there will always be diseases and accidents. Therefore, unless medicine becomes so powerful that it can cure anything, in which case it could cure any neonatal disability, there will always be

adults and children with disabilities. It turns out that the promise of prenatal medicine is not to eliminate disability, but to reduce the number of people with disabilities by reducing the number of people born with disabilities (Blumberg 1994).

2. The widespread use of selective abortion to reduce the number of people born with disabilities has potential effects that have not been considered by people who have little knowledge of disability and/or take its disvalue for granted, including these:
   a. It sends a message to children and adults with disabilities, especially people who have genetic or prenatal disabilities, that "We do not want any more like you." Knowing that your society is doing everything possible to prevent people with bodies like yours from being born is bound to make you feel as though you are not valued and do not really belong, especially when there are so many attitudes and conditions in the society that derogate and/or exclude you. Laura Hershey, who was born with a rare disabling neuromuscular condition, says, "I believe the choice to abort a disabled fetus represents a rejection of children who have disabilities" (Hershey 1994, 30).
   b. It strengthens the widely held belief that life with a disability is not worth living. This belief is usually arrived at in ignorance of the lives of people with disabilities. Remember Anita Silvers's remark . . . that the suicide rate among people with disabilities would be much greater if it reflected the frequency with which non-disabled people report that they would rather be dead than disabled (Silvers 1994, 139). Moreover, the judgement that life with a disability is not worth living usually assumes that the person with a disability will have to live with the present level of prejudice and social exclusion, rather than recognizing that social improvements could make life with a disability much more worth living than it is now. Many people with disabilities, even those with the strongest social-constructionist perspective, admit that there are often heavy personal burdens associated with the physical and mental consequences of disabling physical conditions—such as pain, illness, frustration and unwanted limitation—that no amount of accessibility and social justice could eliminate (Finger 1990; Morris 1991). But there is a crucial difference between not wanting others to suffer from the burdens of a disability and not wanting those who will suffer from them to exist, between wanting to prevent or cure disabilities and wanting to prevent people with those disabilities from being born. For example, I would be terribly sorry to learn that a friend's fetus was very likely to be born with ME, but I would not urge her to abort it. In other words, many people with disabilities, while we understand quite well the personal burdens of disability, are not willing to make the judgement that lives like ours are not worth living. Every life has burdens, some of them far worse than disability.
   c. It might weaken efforts to increase accessibility and opportunities for people with disabilities, because it appears to reduce the social problems of people with disabilities by reducing the number of people with disabilities. Thus, Laura Hershey wonders: "Are expensive, government-funded genetic research projects initiated primarily for the benefit of a society unwilling to support disability-related needs?" (Hershey 1994, 31). If so, we have to ask what will be the social fate of people who already have disabilities and those who, in the future, will become disabled by accident or disease.

d. It might lead to even greater reluctance to commit resources to medical treatment of people with incurable conditions—treatment that makes their lives more comfortable and rewarding. As Mary Johnson says, "Treatments that don't lead to cure are boring to a society whose interest is not in making the lives of cripples comfortable but in ridding society of them altogether" (Johnson 1990, 34).

3. Feminists with disabilities recognize that, under present conditions in most societies, individual parents, especially mothers (who do most of the care-giving work), must provide the extra resources, especially the time and energy, required for raising children with disabilities. Thus many feminists with disabilities support women's right to choose not to give birth to a baby with a disability. Yet we are also aware that most women faced with the knowledge of their fetuses' potential disability are not given adequate information.

   For example, as Lisa Blumberg points out, prospective parents may not be informed that most prenatal tests can only place a diagnostic label on a fetus; they cannot predict the degree of functional disability that the fetus would experience as a child or adult.

   > *A diagnosis of spina bifida, for example, will not indicate whether a child would walk with just some degree of difficulty or use a wheelchair, or whether he or she would be intellectually gifted, have average intelligence or be slightly retarded. Neither would a finding of cystic fibrosis provide guidance on whether a person's lifespan would be eight years or 58 years or somewhere in between (Blumberg 1994, 220).*

   Moreover, prospective parents of a fetus with a potential disability may not be given information about the quality of life that people with those disabilities can and do have, or the services and support available to parents should they choose to have the babies (Morris 1991; Hershey 1994). Too often, potential disability is treated as an "objective" medical matter on which physicians can advise parents without reference to values or the social context. "Rarely are clients encouraged to discuss disability-related concerns with people who are disabled or are parents of disabled children" (Blumberg 1994, 221).

4. Screening of fetuses and selective abortion are likely to begin as voluntary medical procedures but become socially mandatory fairly quickly. Given that so many people believe that being born with a disability is a tragedy, they are likely to blame women for creating a tragedy if they do not undergo all the available medical procedures. Moreover, since most non-disabled people regard people with disabilities as noncontributing burdens on society, women who give birth to babies with disabilities are liable to be blamed for creating drains on social resources. The more women "choose" to screen and selectively abort fetuses, the more blame will be placed on those who give birth to babies with disabilities, the fewer resources will be made available for raising babies with disabilities and the more the element of choice will diminish (Morris 1991).

5. Genetic screening and selective abortion of potentially disabled fetuses might lead to increased tolerance of eugenic policies in general and expansion of eugenic efforts into other areas (Degener 1990; Hershey 1994). This is a particular danger in societies already caught up in myths of control and perfection of the body. Nor is it a baseless

fear when there is strong governmental and scientific support for the multibillion-dollar Human Genome Project in the United States, a long-term scientific effort to map all the genetic material inside the nuclei of human cells. This project is now conceived of primarily as having medical benefits in prediction and prevention of disease and disability (*The Women's Review of Books*, July 1994). Scientific research into genetic contributions to disvalued characteristics is proceeding quickly and with some success. It seems that every month we hear about the discovery of a "gene" for some disease or disability, or for some unwanted propensity of character or personality.

The desire for perfection and control of the body, or for the elimination of differences that are feared, poorly understood and widely considered to be marks of inferiority, easily masquerades as the compassionate desire to prevent or stop suffering. It is not only a matter of being deceived by others, but all too often a matter of deceiving ourselves. It is easy to make the leaps from imagining that I would not want to live in certain circumstances to believing that no one would want to live in those circumstances, to deciding to prevent people from being born into those circumstances, to supporting proposals "mercifully" to kill people living in those circumstances—all without ever consulting anyone who knows life in those circumstances from experience.

Nor is it reassuring to insist that genetic screening, prenatal diagnosis and selective abortion are voluntary individual choices, unlike previous eugenic efforts, which were often coercive. We know how quickly the possibilities offered by medical technology become social necessities in complex consumer cultures (Sherwin 1992). . . .

References

Blumberg, Lisa. 1994. "Eugenics and Reproductive Choice." In *The Ragged Edge: The Disability Experience from the Pages of the First Fifteen Years of the Disability Rag,* ed. Barrett Shaw, 218–27. Louisville, KY: Advocado Press.

Degener, Theresia. 1990. "Female Self-Determination between Feminist Claims and 'Voluntary' Eugenics, between 'Rights' and Ethics," *Issues in Reproductive and Genetic Engineering* 3 (2): 87–99.

Fine, Michelle, and Adrienne Asch, eds. 1988. *Women with Disabilities: Essays in Psychology, Culture and Politics*. Philadelphia: Temple University Press.

Hershey, Laura. 1994. "Choosing Disability." *Ms*. July/August: 26–32.

Hillyer, Barbara. 1993. *Feminism and Disability*. Norman and London: University of Oklahoma Press.

Johnson, Mary. 1990. "Defective Fetuses and Us." *The Disability Rag*. March/April: 34.

Morris, Jenny. 1991. *Pride against Prejudice: Transforming Attitudes to Disability*. Philadelphia: New Society Publishers.

Sherwin, Susan. 1992. *No Longer Patient: Feminist Ethics and Health Care*. Philadelphia: Temple University Press.

The Women's Review of Books. July 1994a. "Biology Is Not Destiny: An Interview with the Women's Community Cancer Project." 11 (10–11): 7–10. Wellesley, MA: The Women's Review.

The Women's Review of Books. July 1994b. "The Politics of Genetics: A Conversation with Anne Fausto-Sterling and Diane Paul." 11(10–11): 17–20. Wellesley, MA: The Women's Review.

Between Body and Culture: Beauty, Ability and Growing Up Female

Carla Rice

Carla Rice is Assistant Professor in Women's Studies at Trent University where she lectures in culture, health and psychology. A leader in the field of body image within Canada, she is founder and former director of community-based initiatives. Her research explores representations and narratives of body and identity across the lifespan.

Of all the concerns young women face growing up in the Western world, their changing relationships with their bodies is one of the most challenging. Young women today receive a confusing range of messages about their bodies in Western culture, from the affirming to the derogatory. These messages can strongly affect a young woman's developing sense of her body as well as her evolving sense of self. However, though body image is an important topic for many women exposed to or immersed in Western culture when they are growing up, all women do not develop the same body image problems. Moreover, not all women experience body issues with the same intensity, nor do they all find similar solutions to the body image problems with which they struggle.

What accounts for such differences among women? Recently, feminists have begun to explore variations in experiences of body among women, asking a number of compelling questions regarding why diverse populations of women relate to their bodies differently. Exploring the significance of differences in race, class, age, size, sexual orientation and disability to women's experiences of their bodies, they are asking how standards of beauty differ across populations of women, and how beauty practices vary from group to group. Do body image issues differ among diverse groups of women? If they do, what are the roots of these variations? How do women vary in their ability to approximate ideals of beauty and how does this affect their life aspirations and choices? And finally, in what different ways do women respond to dominant images of beauty, and why do some embrace these ideals while others reject them? . . .

BODY IMAGE: THE INTERSECTION OF BODY AND CULTURE

. . . What are some of the messages girls receive as they make their way from childhood into adulthood? Most young women growing to maturity in our Western culture internalize destructive messages regarding their developing bodies: between 80 and 90% of North American women come to dislike their bodies or some aspect of the bodies (Hutchinson 1985); over 80% of adolescent girls worry a lot about their appearance (Canadian Teachers Federation 1990); 65% of adolescent girls feel "too fat," and close to half have tried dieting (Day 1990); almost 40% of adult Canadian women engage in yo-yo dieting (Canadian Gallop Poll 1994); and from 15 to 20% develop health-threatening eating problems (National Eating Disorder Information Centre 1989). The current widespread preoccupation with thinness is rooted in a struggle between biology and ideals of beauty, a conflict experienced by a significant number of young women as evidence of their personal failure.

It is interesting that weight and eating problems are presented in the popular media as psychological disorders primarily affecting young, affluent white women. . . .

Researchers are finding that the "rich white girl" stereotype is false. . . . A study conducted through *Essence* magazine found that 65% of African-American women were dieting, and that 21% were engaging in bulimia as a means of weight control (Pumariega et al. 1994). A survey of young Native women found that almost half were dieting, 27% reported that they induced vomiting to lose weight, and 11% have used diet pills (Story et al. 1994). Weight and eating problems also cross class and income lines. Most studies have found that bulimia is more common among poor than affluent women (Gard and Freeman 1996). Feminist researchers exploring eating problems among lesbians and women of colour are finding that a woman's relationship with food and her body is also affected by sexism, racism, class bias and homophobia (Hall 1995; Thompson 1994).

The "rich white girl" stereotype does not fit with the realities of many women who are dealing with eating and weight concerns. Moreover, weight issues are not the only body issues that girls can experience, nor are they necessarily the most salient ones. Girls are faced with the reality of having a female body, which can be experienced as pleasurable or problematic depending on the messages received from others. Weight is only one of the criteria by which girls are assessed. A girl's hair texture and style, her breast and hip size, her eye and skin colour and her body shape and facial features can become focuses of concern, especially when these are evaluated against white ideals of beauty (Camper 1994; Featherston 1994; Rooks 1996). Furthermore, physical differences such as a scar or burn, or visible physical disabilities, become concerns for women when their looks and bodies are compared with the able-bodied beauty ideal (Driedger and D'Aubin 1992; Hahn 1992; Ridington 1989). . . .

GROWING UP FEMALE: LESSONS IN BEAUTY AND BEING A WOMAN

Body Confidence and Mastery

In Western culture, bodies are a primary source of identity. For example, bodies are given a gender, a race and sometimes a disability from birth, and these labels often shape the options and life possibilities of the person in that body (Fanon 1967; L. Davis 1995; Butler 1990). Though many life-shaping identities are assigned to babies from birth, most women who talk about the histories of their bodies do not recall feeling burdened by these labels in early childhood. Instead, they remember feeling a lack of body consciousness, and a lack of concern about their appearance and physical traits. Most say that as young children they acquired a sense of confidence in their bodies, whatever their body type or abilities. Tara, a young Scottish-Italian woman, remembers: "I was really active when I was young. It sort of dwindled when I got older. I never thought there wasn't anything I could do when I was younger. I think most kids probably think that way, though. You're indestructible. You could just do anything."

The First Socializing Messages

Many women learn about societal values regarding having a beautiful and able body as they begin to receive negative messages from other people. Mainly, it is peers and adults who send girls messages that their female bodies are not acceptable. . . .

The education and medical systems often send girls harmful messages about their bodies. One compelling message that most children learn in these systems is that fat is stigmatized

(Feldman et al. 1988). As young as five, they develop extremely negative associations with the idea of obesity—for example, they learn to perceive fat people as lazy, sloppy, ugly, mean and stupid (Staffieri 1967). . . .

Though children of both sexes internalize a prejudice against fatness, the preoccupation with appearance is socialized in girls more than in boys. For example, more girls than boys are put on diets by their parents or caretakers (Pierce and Wardle 1993). Also, parents stress the importance of girls being beautiful and boys being strong; this teaches children of both sexes that girls' bodies are to be worked on and made more beautiful (Freedman 1984). . . .

Media Influences

The popular media reinforce socializing messages and practices concerning weight and beauty. Children watch an average of four hours of television every day. By the time they reach high school, they have watched approximately 15,000 hours of TV and have seen 350,000 advertisements, over half of which stress the importance of being thin and beautiful (Moe 1991). Television images affect a child's developing sense of self: only fifteen minutes of exposure to beauty advertisements is enough to persuade girls that beauty is important to their popularity with boys (Freedman 1984). . . .

The Body as an Instrument of Femininity

Many women experience a period of foment in relation to their bodies, spanning from early adolescence into young adulthood. Though the development of a girl's gender identity begins at birth, it is through adolescence that becoming feminine is "taught and enforced by complex social forces including adults, peers and society at large through books, magazines, the media and even the responses of strangers in public" (Kaschak 1992, 90). As French-Canadian Marie-Claire suggests, the process of learning to be a woman can be both exciting and frightful: "So, I started shaving my legs, so that was something new. And I had to start wearing deodorant, right? Not you had to, but you did, because that's just the way that it worked, right? You had to start wearing a bra. . . . Yeah, it was kind of a mixture of excitement and sort of, ah . . . fear?" A girl learns the rules for proper behaviour and appearance from peers and adults, who often direct the regulation of a girl's body. Some of the tasks she learns include using makeup, removing body hair, concealing odors, experimenting with clothing, styling her hair, managing her period, controlling her sexuality, watching her weight and concealing figure "flaws" (Bartky, 1990). . . .

The Body as a Subject of Public Scrutiny

During the transition from childhood to adulthood, which Western culture identifies as the time of self-experimentation and definition, young women face the greatest external challenges to their body images. For example, many find that while their bodies are changing, they are subjected to unwanted assessment and attention (Lee and Sasser-Coen 1996). . . .

Studies of female and male high school students have shown that young women are much more dissatisfied with their bodies than their male counterparts (Paxton et al. 1991). Weight and appearance become salient issues for young women, who diet more, feel more body consciousness through adolescence and report that their appearance interferes more with social activities than it does for young men (Rodriquez-Tomé et al. 1993). . . .

The Body as an Object of Social Control

Why do some young women develop more serious body dissatisfactions and weight struggles than others? Girls' satisfaction with their bodies is related to their feelings of belonging and of being accepted by others (Paxton 1996). The messages they receive about their developing bodies from their family, peers, communities and the larger culture during this crucial period strongly affect how good they feel about their bodies (Striegel-Moore and Kearney-Cooke 1994). The greater the acceptance and affirmation of a young woman's physicality and sexuality as she moves through adolescence, the more likely she is to develop a positive sense of body. Conversely, the more actively a girl's body is monitored and regulated by adults and peers, the greater the chance she will develop serious body image problems. . . .

The Body as Currency

In adolescence, a girl's body becomes her currency, its value measured according to heterosexual standards of desirability. This means young women develop a negative or positive sense of body as a result of others' assessments of their sexual attractiveness. Gina learned the early lesson that losing weight not only changed how people treated her but also whether they even saw her: "I tell people I was thin for ten minutes once when I was fourteen! I lost quite a bit of weight in three weeks and it was incredible the difference it made in the way that people reacted. All of a sudden those same boys that used to put me down, were clamouring for my attention. . . . It was like they had never seen me before I lost the weight."

Physical traits such as body size and skin colour have a significant impact on the future socioeconomic status, subsequent educational attainment and life chances of young women (Gortmaker et al. 1993; Russell et al. 1992). A range of stresses placed on young women—including changes in their bodies, public reaction to these changes, messages from family, peers and culture about the importance of appearance and assessments of girls' attractiveness—can increase or decrease the probability that they will develop serious body image problems (Levine et al. 1994).

The Body as a Target of Harassment

Harassment is a common source of stress in young women's lives, and often undermines their sense of body esteem. . . .

Many young women experience "body-based" harassment during adolescence. Researchers are only now exploring how this kind of abuse may relate to the development of body image and eating problems (Larkin, Rice and Russell 1996). . . .

The Impact of Violence

Sexual violence also is implicated in the development of serious body image and eating problems. Most studies exploring the possible links between violence and eating problems have documented a significant relationship between sexual and physical assaults and the later development of serious eating issues (Rice and Langdon 1991). This does not mean that all women with eating problems have experienced childhood sexual abuse, sexual assault or partner abuse—only that such violence makes it more likely that women will develop eating concerns (Rice 1996). . . .

Messages from friends, lovers, peers and adults about appearance, ability and desirability can shape young women's perceptions of their bodies and selves. Relationships are an extremely important influence on body image development; young women report that connections with families, peer groups and other support systems can prevent them from, or propel them into, taking drastic action to communicate the stresses to which they are subjected. This discussion demonstrates how young women are united in the lessons they learn in growing up female, and how they typically internalize a desire to be seen as attractive and normal. That being said, bodily standards are experienced differently by women according to their race, ethnicity and physical abilities and this causes them to experience their bodies and the ideals in very different ways.

LESSONS IN COLOUR, RACE AND ETHNICITY

Much of Western feminist work on body image has focused on gender—on the ways in which growing up female places young women at risk for developing body image problems. Yet every woman born in the Western world is also given a racial identity, and the reality of growing up with such an identity shapes her body image in complicated ways. Race is believed by many people to be a biological trait, like sex. However, not all people of a racial group share the same biological traits, nor do they have chromosomes that identify them as genetic members of that group (Zack 1997). This suggests that a person's race is not in their genes—in other words, that race does not have a biological basis beyond superficial physical traits. Many social theorists now agree that race is nothing more than a changing range of attributes that have been labelled as racial—that race, in short, is socially created (Westley 1997). Though race shapes many aspects of an individual's experiences, many researchers believe it is a cultural invention that changes over time and with historical circumstances (Thompson 1996). . . .

Colour Consciousness: Fair Skin versus Unfair Skin

How do Western ideals of beauty affect the body and self-images of women of colour growing up in this culture? Western conceptions of beauty are creating a hierarchy in which women are ranked strictly according to their closeness to the ideal. This hierarchy ranks and divides women across racial groups, separating those who merit visibility and personhood from those who are condemned to invisibility and dehumanization (Derricotte 1997). . . .

Girls who grow up learning that their skin colour and physical features are unfavourably compared to those of Western beauty ideals often feel ashamed and humiliated (hooks 1992b, 1993). . . .

From their early social interactions, children internalize colourist values and learn to rank one another based on Western notions of beauty and colour (Russell et al. 1992). . . .

The internalization of colourist values from childhood and experiences with racial stereotyping, isolation and harassment, drive many women to lighten their skin colour using cosmetics, to straighten their hair with chemicals and hot irons and sometimes even to change their facial features through cosmetic surgery. Although light skin, straight hair and European facial features have privileged some women of colour relative to their peers, continued racism in our culture ensures that a woman's race usually supersedes her skin colour or hair texture when it comes to determining how she is treated in white society.

The Economic Imperative

Women want to be beautiful, and they strive to avoid harassment and stereotyping. Economics is another important reason why women change their hair texture, hairstyle, skin colour, facial features or eye colour. More and more studies are showing that men and women of any race who approximate Western ideals earn significantly higher wages than those who do not (Cohen et al. 1996). In white-dominated institutions or companies, conformity to the acceptable "look" may be necessary to get and keep a job (Buchanan 1993). . . .

Integrationist versus Oppositional Ideals

Beauty rituals that enable women to conform to mainstream ideals have been labeled "integrationist" beauty practices (Mama 1995). Trying to conform to dominant ideals does not mean that a woman wants to be white (Buchanan 1993). The emphasis on fair skin, straightened hair or a small nose is less about black or South Asian women wanting to be white than about them wanting to be attractive. This is especially the case "in a patriarchal world that assumes beauty to be blond and blue-eyed, and makes it imperative for women to be attractive enough to succeed with men" (Mama 1995: 151).

Some women of colour feel caught between two different ideals: the dominant, white ideal, and the ideals of their culture of origin. They are being asked to look and behave in two different ways; they have been told from very early on that they have to conform to two standards of beauty. . . .

Some women cope with the pressures they face concerning their looks and bodies by rejecting mainstream definitions of beauty, and with them, mainstream ideas about what is sexually attractive and feminine. Thus, some women of colour have tried to conform to dominant Western ideals or to the traditional ideals of their culture of origin, and others have tried to create new "oppositional standards." Oppositional ideals are "anti-ideals" of beauty that directly oppose dominant standards and that value the very physical traits that mainstream culture devalues. Oppositional ideals challenge the assumption that women need to conform to mainstream images; in doing so, they offer women of colour alternative notions of beauty. Maria explains how she has used her pride in her indigenous features and heritage to create her own oppositional ideal:

> *I'm a Latin American woman. I have Latin American features. I have an indigenous background, ancestry. I have some indigenous features. It makes me who I am. . . . If you look at indigenous women, they're very strong women. . . . And I look at my own family and my own grandmother and my own mother, despite all the adversities that they've had to face throughout their childhood, throughout their lifespan, I look at their strengths and that's when [I see] the strengths that I learned and I take my strengths and try to blossom them. . . . I would say yes it is important, my appearance to my identity.*

As Maria suggests, oppositional ideals are a source of strength and inspiration for many women. But attempts to conform to oppositional ideals can generate their own problems, especially if the opposing ideal replaces one standard of beauty with another one which is equally narrow (Mama 1995). . . .

RESISTANCE AND RESOLUTION

Many young and adult women find body and self-confidence through a wide range of strategies for resisting dominant beauty ideals. The term resistance is an ambiguous one, "meaning diverse things, translating into different practices and strategies that must be assessed and developed each in its sociohistorical situation" (de Lauretis 1986:3). Resistance can be lived privately or practiced publicly; it can be open and confrontational or quietly subversive; it can be humourous and playful or serious and painful; it can be individually motivated or socially organized in group action. The following are some of the resistance strategies that women have used to counter cultural ideals of the body.

Making Connections

For many women, overcoming struggles with body image involves making connections with people who give them positive messages about themselves and severing relationships with people who are destructive to them. . . .

Talking Back

Another strategy that some women have used is "talking back" to authority as a way of reasserting their human dignity. This can be empowering, but it can also be difficult, especially if a woman is criticized or punished for speaking up. . . .

Rebelling through the Body

Most women learn to regulate their bodies mainly through messages from families, peers and systems, all of which monitor their appearance, body functioning and sexual behaviour. Rebellion against social pressures can take the form of smoking, drinking, tattooing and piercing. It can also involve making radical changes to appearance and defying family, peer or cultural sexual norms. Jan explains: "[Taking risks] meant like going to my friend's mom's and smoking cigarettes and drinking. That's not such a big risk but coming from my family, it was, where that's just not something that you do and get caught. And boys, too. Boys, I remember."

Angela, a young Australian and Vietnamese woman, described how she rebelled by defying her culture's gender norms: "I had to become a bad girl. I was always devious in my own mind, but I smoked, I joined a gang and we ganged up on people. We stole. I developed the same kind of attitude—kind of 'fuck the world I am going to do what I want' attitude." Instead of defying gender norms, Natasha, an Indo-Canadian woman, rebelled against the cultural markers of biological femaleness:

> *If my sister or my mom asked me, "Oh, are you on the rag? Do you have your period now?" I would say "No" when I really was. Why? Because I don't want it to be talked about. I don't want things that make me so much a woman to be talked about, to be pulled out and distinguished. I think it's resistance. I don't want to be seen as a woman. . . . I used to wear sports bras for a long time because I didn't want it so defined. Why should I wear underwire when the sports bras are more comfortable? I think I always maybe wanted to be a guy. Maybe that's why. Because I think I would always want to play with them at school and I would always resist being a woman. I think they got away with a lot. I used to find it unfair. I still find it unfair.*

Kathryn describes making a conscious decision to reject mainstream beauty ideals: "One day I had hair that was longer than yours and straightened. I went to the hairdresser's and she cut it all off to one inch. The hairdresser called my mother and said, 'You know what I'm doing? She wants all of her hair cut off.' That was when the black movement was very big, and I wanted all my hair cut off." Like Kathryn, many women interviewed describe feeling liberated after they defied dominant ideals and began experimenting with oppositional ones. . . .

Questioning Cultural Ideals

The examples I have provided so far have focused on the resistance strategies that are used by the individual to defuse the impact of body ideals or increase their personal agency. Some of the women interviewed have demonstrated their opposition to social values regarding beauty by posing insightful questions concerning the social and cultural roots of their experiences. Feminists have long argued that consciousness raising—reading, speaking and listening to one another—is the best way women have of understanding the female self in society (de Lauretis 1986). Through cultural resistance, women actively challenge taboos regarding female sexual pleasure and female beauty, and develop their own analyses of how their bodies have been manipulated in the culture. Kasha, a woman with Eastern European roots, remarks:

> *Men are allowed to keep their sexuality, whether they're balding or fat. But as soon as a woman breaks out of a mold of what her society considers attractive, that's it. . . . I guess I am looking for an answer. Why? Why can't we look at women who are larger sexually, why is it comical? Is society afraid of sexuality? Is that something people are afraid of? What does it represent that's so horrible and comical? I think people find it comical because they are afraid somehow. This is too big a woman, who's taking up too much space, who's too sexual. So in a way it must represent power and that's why it's being crushed.*

Organizing for Change

There is no question that social change movements have contributed to the world views of many women and have influenced their attitudes and decisions regarding their bodies. The impact of social movements is evident in women's insights into how culture has shaped their experiences of their bodies: these insights would have been impossible before the feminist, black and disability rights movements. Women not only identify the roots of problems and ways of improving their own body and self-images, but also suggest concrete strategies for social change. Some young women have organized events in their high schools. Others have started groups in their universities and colleges. . . .

As women pass through adolescence and move into adulthood, many of them work to resolve their body struggles. They often go through a process of working out problems concerning their feelings about their bodies and their identities. This is a time when they confront confusion about being a woman, being fat, being dark, being disabled or being biracial; a time when they negotiate their own self-definitions. This negotiation often takes place within a woman's family, friendship circles, networks and cultural context(s). This does not mean that she internalizes the values of her parents or of the mainstream culture;

it is more about her developing a positive sense of her body and self out of many conflicting forces. The solutions a woman finds inevitably evolve and change as she becomes pregnant, gains weight and ages. She must confront and respond to changing messages concerning her body and being throughout her life.

CONCLUSION

. . . [In this study,] the women suggest that greater body acceptance is won through the use of shifting strategies, which depend on what avenues for self-assertion are possible in the moment. Solutions to the problem of standards of beauty are always partial. Depending on the social context, women sometimes reinforce one body norm while challenging another. They also employ many different strategies to resist ideals and define themselves, which indicates that freedom exists in the possibility of using many different strategies and practices.

Solutions to the problem of the ideal are as varied as the women who seek them. It is important that we respect and support each woman's responses to this problem, whether or not we agree with those solutions. I offer no final judgments about beauty practices because their implications vary so widely. The only feminist responses I can advocate are these: helping women define and expand options for ways of being in their bodies and their worlds; helping them work through the political, ethical and health-related dilemmas associated with their practices; and helping them choose their most empowering option, given their historical, cultural, personal and bodily realities. The varied experiences of the women I have quoted in this chapter suggest that we must continue to create alternative images of beauty and a broader range of options for all of us, so as to provide every woman with expanded definitions of beauty and womanhood.

References

Asch, A., and M. Fine. 1988. "Shared Dreams: A Left Perspective on Disability Rights and Reproductive Rights." In *Women with Disabilities: Essays in Psychology, Culture and Politics,* edited by M. Pine and A. Asch. Philadelphia: Temple University Press.

Bartky, S. 1990. *Femininity and Domination: Studies in the Phenomenology of Oppression*. New York: Routledge.

Bordo, S. 1993. *Unbearable Weight: Feminism, Western Culture and the Body.* Los Angeles: University of California Press.

Buchanan, K. 1993. "Creating Beauty in Blackness." In *Consuming Passions,* edited by C. Brown and K. Jasper. Toronto: Second Story Press.

Butler, J. 1990. *Gender Trouble: Feminism and the Subversion of Identity.* New York: Routledge.

Camper, C., ed. 1994. *Miscegenation Blues: Voices of Mixed Race Women.* Toronto: Sister Vision Press.

Canadian Gallup Poll. 1994. *Report on the Behaviour and Attitudes of Canadians with Respect to Weight Consciousness and Weight Control.* Toronto: Canadian Gallup Poll Limited.

Canadian Teacher's Federation. 1990. *A Cappella: A Report on the Realities, Concerns, Expectations and Barriers Experienced by Adolescent Women in Canada.* Ottawa: Canadian Teacher's Federation.

Chapkis, W. 1986. *Beauty Secrets: Women and the Politics of Appearance.* Boston: South End Press.

Charmaz, K. 1995. "The Body, Identity, and Self: Adapting to Impairment." *The Sociological Quarterly* 36(4): 657–80.

Cohen, C., R. Wilkes, and B. Stoeltje, eds. 1996. *Beauty Queens on the Global Stage: Gender, Contests and Power.* New York: Routledge.

Collins. 1990. *Black Feminist Thought: Knowledge, Consciousness and the Politics of Empowerment.* Boston: Unwin Hyman.

Collins, T., M. Schneider, and S. Kroeger. 1995. "(Dis)Abling Images." *Radical Teacher* 47: 11–14.

Darwin, C. 1981/1871. *The Descent of Man and Selection in Relation to Sex.* Princeton, NJ: Princeton University Press.

Davis, K. 1995. *Reshaping the Female Body: The Dilemma of Cosmetic Surgery.* New York: Routledge.

Davis, L. 1995. *Enforcing Normalcy: Disability, Deafness and the Body.* New York: Verso Press.

Day, D. 1990. *Young Women in Nova Scotia: A Study of Attitudes, Behaviour and Aspirations.* Halifax: Nova Scotia Advisory Council on the Status of Women.

de Lauretis, T., ed. 1986. *Feminist Studies, Critical Studies.* Bloomington: Indiana University Press.

Derricotte, T. 1997. *The Black Notebooks: An Interior Journey.* New York: W.W. Norton.

Driedger, D. and A. D'aubin. 1992. "Women with Disabilities Challenge the Body Beautiful." *Healthsharing Magazine* 12(4): 35–41.

duCille, A. 1996. *Skin Trade.* Cambridge, MA: Harvard University Press.

Fanon, Frantz. 1963. *The Wretched of the Earth.* New York: Grove Press.

——. 1967/1952. *Black Skin, White Masks,* translated by C. Lam Markmann. New York: Grove Weidenfeld.

Featherston, E. 1994. *Skin Deep: Women Writing on Color, Culture and Identity.* Freedom, CA: The Crossing Press.

Feldman, W., E. Feldman, and J. T. Goodman. 1988. "Culture versus Biology: Children's Attitudes toward Thinness and Fatness." *Pediatrics* 81(2): 190–4.

Freedman, R. 1984. "Reflections on Beauty as It Relates to Health in Adolescent Females." In *Health and the Female Adolescent,* edited by S. Colub. York: Harrington Park Press.

Gard, M., and C. Freeman. 1996. "The Dismantling of a Myth: A Review of Eating Disorders and Socioeconomic Status." *International Journal of Eating Disorders* 20(1): 1–12.

Garland, R. 1995. *The Lye of the Beholder: Deformity and Disability in the Graeco-Roman World.* Ithaca, NY: Cornell University Press.

Gortmaker, S., A. Must, J. Perrin, A. Sobol, and W. Dietz. 1993. "Social and Economic Consequences of Overweight in Adolescence and Young Adulthood." *The New England Journal of Medicine* 329(14): 1008–12.

Hahn, H. 1992. "Can Disability Be Beautiful?" *Social Policy* 18(3): 26–31.

Hall, C. 1995. "Asian Eyes: Body Image and Eating Disorders of Asian and Asian American Women." *Eating Disorders: A Journal of Treatment and Prevention.* 3(1): 8–19.

Harris, A., and D. Wideman. 1988. "Construction of Gender and Disability in Early Attachment." In *Women with Disabilities: Essays in Psychology, Culture and Politics,* edited by M. Fine and A. Asch. Philadelphia: Temple University Press.

Higgins, P. 1992. *Making Disability: Exploring the Social Transformation of Human Variation.* Springfield, IL: Charles C. Thomas.

Hill, A., and R. Bhatti. 1995. "Body Shape, Perception and Dieting in Preadolescent British Asian Girls: Links with Eating Disorders." *International Journal of Eating Disorders* 17(2): 175–83.

hooks, bell. 1992b. *Black Looks: Race and Representation.* Toronto: Between the Lines Press.

——. 1993. *Sisters of the Yam: Black Women and Self-Recovery.* Toronto: Between the Lines Press.

Hutchinson, M. 1985. *Transforming Body Image.* New York: The Crossing Press.

Kaschak, E. 1992. *Engendered Lives: A New Psychology of Women's Experience.* New York: Basic Books.

Larkin, J., C. Rice, and V. Russell. 1996. "Slipping Through the Cracks: Sexual Harassment, Eating Problems and Problems with Embodiment." *Eating Disorders: A Journal of Prevention and Treatment* 4(1): 5–26.

Lee, J., and J. Sasser-Coen. 1996. *Blood Stories: Menarche and the Politics of the Female Body in Contemporary U.S. Society.* New York: Routledge.

Levine, M., L. Smolak, A. Moodey, M. Shuman, and L. Hessen, 1994. "Normative Developmental Challenges and Dieting and Eating Disturbances in Middle School Girls." *International Journal of Eating Disorders* 15(1): 11–20.

Mama, A. 1995. *Beyond the Masks: Race, Gender and Subjectivity.* New York: Routledge.

Moe, B. 1991. *Coping with Eating Disorders.* New York: Rosen Publishing Group.

Moraga, C., and G. Anzaldua, eds. 1983. *This Bridge Called My Back: Writings by Radical Women of Colour.* New York: Kitchen Table Women of Colour Press.

National Eating Disorder Information Centre. 1989. *An Introduction to Food and Weight Problems.* Toronto: National Eating Disorder Information Centre.

Paxton, S. 1996. "Friendships, Body Image and Dieting in Teenage Girls: A Research Report." *National Eating Disorder Information Centre Bulletin* 11(2): 1–4.

Paxton, S., E. Wertheim, K. Gibbons, C. Szmukler, L. Hillier, and J. Petrovich. 1991. "Body Image Satisfaction, Dieting Beliefs and Weight Loss Behaviours in Adolescent Girls and Boys." *Journal of Youth and Adolescence* 20(2): 361–79.

Pierce, J.W., and J. Wardle. 1993. "Self-esteem, Parental Appraisal and Body Size in Children." *Journal of Child Psychology and Psychiatry* 34(7): 1125–36.

Pumariega, A., C. Gustavson, J. Gustavson, P.S. Motes, and S. Ayers. 1994. "Eating Attitudes in African-American Women: The Essence Eating Disorders Survey." *Eating Disorders: A Journal of Prevention and Treatment* 2(1): 6–16.

Rice, C. 1996. "Trauma and Eating Problems: Expanding the Debate." *Eating Disorders: A Journal of Prevention and Treatment* 4(3): 197–237.

Rice, C., and L. Langdon. 1991. "Women's Struggles with Food and Weight as Survival Strategies." *Canadian Woman Studies* 12(1).

Rice, C., and V. Russell. 1995a. "EmBodying Equity: Putting Body and Soul into Equity Education, Part I: How Oppression Is Embodied." *Our Schools, Ourselves* 7(1): 14–36.

——. 1995b. "EmBodying Equity: Putting Body and Soul into Equity Education, Part II: Strategies for Change. *Our Schools, Ourselves* 7(2): 42–54.

——. *EmBodying Equity: Working with Young Women at the Intersections of Body, Self and Society.* Unpublished manuscript.

Ridington, J. 1989. *Who Do We Think We Are? Self-Image and Women with Disabilities.* Toronto: DisAbled Women's Network (DAWN) Canada.

Rodriquez-Tomé, H., F. Bariaud, M.F. Cohen Zardi, C. Delmas, B. Jeanvoine, and P. Szylagyi. 1993. "The Effects of Pubertal Changes on Body Image and Relations with Peers of the Opposite Sex in Adolescence." *Journal of Adolescence* 16: 421–38.

Rooks, N. 1996. *Hair Raising: Beauty, Culture, and African American Women.* New Brunswick, NJ: Rutgers University Press.

Root, M., ed. 1996. *The Multicultural Experience: Racial Borders as the New Frontier.* London: Sage.

Rousso, H. 1988. "Daughters with Disabilities: Defective Women or Minority Women?" In *Women with Disabilities: Essays in Psychology, Culture and Politics,* edited by M. Fine and A. Asch. Philadelphia: Temple University Press.

Russell, K., M. Wilson, and R. Hall. 1992. *The Color Complex: The Politics of Skin Color among African Americans.* Toronto: Anchor Books.

Schiebinger, L. 1993. *Nature's Body: Gender in the Making of Modern Science.* Boston: Beacon Press.

Spitzack, C. 1990. *Confessing Excess: Women and the Politics of Body Reduction.* Albany: State University of New York Press.

Staffieri, J.R. 1967. "A Study of Social Stereotype of Body Image in Children." *Journal of Personality and Social Psychology* 7: 101–4.

Story, M., F. Hauck, B. Broussard, L. White, M. Resnick, and R. Blum. 1994. "Weight Perceptions and Weight Control Practices in American Indian and Alaska Native Adolescents." *Archives of Pediatric Adolescent Medicine* 148: 567–71.

Striegel-Moore, R., and A. Kearney-Cooke. 1994. "Exploring Parents' Attitudes and Behaviours about Their Children's Physical Appearance." *International Journal of Eating Disorders* 15(4): 377–85.

Székely, E. 1988. *Never Too Thin.* Toronto: The Women's Press.

Thompson, B. Carl. 1994. *A Hunger So Wide and So Deep: American Women Speak Out on Eating Problems.* Minneapolis: University of Minnesota Press.

——. 1996. "Multiracial Feminist Theorizing about Eating Disorders: Refusing to Rank Oppressions." *Eating Disorders: A Journal of Treatment and Prevention* 4(2): 104–13.

Tseëlon, E. 1995. *The Masque of Femininity: The Presentation of Women in Everyday Life.* Nottingham: Nottingham Trent University.

Tyagi, S. 1996. "Writing in Search of a Home: Geography, Culture and Language." In *Names We Call Home: Autobiography on Racial Identity,* edited by B. Thompson and S. Tyagi. New York: Routledge.

Wendell, S. 1996. *The Rejected Body: Feminist Philosophical Reflections on Disability.* New York: Routledge.

Westley, K. 1997. "White Normativity and the Racial Rhetoric for Equal Protection." In *Existence in Black: An Anthropology of Black Existential Philosophy,* edited by L. Gordon. New York: Routledge.

Young, I. 1990. *Throwing Like a Girl and Other Essays in Feminist Philosophy and Social Theory.* Indianapolis: Indiana University Press.

Zack, N., ed. 1997. *Race/Sex: Their Sameness, Difference, and Interplay.* New York: Routledge.

The Flight from the Rejected Body

Susan Wendell

Susan Wendell is Professor Emerita in Philosophy and Women's Studies at Simon Fraser University. Her research interests include feminist social and political theory, feminist ethics, feminist epistemology and women and disability. Since 1997, she has been interested in studying the influence of gender, race and class on psychosomatic diagnosis.

In the commercial-media-soaked societies of North America, the body is idealized and objectified to a high degree; these cultural practices foster demands to control our bodies and to attempt to perfect them, which in turn create rejection, shame and fear in relation to both failures to control the body and deviations from body ideals. Implied in any idealization of the body is the rejection of some kinds of bodies or some aspects of bodily life. I use the terms "rejected body" and "negative body" to refer to those aspects of bodily life (such as illness, disability, weakness and dying), bodily appearance (usually deviations from the cultural ideals of the body) and bodily experience (including most forms of bodily suffering) that are feared, ignored, despised and/or rejected in a society and its culture. . . .

Our real human bodies are exceedingly diverse—in size, shape, colour, texture, structure, function, range and habits of movement and development—and they are constantly changing. Yet many cultures, especially modern commercial cultures, do not seem to absorb or reflect these simple facts. Instead, they idealize the human body; the ideals change from time to time, but there always seem to be ideals. Body ideals include not only ideals of appearance, which are particularly influential for women . . . but also ideals of strength, energy, movement, function and proper control; the latter are unnoticed assumptions for most people who can meet them, but they leap to the foreground for those who are sick or disabled. In Canada and the United States, we are bombarded everywhere with images of these ideals, demands for them, and offers of products and services to help us achieve them.

Clearly idealization of the body is related in complex ways to the economic processes of a consumer society. Idealization now generates tremendous profits, and the quest for profit demands that people be reminded constantly of existing body ideals and presented regularly with new ideals. Moreover, never before in history have images of real people who meet the latest cultural ideals of beauty, health and physical performance been so often presented to so many people. Now it is possible for the images of a few people to drive out the reality of most people we actually encounter. (For example, I find that few people realize that the average North American woman is much fatter than the average woman we see on television.) This tends to conflate body ideals with our concept of what is physically "normal," increasing the number of people whose bodies are regarded by themselves and others as abnormal and socially unacceptable.

. . . [O]ther factors are the cultural splitting of mind from body and derogation of the body, strong cultural emphasis on physical appearance, medical ways of seeing and treating the body, sexual exploitation, pressures to perform and some forms of competition. To objectify another person's body is to ignore (at least temporarily) the consciousness that is embodied there and to fail to concern oneself with her/his subjective bodily experience. Objectifying one's own body is more complex; one must, in a sense, split one's consciousness from it and ignore one's inner subjective experience of it in order to regard or treat it as another person might. Widely accepted current forms of objectifying one's own body include treating it primarily as an instrument for accomplishing one's goals, regarding it as a physical object to be viewed, used and manipulated and treating it as a material possession to be maintained, exploited and traded. . . . They all assume and require considerable control of the body in order to maintain its suitability as an object of that type. Observing and participating in constant cultural objectification of other people's bodies encourages us to objectify our own. Some objectification of one's own body is probably inevitable, and not always harmful, but if it becomes the primary mode of experiencing one's body, it is a source of profound alienation from feeling, from nature, from the unconscious, from every aspect of oneself and others that resists control.

THE DISCIPLINES OF NORMALITY

Feminist analyses of the cultural treatment of women's bodies have shaped a great deal of my thinking, and Sandra Lee Bartky has done more than anyone to illuminate for me the social construction of femininity through idealization, objectification and demands for control of the female body. Expanding upon Michel Foucault's account of the disciplinary practices that produce the "docile bodies" required by modern social institutions . . . she has provided a detailed examination of "those disciplinary practices that produce a body which in gesture and appearance is recognizably feminine," including "those that aim to produce a body of a certain size and general configuration; those that bring forth from this body a specific repertoire of gestures, postures and movements; and those directed toward the display of this body as an ornamented surface". . . .Moreover, she has argued that because these disciplinary practices, which include (among other things) dieting, exercise, control of facial expression and careful constraint of movements, removal of body hair, application of skin-care preparations, hairdressing and the "correct" application of cosmetics, are not forced upon women by anyone in particular (indeed, they are often self-imposed, although there are also severe external sanctions), they appear to be natural or voluntary while they wield tremendous power in women's lives:

> *[T]he disciplinary power that is increasingly charged with the production of a properly embodied femininity is dispersed and anonymous; there are no individuals formally empowered to wield it; it is . . . invested in everyone and in no one in particular. This disciplinary power is peculiarly modern: It does not rely upon violent or public sanctions, nor does it seek to restrain the freedom of the female body to move from place to place. For all that, its invasion of the body is well-nigh total:*

> *The female body enters "a machinery of power that explores it, breaks it down and rearranges it." The disciplinary techniques through which the "docile bodies" of women are constructed aim at a regulation which is perpetual and exhaustive—a regulation of the body's size and contours, its appetite, posture, gestures and general comportment in space and the appearance of each of its visible parts. . . .*

I believe that there are also disciplinary practices of physical normality that are in many ways analogous to the disciplinary practices of femininity Bartky describes. Unlike the disciplines of the body described by Foucault, which are specifically linked to participation in certain modern social institutions, such as armies, schools, hospitals and prisons, but like Bartky's disciplines of femininity, the disciplines of normality are "institutionally unbound" . . . internalized by most of us, and socially pervasive. Like the disciplines of femininity, they require us to meet physical standards, to objectify our bodies and to control them.

The disciplines of normality are preconditions of participation in every aspect of social life, yet they are unnoticed by most adults who can conform to them without conscious effort. Children are very aware of the requirements of normality; among children, conformity to standards of normality in body size, carriage, movement, gesture, speech, emotional expression, appearance, scent, ways of eating and especially control of bodily functions such as salivation, passing gas, urination and defecation, are enforced by teasing, taunting and the threat of social ostracism, beginning at an early age. (When I was a child in New York City public schools, peeing in your pants in school or on the playground was one of the most shameful things that could happen to you; nothing you might do deliberately, no matter how morally rotten, could compare in shamefulness.) Those of us who can learn to be or seem "normal" do so, and those of us who cannot meet the standards of normality usually achieve the closest approximation we can manage.

The disciplines of normality, like those of femininity, are not only enforced by others but internalized. For many of us, our proximity to the standards of normality is an important aspect of our identity and our sense of social acceptability, an aspect of our self-respect. We are unlikely to notice this until our ability to meet the standards is threatened in some way. An injury or a prolonged illness often draws the attention of non-disabled people to this previously unnoticed facet of their self-images. For people who already have disabilities, the prospect of more disability can have the same effect. Shame and self-hatred when we cannot measure up to the standards of normality are indications that they are enforced by a powerful internalized disciplinarian.

People who do not appear or act physically "normal" draw attention to the disciplines of normality, just as women who do not practice the disciplines of femininity make them more apparent. In both cases, there are rules at work, but most of us are trying to ignore the existence of the rules, trying to pretend that things are "naturally" and effortlessly the way they seem, not socially enforced. (Consider how rarely anyone admits in public that s/he is depressed, having intestinal cramps, or even just desperate for a toilet, compared to how often you feel that way. Stating such a thing would be at least as embarrassing as a woman's remarking in public that she did not have time to shave her legs.) Moreover, since almost everyone tries to appear as "normal" as possible, those who appear clearly "abnormal" according to their society's standards are constant reminders to those who are currently measuring up that they might slip outside the standards. In this aspect, people with disabilities arouse fear. But they are also reassuring, in that encountering them can make "normals" feel more "normal" by comparison (which in turn may arouse guilt). These reactions are completely understandable, given the disciplines of normality, and they all contribute to the "Otherness" of people with disabilities.

It is not easy to distinguish standards of physical normality from ideals of health, appearance and performance, just as it is not easy to distinguish between feminine body ideals and minimal standards of femininity. One would expect the range of social normality (not medical "normality," which is different) to be considerably broader than the physical ideals of a culture, because otherwise very few people would be considered normal. Nevertheless, in practice, the two are linked. When the ideals of physical health, appearance and performance become more difficult to meet, the social standards of normality follow suit, threatening more of us with the possibility of falling below the minimum required for self-esteem and social acceptability. Moreover, for many people, falling within the "normal" range is not enough, especially when they are constantly pressured and encouraged to try to meet the ideal. By pursuing the cultural ideal, people can raise the standards of normality.

Kathryn Pauly Morgan discusses this phenomenon in relation to plastic surgery for women:

> *In the technical and popular literature on cosmetic surgery, what have previously been described as normal variations of female body shapes or described in the relatively innocuous language of "problem areas," are increasingly described as "deformities," "ugly protrusions," "inadequate breasts," and "unsightly concentrations of fat cells"—a litany of descriptions designed to intensify feelings of disgust, shame and relief at the possibility of recourse for these "deformities." Cosmetic surgery promises virtually all women the creation of beautiful, youthful-appearing bodies. As a consequence, more and more women will be labeled "ugly" and "old" in relation to this more select population of surgically created beautiful faces and bodies. . . . I suspect that the naturally "given," so to speak, will increasingly come to be seen as the technologically "primitive"; the "ordinary" will come to be perceived and evaluated as the "ugly". . . .*

Other ideals can sneak up on us, becoming standards of normality because they enter into a society's competitive structure. For example, when the pace of life increases, stamina becomes more important to participation in every aspect of society, and what was once regarded as an ideal level of energy gradually comes to be regarded as normal. Everyone who cannot keep up is urged to take steps (or medications) to increase their energy, and bodies that were once considered normal are pathologized. In my society, I have noticed that it has become increasingly unacceptable to "slow down" as one ages, when not long ago it was expected.

Bartky argues that the disciplinary practices of femininity "must he understood as aspects of a far larger discipline, an oppressive and inegalitarian system of sexual subordination. This system aims at turning women into the docile and compliant companions of men just as surely as the army aims to turn its raw recruits into soldiers". . . . Here I think there are disanalogies between the disciplines of femininity and those of normality. Although the standards of normality are certainly aspects of the subordination of people with disabilities, and although the disciplines of normality do generate profits in a consumer society (much advertising offers products to help us hide or correct our physical "abnormalities," such as "excess" fat, lack of teeth, lack of hair, flabby muscles and weak bladders), and therefore serve some people's direct interests, they also weigh heavily upon all people without disabilities. Under the disciplines of femininity, women must fear becoming less feminine, but men need not fear becoming women of any kind. Under the disciplines of normality, everyone must fear becoming a member of the subordinated group; everyone who does not die suddenly *will* become a member of the subordinated group. Who does not suffer from these standards?

Some people can have the temporary self-acceptance that comes from believing that their bodies are "close enough" to current body ideals, but this gives them an investment in the ideals and draws them into the endless task of reconciling reality with them. Most people learn to identify with their own strengths (by cultural standards) and to hate, fear and neglect their own weaknesses. Everyone is subjected to cultural pressure to deny bodily weaknesses, to dread old age, to feel ashamed of and responsible for their distance from the ideals and to objectify their own bodies at the expense of subjective bodily awareness. These pressures foster a desire to gain/maintain control of our bodies; conversely, the myth that we can control our bodies encourages us to strive to meet body ideals.

Most people with disabilities cannot even attempt to make their bodies fit the physical ideals of their culture. They may wish for bodies they cannot have, with frustration, shame and sometimes self-hatred; they may reject the physical ideals as narrow, unimaginative and/or oppressive; or, like myself, they may fluctuate irrationally between these points of view. In any case, they must struggle harder than non-disabled people for a self-image that is both realistic and positive, and this is made more difficult by other people's reactions to them. In a society that idealizes the body, people who cannot come close enough to the ideals, and those whose bodies are out of control, become devalued people because of their devalued bodies. . . . Moreover, they are constant reminders to the temporarily "normal" of the rejected body—of what the "normal" are trying to avoid, forget and ignore. . . .

Of course, it is not just from fear of being or becoming abnormal that the rejected body is shunned; it is also shunned from fear of pain, illness, limitation, suffering and dying. Yet the cultural banishment of the rejected body contributes to fear of those experiences by fostering ignorance of them. Even though everyone has or will have experiences of the negative body, if the cultural concept of the "normal" body is a young, healthy, energetic, pain-free body with all parts present and a maximum range of graceful movement, then experiences of the negative body need not be confronted and understood. They belong to those with disabilities and illnesses, who are marginalized, not "ordinary" people, not "us."

People with disabilities and illnesses learn that most people do not want to know about the suffering they experience because of their bodies. Curiosity about medical diagnoses, physical appearance and the sexual and other intimate aspects of disability is common; interest in the subjective experience is rare. . . . This also is understandable. If we tell people about our pain, for example, we remind them of the existence of pain, the imperfection and fragility of the body, the possibility of their own pain, the *inevitability* of it. The less willing they are to accept all these, the less they will want to know. If they cannot avoid confronting pain in our presence, they can avoid us. They may even blame us for being in pain. They may tell themselves that we could have avoided it, in order to believe that they can avoid it. They may want to believe they are not like us, not vulnerable to this; if so, they will cling to our differences, and we will become "the Others." Our shared culture offers this solution and makes the distance between our experiences difficult to bridge. It is not surprising that many people who can, hide their disabilities from everyone but their closest friends.

Are there sources of resistance to the disciplines of normality, analogous to the oppositional discourses and practices (many of them feminist) that Bartky identifies as emerging forms of resistance to the disciplines of femininity? Certainly I see disabled people's revaluing of their own bodies and ways of living, and the forms of culture that are emerging from disability pride, as oppositional discourses and practices. They do weaken the internal hold of the disciplines of normality over those of us who have disabilities. But do they undermine commitment to those disciplines and fear of abnormality in those who meet the social standards of normality or do they only, at best, change some attitudes toward "the Others"? I do not think we can answer that question yet. There has been only a small, recent increase in the general presentation of disability culture, and there is still a flood of cultural idealizations of the body.

FEMINIST IDEALIZATIONS OF THE BODY

Feminists have always criticized the idealization and objectification of women's bodies, recognizing them as sources of exploitation and alienation. They have particularly focused on ideals of appearance, grooming and bodily comportment for women, and on sexual and medical objectifications of women's bodies. Yet feminist movements have expressed their own body ideals, often insisting on women's strength and overlooking the fact that many women's bodies are not strong. We have celebrated those aspects of women's bodily experience that are sources of pleasure, satisfaction and feelings of connection, but we have underestimated the bodily frustration and suffering that social justice cannot prevent or relieve. Feminists have also criticized and worked to undo men's control of women's bodies, without undermining the myth that women can control our own bodies. In one of the most influential feminist books that discussed bodily life, *Of Woman Born*, Adrienne Rich wrote: "In order to live a fully human life we require not only control of our bodies (though control is a prerequisite); we must touch the unity and resonance of our physicality, our bond with the natural order, the corporeal ground of our intelligence". . . .

Until feminists criticize our own body ideals and confront the weak, suffering and uncontrollable body in our theorizing and practice, women with disabilities and illnesses are likely to feel that we are embarrassments to feminism. In a 1992 article in *Ms.*, Canadian feminist filmmaker Bonnie Klein described her experience at a feminist film festival—the first she had attended since being disabled by a stroke.

> *The women who had organized the festival—also Canadian filmmakers—had promised to "accommodate" me, but they make no provision for my needs. I am expected to fit in and keep up. They schedule my films late at night when I am too tired; they do not include me in panel discussions or press conferences; they arrange social events in inaccessible places. I miss the informal personal exchanges catalyzed by the shared film experience.*
>
> *I can no longer move in what had been my world. I feel I have been used for my films, but neglected and made invisible as a person. I feel as if my colleagues are ashamed of me because I am no longer the image of strength, competence and independence that feminists, including myself, are so eager to project. There is clearly a conflict between feminism's rhetoric of inclusion and failure to include disability. My journals reveal that this is the only moment in which I think of suicide. . . .*

References

Bartky, Sandra Lee. 1990. *Femininity and Domination: Studies in the Phenomenology of Oppression.* New York: Routledge.

Foucault, Michel. 1979. *Discipline and Punish.* New York: Vintage Books.

Hannaford, Susan. 1985. *Living Outside Inside. A Disabled Woman's Experience. Towards a Social and Political Perspective.* Berkeley: Canterbury Press.

Klein, Bonnie Sherr. 1992. "'We Are Who You Are': Feminism and Disability." *Ms.* 3 (3): 70–74.

Lessing, Jill. 1981. "Denial and Disability." *Off Our Backs* 11 (5): 21.

Matthews, Gwyneth Ferguson. 1983. *Voices from the Shadows: Women with Disabilities Speak Out.* Toronto: The Women's Press.

Morgan, Kathryn. 1991. "Women and the Knife. Cosmetic Surgery and the Colonization of Women's Bodies." *Hypatia: A Journal of Feminist Philosophy* 6 (3): 25–53.

Rich, Adrienne. 1976. *Of Woman Born: Motherhood as Experience and Institution.* New York: W.W. Norton.

Sheets-Johnstone, Maxine, ed. 1992b. *Giving the Body its Due.* Albany: State University of New York Press.

From Airbrushing to Liposuction: The Technological Reconstruction of the Female Body

Dr. Fabienne Darling-Wolf

Dr. Fabienne Darling-Wolf is an Assistant Professor in the Journalism Department and the Mass Media and Communication program, School of Communications and Theater, at Temple University in Philadelphia.

I started dieting at age twelve. From then on, my childhood memories are tinted by the subtle awareness of the many inadequacies of my less-than-ideal female body. I remember kneeling at the toilet, two fingers stuck down my throat, desperately attempting to purge myself from the guilt of a piece of chocolate cake. I remember my sister teaching me how to apply thinning cream—and developing an incredibly itchy rash thereafter. I remember dying my hair in the company of my mother. I remember only allowing myself to eat one apple per day. I remember spending entire afternoons with my best friend, fixing each other's hair. I remember tearing off the pages of women's magazines that offered an incredible variety of beauty tips, which would require entire days to perform adequately. In a word, I remember being socialized into dominant ideals of femininity.

These memories are both painful and precious. Precious because they represent moments of bonding with my female friends and family members. Indeed, I have found that in many situations beauty rituals can be a means of connecting with other women, even across the significant differences of race, class, culture or age. Painful, because for me these memories represent the beginning of a conscious awareness of the fact that my female body was not only a source of pleasure, but also a source of social control, discrimination and, ultimately, oppression. Numerous feminists suffer from a similar ambiguity. As both victims and critics of dominant representations of femininity, feminist scholars have developed a political understanding of the female body that recognizes it as a crucial site on which culture and ideology are inscribed, as well as a site of struggle against dominant ideology.

In this chapter, feminist interpretations are used to investigate the significance of cultural constructions of the female body and how such constructions can evolve according to the dominant ideology of a specific historical moment. Current conceptions of the female body as controllable through the use of science and technology are far from neutral, and it is important that we, as feminist scholars and activists, continue to develop a critical understanding of the dominant cultural constructions of the female body, including those promoted in popular cultural texts. . . .

NEW AND IMPROVED BODIES

In a culture in which organ transplants, life-extension machinery, microsurgery and artificial organs are commonplace, a new ideal of human freedom from bodily determination has evolved. Susan Bordo links this evolution to the development of postmodern conditions, the progress of consumer capitalism and the proliferation of products and images that are offered to viewers as an array of subjectivities from which each individual is free to choose. Characterized by the rejection of the belief in all-encompassing forces (God the watchmaker) in favour of an understanding of power as increasingly fragmented and dislocated, postmodern ideology constructs the body as under human control. Even nature can be subjected to human will through increasingly sophisticated manipulations. The body itself becomes a crucial site for experimentation either with or against the laws of nature. Supporting Bordo's assertion, Anne Balsamo observes that the female body has become a site for technological intervention, as exemplified by the proliferation of cosmetic surgical techniques.[1] Today the body is conceived as the raw material on which doctors intervene.

Indeed we are increasingly assured that we can escape the natural processes of the body, particularly those of the burdensome female body with its hormone changes, disturbing bulges and unusual organs. Processes such as aging, reproduction, fat accumulation and even death are presented to us in newspapers and magazines as challenges, frontiers to be conquered, rather than natural parts of life. . . .

In popular culture, current representations of the female body certainly follow this dominant ideal. As might be expected, since media sources are foundations where cultural ideals are constructed and perpetuated, media ideals of femininity have undergone an evolution similar to those of society at large. Models have become increasingly thin, and through advertising, we are now offered a variety of solutions to escape the tyranny of our bodies. Advertising has learned to create a wider range of identities, which women are told they can choose from and achieve through consumption (generally of beauty products). The use of such products may even grant women a level of respectability and recognition they may never have otherwise achieved. . . .

. . . [M]edia representations of the ideal female body are facilitated by fairly recent technological developments. The production process of feminine representations has been freed from all biological constraints. While image manipulation, such as airbrushing, has long been possible, the capacity for manipulation afforded by new imaging technology has incredible new proportions. With the stroke of a few keys, digital editing allows magazine editors to correct the too-hairy lip, the too-large breast, the too-slender shoulders, the too-large feet, the too-great or too-slight stature. It allowed film editors to give leading American actor Julia Roberts—deemed too fat—a new body in the movie *Pretty Woman.*[2] Even Kate Moss, Calvin Klein's ultra-thin supermodel, could lose twenty pounds on the computer screen—a clear example of digital imagery moving beyond biological feasibility. Today's supermodels have evolved into cultural icons that bear no relation to real women.

But technology is nevertheless offered as the "real life" solution for women to reach this unrealistic, or unreal, ideal. Advertising offers women a postmodern body on a silver platter. Often using quasi-feminist terminology of women's rights (to a thin, toned body), liberation (from unwanted hair) and freedom of choice (of deodorant), ads for breath fresheners, hair removal devices, liquid diets, cosmetics and plastic surgery services assure women that consumption can free them from the trappings of the body. Technological intervention is often presented as acceptable, or even desirable, in popular cultural texts. . . .

Even the most troublesome markers of ethnicity or race can be remedied with the simplest technological intervention. Where modernity tied the body to the exercising machine, the new ideal comes up with instant solutions. Telling women they can have it all—a high paying job, a family and freedom from embarrassing body odours—advertising constructs multiple identities for women to consume, regardless of the shape, size or colour of the body they happen to be in. Defying the very materiality of the body, this new imagery renders bodies irrelevant, at least on paper.

HOW IRRELEVANT ARE BODIES?

Often argued by postmodernist scholars to be divested of political significance, advertising imagery is sometimes presented as a playful fantasy for viewers' enjoyment—a fantasy that everyone can use in empowering ways. Advertising, however, may not be as neutral and playful as this argument proposes. A sense of freedom of choice is part of the basic ideology of advertising.[3] By constituting viewers as actors and creators of meaning rather than passive receivers, advertising effectively hides the dominant ideology it promotes, becoming more effective in the process. Freedom, independence, pleasure, are reduced to matters of style and consumption, and the choice of advertising is largely illusory. . . .

While the role assigned to technology is often that of transcendence, transformation and control, the technologized object—the raw material—is constructed as inferior or primitive.[4] For instance, Martin argues that doctors conceptualize the female body as a less than satisfactory incubator compared to more technologically mediated reproductive methods. She notes that cesarean sections are often considered superior to vaginal births, which are deemed too stressful for the baby. Moreover, technological intervention on the female body can be justified by the successful production of a healthy child. Women's anger at being forced to undergo a C-section is easily dismissed as irrational if the procedure results in the successful production of a baby in good health.[5] Similarly, female bodies undergoing cosmetic surgery are described by plastic surgeons as the raw material from which doctors create beauty. In *Backlash,* one surgeon told Susan Faludi, "It's very individual. We are sculptors."[6] Again, favouring the skills of the technician or even the artist, the cosmetic surgeon's eye redefines the female body as an object for technological reconstruction.

Such a construction contributes to an ideology—clearly present in the language used by plastic surgeons—of the female body as inherently flawed and pathological. . . . Not all bodies, however, are equally affected by such deformities. The deviant female body naturally requires more attention than the more perfect (white) male body. There has not been any controversy over men's right to access potentially dangerous penile enlargement surgery.

THE "PERFECT" FEMALE BODY

This construction of the female body as flawed, promoted by plastic surgeons and perpetuated in the media, becomes even more disturbing when taking into account what kinds of female bodies are constructed as particularly in need of remedy. On top of the list of candidates for technological correction are too-long Jewish noses, too-flat African-American ones, "Oriental" eyelids[7] and, of course, any sign of aging. Technology is offered as a solution to those unfortunate characteristics that pull women away from the young, white, middle-class ideal. Plastic surgeons recognize that bone structure is different in all racial identities, but they nevertheless evaluate ideal proportions through the measurement of Caucasian faces, promoting one standard based on a Caucasian ideal. . . .

But the discourse of cosmetic surgery is not the only cultural text that constructs ethnicity and race as abnormalities. Numerous feminists have noted that the Western cultural construction of female beauty promoted in the media is largely based on a white, middle-class ideal. As Kobena Mercer reminds us, "an *aesthetic* dimension, concerning blackness as the absolute negation or annulment of 'beauty,' has always intertwined with the rationalization of racist sentiment."[8]. . . .

The current ideal of bodily escape has particularly disturbing implications for those whose bodies are most specifically targeted as deviant—those whose bodies are not white enough, not young enough, not middle-class enough, not thin enough, not abled enough. Furthermore, technological intervention on the numerous "deformities" of race, ethnicity, age or excessive flesh, might also become increasingly difficult to reject. . . .

Fat bodies clearly challenge the ideal of bodily escape. They are blatantly sexual, unapologetically physical, primitive, uncultured, out of control. Consequently, fat bodies are under the most pressure to submit to technological reconstruction. Those who remain fat, or even wiggly, in spite of exercising machines, diet pills, weight-loss programs and liposuction are deemed lacking in moral character. . . . The fat female body in particular raises the specter of an insatiable appetite both sexual and otherwise. In her essay on hunger as ideology, Bordo links the control of women's food intake to the control of female sexuality. Indeed, sexual metaphors permeate advertisements for food. But while men are encouraged to unselfconsciously dig in, "their total lack of control portrayed as appropriate, even adorable,"[9] women are held to a more contained standard. They can only indulge in low-calorie meals, fat-free desserts or Weight Watchers' dinners. Women who exhibit the most control over their bodies, such as anorectics, receive the most praise from society. In fact, food advertisements targeted at women often exploit the characteristic thought processes of eating disorders, including constant thinking about food, or binging and purging. Women judged to exercise too little control receive only contempt, especially from the media.

Of course, in contrast to the dominant stereotype of fat people as lazy and not wanting to "help themselves," those whose bodies do not fit the cultural norm might actually be spending the most time and effort attempting to control their "unruly" bodies through constant dieting, chemical intake or liposuction—the dangerous procedure through which fat is scraped and sucked out of "problem areas."[10] Recognizing this fact, however, would entail admitting the failure of science and technology to fix the abnormality of excess flesh, or admitting that excess flesh is not abnormal at all. In their unabashed physicality, fat bodies remind us too clearly that the current ideal of bodily escape is but a fantasy.

BODIES THAT REACT

Unfortunately, imagery of the body does not stop at the level of the text. In our critiques of cultural constructions of femininity and physical attractiveness, we must keep in mind that we are talking about actual material female bodies and not just theoretical constructs. "Cosmetic surgery is not simply a discursive site for the 'construction of images of women,' but a material site at which the physical female body is surgically dissected, stretched, carved and reconstructed according to cultural and eminently ideological standards of physical appearance."[11] The distinction between imagery and actual female flesh cannot always be ignored. . . .

ON RECLAIMING THE BODY

I do not mean to imply in this essay that women who attempt to conform to the cultural ideal of femininity are passive dopes of dominant ideology. Importantly, in the patriarchal environment in which we evolve, the pain and effort required to fit the ideal might be worth a try. . . .

. . . [W]hile body piercing or tattooing have sometimes been characterized as forms of self-mutilation by feminist scholars,[12] they can also be interpreted as forms of resistance to dominant ideals of femininity. In the small town where I currently live this fact was illustrated by teenagers' vehement protest of a law that would have required parental consent for body piercing for youth under the age of eighteen. Young protesters argued that body piercing was only meaningful as an act of rebellion against parental supervision. While body piercing as oppositional may be somewhat questionable, these teenagers already understood that their bodies were a significant site of struggle against the dominant ideology of their culture. The law was repealed.

Finally, experiences grounded in the female body, including the particular pressures it is subjected to, are also a possible site for connections. My "beauty memories" described at the beginning of this essay are a painful reminder of how disconnected I felt from my own body growing up in a culture particularly obsessed with appearance. And they are also a source of pleasure at the feelings of closeness I experienced in those moments when I shared beauty secrets with other women. I agree with Elspeth Probyn that it can be liberating to be able to play with fashion without being accused of false consciousness. However, I also agree with her when she notes that "we need to question how far playing with style can go before it becomes yet another way of conforming to the dominant ideology of women as objects."[13]

In order to put our bodies to work against the dominant ideology, we need to find ways of reappropriating dominant constructions of the body so that we can define our bodies in our own terms and create more positive imagery and metaphors. For instance, using late-20th-century capitalist ideology, the female body and its monthly cycles could be interpreted as flexibly adjusting to changing conditions in the environment in which it evolves.[14] We must learn to reclaim the female body as a site of political struggle on which feminist claims can be voiced, as a site of "action through transformation, appropriation, parody, and protest."[15] We must also learn to use our bodily instincts and experiences to develop a critical understanding of our own selves and of each other. Female bodies are not simply passive targets of technological reconstruction, or sites for playful experimentation. They are also a potentially powerful source for our developing theories to counteract hegemonic control of women's bodies.

Endnotes

1. Anne Balsamo, *Technologies of the Gendered Body* (Durham, NC: Duke University Press, 1996).
2. Jean Kilbourne, *Slim Hopes: Advertising and the Obsession with Thinness* (Northampton, MA: Media Education Foundation, 1995), video.
3. Judith Williamson, *Decoding Advertisements* (New York: Marion Boyars, 1978).
4. Kathryn Morgan, "Women and the Knife: Cosmetic Surgery and the Colonization of Women's Bodies." *Hypatia* 6 (1991) 47.
5. Emily Martin, *The Woman in the Body* (Boston: Beacon Press, 1992).
6. Susan Faludi, *Backlash: The Undeclared War against American Women* (New York: Corwn, 1991), 216.
7. Anne Balsamo, *Technologies of the Gendered Body* (Durham, NC: Duke University Press, 1996), 62.
8. Kobena Mercer, *Welcome to the Jungle: New Positions in Black Cultural Studies* (New York: Routledge, 1994), 102, emphasis in the original.
9. Susan Bordo, *Unbearable Weight: Feminism, Western Culture and the Body* (Berkeley: University of California Press, 1993), 111.
10. In *Backlash,* Susan Faludi notes that a 1988 congressional subcommittee placed the death toll of liposuction at twenty. She adds, however, that the figures are probably actually higher, as patients' families are often reluctant to report liposuction as the cause of death for fear of accusations of vanity and shallowness on the part of the victim (p. 221).
11. Balsamo, *Technologies of the Gendered Body,* 58.
12. Robin Tolmach Lakoff and Raquel Scherr, *Face Value: The Politics of Beauty* (Boston: Little, Brown and Co. 1984), 161.
13. Elspeth Probyn, "Theorizing through the Body," in Lana Rakow, ed. *Women Making Meaning: New Feminist Directions in Communication* (New York: Routledge, 1992), 86.
14. Martin, *The Woman in the Body.*
15. Morgan, "Women and the Knife," 44.

Feminizing the Mobile: Gender Scripting of Mobiles in North America

Leslie Regan Shade

Leslie Regan Shade is an Associate Professor at Concordia University in the Department of Communication Studies. Her research focus since the mid-1990s has been on the social, policy and ethical aspects of information and communication technologies (ICTs), with particular concerns towards issues of gender, globalization and political economy. The research contributions straddle the line between academic and non-academic audiences, including policymakers and non-profit groups. She is the author of Gender and Community in the Social Construction of the Internet *(Peter Lang, 2002), and co-editor of* Feminist Interventions in International Communication *(with Katharine Sarikakis, Rowman & Littlefield, 2007), two volumes in* Communications in the Public Interest *(edited with Marita Moll, Canadian Centre for Policy Alternatives) and* Mediascapes: New Patterns in Canadian Communication, *2nd ed (with Paul Attallah, Nelson Canada). Articles have also appeared in* Continuum, The Gazette, Canadian Journal of Communication *and* Government Information Quarterly. *She is the former President of the Canadian Communication Association and the former editor of* Computers and Society.

A lively body of feminist research has examined how communication technologies have been gendered through their social uses—often unintended—and their design (Chabaud-Rychter 1994; Cowan 1985; Horowitz & Mohun 1998; Lupton 1993; Olzenziel 1999). The telephone is particularly illustrative. Rakow (1992) and Moyal's (1992) research demonstrated that women's primary use of the telephone was for community bonding and family "kin keeping" while Martin's (1991) study of Bell Telephone during the early 20th century in Canada emphasized its move from a business tool for men to its feminization, achieved via women's labour as operators and their creation of a viable social culture.

Telephone technology and design have changed considerably to appeal to female consumers, reflecting its status as an indispensable domestic artefact, including stylistic trends (colours—plain black to pale hues), design (the Princess telephone) and technological innovations (push-button to portables) (Lupton 1993). The mobile telephone is increasingly designed and marketed to appeal to women and female teenagers. Whether through the creation of features and accessories (ringtones, wallpaper, faceplates, camera phone, wireless synergies) or through branded phones of high-end fashion designers, the design of the mobile reflects a distinctive feminization. This mimics efforts in the 1990s when media corporations and entrepreneurs feminized the Internet through the creation of popular content that privileged and encouraged women's consumption, rather than production or critical analysis (Shade 2002).

Using the concept of the gender script (Rommes 2002; van Oost 2003), this paper sketches the feminization of the design and marketing of mobile phones in the North American context through an analysis of selected print advertisements appearing in women's and teen magazines. Despite their high penetration of broadband, Canada and the United States lag behind other developed countries in their uptake of mobile phones because both countries are well served by solid landline infrastructures. Organisation for Economic Co-Operation and Development (OECD) statistics for 2004 indicate that the United

States had 62 mobile subscribers per 100 inhabitants, and Canada 47; this contrasts with the OECD average of 72, with 109 in Sweden, 102 in the United Kingdom, 96 in Finland and 72 in Japan (OECD, 2005). Unlike Europe and Asia, a distinctive mobile culture is nascent, and marketing the mobile for women and female teenagers in Canada and the United States is thus opportunistic and timely for mobile manufacturers and wireless carriers.

To date, little scholarly research has looked at the marketing of mobiles to women or female teens in North America (unlike studies on Italy and Scandinavia; see Zatta 2003 and Mortberg 2003). Townsend (2000), reviewing early U.S. marketing, notes its importance in shaping ideologies of mobile usage; advertising to women was often marketed to dispel security and to promote domestic "kin keeping" while for men it was "most frequently marketed as a tool of fashion, power, and virility" (p. 6).

GENDER SCRIPTS

Van Oost describes a "gender script" as:

> *the representations and artifacts designers have or construct of gender relations and gender identities—representations that they then inscribe into the materiality of that artifact. Like gender itself, which is defined as a multi-level process, gender scripts function on an individual and a symbolic level, reflecting and constructing gender differences in the division of labor. (2004; p. 195)*

Van Oost used this notion of gender scripts to describe the design history of shavers for men and women, highlighting how the artifacts embodied gender. Indeed, looking at current constructions of the razor we see how gender is overtly built into their design and marketing; just think of the steely-grey and green Mach3 turbo razor for men ("The best a man can get!"), versus the turquoise-blue Venus Divine shaver for women ("Reveal the goddess in you!"). Perhaps coincidentally, Motorola introduced "his" and "her" slim Razr phones—his was jet black, while hers was an "eye-catching tone of pink", and was soon, according to Motorola's promotional material:

> *seeded to a select group of fashion elite and Hollywood "it" girls . . . its shocking measurements make it one of the slimmest phones on the market. Rich functionality, performance excellence and design innovation give the user a total sensory experience—from photo messaging to hands free connections to superlative metallic finishes.* (www.motorola.com/mntoinfo/product/details/0,,128,00.html)

Domestication refers to how technology is incorporated into the everyday patterns of the users, and has been widely used by communication and feminist scholars to study the ways in which family members negotiate technologies within the household (Haddon 2004; Silverstone & Hirsch 1992).

Gender scripts will be used to illustrate several trends with mobiles: the mobile as a new marketing terrain (especially targeting teenage girls) and the mobile as fashion accessory and branded haute couture. It should be emphasized that this paper focuses only on mobile phone design and marketing for women and female teenagers, and does not analyze how mobiles have been "masculinized" as well via design and marketing.

In Canada, Rogers Wireless teamed with MuchMusic (the Canadian equivalent of MTV), for the MuchMusic Edition Phone, with content including "exclusive" private access to MuchMusic updates, a videophone to send and receive video clips, a TuneTracker ("hold your phone up to the music for the song's name and artist") and the MuchMusic Factory, to create individualized ringtones. "Finally, a phone as individual as you are", reads the ad copy, depicting a young teenage girl dancing solo on a stage.

Incorporation and conversion are reflected in ads that highlight the mobile as a tool to coordinate social engagements. mMode from AT&T Wireless combines wireless Internet with e-mail, instant messaging, games and various content (news, weather, sports, entertainment, lifestyle, games, pictures, travel and dining). An ad displays a woman seated at a barstool looking at her mobile, with a smiling man behind her. Says the ad copy: "You can use mMode to make a connection on Match Mobile, then choose a restaurant and find directions to get you there. It will even help you find the nearest ATM in case you want to go Dutch." Samsung's A800 phone is the "perfect dining and traveling companion—it's sleek, stylish, powerful, and it never forgets a face or a name. Besides being a camera phone, it takes dictation and you don't even have to buy it a drink."

Incorporation and conversion are also in play via mobile-casting; one particular example is a venture between Mott's (an apple and fruit juice company owned by parent Cadbury Schweppes) and Epicurious.com (the recipe website for Gourmet Magazine) wherein "Mott's recipe ideas and made-to-order shopping lists [are] beamed directly to your mobile phone." The ad in *Bon Appétit* magazine shows a white, blonde woman in breezy summer white attire, shopping bags in hand, smiling blissfully at her mobile.

MARKETING THE MOBILE TO TWEENS

Teenagers are considered the "sweet spot" for mobile designers. U.S. statistics estimate that "76% of young people ages 15 to 19, and 90% of people in their early 20s regularly use their cell phones for text messaging, ringtones and games, and that enthusiasm has turned wireless data services into a significant business" (Thottam, 2005).

Celebrity branding of mobiles for female tweens is one such trend. Single Touch pioneered the Hilary Duff phone, a prepaid handset featuring preloaded wallpaper and ringtones exclusive to the teen star. Boasting itself as the first phone catering to pre-teen girls, Mattel and Nokia launched the Barbie phone packaged with prepaid minutes, customized ringtones and faceplates (Heller 2005). Marketed alongside the Barbie MyScene toy line, the phones are sold in U.S. mega-retail stores Target, Toys R Us and WalMart. Timothy J. Kilpin, senior vice-president for girls' marketing and design at Mattel, claims the Barbie phone "transcends traditional doll play—it's steeped in entertainment. It allows girls to interact with the brand" (Crockett & Kharif, 2005).

Promotional material positions the phone as a parenting device, deviously aligning its use to rewarding proper behaviour from the child, while maintaining a panoptic gaze:

> *Parents not only have the peace of mind knowing that they are "Always in touch" with their child but they can also stay in control of phone usage by tying your child's good behavior to added minutes via the Reward Board. Just go online [to Single Touch's* www.myscenemobile.com*], set a list of chores which can include making the bed, finishing homework or not arguing with your brother or sister, and place stars on the completed tasks. At the end of the week or month, parents can buy extra minutes according to the child's list of completed tasks.* (www.singletouch. net/brands/msm.htm)

Similarly, MGA's popular Bratz line of nubile dolls has coordinated with Sony Ericsson for the "Bratz Mobile"; features allow parents to control how their children use the phone through restricting outgoing calls to pre-programmed and approved numbers only.

THE MOBILE AS FASHION ACCESSORY AND BRANDED HAUTE COUTURE

Lacohée et al. (2003) argue that "the idea that the mobile is on constant show and is therefore a fashion accessory has fed into an advertising rhetoric of continual upgrading to avoid being shamed" (p. 208). This sentiment was echoed by rapper mogul Sean "P. Diddy" Combs in his comments to the Cellular Telecommunications & Internet Association convention, where he mused on the blending of hip-hop and cell phone culture: "It's not about the minutes or the service . . . it's about how the person is defined" (Rhoads 2005). Likewise, Munich-based fashion house Escada spokeswoman Sabine Eisenreich enthused that the mobile "is not just a functional thing . . . it's become an accessory, like shoes, bags, belts or jewelry" (Rhoads 2005).

Industry market research is aligned with Eisenreich's sentiments; new points of sale for mobile handsets include upscale fashion boutiques that merge haute couture designers with handset companies: Siemens/ESCADA, Nokia/Versace, Nokia/Vertui. Motorola and Samsung have coordinated with designers Diane Von Furstenberg, Anna Sui and Vivienne Westwood. Strategies utilized in the haute couturing of the mobile include co-branding of handset vendors with designers, and handsets incorporating fashion elements. Siemens and Escada launched three limited-edition cell phones; one version, Denim and Diamonds, was decorated in denim, Swarovski crystals and a string of attached pearls. According to an Escada spokeswoman, all 7,000 of the U.S. $1 040 handsets sold out within two months (Rhoads 2005).

Samsung is a vanguard designer for feminized mobiles. In 2002 it launched the red "Ladyphone"—the design mimicked a make-up compact featuring "a biorhythm calculator, a fatness function that calculates a user's height-to-weight ratio, a calendar for keeping track of your menstrual cycle and a calorie-counting function. Enter an activity (cleaning, dish-washing, cooking, shopping) and the time spent, and the phone works out how many calories have been consumed" (*The Economist* 2002). Samsung promotional copy described the Egèo phone as "engraved with a gold rose . . . a beautiful symbol of your aristocratic dignity. Its small and compact design adds a warm glow in your hands like a precious gem" (see www.samsung.com/my/products/gsm/gsm/sgh_a400.asp). Samsung also sponsored the 2002 Britney Spears concert tour. Designer Diane von Furstenberg, exclaiming that the mobile phone had become "part of a woman's body language" (Rhoads 2005), designed her Samsung namesake mobile with a replica of her 1974 Andy Warhol portrait.

CONCLUSION: MOBILIZING GENDER?

Gender scripts can "illuminate how gendered user representations are inextricably part of designing artifacts" (Van Oost 2003, p. 194). The description of mobile advertising in this paper highlights how women have been inscribed as particular users and consumers. Mobiles were first marketed in the 1990s to women as a tool for "remote mothering" (Rakow & Navarro 1993) or as security and safety devices for travel. As mobile penetration increases in North America—particularly amongst young women and tweens, entrepreneurs and telecom companies are counting on cross-media convergence to spark new marketing platforms on the "third screen", while they are also promoted as branded fashion accessories and as status symbols through limited edition haute couture items. The gendered scripts here, through explicit user representations, reinforce women's role as consumer and as object, with uses for sociability, shopping and entertainment. As Kearney argues in her analysis of popular film and television programmes in post-Second World War America, the common trope of the female teenager on the telephone was "not part of an attempt to eliminate teenage girls' independence altogether, as one focused on preventing its further subversion of heterosexual patriarchy" (Kearney 2005, p. 594). Likewise, contemporary marketing of the mobile in North America reinforces femininity and hetero-normativity; the mobile is an extension of one's stylistic sensibility, the gaze is narcissistic and competitive. These instrumental uses certainly contrast with the innovative *keitai* culture in Japan (Ito et al. 2005).

While not disavowing that fashion trends are an intrinsic facet of identity formation (particularly for young women), the challenge now is how to design mobile phones (which are undoubtedly used by many women as a mundane tool both to support domesticity and supplement the increasingly mobile workplace) to more seamlessly integrate domestic functionalities alongside creative, cultural, playful and perhaps even civic modes of communicating. Bell et al., (2005) argue that defamilarizing the known within the domestic context can provoke critical and culturally sensitive perspectives on technology design. Becoming cognizant of how design and marketing incorporate stereotyped gender assumptions through gender scripts is important. While the gender scripts analyzed in this paper accentuate emancipatory uses, other socio-technical networks may conceive of the mobile as less liberating. Where and how are women involved in mobile phone design, production and manufacturing? Feminist interrogations of mobiles must thus also go beyond mere critical assessments of the consumption of mobiles, and focus on the political economic realities in their production.

References

Bell, G., Blythe, M. & Sengers, P. (2005) "Making strange: Defamiliarization and the design of domestic technologies", *ACM Transactions on Computer–Human Interaction*, vol. 12, no. 2, pp. 149–173.

Chabaud-Rychter, D. (1994) "Women users in the design process of a food robot: Innovation in a French domestic appliance company", in *Bringing Technology Home: Gender and Technology in a Changing Europe*, eds C. Cockburn & R. Furst Dilic, Open University Press, Buckingham, pp. 77–93.

Cowan, R. S. (1985) *More Work for Mother: The Ironies of Household Technology from the Open Hearth to the Microwave*, Basic Books, New York.

Crockett, R. O. & Kharif, O. (2005) "Calling preteens with a Barbie phone", *Business Week* [online], 18 Feb., Available at: www.businessweek.com/technologyfcontentffeh200s/tc20050218_4609_tc024.htm

The Economist. (2002) "From cell phones to self phones", 24 Jan., Available at: www.economist.com/business/displayStory.cfm?Story_ID=954329

Haddon, L. (2004) *Information and Communication Technologies in Everyday Life: A Concise Introduction and Research Guide*, Berg, London.

Heller, L. (2004) "Back-to-school: pencils, homework, cell phones?", *DSN Retailing Today*, vol. 44, no. 8, p. 42.

Horowitz, R. & Mohun, A. (eds) (1998) *His and Hers: Gender, Consumption, and Technology*, University Press of Virginia, Charlottesville.

Ito, M, Okabe. D. & Matsuda, M. (eds) (2005) *Personal, Portable, Pedestrian: Mobile Phones in Japanese Life*, MIT Press, Cambridge, MA.

Kearney, M. C. (2005) "Birds on the wire: troping teenage girlhood through telephony in mid-twentieth century US media culture", *Cultural Studies*, vol. 19, no. 5, pp. 568–601.

Lacohée, H., Wakeford, N. & Pearson, I. (2003) "A social history of the mobile telephone with a view of its future". *BT Technology Journal*, vol. 21, no. 3, pp. 203–211.

Lupton, F. (1993) *Mechanical Brides: Women and Machines from Home to Office*, Cooper-Hewitt National Museum of Design, Smithsonian Institute, and Princeton Architectural Press, New York.

Martin, M. (1991) *Hello Central? Gender, Culture, and Technology in the Formation of Telephone Systems*, McGill-Queen's University Press, Montreal.

Mortberg, C. (2003) "Heterogeneous images of (mobile) technologies and services: a feminist contribution", *NORA*, vol. 3, no. 11, pp. 158–169.

Moyal, A. (1992) "The gendered use of the telephone: An Australian case study", *Media, Culture and Society*, vol. 14, pp. 51–72.

Olzenziel, R. (1999) *Making Technology Masculine: Men, Women and Modern Machines in America, 1870–1945*, Amsterdam University Press, Amsterdam.

Organization for Economic Cooperation and Development (OECD) (2005) *OECD ICT Key Indicators*. Available at: www.oecd.oru/sti/ICTindicators

Rakow, L. (1992) *Gender on the Line: Women, the Telephone, and Community Life*, University of Illinois Press, Chicago.

Rakow, L. & Navarro, V. (1993) "Remote mothering and the parallel shift: women meet the cellular telephone", in *Critical Studies in Mass Communication*, 10 Winter, pp. 144–157.

Rhoads, C. (2005) "Cellphone makers, users heed fashion world's call", *Wall Street Journal*, 18 Mar. p. B1.

Rommes, F. (2002) *Gender Scripts and the Internet: The Design and Use of Amsterdam's Digital City*, Twente University Press, Enschede.

Shade, L. R. (2002) *Gender and the Social Construction of the Internet*, Peter Lang, New York.

Silverstone, R. & Hirsch, F. (eds) (1992) *Consuming Technologies: Media and Information in Domestic Spaces*, Routledge, New York.

Thottam, J. (2005) "How kids set the (ring) tone", *Time*, vol. 165, no. 14, p. 40.

Townsend, A. M. (2000) "Life in the real-time city: mobile telephones and urban metabolism", *Journal of Urban Technology*, vol. 7, no. 2, pp. 85–104:

Van Oost, B. (2003) "Materialized gender: How shavers configure the users' femininity and masculinity", in *How Users Matter: The Co-construction of Users and Technology*, eds N. Oudshoorn & T. Finch, MIT Press, Cambridge, MA, pp. 193–208.

Zatta, S. (2003) "Powerful objects for powerful women? Feminine representation in Italian technology advertising imagery", Paper presented at "Gender and Power in the New Europe", *5th European Feminist Research Conference*, Lund University, Sweden, p. 20–24 Aug.

CHAPTER 5

Sexuality

Canadian feminist contributions to sexuality studies are diverse; Canadian feminists speak in many and sometimes oppositional voices. Indeed, as Stevi Jackson and Sue Scott (1996, p. 1) comment, " . . . sexuality has been a contested terrain amongst feminists since the 19th century. No sooner had it been identified as a major area of concern by the modern movement, than significant disagreements began to emerge." We have tried to reproduce material that is reflective of the diversity of contemporary Canadian feminist thinking.

If there is one unifying theme in this set of readings it is the construction of a challenge to the compulsory nature of heterosexuality. Together with gay scholarship and queer theory, feminist theory played a central role in gaining recognition of the socially constructed character of sexuality. Wresting sexuality away from its framing as natural and biological has been a formidable challenge, but it has opened the way for an interrogation of dominant sexual norms. Readings in this chapter explicitly or implicitly draw upon Adrienne Rich's groundbreaking theorization of heterosexuality as an institution ("Compulsory Heterosexuality and Lesbian Existence," 1986). Rich analyzes heterosexuality as a means of ensuring male right of physical, economic and emotional access to women and suggests that heterosexuality is institutionalized, constructed through ideology and physical coercion. The coercion inherent in dominant heterosexuality has been identified most clearly by feminists working on gender violence (see Chapter 3). In this chapter, we represent a range of feminist efforts to theorize sexual identity categories and to analyze their interrelation, their regulation and their consequences. The readings in this chapter interrogate and analyze the changing character of sexual regulation in the present, interrogating heterosexuality from new perspectives, critically analyzing the normalization of gay and lesbian identities, exploring the intersections of race and sexuality and using insights from queer theory to disrupt sexual identity categories.

INTERROGATING HETEROSEXUALITY IN THE PRESENT

Second wave feminist analysts posed lesbianism as a site of challenge to institutionalized heterosexuality. For some lesbian feminists, heterosexual feminism became oxymoronic. To engage in heterosexuality, as Andrea Dworkin (1987) insisted, was to quite literally sleep with the enemy. **Christine Overall**'s now classic piece in this chapter (**"Heterosexuality and Feminist Theory"**) is a reaction to the castigation of heterosexual feminists as "dupes of patriarchy." Overall engages in a social constructionist analysis of heterosexuality, refuting the claim made by some lesbian and radical feminists that heterosexuality is both unchangeable and incompatible with feminism. While defining heterosexuality as an institution that is enforced and arguing that heterosexual privilege must be acknowledged, she contends that choosing lesbianism means the corollary possibility of choosing heterosexuality. In drawing an important distinction between heterosexual practices and the institution of heterosexuality, she suggests that to pose heterosexuality as a choice undermines the compulsory nature of heterosexuality. Resistant heterosexual practices may work to alter the oppressiveness of institutionalized heterosexuality.

Erin Connell ("Desire as Interruption: Young Women and Sexuality Education in Ontario, Canada") and **Melanie Beres ("Moving Beyond 'No Means No': Understanding Heterosexual Casual Sex and Consent")** carry forward the project of interrogating the specific construction of heterosexuality in the present, offering possibilities of resistant heterosexual practices. As Connell contends, women are at risk of sexual violence and sexually transmitted disease; they live their sexualities under the shadow of institutionalized heterosexuality and dominant norms that construct men as active sexual subjects and women as objects of men's desire. At the same time, the sexual revolution of the 1960s, access to birth control and abortion and second wave feminist activisms created the conditions for the assertion of female sexual desire and pleasure. Women negotiate their sexualities within this dialectic of pleasure and danger. Connell engages in an examination of how young women's sexual danger and pleasure are characterized in official discourses, specifically those of school-based sexuality education. As she finds, discourses of victimization and individual morality dominate the Ontario sex education curriculum through its emphasis on abstinence and the negative consequences of sex. Moreover, the curriculum reinforces compulsory heterosexuality and gender specific sexual roles. Echoing Overall's call for practices of resistance, Connell argues for a shift in sex education that would foster the social and sexual subjectivity of adolescent girls and acknowledge the importance of sexual pleasure and experimentation.

Beres engages in a careful examination of how young adults say yes to heterosexual sex. Her work, like Overall's, marks a distinction between the institution of heterosexuality and practices of heterosexuality. In this piece she reflects on the conclusions of a qualitative study that she conducted analyzing how young adults negotiate casual heterosexual encounters. Echoing Connell, Beres finds that dominant heterosexual discourses impact how young men and women position themselves as active or passive subjects. These discourses provide greater potential for male power and Beres notes the absence of a discourse of women's desire, with women often reporting that they engage in sex because it is expected rather than truly desired. Nonetheless, she emphasizes how women are able to carve out spaces of power within a context dominated by masculine ideals of casual sex and relationships. Equally important is her exploration of the ways that young heterosexuals communicate willingness in the context of casual sexual encounters through readings of bodily cues. As Beres argues, these practices remain gendered with men positioned as seeking sex and women positioned as giving sex to men. But as she suggests here, in order to begin to resist the gendered dynamics of heterosexual communication and to develop more ethical sexual practices, we must be attentive to current communication strategies and build on the cultural knowledge that is already in existence.

NORMALIZING THE LESBIAN COUPLE

Feminist historians using social constructionist approaches have argued that lesbianism came into being as a specifically sexual identity with turn-of-the-century science and medicine. Over the course of the 20th century, lesbian cultural and political movements have mobilized on the basis of this identity, challenging its construction as deviant and pathological. Despite this mobilization, and until very recently, lesbianism remained silenced within a culture that defined heterosexuality as natural and paradigmatic. Beginning in the 1990s, activists deployed the Canadian Charter's guarantee of equality to push forward the rights of gay and lesbian people. This equality rights strategy was enormously successful, culminating in the legalization of same-sex marriage in 2005. Same-sex couples, whether married or common law, now enjoy the same rights and responsibilities as heterosexual couples. In a shift of historic proportions, lesbian and gay identities, once stigmatized and silenced, have gained both legal recognition and cultural legitimacy. The threat that same-sex relationship recognition poses to compulsory heterosexuality should not be underestimated. At the same time, **Marianne Valverde ("A New Entity in the History of**

Sexuality: The Respectable Same-Sex Couple") and **Claire Young and Susan Boyd** ("**Losing the Feminist Voice?: Debates on the Legal Recognition of Same-Sex Partnerships in Canada**"), encourage us to think critically about the meaning and implications of this development.

Valverde analyzes the new legal and cultural prominence of the respectable same-sex couple (RSSC). In this thought-provoking piece, Valverde argues that the RSSC is a post-homosexual identity that marks a decisive break with 20th century constructions of homosexuality as a sexual identity. She analyzes media representations and legal texts to demonstrate how the RSSC is thoroughly desexualized, defined not by sex, but instead by domesticity, finance and consumerism. As Valverde suggests, the RSSC works to normalize gay and lesbian identities.

Boyd and Young also contend that the move towards same-sex marriage is profoundly assimilative, incorporating gays, lesbians and queers into a model of normative heterosexuality. While recognizing the enormous symbolic significance of same-sex marriage, the great strength of this article is in bringing feminist critiques of the family to bear on the drive towards marriage. The authors insist that marriage has a history that is deeply intertwined with relations of subordination, reproducing, in particular, women's dependency and inequality. Boyd and Young analyze Canadian debates on same-sex marriage to show how the struggle proceeded on the basis of formal equality, while more radical positions on marriage and the family were silenced. As they argue, to the extent that feminist voices were marginalized, heteronormative discourses on marriage and the family were reinforced, even as same-sex relationships gained recognition. They suggest that same-sex relationship recognition means the uncritical incorporation of gays and lesbians into heteronormative standards, creating hierarchies between good gays and lesbians who embrace coupledom and those who resist. Moreover, returning our focus to neoliberalism, Boyd and Young warn that marriage recognition is consistent with the privatization of social responsibilities: good gay and lesbian citizens will organize themselves into dyadic units built upon financial interdependence.

RACIALIZING SEXUALITY

Feminist efforts to interrogate sexuality have, until recently, failed to explore the complex relationships between race and sexuality. The "lesbian" of lesbian feminism was an ahistorical and abstracted figure, and feminist efforts to contextualize sexuality most often left the lesbian's whiteness untouched. The unstated whiteness of sexual identity categories and the analytic separation of sexuality from race have been critiqued by anti-racist, Aboriginal and third wave Canadian feminist scholars. **Lee Maracle ("Isn't Love a Given?")** and **Cassandra Lord ("The Silencing of Sexuality")** challenge us to move beyond essentialist frameworks and to consider the interconnected nature of race and sexuality.

Maracle's essay seeks to value lesbian sexuality from the perspective of heterosexuality. Maracle is an important Aboriginal Canadian novelist; her fictional and theoretical writings have been central contributions to a developing Aboriginal feminist literature. Maracle situates the negation of Aboriginal women's sexuality in racism, colonization and the resulting destruction of cultures and communities. In this context, she argues, sex becomes little more than physical release. Aboriginal women became constructed as less than fully human, as mere vessels for male gratification. This is a powerful and enduring construction that legitimizes sexual violence against Aboriginal women interrogated by earlier pieces in *Open Boundaries*. As Maracle writes, "[I]n our society it is loving women that is prohibited," so naturally "we are going to hate women who love women." The struggle against compulsory heterosexuality is crucial, she insists, in order to reclaim the "sacred right of women to love and be loved."

Lord's contribution takes up the particular difficulties in "coming out" faced by young black lesbians. Lord is a self-defined third wave feminist, and her article engages in third wave themes of difference, the disruption of identity categories and the importance of theorizing from personal experience. Like Maracle, Lord situates the specific silencing of black lesbians within broader, historical processes rendering black women's sexuality simultaneously invisible, colonized and, as a legacy of slavery, completely commodified. She critiques both the use of the term "lesbian" without racial specificity within white lesbian culture and also the black community's erasure and closeting of lesbianism. Living a divided and separated existence means that the "closet" is a complex space for black lesbians. Lord emphasizes the crucial importance of alternative communities for black lesbians as a means of support and as sites for resisting this politics of silencing.

QUEERING SEXUALITY/DECONSTRUCTING IDENTITIES

If feminist social constructionist approaches to sexuality have succeeded in denaturalizing heterosexuality, in tracing the evolution of lesbian identities, and, in some cases, in racializing sexuality, recent shifts in sexuality studies have pushed the agenda of social constructionism even further. Queer theory takes as its central object of critique the enduring and foundational hierarchical binaries of male/female and heterosexual/homosexual (see Jagose 1996). Mobilizing on the basis of coherent sexual identity categories—for example, gay and lesbian—fails to unhinge these binaries and, in fact, reinforces the privilege and norm of heterosexuality. Judith Butler (1990), for example, has argued powerfully that to assume the identity "lesbian" is both an exclusionary move and one that fails to challenge a heterosexual matrix dependent upon the maintenance of stable boundaries between man and woman, heterosexual and homosexual. For Butler, sex, gender and sexual identity are discursively constructed; heterosexuality and masculine and feminine gender identities appear permanent but are the effect of repetitive performances. Rather than reinforcing the apparent stability of gender and sexual identities, queer theorists advocate a politics of deconstruction and sexual diversity. Through resistant performances (for example, through drag, butch/femme) and nonconformist practices, heteronormativity can be denaturalized and subverted.

Influenced by queer theory and third wave feminist insights, **Amber Dean ("Does a Lesbian Need a Vagina Like a Fish Needs a Bicycle? Or Would the Real Lesbian Please Stand Up")** asks us to consider who qualifies as a lesbian in the present and for what reasons. Dean engages in a genealogy of lesbian identity by tracing the connections between "being a lesbian" and "looking like a lesbian." Appearance, as she highlights, has long been used to signify lesbian identity and to combat lesbian invisibility. But each style, from the butch/femme aesthetics of the post-war period to the androgynous uniform of the 1970s and 1980s, marked a boundary around the category lesbian, excluding those who refused to conform. In the 1990s, she argues, there was a resurgence of butch/femme lesbian aesthetics and increasing challenges to the centrality of white middle-class women's experiences as definitive of feminist and lesbian communities. This produced a shift away from rigid concepts of "what a lesbian looks like" to self-identification and desire for women as definitive of belonging. Dean seeks to problematize boundary policing and at the same time, she asks a provocative question. If, as Butler argues, sex is constructed, is it then possible for a man to be a lesbian? Is the category lesbian infinitely elastic?

The question of boundary policing also preoccupies **Jean Bobby Noble ("Sons of the Movement: Feminism, Female Masculinity and Female to Male (FTM) Transsexual Men")**. In an essay that is both autobiographical and theoretically sophisticated, Noble recalls his journey through lesbian identity and feminist politics to FTM transsexual masculinity. Noble's essay is an example of the new alliance between feminist and transgender theory. As Noble argues, feminism can benefit from an engagement with transgender theory—a theory that sheds important insights on the meanings of man and woman, straight and gay. FTM transsexual men have been viewed with suspicion within some lesbian and feminist circles. If, as some second wave feminists suggested, heterosexual feminists slept with the enemy, FTM transsexual men are sometimes seen as literally having become the enemy by taking on the privileges of masculinity. Yet as Noble contends, FTMs never fully become the kind of man privileged in this culture. FTMs thus have the potential to offer a unique vantage point on both feminism and masculinity and FTM masculinity must be seen as an alternative and pro-feminist embodiment of non-phallic masculinity. This article is a nuanced and complicated piece, demonstrating the proliferation of new sexuality literatures within Canadian feminism and the challenging directions that are now being pursued as feminists seek to problematize gender and sexuality in multiple ways.

Heterosexuality and Feminist Theory

Christine Overall

Christine Overall is a Professor of Philosophy, cross-appointed to Women's Studies, and holds a University Research Chair at Queen's University, Kingston. Her research and teaching are in the areas of feminist philosophy, applied ethics, social philosophy and philosophy of religion. Her most recent books are Thinking Like a Woman: Personal Life and Political Ideas *and* Aging, Death and Human Longevity: A Philosophical Inquiry.

Heterosexuality, which I define as a romantic and sexual orientation toward persons not of one's own sex, is apparently a very general, though not entirely universal, characteristic of the human condition. In fact, it is so ubiquitous a part of human interactions and relations as to be almost invisible, and so natural-seeming as to appear unquestionable. Indeed, the 1970 edition of *The Shorter Oxford English Dictionary* defines "heterosexual" as "pertaining to or characterized by the normal relation of the sexes". . . .[1]

This is, then, the first of what I shall refer to as the paradoxes of heterosexuality: As an expected, supposedly normal characteristic of adult and even pre-adult life, it is so pervasive that it melts into our individual lives; its invisibility as a social condition makes it seem to be just a matter of what is personal, private and inevitable. Heterosexuality is simultaneously the only "real" form of sexuality, and yet (for that very reason) very difficult to perceive. Heterosexuality is transparent, in the way that a piece of plastic wrap is transparent. Yet, like plastic wrap, it has the ability to hold things in place, to keep things down and to provide a barrier to prevent other things from coming in contact with that which it seems to be protecting. . . .

THE INSTITUTION OF HETEROSEXUALITY

. . . By the institution of heterosexuality, or what I shall call for short the heterosexual institution, what I mean is the systematized set of social standards, customs and expected practices that both regulate and restrict romantic and sexual relationships between persons of different sexes in late 20th-century Western culture. . . .

In referring to heterosexuality as an institution, I am rejecting an essentialist or reified view of sexual orientations. Human sexuality is culturally constructed, that is, it is "a social," not [only] a biological phenomenon.[2] There is no reason to suppose that sexual activity and expression are more immune to the effects of enculturation than are other apparently "natural" human activities such as caring for children, or eating. Of course, the fact that sexuality is culturally constructed does not entirely preclude the possibility that some form of sexual expression is innate or "natural," or that we have "biological inclinations" toward some form of sexual activity. But it does imply both that the evidence for such a natural sexuality will be virtually impossible to detect, and that the stronger hypothesis is that there is no such natural sexuality. One cannot even refer to primordial feelings or irresistible passions as natural, since enculturation processes, including the heterosexual institution, help to define what feelings we do and do not, or ought and ought not to have. . . .

. . . [F]or, whatever our inherent proclivities may or may not be, there is undeniably tremendous social pressure toward heterosexuality. This pressure is a part of the heterosexual institution. Indeed, I wonder why, if heterosexuality is innate, there are so many social voices telling us, ad nauseum, that that is what we should be. These voices include the ideology that surrounds heterosexual romance, dating and marriage; the mythology of falling in (and out of) heterosexual love, of flings, crushes, affairs, passions and helpless attractions; the cultural apparatus that purports to assist women to be heterosexually attractive, to be coy, alluring, "sexy" and flirtatious, in order to "find true love" or to "catch a man," and then to maintain his interest once he's caught; the psychotherapies and medical treatments, together with literature ranging from self-help manuals to scholarly treatises, that claim to prescribe the nature and forms of and adjustment to healthy female heterosexuality and the cures or panaceas for its disfunctions; the cultural images, in popular music, paintings, dance crazes, novels, stories, advice columns, films, videos, plays and advertising, that interpret human sexuality and love exclusively in terms of two by two heterosexual pairing; and the predominant instruments of Western social life—the bars, dances, parties, clubs—that recognize only the heterosexual couple. Why is there so much insistence, via these intensive socialization mechanisms, that all women be heterosexual and *learn* to be heterosexual, if that is what we are all naturally inclined to be anyway? So the presence of that strong social insistence upon heterosexuality is, to my mind, one very large piece of evidence that heterosexuality is not innate. But, whether it is or it is not, it is the heterosexual institution that is the subject of discussion in this paper. . . .

THE POLITICS OF HETEROSEXUALITY

. . . My question about the object of the heterosexual institution is akin to questions about the object of other institutions such as the state, the family, the educational system or religion. And one way of starting to answer such questions is by looking to see what individuals or groups of individuals benefit from the institution, what the benefits are, how those benefits are created and distributed and at whose cost the benefits are acquired.

For the past two decades, radical feminists have offered disturbing answers to these questions. They have argued, first, that the heterosexual institution primarily benefits men, not women; and that it affords men easy sexual gratification and material possession of women, as well as reproduction of themselves and their offspring. Second, these benefits are created and distributed through what Adrienne Rich and others have described as the compulsory nature of heterosexuality: female heterosexual desire and activity must be enforced and coerced, through a myriad of social practices in the family, in culture, in religion, education and law.[3] This process has been described as the deliberate recruitment of women into active participation in heterosexuality.[4] Mariana Valverde states:

> *[G]iven the enormous social weight of heterosexism, one cannot accurately describe heterosexuality as merely a personal preference, as though there were not countless social forces pushing one to be heterosexual. People do not generally choose heterosexuality out of a number of equally valid, equally respected lifestyles. . . . As long as certain choices are punished while others are presented as natural, as the norm, it is naive to describe the complicated process of the construction of conformity and/or deviance by reference to a consumer-type notion of personal preference.*[5]

Third, whatever its rewards may be (and they are more than amply celebrated in romantic fiction, films, songs and everyday mythology) the costs for women of providing the benefits of female heterosexuality for men are of two types: First, violence, degradation and exploitation of women's bodies and women's sexuality, through such practices as prostitution, rape and other forms of sexual assault, woman battering, pornography and incest; and second, the deliberately cultivated separation of women from their allies, each other. The operation of the heterosexual institution is a very successful demonstration of the political maxim that to keep a subject group down, it is important to keep its members divided, to prevent them from developing loyalties to each other, and to direct their trust and commitment to members of the oppressor group. In short, the heterosexual institution is the strongest arm and most powerful manifestation of patriarchy; and therefore one of its most important objects is the oppression of women.

As an agent of patriarchal oppression, the heterosexual institution generates a second paradox in heterosexuality: the conjunction of heterosexual privilege and heterosexism. On the one hand, the heterosexual institution grants a certain privilege to heterosexual women that is not possessed by non-heterosexual women. A heterosexual woman is validated for having (or at least wanting) men in her life: the presence of a boyfriend or husband—or even the search for a male partner—confirms that the woman is a "real woman"; that (some) men (sometimes) find her attractive; that, whatever else she might be or feel or think, she is not (so the assumption goes) a "man hater" and therefore beyond the moral pale (even though woman hating is considered a fairly normal part of human civilization). A woman's heterosexuality, visibly demonstrated, shields her from the vicious attacks reserved for non-heterosexual women.

At the same time, heterosexual privilege is coupled with heterosexism, that is, discrimination on grounds of non-heterosexual orientation. Hence, heterosexual privilege has its price: strict conformity to the standards and requirements of heterosexual behaviour and appearance. On the one hand, deviations, even apparent ones, are usually noticed and punished, through verbal and even physical violence, ostracism and the threatened loss of employment, reputation, peace and safety, home, children or financial security. In many instances to be a feminist (regardless of one's sexual activities) is to invite heterosexist vituperation; many people, including some feminists as well as non-feminists, are inclined to regard the word "lesbian" as a dangerous term whose application to oneself undermines one's credibility and acceptability. Yet on the other hand, successful conformity to heterosexual standards of behaviour and appearance may also be painful, and necessitate contortions, self-abasement and continual self-observation in order to regulate one's feelings, speech and behaviour to fit the image of the heterosexual woman. Hence, not only are there tremendous costs for the person who is non-heterosexual, but also the heterosexual woman is in a classic double-bind situation: to avoid the damages of non-conformity, she must incur the damages of conformity. . . .

HETEROSEXUALITY AND CHOICE

In one of my favourite cartoons, a young woman asks her tough and savvy feminist mother, "Ma, can I be a feminist and still like men?" "Sure," replies the mother. "Just like you can be a vegetarian and like fried chicken." When I recounted this joke in an introduction to feminism course, my young female students were disturbed rather than amused. And this is not surprising. To some, the mother's reply may seem to be a reductio ad absurdum of combining feminism and heterosexuality. A good vegetarian, one might think, just does not like fried chicken; or she certainly *ought* not to like it. And if, in a moment of weakness, she does consume fried chicken, then she is either not a good, moral, consistent vegetarian, or, worse still, she is not a vegetarian at all. So also with the feminist. While many of my students hoped that it would be both logically and empirically possible to be a feminist and still like men, or even love them, they also saw considerable tension in being both heterosexual and feminist. Some feminists who love men have expressed both doubt and guilt about the legitimacy of their lives, and some non-heterosexual feminists have encouraged those feelings. . . .

Is, then, a "feminist heterosexuality" possible?[6] To answer that question, it is necessary first to consider the nature of choice. If, as some feminists have argued, heterosexuality in women is coerced, it would seem that no woman chooses to be heterosexual. When there are not several recognized and legitimate options, when there are so many pressures to be heterosexual and when failure to conform is so heavily punished, it is difficult to regard heterosexuality as the genuine expression of a preference. In fact, as one (heterosexual) woman remarked to me, given the damning indictment of heterosexuality that has been presented by some feminists, it might seem that any woman would be heterosexual only if it were *not* a choice.

But this is not all that can be said about the possibility of choosing heterosexuality. For, first, a single-minded focus on the coercive aspects of the heterosexual institution absolves heterosexual women of any responsibility for their sexual practice in a way that seems inappropriate, at least in the case of feminist women, who have had some opportunities to reflect upon the role of heterosexuality in patriarchal oppression. The idea that all heterosexual women (unlike non-heterosexual women) just can't help themselves and are somehow doomed to love and be attracted to men gives too much weight to the view of women as victims, and too little credit to the idea that women can act and make decisions on their own behalf. Moreover, it implicitly imputes to all heterosexual women a sort of false consciousness. Most such women will not see themselves as victims of coercion. Although they may not think of heterosexual practice as a choice they have made, they also do not necessarily feel like helpless victims of the heterosexual institution. But if no woman can choose to be heterosexual, then all heterosexual women either fail to correctly understand their own sexuality, or they can correctly understand their sexuality only by seeing themselves as helpless victims.

On the contrary, I would argue, it is a mistake to summarily dismiss *all* heterosexual women's experience as a failure to understand their own sexuality. Indeed, it is possible that some such women may have actively chosen, rather than fallen into, a life of heterosexual marriage and children . . . and that in their heterosexual relationships, they have control over their own sexuality and share equally in the enjoyment of and participation in their sexual relationships.[7]

I am not saying here only that some heterosexual women may lead exceptional lives in the sense that their relationship with their man (or men) is experienced as egalitarian and uncoercive; I am saying that there is an important sense in which a woman can genuinely and even sanely choose to be heterosexual, although the conditions and opportunities for that choice may be fairly rare. Beyond the claim that heterosexuality is innate (which seems to be an insufficiently grounded essentialist claim) and the claim that heterosexuality is coerced (which seems true in regard to the heterosexual institution as a whole) there is a third possibility: that heterosexuality is or can be chosen, even—or especially—by feminists.

If it is possible to choose *not* to be heterosexual—and most radical feminists have argued that it is—then it is possible to actively choose to be heterosexual. To some degree, each of us is able to make ourselves into the kinds of sexual beings we are, through a process of interpretation and reinterpretation of our past and present experiences and of our feelings and emotions, and through active interaction with other persons, not just passive receptivity to their influence. By choosing one's heterosexuality I mean not merely acquiescing in it, or benefiting from heterosexual privilege, but actively taking responsibility for being heterosexual. Admittedly, most apparently heterosexual women never make, and never have an opportunity to make, such an active conscious choice. In what cases, then, might it be correct to say that a woman has genuinely chosen her heterosexuality? The following remark by Charlotte Bunch provides a crucial insight into the paradoxical answer to that question:

> *Basically, heterosexuality means men first. That's what it's all about. It assumes that every woman is heterosexual; that every woman is defined by and is the property of men. Her body, her services, her children belong to men. If you don't accept that definition, you're a queer—no matter who you sleep with. . . .*[8]

For a heterosexual woman, to start to understand the institution of heterosexuality and the ideology of heterosexism is already to start to leave standard heterosexuality behind. For part of what is customarily meant by the ascription of heterosexuality is its unconscious "perfectly natural" character. Persons who are non-heterosexual never have the luxury of accepting their sexuality in this way. . . .

. . . Marilyn Frye has pointed out that in discussions of sexual prejudice and discrimination one may often hear a statement such as "I don't think of myself as heterosexual"—presumably said by a person who engages in heterosexual activity.[9] Heterosexuals ordinarily extend to others the somewhat dubious privilege of assuming that everyone is like them; since to be sexual is to be *hetero*sexual, "[t]he question often must be *made* to arise, blatantly and explicitly, before the heterosexual person will consider the thought that one is lesbian or homosexual."[10] On the other hand, such persons often perceive non-heterosexuals as being unnecessarily preoccupied with their sexuality, unable to stop talking about it and "flaunting" it to the world. But, Frye suggests:

> *Heterosexual critics of queers' "role-playing" ought to look at themselves in the mirror on their way out for a night on the town to see who's in drag. The answer is, everybody is. Perhaps the main difference between heterosexuals and queers is that when queers go forth in drag, they know they are engaged in theater—they are playing and they know they are playing, heterosexuals usually are taking it all perfectly seriously, thinking they are in the real world, thinking they are the real world.*[11]

The person whose sexual practice is heterosexual and who honestly and innocently states that she does not think of herself as heterosexual shows herself most clearly to be heterosexual in the standard sense. Paradoxically, then, for a woman to firmly and unambiguously affirm her heterosexuality may already begin to leave it behind, that is, to cease to be heterosexual in the unthinking unconscious way she once was: she ceases to participate wholeheartedly in the heterosexual institution, and begins the process of disaffiliation from it.[12] When that sort of reflection takes place, I believe, the woman is beginning genuinely to choose her heterosexuality; and she is choosing heterosexual practice without a concomitant endorsement of the heterosexual institution.

Of course, for such a woman, heterosexuality is still something which is enforced, in Rich's sense; that is, persistent cultural pressures strive to ensure her conformity, and deviance from heterosexuality is penalized, often severely. No amount of awareness of the heterosexual institution can, by itself, change the compulsory nature of heterosexuality, and disaffiliation by one woman will not rock the institution.

Nevertheless, that awareness can make a difference, for the previously unawarely heterosexual woman, in the dimensions of her own sexuality: she can begin the process of shaping her own sexuality, by making decisions and choices based upon an understanding of the power and the limits of the heterosexual institution. For she can explore her own personal history and determine how and when her sense of the erotic became separated from women and connected to men.[13] In so doing, she can no longer regard her heterosexual orientation as something over which she has no power or control, as something which just dominates her sexual feelings and practices. Instead, she can distinguish between sexual passion and attraction, on the one hand, and dependence, need, fear and insecurity on the other. She can become aware of her feelings about women's and men's bodies, and discover whether and/or to what degree she has internalized a socially validated revulsion toward the female body. She can genuinely ask herself whether sexual activity with men is something she wants, or merely something in which she engages. (For, of course, we cannot assume that all women whose sexual practice is heterosexual also enjoy their sexual activities.)

If the answer is no, it is not something she wants, she then has the prospect of choosing to be non-heterosexual. On the other hand, if the answer is yes, she can, in a way, begin to come out as a heterosexual: Not in the heterosexist fashion by which almost all heterosexuals, male and female, ordinarily mark their heterosexuality, but rather in terms of an informed and self-aware feminist evaluation of her life as a heterosexual,[14] renouncing as far as possible the privilege accorded by heterosexuality[15] and recognizing both the different varieties of oppression non-heterosexuals undergo and also the affinities she shares with non-heterosexual women. She can support non-heterosexual women, validate their relationships, and refuse any longer to be complicitous in the erasures they often undergo. She thereby chooses to be heterosexual as a matter of sexual practice, but not as a matter of the exclusive heterosexist alignment or orientation of her life.

Nevertheless, although it may now seem that heterosexuality can be genuinely chosen by women, for some feminists the question may still remain whether it *ought* to be chosen, whether it is ever a good choice, a choice a feminist could responsibly make. Although some heterosexual feminists pride themselves on their "exceptional" heterosexual relationships, relationships which are, apparently, non-oppressive and egalitarian, still, whatever the particular relationship is like, it nonetheless remains *possible* for the man to take advantage of his potential power. All that stands in the way of his using that power is his own good will, while he is not similarly dependent on the woman's good will. And he still benefits, however indirectly, from male hegemony, and "even the advantages that he is in a position to refuse are waiting for him if he changes his mind."[16]

[C]hanging our expectations will [not] by itself change the unequal power relationship. It does not, for instance, change the expectations and behaviour of the man. Neither does it remove the institutional power vested in the male in heterosexual relationships.[17]

Moreover, the woman in such a relationship is still giving her energies very largely to a man, consorting intimately with a member of an oppressor group, and hence, indirectly withholding her energies from a woman. For any woman, heterosexual orientation seems to mean putting men, or at least a man, first. And even while rejecting the heterosexual institution, such a woman also still benefits from heterosexual privilege. Thus, no matter how idyllic her relationship, it seems to fail of its very nature to challenge the status quo, and to reinforce the apparent exclusive loyalty of a woman to her man. Together, the two persons in the relationship still appear to participate in and contribute to the perpetuation of an institution that is oppressive of women, particularly of non-heterosexual women and unattached women of any orientation, as well as of heterosexual women in abusive relationships.[18] And of course having an exceptional relationship does not in any way spare a woman from the worst excesses of the heterosexual institution as they may be visited upon her by men other than her immediate sexual partner(s).

The foregoing observations appear to call into question the *legitimacy* of a woman's deliberately deciding to be heterosexual, and I have only very tentative responses to them. The first involves taking seriously the distinction between the institution of heterosexuality on the one hand, and on the other hand, specific heterosexual relations and the persons who become involved in them. This is the same sort of distinction made by Adrienne Rich in her discussion of motherhood. Rich has urged us to recognize that while motherhood itself is an oppressive institution, mothering particular children may be a delightful, worthwhile, valuable human activity.[19] Similarly, while heterosexuality is an oppressive institution, not all heterosexual relationships are valueless as a result. Glimpsing this possibility might also encourage feminists to make a distinction between what could be called the *institution* of manhood on the one hand and individual men on the other. . . .

. . . [T]his answer, by itself, has of course all the weaknesses of any "individual solution" to problems of oppression. For it depends upon a commitment of the man in the relationship not to avail himself of the power of his position. And so, it must be said, for a woman to actively choose to be heterosexual is an act of faith—faith first of all in the fundamental humanity of the men whom she chooses to love. By actively choosing to be heterosexual, a feminist woman is rejecting the view that male sexuality is inevitably and innately violent and exploitive, and that men are hopelessly fated to engage only in aggressive and oppressive relationships. Although members of the two sexes acquire very different roles, men just as much as women learn to participate in the heterosexual institution. And it is a lesson that men can reject. The heterosexual institution is a social artifact that can be changed, and men themselves may be the allies of women in changing it.

Endnotes

1. *Shorter Oxford English Dictionary*, Addenda (1970), my emphasis.
2. Carole S. Vance and Ann Barr Snitow, "Toward a Conversation about Sex in Feminism: A Modest Proposal," *Signs* 10 (1984) 127.
3. Adrienne Rich, "Compulsory Heterosexuality and Lesbian Existence," in Catharine R. Stimpson and Ethel Spector Person, eds., *Women: Sex and Sexuality* (Chicago: University of Chicago Press 1980) 62–91.
4. Beatrix Campbell, "A Feminist Sexual Politics: Now You See It, Now You Don't," in The Feminist Review, ed., *Sexuality: A Reader* (London: Virago Press 1987) 23.
5. Valverde, 114.
6. The question is taken from the title of Angela Hamblin's article, "Is a Feminist Heterosexuality Possible?," in Sue Cartledge and Joanna Ryan, eds., *Sex and Love: New Thoughts on Old Contradictions* (London: The Women's Press 1983) 105–23.
7. Ann Ferguson, "Patriarchy, Sexual Identity, and the Sexual Revolution," in Nannerl O. Keohane, Michelle Z. Rosaldo, and Barbara C. Geipi, eds., *Feminist Theory: A Critique of Ideology* (Chicago: University of Chicago Press 1982) 159.
8. Charlotte Bunch, "Not for Lesbians Only," in Charlotte Bunch et al., eds., *Building Feminist Theory: Essays from Quest* (New York: Longman 1981) 69.
9. Marilyn Frye, "Lesbian Feminism and the Gay Rights Movement: Another View of Male Supremacy, Another Separatism," in *The Politics of Reality*, 147. Michael Ramberg has pointed out to me that to say "I don't think of myself as heterosexual" could also mean "I am not only heterosexual" or "I will not always be heterosexual."
10. Marilyn Frye, "On Being White: Toward a Feminist Understanding of Race and Race Supremacy," in *The Politics of Reality*, 116, her emphasis.
11. Marilyn Frye, "Sexism," in *The Politics of Reality*, 29, her emphasis.
12. Frye, "On Being White," 127.
13. Marilyn Frye, "A Lesbian Perspective on Women's Studies," in Margaret Cruikshank, ed., *Lesbian Studies: Present and Future* (Old Westbury, NY: The Feminist Press 1982) 197.
14. See Katherine Arnup, "Lesbian Feminist Theory," *Resources for Feminist Research/Documentation sur la recherche feministe* 12 (March 1983) 55.
15. Amy Gottlieb, "Mothers, Sisters, Lovers, Listen," in Maureen Fitzgerald, Connie Guberman, and Margie Wolfe, eds., *Still Ain't Satisfied! Canadian Feminism Today* (Toronto: Women's Press 1982) 238–9.
16. Sara Ann Ketchum and Christine Pierce, "Separatism and Sexual Relationships," in Sharon Bishop and Marjorie Weinzweig, eds., *Philosophy and Women* (Belmont, CA: Wadsworth 1979) 167, 168.

17. Hamblin, 117.
18. See Leeds Revolutionary Feminist Group, "Political Lesbianism: The Case against Heterosexuality," in *Love Your Enemy? The Debate between Heterosexual Feminism and Political Lesbianism* (London: Onlywomen Press 1981) 5–10.
19. Adrienne Rich, *Of Woman Born: Motherhood as Experience and Institution* (New York: Bantam Books 1976).

Moving Beyond "No Means No": Understanding Heterosexual Casual Sex and Consent

Melanie Beres

Melanie Beres is a postdoctoral fellow in the Department of Psychology at the University of Auckland in Aotearoa/New Zealand. Her research interests are in the areas of gender, sexuality and sexual violence. *She wishes to thank SSHRC and the Department of Sociology at the University of Alberta for funding that enabled this research.*

This was a project born out of frustration—frustration with a lack of understanding of "consensual" sex and the ambiguous ways of talking about consent. For me, it seemed counterintuitive that while sexual assault was defined as sex without consent there was so little information regarding how consent is defined and how to understand consensual experiences. There were many debates regarding how to tell if sexual assault has happened, or how to determine if and when there was an absence of consent in the classrooms where I facilitated workshops, and within the legal and sexual violence literature. It struck me as strange that so many discussions were taking place about determining when consent was absent, without any understanding of how to determine if consent is present. In order to develop a thorough understanding of sexually violent and coercive situations, we must also understand sexually non-violent and non-coercive experiences.

This task proved to be more difficult and convoluted than I originally anticipated (and I anticipated it to be quite convoluted). Nicola Gavey (2005) discusses a "complex gray area between what we might think of as mutually consenting sex, on the one hand, and rape or sexual coercion on the other" (p. 136). As a sexual assault educator I believed there was no gray area, that to suggest a gray area was both to deny women the right to speak of certain harmful experiences as violent and to fail to recognize the breadth of sexually violent experiences. Of course, there were times when women regretted having sex, but these experiences fell firmly on the side of consensual sex and were not a concern to me, at least not a concern related to *violence* and *coercion.*

My views have changed considerably since I left my position at the sexual assault centre and all but abandoned my activist work. I am no longer confident that a clear understanding of the division of violence from "consensual" sex is possible, or perhaps even desirable. I am interested in the "spaces in between" consensual and so-called unproblematic sex, and violent or coercive sex, as well as the construction of (women's) sexual desires and willingness to participate in sex, and consent to sex.

THE CONTEXT

Jasper, quiet Canadian mountain town, is the socio-spatial context of my inquiry into heterosexual casual sex and consent: an environment with a reputation as an ideal place to engage in casual sex and as a place where there is a lot of casual sex. In many ways, this context facilitated my access to understandings of casual sex and consent. Due to the open and accepting environment many people were open to talking with me about casual sex, either formally in an interview or informally in a bar or social gathering.

DISCOURSES OF HETEROSEXUAL CASUAL SEX

When negotiating casual sex young adults in Jasper (YAJs) take up subject positions similar to those identified through Hollway's (1984a) description of dominant heteronormative discourses. The male sexual drive discourse is perhaps the most influential in creating the predominant subject positions available to women and men. Men are often positioned as always wanting to engage in casual sex. One participant said it was "inevitable" that he would have casual sex during the summer and another said that any man who says he is not interested in casual sex is lying. . . . Some men were quite active in pursuing casual sex. They looked for women when they were at bars and altered their behaviour in an effort to increase women's interest in them. Other men were less active and talked mostly about experiences when women initiated some contact or when they "just happened" to find a woman they were interested in.

According to Hollway's (1984a) description, women are the objects of the male sexual drive discourse. In Jasper, women often position themselves within the permissive discourse (see Hollway 1984a), where it becomes as acceptable for women as men to engage in casual sex as long as they are participating in, and acting in ways consistent with the male sexual drive discourse. Thus, while it is acceptable for women in Jasper to seek out and initiate casual sex, they cannot be "too" assertive, or take control of the sexual experience, because that is viewed as being too "slutty". Also, it is expected that they participate in male versions of casual sex, meaning that sex includes intercourse. In this way, the male sexual drive discourse is related to what Jackson (1984) refers to as the coital imperative . . .

Women also often position themselves within the have/hold discourse where women are looking to establish lasting and committed relationships. Many women said that one reason why they prefer engaging in sex with other YAJs is because then there is the potential for a relationship to develop. This is consistent with other studies that reported the reasons why women engage in casual sex (see Regan & Dreyer 1999). However, popular ideas about how to begin a relationship with a man often include waiting to have sex, rather than engaging in sex on the first date. This will send the message that you are out to "capture his heart" instead of just out for a night of fun (see Fein & Schneider 1988). Several women I interviewed said that they had a rule that they do not sleep with a man on the first date, waiting at least until the second date; however, this strategy often does not work for them.

In addition to the heteronormative discourses identified by Hollway (1984a) I argue that the YAJs also deployed what I label as the "it just happens" discourse. This discourse suggests that no one is responsible for initiating casual sex; rather there were simply natural urges that take over and result in the couple having sex. . . .

HETEROSEX AND POWER

The radical feminist critique of heterosexuality suggests that heterosexual relations are the primary means by which women's oppression is produced and reinforced (Kitzinger & Wilkinson 1994; Jeffreys 1990; Radicalesbians 1970). Thus, many radical feminists argue that a form of political lesbianism, whereby women forego any and all sexual relationships with men, is the best solution toward ending sexist oppressions. Many feminists see this radical critique of feminism as essentialist and argue that men's patriarchal power is not monolithic, that women can and do have power within heterosexual relations (Allen 2003; Hollway 1984b). The women I spoke with were, with few exceptions, uncritical of the male-dominated discourses of casual sex. They were, however, able to carve out spaces of power; this included choosing partners, limiting and disrupting the masculinist sexual script and taking up the script for their own purposes.

Men and women had the impression that more men than women are interested in engaging in casual sex, even though women in Jasper are viewed as more sexually assertive than women elsewhere. Thus, the impression was that they had a source of power over the men. This echoes some sexual script theorists who argue that women choose when a couple engages in sex (Dworkin & O'Sullivan 2005; Laner & Ventrone 1998; O'Sullivan & Byers 1992; Byers & Heinlein 1989). . . . It is considered unlikely that a man would turn down a woman, while the reverse is considered quite common. The male sexual drive discourse is frequently reproduced and both men and women believe that men do not say no to sex. In some ways men see themselves at the mercy of women who are able to execute a certain level of discretion in choosing men. . . .

Women are aware of the coital imperative and some women report disrupting the script to engage in behaviours other than intercourse to get the sexual activity that they wanted. Some women tell their partners early that they do not want to have sex until they are married and verbally negotiate other forms of sexual activity. Others implied that they are having their period and therefore "cannot" engage in "sex". In order to alter the script and negotiate other forms of sexual activity, it is necessary for women to verbalize their limits early in the interaction to make it clear that intercourse would not take place. One woman subverted the dominant understanding of casual sex in Jasper by taking an active role and a typically "male" subject position. She chose and pursued a man that she was interested in having casual sex with. Thus, women are able to carve out spaces of power within this context dominated by masculine ideals of casual sex and relationships.

However, many of the stories from women echoed stories that Gavey (2005) reported about women's experiences of unwanted sex. Many women are engaging in casual sex without desiring or really wanting it. They desire some sexual activity like kissing and/or cuddling and see having sex as the cost to obtain the sexual contact that they want. For example, some women said that it was sometimes just easier to engage in casual sex than refusing to have sex or that after engaging in certain other sexual behaviours (like groping on the dance floor) sex is expected.

Some women often speak with what Gavey referred to as the "discourse of missing desire". Through their stories, they often do not mention any desire to have casual sex or that they enjoy having sex. Rather, these women speak about having sex because it is expected or because they are looking for a longer romantic relationship with a man.

Through my analysis of the ways that YAJs talk about their casual sex experiences, it is possible to see how power within and control of heterosexual casual sex is not singularly allocated to men or to women. When talking using the "it just happens" discourse men and women both express a lack of control over casual sex, and suggest that the locus of control is located somewhere external to the dyad—in biological drives (for example). The dominant heteronormative discourses outlined by Hollway (1984a) are also operational among YAJs and highlight the way that heterosexual relations are constructed around men's sexual desires and leave little room for female-desired sexual activities. However, within these discourses women locate spaces of power and control.

CONSTRUCTING CONSENT

This project began with a question about the definition of consent, what it is, what it accomplishes and how it is communicated. At the beginning I anticipated developing some sort of understanding of consent in order to answer these questions—something more definitive regarding what consent *is*. Unfortunately (or maybe fortunately) I feel as though I am further away from answering those questions. As an anti-sexual violence activist and educator I placed a large emphasis on the concept of consent as the defining feature of sexual assault. Thus, I felt it was important that people *know* what consent is, and what it is not, in order to communicate more clearly with their partners.

I am no longer convinced that consent is a concept of value in education work or for social understandings of sexualized violence. Understandings of consent seem to be fully embedded within the legal discourse.

Consent's tie to the law and date rape education is also evident in the ways that men and women talk about consent and revert to the "no means no" discourse around date rape. Consent is not a concept that YAJs are thinking about as they engage in casual sex; they do not question consent itself. Instead they are thinking about the comfort level of their partner (although not necessarily out of concern for their partner), wondering what they want to do and trying to have a good time. Thus, consent as a legal concept does not translate into the narratives of YAJs.

GENDERED NATURE OF CONSENT

[S]cholarly conceptions of consent are gendered—authors assume that consent is something women give to men. . . . Overwhelmingly, the women [I interviewed] began by talking about their own willingness and men began by talking about their female partner's willingness to have sex.

This contradicted my understanding of consent and willingness as something that both partners communicate and legal definitions of consent that are gender neutral. . . .

This gendered understanding also reflects the gendered nature of sexual violence. Many more women suffer violence at the hands of men than vice versa. Thus, public awareness campaigns and educational programs focus on women as potential "victims" and men as potential "perpetrators". Women are often taught how to communicate more clearly and assertively while men are taught how to pay attention to women's communication, and to dispel the myth that women "say no" when they mean "yes".

An empirical analysis of gendered practices of consent has not been undertaken in the scholarly literature and this is one of the major contributions of this project. Without explicitly recognizing that consent is often perceived as gendered, education programs have typically taken two approaches to discussing consent: either to discuss it through a legal understanding of consent and thus present it as gender neutral, or to assume a gendered division and talk about how men should read women's consent cues and women can "more assertively" communicate consent, or lack of consent.

By recognizing how consent is gendered both in popular understandings and in practices, it becomes possible to address this assumption within educational programs. Educators can discuss the inadequacy of a gender neutral understanding—it does not reflect hegemonic patriarchal power dynamics that influence sexual relations between women and men (and likely between men and between women). Simultaneously, educators can problematize the gendered assumption of consent and discuss ways of conceptualizing consent that do not reify stereotypical heteronormative discourses.

CONSENT AS THE ABSENCE OF VIOLENCE/COERCION

When I asked YAJs to define consent they most often defined it by the absence of refusal or resistance behaviour. They described ways of refusing or resisting sex and indications that their partner was uncomfortable or did not want sex. These descriptions included not allowing their partner to take their clothes off, withdrawing or becoming tense and saying "no". Thus, sexual violence is defined as its opposite (consent), while sexual consent is also defined as its opposite (resistance). This circular reasoning renders consent almost meaningless as a concept for understanding sexual relations between women and men—sexual violence is then defined as sex when one partner ignores or overcomes the other partner's refusals and resistance behaviours. This is not consistent with the legal definition of consent and is laden with problems that feminist activists have been lobbying to overcome: the resistance requirement.

COMMUNICATING "CONSENT"

So, now I turn my attention to one of the main questions of this project—how do partners know that the other is willing to participate in casual sex? For many YAJs their first inclination was to say that "they just knew", that somehow this knowledge is transmitted to them through "chemistry", telepathy or an innate biological sense. However, upon further probing, most participants were able to articulate subtle cues of communication. This in and of itself is quite important—the participants demonstrated knowledge about the subtle nonverbal behavioural cues and how to read their partner's body language.

Kitzinger and Frith, (1999) argue that men and women are able to understand refusals in everyday contexts and women report refusing sex in ways similar to other types of refusals. Thus, they argue that men should be able to understand sexual refusals. O'Byrne et al. (2006) built on Kitzinger and Frith's argument and demonstrate that men were able to articulate the subtle and conventional ways that women refuse sex. I further this argument by suggesting that men can understand the difference between a refusal and acceptance of sexual activity. Men are able to articulate differences in the ways women behave when they are interested in sex and when they are not interested. These behaviours include breathing, tenseness or relaxedness of a woman's body and the way they participate in the sexual activity. Men expect their partners to actively participate in sex. A lack of active participation is interpreted as an indication of discomfort, in which case they said they slow down, stop, or ask if their partner was "okay".

Women are also able to articulate similar ways of indicating their willingness to participate in casual sex and report many of the same behaviours and cues as did men. Thus, it is likely that men and women are meaning similar things when they discuss "willingness".

Montagna (2000) talked about being an anti-rape educator and working exclusively with men. His initial question to men was how they knew that a woman wanted a kiss:

> *which yields the typical stereotypes of our pop culture: "she looks at you in a certain way," "she moves closer to you," or some intricate combination in which she looks at you, then away, then down, then back at you. The irony is that many men take this as "yes" and never bother to ask what their partner may actually feel like doing. "If all this body language is in place, and you're telling me that you know she wants a kiss," I ask them, "then you have your answer. Where is the risk in asking?" (p. 186)*

The behaviours listed by Montagna (2000) are similar to what I heard male participants saying when I asked them about how they know when a woman is willing to have sex. Montagna argues that this was not good enough and said that the men need to ask. While I fully support initiatives that encourage women and men to communicate more openly with their sexual partners, I am not convinced that this shift is a requirement for ethical and consensual sex. The women and men I spoke with are able to articulate subtle cues used to communicate willingness and they talked about the same cues. This leads me to believe that there is a possibility for a communicative model of sex based on nonverbal cues, that a verbal understanding is not required. However, I am not arguing for a purely nonverbal model of communicative sexuality. Rather I argue that instead of labeling their current communication strategies completely ineffective and attempting to radically change the ways that young people engage in casual sex, educational efforts should build on normative and conventional knowledge that young people already have about consent, and negotiating casual sex. Thus, educators must recognize the types of cues and behaviours that women and men already use to indicate willingness (or consent) to their partner and encourage them to incorporate verbal behaviours into their sexual experiences—especially their casual sex experiences where there may be a greater chance of "miscommunication".

While the prevalence of sexual violence suggests there are serious concerns with heteronormative sexual relationships, I would argue we do not need to radically change the way that people are engaging in sex. Cultural knowledge regarding sexual communication is largely hidden; we seldom talk about how we interpret a partner's behaviours as indications of willingness. Often the most frequently discussed behaviours are public ones (clothing, behaviours in bars). This is unhelpful when it comes down to a sexual interaction and reinforces rape myths. I argue we need to further interrogate the ways that partners communicate sexually and discuss issues related to ethical sex in order to build on the cultural knowledge that is already in existence. By suggesting in the educational workshops given by Montagna (2000) that men do not know how to get consent, men are constructed as irresponsible sexual subjects, which likely creates resistance among workshop participants.

In hindsight, this was also a problem in the workshops I facilitated as coordinator of a sexual assault education program. In these workshops we argued that participants should move to a verbal form of sexual communication. This in itself is not problematic, although implicit in the workshop was the message that their current strategies were irresponsible and immature. This can place the participants in a defensive position, not very conducive to promoting change.

Similarly, Gavey (2005) argues that by instructing women to "say no" in obvious ways we are asking them to act in ways incongruent with norms of everyday conversation. The same could be said for accepting an exclusively verbal negotiation of consent—it contradicts the normative ways of interacting sexually.

Perhaps the problem is that normative and conventional ways of communicating willingness and consent are unclear—at least that is the assumption made by date rape educators and many scholars. I argue that it is not that the communication is unclear and that we need to teach men and women to communicate about sex more overtly, but that we need to learn more about the different ways of communicating consent. I argue that men and women are likely quite aware of the subtle communication patterns; thus we need to start asking tougher questions of those accused of sexual violence and expect them, too, to be able to interpret those cues. It likely is not a miscommunication; it is likely that the men who choose to rape do not want to hear the message and ignore it.

Carmody (2003; 2005) suggests that educators take a sexual ethics approach to date rape education. She found evidence that the adults she interviewed were practicing a sexual ethic, one that resembled Foucault's notion of ethics based on "rapport à soi". She suggests that date rape education should promote ethical ways of interacting, rather than focusing on refusal skills (Carmody 2005). This could be a viable shift and present a way for educators to build on the knowledge and awareness that young people already have about communicating willingness to participate in casual sex, rather than attempting to create major social change and re-write the ways that people engage in casual sex.

In addition to implications for rape prevention education, this study also has legal implications. The Canadian Criminal Code is already progressive and requires that the defendant demonstrate that reasonable steps were taken to ascertain the victim's consent. This study demonstrates that young men and women can articulate and understand a variety of consent cues; thus, these results could be used to help inform standards for determining reasonable steps and for "willful blindness". For example, considering that men and women articulate similar ways of communicating disinterest and interest in sexual activity through subtle body postures, it seems reasonable to incorporate this knowledge into the reasonable steps criteria and expect accused perpetrators to be literate in these communication methods.

CONCLUDING THOUGHTS

This project began as an inquiry focused on consent to heterosexual casual sex. . . . Through this inquiry, I interrogated the ways that dominant heterosexual discourses impact how young workers in Jasper position themselves as active or passive subjects. While these discourses provide greater potential for male power, women produce spaces to exert power over their casual sex experiences. In addition, I questioned how people understand their partner's willingness to participate in casual sex and how they defined consent. Both women and men were able to articulate similar subtle behavioural cues that they use to indicate their willingness to participate in sex. Consent was most often defined in relation to legal discourse and the "no means no" discourse of rape prevention. Consequently, I advocate for a move away from the framework of consent when educating people about sexual violence, and a move towards recognizing the value of their existing knowledge of the normative ways that people accept and refuse sexual activity.

References

Allen, L. (2003). Power talk: Young people negotiating (hetero)sex. *Women's Studies International Forum, 26,* 235–244.

Byers, E.S., & Heinlen, L. (1989). Predicting initiations and refusals of sexual activities in married and cohabitating heterosexual couples. *Journal of Sex Research, 26,* 210–231.

Carmody, M. (2005). Ethical erotics: Reconceptualizing anti-rape education. *Sexualities, 8,* 465–480.

Carmody, M. (2003). Sexual ethics and violence prevention. *Social & Legal Studies, 12,* 199–216.

Dworkin, S. L., & O'Sullivan, L. (2005). Actual versus desired initiation patterns among a sample of college men: Tapping disjunctures within traditional male sexual scripts. *Journal of Sex Research, 42,* 150–158.

Fein, E., & Schneider, S. (1988). *The Rules: Time Tested Secrets for Capturing the Heart of Mr. Right.* New York: Warner Books.

Gavey, N. (2005). *Just Sex? The Cultural Scaffolding of Rape.* New York, NY: Routledge.

Hollway, W. (1984a). Gender difference and the production of subjectivity. In J. Henriques, W. Hollway, C. Urwin, C. Venn and V. Walkerdine (eds.) pp. 227–263. *Changing the Subject: Psychology, Social Regulation and Subjectivity.* New York: Routledge.

Hollway, W. (1984b). Women's power in heterosexual sex. *Women's Studies International Forum, 7,* 63–68.

Jackson, M. (1984). Sex research and the construction of sexuality: A tool of male supremacy? *Women's Studies International Forum, 7,* 43–51.

Jeffreys, S. (1990). *Anticlimax: A Feminist Perspective on the Sexual Revolution.* New York: New York University Press.

Kitzinger, C., & Frith, H. (1999). Just say no? The use of conversation analysis in developing a feminist perspective on sexual refusal. *Discourse & Society, 10,* 293–316.

Kitzinger, C., & Wilkinson, S. (1994). Virgins and queers: Rehabilitating heterosexuality? *Gender & Society, 8,* 444–462.

Laner, M. R., & Ventrone, N. A. (1998). Egalitarian Daters/Traditionalist Dates. *Journal of Family Issues, 21,* 488–500.

Montagna, S. (2000). Men-only spaces as effective sites for education and transformation in the battle to end sexual violence. In J. Gold, & S. Villari (eds.) pp. 181–188. *Just Sex: Students Rewrite the Rules on Sex, Violence, Activism, and Equality.* Lanham: Rowman & Littlefield Publishers Inc.

O'Byrne, R., Rapley, M., & Hansen, S. (2006). "You couldn't say 'no', could you?": Young men's understandings of sexual refusal. *Feminism & Psychology, 16,* 133–154.

O'Sullivan, L., & Byers, E. S. (1992). College students' incorporation of initiator and restrictor roles in sexual dating interactions. *Journal of Sex Research, 29,* 435–446.

Radicalesbians (1970). *The Woman Identified Woman.* Retrieved May 13, 2006 from www.carnap.umd.edu/queer/radicalesbian.htm

Regan, P. C., & Dreyer, C. S. (1999). Lust? Love? Status? Young adults' motives for engaging in casual sex. *Journal of Psychology & Human Sexuality, 11,* 1–24.

Desire as Interruption: Young Women and Sexuality Education in Ontario, Canada

Erin Connell

Erin Connell is a PhD candidate in the Department of Sociology, Carleton University. Her dissertation explores the dominant and contested strategies of Canadian school-based sex education.

INTRODUCTION

Danger and pleasure are terms commonly employed to describe women's experiences of sexuality. Women are at risk for dangers such as sexual violence and coercion, unintended pregnancy and sexually transmitted infections (STIs). Expectations of a compulsory heterosexuality support a double standard of female passivity and male aggression and dominance. Within a master narrative of romance, men are characterized as active subjects with a natural and biologically given desire, and women are both the objects of and in need of protection from this desire. "Bad girls", who risk acquiring a reputation of promiscuity because they experience desire and pleasure, are posited against "good girls", who do not.

Discourses concerned with female desire, agency and subjectivity exist alongside, and sometimes successfully challenge, these dangers, particularly when framed as women's rights and/or human rights. Indeed, the "sexual liberation" of the 1960s resulted in the mass distribution and legal access to the pill, the intra-uterine device and abortion services; more family formation options due to liberalized divorce laws and increasing cohabitation among couples; and a freedom that school and employment offered women in order to experiment sexually (McLaren 1999). The women's movement provided women with the opportunity to discuss and explore the "myth of the vaginal orgasm" as well as female sexual pleasure and danger in consciousness-raising groups. The gay rights movement afforded greater visibility to lesbians and same-sex desire. While the sexual liberation has been described as not fully liberating women (see Hawkes 1996; McLaren 1999), spaces were created, nonetheless, for women to negotiate their sexualities within this dialectic of danger and pleasure.

The danger and pleasure of women's sexual lives are particularly organized according to class, race, ethnicity and culture. A woman's age is also critical. In fact, young women are acutely aware of the dangers and pleasures that shape their sexual lives, as recent ethnographies demonstrate.

In her interviews with young women in both urban and suburban schools, Tolman (2002) described the "sounds of silence" of young girls who avoided addressing the dilemma of desire by simply not having desire; the "dangers of desire" due to the "good girl"/"bad girl" dichotomy; the institution of heterosexuality and master narrative of romance; and the "parameters of pleasure" in which some girls expressed entitlement to sexual desire, although this desire was mired and complicated by the preceding sociocultural barriers. Very few girls in her study staked unapologetic claims to their desire. The dilemma of desire is that girls were aware "of the power, pleasure and possibility embedded in their sexual desire, [but also] feel acutely vulnerable to its dangers" (Tolman 2002, p. 115).

A central concern of this paper is how young women's sexual danger and desire are represented and characterized in official discourses, specifically those of school-based sexuality education. Drawing on Michelle Fine's (1988) four major discourses of sexuality education, I will argue that discourses of victimization and individual morality dominate in the Ontario sexuality education curriculum, while the discourse of desire is largely absent. As such, there is considerable emphasis on danger and insufficient attention paid to pleasure/desire.

FOUR MAJOR DISCOURSES OF SEXUALITY EDUCATION

In her article "Sexuality, schooling, and adolescent females: The missing discourse of desire", Michelle Fine (1988) describes four major discourses of sexuality that characterize national debates over sex education and inform how sexuality is managed in schools.

The first discourse, sexuality as violence, is the most conservative discourse. It equates adolescent heterosexuality with violence, such as abuse, incest, AIDS and coercion, and presumes a causal relationship between official silence about sexuality and a decrease in sexual activity. Proponents of this discourse call for the elimination of sex education and clinics, and urge a complete reliance on the family to dictate appropriate values, mores and behaviour.

The second discourse, sexuality as victimization, emphasizes the need for young women to learn of their vulnerability to potential male predators and the subsequent need to defend themselves against disease, pregnancy and "being used". Females are victims of male desire: males are portrayed as potential predators while females are portrayed as victims. Within this discourse, sex education includes practicing how to say no as well as an emphasis on abstinence, the risks of sex and diseases associated with sex. Proponents of this discourse support sex education with parental consent.

The third discourse, sexuality as individual morality, emphasizes the value of young women's decision-making as long as decisions made are for premarital abstinence and chastity. Within this discourse, sex is a test of self-control and self-respect: individual restraint triumphs over social temptation. Non-interventionists call for the elimination of school-based sex education. Interventionists believe schools should offer sex education by focusing on "good values", although there is no consensus on what comprises "good values"—it varies from sexual restraint to correct and consistent condom use.

While the former three discourses emphasize danger, the fourth discourse is the discourse of desire. The discourse of desire is, according to Fine, largely absent from school-based sexuality programs. Naming desire, pleasure and sexual entitlement (especially that of women) barely exists in the formal agenda of school-based sex education and, if spoken, is immediately followed up with the reminder of consequences. Fine advocates a genuine discourse of desire, and while desire is a complex object that can invoke multiple understandings and meanings, what is key in this discourse is the ability for adolescents to explore what feels good and bad, desirable and undesirable, and grounded in experiences, needs and limits. It would also release females from positions of receptivity—women would be subjects of sexuality, as well as initiators and negotiators. Such a discourse would enable an analysis of the dialectics of victimization/danger and pleasure/desire.

DISCOURSES IN THE ONTARIO CURRICULUM

After assessing the Ontario curriculum and companion Course Profiles, discourses of victimization and individual morality dominate Ontario school-based sexuality education. In fact, they not only dominate, but also mutually reinforce each other.

The term "abstinence", defined in the Ontario Curriculum as "a conscious decision to refrain from sexual intercourse", is first introduced in the Grade 7 curriculum with the following learning outcome: "Students will explain the term abstinence as it applies to healthy sexuality". Building on this, Grade 8 students "will explain the importance of abstinence as a positive choice for adolescents". In Grade 9, "students will describe the relative effectiveness of methods of preventing pregnancies and sexually transmitted diseases [STDs] (e.g. abstinence, condoms, oral contraceptives)" and "will describe the factors that lead to responsible sexual relationships". Similarly, in Grade 10, "students will explain the effects (e.g. STDs, HIV/AIDS) of choices related to sexual intimacy (e.g. abstinence, using birth control)" and "demonstrate understanding of how to use decision-making skills effectively to support choices related to responsible sexuality". Abstinence is presented as a responsible, healthy and positive choice for adolescents. Decision-making is promoted and valued "so long as decisions made are for premarital abstinence" (Fine 1988, p.32). This discourse of individual morality is reinforced with the discourse of victimization—if you make an irresponsible, unhealthy choice, if you do have sex, there will be negative consequences.

Concern regarding the consequences of sexual intercourse is first introduced in the Grade 8 curriculum, where students will "identify symptoms, methods of transmission, prevention, and high-risk behaviours related to common STDs, HIV, and AIDS", "identify methods used to prevent pregnancy" and "apply living skills (e.g. decision-making, assertiveness, refusal skills) in making informed decisions, analyse the consequences of engaging in sexual activities and using drugs". In Grade 9, students are expected to "explain the consequences of sexual decisions on the individual, family, and community" and "demonstrate understanding of how to use decision-making and assertiveness skills effectively to promote human sexuality (e.g., healthy human relationships, avoiding unwanted pregnancies and STDs such as HIV/AIDS)". Grade 10 students will "explain the strategies to promote positive lifestyle choices and relationships with others" and "explain the effects (e.g., STDs, HIV/AIDS) of choices related to sexual intimacy (e.g., abstinence, using birth control)". In Grade 11, students will "demonstrate an understanding of sexual and reproductive health" by exhibiting "an understanding of causes and issues related to infertility". In this case, sexual intercourse is framed as a high-risk behavior with serious consequences: STDs, HIV/AIDS, unintended pregnancy and infertility. "Assertiveness" and "refusal skills" are mechanisms for affirming abstinence and positive lifestyle choices. Adolescents are responsible to their families and communities for their sexual decisions: "the language of self-control and self-respect reminds students that sexual immorality breeds not only personal problems but also community...burdens" (Fine 1988, p.32).

This emphasis on abstinence and the negative consequences of sex within discourses of victimization and individual morality is also reflected in the Course Profiles. Activity 4: Understanding Sexuality Choices and Decisions, in the Grade 10 Course Profile, is an activity about responsible choices and irresponsible choices. The most responsible choices are abstinence and reaffirming abstinence. "Abstainers" demonstrate their trustworthiness and self-control and maintain/reestablish their self-esteem, which is particularly gendered, since it is only sexually active females who "lose" their self-esteem and reputation. In addition, the "effects of saying yes" are all negative—the emphasis is on loss, stress and risk, while pleasure, fun and satisfying curiosity are absent from the discussion. Even the discussion concerning "safer sex" (e.g. using contraception and/or STD prevention) excludes any acknowledgement of pleasure or fun—the use of condoms is described as reducing spontaneity and sensitivity—and is presented solely within a context of responsibility. Similarly, the list of "alternative forms of sexual expression" (non-penetrative sexual activities) is limited to "kissing, hugging, holding hands, touching/massage". What about discussing a broader range of sexual choices and behaviours that may include heavy/deep kissing, masturbation, mutual masturbation, fantasy and oral sex? Desire and pleasure are entirely absent and the focus is one of danger, responsibility and self-control. "In the absence of a way to talk about passion, pleasure, danger, and responsibility, [teachers] fetishize the latter two, holding the former two hostage...the separation is false, judgmental, and ultimately not very educational' (Fine 1988, p.38).

In addition to the emphasis on abstinence and consequences of sex, discourses of victimization and individual morality are also evident in the way gender roles are reproduced:

> *Dawn has been dating an older boy from another school for almost two months. He is very popular and has a reputation for being sexually active with many girls. Dawn knows that they are at a point in their relationship when she has to make a decision regarding whether she wants to be intimate with him. (Case study, Grade 9 Course Profile)*
>
> *Gurpreet is fifteen and is very curious about sex. Her cultural background prohibits sexual intercourse prior to marriage. Her boyfriend, Jassal, has been pressuring her to have sex, and says that he will wear a latex condom. Gurpreet finally agrees. (Case study, Grade 10 Course Profile)*
>
> *Hamid and Jamie are both in their third year of high school and have been dating for four weeks. They have spent most of their dates talking about their families, school, sports, and worldwide events. Currently, their sexual relationship has involved kissing. Hamid believes that they are ready for more acts of sexual intimacy but Hamid has never talked about this with Jamie. When he begins to express himself, he simply begins touching Jamie. She does not feel comfortable with this. Jamie stops his advances and expresses that she feels they are not ready to go any further. Hamid does not understand why she feels this way, as he thought she felt the same way as he did. He moves away and becomes quiet. (Case study, Grade 12 Course Profile)*

These case studies illustrate very gender-specific roles and expectations in intimate relationships. Boys gain popularity with sexual experiences, are curious about sex, put pressure on girls for sex and emotionally withdraw if girls refuse sexual advances. Girls are uncomfortable when it comes to sex and only reluctantly agree to sex. The only girl who is curious about sex in these case studies is Gurpreet but her cultural background prescribes limits and restrictions on her desire. In summary, these case studies reinforce the message that boys are active agents and "studs" with an insatiable appetite for sex, while girls are passive, uninterested in sex and only submit to it under pressure. Boys have desire and girls do not. Indeed, "...female adolescents continue to be educated as though they were potential *victims* of sexual (male) desire" (Fine 1988, p.42). And "what results is a discourse of sexuality based on the male in search of desire and the female in search of protection...a forum for the primacy of male heterosexuality and the preservation of female victimization" (Fine 1988, p. 40). These rigid and stereotyped gender roles are detrimental to the sexual subjectivities of adolescent females. Young women are educated away from positions of sexual self-interest (Fine 1988) because they are the objects and potential victims of someone else's desire. As a result, young men secure certain gains through such subjectivities—sexual desire in males is deemed normal and natural, and males assume a sense of entitlement to sex. But I would also argue that young men suffer from this mis-education. These gendered expectations put enormous pressure on young men to be initiators of sexual activity, while accusing young men of being sexually aggressive is not only detrimental to their self-esteem, but also poses an "anxiety about whether they are behaving within the ethical parameters of what is wrong or right conduct for their putative sexual identities" (Stoltenberg 1989, p. 14).

Finally, discourses of victimization and individual morality are enforced not by what is said, but in what is silenced. Fine (1988) refers to silencing as "a systematic refusal to name issues, particularly issues that cause adults discomfort" (p. 38). There are some clear silences in the Ontario curriculum that include: options for unintended pregnancy, sexual orientation and sexual behaviour.

In 2000, 12 754 Ontario teenagers became pregnant and 7 277 of these pregnancies ended in abortion (Statistics Canada, 2004). However, unintended pregnancy and options for unintended pregnancy (such as abortion) are entirely absent from the curriculum. This not only fails to address the lived realities of a significant portion of young people, but it also fails to acknowledge, in the context of abstinence messaging, how not all young people "just say no" to sex.

Similarly, sexual orientation is absent from the curriculum. It can be argued that with its abstinence (from penile–vaginal sex), consequences (of penile–vaginal sex) and gendered emphasis, the Ontario curriculum supports a (hetero)sex education. Although educators are warned in the Planning Notes of the Grade 10 Course Profile to "be sensitive to differences in sexual orientation" and "be sensitive to the variety of relationships and family structures which exist in society", sexual orientation is not part of the curriculum. In fact, the foundation for a compulsory heterosexuality is established in the Grade 7 curriculum: "students will describe age-appropriate matters related to sexuality (e.g., the need to develop good interpersonal skills, *such as the ability to communicate effectively with the opposite sex*)" (emphasis added). As a result, the silence surrounding abortion options and diversity in sexual orientations denies adolescents information and sends the message that such conversations are taboo (Fine 1988, p. 39).

Finally, a very narrow range of sexual choices and behaviours is described in the curriculum. "Responsible" adolescents will choose abstinence and consider only the following alternative forms of sexual expression: kissing, hugging, holding hands, touching/massage. While these activities can be very sexual, and touching/massage could mean mutual masturbation, such specific language is not used.

With the emphasis on victimization and individual morality, this is "desire as interruption" and evidence of a "discourse of desire that fades rapidly into the discourse of disease" (Fine 1988). The reliance on discourses of victimization and individual morality emphasize the dangers of adolescent sexuality. The discourse of desire is typically not represented in the Ontario curriculum.

This is not to say, however, that implementing a discourse of desire is impossible or unrealistic. Fine states that:

> *In order to understand the sexual subjectivities of young women more completely, educators need to reconstruct schooling as an empowering context in which we listen*

> *to and work with the meanings and experiences of gender and sexuality revealed by the adolescents themselves . . . by providing education, counseling, contraception and abortion referrals, as well as meaningful educational and vocational opportunities, public schools could play an essential role in the construction of the female subject—social and sexual. (1988, pp. 36, 50)*

The acknowledgement of these political and educational contexts is critically important in fostering the social and sexual subjectivity of adolescent girls (and boys, as well, I would argue). Clearly, there needs to be a paradigm shift in the actual content of sexuality education. While it is important to provide information to young people about the dangers and possible negative consequences of sexual activity and to present abstinence as an option, it is equally important to focus on the positive and pleasurable "consequences" of sexual activity. In summary, we must put the sex back into sex education. We should encourage adolescents to explore non-goal-oriented sex (e.g., non-penetrative sex) and sexual self-exploration within their experiences, needs and limits. We need to talk about like, love and lust with adolescents. We need to talk about orgasms, pleasure, thoughts, feelings, sexual expectations and desires. We also need to discuss the sociocultural forces that shape and constrain sexuality and sexual subjectivity. We need to deconstruct gender, gender expectations and gender roles, and foster the subjectivity and agency of both adolescent females and males. We need to challenge compulsory heterosexuality in order to recognize the lived realities of all young people. We need to talk about *both* victimization/danger and pleasure/desire.

For example, Johnson (2002) describes queer heterosexuality, which "entertains wider possibilities for rearranging romance [that] may appeal to the men and women of Generation X more than traditional notions of romance or feminist rejections of it" (p. 48). Queer heterosexuality could be comprised of less restrictive gender roles; non-reproductive sexuality, justified by pleasure alone; recognition of pleasure as a fundamental human need; recognition of heterosexuality as one relationship configuration among many, not the norm; total body integrity for both partners; and non-coital, non-penis-centred eroticism and sex.

And in discussing sexual readiness, we must do more than encourage adolescents to "just say no". In her discussion of girls' sexual readiness, Thompson (1990) explains how young women need an erotic education and that they should be encouraged to ask themselves the following questions:

- Do you get wet when you have a romance or sexual daydream? When you think about kissing or petting? Do your genitals become warm or feel pleasure?
- Do you know where your clitoris is? Have you touched it? Excited it?
- Are you sexually excited when you and your prospective lover are together or making out? Do you have an idea of what an orgasm is? Have you visualized or imagined what it will be like to be naked with someone? To kiss or pet without clothes on? Have you tried it?
- Have you touched your breasts and genitals?
- Have you touched yourself inside?
- If you are considering having intercourse, have you imagined what penetration may feel like?
- Have you looked into the various forms of birth control? Obtained one? Tried using it? Talked with your friends about their experiences?

- Does the idea of having sex with the person you are considering it with excite you?
- Do you think your prospective lover will take the time to pleasure, or learn how to pleasure, you? Stop whatever he or she is doing if you insist? Continue until you want to stop?

From a curriculum perspective, these frameworks could help shape discussions on relationships, communication, decision-making, sexual and gender identity and "safer sex" practices. Moreover, including a "discourse of erotics", a "personal discourse of emotional and bodily feelings concerning desire and attraction and how these were acted upon, as well as what sexual activity was like and how it was engaged in" (Allen 2001, p. 114) is consistent with the type of discussion that interests and motivates young people (Allen 2001, p.118). As such, the inclusion of a discourse of erotics might aid in bridging the knowledge/practice gap—the gap between what young people learn in sexuality education and what they do in practice (Allen 2001, p. 120).

References

Allen, L. (2001) Closing the sex education's knowledge/practice gap: The reconceptualisation of young people's sexual knowledge, *Sex Education*, 1, 109–122.

Fine, M. (1988) Sexuality, schooling, and adolescent females: The missing discourse of desire, *Harvard Educational Review*, 58, 29–53.

Hawkes, G. (1996) *A sociology of sex and sexuality* (Philadelphia, Open University Press).

Johnson, M. L. (2002) Fuck you and your untouchable face: Third wave feminism and the problem of romance, in: M. L. Johnson (Ed) *Jane sexes it up: True confessions of feminist desire* (New York, Four Walls Eight Windows).

McLaren, A. (1999) *Twentieth century sexuality* (Blackwell, Oxford).

Statistics Canada (2004) *Teenage pregnancy, by outcome and age group, count and rate per 1,000 women aged 15 to 19, Canada, provinces and territories, 1998–2000.* Available online at: www.statcan.ca/englishlfreepub/82-22 1-XIE/00604/tables/html/41 1.htm (accessed 9 November 2002).

Stoltenberg, J. (1989) *Refusing to be a man: Essays on sex and justice* (Portland, Breitenbush Books).

Isn't Love a Given?

Lee Maracle

Lee Maracle is a Native Canadian writer whose work is unparalleled in its creativity and scope. Through novels, poetry, drama, performance art and storytelling, she exposes and explores the experience of Aboriginal peoples in Canada. Her work re-imagines centuries-old myth and tradition for future generations, and reflects her antipathy toward sexism, racism and white cultural domination. A graduate of Simon Fraser University, Maracle has held numerous distinguished academic posts, including the Stanley Knowles Visiting Professor in Canadian Studies at the University of Waterloo, the Distinguished Professor of Canadian Culture at Western Washington University, and Writer in Residence at the University of Guelph. She is currently Associate Professor in the Department of English at the University of Toronto, Writer in Residence for the university's Aboriginal Studies Programme, and Traditional Cultural Director for the Indigenous Theatre School.

I am appalled by the fact that I have been asked on numerous occasions to state my position on the question of women and lesbianism. What really appalls me is that the person thinks that I ought to take a position on the sacred right of women to love and be loved. Isn't love a given?

But if I am appalled at being asked, I am doubly appalled and shamed by the fact that the question needs to be answered. We have not come a long way, baby. The prohibition of women's right to choose is all-encompassing in North America. It is the most deep-seated bias in the history of class society. Racism is recent; patriarchy is old.

Colonization for Native women signifies the absence of beauty, the negation of our sexuality. We are the females of the species: "Native," undesirable, non-sensuous beings that never go away. Our wombs bear fruit but are not sweet. For us intercourse is not marked by white, middle-class, patriarchal dominant-submissive tenderness. It is more a physical release from the pressure and pain of colonialism—mutual rape. Sex becomes one more of the horrors of enslavement, driving us to celibacy. The greater the intellectual paralysis, the more sex is required and the more celibacy is desired.

Does this seem incongruous? Yes, but so are paralysis and movement.

Our life is lived out schizophrenically. Our community desires emancipation. The greater the desire, the more surely do we leap like lemmings into the abyss of alcoholism, violence and suicide. We cannot see our enemy, but we know we must have one. We are standing at the precipice of national destruction.

Women kid themselves that traditionally we were this way or that way. In the name of tradition we consent to all kinds of oppressive behaviour from our men. How often have we stood in a circle, the only female Native, and our contributions to the goings-on are not acknowledged?—as though we were invisible. We are the majority of the membership of almost every Native organization at the lowest level, the least heard and never the leaders. It is not for want of our ability to articulate our goals or lead folks, either. We have been erased from the blackboard of our own lives.

What pains me is that I never saw this before. How often do we read in the newspaper about the death or murder of a Native man, and in the same paper about the victimization of a female Native, as though we were a species of sub-human animal life? A female horse, a female Native, but everyone else gets to be called a man or a woman. (I will qualify this by saying that I do not recall the death of a black woman ever being reported. Gawd, Cj, let's hope it is because no black woman ever died on skid row. But we know different, don't we?)

I have been to hundreds of meetings where the male members demand written submissions from female members while giving themselves the benefit of collective discussion and team development prior to any attempt to write it up, thus helping male speakers to sharpen their ideas. Worse, I have watched the chairperson sit and listen to an endless exchange between two male colleagues while a patient woman holds her hand in the air, waiting to be recognized.

It doesn't stop there. This anti-woman attitude by Native males seems to be reserved for Native women. The really big crime is that our men-folk rise when a white woman walks into the room. Native men go to great lengths to recognize her, and of course, where there is controversy, her word is very often the respected one.

We must and will have women leaders among us. Native women are going to raise the roof and decry the dirty house that patriarchy and racism have built on our backs. But first we must see ourselves as women: powerful, sensuous beings in need of compassion and tenderness.

Please bear with me while I try to unravel the tangled roots of this bias against love and choice. We must try to look at why women reject women's rights to choose, and understand why women treat the love between women as some sort of leprous disease that is contagious. I cannot write for women who love women; so far, the only lovers in my life have been men. I can address the feelings of homophobia that preclude our ability to accept lesbians among us.

Homosexuality has been named abnormal. If love were a matter of mathematics, averages and so forth, then that would be a fitting way to look at it, since the majority of us are heterosexual. However, love is a thing of the spirit. It finds its major expression through the heart and body. Since contemporary society is based largely on the economics of class and power, norms and mathematics usually prevail. The nature of love, its spiritual, emotional and physical origins are never considered in the white, male point of view.

When men talk about love between people of the same sex as abnormal, they are not referring to love at all, but to sex. Since we are speaking about love, we will have to ignore the male viewpoint. When women refer to women who love women as unnatural, what they really mean—and this is pathetic—is that it is almost unheard of, and, they agree, it is not allowed. Men loving women is almost unheard of: does its scarceness make it abnormal, unnatural? Any love women can garner for themselves will appear unnatural if women are generally unloved.

Nowhere in the white, male conception of history has love been a motive for getting things done. That is unnatural. They can't see love as the force which could be used to move mountains, change history or judge the actions of people. Love/spirit is seen as a womanly thing and thus is scorned. Women love their sons but men influence, direct and control them. Women love their husbands; men provide for women in exchange for a stable home and conjugal rights and that ever-nurturing womanly love. Men scorn love. We are expected not only to accept this scorn in place of love, but to bear untold suffering at the hands of men. That there is violence in North American homes is taken for granted: "Everyone knocks the wife around once in a while." And does anyone want to admit that very often after a beating on a drunken Friday, a woman is expected to open up to further scorn by moaning and groaning happy sounds while the man who beat her helps himself to her body?

Have you ever heard a man honestly admit that a woman's fear, her surrendering as a result of having been intimidated, excites and arouses him? Rape, ladies and gentlemen, is commonplace in the home. In the home, it is not a crime. What is worse, in our desperate fear of being unloved, a good many women plea for mercy and accept responsibility for the beating and beg forgiveness for imaginary transgressions. Could this be where men get the idea that women "like it, ask for it" when the subject of rape is discussed?

To be quite frank, my friends, if that is how we feel about ourselves, then it is quite likely that we are going to be vitriolic about women who are not victimized in the same way. A woman who has found love apart from men is seen as a traitor, just as a woman who has found the love of a gentle man is seen as undeserving. He, of course, must be a wimp—pussy-whipped. In our society it is loving women that is prohibited.

Sexuality is promoted as the end-all and be-all of womanhood, yet perversely it is often a form of voluntary rape: self-deprecation and the transformation of women into vessels of biological release for men. Our bodies become vessels for male gratification, not the means by which we experience our own sexual wonderment. Any other sexuality is considered abnormal and to be derided. White women spend a lifetime striving for the beauty of large breasts, a small waist, clear skin and that practiced look of submissive stupidity that indicates they will quietly acquiesce to brutal sex.

A woman close to myself and my lover left her husband not too long ago. He beat her on a regular basis for some fifteen years. Between beatings, she told us that he would get on top of her and without ever looking at her, relieve himself of sexual tension. Over the years, she was never sure if, every time he had sex, she had volunteered herself for rape. That is the kind of story I have heard over and over again just too frequently. It is the kind of sex that is going on in too many homes of the nation.

How many women on Saturday night face beer-breathed husbands in the darkness of their rooms, saying, "Please, no," to men who carry on without their consent? They don't scream because they would awaken their own children. Marriages end over a woman's right to say no in her own bedroom. The law says she must allow her husband conjugal rights. This amounts to reducing women's bodies to soft knots in deformed trees.

Divorce alone gives a woman the right to deny her husband rutting privileges on his terms. We certainly cannot go beating our husbands as they do us. We are not usually their physical equals. Before the shame of colonization caught up to us and our men-folk started behaving like lesser white men (the more brutish type), Native men used to respond to flirting from women. Some still do. We used to believe that men responded to women, naturally. We also believed that choice was sacred, and that women were sexually passionate beings. We had better get back to some of the traditions that kept us human.

Nearly every woman in North America, particularly if she is a woman of colour, knows that vacant look of a man who is "getting his rocks off," that phrase unspoken in polite company. Men say it to each other more often than anyone cares to face. The very thing we never bring up in mixed company is that basically men take great pride in referring to sex in just that way: "getting your rocks off," "changing your oil," etc. For those of you who think that feminism or women's liberation has brought about a change in this attitude, just go to a leftist social event and bring up the subject of fucking. There is no way to clear a room more quickly than to ask a man if he "got his rocks off much in high school." He will squirm and deny that he ever put it quite that way. If he merely squirms, like as not he was one of the boys who listened to other boys talking like that on the high school football field and laughed. If he squirms and turns red, he is lying.

Homophobes are quick to vilify love between women because the idea of women loving each other is diametrically opposed to volunteering yourself up for rape. The danger of women who love women, in the decrepit minds of patriarchal males, is that men may be challenged to love women too. No more "getting your rocks off." No more venting your frustrations on your wife. If you've got a problem you'll have to solve it.

What else is there? Some man will have to answer that question. I am not about to help you to be more human; I have enough trouble doing that for myself. It is hard enough to reach inside myself and find my own humanity without carrying your load too.

I didn't always feel that way, as my friend Cj commented:

The Servant

Lee, you make me hysterical
yes, you do
this white man wants to be served
and you trot out your daisy apron
and serve him
in his own language!

Listen to the tone of the women who curse "Damn dyke!" It is filled with resentment and laced with a very mysterious kind of awe. You just know that "Who does she think she is?" follows closely on the heels of that first epithet. If we accept brutal sex as the best we can get, the norm, then naturally we are going to hate women who love women and don't have to put up with the violence that degrades most women in North America. Hate is itself perverse and so of course we get even by referring to dykes and faggots as diseased or mind-sick individuals.

Even the feminist movement has a hard time with love. I have heard it said that lesbianism is "women identifying with women." I admit I am at a loss for words that would embrace the very intimate love between two people who happen to be women. I am at a loss as to how to describe it as anything other than love between Sue and Carol, or whoever they happen to be. But calling it "women identifying with women" feels like a misnomer. Sex, love, intimacy are not about identification, they are bigger, deeper and broader than that. I am at a greater loss to describe the phenomenon here in North America where lesbianism has become a liberating force, as though it were an alternative to love. Having the freedom [to] love, be loved, determine the nature of the physical expression of that love, the power to name it, govern it, is liberating, whether the person you enjoy this freedom with is the same sex as you or different from you. It is just as powerful to enjoy the freedom to love with a man as it is with a woman. What is lacking for all women is the absolute right to be cherished and the absolute freedom to govern our love's expression.

All of our conversations about women who have women lovers are couched in terminology which escapes my comprehension: homosexuality, heterosexuality, lesbianism, homophobia. . . . I have a very simple and straightforward philosophy, learned from my grandmother: "In the end, granddaughter, our body is the only house we will ever truly own. It is the one thing we truly own. . . . What is more, in the end, command of it will only amount to the sacred right of choice."

From my grandmother's words I understand that there is human sexuality, a biological need for sex, and there is love. (All those who are easily embarrassed can put the book down.) Sex is sex. Sex and love are not the same thing and they are not equal. Sex is the one thing that we can enjoy completely on our own. (I suspect that good many women do just that.) Few other animals have the wherewithal to gratify themselves sexually quite like we do. We do not need a partner or lover to have sex. When you upgrade sex to the level of love, you erase love completely.

When someone says she is a lesbian she is saying that her sexual preference is toward women. She is not saying that she does not like or love men. I have heard from women that so-and-so was bitter about her marriage so she went gay. It sounds so dangerously logical and absurd at the same time. It's as though "gay" were some place women go as opposed to, say, "shopping," and that there are only two attitudes women can have toward men, bitter and not bitter. Those who are bitter go gay and those who are not go shopping. The danger of the logic is that rather than respecting women as beings, it consigns them to going toward men or away from the men. It accepts that men and our attitudes toward them determine our sexual being. We get all tangled up in the web of our own misunderstanding and then ascribe that colossal ignorance to someone else.

Sex can sometimes go hand-in-hand with love. If it does, so much the better. But it is not necessary to be in love to enjoy sex. When I first said that in public, an indignant, uncoupled woman said, "Well, sex and love have to go together." I responded brutally:

"Yes, I am going to fuck my mother, my father, my sister, my daughters and all my friends." She didn't mean that.

What she thought is that women cannot have sex without love. Nonsense. I once went to a bar, looked around the room, saw a nice smile with a reasonable male body attached to it, walked over to the table and sat down. After a beer I grabbed hold of the gentleman's arm and let him know that any more of that stuff might impair his performance. To which he responded, "Are you interested in my performance?" I had hold of his hand already so I just nodded. "Why are we still here then?"

We left. The sex was not bad. There was no love, no illusions whatsoever, just the two of us rutting and being gratified.

Sex is good but love is precious. It is our passion and compassion. Love defines our humanity. Focussed, love binds two people together in a relationship that can be lifelong. If we truly loved ourselves as women, the question of who we choose to engage with sexually would be irrelevant. Let us stop elevating rutting to the position of defining our humanity. Despite the pressure of sexually oriented billboards and TV ads, let us stop placing fucking on a plane alongside moral principles which confine women to being sexual vehicles rather than sexual beings.

The result of telling young women that they cannot have sex until they are married and in love is that the shame of desiring sexual gratification will mis-define their lives from pubescence onward. My daughters know, as all girls do, that if they want sex no one can stop them from getting it. It is one of the most available commodities on the market, if you don't mind my cynicism. It is mis-defining their lives around sex that is degrading, and it usually comes from mothers at the behest of fathers. Some mothers, in the interest of equality, try to convince their sons that they should also abstain from sex until marriage.

Pardon my heresy. I taught my children not to confuse love with sex, just as my mother taught me. I wanted them to learn about love from birth on. Surely we do not expect our babies to begin enjoying sex at birth. Is it love then that we seek to deny them? I am convinced that equating sex with love is what is behind all the perversity of child sexual abuse. Some people have taken the bullshit seriously.

The last little note I want to make on sex and sons is a curious one. We are dichotomous in the rearing of our sons and daughters. In order that our sons not grow up to be faggots, we teach them to be macho and to hate girls, loathe all that is gentle, loving and tender. We teach them to pursue sex with girls, who have been taught that sex without love is evil and immoral. We are ashamed when our daughters are discovered to be sexually active, but proud of our sons' sexual proclivity. "He is a real lady-killer." Listen to that: a killer, and we say it with pride.

Love is both a social and personal phenomenon. The dictates of individualism in North America put social love somewhere in the ashcans of the mind. I love men, but I choose one lifelong partner. I love women but sexually I prefer men, so the women I love will be enjoyed at the spiritual level and not the physical. Or the converse, I love men but prefer women sexually, therefore it is men who will be enjoyed on the spiritual level. Sound simple?

Love presumes the right to choose. That means it is no one's business but my own what goes on in my bedroom. Neither my children, my friends, my neighbours nor the world at large has the right to choose my partner. In fact, we don't practice that: our friends and families are notorious for pressuring us into choosing a "suitable" mate. Women influence their children to choose a partner that is compatible with them as mothers. Men extort from their sons the right to direct their choice of a lifelong partner. And yet we make loud noises about our freedom of choice compared to people in places like Africa and India, where arranged marriage is still a reality. In practice, there is little choice in partner selection, right here.

The right to choice is as false in this society as the right to be free. Feminists are fond of analyzing the practices of societies in Africa and pointing out the horrible roles of women in such places. Pointing fingers at the oppression of women elsewhere changes not a damn thing for women here.

Before we force women who love women to parade their intimate affection for all to examine, we should talk about rape—the kind that goes on in the home between partners. Before we ask women to justify themselves, we had better talk about why we hate each other. And before we bestow the right on society to judge women who love women, we had better demand that society rectify itself.

The next time a woman asks me what my position on lesbianism is, I am going to ask her what her position is on her husband "getting his rocks off." If she gives me a straight answer, I am going to tell her that I am absolutely opposed to rape and that forcing a woman to accept my definition of who she may love amounts to rape.

To be raped is to be sexually violated. For society to force someone, through shame and ostracism, to comply with love and sex that it defines, is nothing but organized rape. That is what homophobia is all about. Organized rape.

The Respectable Same-Sex Couple: A New Entity in the History of Sexuality

Mariana Valverde

*Mariana Valverde holds a PhD in Social and Political Thought from York University. After some years of activism and part-time teaching, mainly in Women's Studies, during which she published her first book (*Sex, Power, and Pleasure *[Women's Press, 1985]), she re-entered the academy, and is currently Professor at the Centre of Criminology, University of Toronto. She has published widely in historical sociology, social theory and socio-legal studies, and was elected Fellow of the Royal Society of Canada in 2006. Sole-authored books include:* The age of light, soap, and water: moral reform in English Canada 1880s-1920s *(1991),* Diseases of the will: alcohol and the dilemmas of freedom *(1998), and* Law's dream of a common knowledge *(2003).*

In *The History of Sexuality: Volume I*, Michel Foucault argued that "homosexuality" is a relatively recent invention, distinct from earlier forms of same-sex love and lust. "Homosexuality" could only emerge when European scientific knowledges began to peer into—and construct—an inner "self," a personal identity that the 19th century saw as a matter of physiology and that the 20th century regarded as fundamentally psychological. Sexuality—in the West but not in the East—came to be regarded as that which is most secret and therefore most authentic about "the self," the key, in other words, to personal identity.

Before the rise of modern scientific knowledges, law governed sexuality as a set of acts, mainly distinguishing "unnatural" from "natural" acts. But it is not inappropriate, when making a large-scale generalization, to say, in line with Foucault's famous thesis, that the regulation of the self has been increasingly dominated by the notion of "identity." What you did with various body parts came to be regarded, throughout the course of the 20th century, mainly as a clue about what kind of person you were. And "the homosexual" was probably the most successful of all deviant identities. It was invented at the same time as the hysteric, the nymphomaniac and the kleptomaniac, but unlike these marginal entities/identities, it ended up occupying a very central place in the constitution of 20th-century human beings and social groups. Although subsequent research has shown that Foucault's contrast is far too sharp, the point about the shift from governing sexuality through acts to governing through identities has been generally accepted by historians and social scientists.

But what has happened since the 1970s, when Foucault was writing about sexuality? Let me suggest, half jokingly, but half seriously, that we have been witnesses to a historic event. This is the emergence, in the space occupied by "homosexuality," of a new sexual object/subject: the respectable same-sex couple. If the medieval soldier charged with sodomy was not "a homosexual," as Foucault argued, so too, we can argue, the respectable same-sex couple (to which I am assigning the acronym "RSSC") is not two homosexuals added together.

It certainly seems true that the particular form of the inner self that is "sexuality"—the object of inquiries from 1890s sexology to sex-change clinics—may indeed be now fading.

Young people who would rather be "queer" than "gay" are leading the way. The term "queer" blurs the boundaries of the homosexual self of tormented 1950s autobiographies and medico-legal inquiries. Queer is a purposefully vague name for a nonconformist lifestyle that is "post-homosexual," historically if not biographically. And AIDS discourse has also given rise to a new, post-homosexual object: the man who has sex with men. Contrary to Foucault's discussion of the disciplinary gaze, AIDS experts don't care one bit whether this personage is gay.

But the queer youth and the "man who has sex with men" are marginal by comparison with the legally and culturally prominent figure of the RSSC. This is likely more apparent in Canada, where gay/lesbian marriage began to be legalized as early as 2003, than south of the forty-ninth parallel; but given the speed with which Americans rushed to San Francisco city hall during February of 2004, when gay/lesbian marriage was for a time provided in a more or less legal manner, perhaps the Canadian situation is relevant elsewhere, even in Bush's America.

The pictures that were used in the media are of particular importance for understanding how the RSSC is something new, rather than the addition of two homosexuals. As marriage for gays and lesbians approached legality, around 2003, Canadians were treated to an unprecedented visual display of respectable homosexuality: an extended series of photos displaying not the ashamed and effeminate homosexuals that used to be posed in dark corners in 1960s reportage of seamy gay life, but rather an array of perfect "same-sex" couples, usually shown in the full glare of sunlight, a lighting convention at odds with representations of the classic homosexual. A look at the photographs that are still available, somewhat after the fact, proves enlightening. The first lesson in social semiotics is provided by an analysis focusing on that most important of all signs of marriage, notably, the wedding dress. A number of the lesbian couples who got married at the San Francisco city hall wore wedding dresses. And I can also attest to the presence of wedding dresses from personal experience. I happened to be in San Francisco in mid-February 2004 (where my partner and I were constantly asked if we had come to get married by well-meaning Americans not aware of the fact we could have gotten married in Toronto quite easily, if that was our desire). My partner and I, used to the idea of gay/lesbian marriage but not to the flashier styles of U.S. lesbians, were quite struck by seeing young lesbians in full wedding white waiting for the subway in the Berkeley mass transit station. It was very difficult to tell whether the wedding dresses were being worn in straight-up imitation of marriage or in playful parody. It is quite possible, given the mixed feelings gays and lesbians have about marriage, that the wearers were not themselves very clear about their intentions. By contrast, the available photos of Canadian lesbian couples did not reveal a single wedding dress. All the couples depicted looked earnest and serious, sort of butch, and dressed in office attire: no wedding dresses; no playfulness; no parody; but also, no imitation of marriage. Perhaps Canada really is a more boring and earnest country; the lesbians do seem just to be wanting to get married, as opposed to wanting to dress up and have a really good time.

But what about the male couples? The first thing that one notices is that none of the men in U.S. or Canadian pictures of gay male weddings wear white dresses. Drag queens seem to have vanished from view. Nearly all of the men featured in the newspaper photographs wore shirts and ties; nearly all were middle-class, middle-aged and white.

But perhaps pictures of actual weddings, or rather of that small sample of weddings that happened to be covered by the media, are not representative. I thus turned to another source, the *Toronto Star*'s Pride Day special section, published June 19, 2004. Toronto Pride Day is a significant event because it draws around three quarters of a million people, many of them U.S. gays and lesbians. The local press now covers this event in a boosterish manner, just like any other event that contributes to the local economy and to the local myth that Toronto is the mecca of multiculturalism and tolerance. This special section of Canada's largest circulation daily had two main articles. One featured the 73-year-old homosexual activist, George Hislop, wistfully reminiscing about the days of illegality. This story was obviously meant to represent the ghost of gay lives past. The community's future, by contrast, was embodied not in a young queer person of a transsexual activist, but, predictably, in images of a RSSC. Equally predictable, the couple in question was made up of two middle-class men. The couple is portrayed as totally immersed in the financial and logistical challenges of their upcoming wedding. In what can best be described as a feminist nightmare vision, both are obsessing about the colour scheme, the food, the entertainment and the guest list.

I looked in vain for something that the RSSC might have had in common with Hislop. Sex, perhaps? Foucault would have said that in the end it is sex that holds the RSSC together and links it to both the homosexual of the 1960s and the 18th-century sodomite. But nothing about sex was said or even faintly implied in the article about the gay male couple. The two men who were about to tie the knot seemed to be far too engrossed in the details of their wedding to even think about sex. Other than the RSSC itself, the only people cited in the article are wedding professionals. These entrepreneurs offer up-to-date information about the new consumer niche and advise readers who operate small businesses not to neglect the gay marriage market (the gay marriage market at any rate; lesbian weddings aren't mentioned). Readers (including business people) thus learn from authoritative sources that gay and lesbian couples always pay for their own wedding, with no parental involvement, which is apparently a key marketing point.

The *Star*'s coverage of Pride Day certainly supports the claim that if homosexuality did not die with Foucault in 1984, it is dying or dead now. Hislop, who despite his advanced age likes to shock people by saying he likes boys, probably knows many florists; but he is otherwise wholly unconcerned with weddings and, indeed, with consumption. In the days of homosexuality, activism meant poverty. Hislop, who is still fighting in the courts to get the Canadian government to retroactively include him in the same-sex pension arrangements that have been made available in recent years (his partner died a few years before the cut-off date for same-sex pensions), does not come across as a consumer at all.

But what about law? Putting away the newspaper, I turned to the relevant decisions of the Supreme Court of Canada, the decisions that were key in paving the way for gay/lesbian weddings, in pursuit of the vanishing homosexual. Instead of sexuality, homo or otherwise, I found two non-sexual themes. The two themes that run throughout the decisions are (1) family, and (2) finance/consumption. Conjugality, family and impoverishment were the sole themes of the Court's descriptions of the retirement struggles of James Egan and his partner in the 1995 case *Egan v. Canada*, a landmark decision that first declared that discrimination against gays and lesbians was in Canada just as illegal as discrimination on the basis of race or religion. Neither sex nor sexuality are mentioned in either the majority or the minority *Egan* decision. "Sexual orientation" is the only sex-like term in the Court's text—but this is not a *sexual* identity. As I have argued elsewhere with much more evidence than can be presented here, sexual orientation in Canadian law actually refers not so much to homosexuality as a sexual identity, but to an urban lifestyle, partly political and partly consumerist. But perhaps the desexualization of gay rights in this decision is due to the fact that the *Egan* case was about pension benefits. A couple that has been together forty years is unlikely to have a sexy aura. Perhaps the Egans are not sexual, and hence not homosexuals, by virtue of the fact that they were challenging pension regulations.

So what about the other famous RSSC of Canadian law, then? Another notable Canadian legal case involved a lesbian couple known as "M and H" (to preserve their privacy). A 2001 Supreme Court decision, which stopped short of actually legalizing gay marriage, extended exactly the same recognition of heterosexual common-law couples to lesbian and gay couples, a recognition that involves compulsory support obligations after living together for two years. M and H are two women. They are not elderly. They weren't trying to get their pension. And they were undoubtedly presenting themselves as lesbians when they went to court. They could thus be sexual/homosexual. But their sexuality too is completely erased. Their issue was divorce, or rather, alimony. In a nutshell, M was unemployed or precariously employed, while H owned considerable property. When they split up, M claimed a right to alimony. The Supreme Court eventually ruled that H and others in similar positions did indeed have an obligation to support their ex-partners.

Not infrequently, people divorce for reasons related to sexuality, but this is not contemplated anywhere in the legal texts. The Court's recounting of their relationship is wholly devoted to financial matters. Of course, a claim for alimony is all about money; but nevertheless, some reference to the initial romance might have been found relevant, if only to explain the somewhat careless joining of finances that later caused discord. Let us turn to the Supreme Court text to see if there are any homosexuals.

> *M and H are women who met while on vacation in 1980. It is agreed in 1982 they started living together in a same-sex relationship that continued for at least five years. . . . During that time they occupied a home which H had owned since 1974. H paid for the upkeep of the home. . . . In 1983, M and H purchased a business property*

together. In 1986, they purchased as joint tenants a vacation property in the country. They later sold the business property and used the proceeds to finance the construction of a home on the country property.

As a result of a dramatic downturn in the advertising business in the late 1980s, the parties debt increased significantly. H took a job outside the firm and placed a mortgage on her home to pay for her expenses and those of M. M also tried to find employment but was unsuccessful. . . .

In September of 1992, M and H's relationship deteriorated.

The sheer ordinariness of the details given here is no doubt intended: writing up "the facts" in this dreary-details-of-domestic-life manner furthers the justices' project to normalize same-sex marriage. Amidst the property relations, sex is nowhere to be found; neither is homosexuality. Nobody even inquires whether they sleep together, much less what they do in bed; the famous disciplinary gaze has vanished.

The RSSC of the *Toronto Star* pre-wedding photos and the RSSC of M and H occupy opposite ends of the marital happiness spectrum. But neither entity is made up of two homosexuals. Nobody cares about their sexuality—including, apparently, the parties involved. The nonsexual transactions that make up the everyday fabric of coupledom are what the texts find worth recounting. In the *Star*, one finds that the narrative of the happy Toronto couple is wholly made up of florists' bills and plane tickets for relatives. The narrative of the divorcing couple of the M and H Supreme Court decision, for its part, is made up of joint tenancy agreements and bank loan documents.

The RSSC is still a very new object in the legal (and economic) horizon. It would thus be premature to make any grand claims about its "essence." But it is clear that Hislop's reminiscences of homosexuality and its pleasures and dangers are precisely that—reminiscences. Bank loans, florists' bills, joint bank accounts, renovated gentrified downtown homes and worries about the relatives are the pieces that make up the new, post-homosexual entity that Canadian jurisprudence has helped to fabricate: the respectable "same-sex" couple. Like other proper homosexuals, Foucault is no doubt turning over in his grave.

Losing the Feminist Voice: Debates on the Legal Recognition of Same-Sex Partnerships in Canada

Claire Young and Susan B. Boyd

Claire Young is Senior Associate Dean, Academic Affairs and Professor of Law at the University of British Columbia. She teaches, researches and writes on tax law and policy issues, and is currently engaged in work that focuses on women and tax. Her other research interests include feminist legal theory and sexuality and the law.

Susan B. Boyd is a Professor of Law and holds the Chair in Feminist Legal Studies at the University of British Columbia, where she works in the fields of family law and feminist legal studies. She recently co-edited: Poverty: Rights, Social Citizenship, and Legal Activism *(UBC Press 2007);* Reaction and Resistance: Feminism, Law, and Social Change *(UBC Press 2007); and* Law and Families *(Ashgate 2006).*

Canada has for some time granted legal recognition to unmarried opposite-sex cohabitants, treating them as virtually the same as married couples for many, though not all, purposes. Since the early 1990s, Canada has been challenged to extend this legal recognition to same-sex partners. The ensuing changes can be termed an incredible success story for the lesbian and gay social movements and a challenge to legal heteronormativity. Same-sex cohabitants increasingly, though unevenly across provinces and territories, are now treated like opposite-sex cohabitants. Furthermore, the opposite-sex requirement for legal marriage was challenged and in July 2005 the federal government legalized civil same-sex marriage across Canada. Both opposite-sex and same-sex partners can now choose whether to marry or not. Even if they do not, they may still be ascribed spousal status for various purposes, based on a period of cohabitation.

The extent of these changes to normative ideas about family would have been difficult to foresee even a decade ago, let alone in the 1980s when the lesbian and gay social movement began to use the legal system as a site of struggle (Herman 1994; Smith 1999; Lahey 1999). Same-sex relationship recognition disturbs the assumption that marriage and kinship rest on naturalistic and biologistic notions of reproduction and family. As a result, familial ideology—long critiqued by feminists (e.g., Barrett & McIntosh 1982; Gavigan 1993)—is uprooted from its traditions. The threat that same-sex marriage brings to socially conservative assumptions about family, society and nation cannot be underestimated, nor can resistance to it (Mello 2004). Many lesbians and gays from other countries have looked to Canada as a model for their own jurisdictions, while others have come to Canada to marry (Kitzinger & Wilkinson 2004). The calls by social conservatives for legal protection of the opposite-sex definition of marriage have exposed the fragility of marriage as a historically specific social institution, as opposed to a naturalized, timeless one. As well, essentialist assumptions about the natural complementarity of female and male roles, and their importance in relation to the socialization of children, have been interrupted.

Without diminishing the struggle that lesbians and gay men have endured to secure legal recognition of their relationships, we wish to trouble the evolutionary narrative of progress in this field by investigating the terms on which recent legal struggles have advanced. Judith Butler (2002) has pointed out that the political context surrounding the same-sex marriage debates has led to a dichotomous framing of the "debate" and a perceived demand that a stand be taken either for or against marriage, without problematizing marriage as a social and economic institution. Taking up Butler's call to resist this imposed binary, we suggest that the story of the legal recognition of same-sex relationships is less than fully positive, in the sense that it has proceeded in a way that has rendered invisible important feminist critiques of marriage, familial ideology and the domestication of lesbian and gay relationships (Polikoff 1993; Robson 1994, p. 976). In particular, a diminishing space appears to exist for feminist voices on various issues related to the family and economic security. We will argue that to the extent that feminist voices are marginalized, conservative and heteronormative discourses on marriage and family are reinforced, even as same-sex relationships are recognized.

THE SUCCESS STORY: TRANSFORMING THE LEGAL DEFINITION OF SPOUSE

The enactment of the Canadian Charter of Rights and Freedoms (the Charter) in 1982 and the coming into force of its equality section in 1985 provided a tremendous impetus for court challenges to heterosexist statutory definitions of spouse. Although sexual orientation was not explicitly listed as a prohibited ground of discrimination, in 1995, the Supreme Court of Canada in *Egan v. The Queen* confirmed that it was an analogous ground. Two other groundbreaking cases deserve comment. In 1998, the Ontario Court of Appeal held in *Rosenberg v. Canada (Attorney General)* that the words "or same-sex" should be read into the definition of "spouse" in the Income Tax Act, for the purposes of registration of pension plans (see Young 1998). This ruling effectively extended entitlement to survivor benefits under occupational pension plans to the partners of lesbians and gay men. Then, in 1999, the Supreme Court of Canada rendered the most important judicial decision to date on same-sex spousal recognition in *M. v. H.*, striking down as unconstitutional, an opposite-sex definition of "spouse" in a family-law statute.

In the early 21st century, a renewed struggle for same-sex marriage emerged, having been put on hold in Canada in the mid-1990s in favour of seeking the rights available to unmarried opposite-sex cohabitants. Several successful Charter challenges were raised to the common law rule that defined marriage as between one man and one woman, so that same-sex couples acquired, with startling rapidity, the right to marry in several provinces and one territory. In October 2004, the federal government sought the opinion of the Supreme Court of Canada on whether same-sex marriage for civil purposes was consistent with the Charter and on December 9, 2004, the Supreme Court of Canada held that it was. On July 20, 2005, Bill C-38, the Civil Marriage Act received Royal Assent and was proclaimed, legalizing civil same-sex marriage across Canada. Civil marriage is now defined as "the lawful union of two persons to the exclusion of all others."

PROBLEMATIZING SUCCESS: FEMINIST CRITIQUES OF MARRIAGE AND MARRIAGE-LIKE DYADS

This rapid reversal of state-sanctioned homophobia in the Canadian legal system, and the creative work by many lesbians and gay men and others to achieve this change, is extraordinary. Nevertheless, we want to explore the terms on which the success occurred. We will argue that the more radical perspectives on the institution of marriage, the exclusivity of the nuclear family and familial ideology have been marginalized as the legal embracing of same-sex relationships has progressed.

This dynamic is not entirely surprising. Those participating in the debates about same-sex relationships are a product of their society, which includes still powerful ideologies of the exclusive, nuclear family. Many lesbians and gay men are not inclined to challenge the role that marriage has played in reinforcing unequal relations in society. Indeed, some major proponents of same-sex marriage seek admission to that institution precisely by invoking some of its oppressive features (e.g., Sullivan 1989, p. 22, 1997). A Canadian editorial called "Gays in the 'hood'" (2005) recalled the bourgeois comforts of marriage:

> *By embracing marriage, homosexuals remind others that it is, or should be, the norm for committed couples. It is the best place to experience love, sex and companionship*

together. It is the best place to raise children. Marriage's "till death do us part" pledge of permanence gives people the security they need to give themselves fully to the other. It is one of the ironies of the same-sex marriage debate that conservatives who once condemned the hedonistic, selfish and licentious "gay lifestyle" would now deny homosexuals the right to opt into the bourgeois comfort of marriage.

This approach is geared towards capturing the approval of "middle America" for same-sex relationships, and so endorses key elements of familial ideology. Equally, it raises the possibility that recognition of lesbian/gay relationships in family law may not challenge male economic privilege or the sexual division of labour within the privatized family that has been the subject of feminist critique (see Jacobs 1997, pp. 65–184). The continued exploitation of women's unpaid work coupled with the assigning of responsibility for the costs of social reproduction to the family constitutes an intrinsic component of the capitalist mode of production (Hennessy 2000, p. 64; Picchio 1992). From a feminist and left perspective, failing to challenge at a fundamental level the roles that marriage and family play in social inequality is problematic. Yet this is precisely what has occurred in the debates over same-sex relationship recognition: the familial sphere has been recoded to place less emphasis on the gender-based normative structure of the family and more on its support functions. The family remains the natural site for social reproduction, although new sexual citizens can now participate in it (Cossman 2002a).

This issue raises a broader range of questions about family and gender than marriage alone. As many have pointed out, despite social changes such as the increased participation of married women in the labour force, marriage remains an inherently patriarchal institution, with men viewed primarily as breadwinners and women carrying complementary responsibility for childcare and work in the home. Despite changes to family law, many fought for by feminists, economic remedies available on marriage breakdown have not been especially successful in addressing the inequalities stemming from women's continuing provision of the reproductive labour needed to sustain families, the economy and labour power. Individuals may well within their own marriages challenge traditional norms such as the sexual division of labour, but the socio-legal institution of marriage at a larger level still embodies patriarchal and heterosexual norms. Although the concept of coverture inherent within marriage has been challenged, "its (hetero)sexual performatives remain a key trope in marriage and (to a lesser extent) marriage-like relationships" (Brook 2000, p. 133).

Moreover, the legal institution of marriage has been implicated in racist practices. In Canada, marriage provided a mechanism for the imposition of colonialist and patriarchal norms on Aboriginal communities, with negative consequences for indigenous women (McIvor 2004). Within the American legacy of slavery, the "racialized engendering of marriage had very different consequences for white and black women" (Hennessy 2000, p. 65). Slaves were forbidden to marry and the ideologies of womanhood that prevailed for women in white, bourgeois families were not engendered in the same way for African American women, indeed quite the contrary (Carby 1997; Davis 1983; Roberts 1997). Moreover, miscegenation statutes in the United States prohibiting interracial marriage in some states were not declared unconstitutional until surprisingly recently.

Given these critiques of marriage as an institution that rests—perhaps irretrievably—on profoundly hierarchical social and economic relations, struggles to achieve legal recognition of same-sex relationships may require a normalization of lesbian and gay intimate relationships to appear as marriage-like as possible, in turn leaving intact the hierarchies that are ideologically embedded within marriage. Furthermore, the invocation of the equality rights section of the Canadian Charter has exacerbated this trend, requiring that litigants demonstrate that they have been discriminated against on the basis of sexual orientation. As a result, litigants must compare themselves to others in a relevant category, in a way that tends to suppress differences and emphasize similarities (Iyer 1993, p. 183).

The Charter challenges in Canada have indeed tended to rest on evidence that same-sex couples are virtually the same as heterosexual couples and should, therefore, be given equal legal treatment. The affidavits in the same-sex marriage cases emphasized factors such as joint finances, reciprocal wills, monogamy and the desire to be "just like" other couples, which they would be but for their sexuality.

Successful inclusion in the institution on these terms may well result in the marginalization of those who "deviate" from the relationship pattern that has been "normalized", thus creating a new hierarchy of acceptable and non-acceptable gays and lesbians. As we shall see, submissions to the Canadian House of Commons Standing Committee show it was almost impossible for lesbians and gay men to raise a critique of the institution of marriage in an effective manner.

This dynamic of normalizing same-sex relationships through comparison to a heterosexual norm may also help to explain why same-sex relationship recognition has proceeded relatively quickly: "the threatening possibility of a gender-less sexual desire" is contained by this process and "by a new paradigm of sexual identity that articulated it in a heterogendered frame" (Hennessy 2000, p. 101). As long as the economics work well, "neoliberalism is generally agnostic in relation to same-sex challenges to spousal definitions, insofar as it is not wedded to any particular family form" (Cossman 2002, p. 182). The extent to which the complex social relations of inequality can be challenged under this formal equality rights model inherent within liberal legalism and neoliberalism is limited. Moreover, the heteronormative model that underpins such legal changes may reinforce distinctions between "good" gays and lesbians, who look as much as possible like the traditional nuclear couple, and "bad" gays and lesbians, whose relationships violate familial norms. The neoliberal state is quite happy to accommodate new sexual citizens so long as they adhere to a privatized, familialized heteronormativity (Cossman 2002a, p. 484).

In addition to these normalizing, assimilating trends, expanding spousal recognition to unmarried and same-sex partners has particularly problematic economic implications for already disadvantaged persons, related to neoliberal policies of privatized economic responsibility. Rhetoric in favour of the legal recognition of same-sex partners often ignores the economic disadvantages, as opposed to advantages, that spousal recognition can bring. Class and gender are relevant here: spousal recognition can benefit wealthier couples or couples whose relationships are premised on the economic dependency of one partner, but cause disadvantage to lower income couples.

This policy of privatization of economic responsibilities has accelerated in the neoliberal climate of the past decade. It rests on an assumption that responsibility to redress economic need or dependency should reside in the private sphere of family or charities, rather than be shared with or reside with the collectivity (Boyd 1999; Cossman 2002; Fineman 2000). Given the weaknesses of privatized economic remedies, various authors have instead suggested that benefits such as social assistance should be extended on an individual basis, rather than focusing on adult, sexually intimate relationships as a marker of economic responsibilities (Ettelbrick 1992; Gavigan 1993).

Critiques such as these have led some feminist authors to argue that privileging a sexually intimate adult relationship in laws and social policies is mistaken and that marriage as a legal category should be abolished (Fineman 1995, 2000). For instance, Nancy Polikoff (2000) has argued that marriage as a legal institution fails to envision a truly transformatory model of family for all people and is problematically embedded in liberal notions of equality and choice.

CANADIAN COMMITTEE HEARINGS ON SAME-SEX MARRIAGE (2003)

It is not surprising that when the committee held hearings on same-sex marriages in 2003, based on a Department of Justice (Canada) discussion paper (2002), interest was intense. No fewer than 362 briefs were presented and 444 witnesses appeared, more than 20 times the number of witnesses at the Bill C-23 (Modernization of Benefits and Obligations Act) hearings. Of those witnesses, 265 supported same-sex marriage, 163 opposed it, and 16 took no position. The discussion paper actually offered three options—retaining the opposite-sex definition of marriage, expanding legal marriage to same-sex partners and abolishing marriage as a legal (though not religious) category, instead introducing a registration system. Most witnesses at the hearings focused on the first two options, retaining the status quo or eliminating marriage's opposite-sex definition.

The briefs and testimony presented to the committee by supporters of same-sex marriage were based on formal equality: lesbians and gay men should be allowed to marry partners of the same sex because to deny them the same marriage rights as heterosexual persons is discriminatory and contravenes the Charter. The rationale was that same-sex couples should be given the same choice to marry as heterosexual couples because their relationships are similar. Some witnesses also emphasised that allowing same-sex couples to marry would strengthen marriage and the family. All of these arguments are based on liberal legalism, looking to law to remedy a discriminatory situation whereby likes are treated in an unlike manner. They draw on liberal notions of "formal equality" and "choice"—an attractive concept in neoliberal times and one that is ascendant in family law (Boyd & Young 2004). They also reinforce the normative status quo, in this case, the primacy of the exclusive, nuclear family. Although a few witnesses raised feminist concerns about marriage, most did so after endorsing the formal equality approach.

ARGUMENTS FOR SAME-SEX MARRIAGE

It's the Law

"It's the Law" was the phrase used by E.G.A.L.E. throughout the same-sex marriage debates, building on its argument in 2000. E.G.A.L.E.'s Director of Advocacy stated that "[we] have a constitution that requires that all Canadians be treated equally under the law. Opposite-sex couples can get married. Same-sex couples can't. That's not equality. It's discrimination, and it's prohibited by the Charter of Rights." Obviously the Charter has provided enormous support for the equality arguments of Canadian lesbians and gay men, but as discussed above, equality rights discourse is based on comparisons. Arguing that same-sex couples are the same as heterosexual couples, and thus should be entitled to legally marry, leaves virtually no room for critical analysis of the institutions of marriage and family, and their relationship to the political economy and social relations of inequality. This constrained level of debate can produce problematic practical consequences for already disadvantaged groups and reinforce existing disadvantage.

CHOICE

The rhetoric of choice so often associated with liberalism also played a significant role in the written and oral submissions of supporters of same-sex marriage. For the Canadian Union of Public Employees marriage was "about equality, choice and ending the discrimination we know all too well" while the New Democratic Youth of Canada stated, in a rare allusion to the fact that not all lesbians and gay men embrace the institution of marriage, that "while some same-sex couples may not hold marriage as an option for them personally, the general consensus of the L.G.B.T. communities is that people should at least be allowed the choice."

Arguments based on the freedom to choose, located as they are in the liberal paradigm, are attractive and easy to make. The choice to marry is typically viewed as the exercise of an individual right, isolated from broader social structures that favour certain social relationships and determine how they should be regulated. Yet the individual "choice" to marry is actually shaped by the powerful familial ideologies encouraging dyadic adult commitments within nuclear family settings, and is therefore not completely free or unfettered, nor innocent of being implicated in social relations of power and hierarchy. Familial ideology renders "normal" and desirable the choice to enter a dyadic relationship and bolsters these choices via the ideal liberal contract—the contract of marriage (Phelan 2001, p. 74).

SAMENESS

Images of sameness and assimilation permeated many of the pro-same-sex marriage submissions in Canada, often invoking traditional norms of family. Again and again, the point was made that lesbian and gay relationships mirror those of heterosexual couples.

E.G.A.L.E.'s brief contained a series of "portraits" of lesbian and gay couples, again focusing on how similar to heterosexual couples they were in relation to attributes such as monogamy, love, fidelity, sharing of property, being viewed by others as a couple and longevity of relationship. It is not especially surprising that these images were put forward. As we know, (formal) equality discourse lends itself to arguments based on comparisons and demonstrating sameness while at the same time obscuring diversity. In this context the obvious comparator for lesbian and gay couples is heterosexual couples. But the results can be problematic. First, even the concept of the typical heterosexual couple as monogamous and in a long-term relationship in which virtually all property is shared is somewhat artificial, and certainly an idealized norm rather than a representation of reality. Second, the research on the dynamics of same-sex partnerships remains at an early stage (Ambert 2003) and it is unclear what similarities and differences exist. At the same time, using the idealized heterosexual model as the comparator serves to "other" those who do not fit the mould. Those individuals—whether heterosexual or not—who do not fit within the dyadic marriage model will be left out in the cold. For instance, those who rely on the collective for support in fields such as health, poverty, transport and migration will suffer unless wider discussion ensues about the broader redistribution of responsibilities rather than a simple fetishizing of romantic coupledom (Cooper 2001, p. 96).

MARRIAGE AND FAMILY STRENGTHENED

While many who opposed same-sex marriage argued that permitting lesbians and gay men to marry would weaken the institution, many proponents argued the exact opposite. Under both approaches, the significance of dyadic marriage and the nuclear family was bolstered.

Speaking for the Foundation for Equal Families, Michelle Douglas said that "[t]he foundation believes that equal marriage will in fact strengthen the institution of marriage by expanding the range of loving couples who subscribe to its tenets". Another witness alluded to the benefits of marriage to the family when she said "[t]here are also clear advantages for the children." But she continued in a broader vein, stating that "[b]enefits to Canada, to the state, include the promotion of intra-family solidarity, the empowerment and solidarity of couples and families and certainly a reduced social burden for the state." Bureau was the only witness to comment explicitly on the "benefits" that would accrue from the privatization of economic responsibility within the family, reinforcing the tendency to look inwards to the family for support under the neoliberal approach of privatized self-reliance.

MARRIAGE AS THE GOLD STANDARD

One option presented in the Canadian Department of Justice Discussion Paper on Same-Sex Marriage was to permit lesbians and gay men to enter civil unions or registered domestic partnerships (R.D.P.s) instead of the right to legally marry. One might have thought that these options would attract support, since they avoid the ideological trappings of marriage. However, those who supported same-sex marriage either rejected civil unions or R.D.P.s outright, or in some cases, rejected them unless same-sex marriage was also legalized. For example, E.G.A.L.E. stated that "[g]iven the social imprimatur of marriage and the stigma still attached to homosexuality, registered domestic partnerships could only be interpreted as official, government sponsored, second class status."

For most supporters of same-sex marriage, there appeared no interest in accepting anything other than marriage. The symbolic importance of marriage was thus reinforced, even as arguments were made for challenging its heterosexual premises.

THE FEMINIST OR PROGRESSIVE VOICE

None of the Canadian briefs and submissions discussed so far included critiques of marriage, and perhaps understandably: it is very difficult to argue for inclusion in an institution while at the same time raising problems inherent within it. However, a few witnesses tried to walk that fine line. For example, while endorsing same-sex marriage, Lise Gotell also raised concerns with the terms on which the debate was framed. She was careful to point out that allowing same-sex marriage would simply result in formal equality for lesbians and gay men and would not lead to substantive equality. It would not, for example, eliminate homophobia, just as ending racial segregation in the United States had not eliminated racism. No committee member engaged with Gotell's concerns about the incompleteness of marriage as a tool by which to achieve equality.

West Coast Legal Education and Action Fund (L.E.A.F.), a group seeking equality for women, attempted to break free from the formal equality model and introduce a more nuanced feminist analysis, raising the larger issue of the role that marriage has played in "enforcing women's economic inequality, allowing women's victimization by domestic violence and devaluing the important work of caregiving." Only one committee member engaged with these gender issues and then not in a spirit that accorded with the group's recommendation. Vic Toews (Canadian Alliance) used the concerns expressed by West Coast L.E.A.F. to suggest that marriage not be extended to same-sex couples. He asked "are we certain enough about what we're doing with this particular institution, given the history we've had with divorce and the impact of divorce and the 'feminization of poverty', as one witness put it here? Don't we have to worry about those kinds of things?"

The transcripts reveal how little room existed for any position other than absolute opposition to same-sex marriage or complete support for it. The questions and comments by the committee members clearly demonstrated that they were not prepared to engage in a more nuanced debate. Any more nuanced an approach might be taken as evidence by opponents that the concept of same-sex marriage is indeed flawed and should not go forward. Most lesbians and gay men and feminists were unwilling to take that risk.

The most radical analysis was offered by Gary Kinsman, who called for the abolition of state sanctioned marriage. He addressed the patriarchal nature of marriage, noting that marriage is the most privileged of social relations and that state institutionalized recognition of marriage is itself a state practice of discrimination against other forms of social and sexual relationships, such as single-parent-headed households. He suggested that there should be recognition of and support for individuals "on the basic principles of social justice, on the basis of democracy, autonomy, equality, consent, choice and the redistribution of wealth to those living in poverty and hardship." Members of the committee appeared confused by Kinsman's testimony, which did not fall easily into an argument for or against same-sex marriage. No committee member addressed his position directly or challenged him on its implications. Ideas about the abolition of marriage and regulating social relationships by use of other markers seemed to be outside the imagination of the committee, and indeed, most witnesses.

ARGUMENTS AGAINST LEGALIZING SAME-SEX MARRIAGE: HETEROSEXUAL ANXIETY

Most of those who opposed same-sex marriage tried to cast same-sex couples as the antithesis of heterosexual couples in terms of their relationships and lifestyle, often in clearly homophobic terms. Underpinning their opposition to same-sex marriage was a neoconservative view of marriage and the family as inherently patriarchal and hierarchical institutions. For them, the imperviousness of marriage and the family to the critique of feminists and others was crucial to the health of society and the nation. These interventions represented a "performance of heterosexuality", revealing the anxiety of many men (and women) in society about the fact that "being straight" is an increasingly contested status, as is masculinity (Collier 1996).

The main opposition to same-sex marriage was based on a belief that allowing lesbians and gay men to marry would lead to the demise of marriage, the family and society.

Opponents of same-sex marriage first went to great lengths to argue that lesbian and gay relationships were the antithesis of heterosexual relationships in every way. Their vision of the nature of the heterosexual married couple's relationship was highly idealized: marriage is a monogamous union of two people who have children and remain together until death. In their attempt to preserve marriage as a heterosexual institution, opponents made extremely homophobic statements that clearly disturbed some committee members. For example, Réal Ménard (Bloc Québecois) responded to the submissions by members of the Cosmas and Damian Society by saying, "I am a bit surprised by your presentation, because it gives the impression that homosexuals are full of unchecked desires, who do nothing but have sex and who are entirely incapable of being parents. I am all the more surprised by the basis of your presentation since you are presenting yourselves as professionals." The attack by opponents "othered" same-sex relationships in terms that reinforced the values and essentialist gender roles underlying traditional views of heterosexual marriage. Ménard's response in turn normalized same-sex relationships.

Many witnesses also argued, ignoring the "gayby boom" (Kelly 2004, p. 134), that because lesbian and gay couples could not procreate, they should not be allowed to marry. As Dr. Franklin Pyles of the Evangelical Fellowship of Canada said, "the conjugal relationship is essentially a procreative act. Marriage encourages procreation. It is the place where procreation is to occur."

Second, many witnesses who opposed same-sex marriage gave evidence about how the "lifestyle" of lesbians and gay men was so debauched that they should not be permitted to marry, focusing mainly on negative, stereotyped perceptions of the gay male lifestyle. Rita Curley of the St. Ignatius Martyr Council said, using the quintessential slippery slope argument, "[t]o redefine marriage to be inclusive of homosexuality is to create a new morality in which homosexuality is not merely tolerated but is normalized and would branch out into sexual activity with babies, children of both sexes, and with animals."

A third theme was that permitting lesbians and gay men to marry would lead to the demise of society and, for some, the end of civilization. Some witnesses argued that permitting same-sex marriage would lead to polygamy, legalization of incest, or marriage between two sisters or brothers. Gwen Landolt said during a heated exchange with the Chair of the Committee:

> *Now you say polygamy is illegal, and incest is illegal—all of those things. But marriage is an institution that has been historically there before the common law. That is the principle, and you're going to change it fundamentally and reform it. This is the whole point of what I'm getting at: Is marriage to be as it always has been, for the purposes I've already said many times today, or are you going to open it up to any kind of relationship, legal or illegal? Because in principle, you cannot open marriage up to homosexuals or lesbian couples unless you open it up in principle to all sorts of other relationships.*

In June 2003, the Standing Committee voted by a margin of only one to recommend to the federal government that it not appeal the ruling by the Ontario Court of Appeal in *Halpern v. Canada* redefining marriage as being between "two persons". Perhaps due in part to the heated political backdrop to the same-sex marriage hearings of 2003, the dichotomous framing of the debate for or against marriage (Butler 2002) was deeply entrenched with those who tried to offer analysis that problematized the dichotomy barely being acknowledged.

CONCLUSION

By and large, the debates about recognizing same-sex relationships as spousal in Canadian law operated within a narrow paradigm. A formal equality paradigm was used by those in favour of legal recognition. Meanwhile, resistance to such legal recognition generally reflected the extent to which marriage was seen by conservative forces as the last bastion of state enforced reinforcement of the special significance of heterosexual couples. Moreover, those in favour of formal equality argued that nothing less than marriage will do, thus reinforcing marriage as the "gold standard". Virtually no critiques of marriage or familial ideology, nor links to its relationship to unequal power, domestic abuse, economic dependency and poverty were raised, nor could they be "heard".

At one level, Canada's legalization of civil same-sex marriages makes perfect sense. Marriage is, in some sense, an individualistic act that fits well within the current neoliberal climate in Canada: everyone for herself, preferably in a dyadic family unit, not relying on the community unless absolutely necessary. Other legalized dyadic relationships such as common law partnerships also marry well with neoliberalism. Feminist critiques have long exposed this ideology of marriage and the nuclear family (Barrett & McIntosh 1982) and the difficulty of challenging this social construction from within (Hennessy 2000, p. 97). More recently, it has been pointed out that emphasizing marriage as a key social struggle and goal has implications for citizenship. On the one hand, extending marriage rights to same-sex couples will "change cultural assumptions about who may and does love whom, about the meaning of reproductivity and parenting" (Phelan 2001, p. 158). On the other hand, assumptions about the relationship between kinship and citizenship may not change as a result of extending the definition of family: "[W]e run the risk of reconsolidating the idea of the responsible citizen as economically independent—or at least married to a provider—thus removing the burden of notice and care from other citizens" (Phelan 2001, p. 158).

The struggle for the legal redefinition of marriage to include same-sex partners in Canada, in many ways so radical, has embodied this constraint; the responsible lesbian or gay citizen of the future may well be a married one. As Butler puts it, "options outside of marriage are becoming foreclosed as unthinkable" (2002, p. 18). The neoliberal choice model that enables same-sex marriage certainly is preferable to a neoconservative space that would continue to endorse restrictive definitions of marriage and family. Moreover, given the security of legal recognition of their relationships, lesbians and gay men may feel secure enough in their legal rights to undertake the kind of critical analysis of marriage and familial ideology that we have argued has been undermined. As others have observed, "citizenship is never wholly disciplined, but may simultaneously retain 'an unruly edge'" (Cossman 2002a, p. 487; Stychin 2001, p. 290). In order to engage this unruly edge, however, lesbians and gay men—indeed all citizens—will have to return their gaze to the "other"—those who do not fit the mould of the responsible citizens of neoliberalism. Given that Canada has legalized same-sex marriage for the whole country, we can study whether or not this broader gaze—arguably a feminist gaze—is achievable.

References

Ambert, A., *Same-Sex Couples and Same-Sex Parent Families: Relationships, Parenting, and Issues of Marriage* (The Vanier Institute of the Family, 2003), www.vifamily.ca/library/cft/samesex.pdf.

Barrett, M. & McIntosh, M, *The Anti-Social Family* (London: Verso, 1982).

Boyd, S.B., "Family, Law and Sexuality: Feminist Engagements", *Social & Legal Studies* 8/3 (1999), 369–390.

Boyd, S.B. & Young, C.F.L., "Feminism, Law, and Public Policy: Family Feuds and Taxing Times", *Osgoode Hall Law Journal* 42/4 (2004), 545–582.

Brook, H., "How to do Things with Sex", in *Sexuality in the Legal Arena*, eds. C. Stychin & D. Herman (London: The Athlone Press, 2000), 132–150.

Butler, I., "Is Kinship Always Already Heterosexual?", *Differences: A Journal of Feminist Cultural Studies* 13/1 (2002), 14–44.

Carby, H.V., "White Woman Listen! Black Feminism and the Boundaries of Sisterhood", in *Materialist Feminism: A Reader in Class, Difference, and Women's Lives*, eds. R. Hennessy & C. Ingraham (New York & London: Routledge, 1997), 110–128.

Collier, R., "Coming Together'? Post-Heterosexuality, Masculine Crisis and the New Men's Movement", *Feminist Legal Studies* 4/1 (1996), 3–48.

Cooper, D., "Like Counting Stars?: Re-Structuring Equality and the Socio-Legal Space of Same-Sex Marriage", in *The Legal Recognition of Same-Sex Partnerships: A Study of National European and International Law*, eds. R. Wintemute & M. Andenæs (UK: Hart Publishing, 2001), 75–96.

Cossman, B., "Family Feuds: Neo-Liberal and Neo-Conservative Visions of the Reprivatization Project", in *Privatization, Law, and the Challenge to Feminism*, eds. B. Cossman & J. Fudge (Toronto: University of Toronto Press, 2002), 169–217.

Cossman, B., "Sexing Citizenship, Privatizing Sex", *Citizenship Studies* 6/4 (2002a), 483–506.

Davis, A,Y., *Women, Race, and Class* (New York: Vintage, 1983).

Department of Justice, Canada. *Marriage and Legal Recognition of Same-Sex Unions: A Discussion Paper* (Ottawa: Department of Justice, November 2002).

Editorial, "Gays in the 'hood' ". *Globe and Mail*, 31 January 2005, A12.

Ettelbrick, P., "Since When is Marriage a Path to Liberation?", in *Lesbian and Gay Marriage: Private Commitments, Public Ceremonies*, ed. S. Sherman (Philadelphia: Temple University Press, 1992), 20–26.

Fineman, M.A., *The Neutered Mother, the Sexual Family and Other Twentieth Century Tragedies* (New York: Routledge, 1995).

Fineman, M.A., "Cracking the Foundational Myths: Independence, Autonomy, and Self-Sufficiency", *Journal of Gender, Social Policy and the Law* 8/1 (2000), 13–30.

Gavigan, S.A.M., "Paradise Lost, Paradox Revisited: The Implications of Familial Ideology for Feminist, Lesbian and Gay Engagement to Law", *Osgoode Hall Law Journal* 31 (1993), 589–624.

Hennessy, K., *Profit and Pleasure: Sexual Identities in Late Capitalism* (New York: Routledge, 2000).

Herman, D., *Rights of Passage: Struggles for Lesbian and Gay Legal Equality* (Toronto: University of Toronto Press, 1994).

Iyer, N., "Categorical Denials: Equality Rights and the Shaping of Social Identity", *Queen's Law Journal* 19/1 (1993), 179–207.

Jacobs, M.P., "Do Gay Men Have a Stake in Male Privilege? The Political Economy of Gay Men's Contradictory Relationship to Feminism", in *Homo Economics: Capitalism, Community, and Lesbian and Gay Life*, eds. A. Gluckman & B. Reed (New York: Routledge, 1997), 165–184.

Kelly, F., "Nuclear Norms or Fluid Families? Incorporating Lesbian and Gay Parents and Their Children into Canadian Family Law.", *Canadian Journal of Family Law* 21 (2004), 133–178.

Kitzinger, C. & Wilkinson, S., "The Re-Branding of Marriage: Why We Got Married Instead of Registering Civil Partnership", *Feminism and Psychology* 14/1 (2004), 127–150.

Lahey, K., *Are We Persons Yet?: Law and Sexuality in Canada* (Toronto: University of Toronto Press, 1999).

McIvor, S.D., "Aboriginal Women Unmasked: Using Equality Litigation to Advance Women's Rights", *Canadian Journal of Women and the Law* 16/1 (2004), 106–136.

Mello, M., *Legalizing Gay Marriage* (Philadelphia: Temple University Press, 2004).

Mossman, M.J., "Running Hard to Stand Still: The Paradox of Family Law Reform", *Dalhousie Law Review* 17 (1994) 5–34.

Phelan, S., *Sexual Strangers: Gays, Lesbians, and Dilemmas of Citizenship* (Philadelphia: Temple University Press, 2001).

Phipps, S.A. & Burton, P.S., "Sharing Within Families: Implications for Measurement of Poverty Among Individuals in Canada", *Canadian Journal of Economics* 28/1 (1995), 177–204.

Picchio, A., *Social Reproduction: The Political Economy of the Labour Market* (New York: Cambridge University Press, 1992).

Polikoff, N., "We Will Get What We Ask For: Why Legalising Gay and Lesbian Marriage Will Not Dismantle the Structure of Gender in Every Marriage", *Virginia Law Review* 79 (1993), 1535–1550.

Polikoff, N., "Why Lesbians and Gay Men Should Read Martha Fineman", *Journal of Gender, Social Policy, and Law* 8 (2000), 167–176.

Roberts, D., *Killing the Black Body: Race, Reproduction, and the Meaning of Liberty* (New York: Pantheon Books, 1997).

Robson, R., "Resisting the Family: Repositioning Lesbians in Legal Theory", *Signs* 19/4 (1994), 975–996.

Smith, M., *Lesbian and Gay Rights in Canada: Social Movements and Equality Seeking. 1971–1995* (Toronto: University of Toronto Press, 1999).

Stychin, C., "Sexual Citizenship in the European Union", *Citizenship Studies* 5 (2001), 285–320.

Sullivan, A., "Here Comes the Groom: A (Conservative) Case for Gay Marriage", *The New Republic*, 3893. 28 August 1989. 20.

The Silencing of Sexuality

Cassandra Lord

Cassandra Lord is a PhD candidate and Teaching Assistant at the University of Toronto where she is pursuing her interests in feminist/gender studies, anti-racist theory and practice, queer theory and critical geography. She has also worked in the field of human resources in the areas of benefits and salary compensation at PricewaterhouseCoopers LLP over the past 12 years. In 2002, Cassandra received the City of Toronto Community Service Volunteer Award for developing the Black Queer Youth initiative, a program of

Supporting Our Youth. She has served on the boards of the Lesbian, Gay, Bisexual Youthline, Fireweed, a feminist collective, and is currently a member of the board of the Lesbian and Gay Community Appeal Foundation.

There are many times I have felt silenced in talking about my sexuality, which is often the result of the negative responses I have received from friends, family, community and also from society, when the term "lesbian" is mentioned. Depending on my location, it becomes even more distressing when I have to constantly negotiate my sexual identity with my race and class position. The silencing of black lesbian sexualities continues to exist outside as well as inside various black communities, and in many ways is influenced by race, class and gender stereotypes about black women's sexuality. These factors, along with social and cultural factors, contribute to this silencing.

In her essay "Black (W)holes and the Geometry of Black Female Sexuality," Evelynn Hammonds points out that "black women's sexuality is often described in metaphors of speechlessness, space, or vision, as a 'void' or empty space that is simultaneously ever visible (exposed) and invisible and where black women's bodies are always already colonized."[1] Through the historical legacy of slavery, black women's bodies were exposed on auction blocks and viewed as commodities that could be bought and sold at the slave master's request. As a result, black women's bodies, even more than white women's, were constructed as sexual commodities, with no intrinsic non-commercial value. This distorted view continues to reinforce negative stereotypes about black women's sexuality. Black lesbians have shared in this history, with the added oppression of being forced into denying our sexual orientation. This denial has forced some of us to remain in hiding, not only from our families but also from ourselves.

The well-known "closet" often functions in ambiguous ways: it acts as a protective skin from society at large, but at the same time contributes to the multiple oppressions we face as black lesbians. We are sometimes forced into the "closet" by white lesbians, who focus on their sexual oppressions but fail to recognize how these oppressions, as well as how racism, operates in the lives of lesbians of colour. This is made evident by black lesbian theorist Ekua Omosupe in "Black/Lesbian/Bulldagger" when she writes that "the term 'lesbian' without racial specificity, focuses on and refers to white lesbian culture."[2] . . .

Race also functions as a factor in the relationships we choose to form with other lesbians . . . If black lesbians choose to have relationships with white women, we are viewed as committing a double act of betrayal: becoming traitors to the black race and at the same time preventing its continuity.

As a black lesbian, I am very familiar with the term "double life," as this is how I have existed for most of my adult life. Leading two separate lives is a difficult thing, as you have to negotiate your sexuality based on whether you live at home or on your own. As a friend told me, "If you live at home it is even more difficult, telephone calls are censored, 'she' is replaced by 'he,' you also have to make sure at all times that your personal space is made lesbian free." Family and community gatherings are also the places where you are expected to leave the other part of you behind. On one occasion, before my family headed off to my aunt B's house for a celebration, I was warned by my mother to not bring up issues concerning feminism or lesbianism, as the family will not understand. Audre Lorde best describes the dilemma we feel as lesbians in *Sister Outsider:* "Being an open lesbian in the black community is not easy . . . being closeted is even harder."[3]

The most difficult thing about coming out as lesbian is your parents' denial of your sexuality. My mother's denial of my lesbianism is exemplified by responses such as "don't worry, you'll grow out of it; it's just another phase." I think that by ignoring this part of me, she is trying to find a way of accepting my lesbianism. She does not understand that I am almost thirty and I don't expect or want to grow out of this. Donna Allegra writes in "Lavender Sheep in the Fold," that her parents' denial of her sexuality was also coupled with the hope that she would also grow out of this phase. It was an experience akin to her vegatarianism: "After 10 years of my being a vegetarian, my mother had asked . . . but wouldn't you like some meat, dear? And after 20 years, my father says you still on that no meat-eating kick?"[4] The lack of acceptance of our sexual orientation by our families is influenced by how lesbianism is viewed in black communities. bell hooks speaks to this issue when she states, "Black communities may seem more homophobic than other communities because there is a tendency for individuals in black communities to verbally express in an outspoken way anti-gay sentiments."[5]

The creation of alternative communities helps black lesbians develop support and, at the same time, reinforce positive affirmations of sexual identity. The importance of such communities is stressed by Audre Lorde in *Zami: A New Spelling of My Name:* "We tried to create a community . . . [to] survive within a world we correctly perceived to be hostile to us."[6] In these communities, friendships as well as relationships were formed, and this acted as a wider social network for meeting new people.

Lesbian communities were also established across racial boundaries in the 1950s, which is described in the book *Boots of Leather, Slippers of Gold.* "Black and white lesbians," the authors write, "began to interact on a regular basis and to participate in a shared culture."[7] Although communities based on shared experiences continue to exist, there is also the need for subcommunities within these groups to be formed, as the larger community in which they are located may not be able to address certain concerns. In "Man Royals and Sodomites: Some Thoughts on the Invisibility of Afro-Caribbean Lesbians," Makeda Silvera writes: "The white lesbian organisations/groups have barely (some not at all) begun to deal with or acknowledge their own racism, prejudice, and biases."[8] I have experienced feeling marginalized in certain women's collectives, where I may be the only woman of colour within the group who is also lesbian. There is the problem that, when issues are raised about black women or black lesbians, I am placed in a position where I am looked upon as being the voice for all black women. As a result, it is sometimes easier to be part of a group of similar racial histories because you are able to speak for yourself.

The function of the "closet" and the reasons many black lesbians are afraid of coming out is an area where critical attention must be placed in order to understand how "silencing" functions within black communities. We will only be able to break this silence when we are able to speak freely about our experiences as black lesbians, wherever we are.

Endnotes

This essay was originally published in a different form in Tiphanie Gundle, ed., *Oshun's Light: Rebirth of Anansi* (Saint Bani Press, May 2000).

1. Evelynn M. Hammonds, "Black (W)holes and the Geometry of Black Female Sexuality," *differences* 6, nos. 2/3 (Summer/Fall 1994), 132.
2. Ekua Omosupe, "Black/Lesbian/Bulldagger," *differences* 3, no. 2 (Summer 1991), 108.

3. Audre Lorde, *Sister Outsider* (Trumansburg, NY: Crossing Press, 1984), 99.
4. Donna Allegro, "Lavender Sheep in the Fold," in Moore, ed., *Does Your Mama Know? An Anthology of Black Lesbian Coming Out Stories* (Decatur, GA: Red Bone Press, 1997), 158.
5. bell hooks, *Talking Back: Thinking Feminist, Thinking Black* (Boston, MA: South End Press, 1989), 122.
6. Audre Lorde, *Zami: A New Spelling of My Name* (Watertown, MA: Persephone Press, 1982), 179.
7. Elizabeth Lapovsky Kennedy and Madeline D. Davis, *Boots of Leather, Slippers of Gold: The History of a Lesbian Community* (New York, NY: Penguin Books, 1993), 117.
8. Makeda Silvera, "Man Royals and Sodomites: Some Thoughts on the Invisibility of Afro-Caribbean Lesbian," in Moore, ed., *Does Your Mama Know?* 182.

Does A Lesbian Need a Vagina Like a Fish Needs a Bicycle? Or, Would the "Real" Lesbian Please Stand Up!

Amber Dean

Amber Dean is working on her PhD in English at the University of Alberta, although she continues to be most at home in Vancouver where she teaches Women's Studies courses at Capilano College in the summertime. Her work has been published in Canadian Woman Studies *and* Review of Education/Pedagogy/Cultural Studies *(forthcoming), and she is currently co-editing a special issue of* West Coast Line *on representations of murdered and missing women.*

About five years ago I stumbled upon a comic strip from Alison Bechdel's brilliant *Dykes to Watch Out For* series that (like so many of her comedies) made me laugh out loud and then shake my head in wonderment at her ability to so compellingly bring forward the very debates I'd found myself having with friends only weeks or days or maybe even hours before. This particular strip, "I.D. Fixé?" (Bechdel 58–59), starts out as a debate about who "qualifies" as a dyke, and by the end of the strip leaves the reader pondering the ongoing relevance of identity categories *period* in the present "post-"(insert favourite now-under-fire-brand-of-theorizing-or-category-of-identity here) world. I was particularly struck by main character Sparrow's insistence that sleeping with a man need not entail renouncement of her "dyke" status (she self-identifies as a "bi-dyke" in the strip), while her boyfriend Stuart asserts that he considers himself to be "a butch lesbian in a straight man's body." The comic also points out how trans-identified people have the subversive potential to put identity categories into a tailspin, but (still, and perhaps stubbornly) identifying as a dyke myself, I am more intrigued by the questions the strip raises about who "qualifies" as a lesbian these days and for what reasons.

Around the same time, I came across a personal ad in the notoriously gender-bending lesbian sex magazine, *On Our Backs*, in which the writer insisted that only "real lesbians" need reply: according to the author of this ad, a "real" lesbian is apparently a "professional woman who's childless, financially secure, spiritual, intelligent and likes working out and reading" and is definitely not a "Bi." Hmm, I wondered, am I missing something here? When I came out, did somebody forget to send me some important guidelines that spell out exactly what qualifies one as a "real" lesbian? Or, if I *am* a real lesbian, would I just *know* the guidelines without needing to be told? Does Bechdel's Sparrow—complete with long hair, make-up, flowing dresses and boyfriend—qualify as a "real" lesbian? Not according to the author of the *On Our Backs* personal ad, but what about to others? What about Stuart, the "butch lesbian in a straight man's body"—would he qualify as a lesbian in *anyone's* eyes but his own? And who gets to decide whether one "qualifies" as a lesbian or not, anyway? In this paper, I attempt to think through some of these questions.

TO BE VISIBLE

When I first started to explore my lesbianism in the mid-1990s, I had long spiraling hair and liked to wear full-length skirts or flowing dress pants with V-neck blouses or sweaters and, often, long dangly earrings. I applied perfume, makeup and hair products daily as part of my beauty regimen. As I tried to break into the lesbian scene, I sometimes wondered if my appearance was a barrier. Did my looks somehow disqualify me as a lesbian? Similarly, a subject in Julie Melia's essay on the lesbian "continuum of resistance" describes a long-haired friend of hers who worried she "wasn't a real dyke because of her hair" (551). This connection between *looking like* a lesbian and *being* a lesbian—between appearance and identity—seems to be a common theme. A subject from Anthony Freitas, Susan Kaiser and Tania Hammidi's study on visibility issues in queer communities tells us that "if you feel you are a part of the greater lesbian community, it is important to look like you identify with that community" (99). In their short film *What Does a Lesbian Look Like?* Winnipeg performance artists Shawna Dempsey and Lorri Millan poke fun at the controversy and uneasiness surrounding what it means to "look like a lesbian": "Is she butchy, ball-busting, bad-assed with facial hair?" they ask. "Or does she strut her stuff, show some thigh, and leave a trail of kisses with her lipstick?" The question of what a lesbian looks like has been hotly contested, and has at times been used as a standard for judging who qualifies as a "real" lesbian and who does not. How much does being visibly identifiable as a lesbian relate to the question of who "qualifies" as a lesbian?

A week after my first sexual experience with a woman, I bought my first pair of cargo pants and played seriously with the idea of cutting my hair short and maybe getting a nose ring. My last lesbian lover, who was in a relationship with a man prior to me, cut her long hair drastically short within the first two weeks of our relationship. We had a running joke about who looked "dykey-er." Not long after that relationship ended, I decided it was time to (once again) go back to short hair in an effort to look more "like a lesbian." Of course, my idea of what a lesbian "looks like" is largely shaped by my own race and class backgrounds: being white, from a middle-class background and coming to my lesbianism largely through my engagement with feminism in an academic environment, I can't help but suspect that my notion of lesbian appearance is shaped by the lingering influence of 1970s lesbian feminism. My ability to conform to this narrow notion of what a lesbian "looks like," then, is unquestionably influenced by my race and class privilege.

The subjects in Melia's study point out that there is a tendency to dramatically alter one's appearance shortly after starting to self-identify as a lesbian (550, 554). Thus I remain convinced that appearance is still intimately connected to my own and many other lesbians' sense of our identities as lesbians.

Visibility, then, is perhaps related as much to desire as it is to identity: being visible as a lesbian allows me to communicate my desire to others, just as being able to visibly identify other women as lesbian facilitates my desire for those women. My appearance is also a way for me to communicate to the rest of the world that I am different and proud of my difference. When I first came out I was eager to signal my resistance to heteronormativity and my willingness to take on whatever challenges I might have to face as a result of my difference, even if this meant harassment or personal attacks.

Although some postmodernist theorizing has encouraged a shift from thinking in terms of visible/invisible bodies to terms of marked/unmarked ones, Lisa M. Walker chooses to continue to use the former, despite the "lack of clarity" she perceives in these terms (868, fn). As she points out, the term "unmarked" is used to describe the normative body in theory, but "invisible" refers to those bodies that are not normative, and so the two sets of terms fail to "map directly onto each other" (868). She argues that a focus on visibility among several so-called minority groups has become a "tactic of late twentieth-century identity politics" (868). Melia points to how queer activists have privileged appearance and style as "a key part of resistance" (548), and the prevalence of the popular slogan *visibility = life* on the t-shirts of some gay and lesbian activists has also been noted (Freiras et al. 84). Clearly, visibility—looking "like a lesbian"—has historically been and remains an important aspect of many lesbians' identities, and hence gets tied to debates about who qualifies as a "real" lesbian.

So what *does* a lesbian look like? Although many have suggested that at various points in history there is an identifiable (normative) lesbian appearance, or very specific standards of dress and style, what a lesbian *actually* looks like depends a great deal (of course) on the historical period, on her personal preferences, and/or on her desire to conform to these standards (Melia; Freitas et al.; Myers, Taub, Morris and Rothblum). It also depends a lot on her race or ethnicity, class, ability and age. As soon as a categorical "lesbian uniform" is posited it becomes important to think about who is being excluded through this categorization of lesbian appearance. There are numerous testimonies, for example, of the unhappiness suffered by women who identified as femmes but abandoned this style (and, for a time, a femme identity) in order to continue to "qualify" as a lesbian during the heyday of the lesbian-feminist 1970s (see Millersdaughter; Faderman).

Similarly, many lesbians write about how being of colour or being from a working class background has resulted in their exclusion from gay and lesbian communities that privilege whiteness and middle- or upper-class visibility (Allison; Feinberg; Khan; Law). These exclusions have caused some lesbians to struggle with their allegiance to lesbian communities, wondering whether they would have to forgo their racial or class allegiances in order to be "visible" as lesbians. Surina Khan articulates this struggle when she writes: "When I came out I identified only as a lesbian. It didn't occur to me to identify as a Pakistani lesbian" (130). Only after many years of struggling with her various identities and the intersecting impacts of racism and homophobia—often experienced *within* her queer and Pakistani communities—was Khan able to come out as and embrace a Pakistani lesbian identity.

The dominant construction of what a lesbian "looks like" was developed, according to Deke Law, "by white women in response to sexism in the U.S. Left and in the gay men's movement, with an apparently rigid definition for membership" (144). Law insists we must critique this construct because, whether it is expressed "through clothes, politics, or space, there is an implicit understanding that all lesbians are alike in fundamental ways" (144). This assumption has frequently resulted in the exclusion of femmes, trans-identified people, lesbians of colour, working class, disabled and older lesbians from the category of "lesbian," which has seriously undermined the revolutionary potential of lesbian politics.

For most lesbians in the 1950s, appearance was central to both identity and community. As described so poignantly by Leslie Feinberg in her autobiographical novel *Stone Butch Blues*, in the 1950s there were butches and femmes, and femmes partnered with butches, period. Feinberg writes about primarily working-class lesbians, and in her novel any lesbian who strayed outside of the butch-femme formation in the 1950s and early 1960s was ostracized and failed to qualify as a "real" lesbian. At this time butch-femme was a way of life for many lesbians, but a butch or a femme was defined as much by appearance as by behaviour, sexual preference or preferred roles in sex acts (Myers et al.).

With the rise of second wave feminism in the late 1960s and throughout the 1970s, butch and femme came under fire. A new breed of feminist lesbians, mostly middle-class, mostly academic and mostly white, decried the "old ways" of butch-femme (Faderman). They believed the butch-femme configurations of most lesbian relationships up to that time were merely an attempt to mirror heterosexual relationships, right down to "appearing" like a "man" or a "woman." Claiming that she wanted to break with the trappings of patriarchy entirely, the new lesbian feminist did her best to achieve an appearance that was completely androgynous, similar to the style previously known as butch (Faderman). The pressure to conform to this regulation of appearance was enormous for those who still wanted to count as "real" lesbians and wanted a place in the lesbian feminist community. The 1970s "lesbian uniform" most prevalently accepted and adhered to was created to signal this desire for androgyny: "Flannel shirts, blue jeans, work boots, no jewelry or makeup, and short hair became *de rigeur*" (Myers et al. 21). Indeed, as recently as 1997, some women interviewed by Anna Myers, Jennifer Taub, Jessica Morris and Esther Rothblum indicated that their extremely butch or extremely femme appearances still drew hostility from other lesbians. Clearly, such a "uniform" posed significant visibility barriers for any lesbian wanting to represent other aspects of her identity.

In the 1980s and 1990s butch-femme made a comeback. It was once again becoming acceptable among most lesbians to claim a butch or femme identity, and to construct one's appearance accordingly. Lesbians who had suppressed their femme-ness and conformed to the androgynous dress code of the 1970s now re-embraced their "femmes within" and reclaimed dresses and makeup. The term "lipstick lesbian" was no longer necessarily a pejorative (Clark 488). Similarly, challenges to the centrality of white, middle-class women's experiences in feminist and lesbian communities made by women of colour, working-class women, women with disabilities and more recently by older women, helped to increase awareness about racism, classism, ableism and ageism within these communities (although there is still much work to do). This made it easier for lesbians to dress in ways that also reflect other aspects of our identities without (perhaps) the same level of hostility about our claims to lesbianism. The qualifications for a "real" lesbian shifted from rigid concepts of what a lesbian "looks like" to the more straightforward qualifier of one woman's attraction to or desire for another woman. Indeed, Jacquelyn Zita tells us that "lesbians are customarily defined by a preference for sexual encounters generally involving four breasts, two vaginas and two clitorises, among other things" (112).

But while some have (re)claimed butch or femme styles and challenged rigid "lesbian uniforms," there still exists some consensus among the lesbians participating in at least one study about what constitutes "conventional dyke style—jeans, T-shirt, boots" (Melia 550) with short hair and no makeup. While I am hesitant to suggest that this "conventional dyke style" has anything to do with who qualifies as a "real" lesbian, I am also struck by the fact that I (one who knows better) still make an effort to conform to this style when I really want to "look like a lesbian," even though I know that not all—not *nearly* all—lesbians conform to these conventions.

Debates about what a lesbian "looks like" in the 21st century have been rekindled by the increasing appearance of lesbians in popular culture. The TV drama *The L Word*, the first ongoing program to focus almost exclusively on lesbian life, has kicked off heated debates about whether the show's characters look enough like lesbians. I confess that until recently I refused to watch the program out of disdain for the so-called representation of lesbianism apparent in the show's advertisements: a group of thin, long-haired, extremely well-coifed, predominantly white women in expensive tailored suits and high heels is a far cry from what I would consider to be a grand achievement of lesbian visibility (which tells you something about my assumptions). But some dyke friends have told me that they really like the show and find it does a good job of representing lesbian life, so I decided to rent the first season to see if my assumptions would be challenged.

In the first couple of episodes of *The L Word*, I was genuinely surprised at the derision directed towards the show's only almost-butch character, Shane, who is informed that everything about the way she dresses "screams dyke" and is therefore embarrassing to some of the other characters. Shane, despite making some gestures towards butch style, still has long hair, is painfully thin and frequently wears make-up and low-cut, femme-like outfits, yet in one episode she is (unconvincingly) mistaken for a gay man. As Karen X. Tulchinsky notes in her primarily positive review of the show in the feminist magazine *Herizons*, *The L Word* "has been criticized . . . for not representing 'real lesbians'" (17) since most of the main characters are thin, femme, wealthy women who live in fancy homes and drive sporty ears. Rather than protesting whether a femme woman "qualifies" as a lesbian, though, I believe critics of *The L Word* (including myself) are primarily concerned with the lack of diversity among the characters: in other words, it's not the presence of femme lesbians so much as the predominance of femme style (and a very narrow representation of femme at that) at the expense of all other visible signifiers of lesbianism that is at issue.

In Canada, the feminist press has (surprisingly) been kinder to the show than the queer press: in queer bi-weekly *Xtra! West*, columnist Ivan E. Coyote points out that some of the show's advertising is specifically directed towards straight men, using the show's graphic lesbian sex to encourage a straight male audience to tune in to the show "right after the *Trailer Park Boys*." Coyote, a high-profile Vancouver butch lesbian, was hired to teach the program's actors about how to look and act like more "authentic" lesbians, but was disappointed to note the significant absence of crew-cuts, boots, belts or butches among the actresses. Not to mention the entire exclusion of working-class lesbians, which Coyote argues is a gross misrepresentation of the fact that most lesbians don't have the luxury of driving fancy cars since women still bring home so much less, on average, than men. Still, the debates that the show incites about what a lesbian looks like indicate that a connection between appearance and identity is still highly relevant to many lesbians today.

Elizabeth Wilson (1990) argues that changes in style among lesbians are partly a reflection of changing styles for women as a whole. The butch-femme styles of the 1950s, she suggests, may have come about because it was becoming more and more difficult for lesbians to achieve a look that marked their difference from straight women, as mainstream fashion styles themselves became more relaxed. Pointing to how changes in mainstream fashions for women have made it more difficult to visually separate lesbians from straight women, Wilson laments "it's so hard to look deviant these days" (73). Indeed, short hair, no makeup, or clothing that would more traditionally be considered "mannish" can no longer automatically be assumed to be signs that are indicative of a lesbian, as "many of the signifiers of lesbian identity have become trendy in the avant-garde heterosexual community" (Inness 174). While some lesbians feel proud to see styles that we feel some ownership of adopted by a more mainstream audience, we are also faced with an identity challenge. After all, if there is no longer any sure way to "look like a lesbian," how will we know who the lesbians *are*?

VISIBILITY PROBLEMS

Despite the importance of appearance to an individual and communal sense of identity for many lesbians, several writers have raised some serious problems stemming from a connection between appearance and identity (Melia; Freitas et al.; Walker). Walker, for example, argues that privileging visibility as central to a lesbian identity causes an erasure of those lesbians whose appearance might not conform to the generally accepted standards of what a lesbian "looks like." Such an erasure or dismissal causes some lesbians to struggle precisely with this question of whether we qualify as "real" lesbians or not, putting our sense of identity in crisis and sometimes resulting in our ostracism from lesbian communities. Walker argues that these problems tend to be most profound in relationship to lesbians who—like Sparrow in the comic strip—can "pass" for straight: "Because subjects who can 'pass' exceed the categories of visibility that establish identity, they tend to be regarded as peripheral to the understanding of marginalization" (868). Shuffling those who can "pass" to the sidelines of lesbian communities results in a further marginalization of such women within our already marginalized communities and constitutes a use of oppressive tactics for the purposes of "lesbian" boundary maintenance.

Although those in queer communities who hold tightly to the *visibility = life* philosophy view passing for straight as perhaps the greatest threat to gay or lesbian identities, women who pass as straight may do so for a variety of reasons. A lesbian who shapes or adorns her body in a way that does not make her easily identifiable as such often causes others (both lesbian and straight) to react with "uneasiness, anger, or even terror" (Inness 161). Yet Melia points out the many dangers some lesbians still face if we choose to always overtly assert our lesbianism, ranging from loss of employment to harassment or assault. She argues that a "continuum of resistance" (556) should be used to expand our understanding of how passing can sometimes be a subversive strategy for lesbians. Sherrie A. Inness insists that passing at some point is inevitable for all lesbians, and argues that the roll of the onlooker is essential in determining whether a lesbian will "pass" in a given situation—in other words, whether a lesbian will "pass" in a given situation may have little to do with whether she *herself* desires to pass.

Historically, the backlash from within lesbian communities against the lesbian whose style preference is more traditionally feminine has been rooted in femme women's abilities to more easily pass as heterosexual. For some lesbians the fact that a femme (or a bi-dyke, for that matter) can pass more readily as straight is considered a sign that femmes and bi-dykes are less committed to lesbianism or less willing to risk being identified as a lesbian, possibly out of a fear of the various ways in which lesbians are oppressed. An outright decision to pass as straight in some areas of her life may have drastic consequences for a lesbian—as a subject from Melia's research explains, "you lose friendship and community" (551). However, a closer theoretical examination indicates that femme lesbians, bi-dykes, or lesbians who, consciously or not, pass as straight in some areas of our lives, may pose a deeper threat to heteronormativity than a first glance allows. After all, there is a desire not only among some lesbians but also among many people who identify as straight to be able to visually identify a lesbian in order to ensure her exclusion from the realm of "normal," or, in the Butlerian sense, from the realm of "bodies that matter." Disruptions of what a lesbian "looks like" have the potential to confound those people who would like to continue to define the lesbian body as deviant.

So the lesbian who some would argue fails to "qualify" as a lesbian because she differs in appearance from what is *expected* of a lesbian actually has as much, if not more, potential to disrupt heteronormativity than the lesbian who looks like what she is: for some, a good argument to suggest that women like Bechdel's bi-dyke Sparrow have just as much entitlement to the signifier "lesbian" as women who have short hair, wear t-shirts, jeans and boots, swear off make-up, and have sex strictly with other women.

THE LESBIAN "BODIES THAT MATTER"

Judith Butler's theories on how certain bodies come to "matter" can be helpful in articulating how lesbians who sometimes pass as straight can present a significant challenge to heteronormativity. Although Walker has argued the limitations of Butler's earlier writings in defining the subversive potential embodied by lesbian femmes (884), in *Bodies that Matter* there are several passages that indicate Butler's belief in such a potential. For example, Butler insists that she does not wish to suggest the masculinized (or butch) lesbian and feminized fag are the "only two figures of abjection," or only two figures excluded from the category of bodies that come to matter in our society (103). Rather, she goes on to tell us that to take these two figures as the only "figures of abjection" causes us to lose sight of those figures that incorporate "precisely the kind of complex crossings of identification and desire which might exceed and contest the binary frame itself" (103). The femme "bi-dyke" would certainly be a figure for such "complex crossings."

But if there is no set definition of what a lesbian "looks like," then what sort of body "qualifies" as a lesbian body? In the 1970s, the acceptable construction of what a lesbian looked like involved, as I have discussed, appearing as androgynous as possible. Yet such restrictions on who qualifies as a lesbian are comparable to the oppressive tactics used to measure who qualifies as "human" (white heterosexual men), or as a "body that matters." The more relaxed standards for what a lesbian looks like in the late 1980s and 1990s are partly a response to a growing awareness of the fragmentation caused by the strict "lesbian policing" (Freitas et al. 99), or pressures from within lesbian communities to conform to normative standards for appearance. According to Butler, we have to adopt certain positions or categories (e.g. "Lesbian") while at the same time contesting or being open to contestation of the boundaries or limits of these categories, in order to develop a more "complex coalitional frame" (115). This frame would allow women to maintain different aspects of our identities (for example, our race and class backgrounds) without needing to privilege one at the expense of another. Such an understanding of how change occurs certainly encompasses the negotiations within lesbian communities over who qualifies as a "real" lesbian that have been taking place throughout the last few decades.

Still, Butler warns us to be aware of instances when "denaturalizing parodies," such as the parodies of masculinity and femininity encompassed by butch and femme, reiterate norms without questioning them (231). The subversive potential in both butch and femme, and indeed in lesbianism itself, lies in the challenge these identities pose to heteronormativity, or an understanding of heterosexuality as natural, normal, or the only sexual choice available. Butch and femme appearances can denaturalize gender, sex and sex roles by showing how they are constructed rather than natural. But if at any point butch lesbians, femme lesbians or lesbians in general create or "police" norms of our own, without at least being open to exceptions to or contestation of these norms, Butler warns that our radical or subversive potential will be diminished.

But if there can be no boundaries to the category "lesbian," no directives for what a lesbian "looks like" (or who she necessarily sleeps with), is there *such a thing* as a lesbian? Or could *anyone* be a lesbian?

Certainly some postmodernist theorizing might lead us to think so. As Cathy Griggers explains, "lesbians in the public culture of postmodernity are subjects-in-the-making whose body of signs and bodies as signs are up for reappropriation and revision" (123). In the past few years, the place of trans-identified people within lesbian communities has been a source of much debate. Zita makes note of the following signs surrounding what she calls the "precious little lesbian space there is in the world:" "Women only. Lesbians only. Women-born-women only. Genetic female dykes only. No boys over the age of twelve" (122). Yet most lesbian communities have slowly started to accept that trans-identified people can and should "qualify" as lesbians if they desire to identify as such. But what about someone like Bechdel's Stuart, meaning an anatomically male human being with a penis, testes, male secondary sex characteristics and no plan to alter any of these, whose gender identity is also masculine and who would unquestioningly be interpreted by onlookers to be, without hesitation or doubt, a man? In Bechdel's comic strip, Stuart makes a claim to a lesbian identity. Could Stuart qualify as a "real" lesbian? Should he?

THE MALE LESBIAN (?)

Can a man "qualify" as a lesbian? This is perhaps the most difficult identity question that a feminist-postmodernist-lesbian has to ponder. For some lesbians, of course, the question is also an absurd one, and may understandably seem highly irrelevant in the context of trying to survive, support a family and deal with the day to day pressures of being an out lesbian in a homophobic culture.[1] But the male lesbian keeps popping up on our radar: five years ago there was Bechdel's Stuart, and today we're confronted with "Lisa," a "lesbian-identified-male" who becomes one of the main characters' "lesbian lover" during the first season of *The L Word*. Hence I remain persuaded of the importance of the figure of the male lesbian to lesbian and feminist theorizing and politics, and as such I will flesh out his theoretical and political significance in this section.

A belief in the constructed-ness of gender forms the basis of many feminist theories. A belief in the constructed-ness of sex follows close behind, and has been argued by Butler and adopted by many feminist and postmodernist theorists. If sex is a construct, then a deconstruction would certainly allow the possibility of a male lesbian, since the category "male," and, for that matter, the category "lesbian," no longer hold the same meaning. After all, Butler has insisted that it is "unclear to [her] that lesbians can be said to be 'of' the same sex" (65–66). But is the possibility of a man wanting to represent himself as a lesbian not antithetical to almost everything that lesbianism has stood for or tried to accomplish in the last few decades? Yet if the category of "lesbian" can stretch (as it mostly has and certainly must) to include those who fail to "look like" a lesbian (i.e., femme lesbians) or to always "act like" a lesbian (i.e., bi-dykes), or to those who resist narrow and essentialist meanings of the signifier "woman" (i.e. trans-identified people), what recourse (if any) do we have to argue that a man cannot "qualify" as a lesbian?

Opening the definition of "lesbian" to include women whose appearances stray from the androgynous "lesbian uniform" discussed before seems to be a far cry from opening the definition to include men. But at the same time there is certainly precedence, even within lesbian communities, for such an opening to occur. In the 1970s some lesbians tried to desexualize lesbianism, arguing that instead of being defined by her desire to have sex with other women, a lesbian was defined merely by her "woman-centeredness" or her political commitment to other women.[2] Given such a definition of lesbianism, I certainly know a few men who could qualify. Indeed, Adrienne Rich's notion of the lesbian continuum, long hailed as the cornerstone of lesbian theorizing, contributed to a de-sexualizing of lesbianism in its attempt to marry feminist and lesbian thought. Monique Wittig has often been quoted for her infamous pronouncement that "lesbians are not women" (qtd. in Wiegman 16), leaving us to beg the question: "Can they be men?" And, in one of the only existing theoretical writings on male lesbians, Zita suggests that a male who is willing to relinquish the significance of his penis and also ask others to do so, or who is willing to engage in "sex acts, mutually interpreted as 'female' sex acts" (120), might have grounds to consider himself a lesbian and ask others to do so as well.

However, many (or most?) women who identify as lesbian might oppose the idea of men qualifying as "real" lesbians (well, for sure the woman who wrote the personal ad in *On Our Backs* would, anyhow). As Zita points out, "[t]he 'male lesbian' seems to be an oxymoron. Yet I have met more than a few. Other lesbians report similar encounters. Is there a problem here?" (107). How much weight does the opinion of other lesbians carry in the ability of a man to self-identify as lesbian? Well, Sherrie Inness argues that the role of the onlooker is essential in determining whether a lesbian will "pass" in a given situation. Similarly, in critiquing Judith Butler's work, Susan Bordo argues that "subversion of cultural assumptions is not something that happens in a text or to a text. It is an event that takes place (or doesn't) in the 'reading' of the text" (8). What is the likelihood that observers of the text of man-as-lesbian will read "Lesbian"? How would a man signify his lesbianism to an audience for which such a reading would basically be implausible?

Still, some men wanting to qualify as lesbians might find acceptance in a community of postmodernist-dykes willing to interpret the representation or "text" he is creating in the manner that he wants them to (think of Ginger's half-hearted acknowledgement of Stuart's lesbian potential when she grumbles that he could be "*Soft* butch. *May*-be" in the Bechdel comic, or of the main characters' apparently unquestioning acceptance of "Lisa" in *The L Word*). Would such a man then qualify as a lesbian? Zita argues that even if such acceptance is found, the man who wishes to identify as lesbian is unable to control the readings of his (male) body undertaken by the outside world. "When these readings numerically outnumber the less frequent 'lesbian' attributions in the charmed circle," she argues, "this external world definitively 'sexes' his body" (125). "Lisa," the lesbian-identified-male from *The L Word*, passes as lesbian only with the support of the show's lesbian community: outside of that community he is clearly not read as lesbian, as his confused encounter with a straight male in episode 10 makes clear. Zita points out that the outside world's reading of the subject's body as "male" also determines his access to certain types of privilege inaccessible to a subject read as "woman" or "lesbian," even if such readings occur against his will.

There seem to be potentially significant political consequences of both including and excluding men from the category "lesbian": the consequences of excluding them risks reproducing the kind of lesbian policing that has also at times (and ongoingly) excluded large numbers of women on the basis of other forms of difference. Yet the consequences of including men in the category of "lesbian" in the present might result in an undermining of lesbian political organizing, since, as discussed, men are seldom likely to be read as "lesbian" outside of a potentially small, welcoming circle at the present moment in time.

So, can a man qualify as a lesbian—or should he? This is, at present, perhaps a question better left unanswered, although certainly an important one to ask. For a related question we would have to ponder would of course be whether the very category of "lesbian" is still relevant, important, essential or meaningful. Consider the assertion of Sparrow, in Bechdel's comic strip, that perhaps now "identity is so much more complex and fluid than these rigid little categories of straight, gay, and bi can possibly reflect" (58–59). After providing a framework for understanding how some postmodernist theorizing has made it possible for a man to qualify as a lesbian, Zita concludes by providing us with tools for a continued exclusion of men from this category. While she agrees that readings that confer a sex to a given body, regardless of the wishes of the subject, may be "utterly constructed and arbitrary," she nevertheless reminds us that they are also "encumbering" (125).

Perhaps for the present, it might be more politically expedient for a man wishing to identify as a lesbian to instead focus his energy on deconstructing masculinity and the many restrictions that construct places on his behaviour and identity. Such a critique of masculinity might even undercut the need some men might feel to identify as lesbian, since the desire to claim a lesbian identity might stem in large part from a rejection of hegemonic constructions of masculinity ("Lisa" makes this point in the *The L Word* when he insists that straight white men represent "everything that's wrong in the world"). However, it is equally important that we remain open to contestation of the boundaries of the category "lesbian," perhaps always with the vision of a time when it will be commonly or popularly accepted that there are more than two genders, more than two sexes, more than two sexualities—in short, what Zita describes as "a number of different ways to inhabit the body" (123). But until we have gone further in popularizing the notion that gender, sex and sexuality are constructed, it might be more politically astute for a man who wants to qualify as a lesbian to identify himself instead as what Zita has coined a "lesbian-identified-non-lesbian-hating-male" (123).

While it may be necessary in the current political context to continue to raise questions and debate about men who wish to represent lesbianism, it is absolutely essential that we maintain a vision for a future in which such policing of the boundaries of lesbianism will become unnecessary or perhaps irrelevant. As Butler suggests, "it may be only by risking the *incoherence* of identity that connection is possible" (113, emphasis in original). Because we live in an imperfect world, it is at times politically necessary to create and maintain a working definition of "lesbian," while always remaining open to contestation of who "qualifies" as a lesbian. But perhaps in the "post-postmodern" period, the male lesbian will have his day.

Endnotes

1. Thanks to an anonymous reviewer for reminding me of this fact.
2. Thanks to an anonymous reviewer who pointed out that there was also an effort among some lesbian feminists in the 1970s to define a "real lesbian" as a woman who had *never* had sex with a man. Clearly, these debates from the 1970s are still reverberating in our communities today.

References

Allison, Dorothy. *Two Or Three Things I Know for Sure*. New York: Dutton, 1995.

Bechdel, Alison. "I.D. Fixé?" *Post-Dykes To Watch Out For*. New York: Firebrand, 2000. 58–59.

Bordo, Susan. "Postmodern Subjects, Postmodern Bodies." *Feminist Studies*, 18(1) (1992): 159–176.

Butl¢r, Judith. *Bodies that Matter: On the Discursive Limits of "Sex."* New York: Routledge, 1993.

Clark, Danae. "Commodity Lesbianism." *Out In Culture: Gay. Lesbian, and Queer Essays on Popular Culture*. Eds. Corey K. Creekmur and Alexander Dory. Durham: Duke University Press, 1995. 486–500.

Coyote, Ivan E. "The B-Word: Parts land 2." *Xtra! West*, Feb. 17 and Mar, 17, 2005. Online: www.xtra.ca. Date accessed; 05/04/05.

Faderman, Lillian. "The Return of Butch & Femme: A Phenomenon in Lesbian Sexuality of the 1980s and 1990s." *Gentler in the 1990s*. 2nd Edition. Eds. F. D. Nelson and B. W. Robinson. Toronto, Nelson Canada, 1995. 40–57.

Freitas, Anthony, Susan Kaiser and Tania Hammidi. "Communities, Commodities, Cultural Space, and Style." *Journal of Homosexuality* 31(1/2) (1996): 83–107.

Feinberg, Leslie. *Stone Butch Blues: A Novel*. New York: Firebrand Books, 1993.

Griggers, Cathy. "Lesbian Bodies in the Age of (Post)Mechanical Reproduction." *The Lesbian Postmodern*. Ed. Laura Doan. New York: Columbia University Press, 1994. 118–133.

Inness, Sherrie A. *The Lesbian Menace: Ideology, Identity and the Representation of Lesbian Life*. Amherst: University of Massachusetts Press, 1997.

Khan, Surina, "Color Me White." *This Is What Lesbian Looks Like*. Ed. Kris Kleindienst. New York: Firebrand Books, 1999. 127–135.

The L Word. Dir. Rose Troche. Los Angeles, CA: Showtime Networks Inc., 2004.

Law, Deke. (1999). "Evolution." *This Is What Lesbian Looks Like*. Ed. Kris Kleindienst. New York: Firebrand Books, 1999. 137–145.

Lorde, Andre. "The Master's Tools Will Never Dismantle the Master's House." *Sister Outsider: Essays and Speeches*. Freedom, CA: The Crossing Press, 1996. 110–113.

Melia, Julie. "An Honest Human Body: Sexuality and the Continuum of Resistance." *Women's Studies International Forum* 18 (5/6) (1995): 547–557.

Millersdaughter, Katherine. "A Coincidence of Lipstick and Self-Revelation." *Femme: Feminists, Lesbians and Bad Girls*. Eds. Laura Harris and Elizabeth Crocker. New York: Routledge, 1997. 119–130.

Myers, Anna, Jennifer Taub, Jessica Morris and Esther Rothblum. "Beauty Mandates and the Appearance Obsession: Are Lesbians Any Better Off?" *Looking Queer: Body Image and Identity in Lesbian, Bisexual, Gay, and Transgender Communities*. Ed. Dawn Atkins. New York: Haworth Press, 1998. 17–26.

Rich, Adrienne. "Compulsory Heterosexuality and Lesbian Existence." *Signs: Journal of Women in Culture and Society*, 5, (Summer 1980): 631–60.

Tulchinsky, Karen X. "Drama Queers." *Herizons: Women's News and Feminist Views* (Spring 2005): 16–18 & 45.

Walker, Lisa M. "How to Recognize a Lesbian: The Cultural Politics of Looking Like What You Are." *Signs* 18(4) (1993): 866–890.

What Does A Lesbian Look Like? Dir. Shawna Dempsey and Lorri Millan. Finger in the Dyke Productions/Much Music, 1994.

Wiegman, Robyn. "Introduction: Mapping the Lesbian Postmodern." *The Lesbian Postmodern*. Ed. Laura Doan. New York: Columbia University Press, 1994. 1–22.

Wilson, Elizabeth. "Deviant Dress." *Feminist Review* 35 (Summer 1990): 66–73.

Zita, Jacquelyn N. "Male Lesbians and the Postmodernist Body." *Hypatia* 7(4) (1992): 106–127.

Sons of the Movement: Feminism, Female Masculinity and Female To Male (FTM) Transsexual Men

Jean Bobby Noble

Jean Bobby Noble (PhD, York University) is an Assistant Professor in the new Sexuality Studies program housed in the School of Women's Studies at York University (Toronto, Canada). His research focuses on sexuality, gender, transgender/transsexuality, anti-racist whiteness and popular culture through a cultural studies approach. Bobby has published numerous articles and is the author of the book Masculinities Without Men? *(University of British Columbia Press, Winter 2004), selected as a Choice Outstanding Title, 2004; a co-editor of* The Drag King Anthology, *a 2004 Lambda Literary Finalist (Haworth Press 2003); and has just published a new monograph called* Sons of the Movement: FTMs Risking Incoherence in a Post-Queer Cultural Landscape *(Toronto, Women's Press, 2006).*

In my first department meeting as a professor in an unnamed university, one held during a long and very successful academic strike on our campus, the department was attempting to address the gender imbalance amongst its rank of full professors. Given that many of the full professors are male, the department was taking the very important step of finding a remedy to this situation. One senior professor (but not full professor), a woman who teaches, amongst other things, feminist theory, made the very curious claim that given how easy it is these days to change one's gender—and this even after Ontario government delisted sex reassignment surgeries—that she would volunteer to do so if it would allow her to help to step into the pay increase that accompanied a full professorship. A friendly round of laughter ensued, in which all seemingly agreed that this was indeed an easy process and the meeting continued. I sat a little dumbfounded that, in the midst of a unionized labour action on the campus, a locale which has been remarkably progressive in its inclusion of trans issues in its mandate, and in the face of both the aggressive delisting of sex reassignment procedures and the sad reality that male professors still outranked the female, white outranking the professors of colour, any of these matters would be so easily the source of laughter amongst faculty. This work, in part a response to these comments, attempts to look at the most recent current border war in this political conjuncture of feminist theory and activism, as well as trans, queer and gay, lesbian, bisexual and anti-racism social movements.

The title of this paper references Julia Greet's 1991 essay called "Daughters of the Movement: The Psychodynamics of Lesbian S/M Fantasy," a paper which theorized the dynamics of the sex war that raged throughout the 1980s between feminism and sex radicals. These debates, conflicts and extremely acrimonious battles circulating around questions of feminist sexual practices began, so our mythologies tell us, around several very early events: the publication of *Heresies #12: The Sex Issue* (1981), and the 1982 Barnard College conference entitled "The Scholar and the Feminist IX" (Vance 1989). In fact, Patrick Califia has suggested that the opening missives of the sex wars were fired as early as 1977–1979 in San Francisco (Califia 1982). The sex wars seemed to end shortly after the publication of Judith Butler's paradigm shifting treatise *Gender Trouble*, a text which, again, as our mythologies have it, co-parented the spawn of the sex wars: *Queer Theory* (1990). Greet's paper also made important interventions in these debates, arguing that one of the most consistent tropes in lesbian s/m writing was the motif of the good feminist mother and the "bad" irreverent daughter (Greet 1991). I borrow my title from Greet's work to secure the argument of this paper in a history of feminist acrimony which seems, through even just a cursory look at intellectual and political histories, to be quite productive rather than futile.

I focus on the most recent border war within feminism/women's studies: that of transsexuality. But I want to locate both the argument of this essay as well as its content within feminist histories of acrimony.

In her book, *Am I That Name? Feminism and Category of "Women,"* Denise Riley makes a similar assertion (1988). Arguing that feminism needs to refuse to locate itself in categorical and essentialist foundations, Riley suggests instead that feminism might entertain the possibility of contingency, indeterminacy and instability as a willful epistemology and politic. Given that these passionate fictions of gender, sexuality, embodiment, class, race, nation, ethnicity are all historically specific and enmeshed with the lived histories of other concepts, as for instance the social, the subject, constructions of power, the mind, the soul, the body, capitalism and economies, then, Riley asks: why does feminism attempt to secure its politics to a fixed and ahistorical essence of gender? Leaving behind the "why" question, Riley and others argue that any strategy that attempts to ensure victory through fixity rather than flexibility cannot win in the long run. If the sex/gender system and its rhetorics of biological determinism work by stabilizing gender essences, then why attempt to build a politic on that same supposed self-evidence of the body? Such corporeal self-evidence is precisely the stakes of the border skirmish under discussion in this paper.

I also evoke the concept of history here for another reason. I want to articulate this work within my own personal history as a white transsexual man—inside the feminist movement. Like many transsexuals—and despite a panic to the contrary—I come to this current border war with a long feminist history: I came out as a working-class lesbian in my last year in high school, 1978. I had found the word lesbian in the very important feminist book *Lesbian Woman* by Del Martin and Phyllis Lyon (1972), and after asking myself "am I that name?", I answered "yes." After a brief stay in Toronto in the late 1980s, I made my way west to Edmonton, Alberta where I spent almost a decade working inside the lesbian feminist movement. My pre-academic resume details much of this work: I worked almost four years with the Edmonton Rape Crisis Centre; I was part of the lesbian caucus of the Alberta Status of Women Action Committee; I organized and took part in far too many *Take Back the Night* Marches. I was one of a very small group of people to organize and march in Edmonton's first Gay Pride Parade (about 1987: there were seven of us; we walked for a block and then ran for our lives). I started and sustained through two Edmonton winters a sex worker advocacy group called the Alliance for the Safety of Prostitutes, a group which met, during the coldest winter nights, in the only gay bar in Edmonton. I was "the" out lesbian for many television and radio interviews and published many activist articles, pamphlets and tracts in a variety of feminist and lesbian feminist newspapers and magazines. I've helped build many parts of our activist movement long before I entered university and claim this history quite proudly.

I don't find my home in the word lesbian any longer (although that's often my dating pool) but I want to be very clear that I'm not here—as a transsexual man—knocking at the door of the feminist movement asking to be let in. I have been in, of, and indeed, have been the feminist movement and in my work on masculinity, and in my burgeoning identity as a transsexual man, I continue to wear that banner with a great sense of history and with a great deal of pride, if not frustration some days. I belabour this very personal introduction because I want to make it clear here that instead of imagining that female-to-male transsexual men are inside the Trojan horse when we come to the feminist movement, we need to rethink our movements to understand that trans men are actually inside the belly of the beast when we leave feminist spaces. We are, like many other men, sons of the movement and feminism has much to gain by claiming its masculine progeny.

That there are triangulated border wars between women's studies, lesbian butches and female to male transsexual men (FTMs) is by now almost cliche. Those border wars within feminism and women's studies over the subjects of what I'm calling No Man's Land—female masculinity, transsexual masculinity and masculinity studies—are, I'm going to argue, absolutely vital, not dangerous, to the future of feminism.

Such a belief—that thinking masculinity (trans or otherwise) in the context of feminism is its undoing—is the grammar of continued feminist scholarship; for instance, Tania Modleski's book, *Feminism Without Women: Culture and Criticism in a 'Postfeminist' Age* (1991). Confusing feminist deconstruction with anti-feminist "postfeminism," Modleski rightly queries the stakes of a deconstructive feminism but wrongly draws conclusions which are, at the very least, trans-phobic in their oversights. Modleski's book is curious. On the one hand, she interrogates the ideologies of texts that proclaim or assume the advent of post-feminism but draws inevitable conclusions when she argues, on the other hand, that these are texts that are instead engaged in negating the critiques and undermining the goals of feminism—in effect, delivering us back into a pre-feminist world (3). Modleski's invocation of a simultaneous post- and pre-feminism suggests, rhetorically and self-servingly, that feminism hasn't occurred at all yet and supports her assertion that a progressive, theoretically sophisticated and politically effective feminism needs to return to its own limited and historically bound moment of origins, something third wave feminism is attempting to and needs to transcend. This temporality is reiterated in the final sentence of the book: "The post-feminist play with gender in which differences are elided can easily lead us back into our pre-gendered past where there was only the universal subject—man" (163).

In fact, the word "transgender" appears only once—the last paragraph of the book—to reference the failure of queer politics and theory, as well as feminist masculinity studies, to "break free of restrictive gender roles" (1991, 163). Work such as Modleski's holds out much deconstructive promise but fails to supercede its own limited essentialist frameworks. The result is the complete erasure of the productive possibilities for feminism of a politic located within No Man's Land and a reconsolidation of a categorically conservative identity politic.

But these reconsolidations are not limited to feminist theory. Queer theorist Judith Halberstam and trans theorist C. Jacob Hale document similar border skirmishes in "Butch/FTM Border Wars," their essay in The Transgender Issue of *GLQ, A Journal of Lesbian and Gay Studies*, but they examine these border wars as they emerge between transsexual/transgender politics and queer theory (1998). Attempting to rearticulate an argument from an earlier controversial essay, Halberstam, in particular, queries the space between lesbian masculinity and transsexual men. That earlier essay, "F2M The Making of Female Masculinity," generated a great deal of debate when Halberstam argued that within postmodern economies of gender, all genders are fictions of a body taking its own shape . . . for some an outfit can be changed; for others skin must be resewn. There are no transsexuals" (1994, 210–12). In the *GLQ* essay, Halberstam addresses the controversy generated by the earlier essay by suggesting that part of the stakes of each essay is the stabilization of the terms—transsexual, transgender and butch—as unique and distinct identities, each separate from the other. Instead, Halberstam writes, "One of the issues I want to take up here is what model of masculinity is at stake in the debates . . . and what, if anything, separates butch masculinity from transsexual masculinities, suggesting instead that what has been at stake in the border wars are the terms of gendered embodiment itself (288). Halberstam gestures to the strategic deconstructive experiences of transsexual masculinity although, as I will argue later, she resorts back to categorical determinism when coining the phrase female masculinity.

Clearly, what interests me about these debates is less the veracity or authenticity of these conversations (presuming such things are even possible or valued), but rather the way that these terms flag shared feminist histories, or histories of the ideas about gender and sexuality. That is, these movements—feminism, gay, lesbian and bisexual movements, the pro-feminist men's movement and trans movements—each remind us that becoming any gender is a socially constructed process that is ongoing, contingent, non-foundational and self-producing. That is, articulating oneself as a subject (engendered, racialized, sexed, nationed, classed, etc.) is the process through which we learn to identify our "I" relative to bodies, power grids, as well as culturally available categories, like pronouns, and then attempt to became that configuration (echoing Riley's question, "is my "I" that name"?). Bound within this process are, of course, two axioms which are coterminous with those of feminism: first, not all selves are commensurate with, and reducible to, the categories, pronouns and, indeed, bodies intelligible in the sex/gender system; and second, not all incongruities are equal, and although we cannot always know in advance how they will be different, we certainly do need to anticipate and correct for the ideological work these differences are doing within our social justice movements (Sedgwick 1990, 21).

These incongruities amongst the subjects flagged by the phrase female masculinity are radically de-emphasized in Judith Halberstam's extremely important book *Female Masculinity* (1998). Besides being the source of my book's title *Masculinities Without Men?* (2003), it is, after *Boots of Leather, Slippers of Gold*, (Kennedy and Davis 1994) the first book-length study of subjects heretofore neglected in academic inquiry. *Female Masculinity* makes several important interventions in sexuality and gender studies. First, after coining the phrase female masculinity, which works through juxtaposition—in other words through categorical indeterminacy—Halberstam produces and then deconstructs the subjects who are now visible through that oxymoron. Halberstam herself notes the misrecognition which has collapsed the very significant differences between subjects hailed by the phrase female masculinity—butch masculinity, transsexual masculinity, transgendered subjects, drag kings and so on. She argues, as remedy, that while these subjectivities might appear to be similar, each has different representational and discursive histories. Where some of the work theorizing these subjects challenges a binary or two-genders system by positing a third gender, Halberstam's work instead gives us multiple engenderings. That is, her work is most potent when she suggests that instead of conceptualizing female masculinity and lesbianism as coterminous and thus, as a singular figure between masculinity and femininity, our analytical findings are richer when female masculinity itself is understood as multiple, contradictory and inherently plural.

But another important goal of Halberstam's work is that of distinguishing female masculinity as distinct from male masculinity, or as she says in an oft-quoted expression, "conceptualizing masculinity without men" (1998, 2). In the end, she wants to make masculinity safe for women and girls, even heterosexual women, so that with more gender freedom, perhaps even men will be able so re-create masculinity using her model of female masculinity. A number of critics have read the phrase "masculinities without men" to suggest that it means without relation to men. For instance, in his review for the *Journal of Men's Studies*, Daryl B. Hill comments that the assertion that "[female] masculinity is 'masculinity without men' is problematic." What Hill seems to be identifying here is how Halberstam's work, like my own, is predicated upon a rupture or distinction between masculinity and men. If the term men is successful for both an ideology and as a signifier, then the referent it imagines itself marking is the male body, complete with penis as supposedly self-evident referent. If, however, the term masculinity accomplishes its work, then men no longer references a self-evident penis. What it references instead is that same sex/gender system which feminism has identified and critiqued, only now we see it operating on a new site, masculinity. Men collapses the distinction between signifier and referent whereas "masculinity" not only reasserts it, but suggests that the possession of a conventionally defined penis has nothing to do with securing manhood. Masculinity is a free-floating signifier, detached from that referent. So, when we posit that sometimes masculinity has nothing to do with men, we are not necessarily arguing literally that female masculinity is not related to male masculinity. Instead, the argument is that masculinity now has nothing to do with the male body as it has been conventionally defined. Both trans and female masculinity are each non-derivative forms of manhood where that subject is no longer secured or privileged by a referent.

That said, the irony of Halberstam's accomplishment is that it is achieved through a series of problematic disavowals. First, and perhaps less immediately significant but still glaringly problematic, is the question of the taxonomizing impulse which organizes Halberstam's inquiry. That this categorical imperative is confusing has already been noted in a number of reviews. *Female Masculinity* suffers from an "excessively schematic taxonomy . . . characteristic of gay and lesbian identity politics where the solution to the problem of categorical thinking is to come up with still more categories" (Hill 2002). Why Halberstam chooses this particular tactic is puzzling. But what seems clear is the effect of this impulse: *Female Masculinity* is a text primarily concerned with lesbian masculinity; I hope to articulate a post-identity politic, and, post-queer, anti-heteronormative, that is, counter-cultural trans-masculinity. What Halberstam's categorical imperative accomplishes is that it produces an odd alignment of sex and gender which is most powerful when it refuses categorization altogether. What I want to offer through FTM transsexual men is a feminist refusal of essentialist categorical schemas. Post-queer—that is, transgendered and/or transsexual but not gay and/or lesbian subjects are, by definition, newly configured masculine subjects and bodies which deconstruct—in the flesh—the terms of hegemonic gendered embodiment and do so in proximity to masculinity.

These relationships amongst men of different genders within similar class, racial, sexual orientations etc., are the deconstructive stuff, as it were, of transsexual masculinity. Halberstam suggests and declares a performative indifference toward male masculinity, which she hopes will pass as an affirmation of female masculinity. Such affirmations, Halberstam writes in *Female Masculinity*, begin not by subverting masculine power or taking up a position against masculine power but by turning a blind eye to conventional masculinities and refusing to engage [...] power may inhere within different forms of refusal: "Well, I don't care" (1998, 9). I, on the contrary, am interested in taking up power precisely in and as a male subject, although one schooled, as I have alluded in the beginning, as one of the sons of lesbian-feminism. The subjects I am theorizing, not lesbian men but FTM tranny men and boys, are subjects who find power not by feigning indifference but rather by cultivating proximity, identification, similarity with other subjects of masculinity. Can we entertain the possibility that sometimes, as my first epigraph suggests, some lesbians actually do want to become men? The argument that female masculinity does not take notice of, or is not influenced by, or does not reciprocate or return the gaze to male masculinity cannot be supported. Each instance of masculinity is informed, influenced, mentored and otherwise learns to become itself from other men in his class or race. FTM tranny guys—either as transgendered or transsexual—not only have to directly "engage" the men around them, they must also, to turn a cliched phrase, embrace the boy within himself in order to move closer to becoming him. Halberstam's "I don't care" might work as a rhetorical disavowal but, like all disavowals, moments where subjects cannot know what it is they both already know and are always already constituted by, it certainly begs the question of psychic proximity to and identification with masculinity, not distance.

Still, proximity and repetition, together with a critical and strategic distance, are often crucial for those of us who want to become political men. I want to suggest that masculinity simultaneously needs to be reconfigured as a deconstructive fiction as well. Such deconstructions must be predicated upon two things: an intersectional model of thinking identity and a permanent rupture or distinction between "masculinity" and "men," and also a strategic necessity of that rupture. Given the first premise of intersectional theories of social construction, each subject of any identity is also articulated in and through different classes, races, ethnicities, abilities, sexualities and bodies at the same time. These relationships amongst trans men of different genders within similar class, racial, sexual orientations, are not only the stuff, as it were, of transsexual masculinity but they remain the measure of its critical potential as well. Let me come at this from a very real fear and criticism within the context of feminism about these transitions into masculinity. One of the most frequent critiques I hear about FTMs is the assertion that by "crossing over this divide," that is, by transitioning and therefore becoming men, FTM transsexual men are now living a kind of privilege not accorded to lesbians or biological women and so, as a result, are somehow betraying their feminist sisters. I have been troubled by this critique—that of crossing over—but it has been only quite recently that I have been able to discern what is at stake in its metaphors. While I recognize that the presence of masculinity in feminism has been complex, the topography of this metaphor recognizes only one singular battlefield (to continue to use a troubling metaphor). That is, part of what this criticism does is to reduce the complex distributional matrix of power to the site of gender only. If there is only one side that is good, and one side that is bad, then we are back to models of thinking which are singular and non-intersectional. And so this model of thinking paints masculinity with one simple brushstroke as "bad" and antithetical to feminism. If our model of feminist critical practice privileges a singular mono-linguistic identity only (gender), then FTM transsexual men have betrayed the cause. But, within the intersectional models of identity—where we understand power being distributed through a matrix of identities simultaneously—this criticism of FTMs cannot hold.

What this criticism actually reveals when it seeks and thinks it finds privilege accruing to gender is, first, its own inability to think intersectionally and second, its complete erasure of whiteness as a mark of power. Let me phrase this differently; when we think we are seeing FTM transsexual male privilege, what we are actually seeing, I suggest, is whiteness modifying masculinity to give it power. If, for instance, transgendered "women" of colour transit into FTM transsexual masculinity, we would be remiss to suggest that this FTM is transitioning into a privileged gender position in our culture. We cannot say in good conscience that a transsexual man of colour has more power than a white born female, heterosexual feminist, can we? So, if I have more power as a white transsexual man than I had as a transgendered and extremely masculine lesbian, is it not the cause that my whiteness is articulating power through my gender? Especially when we consider that FTM transsexual surgeries are not producing passable bodies; they are producing intersexual bodies that are outside of our gender taxonomies. Whiteness, as so many have told us, works invisibly to modify and articulate identity; but white supremacy also works aggressively to de-privilege particular groups of men in our culture while distributing power quite happily to others. These criticisms, of FTM transsexual men, that is, are bound within non-intersectional models of thinking identity within white supremacy, which either tell us more about the anxieties of whiteness or tell us a great deal about the limitations of our theoretical paradigms.

Having said that, it is important to acknowledge here that some groups of men do have more privilege than others. To be sure, white middle- to upper-class men have more power; heterosexual more than queer; bio men more than trans men. It is not at all my intention to suggest otherwise. But, can we not also suggest that embodiments of masculinity are privileged differently in proximity to hegemonic imperatives of the sex/gender system? That is to say, one of the other things that worries me about this categorical dismissal of FTM transsexual men is the way in which it also tells us something about how we are thinking about the transitional process itself. For FTMs, more than MTFs, the transitional process is one fraught with categorical indeterminacy. FTMs almost never fully become men; they stay in the place of transit even if some strike a hegemonic bargain with masculinity that is similar to that of whiteness. That is, to be a trans man means to accept and to allow others to accept, as James Baldwin suggests about whiteness, a hegemonic mobilized fiction, albeit a powerful one. "White people are not white," suggests Baldwin: "part of the price of the white ticket is to delude themselves into believing that they are" (xiv). That is, they accept the hegemonic bargain which traffics in a fantasy of primary, pre-colonial, universal and racially unmarked whiteness. Baldwin is in conversation with historical thinkers like Sojourner Truth, W.E.B. De Bois, but also contemporary theorists like bell hooks, Ruth Frankenberg, Chandra Mohanty, Gloria Anzaidua and many more women who argue that there is no such thing as pure, categorical whiteness. The existence of the now newly configured non-intersectional white race produces the unconscious (at best) willingness of those assigned to it to place their racial interests above class or any other interests they hold. Whiteness, in other words, is bound by and is, in effect, secured by its imperative of universal, categorical singularity (that it, non-intersectionality). Entrance into this fictionality of whiteness is purchased through an ideological belief in naturalized whiteness.

Kessler and McKenna suggest something similar in their early work, *Gender: An Ethnomethodiological Approach* (1978). They argue that the perception of a fixed gender role is one interactionally and pragmatically coded by the external signifiers of gender. "Gender attribution is a complex, interactive process," they write, "involving the person making the attribution and the person she/he is making the attribution about" (6). The "reading" of a body as gendered, they suggest, involves presenting gender signifiers within an economy where the signifiers accrue toward the appearance of a coherently gendered body. Becoming a transsexual man, however, means occupying the permanent space of becoming [to transit: n. & v., going, conveying, being conveyed, across or over or through, passage route . . .] that is, it is a permanent place of modulation of what came before by what comes after, never fully accomplishing either as an essentialist reality. For me, as an example, this permanent state of becoming means also failing to become the kind of man privileged in our culture. I have lived for more than thirty years as a lesbian feminist first and this training ground has made me one of the best, although admittedly, always already and strategically failed heterosexual men you are likely to find. One of the things that has been key for me in this transition is a refusal of what we've identified in feminism as the hegemonic imperatives of adult manhood. Along with John Stoltenberg; the "Michaels" Kimmel and Kaufman; Stuart Hall and so many other very political pro-feminist men, I have refined, and continue to refuse, the privileges of becoming a man in the hegemonic ways this category is constructed. Instead, I have opted to occupy the pre-man space of boy/boi, a space of what I argue elsewhere as a productive failure. I have done this, by, among other things, maintaining the discursive space of "F" on my drivers license, living and working in lesbian and queer circles, working against white supremacy, capitalism and so on. These juxtapositions between how I present, my categorical refusal to be fully "manned" either in language or in body (Bob or Robert vs. my boi name of Bobby), but also my refusal to step into the discursive space of "M" to match my gender presentation, signal the critical, political but also discursive space of tranny masculinity for me outside of the clinical and medicalized treatment of transsexual bodies. This often puts me, in daily practice, into some very interesting positions, where my presentation trumps the "F" but where my political refusal of manhood—taking up space for instance in male ways; or jockeying for position with other men for the alpha male position; or allying myself with anti-racist practice; or encouraging other men, as an educator, to remain boys instead of becoming manly men; but most importantly, refusing power (not responsibility) if women, and/or men of colour and/or gay men are present to step into that power instead—allows me a daily deconstructive practice that aggressively refuses the hegemonic fantasy of manhood. Part of what I am trying to say here is that there are many different ways of being masculine; there are many different subject positions available for men, some of which have more power than others. If this is true, then there are many different subject positions for FTMs to transit into (masculinity as modulated by power). As a tranny-man, then, it is my constant practice to refuse that hegemonic bargain by refusing to become a man. What I seek as a trans-man is radical modulation and categorical indeterminacy rather than categorical privilege. The trans space of masculinity needs to be reconfigured as a concept of negative space, which, like any other concept of negative space, is only as effective as the things on either side of it. As a critical practice, then, we might embody a disidentified space of woman, yes, but the space of disidentification only means in so far as it informs the simultaneous refusal to become a hegemonic man at the same time. It is the relation that matters here: hence, the need to think paradox: I'm a guy who is half lesbian.

My own work on and through these border wars of feminism, FTM masculinities and male masculinities does not just map these proximities; I advocate for the social, psychic and political necessity of those relationships. Post-queer relationships amongst men are often at different angles to each other politically—even though we are not likely to see the masculine version of the television show "Will and Grace" (could we even imagine, let's say, "Bubba and Butch" or "Spike and Mike")—the space between men and butches or between men and FTMs—male masculinity and female masculinity. Female to male transsexual bodies are bodies that not only matter—need to matter a great deal to feminism—but these are bodies that defy matter. Both female and trans masculinities have much to offer a gender politic in addition to the necessary reconceptualizations and deconstructions of masculinity, these subjects, especially trans masculinity, offer us a new way to defamiliarize heterosexuality. To be sure, politicized transed-men can embody a feminist anti-normative heterosexuality and more often than not queer both it and masculinity [if by queer we mean pervert, challenge, deform]. That, it seems to me, is a project that feminism might want to embrace to stay vital in the 21st century.

References

Baldwin, James. *The Price of the Ticket: Collected Nonfiction 1948–1985.* New York: St. Martin's Press, 1985.

Butler, Judith. *Gender Trouble: Feminism and the Subversion of Identity.* New York: Routledge, 1990.

Califia, Patrick. "A Personal View of the History of the Lesbian S/M Community and Movement in San Francisco," *Coming to Power.* Samois, ed. Boston: Alyson, 1982, 2nd. Ed., pp. 243–81.

Greet, Julia. "Daughters of the Movement: The Psychodynamics of Lesbian S/M Fantasy," *Differences. A Journal of Feminist Cultural Studies. Lesbian and Gay Sexualities.* 3.2 (1991): 135–59.

Elliot, Patricia. "A Psychoanalytic Reading of Transsexual Embodiment." *Studies in Gender and Sexuality.* 2.4 (2001): 295–325.

——and Katrina Roen. "Transgenderism and the Question of Embodiment," *GLQ: A Journal and Gay Studies.* 4.2 (1998): 231–61.

Gardinée, Judith K. *Masculinity Studies and Feminist Theory: New Directions.* New York: Columbia University Press, 2002.

Halberstam, Judith. "F2M: The Making of Female Masculinity," *The Lesbian Postmodern.* Laura Doan, ed. New York: Columbia University Press, 1994, pp. 210–28.

——. *Female Masculinity.* Durham and London: Duke University Press, 1998.

——. "Transgender Butch: Butch/FTM Border Wars and the Masculine Continuum." *GLQ: A Journal of Lesbian and Gay Studies. The Transgender Issue.* 4.2 (1998): 287–310.

Halberstam, Judith and Jacob Hale. "Butch/FTM Border Wars: A Note on Collaboration," *GLQ: A Journal of Lesbian and Gay Studies. The Transgender Issue* 4.2 (1998): 283–85.

Heresies: A Female Publication on Arts and Politics. Sex Issue 3.4 (1981)

Hill, Darryl B. Female Masculinity. (Book Review). *The Journal of Men's Studies.* Winter 10.2 (2202): 237.

Jardine, Alice and Paul Smith. Eds. *Men In Feminism.* New York: Methuen, 1987.

Kessler, Suzanne J. and Wendy McKenna. *Gender: An Ethnomethodological Approach.* Chicago: University of Chicago Press, 1978.

Kennedy, Elizabeth Lepovsky and Madeline D. Davis. *Boots Of Leather, Slippers Of Gold: The History Of A Lesbian.* New York: Penguin Books, 1994.

MacDonald, Eleanor. "Critical Identities: Rethinking Feminism Through Transgender Politics." *Atlantis* 23.1 (Fall/Winter 1998): 3–12.

Martin, Del and Phyllis Lyon. *Lesbian Woman.* San Francisco: Glide Publications, 1972.

Minkowitz, Donna. "Love Hurts," *Village Voice.* April 19, 1994: 24–30.

Modleski, Tania. Feminism Without Women: Culture And Criticism In A "Postfeminist" Age. New York: Routledge, 1991.

Noble, Jean Bobby. *Masculinities Without Men?* Vancouver: UBC Press, 2003.

Riley, Denise. "Am I That Name?": Feminism And The Category Of "Women" In *History.* Houndsmills, Basingstoke, Hampshire: Macmillan Press, 1988.

Schacht, Steven P. and Doris W. Eking, Eds. *Feminism And Men: Reconstructing Gender Relations.* New York: New York University Press, 1998.

Sedgwick, Eve Kosofsky. "Gosh, Boy George, You Must Be Awfully Secure in Your Masculinity!" *Constructing Masculinity.* Maurice Berger, Brian Wallis, and Simon Watson. eds. New York and London: Routledge, 1995, pp. 11–20.

——. *Epistemology of the Closet.* Berkeley and Los Angeles: University of California Press, 1990.

Striker, Susan. "The Transgender Issue: An Introduction." *GLQ: A Journal of Lesbian and Gay Studies.* 4.2 (1998): 145–58.

Vance, Carole S. ed. *Pleasure and Danger: Exploring Female Sexuality.* London: Pandora Press, 1989.

Film And Video

"Boys Don't Cry." [videorecording] Dir. Kimberly Peirce. Beverly Hills, CA: Twentieth Century Fox Home Entertainment, USA 1999.

"The Brandon Teena Story." [videorecording] Dir. Susan Muske and Greta Olefsdottir. New York: Zoeitgeist Films, USA 1998.

Bibliography

Amnesty International. (2004). *Stolen sisters: A human rights response to discrimination and violence against Indigenous women in Canada*, 4 October 2004. www.amnesty.ca/resource_centre/reports/view.php?load=arcview&article=1895&c=Resource+Centre+Reports

Arscott, J., & Tremblay, M. (1999). Il reste encore des travailles à faire: Feminism and political science in Canada and Quebec. *Canadian Journal of Political Science, XXXI*, 125–151.

Bartky, S. L. (1990). *Femininity and domination.* New York, NY: Routledge.

Bauer, D. (2002). Academic housework: Women's Studies and second shifting. In R. Wiegman (Ed.), *Women's Studies on its own* (pp. 245–257). Durham, NC: Duke University Press.

Bird, E. (2001). Disciplining the interdisciplinary: Radicalism and the academic curriculum. *British Journal of Sociology of Education, 22,* 463–478.

Blee, K. (2002). Contending with disciplinarity. In R. Wiegman (Ed.), *Women's Studies on its own* (pp. 177–182). Durham, NC: Duke University Press.

Bordo, S. (1993). *Unbearable weight: Feminism, Western culture and the body.* Berkeley, CA: University of California Press.

Boxer, M. (1998). *When women ask the questions: Creating women's studies in America.* Baltimore, MD: Johns Hopkins University Press.

Braithwaite, A., Heald, S., Luhmann, S., and Rosenberg, S. (2004). *Troubling women's studies: Pasts, presents and possibilities.* Toronto, ON: Sumach Press.

Brodie, J. (1995). *Politics on the margins: Restructuring and the Canadian women's movement.* Halifax, NS: Fernwood Publishing.

——. (1997). Meso-discourses, state forms, and the gendering of liberal-democratic citizenship. *Citizenship Studies, 1*(2), 223–240.

Bromley, V. and A. Ahmad. (2006). Wa(i)ving solidarity: Feminist activists confronting backlash. *Canadian Woman Studies, 25*(3/4), 61–71.

Brossard, N. (2005), *Fluid Arguments*. Toronto: Mercury Press.

Brown, W. (1997). The impossibility of women's studies. *differences, 9*(3), 79–101.

CAUT. (2007). *Almanacs of post-secondary education in Canada*. Ottawa: Canadian Association of University Teachers. www.caut.ca/en/publications/almanac/default.asp

Doe, J. (2004). *The story of Jane Doe: A book about rape*. Toronto, ON: Vintage Canada.

Dworkin, A. (1974). *Woman hating.* New York, NY: Dutton.

——. (1987). *Intercourse*. New York, NY: Free Press.

Eichler, M. (1990). *What's in a name?* Toronto, ON: Department of Sociology in Education, Ontario Institute for Studies in Education.

Elliot, P., & Mandell, N. (1998). Feminist theories. In N. Mandell (Ed.), *Feminist issues: Race, class and sexuality* (pp. 2–25). Scarborough, ON: Prentice Hall.

Gabriel, C. and Scott, K. (1993). "Women's Press at Twenty: The Politics of Feminist Publishing." In L. Carty (Ed.), *And we rise: Feminist mobilizing in contemporary Canada* (pp. 25–52). Toronto, ON: Women's Press.

Green, J. (2007). "Taking account of Indigenous feminism." In J. Green (Ed.), *Making space for Indigenous feminism*. London, UK: Zed Books.

Haraway, D. (1988). Situated knowledges: The science question in feminism and the privilege of partial perspective. *Feminist Studies, 3,* 575–599.

Heald, S. (1985). Social change and legal ideology: A critique of the new sexual assault legislation. *Canadian Criminology Forum, 7,* 117–127.

hooks, b. (1997). Feminism: A movement to end sexist oppression. In S. Kemp, and J. Squires (Ed.), *Feminisms* (pp. 22–26). Oxford and New York: Oxford University Press.

Huffer, L. (1995). An Interview with Nicole Brossard, Montreal, October, 1993. *Yale French Studies*, 87: 115-121.

Hunter College Women's Studies Collective. (1995). *Women's realities, women's choices: An introduction to Women's Studies*. New York, NY: Oxford University Press.

Jackson, S., & Scott, S. (Eds.). (1996). *Feminism and sexuality: A reader*. New York, NY: Columbia University Press.

Jagose, A. (1996). *Queer theory: An introduction*. New York, NY: New York University Press.

Johnson, H. (2006). Measuring Violence Against Women: Statistical Trends. *Statistics Canada Catalogue no. 85-570-XIE*. www.statcan.ca/english/research/85-570-XIE/85-570-XIE2006001.pdf

Karpinski, E. (1998). Communication across difference: Conflict and community building in Women's Studies programme. *Atlantis*, *22*:2, 137–40.

Kemp, S., & Squires, J. (1997). Introduction. In S. Kemp & J. Squires (Eds.), *Feminisms* (pp. 3–12). London, UK: Oxford University Press.

Lamoureux, D. (1987). Nationalism and feminism in Quebec: An impossible attraction. In H.J. Maroney and M. Luxton (Eds.), *Feminism and Political Economy* (pp. 51–68). Toronto, ON: Methuen.

Lorde, A. (1984). The master's tools will never dismantle the master's house. In *Sister outsider: Essays and speeches*. Trumansburg, NY: Crossing Press.

Maroney, H. J., & Luxton, M. (1987). From feminism and political economy to feminist political economy. In H. J. Maroney & M. Luxton (Eds.), *Feminism and political economy* (pp. 5–28). Toronto, ON: Methuen.

Nussbaum, M. C. (1999, February 22). The professor of parody: The hip defeatism of Judith Butler. *The New Republic*, 37–45.

O' Grady, K. (2006). Status of Women Canada cuts a loss for a healthy democracy. Canadian Woman Studies, *25*(3/4): 79–80.

Pryse, M. (2000). Trans/feminist methodology: Bridges to interdisciplinary thinking. *NWSA Journal, 12,* 105–116.

R. v. Ewanchuk, 1 S.C.R. 330. (1999). Judgments of the Supreme Court of Canada. www.scc.lexum.umontreal.ca/en/1999/1999rcs1-330/1999rcs1-330.html

R. v. Morgentaler, 1 S.C.R. 30. (1998). Judgments of the Supreme Court of Canada. www.scc.lexum.umontreal.ca/en/1988/1988rcs1-30/1988rcs1-30.html

Rich, A. (1986). Compulsory heterosexuality and lesbian existence. In *Blood, bread and poetry: Selected prose 1979–1985* (pp. 23–75). New York, NY: W.W. Norton and Company.

Rudy, S. (2005). Nicole Brossard in English: Editor's Introduction. In Nicole Brossard, *Fluid Arguments* (pp. 9-19). Toronto: Mercury Press.

Statistics Canada. (2004). *The General Social Survey: An Overview*. Ottawa, ON: Housing, Family and Social Statistics Division, Statistics Canada. www.statcan.ca/bsolc/english/bsolc?catno=89F0115XIE2004001&ISSNOTE=1

Vickers, J., P. Rankin & C. Appelle. (1993). *Politics as if women mattered: A political analysis of the National Action Committee on the Status of Women*. Toronto, ON: University of Toronto Press.

Wendell, S. (1996). *The rejected body: Feminist philosophical reflections on disability*. New York, NY: Routledge.

Yee, Shirley. (1997). The "women" in Women's Studies. *differences, 9*(3), 46–64.

Feminist Publications

- Resources for Feminist Research
  www.oise.utoronto.ca/rfr
- Atlantis
  www.msvu.ca/atlantis
- Canadian Woman Studies
  www.yorku.ca/cwscf
- Canadian Journal of Women and the Law
  www.utpjournals.com/cjwl/cjwl.html

Feminist Presses

- Inanna Publications
  www.yorku.ca/inanna
- Toronto Women's Press
  www.cspi.org/womenspress
- Sister Vision Press
- Sumach Press
  www.sumachpress.com

Academic Associations

- Canadian Women's Studies Association/ L'association canadienne des études sur les femmes
  www.yorku.ca/cwsaacef
- Canadian Research Institute for the Advancement of Women (CRIAW)
  www.criaw-icref.ca
- Canadian Women's Movement Archives (CWMA)
  www.biblio.uottawa.ca/content-page.php?g=en&s=archives&c=src-cwma-acmf
- Canadian Congress for Learning Opportunities for Women (CCLOW)
  www.nald.ca/cclow
- National Association of Women and the Law (NAWL)
  www.nawl.ca

Suggested Readings

Chapter One: Who is the Woman of Canadian Women's Studies? Theoretical Interventions

Anderson, H. (2006). Performing postfeminism: Escaping identity politics? *Atlantis*, *30*(2), 114.

Anderson, K. (2001). *A recognition of being: Reconstructing native womanhood*. Toronto, ON: Sumach Press.

Arneil, B. (2007). *Sexual justice/cultural justice : Critical perspectives in political theory and practice*. London; New York: Routledge.

Baker, E. (2005). Loving Indianess: Native women's storytelling as survivance. *Atlantis*, *29*(2), 111.

Bannerji, H. (2000). *The dark side of the nation: Essays on multiculturalism, nationalism and gender*. Toronto, ON: Canadian Scholars' Press.

Bannerji, H. (Ed.). (1993). *Returning the gaze: Essays on racism, feminism and politics*. Toronto, ON: Sister Vision.

Bannerji, H., Carty, L., Dehli, K., Heald, S., & McKenna, K. (1991). *Unsettling relations: The university as a site of feminist struggles*. Toronto, ON: Women's Press.

Bannerji, K. (1998). The politics of identity "alternatives" or opposition? In W. Waring (Ed.), *By, for and about feminist cultural politics* (pp. 79–83). Toronto, ON: Women's Press.

Boivin, M. (1999). The category of "woman/women" in discrimination based on sex. *Canadian Journal of Law and Society*, *14*, 203–243.

Braithwaite, A. (2002). The personal, the political, third wave and post feminisms. *Feminist Theory*, *3*, 335–344.

Braithwaite, A. et. al. (2004). *Troubling women's studies: Pasts, presents and possibilities*. Toronto ON: Sumach Press.

Brodribb, S. (1992). *Nothing ma(t)ters: A feminist critique of postmodernism*. Toronto, ON: Douglas and McIntyre.

Brossard, N. (1985). *The aerial letter*. Montreal, QC: Women's Press.

Calliste, A. M., Dei, G., Sefa, J., & Aguiar, M. (2000). *Anti-racist feminism: Critical race and gender studies*. Halifax, NS: Fernwood Publishing.

Code, L. (1993). Feminist theory. In S. Burt, L. Code & L. Dorney (Eds.), *Changing patterns: Women in Canada* (pp. 19–57). Toronto, ON: McClelland and Stewart.

Cohen, M., Ritchie, L., Swenarchuk, M., & Vosko, L. (2001). Globalization: Some implications and strategies for women. *Canadian Woman Studies/Les Cahiers de la Femme*, *21/22*(4/1), 6–41.

Deliovsky, K. (2002). The more things change... Rethinking mainstream feminism. In N. Wane, K. Deliosvsky & E. Lawson (Eds.), *Back to the drawing board: African-Canadian feminisms* (pp. 54–84). Toronto, ON: Sumach Press.

Dua, E., & Robertson, A. (Eds.). (1999). *Scratching the surface: Canadian anti-racist feminist thought*. Toronto, ON: Women's Press.

Elliot, P. (1991). *From mastery to analysis: Theories of gender in psychoanalytic feminism*. Ithaca, NY: Cornell University Press.

Elliot, P. (2004). Who gets to be a woman?: Feminist politics and the question of trans-inclusion. *Atlantis*, 29(1), 13.

Elliot, P., & Mandell, N. (1998). Feminist theories. In N. Mandell (Ed.), *Feminist issues: Race, class and sexuality* (2nd ed.) (pp. 2–25). Scarborough, ON: Prentice-Hall.

Findlay, B. (2003). Real women: Kimberly Nixon v. Vancouver rape relief. *University of British Columbia Law Review*, *36*, 57–76.

Gayle, N. A. (1993). Black women's reality and feminism. In D. Currie & V. Raoul (Eds.), *Anatomy of gender: Women's struggle for the body* (pp. 232–242). Ottawa, ON: Carleton University Press.

Green, J.A. (Ed.). (2007). *Making space for Indigenous feminism*. Black Point, NS: Fernwood.

Hamilton, R. (2005). *Gendering the vertical mosaic : Feminist perspectives on Canadian society* (2nd ed.). Toronto, ON: Pearson Prentice Hall.

Jhappan, R. (1996). Post-modern race and gender essentialism or a post-mortem of scholarship. *Studies in Political Economy*, *51*(Fall), 15–64.

Karpinski, E. C. (1999). Choosing feminism, choosing exile: Towards the development of transnational feminist consciousness. In A. Heitlinger (Ed.), *Émigré feminisme: Transnational perspectives* (pp. 17–29). Toronto, ON: University of Toronto Press.

King, A. E., & Hyman, A. (1999). Women's studies and the internet: A future with a history. *Resources for Feminist Research*, *27*(1/2), 13.

Lakeman, L. (2006). Sustaining our resistance to male violence: Attacks on women's organizing and Vancouver rape relief and women's shelter. *Canadian Woman Studies*, *25*(1/2), 129.

MacDonald, G. M., Osborne, R. L., & Smith, C. C. (2005). *Feminism, law, inclusion: Intersectionality in action*. Toronto: Sumach Press.

Marshall, B. (1994). *Engendering modernity: Feminism, social theory and social change*. Boston, MA: Northeastern University Press.

Massaquoi, N. (2004). An african child becomes a black Canadian feminist: Oscillating identities in the black diaspora. *Canadian Woman Studies*, *23*(2), 140.

Mayeda, G. (2005). Re-imagining feminist theory: Transgender identity, feminism, and the law. *Canadian Journal of Women & the Law*, *17*(2), 423–472.

Namaste, V. K. (2005). *Sex change, social change : Reflections on identity, institutions and imperialism*. Toronto, ON: Women's Press.

Ouellette, G. J. M. W. (2002). *The fourth world: An indigenous perspective on feminism and Aboriginal women's activism*. Halifax, NS: Fernwood Publishing.

Pagé, G., & Lampron, É. (2006). Strangers in an estranged world: Two radical feminists in the academy. *Canadian Woman Studies*, *25*(3/4), 72.

Perreault, J. (1995). White feminist guilt, abject scripts, and (other) transformative necessities. In R. Mika & F. Wah (Eds.), *Colour: An issue* (pp. 226–238).

Philip, M. N. (1992). *Frontiers: Selected essays on racism and culture*. Stratford, ON: Mercury Press.

Razack, S. (1996). Beyond universal women: Reflections on theorizing differences among women. *University of New Brunswick Law Review*, *45*, 209–227.

Razack, S. (2007). The 'Sharia law debate' in Ontario: The Modernity/Premodernity distinction in legal efforts to protect women from culture. *Feminist Legal Studies*, *15*(1), 3–32.

Shteir, A. B. (2002). Women's studies in focus: The women's studies PhD: Report from a conference [the PhD in women's studies: Implications and articulations, Emory University, October 2001]. *Atlantis*, *27*(1), 53.

Strong-Boag, V., Grace, S., Eisenberg, A., & Anderson, J. (Eds.). (1998). *Painting the maple: Essays on race, gender, and the construction of gender*. Vancouver, BC: University of British Columbia Press.

Trimble, S. (2005). Playing Peter Pan: Conceptualizing "bois" in contemporary queer theory. *Canadian Woman Studies*, *24*(2/3), 75.

Wane, N. N., Deliosvsky, K., & Lawson, E. (2002). *Back to the drawing board: African-Canadian feminisms.* Toronto, ON: Sumach Press.

Webber, M. (2006). "I'm not a militant feminist": Exploring feminist identities and feminist hesitations in the contemporary academy. *Atlantis, 31*(1), 55.

White, M. A. (2007). Undoing gender. *Atlantis, 31*(2), 111.

Wiebe, B. (2006). Radical ambivalence: Engaging poststructurally with performance, (re)envisioning the political. *Atlantis, 30*(2), 100.

Chapter Two: The Changing Context of Activisms

Abu-Laban, Y., & Gabriel, C. (2002). *Selling diversity: Immigration, multiculturalism, employment equity, and globalization.* Peterborough, ON: Broadview Press.

Andrew, C., & Rogers, S. (Eds.). (1997). *Women and the Canadian state.* Montreal, QC: McGill-Queen's University Press.

Armstrong, P., & Armstrong, H. (1994). *The double ghetto: Canadian women and their segregated work* (Rev. ed.). Toronto, ON: McClelland and Stewart.

Ayotte, D., & Gullion, J. (2006). Saying the F-word: Feminism, indie-rock style. *Canadian Woman Studies, 25*(3/4), 137.

Backhouse, C., & Flaherty, D. (Eds.). (1992). *Challenging times: The women's movement in Canada and the U.S.* Montreal, QC: McGill-Queen's University Press.

Bakan, A. B., & Kobayashi, A. (2000). *Employment equity policy in Canada: An interprovincial comparison.* Ottawa, ON: Status of Women Canada.

Baker, M. (2001). *Families: Labour and love.* Vancouver, BC: University of British Columbia Press.

Bakker, I. (1998). *Unpaid work and macroeconomics: New discussions, new tools for action.* Ottawa, ON: Status of Women Canada.

Balfour, G., & Comack, E. (Eds.) (2006). *Criminalizing women : Gender and (in)justice in neo-liberal times.* Halifax, NS: Fernwood Publishing.

Bannerji, H. (2003). Demography and democracy: Reflections on violence against women in genocide or ethnic cleansing. *Resources for Feminist Research, 30*(3/4), 93.

Bannerji, H., & Mojab, S. (2003). Women in a world of war and militarization. *Resources for Feminist Research, 30*(3/4), 7.

Bashevkin, S. (1998). *Living through conservative times: Women on the defensive.* Chicago, IL: University of Chicago Press.

Bashevkin, S. (2000). In the shadow of free trade: Nationalism, feminism and identity politics in contemporary English Canada. *Journal of Canadian Studies, 35*, 109–127.

Bezanson, K. (2006). Gender and the limits of social capital. *Canadian Review of Sociology & Anthropology, 43*(4), 427–443.

Bezanson, K., Carter, E., & Canada. (2006). *Public policy and social reproduction.* Ottawa, ON: Status of Women Canada.

Blackford, K., Garceau, M. L., & Kirby, S. (Eds.). (1999). *Feminist success stories/celebration nos réussites feministes.* Ottawa, ON: University of Ottawa Press.

Boyd, S. B. (2003). *Child custody, law, and women's work.* Toronto, ON: Oxford University Press.

Briskin, L., & Eliasson, M. (Eds.). (1999). *Women's organizing and public policy in Canada and Sweden.* Montreal, QC: McGill-Queen's University Press.

Brockman, J. (2001). *Gender in the legal profession: Fitting or breaking the mould.* Vancouver, BC: University of British Columbia Press.

Brodie, J., (Ed.), (1996). *Women and Canadian public policy.* Toronto, ON: Harcourt Brace.

Brodie, M. J., Bakker, I. C., & Canada. (2007). *Canada's social policy regime and women.* Ottawa, ON: Status of Women Canada.

Brodsky, G., & Day, S. (2002). Beyond the social and economic rights debate: Substantive equality speaks to poverty. *Canadian Journal of Women and the Law, 14*, 185–222.

Bromley, V., & Ahmad, A. (2006). Wa(i)ving solidarity: Feminist activists confronting backlash. *Canadian Woman Studies, 25*(3/4), 61.

Buckley, M., & West Coast Women's Legal Education and Action Fund (2001). *Transforming women's future: An activist's guide to equality rights theory and action.* Vancouver, BC: West Coast Women's Legal Education and Action Fund.

Busby, K., & Comack, E. (2006). *Locating law: Race/class/gender/sexuality connections* (2nd ed.). Halifax, NS: Fernwood Publishing.

Campbell, L. (2005). Grrls plugged in: How canadian rural young women are using the internet. *Canadian Woman Studies, 24*(4), 167.

Canada. Parliament. House of Commons. Standing Committee on the Status of Women. (2007). *The impacts of funding and program changes at Status of Women Canada : Report of the Standing Committee on the Status of Women*. Ottawa, ON: Standing Committee on the Status of Women.

Carver, L. (2004). Re-thinking workfare. *Canadian Woman Studies, 23*(3/4), 143.

Chappell, L. A. (2002). *Gendering government : Feminist engagement with the state in Australia and Canada*. Vancouver, BC: UBC Press.

Chunn, D.E., S. B. Boyd & H. Lessard. (Eds.). (2007). *Feminism, law and social change: (Re)action and resistance*. Vancouver, BC: University of British Columbia Press.

Cohen, M. G., & Brodie, M. J. (Eds.) (2007). *Remapping gender in the new global order.* London; New York, NY: Routledge.

Comack, E., & Balfour, G. (2004). *The power to criminalize : Violence, inequality, and the law*. Halifax, NS: Fernwood Publishing.

Connelly, P., & Armstrong, P. (Eds.). (1992). *Feminism in action: Studies in political economy*. Toronto, ON: Canadian Scholar's Press.

Cossman, B., & Fudge, J. (Eds.) (2002). *Privatization, law, and the challenge to feminism*. Toronto, ON: University of Toronto Press.

Crawford, C. (2004). African-Caribbean women, diaspora and transnationality. *Canadian Woman Studies, 23*(2), 97.

Das Gupta, T., & Iacovetta, F. (2000). Whose Canada is it? Immigrant women, women of colour and feminist critiques of multiculturalism. *Atlantis, 24*(2), 1–27.

Deerchild, R. (2003). Tribal feminism is a drum song. In K. Anderson & B. Lawrence. (Eds.), *Strong women stories: Native vision and community survival* (pp. 97–105). Toronto, ON: Sumach Press.

deGroot, J., & Turnbull, L. A. (2006). Femme fiscale brings women's voices to the legislature. *Canadian Woman Studies, 25*(3/4), 173.

Demczuk, I. (2002). *Recognition of lesbian couples: An inalienable right*. Ottawa, ON: Status of Women Canada.

Descarries-Belanger, F., & Roy, S. (1991). *The women's movement and its currents of thought*. Ottawa, ON: Canadian Research Institute for the Advancement of Women.

Dixon, E. R. (2001). *Canada and the Beijing Conference on Women.* Vancouver, BC: University of British Columbia Press.

Dobrowolsky, A. (1998). "Of special interest": Interest, identity and feminist constitutional activism in Canada. *Canadian Journal of Political Science, 31*, 707–742.

Dobrowolsky, A. Z. (2000). *The politics of pragmatism: Women, representation, and constitutionalism in Canada*. New York, NY: Oxford University Press.

Dobrowolsky, A. Z., & Hart, V. (Eds.) (2003). *Women making constitutions*. Basingstoke, Hampshire; New York. N.Y.: Palgrave Macmillan.

Doucet, A. (2004). Fathers and the responsibility for children: A puzzle and a tension. *Atlantis*, *28*(2), 103.

Doyle-Bedwell, P. E. (2003). Mi'kmaq women and our political voice. *Atlantis*, *27*(2), 123.

Driedger, I. F., & Batres, E. G. (Eds.). (1996). *Across borders: Women with disabilities working together.* Charlottetown, PE: gynergy books.

Drolet, M. (1999). *The persistent gap: New evidence on the Canadian gender wage gap.* Ottawa, ON: Statistics Canada.

Drolet, M. (2002). New evidence on gender pay differentials: Does measurement matter? *Canadian Public Policy*, *28*, 1–16.

Duffy, A., Mandell, N., & Pupo, N. (1989). *Few choices: Women, work and family.* Toronto, ON: Garamond Press.

Eichler, M. (1997). *Family shifts: Families, policies and gender equality.* Toronto, ON: Oxford University Press.

Everitt, J. (1998). Public opinion and social movements: The women's movement and the gender gap in Canada. *Canadian Journal of Political Science*, *31*, 743–765.

Faraday, F., Denike, M., Stephenson, M. K., Moreau, S., Baines, B., McIntyre, S., et al. (2006). *Making equality rights real: Securing substantive equality under the Charter.* Toronto, ON: Irwin Law.

Ferguson-Hood, S., & Walker, M. T. (2006). Safe haven: The story of a shelter for homeless women. *Canadian Woman Studies*, *25*(1/2), 210.

Fiske, J. (2000). By, for, or about?: Shifting directions in the representations of Aboriginal women. *Atlantis, 25*(1), 11–27.

Fitzgerald, M., Guberman, C., & Wolfe, M. (Eds.). (1982). *Still ain't satisfied: Canadian feminism today.* Toronto, ON: Women's Press.

Freiler, C. (2001). *Mothers as earners, mothers as careers: Responsibility for children, social policy and the tax system.* Ottawa, ON: Status of Women Canada.

Fudge, J. (2000). The paradoxes of pay equity: Reflections on the law and the market in Bell Canada and the Public Service Alliance of Canada. *Canadian Journal of Women and the Law, 12*, 313–344.

Fudge, J. (2001). Flexibility and feminization: The new Ontario Employment Standards Act. *Journal of Law and Social Policy*, *16*, 1–22.

Giles, W. M., & Arat-Koc, S. (Eds.). (1994). *Maid in the market: Women's paid domestic labour*. Halifax, NS: Fernwood Press.

Gosselin, C. (2006). Remaking waves: The Québec women's movement in the 1950s and 1960s. *Canadian Woman Studies*, *25*(3/4), 34.

Gotell, L. (1995). Litigating feminist "truth." *Social and legal studies*, *4*(1), 99–131.

Gotell, L. (2002). Towards a democratic practice of feminist litigation: LEAF's changing approach to sexual equality. In R. Jhappan (Ed.), *Women's legal strategies in Canada* (pp. 135–174). Toronto, ON: University of Toronto Press.

Greaves, L. (2002). *A motherhood issue: Discourses on mothering under duress.* Ottawa, ON: Status of Women Canada.

Green, J. A. (Ed.) (2007). *Making space for indigenous feminism.* Black Point, NS: Fernwood Publishing.

Hines, J. N. (2004). The social policy snare: Keeping women out of university. *Canadian Woman Studies*, *23*(3/4), 138.

Jeffries, F. (2006). Organizing on the "factory on wheels": The bus riders' union and anti-racist feminism for the 21st century. *Canadian Woman Studies*, *25*(3/4), 127.

Jhappan, R. (1998). The equality pit or the rehabilitation of justice. *Canadian Journal of Women and the Law, 10*, 60–107.

Krosenbrink-Gelissen, L. E. (1993). The native women's association of Canada. In J. Frideres (Ed.), *Native peoples in Canada* (pp. 335–364). Scarborough, ON: Prentice-Hall.

Lambert, L. A. (2006). When Martha met goliath: Feminists and the state in Alberta. *Canadian Woman Studies*, *25*(1/2), 39.

Latchmore, V., & Marple, L. (2005). LGBTQ activism: Small town social change. *Canadian Woman Studies*, *24*(4), 55.

Lochhead, C., & Scott, K. (2000). *The dynamics of women's poverty in Canada*. Ottawa, ON: Status of Women Canada.

Lunny, D. (2006). Out of Canada: The pedagogy of transnational feminist activism. *Canadian Woman Studies*, *25*(3/4), 85.

Luxton, M. (Ed.). (1997). *Feminism and families.* Halifax, NS: Fernwood Publishing.

Luxton, M., & Bezanson, K. (2006). *Social reproduction: Feminist political economy challenges neo-liberalism.* Montreal: McGill-Queen's University Press.

Luxton, M., Rosenberg, H., & Arat-Koc, S. (Eds.). (1990). *Through the kitchen window: The politics of home and family.* Toronto, ON: Garamond Press.

MacDonald, G. M., Osborne, R. L., & Smith, C. C. (Eds.). (2005). *Feminism, law, inclusion : Intersectionality in action*. Toronto: Sumach Press.

Majury, D. (2002). Charter Canadian Charter of Rights and Freedoms, equality rights, and women: Equivocation and celebration. *Osgoode Hall Law Journal*, *40*, 297–336.

Mandell, N., & Duffy, A. (Eds.). (2000). *Canadian families: Diversity, conflict and change.* Toronto, ON: Harcourt Brace.

Manfredi, C. P. (2004). *Feminist activism in the Supreme Court*. Vancouver, BC: UBC Press.

Mathen, C. (2004). Transgendered persons and feminist strategy. *Canadian Journal of Women & the Law*, *16*(2), 291–316.

McIvor, S. D. (2004). Aboriginal women unmasked: Using equality litigation to advance women's rights. *Canadian Journal of Women & the Law*, *16*(1), 106–136.

McKeen, W. (2004). *Money in their own name : The feminist voice in poverty debate in Canada, 1970–1995*. Toronto: University of Toronto Press.

McPhedran, M. (2006). Creating trialogue: Women's constitutional activism in Canada. *Canadian Woman Studies*, *25*(3/4), 5.

Monture, P. (1993). A vicious circle: Child welfare and the First Nations. *Canadian Journal of Women & the Law*, *3*, 1–17.

Mosher, J., & Evans, P. (2006). Welfare policy: A critical site of struggle for women's safety. *Canadian Woman Studies*, *25*(1/2), 162.

Napoleon, V. (2005). Aboriginal self determination: Individual self and collective selves. *Atlantis*, *29*(2), 31.

Newman, J. A., & White, L. A. (2006). *Women, politics, and public policy: The political struggles of Canadian women*. Toronto, ON: Oxford University Press.

Neysmith, S. M. (2000). *Restructuring caring labour: Discourse, state practice, and everyday life.* Toronto, ON: Oxford University Press.

Ng, R. (1996). *The politics of community services: Immigrant women, class and state.* Halifax, NS: Fernwood Publishing.

O'Grady, K. (2006). Status of women Canada cuts a loss for healthy democracy. *Canadian Woman Studies*, *25*(3/4), 79.

Ollivier, M., Bobbins, W., Beauregard, D., Brayton, J., & SauvÉ, G. (2006). Feminist activists on-line: A study of the PAR-L research network. *Canadian Review of Sociology and Anthropology*, *43*(4), 445–463.

Pate, K. (2006). Advocacy, activism and social change for women in prison. *Canadian Woman Studies*, *25*(3/4), 81.

Peckford, N. (2006). FAFIA's CEDAW campaign: 25 years, ready or not? *Canadian Woman Studies*, *25*(3/4), 117.

Pellatt, A. (2000). Equality rights litigation and social transformation: A consideration of the Women's Legal Education and Action Fund's intervention in *Vriend v. R. Canadian Journal of Women & the Law,* *12*, 117–146.

Pelletier, R., & Tremblay, M. (2003). Feminist women in Canadian politics: A group ideologically divided? *Atlantis*, *28*(1), 80.

Power, E. M. (2005). The unfreedom of being other: Canadian lone mothers' experiences of poverty and "Life on the cheque". *Sociology*, *39*(4), 643-660.

Pulkingham, J., & Van der Gaag, T. (2004). Maternity/parental leave provisions in Canada: We've come a long way, but there's further to go. *Canadian Woman Studies*, *23*(3/4), 116.

Rankin, L. P., & Vickers, J. (2001). *Women's movements and state feminism: Integrating diversity into public policy*. Ottawa, ON: Status of Women Canada.

Rankin, L. P., & Wilcox, K. D. (2004). De-gendering engagement?: Gender mainstreaming, women's movements and the Canadian federal state. *Atlantis*, *29*(1), 52.

Rebick, J. (2005). *Ten thousand roses: The making of a feminist revolution*. Toronto: Penguin Canada.

Rodgers, S., & McIntyre, S. (Eds.). (2006). *Diminishing returns: Inequality and the Canadian Charter of Rights and Freedoms*. Markham, ON: LexisNexis Butterworths.

Roy, C. (2006). The irreverent raging grannies: Humour as protest. *Canadian Woman Studies*, *25*(3/4), 141.

Sawer, M., & Vickers, J. (2001). Women's constitutional activism in Australia and Canada. *Canadian Journal of Women & the Law*, *13*, 1–36.

Scott, S. (2007). *All our sisters: Stories of homeless women in Canada*. Peterborough, ON: Orchard Park, NY: Broadview Press.

Scott-Dixon, K. (1999). Ezines and feminist activism: Building a community. *Resources for Feminist Research*, *27*(1/2), 127.

Sheehy, E. A., & McIntyre, S. (Eds.). (2006). *Calling for change: Women, law, and the legal profession*. Ottawa: University of Ottawa Press.

Statistics Canada. (2000). *Women in Canada, 2000: A gender-based statistical report*. Ottawa, ON: Statistics Canada.

Stratford, H. (2002). Micro-strategies of resistance. *Resources for Feminist Research*, *29*(3/4), 223.

Tastsoglou, E., & Dobrowolsky, A. Z. (Eds.). (2006). *Women, migration, and citizenship : Making local, national, and transnational connections*. Aldershot, England; Burlington, VT: Ashgate.

Thorpe, J. (2005). Redrawing national boundaries: Gender, race, class, and same-sex marriage discourse in Canada. *Canadian Woman Studies*, *24*(2/3), 15.

Timpson, A. M. (2001). *Driven apart: Women's employment equity and child care in Canadian public policy*. Vancouver, BC: University of British Columbia Press.

Tremblay, M., & Andrew, C. (Eds.). (1998). *Women and political representation in Canada*. Ottawa, ON: Women's Studies and University of Ottawa Press.

Tremblay, M., & Pelletier, R. (2000). More feminists or more women?: Descriptive and substantive representations of women in the 1997 Canadian federal elections. *International Political Science Review*, *21*(4), 381–405.

Tyyskä, V. (2001). *Women, citizenship and Canadian child care policy in the 1990s*. Toronto, ON: Childcare Resource and Research Unit, The Centre for Urban and Community Studies, University of Toronto.

Voyageur, C. J. (2007). *Firekeepers of the twenty-first century: First nations women chiefs*. Montreal: McGill-Queen's University Press.

Warner, T. (2002). *Never going back: A history of queer activism in Canada*. Toronto, ON: University of Toronto Press.

Whitfield, G. (2006). From riot grrrl to radical: Reflections from a working-class feminist. *Canadian Woman Studies*, *25*(3/4), 185.

Wiegers, W. (2002). The framing of poverty as "child poverty" and its implications for women. Ottawa, ON: Status of Women Canada.

Williams, T. (1990). Re-forming "women's" truth: A critique of the royal commission on the status of women. *Ottawa Law Review, 22*, 725–729.

Wilson, S., Sengupta, A., & K. Evans. (Eds.). (2005). *Defending our dreams: Global feminist voices for a new generation*. London; New York: Zed Books.

Wilson, S., Silver, S., & Shields, J. (2004). Job restructuring and worker displacement: Does gender matter? *Canadian Woman Studies, 23*(3/4), 6.

Wine, J., & Ristock, J. (Eds.). (1991). *Women and social change: Feminist activism in Canada*. Toronto, ON: James Lorimer.

Young, L. (2000). *Feminists and party politics*. Vancouver, BC: University of British Columbia Press.

Young, M. et. at. (Eds.). (2007). *Poverty: Rights, social citizenship, and legal activism*. Vancouver: UBC Press.

Chapter Three: Engendering Violence

Bannerji, H. (2002). A question of silence: Reflections on violence against women in communities of colour. In K. M. J. McKenna & J. Larkin (Eds.), *Violence against women: New Canadian perspectives* (pp. 353–371). Toronto, ON: Inanna Publications and Education Inc.

Bannerji, H. (2003). Demography and democracy: Reflections on violence against women in genocide or ethnic cleansing. *Resources for Feminist Research, 30*(3/4), 93.

Batacharya, S. (2006). A fair trial: Race and the retrial of Kelly Ellard. *Canadian Woman Studies, 25*(1/2), 181.

Bilge, S. (2006). Behind the "culture" lens: Judicial representations of violence against minority women. *Canadian Woman Studies, 25*(1/2), 173.

Bold, C., Knowles, R., & Leach, B. (2002). Feminist memorializing and cultural countermemory: The case of Marianne's park. *Signs: Journal of Women in Culture & Society, 28*(1), 125.

Buckle, S. (2006). Remembering women murdered by men-memorials across Canada. *Canadian Woman Studies, 25*(1/2), 208.

Canadian Council on Social Development, & Canada. Sectoral Involvement in Departmental Policy Development. (2004). *Nowhere to turn?: Responding to partner violence against immigrant and visible minority women: Voices of frontline workers.* Ottawa,ON: Canadian Council on Social Development.

Comack, E. (1993). *Feminist engagement with the law: The legal recognition of the battered woman.* Ottawa, ON: Canadian Research Institute for the Advancement of Women.

Crawford, M., & Gartner, R. (1992). *Woman killing: Intimate femicide and Canada 1974–1990.* Toronto, ON: Ontario Women's Directorate.

Currie, D. (1990). Battered women and the state: From failure of theory to the theory of failure. *Journal of Human Justice, 1*, 77–96.

Doe, J. (2003). *The story of Jane Doe: A book about rape*. Toronto, ON: Random House.

Downe, P. J. (2006). Two stories of migrant sex work, cross-border movement and violence. *Canadian Woman Studies, 25*(1/2), 61.

Faulkner, E. (2006). Homophobic sexist violence in Canada: Trends in the experiences of lesbian and bisexual women in Canada. *Canadian Woman Studies, 25*(1/2), 154.

Flaherty, M. (1997). Inuit women and violence. In C. Andrew & S. Rogers (Eds.), *Women and the Canadian state* (pp.180–184). Montreal, QC: McGill-Queen's University Press.

Gotell, L. (2002). The ideal victim, the hysterical complainant, and the disclosure of confidential records: The implications of the

Charter for sexual assault law. *Osgoode Hall Law Journal, 40*, 251–295.

Gotell, L. (2007). The discursive disappearance of sexualized violence: Feminist law reform, judicial resistance and neo-liberal sexual citizenship. In Chunn, D.E., S. B. Boyd & H. Lessard. (Eds.), *Feminism, law and social change: (Re)action and resistance* (pp. 127-163). Vancouver, BC: University of British Columbia Press.

Hill, D. M. (2003). She no speaks and other colonial constructs of "the traditional Woman." In K. Anderson & B. Lawrence (Eds.), *Strong women stories* (pp. 106–116). Toronto, ON: Sumach Press.

Johnson, H. (1996). *Dangerous domains: Violence against women in Canada.* Scarborough, ON: Nelson.

Kaufman, M. (1989). The construction of masculinity and the triad of men's violence. In M. Kimmel & M. Messner (Eds.), *Men's lives* (pp. 13–25). Boston, MA: Allyn and Bacon.

Kevorkian, N. S. (2006). Violence in the name of honor: Theoretical and political challenges. *Canadian Woman Studies*, *25*(1/2), 202.

Kirk, J., & Taylor, S. (2006). Ending violence against women and girls in conflict contexts: Canadian efforts and experiences. *Canadian Woman Studies*, *25*(1/2), 139.

Lakeman, L. (2006). Sustaining our resistance to male violence: Attacks on women's organizing and Vancouver rape relief and women's shelter. *Canadian Woman Studies*, *25*(1/2), 129.

Lessard, H. (1999). Farce or tragedy? Judicial backlash and Justice McClung. *Forum Constitutionnel, 10*(3), 65–72.

Levan, A. (1996). Violence against women. In J. Brodie (Ed.), *Women and Canadian public policy* (pp. 319–354). Toronto, ON: Harcourt Brace.

Malette, L., & Chalouth, M. (Eds.). (1991). *The Montreal massacre* (M. Wildeman, Trans.). Charlottetown, PE: gynergy books.

Martin, S. L. (2006). Bearing witness: Experiences of frontline anti-violence responders. *Canadian Woman Studies*, *25*(1/2), 11.

Mathen, C. (2004). Transgendered persons and feminist strategy. *Canadian Journal of Women & the Law*, *16*(2), 291–316.

Minaker, J. C. (2001). Evaluating criminal justice responses to intimate abuse through the lens of women's needs. *Canadian Journal of Women & the Law*, *13*(1), 74–106.

Namaste, V. K. (2000). *Invisible lives: The erasure of transseuxal and transgendered people.* Chicago, IL: University of Chicago Press.

Peter, T. (2006). Mad, bad, or victim?: Making sense of Mother–Daughter sexual abuse. *Feminist Criminology*, *1*(4), 283–302.

Peter, T., & Comack, E. (2005). How the criminal justice system responds to sexual assault survivors: The slippage between "responsibilization" and "blaming the victim.". *Canadian Journal of Women & the Law*, *17*(2), 283–309.

Razack, S. (1994). What is to be gained by looking white people in the eye. *Signs*, *19*, 894–923.

Razack, S. (1998). Race, space, and prostitution: The making of the bourgeois subject. *Canadian Journal of Women & the Law*, *10*, 338–376.

Razack, S. (2005). How is white supremacy embodied? Sexualized racial violence at Abu Ghraib. *Canadian Journal of Women & the Law*, *17*(2), 341–363.

Ristock, J. (1991). Beyond ideologies: Understanding violence in lesbian relationships. *Canadian Woman Studies*, *12*, 74–79.

Ristock, J. (2005). Taking off the gender lens in women's studies: Queering violence against women. *Canadian Woman Studies*, *24*(2/3), 65.

Roberts, J., & Mohr, R. (Eds.). (1994). *Confronting sexual assault: A decade of legal and social change.* Toronto, ON: University of Toronto Press.

Sajnani, N., & Nadeau, D. (2006). Creating safer spaces for immigrant women of colour: Performing the politics of possibility. *Canadian Woman Studies*, *25*(1/2), 45.

Tutty, L. M., & Goard, C. (2002). *Reclaiming self: Issues and resources for women abused by intimate partners.* Halifax, NS: Fernwood Publishing.

Walker, G. (1990). *Family violence and the women's movement.* Toronto, ON: University of Toronto Press.

Welsh, S., Carr, J., Macquarrie, B., & Huntley, A. (2006). "I'm not thinking of it as sexual harassment": Understanding harassment across race and citizenship. *Gender & Society*, *20*(1), 87–107.

White, C., & Goldberg, J. (2006). Expanding our understanding of gendered violence: Violence against trans people and their loved ones. *Canadian Woman Studies*, *25*(1/2), 124.

Wright, J. (2001). Consent and sexual violence in Canadian public discourse: Reflections on *Ewanchuk. Canadian Journal of Law and Society, 16,* 173–204.

Chapter Four: The Body: Reproduction and Femininity

Achilles, R. (1994). *Donor insemination: An overview.* Ottawa, ON: Royal Commission on New Reproductive Technologies.

Ariss, R. (1998). Prenatal diagnosis in the Baird report. *Dalhousie Law Journal, 21*, 370–407

Bell, M. (2006). Re-forming the anorexic prisoner: Inpatient medical treatment as the return to panoptic femininity. *Cultural Studies<=> Critical Methodologies*, *6*(2), 182–307.

Boyd, S. C. (2001). Feminist research on mothers and illegal drugs. *Resources for Feminist Research*, *28*(3/4), 113.

Boyd, S. C. (1999). *Mothers and illicit drugs: Transcending the myths.* Toronto, ON: University of Toronto Press.

Brand, D. (1994). This body for itself. In D. Brand (Ed.), *Bread out of stone* (pp. 25–49). Toronto, ON: Coach House Press.

Brodribb, S. (1984). *Reproductive technologies, masculine dominance and the Canadian state.* Toronto, ON: Occasional Papers in Social Policy Analysis, Department of Sociology, Ontario Institute for Studies in Education.

Brownridge, D. A., & Halli, S. S. (2001). *Explaining violence against women in Canada.* Lanham, MD: Lexington Books.

Burfoot, A. (2006). Cyberfeminism and artificial life. *Resources for Feminist Research*, *31*(3/4), 137.

Burstyn, V. (1991). A technological handmaid's tale: The new productive technologies. Ottawa, ON: Brief for National Action Committee on the Status of Women to the Royal Commission on New Reproductive Technologies.

Campbell, L. (2005). Grrls plugged in: How Canadian rural young women are using the internet. *Canadian Woman Studies*, *24*(4), 167.

Currie, D. H., Kelly, D. M., & Pomerantz, S. (2007). Listening to girls: Discursive positioning and the construction of self. *International Journal of Qualitative Studies in Education (QSE)*, *20*(4), 377–400.

Currie, D., & Raoul, V. (Eds.). (1992). *Anatomy of gender: Women's struggle for the body.* Ottawa, ON: Carleton University Press.

Devaro, E. (1998). Consideration of context in the case of disability rights activism and selective abortion. *Health Law Review, 6*(3), 12–19.

Driedger, D. (2003). In sickness and employment: Women living and working with chronic illness. *Resources for Feminist Research*, *30*(1/2), 125.

Driedger, D. (2006). When the body protests: New versions of activism. *Canadian Woman Studies*, *25*(3/4), 188.

Emberley, J. (2002). Body, interrupted: Textual montage, traumatized bodies, and the disciplining of knowledge. *Resources for Feminist Research*, *29*(3/4), 69.

Harris, J. (2005). Lesbian motherhood and access to reproductive technology. *Canadian Woman Studies*, *24*(2/3), 43.

Heyes, C. J. (2007). Cosmetic surgery and the televisual makeover. *Feminist Media Studies*, *7*(1), 17–32.

Heyes, C. J. (2007). Normalisation and the psychic life of cosmetic surgery. *Australian Feminist Studies*, *22*(52), 55–71.

Kelly, D. M., Pomerantz, S., & Currie, D. H. (2006). "No boundaries?" Girls' interactive, online learning about femininities. *Youth & Society*, *38*(1), 3–28.

Kirby, S., & Huebner, J. (2002). Talking about sex: Biology and the social interpretations of sex in sport. *Canadian Woman Studies*, *21*(3), 36.

Kramar, K. J. (2005). *Unwilling mothers, unwanted babies : Infanticide in Canada.* Vancouver, BC: UBC Press.

McDaniel, S. (1998). Women's roles and reproduction. *Atlantis*, *14*, 1–12.

McDonnell, K. (2003). *Not an easy choice: Reexamining abortion.* Toronto, ON: Second Story Press.

Meagher, M. (2003). Jenny Saville and a feminist aesthetics of disgust. *Hypatia*, *18*(4), 23-41.

Ministers Responsible for the Status of Women. (1999). *Preventing violence against women: A strategic framework.* Ottawa, ON: Federal/Provincial/Territorial Status of Women Ministers.

Mire, A. (2001). Skin-bleaching: Poison, beauty, power and the politics of the colour line. *Resources for Feminist Research*, *28*(3/4), 13.

Morgan, J. (2000). Foetal imaginings: Searching for a vocabulary in the law and politics of reproduction. *Canadian Journal of Women & the Law*, *12*(2), 371-405.

Nadeau, D., & Young, A. E. (2005). Decolonising the body: Restoring sacred vitality. *Atlantis*, *29*(2), 13.

Newbery, L. (2002). "Mirror, mirror on the wall, who's the fairest one of all?": Troubling gendered identities. *Resources for Feminist Research*, *29*(3/4), 19.

Overall, C. (1987). *Ethics and human reproduction: A feminist analysis.* Boston, MA: Allen & Unwin.

Paterson, S.L. (2007). Ontario midwives: Reflections on a decade of regulated midwifery. *Canadian Woman Studies*, *24*(1), 153.

Porter, M. (2006). First blood: How three generations of Newfoundland women learned about menstruation. *Atlantis*, *31*(1), 45.

Rice, C. (2007). Becoming "the fat girl": Acquisition of an unfit identity. *Women's Studies International Forum*, *30*(2), 158–174.

Roy, V. J. (2005). The erasure of Ms G: The cultural specificity of substance abuse and adjudication without imagination. *Canadian Journal of Law and Society*, *20*(1), 107.

Royal Commission on New Reproductive Technologies. (1993). *Proceed with care* (final report), Vol. 1 & 2. Ottawa, ON: Department of Government Services, Canada.

Spitzer, D. L. (2003). Panic and panaceas: Hormone replacement therapy and the menopausal syndrome. *Atlantis*, *27*(2), 6.

Story, L. (2003). A head start in life?: Prenatal parenting and the discourse of fetal stimulation. *Atlantis*, *27*(2), 41.

Walks, M. (2004). Womb is womb, but is birth birth? *Canadian Woman Studies*, *24*(1), 68.

White, P., & Neverson, N. (2002). Muscular, bruised, and sweaty bodies...: This is not Barbie territory. *Canadian Woman Studies*, *21*(3), 44.

Williamson, J. (with Bell, L.). (1998). Public warning: An interview with Shawna Dempsey and Lori Millan. *Tessera, 2,* 56–77.

Chapter Five: Sexuality

Allen, C., & Elwin, R. (1993). *Getting wet: Tales of lesbian seduction*. Toronto, ON: Women's Press.

Bell, S. (1994). *Writing and re-writing the prostitute body*. Bloomington, IN: Indiana Press.

Beres, M. A. (2007). "Spontaneous" sexual consent: An analysis of sexual consent literature. *Feminism & Psychology*, *17*(1), 93–108.

Bisexual Anthology Collective. (1995). *Plural desires: Writing bisexual women's realities*. Toronto, ON: Sister Vision.

Bociurkiw, M. (2005). It's not about the sex: Racialization and queerness in Ellen and the *Ellen Degeneres Show*. *Canadian Woman Studies*, *24*(2/3), 176.

Boyd, S. B. (1999). Family law and sexuality: Feminist engagements. *Social and Legal Studies, 8*, 369–390.

Brock, D. R. (1998). *Making work, making trouble: Prostitution as a social problem*. Toronto, ON: University of Toronto Press.

Burgess, A. (2005). Queering heterosexual spaces: Positive space campaigns disrupting campus heteronormativity. *Canadian Woman Studies*, *24*(2/3), 27.

Busby, K. (1994). LEAF and pornography: Litigating on equality and sexual representations. *Canadian Journal of Law and Society, 9*, 165–92.

Cameron, M. (2005). Two-spirited aboriginal people: Continuing cultural appropriation by non-aboriginal society. *Canadian Woman Studies*, *24*(2/3), 123.

Carter, C., & Noble, J. (1996). Butch, femme and the woman-identified woman: Ménage à trois of the 1990s. *Canadian Woman Studies, 16*(2), 24–29.

Cossman, B. (2002). Sexing citizenship, privatizing sex. *Citizenship Studies*, *6*, 483–506.

Cossman, B., Bell, S., Gotell, L., & Ross, B. L. (1997). *Bad attitude/s on trial: Pornography, feminism, and the Butler decision*. Toronto, ON: University of Toronto Press.

Creet, J. (1991). Daughter of the movement: Psychodynamics of lesbian S/M fantasy. *differences, 3*, 135–159.

Curtis, B., & Hunt, A. (2007). The fellatio "Epidemic": Age relations and access to the erotic arts. *Sexualities*, *10*(1), 5–28.

Demczuk, I. (2002). *Recognition of lesbian couples: An inalienable right*. Ottawa, ON: Status of Women Canada.

Elliot, P. (2004). Who gets to be a woman?: Feminist politics and the question of trans-inclusion. *Atlantis*, *29*(1), 13.

Epstein, R. (2005). Queer parenting in the new millennium: Resisting normal. *Canadian Woman Studies*, *24*(2/3), 6.

Faulkner, E. (2006). Homophobic sexist violence in Canada: Trends in the experiences of lesbian and bisexual women in Canada. *Canadian Woman Studies*, *25*(1/2), 154.

Goldie, T. (2000). *Queer nation?* Toronto, ON: Robarts Centre for Canadian Studies.

Goldie, T. (2001). *In a queer country: Gay and lesbian studies in the Canadian context*. Vancouver, BC: Arsenal Pulp Press.

Hogan, M. (2005). Radical queers: A pop culture assessment of Montréal's anti-capitalist Ass Pirates, the Pantheres Roses, and Lesbians on Ecstasy. *Canadian Woman Studies*, *24*(2/3), 154.

Jeffrey, L. A., & MacDonald, G. M. (2006). *Sex workers in the Maritimes talk back*. Vancouver, BC: UBC Press.

Kerr, R. (2006). *Lesbian plays: Coming of age in Canada*. Toronto, ON: Playwrights Canada Press.

Kim, N. (2000). Much to do about something: Destabilizing law's support of dominant ideologies in the context of lesbian mother custody claims in Canada. *Dalhousie Journal of Legal Studies*, *9*, 73–119.

Lacombe, D. (1994). *Blue politics: Pornography and the law in the age of feminism*. Toronto, ON: University of Toronto Press.

Lahey, K. A. (1999). *Are we "persons" yet? Law and sexuality in Canada*. Toronto, ON: University of Toronto Press.

Lebel, S. (2005). Camping out with the lesbian national parks and services. *Canadian Woman Studies*, *24*(2/3), 182.

Lenon, S. J. (2005). Marrying citizens! Raced subjects? Re-thinking the terrain of equal marriage discourse. *Canadian Journal of Women & the Law, 17*(2), 405–421.

MacPhee, M., & Hogan, M. (2006). The role of Montréal's Dykes on Mykes radio show. *Canadian Woman Studies*, *25*(3/4), 193.

Magnet, S. (2005). Erasing queerness/constraining disability: Film representations of queers with disabilities in *Frida* and *Double the Trouble, Twice the Fun*. *Canadian Woman Studies*, *24*(2/3), 171.

Martin, N. K. (2007). Porn empowerment: Negotiating sex work and third wave feminism. *Atlantis*, *31*(2), 31.

Martindale, K. (1998). What makes lesbianism thinkable: Theorizing lesbianism from Adrienne Rich to queer theory. In N. Mandell (Ed.), *Feminist issues: Race, class and sexuality* (pp. 55–76). Scarborough, ON: Prentice-Hall.

Mathen, C. (2004). Transgendered persons and feminist strategy. *Canadian Journal of Women & the Law*, *16*(2), 291–316.

Mayeda, G. (2005). Re-imagining feminist theory: Transgender identity, feminism, and the law. *Canadian Journal of Women & the Law*, *17*(2), 423–472.

Namaste, V. K. (2005). *Sex change, social change : Reflections on identity, institutions and imperialism*. Toronto: Women's Press.

Napoleon, V. (2002). Raven's garden: A discussion about aboriginal sexual orientation and transgender issues. *Canadian Journal of Law and Society*, *17*(2), 149.

Ne ville, S. (2007). Female chauvinist pigs: Women and the rise of raunch culture. *Atlantis*, *31*(2), 109.

Noble, B. (2007). The "P" word: Trans men, stone butches, and the politics of penetration. *Atlantis*, *31*(2), 16.

Noble, J. B. (2005). Strange sisters and boy kings: Post-queer tranz-gendered bodies in performance. *Canadian Woman Studies*, *24*(2/3), 164.

Noble, J. B. (2006). *Sons of the movement : FtMs risking incoherance on a post-queer cultural landscape*. Toronto, ON: Women's Press.

Payne, K. (2007). From abject to subject: Some thoughts on sex work as a missing link in the feminist understandings of sexuality. *Atlantis*, *31*(2), 53.

Rankin, P. (2000). Sexualities and national identities: Re-imagining queer nationalism. *Journal of Canadian Studies*, *35*, 176–196.

Rich, R. (1999). Anti-porn: Soft issue, hard world. In K. Armatage, K. Banning, B. Longfellow & J. Marchessault (Eds.), *Gendering the nations: Canadian women's cinema* (pp. 62–75). Toronto, ON: University of Toronto Press.

Ristock, J. L., & Taylor, C. (1998). *Inside the academy and out: Lesbian/gay/queer studies and social action*. Toronto, ON: University of Toronto Press.

Ristock, J., & Taylor, C. (Eds.). (1998). Sexualities and feminisms (special issue). *Atlantis, 23*(1).

Ross, B. (1991). Sex, lives and archives: Pleasure/danger debates in 1970s lesbian feminism. In S. Kirby (Ed.), *Women changing academe* (pp. 89–112). Winnipeg, MN: Sororal Publishing.

Ross, B. (2003). Taking it off, putting it on: Women in the strip trade. *Canadian Journal of Women & the Law*, *15*(2), 378-382.

Salah, T. (2007). Transfixed in lesbian paradise. *Atlantis*, *31*(2), 24.

Shaver, F. M. (2005). Sex work research: Methodological and ethical challenges. *Journal of Interpersonal Violence*, *20*(3), 296-319.

Stone, S. D. (Ed.). (1990). *Lesbians in Canada*. Toronto, ON: Between the Lines.

Thorpe, J. (2005). Redrawing national boundaries: Gender, race, class, and same-sex marriage discourse in Canada. *Canadian Woman Studies*, *24*(2/3), 15.

Turcotte, L. (1996). Queer theory: Transgression and/or regression. *Canadian Woman Studies, 16*, 118–121.

Valverde, M. (1989). Beyond gender dangers and private pleasures: Theory and ethics in the sex debates. *Feminist Studies*, *15*, 237–254.

Warner, T. (2002). *Never going back : A history of queer activism in Canada*. Toronto, ON: University of Toronto Press.

Index

A

Aboriginal Justice Inquiry, 193
Aboriginal women
  and child welfare system, 210
  children in Native cultures, 48–49
  and colonization, 14–15, 48–50, 75, 133–137, 192, 290, 302
  dehumanization of, 49, 214
  deprecation by Native males, 75, 290
  diseases introduced by Europeans, 210
  eating problems, 234
  education, 210
  employment, 210
  family, attack on, 49
  feminist action, 75
  feminist thought, 7
  gap in law on property division, 208
  healing, struggle for, 49–50
  human rights violations, 49, 208
  imprisonment, 132–140
  inequality of status, 208
  and justice reform, 132–140, 211
  life expectancy, 85
  "motherhood" concept, 48–49
  oppression, 132, 133, 134–137, 290
  organization of, 75
  Pamela George, murder of. *See* George Murder
  police attitudes, 192, 193, 211, 212–213
  positions on self-government, 40–41
  poverty, 85, 210
  prostitution and, 194
  racism against, 210
  rendering in history and perception today, 209–210, 214
  residential schools, 49
  resistance to genocide, 49–50
  safety and security, 207–215
  sexual violence towards, 192, 193
  single mothers, 79
  social and economic marginalization, 211
  subordination by Indian Acts, 40
  in traditional Aboriginal society, 48–49, 209
  in Vancouver's sex trade, 213
  victimization of, 208, 211, 290
  violence against, 72, 75, 85, 192, 208, 211, 212–214
  see also George murder
"Aboriginal Women and Justice Reform" (Monture), 75–76, 132–140
abortion
  see also feminist disability perspective
  access issues, 223–224, 227–228
  Bill C–150, 226
  CARAL study, 223–224
  central issue in second wave Canadian feminism, 223
  decline in services, 227–228
  decriminalization, 223
  feminist disability analyses of, 224, 228–232
  genetic screening, 229, 231, 232
  medical procedure, recognition as, 226
  Morgentaler decision. *See* *Morgentaler* decision
  no discussion in, 287
  rights of mothers and fetuses, 228–232
  sex education, 287
  struggles over, 223–224
"Abortion" (Wendell), 228–232
abstinence
  supported in Ontario curriculum, 285–287
  teaching leads to shame, 294
abuse. *See* violence against women; wife abuse
academic feminism
  see also Women's Studies
  associations, 4–5
  second wave. *See* second wave feminism
  self-criticism needed, 67
  third wave. *See* third wave feminism
  and women's studies, 2, 55
The Accused (film), 222n
activism. *See* feminist activism
advertising of beauty products and services, 252–253
Advisory Council on the Status of Women, 119, 121
Afghan women
  bombing as emancipation, 143, 147
  problems with images of, 147
Allegra, Donna, 313
alternative political spaces, 108–112
analytic tools
  class, 6, 7, 9
  described, 5–8
  feminism, 5–6, 7–8
  gender, 6, 12, 121–123
  interdisciplinarity, 6
  race, 5, 6, 7, 8
anti-essentialist feminism
  see also immigrant women; women of colour
  critique posed by, 12
  trans-theory and, 27
  women, construct of, 11–12, 19–27
anti-feminism, and the third wave, 58, 68
anti-racist feminism
  see also Aboriginal women; immigrant women; women of colour

Canadian anti-racist feminist thought, 14, 34–48
challenges posed by, 13–14
common sense (Gramsci), 29–30
defining, 35
described, 7, 13–14
development of, 35–36
divergent approaches, 36, 37–39
diversity and complexity, 14
epistemological differences, 36, 39
exclusion from Canadian feminist historiographies, 35
interconnections, prioritization of, 36
political economy approach, 36, 37, 38–39
race and gender connection, 35–36, 39
racialization process, focus on, 14, 35
references, 41–48
standpoint methodology, 14, 36, 37, 38, 39
synthesis, lack of, 41
third wave feminism and, 36–41
anti-violence workers, 220, 221n
Armstrong, Hugh, 74, 86–95
Armstrong, Jeanette, 48–50, 74
Armstrong, Patricia, 74, 86–95
Asch, Adrienne, 228–229
"Assessing Gender Equality" (Status of Women Canada), 71–72, 78–86

B

backlash arguments, 171, 174–175
Bailey, Cathryn, 160, 161
Balsamo, Anne, 252
Bannerji, Himani, 13, 28–34, 38
Bartky, Sandra Lee, 246, 248
beauty
see also body image
colourist values, internalization, 237
cultural ideals, questioning, 240
economic imperative, 236, 238
integrationist ideals, 238
norms, 224
oppositional ideas, 238
resistance to dominant ideals, 225, 239–241
rituals as connection, 252, 255–256
Western ideals, and women of colour, 31, 225, 237–238, 254
Bell, Brandi, 77, 156–163
Beres, Melanie, 263, 264, 275–282
"Between Body and Culture: Beauty Ability and Growing Up Female" (Rice), 233–245
Bill C-38, 301
Bill C-49, 110, 111
Bill C-150, 226
black women
see also women of colour
black lesbian sexualities, silencing, 265, 266, 311–314
sexuality commodified as legacy of slavery, 266, 312
blogs and websites as feminist forums, 77
the body
see also body image
abortion. *See* abortion
beauty norms, 224
confidence of young children, 234
control and mastery, 225
cultural constructions, 184, 223, 251–256
as currency, 236, 238
disciplinary practices, 224, 225, 246–250
diversity of, 245
economics and, 226, 228
escape from natural processes of, 252
fat bodies, and ideal of bodily escape, 254–255
feminist disability perspective. *See* feminist disability perspective
feminist idealizations, 225, 250
harassment, target of, 236
idealization of, 245–246
as identity, 234
as instrument of femininity, 235
media influences, 235, 253
medical concept, 253–254
objectification of, 245–246
organizing for change, 240–241
"perfect" female body, 254
plastic surgery, 248, 252, 253
popular culture, representations in, 252
positive imagery needed, 256
public scrutiny, subject of, 235
reactions, 255
rebelling through, 239–240
reclaiming, 255–256
relevance of, 253–254
resistance strategies, 239–241
resolving body struggles, 240–241
social control, object of, 236, 252
societal values, 234–235
technological interventions, 225, 252–255
body-based harassment, 236
body image
see also beauty; the body
connections, making, 237, 239
and consciousness-raising, 240
cultural ideals, 233, 234, 237–238, 240, 245
eating disorders, 233–234, 236–237, 251
negative messages, 225, 233, 234–235
race and, 225, 237–238, 254
resistance strategies, 239–241
"rich white girl" stereotype, 233–234
violence, impact of, 236–237
young women vs. young men, 235
body piercing as resistance, 255
Bordo, Susan, 223, 252, 322
Boyd, Susan B., 265, 299–311
Braithwaite, Ann, 50–57
Brodie, Janine, 71, 95–104
Brossard, Nicole, 7, 16–18
budget cuts, 5, 71
Bunch, Charlotte, 271
Butler, Judith, 8, 266, 300, 320, 321, 323

C

Campbell, Kim, 110, 111
Canada
 see also neoliberalism
 anti-racist feminist thought, 14, 34–48
 gendered division of labour. *See* gendered division of labour
 health-care system, 100
 lesbian and gay equality, evolution of, 298, 301
 liberal democratic state, 116–118
 neoliberalism, impact of, 95–104
 Quebec feminism, 7
 women's movements in. *See* women's movements
Canada Health Act, 226
Canadian Abortion Rights Action League (CARAL), 223–224, 226–228
Canadian Advisory Council on the Status of Women. *See* Advisory Council on the Status of Women
"Canadian Anti-Racist Feminist Thought: Scratching the Surface" (Dua), 34–48
Canadian Charter of Human Rights and Freedoms
 abortion litigation, 226
 equality section, 301, 303
 Morgentaler decision, 226
 rights of gays and lesbians, 264
 same-sex marriage, 264, 301
Canadian Women's Studies. See Women's studies
Canadian Women's Studies Association/L'association canadienne des études sur les femmes (CWSA), 4–5
caring work, 74, 79, 87–91, 102
Carter, Sarah, 192
Charlottetown Accord (1992), 110
Charter. See *Canadian Charter of Human Rights and Freedoms*
child welfare system, and Aboriginal families, 210
childcare, 127–132
 attacks on, 127–128
 "Choice in Childcare Allowance," 75, 129
 Code Blue, 130
 comparisons with other countries, 128
 Conservative opposition to regulated childcare, 130
 and domestic workers, 88, 92–93
 federal-provincial agreements cancelled, 129
 government funding of, 129
 improvement, necessity of, 74, 75
 Multilateral Framework on Early Learning and Childcare (2003), 129
 national program, failure to establish, 74–75
 national standards lacking, 128
 Task Force on Childcare (1986), 128
 woman-led activism, 128, 130
children. *See* childcare; immigrant girls
choice, and heterosexuality, 270–274, 293, 294–295
"Choice in Childcare" allowance, 75, 129
citizens' fora, 73, 108–111
citizenship regime, restructuring, 116, 117, 121
class
 and gendered violence, 165
 Marxist critique of ideology, 33
 relationship with race and gender, 32, 33, 34
 and same-sex couples, 265, 297, 299
Coalition Against Free Trade, 120
Code Blue for Child Care, 130
colonialism
 prisons and, 75, 133–137
 violence in, 145
 War on Terrorism, 141
colonization
 see also George murder
 Aboriginal women, 14–15, 48–50, 133–137, 192, 213, 290, 302
common sense, Gramsci's notion, 29–30
community-based activism, 150–155
community building, 2
Conflict Tactics Scale, 173, 175
Connell, Erin, 263–264, 283–289
consent
 absence of violence, 279
 communicating, 279–281
 concept, 278
 defined, 167
 determining, 202–207
 gendered nature of, 278–279
 implied consent rejected as defence, 202–207
 issue in most rape cases, 219, 221
 "only yes means yes," 202–207
constitutional conferences, 110–111
Correctional Service of Canada, 135, 136
cosmetic surgery, 248, 252, 253, 254, 255
Court system, discriminatory, 211
Criminal Code, 281
criminal law reforms
 Bill C-49, 110, 111
 Ewanchuk case, 167, 202–207
 sexual assault, 167
 sexual history evidence, 167
critiques
 anti-essentialist feminism, 12
 anti-racist feminism, 13–14
 exclusionary practices, 13
 Marxist critique of ideology, 33
 transsexuality and critiques of essentialism, 24
Crow, Barbara, 1–9
cultural construction
 the body, 184, 223, 251–256
 femininity, 224, 225
 sexuality, 268
cultural products, 158
culture
 and the body, 233, 234, 237–238, 240, 245
 genocide of Aboriginal culture, 49–50
 and reproduction of racism, 13, 31
Cummings, Joan Grant, 62

cutbacks in government funding, 71, 73, 120, 121
cyberspace and third wave feminism, 66

D

Dalton, Russell, 112
Darling-Wolf, Fabienne, 225–226, 251–256
daycare. *See* childcare
de-gendering of violence, 165–166, 170–176
Dean, Amber, 266–267, 314–325
Decade of Women (1976–85), 97
decentralization and neoliberalism, 100–101
democratic revitalization and reform, 73, 105–112
demographic trends, 78–79
"Desire as Interruption: Young Women and Sexuality Education" (Connell), 283–289
disabilities. *See* feminist disability perspective; women with disabilities
disciplines of normality, 225, 247–250
discrimination, by race. *See* racism
"Discussions with Radical Young Women" (Plyler), 77, 149–156
disease, spread of, 93
distance-normalizing language, 66
diversity of perspectives, 65
division of labour. *See* gendered division of labour
divorce and wife abuse, 292
Dobrowolsky, Alexandra, 104–115
"Does a Lesbian Need a Vagina Like a Fish Needs a Bicycle? Or Would the 'Real' Lesbian Please Stand Up!" (Dean), 266–267, 314–325
"Does No 'No' Mean Reasonable Doubt? Assessing the Impact of *Ewanchuk*" (Ruparelia), 202–207
domestic labour in Canada, 88, 92–93
    see also childcare; gendered division of labour
domination systems, 9, 11
    see also gendered violence; racism
    racism as, 182, 187
double standards, 283
Dua, Enakshi, 13, 14, 34–48
Dubois, Ellen, 59
Duncombe, Stephen, 156, 157, 160

E

earnings and income trends, 81
eating disorders, 233–234, 236–237, 251
economic issues, and women's groups, 119
economic responsibilities, privatization of, 303, 306
education
    Aboriginal women, 210
    sex courses. *See* sex education
    women university graduates, 79
E.G.A.L.E., 305–306
Egan case, 298, 301
electoral system reforms, 107
employment (women's)
    Aboriginal women, 210
    domestic labour, 88, 92–93
    earnings and income trends, 81
    gendered workforce. *See* gendered division of labour
    and globalization, 91–93
    paid work trends, 80
    participation of women. *See* labour force participation
    unpaid work, 80–81, 87–88
    wage gap. *See* income gap
empowerment for women prisoners, 75, 135
equality
    changing legal definition of "spouse," 301
    Charter section, 301, 303
    Criminal Code revisions on sexual assault, 167
    equal pay, struggle for, 119
    law as tool for advancing, 2
equality litigation
    Egan case, 298, 301
    Ewanchuk case, 167, 202–207
    M. v. H., 298–299, 301
    sexual orientation, 298
    spousal recognition, 301
"Erasing Race: The Story of Reena Virk" (Jiwani), 166, 180–190
essentialism
    see also anti-essentialist feminism
    analysis of male violence against women, 165, 166
    in feminist theory, 12–13, 19–27
    transsexuality and, 24
ethnicity and body image, 237–238
eugenics
    see also feminist disability perspective
    and abortion, 231–232
    and RTs, 224
Ewanchuk case, 167, 202–207

F

the family
    see also same-sex marriage
    Aboriginal traditions, 48–49
    attack on Aboriginal families through residential schools, 49
    changing trends and increasing diversity, 79
    feminist critiques, 265, 300, 301–304
    gender inequalities, 292
    immigrant domestic workers and white families, 93
    patriarchal bias in literature, 102–103
    same-sex marriage, 300, 302
    single mothers, 79, 82, 83, 101, 103
    violence, protection from, 102
    work-family stress, 79
the female body. *See* the body
female masculinity, 328–330
femininity
    body as instrument of, 235
    body piercing as resistance, 255
    cultural constructions, 224, 225
    disciplinary practices, 246–247, 248–249
    normative standards, 224
    resistance to dominant ideals, 255
    social construction, 246

feminism
backlash against, 120–121, 122
core issues continuing, 60–61
diversity and boundary-crossing, 7
first wave, 58
impacts of neoliberalism, 7–8, 71, 95–104, 116–118, 119–121
knowledge as situated and engaged, 2
radical, 77, 149–156
second wave. *See* second wave feminism
spread of First World ideas, 93
standpoint feminism, 11, 14
third wave. *See* third wave feminism
and transsexuality. *See* transsexuality
wave metaphor, 8, 58–64, 68
and young women, 77, 149–156, 156–163
"Feminism in Waves: Re-Imagining a Watery Metaphor" (Sawchuk), 58–64
feminist academics. *See* academic feminism
feminist activism
Aboriginal women, 7
critiques of marriage, vs. same-sex marriage, 300, 301–304
equality litigation. *See* equality litigation
neoliberalism and, 5, 7–8, 71, 95–104, 116–118, 119–121
opposition to corporate globalization, 122–123
Royal Commission on the Status of Women in Canada, 96, 118, 127
and trade issues, 116–118
and Women's Studies, 2
feminist disability perspective
abortion, 224, 228–232
the body, 225
eugenics policies, 231–232
genetic screening, 229, 231, 232
information, need for, 231
literature, summary of, 229–232
mandatory procedures, 231
selective abortion, and devaluation of disability, 230–232
feminist heterosexuality, possibility of, 270–273
feminist idealizations of the body, 225, 250
feminist organizations. *See* women's movements
feminist political economy
trade issues, 115–118
transformative, 104–115
feminist publishing, 4
feminist scholarship. *See* academic feminism; Women's Studies
feminist theory
anti-racist feminist theory, 13–14
see also anti-racist feminism
described, 6
erasure of non-white women, 13, 31–32
essentialism, 12
gender relations, moving beyond, 6
and heterosexuality, 267–275
project of, defined, 6
second wave feminism, 11, 12
sexuality. *See* sexuality
state theory, 7–8
third wave feminism. *See* third wave feminism
Western theoretical frameworks, dominance, 13–14
feminist writing, 16–18
anti-racist feminist thought, 14, 35–36
attack on power relationships, 17
feminist disability perspective, 228–232
politicization of feminist thought, 16–17
silence, concept of, 28–29
"Feminizing the Mobile: Gender Scripting of Mobiles in North America" (Shade), 225, 257–262
fetus, rights, 228–232
see also abortion
Fine, Michelle, 228–229, 284, 287–288
Fireweed (magazine), 28
First Nations. *See* Aboriginal women
First World/Third World relationships, 92–93, 94
"The Flight from the Rejected Body" (Wendell), 245–251
Foucault, Michel, 34, 246, 296
free trade, 92
feminist opposition, 116
Free Trade Agreement, 98, 117, 120
Friendly, Martha, 74–75, 127–132
"From Airbrushing to Liposuction: The Technological Reconstruction of the Female Body" (Darling-Wolf), 225–226, 251–256
FTM (female-to-male) transsexuals, 330–333

G

Gabriel, Christina, 72–73, 115–127
gay rights movement
see also same-sex marriage; spousal recognition
Charter's guarantee of equality, 264
greater visibility for same-sex desire, 283
gender
analytic tool, 6, 12, 121–123
challenges to conventional usages, 8
constructed-ness of, 321
perception of, 332
race, class and sexuality in gendered violence, 165, 196
and race, connection, 6, 9, 331
same-sex couples. See same-sex marriage; spousal recognition
gender-denying messages, 170–173, 175
gender equality and trade relations, 115–118
gender essentialism
analysis of male violence challenged, 165, 166
anti-essentialist critiques, 12
and second wave feminism, 11, 12
and third wave feminism, 12

"Gender Politics and Social Policy in Canada" (Brodie), 71, 95–104
gendered division of labour, 74, 87–88, 90, 93–94
caring work, 74, 88–91, 93
lumping, 87–88
slicing, 88–90
trade relations, 115–118
gendered paradoxes, neoliberalism, 103–104
gendered racism, 210
gendered violence
see also violence against women
"degendering" response to reforms, 165–166, 170–176
Pamela George murder. *See* George murder
power relations, 165
race, gender, class and sexuality, 165
gendered wage gap. *See* income gap
General Social Survey on Spousal Violence
equalizing all violence, 173
findings, 165, 172
severity far greater for women, 165
suggestions of equal violence, 172
women more frequent victims, 172–173
genetic screening, 229, 231, 232
genocide
of Aboriginal culture, 49
of the family, 48, 49
resistance to, 15, 49, 50
George murder, 190–201
the accused, background, 193, 194–195
Crown, failure to challenge "racial space," 198
defence at trial, 191, 197
dehumanization of Pamela George, 192, 196–197
described, 190–191
finding of manslaughter, 191–192
as gendered racial violence, 191, 192
George seen as rightful target, 196
masking of violence, 192
Osborne murder, parallels with, 193, 195
prostitution, racially bounded space, 192, 196–198
racial aspects of, 192–193
racism, emergence of, 198–199
girl-on-girl violence, media emphasis in Virk murder accounts, 184, 185
global feminism
see also September 11th aftermath
First World/Third World relationships, 92–93, 94
Third World Women, 91–93, 94
trade issues, 115–118
United Nations, diminished power of, 141
United States, power of, 145, 148
Western ideals of beauty, 237–238
globalization, 74, 91–94
contradictions within, 94
disease, spread of, 93
First World practices, spread of, 93
gendered division of labour, 91–93
and neoliberalism, 115–116, 117, 122
protests against, 74, 93–94, 122–123
shared international perspectives, 93
slicing, 93
structural adjustment programs, 91
terrorism and, 94
transnational corporations, 91, 93, 94
women's paid work, 91–93
Gotell, Lise, 1–9
governance, new philosophy of. *See* neoliberalism
government. *See* state policy
Gramsci, Antonio, 29–30, 33

H

Halberstam, Judith, 328–330
Halpern v. Canada, 308
Hammonds, Evelynn, 312
harassment
"body-based," 236
statistics on criminal harassment, 85
Harper, Anita Olsen, 75, 207–215
Harper, Stephen, 75, 129, 130
hate groups, 185
healing lodge, 137, 138n
health-care system, 100
health statistics for women and men, 85
heteronormativity
lesbianism as challenge to, 320, 321
same-sex marriages compared to, 303
heterosexism, 269–270
heterosexuality
awareness of, 272
benefits for men, 269
and choice, 270–274
communication strategies, 264, 279–81
compulsory, 263, 264, 272
costs for women, 269
dominant sources, 276–279, 281
feminist heterosexuality, 270–273
and feminist theory, 267–275
and heterosexism, 269–270
as institution, 263, 264, 268, 273, 274
meaning of, 267
as men first, 271
paradoxes of, 264, 267–268
politics of, 269–270
privileges for women, 270, 273
radical feminism and, 269, 277
in sex education, 264, 287
social construction of, 263
social pressure towards, 266
"Heterosexuality and Feminist Theory" (Overall), 263, 267–275
Heyes, Cressida, 12–13
Highway of Tears Symposium (2006), 213
homophobia
and patriarchy, 292
and rape, 292, 295
homosexuality

see also gay rights movement; lesbian; lesbianism; same-sex marriage
love and sex, 290–295
hooks, bell, 313
husband abuse, 170–179
acceptance of, 174–175
claims of equal violence, 172–176
gender-neutralizing message, 170–173, 175–176
situating, 173–175

I

identity and sexuality, 296
identity question in feminist writing, 18
imaging technology, 253
immigrant girls
experiences of abuse hidden, 182
internalization of dominant values, 181, 182, 186
patriarchy, 181
rejection by dominant society, 181, 184
strain with own culture, 181, 182
immigrant women
see also women of colour
common sense, Gramsci's notion, 29–30
discomfort with feminist discourse, 31–32
as domestic workers, 92–93
feminist thought, 7, 31–34
internalization of dominant culture, 181, 183
in labour force, 89
low-income status, 84
as outsiders, 76, 146, 181, 184
paid work and, 84, 89, 92–93
silence or gaps, 28–29, 30, 31–32
violence against, 166, 181, 183–187
vulnerable status post 9/11, 141, 144
imperialism of U.S., 141, 142–143
implied consent rejected as defence, 202–207
income gap, 80, 81, 87, 92–93
continuance of, 72
gendered division of labour, 87–88
hourly wages (M/F, 1997–2003), 80
occupational segregation, 80
between rich and poor, 101, 105
university graduates, 79
Indian Acts, 40, 209
individualization, 73–74, 102–103, 117
inequality, increasing, 93
integrationist beauty practices, 238
interdisciplinarity, 6
International Monetary Fund, 91
International Year of Women (1975), 97
"Intersecting Identities and Inclusive Institutions" (Dobrowolsky), 104–115
"Introducing Racism: Notes towards an Anti-Racist Feminism" (Bannerji), 13, 28–34
"Invocation: The Real Power of Aboriginal Women" (Armstrong), 15, 48–50
Iraq war
Canadian military contracts, 151
U.S. attacks, 142
"Is Canada Peaceful and Safe for Aboriginal Women?" (Harper), 207–215
"Isn't Love a Given?" (Maracle), 265–266, 289–295

J

Jacobs, Beverley, 213
"Jane Doe," 216–222
Jiwani, Yasmin, 166, 180–190
June 30th Committee, 151

K

Klein, Bonnie, 250
Klein, Naomi, 94
Kummerfield, Steven. *See* George murder

L

The L Word (TV show), 318, 321, 322–323
labour force participation
gendered division of labour, 87–88
growth in, 80
occupational segregation, 80
wage gap. *See* income gap
labour market
law reforms. See criminal law reforms
Lawrence, Errol, 29–30
Legal Education and Action Fund (L.E.A.F.), 306–307
legislatures, women in, 104–105
lesbianism
see also lesbians
from a heterosexual perspective, 265, 289–295
challenge to heteronormativity, 320, 321
historical perspective, 264
radical feminist view, 277
lesbians
see also lesbianism
appearance, 266–267, 315–320, 322
black lesbian sexualities, silencing of, 265, 266, 311–314
"bodies that matter," 320–321
challenges to white middle-class reality, 266–267, 316
desire for another woman as qualifier, 267, 317
Egan case, 301
lesbian identities, 266–267, 315–325
male lesbians, 26, 321–323
in popular culture, 318
postmodernist theorizing, 321
same-sex marriage. *See* same-sex marriage
spousal recognition. *See* spousal recognition
visibility problems, 319–320
liberal democratic state in Canada, 105, 116–118
liposuction, 255, 256n
litigation, equality. *See* equality litigation
Lord, Cassandra, 265, 266, 311–314
Lorde, Audre, 9, 68, 312, 313
"Losing the Feminist Voice: Debates on the Legal Recognition of Same-Sex Partnerships" (Young and Boyd), 265, 299–311

love
bias against, 291
distinguished from sex, 291, 292, 293, 294
feminist movement and, 293
and right to choose, 293, 295
between women, 292, 294, 295
lumping, 74, 87–88

M

Macdonald, Laura, 72–73, 115–127
"magical signs," 53, 55, 56
mainstream women's movements. *See* women's movements
male breadwinner, 96
male lesbians, 26, 321–323
male-on-male violence, 221n
"Managing Trade Engagements?" (Gabriel and Macdonald), 72–73, 115–127
Maracle, Lee, 265–266, 289–295
markets replacing states, 93
marriage
see also same-sex marriage
conjugal rights and Aboriginal women, 208
feminist critiques of, 302, 304, 307
marriage cases, 301
patriarchal nature, 302, 307
racism and, 302
redefined as between "two persons," 308
symbolic importance, 306
Martin, Paul, 129
Marxist critique of ideology, 33
masculinity
aggressiveness, 194
cultural constructs, 225, 323
female masculinity, 328–330
male lesbians, 321–323
sports masculinities, 194, 200n
transsexual, 267, 328–330
media
erasure of racism as factor in Virk murder, 180–181, 183–187
feminism seen as irrelevant, 77
images of ideal female body, 235
justifications for War on Terror, 144
memoirs and histories, present vs. past, 52
men
benefits from a sexist society, 218
domination practices, 193–197, 290, 292
heterosexuality as men first, 264, 271, 273
identity of, 194
and love, 291, 292–294
sex education, 287
sports masculinities, 194
Mercer, Kobena, 254
Millet, Kate, 59
Minaker, Joanne, 165–166
Montagna, S., 280
Monture, Patricia A., 75–76, 132–140
Morgan, Kathryn Pauly, 248
Morgentaler decision
decriminalizing abortions, 223
described, 223, 226
as first step, 223
limitations on, 223, 226
symbolic gains, 223
Morris, Jenny, 229
motherhood
Aboriginal women, 48
and poverty, 101, 103
single mothers, 101, 103
"Moving Beyond 'No Means No'" (Beres), 263, 264, 275–82
MTF transsexuals. *See* transsexuality
Mulroney, Brian, 72, 97, 98, 105, 111, 120, 226

N

National Action Committee on the Status of Women (NAC), 71, 96–97
clash with federal government, 72, 120–121, 174
early years, 118–119
funding cut, 120
opposition to free trade, 120
Native women. *See* Aboriginal women
Native Women's Association of Canada (NWAC), 75, 137, 211–212
neoliberalism
see also welfare state
change from postwar model of state and society, 116–118
child care agreements cancelled, 127–128, 129
cutbacks by Harris government in Ontario, 153
decentralization, 100–101
effects of, 72, 95–104
and feminist activism, 5, 8, 71, 95–104, 116–118, 119–121
and globalization, 115–116, 117, 122
health-care system, 100
income gap and poverty, 97, 98, 101, 102–103
individualization, 73–74, 102–103
and performativity, 98–99
principal axioms of, 98
privatization, 99–100
restructuring of citizenship regime, 116, 117, 121, 123
networking, 111–112
Noble, Jean Bobby, 267, 325–334
non-white women. *See* Aboriginal women; immigrant women; women of colour
normality, disciplines of, 225, 247–250
North American Free Trade Agreement (NAFTA), 98, 117

O

occupation and war, 150–151
Office of Equal Opportunity, 97
Omosupe, Ekua, 312
Ontario Coalition Against Poverty (OCAP), 153
oppositional beauty ideals, 238, 250
Ordas, Jeanette, 158, 160
"Origin Stories and Magical Signs in Women's Studies" (Braithwaite), 50–57
Osborne, Helen Betty, 193, 195
"Other" cultures, dominant framing as deviant, 185–186, 192, 199
Overall, Christine, 263, 267–275

P
paid work
  trends, 80
  wage gap. *See* income gap
patriarchy
  Aboriginal women, 210, 290–291
  feminist critique, 11
  immigrant girls, 181
  violence against women, 192
peer culture, rejection of "others," 184, 186
performativity, and neoliberal state, 98–99
Phillips, Susan, 110
physical normality, disciplinary practices of, 225, 247–250
Pinterics, Natasha, 15–16, 64–70
plastic surgery, 248, 252, 253, 254, 255
Plyler, Jennifer, 77, 149–156
police
  attitudes towards aboriginal women, 192, 193, 211, 212–213
  training in family violence, 219
political economy. *See* feminist political economy
political equality, 104–106
political party system, 107–108, 111
political prisoners, 154
politics of liberating women, 104–115
politics of transformation, 108–112
popular culture, ideal female body, 252
post-feminism, and the third wave, 68
postmodernist theorizing on lesbians, 321
postwar to neoliberal model of state–society relations, 116–118
poverty
  Aboriginal women, 84, 85, 210
  and child welfare system involvement, 210
  "high risk" groups, 101
  and neoliberalism, 97, 98, 101, 102–103
  and sexism, 153
  single mothers, 101
  statistics, 81–84, 101
  women and, 72, 81–84
power relations, 1
  heterosexual relations, 264, 271, 273
  prostitution, 194
prison
  and colonialism, 75, 133, 134–137
  empowerment, 135
  and gender oppression, 135
  healing lodge, 137, 138n
  importance of physical space, 135, 137
  power, control and isolation, 134–135
  social function, 134
  Task Force on Federally Sentenced Women, 75–76, 133–137
privatization, 92, 93
  of economic responsibilities, 303, 306
  and neoliberalism, 99–100
"Project Thread," 151–152
Project Threadbare, 151–152, 155
prostitution
  and racism, 192, 196–198
  and violence against women, 194–198
public sector
  childcare and, 74–75, 128, 129
  cutbacks, impact of, 71, 73, 120, 121
  and employment, 92
  regulation, withdrawal from, 92
  restructuring, 116, 117, 121, 123
  women's issues and, 106–107, 117, 121
Purvis, Jennifer, 60

Q
Quebec feminism, 7

R
R. v. C.R.N., 206
R. v. O.(M.), 203–204
R. v. S.D.P., 204–205
race
  as analytic tool, 7, 8
  and body image, 237–238, 254
  discourses, importance of, 39
  erasure of non-white women in feminist theory, 13
  and gender, connection, 35–36, 39, 182
  and gendered violence, 192–193
  and lesbianism, 266, 311–314
racial profiling, targeting immigrants of colour, 76
racialization
  of colonized women. *See* colonialism; colonization
  of sexuality, 265–266
  and War on Terror, 76, 143
racism
  absences or silences, 28–29, 30, 31–32
  against Aboriginal women, 210, 291
  anti-racist feminist theory. *See* anti-racist feminism
  "common sense" racism, 29–30
  culture, hegemonic role in reproducing racism, 13, 30–31
  denial by mass media, 180–181, 183–187
  elimination, impossibility of, 30–31
  in everyday life, 30, 31
  gendered, 210
  George murder, 198–199
  political correctness and racist perceptions, 30
  and prostitution, 192, 196–198
  reduced to cultural conflict, 166, 181–182
  a system of domination, 182, 187
  systemic in Canada, 166, 181, 182, 185, 186, 187, 211, 217
  in Virk murder, erasure by media, 180–181, 183–187
  in Virk murder, no mention in sentence, 186
  and white feminist discourse, 31, 32
radical feminism, movements, 77, 149–156
radical social constructionism, 8
rape

anti-violence workers, 220, 221n
domestic rape, 219, 292
and homophobia, 295
rising incidence of, 218–219
training and education needed, 220
victims, 217
rape crisis centres, 167, 217
Raymond, Janice, 23, 24
Razack, Sherene, 133
registered partnerships, rejected as option to same-sex marriage, 306
reproductive issues. *See* abortion
residential schools, 49
"The Respectable Same-Sex Couple," 264–265, 295–299
Rice, Carla, 224–225, 233–245
Rich, Adrienne, 250, 273, 322
"rich white girl" stereotype, 233–234
"Riding the Feminist Waves: In with the Third" (Pinterics), 15–16, 64–70
"Riding the Third Wave: Women-Produced Zines and Feminisms" (Bell), 77, 156–163
Riot Grrl movement, 77, 157, 162n
Rosenberg case, 301
Royal Commission on the Status of Women, 96, 118, 127
Ruparelia, Rakhi, 202–207

S

same-sex marriage
see also spousal recognition
arguments against, 307–308
arguments for, 304–306
Canadian committee hearings (2003), 304–308
"choice," 305
civil unions rejected as option, 306
comparison to a heterosexual norm, 303
family "recoded," 302
and feminist critiques of marriage, 300, 301–304
heterosexual norms supported, 297, 305–306
incompleteness as tool for equality, 306–307
legalized, 264, 296–297, 300, 301
marriage bolstered by, 306
marriage cases, 301
neoliberalism, fit with, 309
post-homosexual identity, 265
privatization of economic responsibilities, 303, 306
respectable same-sex couple (RSSC), 264–265, 295–299
"sameness" approach, 305–306
Sawchuk, Kim, 58–64
second wave feminism
abortion, decriminalization of, 223
apex of political influence, 71, 95, 96–97
criticisms of, by third wave feminism, 8, 11–12, 60
and lesbianism, 317
political muscle, and neoliberalism, 95–104
protest movement, 58
"sameness", theorizing of, 11, 12
state-society relationships, postwar, 116
struggle for political representation, 73
third wave feminism, criticisms of, 60
vulnerability of victories, 97
welfare state, effect of, 7, 72, 96–97
The Second Wave (magazine), 59
September 11th aftermath
racialism and racial profiling, 141, 143
U.S. foreign policy, 141–143
"War on Terrorism" launched, 141, 142–143, 144
sex
distinguished from love, 291, 292, 293, 294
and men, 292, 294–295
social construction, 265–266
sex education, 264, 283–89
danger emphasized, 284, 285–87
discourse of desire needed, 264, 284, 286, 287–89
gender-specific roles reinforced, 286–87
sexual orientation absent, 287
support of abstinence, 285–287, 294
unintended pregnancy not mentioned, 287
sex trade workers in Vancouver, missing, 212–213
sexism
femininity, creation of, 224, 225, 246
heterosexism, 269–270
masculinity, creation of, 225, 323
in organizations and communities, 155
and poverty, 153
rape as a tool of, 218
sexual assault
see also violence against women
cases following *Ewanchuk,* 203–207
determining consent, 202–207
Ewanchuk case, 202–203, 207
exercise of power and control, 206
impact of *Ewanchuk,* 202–207
sexual history evidence, 110, 111, 219–221
sexual orientation, silence in Ontario curriculum, 287
sexuality
cultural construction of, 268
danger and pleasure, 264, 283
desire and pleasure for women, 264, 283, 284
double standard, 283
as form of voluntary rape, 292
and gendered violence, 284
heterosexuality. *See* heterosexuality
individual morality, 284, 285, 287
lesbians. *See* lesbianism; lesbians
and personal identity, 296
race and, 265–266

sexual liberation of 1990s, 264, 283
transsexuality. *See* transsexuality
as victimization, 284, 285, 287
women breaking out of mold, 240
Shade, Leslie Regan, 225, 257–262
silence
black lesbian sexuality, 265, 266, 311–314
women of colour in feminist writing, 28–29, 30, 31–32
"The Silencing of Sexuality" (Lord), 265, 266, 311–314
Silvera, Makeda, 313
single mothers, 79, 82, 83, 101, 103
Sisters in Spirit campaign, 75, 211–214
slicing
described, 88–90
globalization, 74, 93–94
Snider, Laureen, 165–166
social conservatism. *See* neoliberalism
social construction
of femininity, 246
heterosexuality, 263
sexuality, 268
"women," 8, 19–21
social justice, 1, 6, 77, 149–156
social movements, 110, 111
social normality, range of, 248
social responsibilities, privatization of, 92, 93
social welfare
see also welfare state
cuts by Harris government in Ontario, 153
soul and sexuality, 24
"Special Report to Celebrate the 15th Anniversary of the Decriminalization of Abortion; Protecting Abortion Rights in Canada" (CARAL), 223–224, 226–228
Spigel, Lynn, 60
sports masculinities, 194, 200n
spousal recognition
see also same-sex marriage
class and gender, 303
historical development, 296–299
litigation successes, 301
M. v. H., 298–299, 301
stalking, 85
standpoint feminism, 11, 14
standpoint methodology, 14, 36, 37, 38, 39
state policy
see also public sector
backlash against feminism, 120–121, 122
change to neoliberal model, 116–118
childcare agreements cancelled, 127–128, 129
economic conservatism, 120–121
and "family," 102
neoliberalism. *See* neoliberalism
state feminism, 116–117
trade issues, 115–118
Status of Women branch (Privy Council Office), 97
Status of Women Canada (SWC), 5, 119–120, 121, 122, 124
"Assessing Gender Equality," 71–72, 78–86
budget cuts, 5, 71
funding for Sisters in Spirit, 212
stereotyping, 146–147, 209
"Stolen Sisters" report, 211
structural adjustment programs, 91, 92
Sumoud (political prisoner solidarity group), 154
systemic racism, 166, 181, 182, 185, 186, 187, 211

T

Taliban regime, 147
Task Force on Child Care (1986), 128
Task Force on Federally Sentenced Women (1990), 133–137
focus on Aboriginal women, 137
tattooing as resistance, 255
Ternowetsky, Alex. *See* George murder
terrorism
and globalization, 94
September 11th aftermath. *See* September 11th aftermath
"Thinking It Through: Women, Work and Caring in the New Millennium" (Armstrong and Armstrong), 86–95
third wave feminism
actions, 66, 76–77, 149–156
alternative communities, 266, 313
as amalgamation of different theoretic streams, 64
and anti-feminism, 58, 68
and anti-racist feminist thought, 36–41
challenges posed by, 8, 16
coalition building, 65
criticisms of, by second wave feminism, 60, 67–68
and cyberspace, 66
definitional moment of, 15
divergent personal narratives, use of, 65
greater acceptance, emphasis on, 65
networking, 65, 157
origins of, 158
post-feminism and, 15, 68
second wave feminism, criticisms of, 60, 65, 66–67
and sexual definitions, 15, 67
social justice movements, 77, 149–156
strategic defiance, 15
synthesis, emphasis on, 65
theories of, 65–66
younger women's activism, 76–77, 149–156
zines. *See* zines
Third World countries, 91–93, 94
Third World women. *See* global feminism
Thobani, Sunera, 76, 140–149
Toronto Pride Day, 297–298
trade agreements, 72, 92, 117
trade issues
and feminist activism, 116
gender equality, 115–118
transformative feminist political economy, 104–115
transgender theory, 267
transgendered people. *See* transsexuality
transnational corporations, 91, 93, 94

transsexuality
  ambivalent attitudes towards, 23, 267
  challenges to boundary of "women," 13, 23–27, 325–333
  essentialism, 24
  exclusionary practices, critique of, 13
  feminist position, 24, 326, 327–328, 331
  FTMs, 330–333
  gender role, 332
  identity, 330–331, 332
  male lesbians, issue of, 26
  reconfiguring masculinity, 330
Trimble, Linda, 107
truth claims
  in contemporary Canada after Thobani's speech, 76, 140–149
  dehistoricizing September 11, 144
  justifications for War on Terror, 141, 142–143, 144
  media reports of Thobani's speech, 143–144
  post 9/11 context, 76
  public discussion closed down, 141
  vulnerable status of immigrants, 141, 144

U

"The Ultimate Rape Victim" (Doe), 216–222
United Nations, diminished power of, 141
United States
  colonialism, 141, 144
  foreign policy, post-September 11th, 141
  foreign policy record, 142
  fundamentalist and racialized ideology, 142–143
  public opinion, manipulation of, 141, 142–143

V

Valverde, Mariana, 264–265, 269, 295–299
violence, systemic, 211
violence against women
  1992 Criminal Code revisions, 167
  Aboriginal women, 72, 75, 85, 192, 208, 211, 212–214, 292
  backlash, 165, 166, 170–172
  beliefs in 1970s, 170–171
  and body image, 236–237
  consent, defined, 167
  criminal law reform. *See* criminal law reforms
  de-gendering, response to feminists, 165–166, 170–176
  equating verbal and physical violence, 173, 175
  essentialism inadequate, 165, 166
  immigrant girls and women, 180–190
  impact of *Ewanchuk* case, 202–207
  legal responses to, 167–168
  men as victims of abuse. *See* husband abuse
  murder of Pamela George. *See* George murder
  murder of Reena Virk. *See* Virk murder
  patriarchy, 181, 192
  power-neutral models of "wife abuse," 171–172
  prostitution and, 194–198
  racism. *See* racism
  rape, 216–222
  severity of women abuse, 165
  sexual assault law reforms, 167, 202–7
  spousal violence survey. *See* General Social Survey on Spousal Violence
  stalking, 85
  Status of Women Canada report, 85
  systemic causes obscured, 166, 180, 181, 185, 186
  third wave feminism, critical analysis of, 166
  wife abuse. *See* wife abuse
Virk murder, 166, 180–190
  see also immigrant girls
  racism absent in sentencing decision, 186
  racism not discussed by media, 180–181, 183–187
visible minority women. *See* immigrant women

W

wage gap. *See* income gap
"War and the Politics of Truth–Making in Canada" (Thobani), 76, 140–149
War on Terror
  closing down of debate, 76
  racial profiling, targeting immigrants of colour, 76
  rhetoric before attack on Afghanistan, 142–143
  rooted in colonialism, 141
wave metaphor, 8, 58–64, 68
weight. *See* body image
welfare state, 7, 100, 102, 103, 117–118
  see also neoliberalism
  dismantling of, 7–8, 101, 174
  support for women's movement, 7, 72, 96–97
Wendell, Susan, 228–232
Western society
  beauty and body image. *See* beauty; body image
  fundamentalist and racialized ideology, 142–143
  Western theoretical frameworks, dominance of, 13–14
"Why Women Still Ain't Satisfied" (Friendly), 74–75, 127–132
wife abuse
  see also violence against women
  divorce to end, 292
  politicization of, 165
  power-neutral models of, 171–172
  and sexual tension, 292
Wittgensteinian-feminist view, 12–13, 19–27
women
  Aboriginal women. *See* Aboriginal women
  boundaries, fluidity, 19–27
  characteristics, no definitive set, 8, 21
  defiance of cultural norms, 239–240
  definition a political activity, 22–23
  demographic trends, 78–79

as dependents, 96
education trends, 79
feminist attitudes to transsexuals, 23–24
health, 85
immigrants. See immigrant girls; immigrant women
in politics, 73, 104–115
as property, 209
right to choose, 291
sexual desire and pleasure, 264, 283, 294
social construct of, 8, 19–21
in universities. *See* academic feminism; Women's Studies
university graduates, 79
violence against. *See* violence against women
work. *See* labour force participation

women of colour
see also immigrant women
anti-racist feminist thought, 14, 38–39
black lesbian sexualities, silencing of, 265, 266, 311–314
colourist values, internalization of, 237
defiance of cultural norms, 239–240
feminist thought, erasure from, 13–14, 31–32
integrationist *vs.* oppositional ideals, 238
leadership positions, 76
and Western ideals of beauty, 237–238

women of Women's Studies
all women as one, 11
anti-racist feminism. *See* anti-racist feminism
essentialism, 12
native women and colonization, 192, 290
second wave feminism, 11
third wave feminism, 35
and transsexuality, 13, 23–27, 325–33
Wittgensteinian-feminist view, 12–13, 19–27

women with disabilities
see also feminist disability perspective
and disciplines of normality, 247–250
and feminist idealizations of the body, 225
gaining government support, 150–151
genetic screening and selective abortion, 229–232
low-income status, 84
and physical ideals, 249
subjective experience, rarity of interest in, 249

women's movements
see also feminist activism
achievements of, 96–97, 223
attacked as advocacy groups, 106–7, 117, 121
changes and developments, 57
economic issues, 119
empowering days in 70s and 80s, 71, 96–97, 118–119
federal government, collision with, 5, 71, 72–73, 119, 120–121
Free Trade Agreement, opposition to, 120
government funding and, 71, 97, 116, 119, 120–121
grassroots, movement away from, 118–125
legal responses to violence against women, 167–168
and lesbianism. *See* lesbianism; lesbians
NAFTA, opposition to, 98, 117
next stage of, 68
opposition to war, 76, 140–149
previously silenced women, leadership of, 76
and Royal Commission on the Status of Women, 118, 119
sexual pleasure and danger explored, 283
single issue focus, in 80s, 119
social programs and, 7
and Women's Studies, 54–55

Women's Program in citizenship branch (Secretary of State), 97, 119

Women's Studies
see also academic feminism
academic feminism and, 55
achievements, 1–5
activism, combination with, 2
ambiguity about itself, 1, 8
analytic tools, 5–8
challenges, continuing, 9
changes in, 54
changing directions, 8
characteristics in Canada, 6–7
constructionist views, 8
cross-listing, 3–4
curriculum shifts, 3
definitions shifting, 1
development of, 3–5
diversity in, 2–3, 7
feminist activism, 2
first undergraduate course in Canada, 3
growth in, 4
as institutional arm of women's movement, 1
institutionalization of, 4–5
interdisciplinarity, 6
"origin stories" in, 50–57
phallocentric knowledge, critique of, 1
political roots, 1, 2
problems, 3–4, 5
self-reflection, need for, 11, 51–52
social justice, emphasis on, 1, 6
transformation, emphasis on, 1
wave metaphor, 8
women of Women's Studies. *See* women of Women's Studies

Women's Studies regional chairs, 5

women's work
see also childcare; domestic labour; employment (women's)
caring work, 74, 79, 87–91, 102
lumping, 74, 87–88
slicing, 74, 88–90, 93

"womyn-born-womyn", failure as category, 25

Woodhull, Winnie, 60

work. *See* employment (women's)

work-family stress, 79

workforce. *See* gendered division of labour
World Bank, 91
World March Against Poverty and Violence Against Women, 123
World Trade Organization, 91

Y
Young, Claire, 265, 299–311
Young, Lisa, 107–108
young women
 activists, 150–155
 and body image. *See* body image
 and feminism. *See* third wave feminism

Z
Zerilli, Linda, 26–27
zines, 66, 77, 156–163
 content, 156, 157
 cultural production, 77, 158–160, 160, 161
 definitions, 156
 feminism and, 160–162
 history, 156
 networking, 157
 opposition to mainstream culture, 156–157
 Riot Grrl, 77, 157, 162n
 style and content, 158–160
 women-produced, 157, 161
Zita, Jacquelyn N., 26, 321, 322, 323